Reginald L. Cook
Middlebury
1936

AMERICAN
FICTION

AMERICAN FICTION

An Historical and Critical Survey

BY

ARTHUR HOBSON QUINN

Author of

"*A History of the American Drama from the Beginning to the Civil War,*"
"*A History of the American Drama from the Civil War to the Present Day,*"
"*The Soul of America*"

STUDENTS' EDITION

D. APPLETON-CENTURY COMPANY

INCORPORATED

NEW YORK   LONDON

TO

H. McK. Q.

WHO HAS HELPED ME WITH SO MANY OF THESE PAGES,

I DEDICATE THEM ALL

PREFACE

In this survey of American fiction, planned twenty years ago and interrupted first by administrative duties and then by productions in other fields, I have made the daring attempt to treat in one volume both the novel and the short story. It seemed to me impossible to paint a complete picture of the development of our fiction without a discussion of Irving, of Poe, and of Bret Harte, who have so profoundly influenced the novelists, and since so many of our novelists have begun with the short story, any thorough consideration of their work must necessarily include both forms. It has, however, obviously been impossible to treat the great mass of American writers of short stories, and I have had rigorously to limit my discussion to those whose preëminence is unquestioned.

Indeed the problem of selection has been the most insistent. This survey is both historical and critical, for the distinction between the literary historian and the critic is superficial, since any history to be valuable must be critical. A history of American fiction must, first, make clear the tendencies and development of an artistic form; second, show its relation to American life, social, economic, and political; third, establish certain fundamental laws of fiction. I have had, therefore, in the earlier periods when fiction was becoming established, to treat authors who illustrated these tendencies even if they were not relatively more important than later writers who must be omitted if this survey is not to be merely a list of names and dates. I have felt it also to be my duty to call attention to writers of distinction who have been neglected by present readers and critics, owing frequently to the difficulties of access to their works or in not a few cases to their being ahead of their times. The tendency of publishing houses to permit some of the best American novels to go out of print is one of the most regrettable features of today. I have chosen, therefore, to limit the types of fiction as well as the number of writers, omitting juvenile fiction and refraining from such interesting social developments as the dime novel or the detective story. I trust that the more extended treatment of those I have chosen will compensate the reader for these omissions. I have also, for reasons given in detail in Chapter XXXIII, felt it unwise to include any writer who began his work since 1920. We are too near this disturbed period to see it in its proper perspective. But, on the other hand, I have brought the discussion of all the living writers whom I have included, down to the present year. It has been a satisfaction to note that in making these decisions the historian and the critic are in agreement!

One of my many problems has been the proper indication of the dates of first publication. In the cases of novels, and of collections of short stories the date given immediately after the title is that of book publication. With the short stories, many of which appeared only in periodicals, it was not possible to give the magazine and date of first publication without seriously disturbing the appearance of the text. In certain cases, such as Poe and Hawthorne, where the stories are easily available, I have given the date of periodical publication immediately after the title. I have, in general, placed in footnotes the dates and places of the periodical publication of short stories, first, when they were not afterwards published in book form; second, when the periodical appearance anticipated book publication by some years or is otherwise of historic importance; third, when collected editions are out of print and the stories may be found most conveniently in the magazines. There are also certain novels which come under this last category, and I have never felt it necessary to be a slave to uniformity or to hesitate to give information in some cases because it was not universally available. I have printed in italics the titles of novels, of novelettes and of other longer narratives whose nature sets them apart from the short story. Short stories have been enclosed in quotation marks.

So many friends have helped in the progress of this work that it seems almost invidious to mention any, since my recognition must necessarily be incomplete. My greatest debt is to Dr. David H. Stevens, Director of the Humanities Division of the Rockefeller Foundation, whose interest in American letters prompted him to offer to the University of Pennsylvania the means through which I obtained a leave of absence which made the completion of the book possible. I appreciate also the promptness with which President Gates accepted the grant and Vice-President McClelland made the arrangements for my release from duty, and I am grateful for the grant made by the Research Committee of the University for expenses connected with the preparation of the work. My colleagues in the Department of English have as always been helpful, especially Professor Child, Dean Musser, Professor Baugh, Professor Bradley, Mr. Edward

H. O'Neill and Dr. T. E. M. Boll. Mr. O'Neill's wide knowledge of American biography has been of invaluable service.

I only wish it were still possible to thank Mr. Howells, Dr. Weir Mitchell, Mr. James Lane Allen, Mr. George W. Cable, Mr. Hopkinson Smith, and Mr. Thomas Nelson Page for the valuable assistance they rendered me when a young man in the interpretation of the less obvious phases of their work. Happily it is not too late to render a similar acknowledgment to Miss Glasgow, Miss Cather, Mrs. Fisher, Miss Gale, and Mr. Garland. For their interest in making my chapter on Marion Crawford authentic, I am grateful to Madame Elizabeth Tomassetti and Mother Clare Marion-Crawford. Mr. Barton Currie, Mr. Charles Norris, Mr. Charles C. Sellers have also given me valuable information.

I should be ungrateful if I did not record my unusual obligation to Mr. Seymour Thompson and his associates in the Library of the University of Pennsylvania. Without Mr. Thompson's assistance in the building up of the resources of the Library in American fiction and without the constant skill and courtesy of his assistants, my work would often have been at a standstill. Should I mention them all here I should be calling the roll of the Library force. Among the correspondents in other libraries, I am especially indebted to Mr. V. Valta Parma and Mr. M. A. Roberts of the Library of Congress, Mr. H. V. Lydenberg and Mr. K. D. Metcalf of the New York Public Library, Mr. Clarence S. Brigham and Mr. R. W. G. Vail of the American Antiquarian Society, Mr. Austin Gray of the Library Company of Philadelphia, and Mr. A. C. Carty of the Athenaeum Club.

From my wife and children, as in all my undertakings, I have received invaluable criticism and assistance.

A. H. Q.

University of Pennsylvania

ACKNOWLEDGMENTS

I WISH to acknowledge here the cordial co-operation of authors, publishers and others controlling copyrights who have permitted the use of quotations as follows:

To the D. APPLETON-CENTURY COMPANY, from the work of Weir Mitchell, Joel Chandler Harris, Henry B. Fuller, Anne Douglas Sedgwick, Edith Wharton, Stephen Crane, Brand Whitlock and Thomas A. Janvier.

To CASSELL AND CO., LTD., London, from *Shadows on the Rock* and *Obscure Destinies*, by Willa Cather.

To DOUBLEDAY, DORAN AND COMPANY from "The Gift of the Magi" in *The Four Million* by O. Henry, copyright 1905, 1933; from "Brother Rabbit's Cradle" and "How Craney Crow Lost His Head" in *Told by Uncle Remus* by Joel Chandler Harris, copyright 1905; from *Penrod*, copyright 1914, and *The Magnificent Ambersons*, copyright 1918, by Booth Tarkington; from *The Octopus*, copyright 1901, 1929, *The Pit*, copyright 1903, 1931, and *The Responsibilities of the Novelist*, copyright 1903, 1931, by Frank Norris.

To MISS ELLEN GLASGOW and DOUBLEDAY, DORAN AND COMPANY, from the Old Dominion Edition of *The Deliverance*, copyright 1904, 1930; *The Romance of a Plain Man*, copyright 1909, *The Miller of Old Church*, copyright 1911, 1928, *Barren Ground*, copyright 1925, 1933, *They Stooped to Folly*, copyright 1929, *The Sheltered Life*, copyright 1932. To MISS GLASGOW and HARCOURT, BRACE AND COMPANY from *Vein of Iron*.

To DODD, MEAD AND COMPANY from *The Cardinal's Snuff Box*, by Henry Harland.

To HAMLIN GARLAND from *Main Travelled Roads*, *Cavanagh Forest Ranger*, *Crumbling Idols* and *Roadside Meetings*.

To HARCOURT, BRACE AND COMPANY from *Vein of Iron* by Ellen Glasgow; from *Main Street* by Sinclair Lewis.

To HARPER AND BROTHERS from *Those Extraordinary Twins* by Mark Twain; from *For the Major* and *East Angels* by Constance Fenimore Woolson; from "In Butterfly Time" in *A Humble Romance*, and from *Jerome* and *The Love of Parson Lord* by Mary Wilkins Freeman; from *Dr. Warwick's Daughters* by Rebecca Harding Davis; from *The Cliff Dwellers* by Henry Blake Fuller; from *The Awakening of Helena Richie* and *The Iron Woman* by Margaret Deland; from *A Kentucky Cardinal* and *Aftermath* by James Lane Allen; from *From the South of France* by Thomas A. Janvier; from *In the Stranger People's Country* by Charles Egbert Craddock.

To WM. HEINEMANN LTD., London, from *A Lost Lady*, *The Professor's House*, and *Death Comes for the Archbishop* by Willa Cather.

To HENRY HOLT AND COMPANY from *The Honorable Peter Sterling* by Paul Leicester Ford.

To MISS MILDRED HOWELLS and JOHN MEAD HOWELLS from *The World of Chance*, copyright 1893 by Harper and Brothers, copyright 1921 by Mildred Howells and John Mead Howells; from *Annie Kilburn*, copyright 1888 by Harper and Brothers, copyright 1915 by W. D. Howells; from *Criticism and Fiction*, copyright 1891 by Harper and Brothers, copyright 1918 by W. D. Howells; from *The Rise of Silas Lapham*, copyright 1884 by Houghton, Mifflin and Company, copyright 1912 by W. D. Howells.

To HOUGHTON MIFFLIN COMPANY by special arrangement, from *Their Wedding Journey* and *The Rise of Silas Lapham* by William Dean Howells; from *Chita*, *Youma*, *Kokoro*, and *A Japanese Miscellany* by Lafcadio Hearn; from *The Country of the Pointed Firs* and *Deephaven* by Sara Orne Jewett; from *The Little French Girl*, *Adrienne Toner* and *Philippa* by Anne Douglas Sedgwick; from *Alexander's Bridge* by Willa Cather; from *Bayou Folk* by Kate Chopin; from *John Ward Preacher* by Margaret Deland; from *But Yet a Woman* by Arthur Sherburne Hardy.

To ALFRED A. KNOPF, INC. from *The Monster* by Stephen Crane; from *Linda Condon* by Joseph Hergesheimer; from *A Lost Lady*, *The Professor's House*, *Death Comes for the Archbishop*, *Shadows on the Rock* and *Obscure Destinies* by Willa Cather; from *Portage, Wisconsin and Other Essays* by Zona Gale.

To ROBERT M. MCBRIDE AND COMPANY from *Figures of Earth* by James Branch Cabell.

To MACMILLAN AND COMPANY, LTD., London, from *The Lesson of the Master* by Henry James.

To THE MACMILLAN COMPANY from *The Lesson of the Master* by Henry James; from *The Mettle of the Pasture*, *The Bride of the Mistletoe*, and *The Doctor's Christmas Eve* by James Lane Allen; from *Birth* by Zona Gale; from *Dear Old Templeton* by Alice Brown; and for the co-operation of the firm in securing permissions to quote from the work of Marion Crawford.

To MISS L. MAY MERRIAM from *My Friend Prospero* by Henry Harland.

To the heirs of Francis Marion Crawford, MADAME ELIZABETH TOMASETTI and MOTHER CLARE MARION-CRAWFORD and to PEASLEE AND BRIGHAM, Attorneys, from *To Leeward, Saracinesca, Marzio's Crucifix, Via Crucis, The Three Fates* and *The Novel, What It Is*, by F. Marion Crawford.

To CHARLES SCRIBNER'S SONS from *Free Joe and the Rest of the World* by Joel Chandler Harris; from "What Mrs. Fortescue Did" in *More Short Sixes* by H. C. Bunner; from *Seth's Brother's Wife* by Harold Frederic;

from *Rudder Grange*, *The Late Mrs. Null*, "The Transferred Ghost" in *The Lady or the Tiger and Other Stories*, and from "The Griffin and The Minor Canon" in *The Bee Man of Orn* by Frank R. Stockton; from *The Beast in the Jungle* and the introduction to *The Portrait of a Lady* (New York Edition) by Henry James and from *The Letters of Henry James* edited by Percy Lubbock; from "Meh Lady" in *In Ole Virginia* by Thomas Nelson Page; from *Colonel Carter of Cartersville* by F. Hopkinson Smith; from "The Derelict," "The Mind Reader" and "The Reporter Who Made Himself King" by Richard Harding Davis; from *The House of Mirth*, *Tales of Men and Ghosts*, "Bunner Sisters" in *Xingu and Other Stories* and *The Writing of Fiction* by Edith Wharton.

To SIMON AND SCHUSTER INC., from *A Gallery of Women* and *The Genius* by Theodore Dreiser.

CONTENTS

New York; his novel of spiritual disintegration in *The Damnation of Theron Ware*—Joseph Kirkland's fiction of pioneer life in Illinois—Hamlin Garland's uncompromising depiction of the hardships of the farmer in Wisconsin and the Dakotas; of literary and artistic life in Chicago; his romances of the Far West; his return to realism in his autobiographical accounts beginning with *A Son of the Middle Border*—Margaret Deland's study of ethical and religious problems in her early fiction— Her picture of the small Pennsylvania town in *Old Chester Tales* and *Dr. Lavendar's People;* her description of moral and spiritual conflict in *The Awakening of Helena Richie* and *The Iron Woman*—The achievement of the group.

Allen's distinction from the other writers of Southern romance— His early short stories of Kentucky—The idealistic novelettes, *A Kentucky Cardinal* and *Aftermath*—His realistic studies of the hemp fields of Kentucky and patrician Kentucky life—He begins a trilogy of mature passion with *The Bride of the Mistletoe*—Its reception and his fiction dealing with nature— His later realistic short stories—His descriptive power and his analysis of American life.

The nature of the historical novel—The persistence of the type— Lew Wallace's romances of foreign life—Jane G. Austin's novels of colonial New England—Mary Hartwell Catherwood's stories of early Canada—The historians turn to politics—Henry Adams' *Democracy* and John Hay's *Breadwinners*—Mrs. Burnett's *Through One Administration*—Edward Bellamy's romances of the past and the future—The historical novel becomes a vogue—James Maurice Thompson—Paul Leicester Ford's political and historical fiction—Winston Churchill's historical novels, leading to his critical studies of political corruption— Mary Johnston's treatment of colonial Virginia and the Civil War—Owen Wister's celebration of the passing of the cowboy —The mass of second rate fiction at the turn of the century— The steady continuation of the impulse during the twentieth century—Caroline Dale Snedeker's novels of Greek life, John T. McIntyre's novels of Philadelphia.

Hearn's training in New Orleans—His descriptions of the islands of the Caribbean Sea—His *Two Years in the French West Indies*—His remarkable picture of the half-breed in *Youma*— His interpretation of the spirit of the Japanese race, its social organization and religious beliefs; of its supernatural legends— The quality of his style—John Luther Long's contrasts between

in *Birth*; of the unmarried woman in *Miss Lulu Bett*; her short
stories—Rights and duties in the fiction of Dorothy Canfield;
her short stories of character in New England and in France;
her depiction of marriage in *The Deepening Stream*; Susan
Glaspell's novels of escape from provincialism—The new conception of feminine independence in the fiction of this group.

AMERICAN FICTION
AN HISTORICAL AND CRITICAL SURVEY

CHAPTER I

THE FOUNDATIONS OF AMERICAN FICTION

THE impulse to tell a story is perennial, and the delight in hearing one is among our earliest instincts. Like all literary forms, the novel and the short story are the fruition of a long course of development and, in the childhood of the race as in the childhood of the individual, the events rather than the characters enchain the attention. As we grow more sophisticated, the acid test of greatness in fiction becomes the creation of character, and the novel emerges out of the romance, while the short story springs from the union of the prose tale and the character essay.

The novel in a formal sense begins in America at the end of the eighteenth century. It is perhaps natural that it should have been preceded by the chronicle of adventure, the sermon, the diary, the history, the essay, and verse of various kinds. That the drama preceded it, however, is not so easy to explain. Probably the great succession of British novelists from Defoe to Sterne discouraged Colonial competition, while Thomas Godfrey, our first playwright, had no such contemporary rivals in British drama. It is certain that when the first formal efforts at novel writing appeared in this country, it was at a dull moment in the history of the British novel. The great age of the realists had closed with *Humphrey Clinker*, in 1771, and while *Evelina* had appeared in 1778, the field was more open to American competition.

In fact, even before the formal beginning of the novel in America, there had been created in the work of Benjamin Franklin and Francis Hopkinson fiction in all but name, far surpassing in quality the chronicles of scandal which followed in the last two decades of the eighteenth century. The character sketches of Franklin in the *Letters of a Busybody* are of course definite imitations of the British character sketches in the *Spectator*, but his *Bagatelles*, written between 1778 and 1785, strike a distinct note. "To Madame Helvetius" is almost a short story in the modern sense. The conception of Franklin in Paradise, conversing with the shade of Helvetius concerning the living Madame Helvetius, when suddenly the French philosopher introduces his new celestial spouse, who turns out to be Mrs. Franklin, is built up into a situation any writer of fiction might envy. The final remark, addressed to the living Madame Helvetius,

> Indignant at this refusal of my Eurydice, I immediately resolved to quit those ungrateful shades, and return to this good world again, to behold the sun and you. Here I am; let us avenge ourselves!

sounds across many years to tell the admirers of "O. Henry" that there is nothing new under the sun.

The fictional impulse is seen quite as clearly in the work of Francis Hopkinson. Some enthusiasts have even claimed that his *Pretty Story* (1774) is the first American novel. It is not that, but, while its object is the political satire of Great Britain and its method is allegory, there is real character drawing in the description of King George as the old nobleman who tyrannizes over his Colonial children of the "new farm" and who in his turn is ruled by his wife and his steward, who represent Parliament and Lord North. Hopkinson's clear and vigorous style and his imaginative handling of the material are revealed even in brief sentences like "Now the custom in his family was this:—that at the end of every seven years his marriage became null and void, at which time his children and grandchildren met together and chose another wife for him, whom the old gentleman was obliged to marry under the same articles and restrictions as before," or in the final warning, "These harsh and unconstitutional proceedings of the overseer, so highly irritated *Jack*, and the other families of the new farm, that * * * * * *.
Cetera desunt."

Another of Hopkinson's satires, in his *Letter Written by a Foreigner*, paints so vivid a picture of the British manufacturer who "believes in the Athanasian creed, honours the King and makes pin-heads," and who, comparing his map of England, four feet square, with that of North and South America, two feet square, dismisses the Colonies from his mind, that he remains in memory long after the characters in many a novel. No one who has read Hopkinson's manuscript letters, in which he dramatizes even his children's actions, can fail to realize that one of fiction's natural artists was lost when he turned to law and to the service of his country.

Hopkinson's example was followed by Jeremy Belknap, whose *The*

Foresters, an American Tale, ran through several numbers of *The Columbian Magazine,* beginning in June, 1787, and was published, with a few changes, in 1792. It gives an allegorical account of the settlement of America, the Revolution, the adoption of the Constitution, and the French Revolution. Belknap's style is lively, and the book has some value now as a representative of contemporary opinion. The fashion for epistolary romances is illustrated by Belknap's simple device of beginning his chapters in book form with "Dear Sir" from which the earlier form had been free.

The device of letter writing is employed, too, by Mrs. Ann Eliza Bleecker, who wrote her *History of Maria Kittle* in 1781,[1] although it was published posthumously in 1793. In date of composition it is the earliest of the fictional treatments of the Indian written in America. The entire narrative is concerned with the captivity of Mrs. Kittle, who lives at Tomhannock, New York, following the murder of her child, her brother-in-law, and his wife, in peculiarly revolting circumstances, and the burning of her little daughter, all in the absence of her husband, who returns to find his home in desolation. Since the story is laid during the French and Indian War, she is taken to Montreal, and her husband, enlisting in the British army, eventually rejoins her. This tale, for it is hardly a novel, being only twelve thousand words in length, owes its main interest to the fact that it is based on Mrs. Bleecker's own experiences during the advance of Burgoyne's army. Outside of one chief who has promised to protect her, and who indeed does save her from death, the Indians are not individualized, but their actions have a reality which is bloodcurdling. Mrs. Bleecker does not spare us, for when Kittle returns, "He picked up the calcined bones of his once beautiful Anna." Surely realism was on the way!

How insecure and tentative were the earliest attempts at fiction may be seen by examining the pages of the magazines of this period. Eastern romances and moral tales, clipped from British magazines, appear constantly, varied occasionally by "an original American novel," such as *Amelia, or the Faithless Briton,* printed first in the *Columbian Magazine* for October, 1787, though not issued in book form until 1798. It is called on the title page "a novel," but it is hardly that, for its seven

---

[1] Letter of Mrs. Bleecker to Miss V——, Oct. 19, 1781: see *Posthumous Works of Ann Eliza Bleecker in Prose and Verse* (New York, 1793), where the story first appears in book form. It was first printed in *New York Magazine or Literary Repository* (I and II, 1790–1791).

thousand words deal with one series of incidents, while its lack of characterization excludes it from the category of the short story. Yet *Amelia* has its interest, notwithstanding its absurdities which bring the heroine, her father, Horatius, her brother, Honorius, and her seducer, Doliscus, a British officer, all together in London, most of them at the same inn. Her family honor is avenged in the duel which sends Doliscus to his death, while Honorius, in cheerful disregard of his parole, returns to America in the nick of time, so that he may perish at the battle of Monmouth. Writers of the adventure story of today might envy the cool courage of the anonymous author, who leads his characters exactly where he wants them and before whom military regulations are as nothing. If the references to "our sex" mean anything, the anonymous author was a man; and there is a certain virility in the absence of those morbid details of seduction which mark so many of the novels by the women novelists of this period. What makes *Amelia* historically significant, however, is the fact that it leads the procession of moral tales by which a suffering heroine is made the innocent victim of seduction; that the Revolution is made the background of a story apparently for the first time, and, while no battles are described, the war provides a reason for the presence of Honorius in London in the only probable incident in the story. While the narrative is reminiscent in plot, of course, of *The Vicar of Wakefield*, the tone is decidedly American.

Indeed the authors of the short moral tales which stud the pages of the magazines were determined to give them a native flavor. "The Story of Altamount and Arabella," by "Juba," [2] is "founded on facts which occurred in New Jersey during the Late War," but the war is simply a place to which the author sends the hero to get him out of the way. In "The History of Miranda and Cleander," [3] Cleander leaves the army and rushes on the Indians who have killed Miranda. The Indians, however, are not individuals. Stilted and absurd as such tales were, they reveal the tendency to write upon American material which was later to achieve results.

The first novel of full length written in America by an American was *The Power of Sympathy; or, The Triumph of Nature*, published anonymously in Boston in 1789. It is a history of scandal, sugar-coated with moral reflections. Harrington, the hero, falls in love with Harriot,

---

[2] *Universal Asylum and Columbian Magazine*, V (Nov., 1790), 308.
[3] *Universal Asylum and Columbian Magazine*, V (Dec., 1790), 374.

who proves to be his half-sister, by an earlier amour of his father. Harriot dies of grief, and Harrington appropriately commits suicide. A purely gratuitous scandal is introduced in the correspondence between Harriot and her confidante, Myra, by the extended relation of an amour between a Mr. Martin and his sister-in-law, Ophelia, which results in Ophelia's suicide. The career of Elizabeth Whitman, which was to be made the basis of a later novel, is given in an extended footnote and probably was the inspiration for *The Power of Sympathy*. It has been attributed to Mrs. Sarah Wentworth Morton, a Bostonian, the acknowledged author of two poems, *Beacon Hill* and *Ouabi*. Her authorship has been challenged, and indeed it rested so largely in tradition that it should be considered more than doubtful, especially since the Martin scandal was connected with her own family. The novel may have been written by William Hill Brown, a playwright and the known author of a posthumously printed novel, *Ira and Isabella* (1807), but the evidence is not conclusive,[4] and *The Power of Sympathy* must remain for the present at least anonymous.

Hardly a novel, for the thin narrative which takes Osander and his sister, Rozella Bloomsgrove, through their early lives is merely a thread upon which the author hangs epistolary lectures upon education and morality, the *Memoirs of the Bloomsgrove Family* (1790), by Enos

---

[4] For extended discussion of the authorship of the novel see A. W. Brayley, "The Real Author of *The Power of Sympathy*," *The Bostonian*, I (Dec., 1894), 224–233, who first suggested William Hill Brown; Milton Ellis and Emily Pendleton, *Philenia, the Life and Works of Sarah Wentworth Morton*, Univ. of Maine Studies, Second Series, No. 20 (Orono, Dec., 1931); and Milton Ellis, "The Author of the First American Novel," *American Literature*, IV (Jan., 1933), 356–368, which is the best résumé. Professor Ellis has shown that the novel was not attributed to Mrs. Morton till long after her death, and then on hearsay evidence, that she was a woman of refinement, who would probably not have dragged a family scandal into print, and that the case for her authorship fails because there is no evidence of value to substantiate it. His attempt to prove that William Hill Brown was the author is, however, not so successful. Direct evidence rests largely upon the testimony of an elderly woman, Mrs. Rebecca Thompson, niece of Brown. The similarity of the plot of *Ira and Isabella* to that of *The Power of Sympathy* may be an argument either for or against his authorship. In *Ira and Isabella* both the hero and heroine are illegitimate; they are married before the disclosure of their supposed fraternal relation, through Dr. Joseph's paternity, which turns out to be false so far as Ira is concerned. All ends happily, even in the family life of Mr. Savage, who acknowledges that he is Ira's father in a scene which for absurdity can hardly be surpassed. The style of *Ira and Isabella* seems to the present writer quite different from that of *The Power of Sympathy*. That *The Power of Sympathy* was widely discussed at the time if its publication is indicated by a farce, *Occurrences of the Times; or, Transactions of Four Days, Viz—from Friday the 16th to Monday the 19th January, 1789*, in which the attempts of "Sidney" to suppress the publication are satirized. The author is referred to as "he" and his name is indicated by five dots, which might point to Brown.

Hitchcock, D.D., is as proper as *The Power of Sympathy* is scandalous. The two little angels who are brought up at Tusculum by the "respectable Mr. Bloomsgrove" are too perfect to breathe, and his method of instruction and his whole outlook on life are artificial. Lord Kames, Madame de Genlis, Mrs. Capone, and others are the sources of his inspiration, but Rousseau he questions rather severely, and even about Richardson he is not quite certain. Fielding and Smollett he is even less disposed to favor, and the novel of sentiment of his time he quite rightly denounces, though not upon æsthetic grounds. Some of the most delightful features of this book are the incursions of Mr. Bloomsgrove into history for the benefit of his admiring circle. Of Catherine of Russia he says: "In her were united virtue, with beauty; piety with poverty; humility and great benevolence, with great prosperity," and he then proceeds to a biography of the Empress at the conclusion of which the young ladies, quite naturally, "sat in silent astonishment."

Before *The Power of Sympathy* appeared, a much more important novel was projected in the mind of the author, even though he did not publish it until 1792. Hugh Henry Brackenridge, born in Scotland in 1748, came to York County, Pennsylvania, in 1753, was educated at Princeton, and had an active career as chaplain in the army, dramatist, poet, judge, and editor, until his death in 1816. His novel, *Modern Chivalry; or, The Adventures of Captain Farrago and Teague O'Regan*, appeared in installments from 1792 to 1815. In 1788 Brackenridge had begun to write a satire in verse, in imitation of *Hudibras*, and he published two cantos of this as an appendix to the complete edition of 1815. They prove without question that he was wise in preferring prose as a vehicle for *Modern Chivalry*.

The constant revisions which have made *Modern Chivalry* the despair of bibliographers,[5] arose from the nature of the book. It is a picaresque romance, in which Brackenridge starts the hero, Captain Farrago, and his Irish servant, Teague O'Regan, on their wanderings from their home in western Pennsylvania, and since the book is simply a collection of episodes, the conclusion was constantly postponed. The object is satire, and Brackenridge left few institutions of his day untouched by his shrewd and penetrating insight into pretence and hypocrisy. The law-

[5] See, however, Bibliography in Newlin, C.M., *The Life and Writings of Hugh Henry Brackenridge* (1932), pp. 319–327.

yers, the clergy, the physicians, the scientists, the politicians, are the types most severely ridiculed. Brackenridge uses as a satiric weapon the servant, Teague O'Regan, who has been sold to the Captain as a "redemptioner," a device by which many immigrants repaid their passage money to the New World. Teague is ignorant but ambitious, and when the Captain and he come to a town in which an election for the legislature is being held, he is flattered by the desire of the populace to choose him. Captain Farrago persuades him to refuse, but the incident has given Brackenridge an opportunity to poke fun at the haphazard selection of legislators. Brackenridge was a Democrat, but a patrician Democrat of the type which was to flower in Cooper, and he had no illusions concerning popular government. Teague is offered membership in the order of the Cincinnati, in the American Philosophical Society, and in the ministry; and when he is lost in Philadelphia, Captain Farrago pays a visit to the University of Pennsylvania, under the suspicion that the newly elected professor of Greek may be his servant. Amusing are the descriptions of Teague's performance of "Darby" at the theatre, and his various amatory scrapes are naturally employed to satirize the susceptibility of the sex at a time when the author seems to have been justified, at least by the testimony of the feminine novelists. Teague becomes a revenue officer, and Brackenridge, who had been accused unjustly of complicity in the Whiskey Insurrection of 1793–1794, but was exonerated by Alexander Hamilton, satirizes not only the methods of appointment, but, after Teague is tarred and feathered by the insurgents, pays his compliments again to his old friend, the American Philosophical Society, by the account of two members who discover in Teague a new species of animal and solemnly describe him. They then send him to France, and in the second part of the novel (1804–1805), after a brief description of Teague's adventures there, he returns to conduct a contest between the adherents of "Peter Porcupine" and those of an opponent, who imports a pole cat to offset Porcupine's scurrility of language.

The excesses of democracy are made the main subject of attack in the second part. The people are right "only so far that the majority generally mean right" is his belief. There is much criticism of legal procedure also, and Teague is used as before for satirical purposes, being made a judge. The second part has not the vitality of the first, as Brackenridge lets his narrative fall more and more into the form of an essay.

In the first part he used his two characters more adroitly, and aimed his shafts at institutions through them. In the second part he attacks the institutions directly, and since satire unsupported by the interest of fiction rarely holds its place, the first part of *Modern Chivalry* is still read and the remainder is usually forgotten. Yet it well repays reading, for it represents the early pioneer spirit at its best. "It is Tom, Dick and Harry in the woods that I want to read my book," Brackenridge says. His descriptions of democracy and his reasons for being a Democrat are interesting; especially his prophecy that the term Republican "is now considered cold and equivocal, and has given way pretty generally to that of democratic republican. In a short time it will be simply the democracy and democrat."

His liberal policy toward the immigration that was building up the West is shown in such a passage as:

We had half Europe with us, in our revolution. We had all Ireland, the officers of government excepted, and even some of these. I therefore do not like to see an Irishman obliged to perform a quarantine of the intellect.

His description of the Indians is only incidental to the amusing account of Teague's attack upon them while he is really running away, and his consequent nomination as a Major General. But Teague appears only occasionally. Brackenridge's satire, evidently inspired by his reading of Erasmus Darwin's *Temple of Nature* and *Zoönomia,* is directed against those who trace a kinship between man and the lower animals and believe "that man may have been originally a crayfish, or a flying squirrel." The mob solemnly discuss electing animals to the legislature, and two New England men put Teague in a panther's skin and make him prove that a panther can talk. Brackenridge hits New England more than once—his description of the two enterprising Connecticut youths who, hearing that the Canadian government is offering prizes for American scalps, manufacture them out of the skins of muskrats and martens, is amusing.

His style is far above that of his feminine rivals; that he was a conscious artist is shown in his statement:

Language being the vestment of thought, it comes within the rules of other dress; so that slovenliness, on the one hand, or foppery, on the other, is to be avoided in our attire, so also in our speech and writing. Simplicity in the one and the other is the greatest beauty.

His satiric method, which was not confined to Teague's adventures, is revealed in a passage attacking half-way measures in dealing with slavery:

In the phrenzy of the day, some weak-minded powers in Europe begin to consider what is called the African trade as a moral wrong, and to provide for a gradual abolition of it. If they will abolish it, I approve of its being done gradually; because, numbers being embarked in this trade, it must ruin them all at once, to desist from it. On this principle, I have always thought it a defect in the criminal codes of most nations, not giving license to the perpetrators of offences, to proceed, for a limited time, in larcenies, burglaries, &c., until they get their hands out of use to these pursuits, and in use to others. For it must be greatly inconvenient to thieves and cut-throats, who have engaged in this way of life, and run great risks in acquiring skill in their employment, to be obliged all at once to withdraw their hands, and lay aside picking locks, and apply themselves to industry in other ways for a livelihood.

Brackenridge's model in *Don Quixote* is obvious, and his method was affected, of course, by the great English satirists of the eighteenth century, but there is an originality and a vigor in the book which carried it into great popularity, especially in the West, where his name became a household word for half a century.

It is rather striking that in 1793 the West should be the scene of another novel, Gilbert Imlay's *The Emigrants, etc.; or, The History of an Expatriated Family, Drawn from Real Characters, Written in America.* Imlay was born in this country in 1754 and fought in the Revolution, but, notwithstanding his title page, doubt has been thrown upon his stay in this country after 1786.[6] His later romantic union with Mary Wollstonecraft and his association with James Wilkinson have given him considerable notoriety, but his chief claim to our notice lies in the fact that he knew about the country he describes at first hand.[7] *The Emigrants* is a novel with several purposes—to show the superior merits of the social organization in the United States to that of Great Britain, to advocate divorce, and to champion the rights of women by describing the condition in which the British law placed them when their husbands proved unfaithful. It is laid in or near Pittsburgh, though as it is told by letters, some of it takes place near Louisville, in Philadelphia and in

[6] Rusk, R. L., *The Adventures of Gilbert Imlay*, Indiana University Studies, Vol. X, No. 57 (March, 1923). Emerson, O. F., "Notes on Gilbert Imlay," *Publications of Modern Language Association*, XXXIX (June, 1924), 406–439.

[7] See Hall's tribute to Imlay's accuracy in his *Sketches of History, Life, and Manners in the West* (Philadelphia, 1835), Vol. II, pp. 97–106.

England. The T——n family, consisting of a London merchant, his wife, three daughters and a son, migrate to Pittsburgh. Caroline is the usual sentimental heroine, who goes into raptures one moment and is the next in the depths of misery. From her various dangers, which include capture by the Indians, who have treated her with "the utmost delicacy and respect," she is saved by Captain Arlington, who moves rapidly from Philadelphia to Louisville, via Pittsburgh and the West. The Indians are not characterized, but they do appear as living beings. Among other contributions to the progress of the novel they scalp Caroline's uncle, P—— P——, who has left England on account of the persecutions consequent upon his rescue of Lady B—— from her cruel husband. Their seven children likewise fell a prey. *The Emigrants,* apart from its scene and in spite of the absurdity of its style, has an historical interest as a combination of the novel of adventure, the sentimental novel of intrigue, and the fiction of social reform. Although there is no sound evidence that Imlay had met Mary Wollstonecraft before he wrote it, he might easily have read her *Rights of Women* and in his turn he may have influenced Godwin, Southey, Coleridge, Brockden Brown, and others by his plan for a social paradise outlined in his third volume and laid in the Western wilderness.

Another picaresque novel with a vigorous satiric note was written by that interesting playwright, poet, novelist, soldier and jurist, Royall Tyler (1757–1826), whose comedy, *The Contrast* (1787), was not only often played in its own day but has been revived with success by nearly every college dramatic society of today. Some of this dramatic quality appears in *The Algerine Captive; or, The Life and Adventures of Dr. Updike Underhill,* published in 1797 and republished in London in 1802. In the preface he speaks of his desire to write of the manners and customs of his native country, striking a similar note to that of the Prologue in *The Contrast.* The novel is supposedly written by Dr. Updike Underhill, a native of New England, who, after paying his respects to the futility of his college education, studies medicine. Tyler uses his hero to satirize the quackeries of medical practitioners in New England and the South, and then turns his invective against slavery, both at home and in Africa. Dr. Underhill gives a vivid picture of the miseries of the victims on the slave ships, and then, being left in Africa, he is captured by the Algerines and sold into slavery himself. His account of his sufferings in Algiers is based upon the supposed adventures of an uncle of Tyler who was never recovered from the Mediterranean pirates though a large ransom was offered. Underhill's resistance to the temptations of Mohammedanism is made the occasion of satire upon those professors of Christianity in America who do not live up to their own standard. Underhill finally returns to his own country. In the preface the author speaks of the increase in the reading of fiction during an imaginary absence of seven years:

When he left New England, books of biography, travels, novels and modern romances, were confined to our sea-ports; or, if known in the country, were read only in the families of clergymen, physicians, and lawyers: while certain funeral discourses, the last words and dying speeches of Bryan Shaheen, and Levi Ames, and some dreary somebody's Day of Doom, formed the most diverting part of the farmer's library. On his return from captivity, he found a surprising alteration in the public taste. In our inland towns of consequence, social libraries had been instituted, composed of books designed to amuse rather than to instruct, and country booksellers, fostering the new-born taste of the people, had filled the whole land with modern travels, and novels almost as incredible.

The Algerine Captive was vastly better than another story of adventure, *Fortune's Football: or, The Adventures of Mercutio* (1797–1798) by James Butler (1755?–1842). Butler was an Englishman who lived near Harrisburg, Pennsylvania, where the book was published.[8] It is merely another wild tale of an English gentleman who, after losing a fiancée by death and a mistress by a cannon ball from a pirate ship, is pressed by a British ship and reaches Quebec but never touches the United States. The author pauses twice in the novel to denounce British tyranny toward America, but otherwise the various adventures of Mercutio in Spain, Italy, or Russia, unlimited by geography or probability, are conducted strictly in accordance with the conventions of the earlier British romance of adventure, especially in the constant interruptions of friends who are invited to tell the stories of their adventures. The book could just as well have been written if James Butler had never been in the United States, and is interesting only as a contrast to Tyler's novel.

The novels of domestic life which followed *The Power of Sympathy* are of interest historically as an example of the depths from which the

---

[8] See Andrew Banks, *History of that Part of Susquehanna and Juniata Valleys, Embraced in the Counties of Mifflin, Juniata, Perry, Union and Snyder in the Commonwealth of Pennsylvania* (Philadelphia, 1886), Vol. I, p. 790.

American novel arose, and as an illustration of the taste of that time. The novel readers, who were largely feminine, indulged vicariously in those excursions into the quicksands of immorality from which they were presumably guarded in real life by standards which are complacently assumed by the superficial observer to have been higher than our own. It is easy to dismiss these novels as unreal and unrepresentative of actual life. But to the social historian who reads between the lines they are not negligible, and to those possessed of a sense of humor, their perusal will not be without reward.

The novel of disaster had a remarkable example in *The Hapless Orphan; or, Innocent Victim of Revenge* (1793), by "an American Lady." Upon the head of the heroine, Caroline Francis, of Philadelphia, fell nearly every species of misfortune possible to an orphan, left by the death of her uncle and aunt "exposed to the attack of every seducer." Caroline, however, is not the ordinary helpless "female" of this species of novel. She not only resists any such assaults upon her virtue but she bears up pluckily against the deaths of nearly all her friends and succumbs only at the end of the second volume to the kidnappers who have been pursuing her throughout most of the book. For the conventional male villain, the author substitutes Eliza, whose lover Caroline has attracted and led to suicide, and who never rests until she brings her rival's corpse to the dissecting room. Yet notwithstanding the absurdities of the book, Caroline Francis remains one of the few living characters in this species of fiction. Her sensible remarks on nervous women and her attacks on silly romances are worth reading, and her direct and moving appeal for advice to the one woman she can trust, when Captain Evremont, her fiancé, misled by Eliza's machinations, breaks their engagement, proves that the author knew how to write. She must have been acquainted with the United States Army, for nearly all her male characters are drawn from the officers who were fighting in 1790 against the Indians, and the description of the movements of the forces in Ohio portrays quite accurately the incompetence of some of the leaders of that campaign.

Of all the early writers of domestic fiction, Mrs. Susanna Haswell Rowson achieved the widest popularity. Her great vogue is indeed the most interesting feature of her career, for it reveals the large audience which in America read with avidity the kind of fiction she wrote with such facility. Born in Portsmouth, England, in 1762, she came to Boston with her father, Lieutenant Haswell, of the British army, in 1769 and grew up at Nantasket. Being deported with her father in 1777, she returned to England, married William Rowson, a bandmaster and merchant; then, losing her small fortune, she began to write novels and became an actress. An opportunity to join the splendid company which Thomas Wignell was building up at the Chestnut Street Theatre brought her to Philadelphia in 1793. In 1797 she joined the Federal Street Theatre Company in Boston and, after leaving the stage in 1798, she kept a very successful school for girls in Boston for many years, dying in 1824. Of her early fiction [9] *The Inquisitor; or, Invisible Rambler*, written in England (1788), and concerned with a man who possesses a ring which renders him invisible at will, is a confessed imitation of Sterne. Her most famous novel, published in England in 1791,[10] and known first as *Charlotte; a Tale of Truth* and later as *Charlotte Temple*, has had a tremendous vogue in this country, 161 editions being listed in 1933. The account of Charlotte's career, which proceeds through her seduction by a British officer to her abandonment and death in New York City, is stilted in language and sentimental in tone. Its great vogue must be attributed to that quality which delights in reading of the misery of others which by contrast makes us satisfied with our own lot.[11]

Perhaps the most interesting aspect of Mrs. Rowson's fiction consists in its reflection of the current standards of morality. She wrote her stories primarily for morality's sake and published her collection of short tales, *Mentoria; or, the Young Lady's Friend* (1791), because she believed that her young charges should not read the novels then being written. Yet she inserts a novelette, *Marian and Lydia*, which contains a situation in which Sir George Lovemore is only prevented from incest with his own daughter by the author's violent intervention! *Rebecca; or, the Fille de Chambre* (1792?) is of more interest to us on account of the picture of her own life during the Revolution and the sufferings her father underwent on account of his fidelity to what she naïvely calls "the best of sovereigns." Mrs. Rowson seems to have harbored no resent-

---

[9] See list in *A Memoir of Mrs. Susanna Rowson*, by Elias Nason (Albany, 1870), p. 36; or better, *Susanna Haswell Rowson, a Bibliographical Study* by R. W. G. Vail (Worcester, 1933).

[10] No copy of the 1791 edition seems to be extant, but its existence is evident from reviews.

[11] For a painstaking description of the individuals on whose history the novel was based, together with a picture of Charlotte's tomb, see Introduction to F. W. Halsey's edition of *Charlotte Temple* (New York, 1905).

ment for this treatment but was more affected by the kindness displayed by certain neighbors who helped them. Indeed, she embalmed them, by their real names, in the novel and even added a footnote containing the names of other friends. There is quite a touch of verity in the scenes at sea and in America, and Rebecca excites more respect than Charlotte, for she acts at times with courage and decision. The satiric picture of the heartless conduct of her mistress, Lady Ossiter, after her mother's death, is not bad by any means.

Naturally those novels of Mrs. Rowson which were written in America are of most interest to us. *Trials of the Human Heart, a Novel in Four Volumes,* was published in Philadelphia in 1795 with an imposing list of subscribers. The story is told by letters from Meriel Howard to Celia Shelburne, who is in a convent. Meriel is the supposed daughter of a man who tries to commit incest—a favorite theme with Mrs. Rowson. Every misery is heaped on her. Her parents die; her brother is a cad; and when she becomes engaged to Rainsford, whom she loves, her cousins, the Mossops, conspire to deceive her and him without apparent motive. After losing £4000, inherited from her grandmother, she tries to get work. Fortunately or unfortunately for her, she has an undoubted attraction for any man, single or married, who comes near her, but she stalks through all dangers, including a house of ill fame, unsullied. At the same time, in her relations with the Belchers and Mrs. Moreton, she skirts the edge of danger with her eyes at least half open; one of the evidences of Mrs. Rowson's skill lies in the way she makes Meriel reach out for human sympathy in her lonely existence. Saved by a friend who suddenly appears from nowhere, she meets Rainsford again, married however, and, in order to save him from remorse and his wife from unhappiness, Meriel deceives him for a time as to her real character. Through her marriage with Rooksby, whom she does not love, and other miseries, including a wreck in the English channel, she keeps up her spirits and finally finds her real father and mother and is married to Rainsford, conveniently widowed. Mrs. Rowson is nothing if not generous. The story of Meriel's mother is a romance in itself, including her union with the Sultan of Turkey, but we are hastily assured "without once receiving a visit from him, or being solicited to entertain him in an improper manner"!

The most extraordinary novel by Mrs. Rowson, and the one most significant in this study on account of its use of American material, was

Reuben and Rachel; or, Tales of Old Times, published in 1798 when she had become thoroughly acclimated. Fortified by a cursory glance over the history of the world, she produced a romance which proceeds with unruffled steps from Christopher Columbus through ten generations of his descendants until the heroine reaches Philadelphia about 1700. To her inventive powers the creation of letters from Columbus to his wife is nothing; nor does she bother about mere fact, time or place, for after she has led him through an imaginary conquest of Peru, she calmly tells us that he sailed back to the islands of the Caribbean Sea, thus anticipating the Panama Canal by some years. After grafting a Peruvian princess and an English gentleman upon the stock of Columbus, she plunges her third heroine, Columbia, into the religious wars of Queen Mary's reign and makes her, among other things, the mother of Sir Ferdinando Gorges. This adventurer, who played a considerable rôle in early New England history, appeared later several times in American literature, but Mrs. Rowson alone furnishes him with so distinguished an ancestry.

As she truly remarks in Chapter XV, "A century when past is but a moment," and we are rushed through three more generations to arrive with Edward Dudley in New Hampshire in 1645. Here Mrs. Rowson, probably for the first time in American fiction, makes the Indian an individual. William Dudley, Edward's son, having been captured by the Indians, becomes a chief and marries Oberea, a maiden of the tribe. His son, Reuben, returns to England, marries Cassiah Penn, and by the end of the first volume we arrive at the twins, Reuben and Rachel, who give title to the story. Reuben Senior is lost at sea, and since his affairs are somewhat involved, owing to Mrs. Rowson's delightfully inconsequential business arrangements, young Reuben comes back, this time to Philadelphia. Being cheated, temporarily, out of his property, he enlists in the war with the Indians and is about to be killed, when he is saved by Eumea, an Indian girl who, of course, loves him. She does not get him, however, for his sister Rachel, after suffering the usual round of miseries in England which Mrs. Rowson serves out to her heroines, turns up with his childhood's sweetheart, Jessy Oliver. The renunciation by Eumea of her happiness is a gem:

"God of the Christians," said she fervently, "make them forever happy. Wife of Reuben, thou art a happy woman, for thy husband is a man of honour. He saw the weakness of a poor unprotected Indian maid, he pitied her folly, but took no advantage of it."

Jessy was affected by the simple yet fervent address. Reuben took the hand of Eumea, and would have made her sit down, but she refused.

"No! no!" said she, "Eumea will rest no more, know peace no more. I had raised a deity of my own, built an altar in my bosom, and daily offered the sacrifice of a fond, an affectionate heart; but the days are past, I can worship no longer without a crime. Farewell," said she, enthusiastically clasping her hands, "do not quite forget the poor, poor Eumea!"

After refusing a few titles and a good deal of money, in order to remain American citizens, Reuben and Rachel settle down in Philadelphia. A mere outline, however, cannot do justice to this mixture of the historical romance, the story of adventure, and the novel of sentiment and intrigue. Despite all its absurdities, she showed in this novel the calm courage of the real romancer, and while her knowledge of Indian life must have been at second hand, her rapid sketches of Quaker Philadelphia have some verity. This novel, also, reveals most distinctly that dramatic sense which was expressed even more clearly in her one extant play, *Slaves in Algiers*.

In *Sarah; or, the Exemplary Wife*, appearing first as *Sincerity* in the *Boston Weekly Magazine* in 1803–1804, and published in book form in 1813, Mrs. Rowson portrayed the struggles of a wife, charming as usual, and beset with many difficulties. These are based, as before, upon her own history, and reflect her courage and capacity. The novel is told by letters passing between Sarah and her confidante, Anne. Having cleared the decks of Sarah's parents and sent her brother to India, Mrs. Rowson denudes her heroine of any resources by her payment of her father's debts, again reflecting her own experience. Sarah becomes a teacher, first at Mrs. Harrop's school and later at Mrs. Beaumont's home, and then illness sets in, and she marries Darnley more as a last resort than for affection. With a nobility that is not imaginary, for Mrs. Rowson herself brought up her husband's natural son, Sarah permits Darnley's mistress and her child to live with them. But Darnley leaves her and she goes to Dublin as a governess, only to meet ill treatment and to rest under suspicion of immorality, largely on account of the people with whom she lives. She dies in London, eventually, of tuberculosis, her brother returning too late to save her.

Mrs. Rowson's last novel was a sequel to *Charlotte*, called *Charlotte's Daughter; or, The Three Orphans*, printed in 1828 in Boston, after the author's death, with a memoir of her. Lucy, Charlotte's daughter, is prevented from marrying the man she loves by the discovery that he is the son of Montraville, who had betrayed her mother. The resemblance of the plot to that of *The Power of Sympathy* is apparent. *Charlotte's Daughter* has not the interest of her other novels written in America, though it is not quite so hopelessly sentimental as its more famous predecessor.

Notwithstanding their obvious faults, Mrs. Rowson's novels are of real significance in the history of English and American fiction. She had a knack of compelling interest and a power of description, evident for example in scenes like the passage of the Irish Sea in *Sarah*. More important, she was, if not the creator, a vivid portrayer of the virtuous woman adventuress. While the influence of Richardson is of course apparent, her creations are not, like Pamela and Clarissa, passive recipients of persecution. She passed on to several of her heroines her own courage and resourcefulness, which are cheering in days when "females" were supposed to faint in any crisis. Before Elizabeth Bennet had routed Lady de Bourgh in *Pride and Prejudice,* and long before Jane Eyre lived, Rebecca and Meriel had broken through the conventionality of an age which demanded that a gentlewoman should do nothing for herself. While Fanny Burney undoubtedly is one of her models, Evelina would not have met such trials with the same daring or capacity. Mrs. Rowson had to live through a great many trials before she wrote about them. One of the earliest of femininists, as her amusing epilogue to *Slaves in Algiers* proves her, Mrs. Rowson's accomplishment in the creation of her heroines is all the more remarkable because she knew so well the constitution of the English social life she depicts. It was based upon the supremacy of the male, and she accepts it. That is why, with a sure instinct, she lays the scenes of her novels largely in England, even after she had become naturalized in America. The most severe criticism of her work lies in its implicit acceptance of a cold-blooded, eighteenth-century morality, British in essence, which permitted a man of wealth to purchase any virtue he desired and accepted as inevitable the hard lot of any woman without friends or money, whom a single mistake might destroy. It would be comforting for an American to dismiss her work as foreign in tone and as unrepresentative of American character and manners. But its great popularity must unfortunately give us pause.

By the time *Charlotte's Daughter* appeared, much had happened in the development of fiction. *The Coquette; or, The History of Eliza Wharton* (1797), by Hannah Foster of Massachusetts (1758–1840), created a character who is as real as any of Mrs. Rowson's progeny and forms another "horrible example." In the letter Eliza writes to her honest if tiresome wooer, offering her hand to him after she has been led astray by a roué who is already married, she reveals the woman who is no longer merely a "female" acted upon by others but at least the moving spirit in her own destiny. *The Coquette,* based upon the career of Elizabeth Whitman of Hartford, was very popular and was republished as late as 1874. It was dramatized also, but there is no evidence that the play was produced.[12]

It would be idle to record all the feminine imitators of Mrs. Rowson. Occasionally, as in *Emily Hamilton* (1803), "by a Young Lady of Worcester County," probably Eliza Vicery, a little variety is provided by a minor character, Eliza Anderson, who is jilted and, instead of dying, writes a sarcastic and spirited letter to her former fiancé. But most of them are hopeless and sporadic. The nearest approach to a professional novelist was Mrs. Sally Sayward Barrell Keating Wood (1759–1854), who seems to have been the first writer of fiction in Maine. Mrs. Wood had morality in her eye, for her first story, *Julia, and the Illuminated Baron* (1800), laid in France and Spain, combats atheism as taught by the Illuminati. *Julia* is a mixture of the Gothic romance, the seduction story, and the moral tale. As Mrs. Wood explains in the introduction, "an aversion to introducing living characters, or those recently dead, rendered Europe a safer, though not a more agreeable theatre" than her own country. She selected the Illuminati for attack since the world was, according to her, becoming "by profession as well as by precept, infidels." The description of the orgies of the Illuminati by one of its feminine associates, who "though dead to virtue was not entirely lost to decency," will repay anyone who has the courage to read the involved history of the de Launa and Alvada families. A glowing reference to Mrs. Morton, "the darling daughter of the muses," whom the hero, Colwort, meets on a visit to America, contains incidentally no reference to her as a novelist, which to a writer of fiction like Mrs. Wood would have been natural had Mrs. Morton's name been associated then

---

[12] Efforts have been made to identify her betrayer as Pierrepont Edwards, but the evidence seems inconclusive. See Mrs. C. H. Dall, *The Romance of the Associations; or, One Last Glimpse of Charlotte Temple and Eliza Wharton* (Cambridge, 1875).

with *The Power of Sympathy*. Of more interest is her attack upon the
native desire for the quick amassing of riches, in *Dorval; or, the Speculator* (1801). The miseries into which the Morely and the Dunbar families are plunged by the machinations of Dorval, the villain, are due to
their speculations in Georgia lands. Aurelia Morely, the heroine, is a
girl of some spirit, who meets the death of her reputed father in prison,
the murder of her aunt, and the discovery of her own illegitimacy, with
a courage that keeps the reader interested, until the final rain of bless-
ings in the shape of her real father and brother, both of whom save
her life, ends the novel in a maze of absurdity. As usual, the description
of manners and customs is of interest. The spectacle of Mary Woodly,
Aurelia's real mother, dying of smallpox while pressing the hand of
Aurelia and distributing her personal belongings to friends and servants,
is quite in keeping with the facts. Mrs. Wood was not in any sense
parochial. *Amelia; or, the Influence of Virtue: an Old Man's Story*
(1802?) is laid in England and France and traces the tremendous moral
effect of an irritating paragon upon all who know her. Yet again, there
are scenes such as that in which her husband's mistress sends Amelia his
child to shelter which are so delightfully absurd that the reader is
almost repaid. In *Ferdinand and Elmira* (1804), Mrs. Wood lays the
scene in Russia and Poland, about 1750, but though the miseries are
again heaped upon the hero and heroine with some skill, the book has not
the interest of *Dorval*, or of her two short stories, published as *Tales of
the Night* (1827). The vivid description of the Arnold family, storm-
stayed in a deserted mansion in Maine, reveals an ability on Mrs. Wood's
part which makes us regret that she did not write more often about what
she knew.

By 1808, when Tabitha Tenney wrote her amusing satire upon the
whole species, *Female Quixotism, Exhibited in the Romantic Opinions
and Extravagant Adventures of Dorcasina Sheldon*, the heroine, who
rejected a fit suitor because he did not make love in a manner pre-
scribed by the romances, only to fall a prey to an adventurer and to be
made the sport of the neighborhood, had become a subject for mirth.
She was undoubtedly inspired by the work of Charlotte Lennox, an
American only by birth, whose novels and plays were written in England where her life was spent. In *The Female Quixote; or, The Adventures of Arabella* (1752), Mrs. Lennox had satirized the earlier novels
of false sentiment by the same methods, and both books are amusing

even today. Mrs. Lennox indeed lays a portion of two of her novels, *The Life of Harriot Stuart* (1751) and *Euphemia* (1790) in America, and the memories of her childhood when, as the daughter of a British officer, she lived at a fort near Albany, give a certain vividness to her descriptions of the Indians. Her novels, however, were completely British in tone. America is a colony and her characters return to England as their native home.

The sentimental novel did not, however, die out. Helena Wells, who is described upon the title page of her two volume novel *The Stepmother* (1799) as "of Charleston, South Carolina," is an illustration of the American loyalist who seems to have left Charleston with the British army and to have lived in London as a governess. *The Stepmother*, which called for a second edition, is laid in England, and, while painfully moral, is not bad reading, if only for the pleasure in following the career of the heroine, who, according to her own unbiased account, is one of the most perfect of beings. Her complacency in reviewing her probity in refusing to marry the man she loves because she has neither property nor position, and he has both, is unmarred by his consequent insanity and death. Her own marriage to a widower, and her methods of bringing up his daughters will reward the curious. In the introduction, the authoress criticizes the romances of the time and tells us that her novel of domestic life is written to counteract the tendency toward such horrors.

The climax of absurdity in the domestic novel was probably reached in *The Gamesters; or, Ruins of Innocence* (1805) by Caroline Matilda Warren, which was reprinted as late as 1828. From the beginning, when "The brittle thread of life was broken and the amiable Mrs. Anderson suddenly dropped into eternity," through all the seductions and other miseries, the authoress resolutely preserves her high flown language. Few females escape her. She is ruthless, for, to quote one of the characters, Williamson, "My daughter, the young, the beautiful Celestia, was seduced and then abandoned by the traitor Theodore. It is needless to mention particulars; suffice it to say, *she was ruined*."

To the historian, the manner in which the older types of fiction recur is of real significance. The chivalric romance is illustrated by two novels by "A Young Lady of the State of New York," *The Fortunate Discovery; or, The History of Henry Villars* (1798) and *Moreland Vale; or The Fair Fugitive* (1801). The Revolution is touched on lightly in the first, but both, although laid in New York State, might be laid anywhere. They are completely imitative of English sentimental fiction; all of the "gentlemen" have property and the student of social history might easily be misled into believing that they represent a native condition, if their prototypes were not so clear. But most remarkable is the constant interjection of romantic adventures of minor characters, none of whom is able to resist the temptation to tell the story of his life.

The borderline between fiction and biography, easily crossed in the sentimental novel, was also not clearly marked in the romance of adventure. *The Female Review* (1797) purports to be the account of a real person, Deborah Sampson, who became a soldier in the Continental army, and served for over two years without her sex being discovered. Although the appendix contains testimonials from her officers and her portrait is given as a frontispiece, no calm reader can believe in the reality of some of her exploits and the impulse which led to her elaborate defence by the biographer is a bit confused with his evident desire to skirt the edge of danger in the descriptions of her relations with both sexes. But the book has quite a good deal of vigor in certain narrative passages, such as those which tell of the British attack on Bunker Hill.

No lover of unconscious humor can afford to neglect another anonymous romance of adventure, *The History of Constantius and Pulchera; or, Virtue Rewarded* (1795). For sheer absurdity it is hard to match this tale, which takes its heroine through shipwreck, imprisonment by the British, hunger and fever, in none of which is her sex discovered, for she has donned the uniform of a lieutenant, which gives her instantly the capacity to command a vessel. It is only when she meets her beloved Constantius in Bordeaux that she gives way, "and her pillow was wet with the choicest tears that ever flowed within the realms of France." *Constantius and Pulchera* was reprinted as late as 1821.

The foundations of American fiction were laid in the domain of adventure, whether among the perils of our Western frontier, the wilds of Africa, or the purlieus of British society. The most universal motives, those of love and of self-preservation, are constantly employed, which accounts for the wide popularity of books like *Charlotte Temple*. Its models were largely British, especially the novels of sentimentality, although there is a possibility of French influence, when the large number of importations of French literature are considered.[13] Judged by the taste of today, the satiric fiction of Franklin, Hopkinson, Brackenridge and Tyler best repays reading, for it was based upon observation of real life and has at times an imaginative quality. But satire alone cannot keep fiction alive, and the contemporary popularity of *Modern Chivalry* and its present neglect only prove again how, from its day to that of *Main Street*, the American people have liked to read a book which makes fun of themselves, and that their grandchildren will pass on to something more enduring.

[13] See Howard M. Jones, "The Importation of French Literature in New York City," *Studies in Philology*, XXVIII (October, 1931), 235–251.

CHAPTER II

CHARLES BROCKDEN BROWN AND THE ESTABLISHMENT OF ROMANCE

THE foundations of American fiction were laid by writers who, with few exceptions, were the creators of one novel, or were sporadic in their efforts. In the work of Charles Brockden Brown, however, we have the professional man of letters, with an achievement which may be estimated in terms both of quality and quantity.

That he wrote romances was of course inevitable. But in speaking of his work as romantic, it is important to employ this misused term correctly. Much confusion would be avoided if the name "romantic" were kept to describe the material of a novelist who rejects the familiar in order to secure the interest which is given to the strange or the new. Its antithesis is not "realistic" but "classic," if again we use that term, in its proper sense, to signify that material which attracts a reader through his familiarity with it and allows him to exercise the faculty of recognition, just as the romantic material kindles the faculties of wonder and surprise. "Realistic" and "idealistic" should be preserved for the methods of treatment, for they adequately describe, on the one hand, a faithful depiction of life, and, on the other, a heightened portraiture which emphasizes one trait, often to the exclusion of others. Fiction may be romantic in its selection of material, and either realistic or idealistic in its treatment. Usually romantic material and idealistic treatment are united, as in *Ivanhoe* or *The Last of the Mohicans,* and classic material and realistic treatment, as in *Silas Marner* or *The Rise of Silas Lapham;* but when the unexpected combinations occur, as in *The Scarlet Letter*—where selection of romantic material is developed through the realistic portrayal of character, or in *Bleak House*—where familiar life is depicted through types as well as individuals, we often have the greatest productions of fiction.

True romance, while it deals with the unusual, is not an inartistic departure from truth, but is based upon truth, for when it is a deliberate departure from exact fact, the result is often the discovery or the suggestion of a truth more profound than fact. By the time Brown began to write *Wieland*, romance in English fiction had passed from the absurd impossibilities of *The Castle of Otranto* into the prosaic explanations of *The Mysteries of Udolpho*, and the tentative approach in the work of American novelists to new fields, such as Indian warfare, the frontier, and the history of the Revolution, has been already noted.

Charles Brockden Brown was born in Philadelphia, January 17, 1771. He was a great reader, and matured rapidly from an intellectual point of view. Those who are disconcerted at the precocity of his heroes forget that Brown saw nothing improbable in the language of Arthur Mervyn, for at the age of ten he apparently talked in the same way. The extraordinary activity of his mind was fostered by his custom of taking long walks in the neighborhood of Philadelphia, where the habit of brooding over ideas drawn from his reading resulted in abstractions often powerful and often absurd.[1] This quality again was transferred to his heroes, as well as the tendency toward tuberculosis which led to the solitary rambles in the open air. Brown was educated by reading; he speaks scornfully of the routine of college training, which he never had; what he needed most was advice which would have taught him some principles of construction. He was greatest at planning and, while his projected epics on the discovery of America, on the conquest of Peru and on the conquest of Mexico, which he had outlined at the age of sixteen, did not materialize, they show his preference for American scenes.

It is not surprising that the first native professional novelist in the United States should have hesitated before he devoted himself to the sphere in which his real strength lay. Novels, like plays, were still frowned upon by a large part of the respectables of the time. Seventeen years later Scott was to publish *Waverley* anonymously. The profession of the novelist in America simply did not exist, and Brown's first claim to our consideration rests upon his foundation of that profession.

To understand him thoroughly one must read his journals, his beginnings in essay and essay-like fiction, recorded in the magazines or in the sympathetic biography by his friend William Dunlap, who was

---

[1] "Overpowered with fatigue, I am prompted to seek relief in walking, and my mind untuned and destitute of energy, is lost in a dreary confusion of images." Letter V, *Weekly Magazine*, II (May 5, 1798), 11.

endeavoring to lay the foundations of our drama. Brown's extended visits to New York brought him into contact with the group of writers who formed the Friendly Club, and gave him inspiration for the large amount of work which he accomplished from 1797 to 1800. His letters then and later, to Dunlap, to John Howard Payne, as well as his deep friendship for Elihu Hubbard Smith, reflect that mutual encouragement which was building up, under such discouraging circumstances, the beginnings of national literature.

In *The Man at Home*, published anonymously in *The Weekly Magazine* from February 3 to April 28, 1798, Brown introduces the pestilence of 1793 and, in the relation of the death of M. de Moivre and the miseries of his daughter, points forward to incidents later developed in *Arthur Mervyn* and *Ormond*. The teller of the story finds a manuscript account of the Revolution, but Brown, after exciting our interest, stops the narrative. The fragment shows his methods, just as his *Alcuin, a Dialogue on the Rights of Women* (1798), reprinted in part in the *Weekly*, with additions, reveals his Federalist leanings and shows his interest in reforming the institution of marriage, although, as is usual in such discussions, he provides no remedy or substitute. That he never completed a projected romance, of which Dunlap gives sample passages, is not to be regretted. While the letters passing from "Jessy" to "Sophia" or "Julia" reveal some knowledge of feminine psychology, they are not really interesting.

That Brown was prompted by native inspiration is shown in a letter by "Speratus," which is probably his. He speaks of a new work to be projected by him and continues:

To the story telling moralist the United States is a new and untrodden field. He who shall examine objects with his own eyes, who shall employ the European models merely for the improvement of his taste, and adapt his fiction to all that is genuine and peculiar in the scene before him, will be entitled at least to the praise of originality.[2]

Of the many forms which romance may assume, Brown used chiefly the deliberate selection of remarkable incidents of contemporary life. His first completed story, *Wieland* (1798), was based in part upon an actual occurrence. A farmer in Tomhannock, New York, suddenly went crazy under the influence of two angels whom he saw in a bright light

[2] *Weekly Magazine*, I (March 17, 1798), 202.

and who urged him to "destroy his idols." He killed his horses, then his children and his wife, and, visiting his sister with apparent intent to destroy her, was captured and confined as a lunatic. What makes the novel important, however, is not one incident, but the portrayal of the soul of Wieland. When he was quite young his father was killed, apparently by a supernatural agency, because he had failed to obey a mysterious command which produced in his soul a dreadful conflict. Wieland's life, however, passed peacefully on the outskirts of Philadelphia, with his wife Catherine, his children, and his sister Clara, who is the narrator of the story. Clara describes the effects of a mysterious voice which is heard by herself, her brother Wieland, and Henry Pleyel, his brother-in-law, with whom she is in love. It resounds especially in her own room, upon a terrace, and in the "Temple," which Wieland's father had built. It warns Wieland not to go to Lusatia to claim a great inheritance; it convinces Henry Pleyel of Clara's illicit relationship to a certain Carwin, who has taken up his abode in the neighborhood. It appears to save her from evil, and yet it plunges her into misery. Brown shows his ability in working up to a climax. Wieland, brooding over the messages he has received and animated by the memory of his father's death, is ripe for the reception of abnormal suggestions. They come from the same voice, which tells him, "Thy prayers are heard. In proof of thy faith, render me thy wife. This is the victim, I chuse. Call her hither, and here let her fall." He kills his wife and his children, and goes to Clara's house to kill her. She is warned, as she enters the house, in a scene which shows Brown's ability to write effective narrative:

I have said that I cast a look behind. Some object was expected to be seen, or why should I have gazed in that direction? Two senses were at once assailed. The same piercing exclamation of *hold! hold!* was uttered within the same distance of my ear. This it was that I heard. The airy undulation, and the shock given to my nerves, were real. Whether the spectacle which I beheld existed in my fancy or without, might be doubted.

I had not closed the door of the apartment I had just left. The stair-case, at the foot of which I stood, was eight or ten feet from the door, and attached to the wall through which the door led. My view, therefore, was sidelong, and took in no part of the room.

Through this aperture was an head thrust and drawn back with so much swiftness, that the immediate conviction was, that thus much of a form, ordinarily invisible, had been unshrowded. The face was turned towards me. Every muscle was tense; the forehead and brows were drawn into vehement expression; the lips were stretched as in the act of shrieking, and the eyes emitted sparks, which, no doubt, if I had been unattended by a light, would have illuminated like the coruscations of a meteor. The sound and the vision were present, and departed together at the same instant; but the cry was blown into my ear, while the face was many paces distant.

Wieland is confined but escapes, and Clara is saved once more from him by Carwin's powers as a ventriloquist.[3] To some critics, this natural explanation of the mysterious voice is irritating. But when Brown used the device, it had not been so definitely associated with trickery, and the scene in which Carwin through its use strips Wieland of the illusion that had lifted him into a state of moral ecstasy and brings him to suicide is masterly. Clara marries Pleyel ultimately, and Carwin sinks out of sight.

The theme of ventriloquism was treated again in the fragment *Carwin the Biloquist*, published in Brown's magazine (1803–1805) but according to Dunlap's Diary, being in manuscript in 1798. This is an account of the early life of Carwin, who is led to the exercise of his power by an echo heard in his youth. The main interest of the fragment lies, however, in the relations of Carwin to his benefactor, Ludloe, who takes him to Dublin and who is about to initiate him into the secrets of a mysterious society, when the account ceases. The terror which Carwin feels for the possible results of his determination to conceal his exercise of "biloquial" power, knowing that this concealment will render him liable to death if discovered, is not badly done.

Brown's concern with native material is illustrated most definitely, perhaps, by his picture of the yellow fever, in *Arthur Mervyn, or, Memoirs of the Year 1793*, which began to appear in the *Weekly Magazine* in June, 1798, but remained a fragment, owing to the suspension of the journal in August, and was published in two parts in 1799 and 1800. The fever is not merely a background; it makes probable the sudden disappearance and reappearance of the characters, and creates that atmosphere of confusion, in which anything may happen, which suited admirably the peculiar gifts of Brown. Moreover, the brooding sense of terror which hangs over the city is an accessory to romance. The romantic material and the highly idealized characters are held in check by the realistic description of the plague, not to be surpassed until Weir

---

[3] Brown does not use this term. He speaks of Biloquism or ventrilocution, the idea of which he seems to have obtained by reading the work of the Abbé de la Chappelle.

Mitchell wrote *The Red City*. The description of the fugitives as Mervyn enters the city, the loathsome details of the hospital, tie the novel to earth. Brown had escaped the plague in Philadelphia in 1793, but he had suffered from it in 1798 in New York, and he simply transferred his experience to his native city. He was exposed to the infection through the generous action of his friend Elihu H. Smith, the physician and playwright, who took an Italian, Dr. Scandella, into the house where both the friends were living. Brown used the incidents of Scandella's death in *Arthur Mervyn*.

The plot of *Arthur Mervyn* is the most complicated of all Brown's novels. It is told partly by Dr. Steevens and partly by Arthur Mervyn, a boy of nineteen whom Steevens finds near his door, stricken with the fever. Suspicion being cast upon Mervyn, he is practically required to give an account of himself. He has had startling adventures, mainly in connection with a certain Welbeck, who has betrayed, robbed or murdered nearly every one of his associates. Arthur Mervyn is one of those imperturbable heroes who acts with courage and resourcefulness in all emergencies, but, unlike the striplings of Gothic romance, he fights with his brain rather than his sword. When he faces the brutal uncle of Eliza Hadwin, the girl of fifteen who worships him and whose farm he is trying to save, his clever handling of a man who could have crushed him is a relief from the methods of earlier and later romancers who would have made him, in defiance of all probability, knock his enemy down with one blow.

The influence of *Caleb Williams*, by William Godwin, is more evident in *Arthur Mervyn* than in *Ormond*. Arthur is propelled by an insatiable curiosity disguised, even to himself, as benevolence, and he preserves an almost painfully virtuous attitude toward life, as Caleb does. But he has a loyalty even to Welbeck, to which Caleb is a stranger, and Brown endows him with a reticence in the telling of his relations with women which is refreshing. His solemn announcement to Eliza Hadwin that he is destined to grow in intellectual stature to a height to which she cannot follow him is, of course, absurd, but his ignorance of his attraction for all the other women, except Mrs. Wentworth, who thinks he is a lunatic, is not the least of his merits. In her eyes, which were those of the eighteenth century, anyone who tried to benefit others without reward was a lunatic. But here, as in Eliza Hadwin's vigorous putting of the woman's position, Brown was in advance of the social and humanitarian progress of the time. With all its inconsistencies and lack of unity, *Arthur Mervyn* holds our interest through two volumes, and the central character remains of all his creations longest in our memory.[4] And it must always be remembered that when Hawthorne placed the bust of its creator in his Hall of Fantasy, with Homer, Shakespeare, Fielding and Scott, it was as "the author of *Arthur Mervyn.*"

According to Dunlap, *Ormond* (1799) was completed in December, 1798, while *Arthur Mervyn* was still in the making. The yellow fever is once more used as a background, but while the details are told with Brown's usual realistic portraiture, the pestilence is used only as a means of heightening the difficulties of Constantia Dudley and her father. Constantia, who excited such warm praise from Shelley, combines the qualities of a real woman with those of an ideal heroine. She meets calamity with energy, and, while her calm disregard of Ormond's desertion of his mistress, Helena, and the latter's suicide, seems at first incredible, it accords with her usual acceptance of the accomplished fact. Constantia's growing interest in Ormond, who loads her with benefits, is no more out of keeping than is her final defence of her honor in the lonely dwelling where he meets death at her hands. Ormond, on the contrary, is so much a bundle of oddities that he hardly comes alive. Brown tried to draw in Ormond a superman, strong and completely selfish, but his hero remains an abstraction, whose conversation is usually absurd. The supposed resemblance to Godwin's Falkland in *Caleb Williams* is slight. Falkland is much more human, and the fundamental differences between the characters are greater than any superficial resemblances.

In *Edgar Huntly* (1799) Brown once more based his novel upon a human aberration from the normal, that of sleep-walking. At the very beginning he drew with uncommon power the picture of the sleep-walker, Clithero, through the eyes of Edgar Huntly. At the same time, he secures sympathy with Clithero and establishes the sense of the wonderful. Notice the directness of language:

He stopt, the spade fell from his hand, he looked up and bent forward his face towards the spot where I stood. An interview and explanation were now, me thought, unavoidable. I mustered up my courage to confront and interrogate this being.

---

[4] See Brown's defence of the probability of certain incidents in his letter to his brother, February 15, 1799, printed in Dunlap's *Life*, Vol. II, pp. 98–100.

He continued for a minute in his gazing and listening attitude. Where I stood I could not fail of being seen, and yet he acted as if he saw nothing. Again he betook himself to his spade, and proceeded with new diligence to fill up the pit. This demeanor confounded and bewildered me. I had no power but to stand and silently gaze upon his motions.

The pit being filled, he once more sat upon the ground, and resigned himself to weeping and sighs with more vehemence than before. In a short time the fit seemed to have passed. He rose, seized the spade, and advanced to the spot where I stood.

Again I made preparation as for an interview which could not but take place. He passed me, however, without appearing to notice my existence. He came so near as almost to brush my arm, yet turned not his head to either side. My nearer view of him made his brawny arms and lofty stature more conspicuous; but his imperfect dress, the dimness of the light, and the confusion of my own thoughts, hindered me from discerning his features. He proceeded with a few quick steps along the road, but presently darted to one side and disappeared among the rocks and bushes.

The story of Clithero, which he is required to tell, because he is under suspicion of the murder of Waldegrave, the brother of Huntly's fiancée, is a novel in itself, and is woven into the main narrative with more skill than is usual with Brown. The search which Huntly institutes for this strange being, who is haunted with the sense of guilt for the murder of the mistress whom he had loved, leads to one of the best passages in Brown's novels, that in which Huntly finds himself at the bottom of a pit, without any memory of recent events. The reader suspects that Huntly has become a sleep-walker, but Brown's art is such that, although the motive has been introduced earlier, there is no prosaic explanation as there was in *Wieland*. Huntly's description of the pit proceeds by that effective method of denying the natural order which Poe was to use so often. The following events, including his escape from the Indians who are at the mouth of the cave, his rescue of the captive, his killing of the Indians, his flight down and across the Delaware, finally come to a point where credulity begins to cease. The last part of the novel is not up to the level of the beginning. But the Indians, including "Old Deb," are painted in real colors, and the motive of revenge for Huntly's parents who have been their victims is introduced sufficiently well. This element in the story was its germ, as the fragment published in his *Monthly Magazine* [5] indicates.

Clara Howard (1801) and *Jane Talbot* (1801) are not to be ranked

[5] I (April, 1799), 21–44.

with the four other completed romances. The first is the expansion of a minor incident in *Edgar Huntly*, and both are love stories, for which Brown had no especial talent. In fact, the characters seem absurd, especially in their letters and conversations. The establishment of the wonderful in terms of the natural is absent from both of them, and while one cannot help sympathizing with Philip Stanley, bewildered between two women, each apparently trying to renounce him in favor of the other, while they are really holding on to him at the same time, one soon loses patience even with him.

Of more interest are the fragments, in some cases of considerable length, which reveal Brown's power in other directions. *Thessalonica* [6] is a vivid description of the massacre of the people of this Roman city about 400 A. D. and shows not only Brown's ability to sketch the development of a great tragedy from a trivial occurrence, but also proved his power to visualize an historic period. The power was evidenced even more clearly in the *Sketches of a History of Carsol*, which Dunlap states was written later than 1800. It is an account of an imaginary kingdom, laid in an island in the Mediterranean, which goes back to pre-Roman days and has been governed successively by Romans, Vandals, Saracens and the descendants of Charles Martel. The interest which Brown excites in the purely imaginary history is due to the singular air of reality which he succeeds in creating, and to the direct style, free from his usual eccentricities. So plausible is his narrative method that it seems as though there should have been such a country. By constantly referring to actual sovereigns of other countries as contemporary, he gives an additional sense of historic accuracy. His social ideas have here an outlet, also. His ideal seems to be that of a despotism ruled by a virtuous and enlightened prince, who subdues the barons and secures uniformity and harmony in religious and economic life. Belonging to the same category, but not quite so successful, are the *Sketches of a History of the Carrils and Ormes*, an account of an imaginary earldom in England. Evidently not revised, for there are many inconsistencies, it afforded Brown another opportunity to express his ideals of society, and it reveals a knowledge of architecture of respectable proportions.

The most striking characteristics of Brown are his remarkable inventive power, his ability at description and narration, his sympathy and understanding of human beings laboring under powerful emotions, and

[6] *Monthly Magazine*, I (May, 1799), 99–117.

the art with which he made even the impossible seem probable. No one save a superman could have survived the exploits of Edgar Huntly and Arthur Mervyn, but we forget these facts as we read. His achievement can be realized only by those who study not only his completed novels, all composed in three years, but also the shorter tales, essays and criticism with which, usually anonymously, he filled the pages of *The Weekly Magazine* and *The Monthly Magazine*. His wide interest, in topics native and foreign, is revealed also in his later editorship of *The Literary Magazine and American Register* (1803–1807), although by this time his period of fiction was largely over.

He was, to use his own expression in *Edgar Huntly*, a "moral painter." His fine spirit, shot through with aspirations for the best in thought and life, poured itself out not only in the pleas for right living which too often impede the progress of his narrative, but, more effectively, in the creation of his characters. They are the incarnations of his love of duty which seeks no reward but the securing of an invincible self-respect. Brown knew, however, that rectitude was not enough to secure for his characters interest and sympathy. He endowed them, therefore, with courage, a love of adventure and, above all, curiosity. The importance of this quality in fiction lies in its being an active, even a driving force. It is not an endearing trait—as he remarks in *Edgar Huntly*, "Curiosity, like virtue, is its own reward." But without it, Clara Wieland, Arthur Mervyn, Constantia Dudley, Edgar Huntly, would be impossible. It keeps the novels moving rapidly, for notwithstanding all dangers and rebuffs, his characters dare fever and famine, savages and supermen, lofty mountains and dim vaults, to find out what they wish to know. Brown imbued his characters with curiosity deliberately. He remarks in his first book, *Alcuin*, "But though we may strive, we can never wholly extinguish, in women, the best principle of human nature, curiosity."

Brown's novels are a protest against the tyranny of narrow minds. In the same magazine in which vehement protests were printed against Thomas Jefferson's candidacy for the Presidency because of his attitude toward orthodox religion, Brown was contending in *Arthur Mervyn* for the intellectual rights of the individual. Arthur Mervyn "could not part with the privilege of observing and thinking for himself," and the same character remarks, apropos of certain slanders circulated in his town, "It was sufficient that the censure of my neighbors was unmerited, to make me regard it with indifference." Wieland and his sister, Constantia and her father, Ormond, Achsa Fielding, Edgar Huntly all arrange their lives without reference to public or private criticism. They suffer in consequence, but it is to be noticed that Eliza Hadwin, who is perhaps closest to the average woman in her nature, is left at the end of *Arthur Mervyn* unrewarded for her obedience and a prey to her emotions. It is easy to attribute this tendency to revolt to his reading of Godwin and his school, but to attribute to foreign inspiration such an impulse on the part of an American novelist who was born three years before Lexington was fought and who grew up in the atmosphere of the last two decades of the eighteenth century in Philadelphia and New York is really unnecessary. That the influence in the case of Godwin and Brown was mutual has often been shown.[7]

That Brown was conscious of his native inspiration is evident. In the preface to *Edgar Huntly* he says:

America has opened new views to the naturalist and politician, but has seldom furnished themes to the moral painter. That new springs of action, and new motives to curiosity should operate; that the field of investigation, opened to us by our own country, should differ essentially from those which exist in Europe, may be readily conceived. The sources of amusement to the fancy and instruction to the heart, that are peculiar to ourselves, are equally numerous and inexhaustible. It is the purpose of this work to profit by some of these sources; to exhibit a series of adventures, growing out of the condition of our country, and connected with one of the most common and wonderful diseases or affections of the human frame.

One merit the writer may at least claim; that of calling forth the passions and engaging the sympathy of the reader, by means hitherto unemployed by preceding authors. Puerile superstition and exploded manners; Gothic castles and chimeras, are the materials usually employed for this end. The incidents of Indian hostility, and the perils of the western wilderness, are far more suitable; and, for a native of America to overlook these, would admit of no apology. These, therefore, are, in part, the ingredients of this tale, and these he has been ambitious of depicting in vivid and faithful colors. The success of his efforts must be estimated by the liberal and candid reader.

Too much stress entirely has been laid upon the foreign influences upon Brockden Brown. The supposed resemblance of *Wieland* to Schiller's *Der Geisterseher* vanishes upon a reading of them both. He knew German literature, but to call his novels "Gothic" is a facile but not significant classification. His mention of the novels of "Mademoiselle

[7] See Godwin's Introduction to his own novel, *Mandeville*.

Scuderi" as powerfully affecting the nature of Stephen Calvert might be misleading if he did not also give us the names of the leading characters, "Statira, Lysimachus and Perdiccas," [8] which are found in the novels not of Scuderi but of La Calprenède.

The most serious criticisms that must occur to readers of Brown's novels are, first, the lack of unity in construction and, second, the stilted language often used by the characters. The first defect arose partly through the very wealth of his imagination, which presented enough material for three novels in one. But it came also from his association with periodical literature. If those portions of *Arthur Mervyn* which appeared in *The Weekly Magazine* are read, it will be noticed that, so far as possible, the installments end in such a manner as to pique the curiosity of the reader. That Brown began to publish his fiction before it was completed is shown not only here, but in his *Memoirs of Stephen Calvert,* whose progress through *The Monthly Magazine* was interrupted in May, 1800, and a note inserted which is little better than an advertisement.

The effect upon his work was on the whole unfortunate. The stopping of the dramatic scene in *Ormond,* when Constantia kills Ormond in defence of her honor, and the return to Sophia's narrative with the words, "It will be requisite to withdraw your attention from this scene for a moment and fix it on myself," is artificial to say the least. In any criticism of his novels for their lack of unity, the fact that they were written with the possibility of periodical publication in mind, must not be overlooked.

His style, while no one would care to defend it in its pompous moments, is to be judged again in the light of the delusion current at the time that the expression of moral truth endowed the fictional character who possessed it with a dilated vocabulary. Indeed, a supreme artist like Jane Austen was not entirely free from this opinion. Brown could write direct and stirring narrative, or vivid descriptions of scenery, but he seemed to lose his skill as soon as his characters open their mouths. Here again the fact that practically all his work is communicated by one character to another in letters had a tendency to add to its formality.

Brown's later activities as editor and his writings on public questions fall outside our province. They show his ability as a close reasoner, and

[8] William Dunlap, *Life of Charles Brockden Brown,* Vol. II, p. 389.

his prophecy of our future continental expansion reveals his imaginative power. He died on February 22, 1809, a victim to tuberculosis.

Brown's influence upon later writers was noteworthy. Thomas Love Peacock has made clear the deep impression his fiction made upon Percy Shelley:

> Brown's four novels, Schiller's *Robbers* and Goethe's *Faust* were, of all the works with which he was familiar, those which took the deepest root in his mind and had the strongest influence in the foundation of his character. . . .
> Nothing so blended itself with the structure of his interior mind as the creations of Brown. Nothing stood so clearly before his thoughts as a perfect combination of the purely ideal and possibly real as Constantia Dudley.[9]

Brown's general influences upon Shelley's immature prose romances, *Zastrozzi* (1810) and *St. Irvyne,* are purely conjectural, since we do not know exactly when he read Brown's works. The habits of the characters like Verezzi, who takes long walks in the woods, runs several miles after escaping from a cave, and is prompted by an unusual curiosity, and the escape of Wolfstein and Megalena from the robbers' cave might have been prompted by Brown's novels. But they also might be due to other influences. Since we know from Peacock's testimony that "the summer house in *Wieland* made a great impression on Shelley," "the altar and the temple bright" in *Rosalind and Helen* seems more definite an inspiration. The vivid description of the pestilence in *The Revolt of Islam,* Canto X, especially those stanzas which describe the immolation by the sufferers of their own "infidel kindred" to appease the god, and the influence of terror which produced death even without infection, may owe its inspiration to Shelley's memories of *Wieland, Ormond,* and *Arthur Mervyn.*

In the list of books read by Mary Wollstonecraft Shelley in 1815, *Wieland* and *Ormond* appear,[10] and in her romance of *The Last Man* the description of the pestilence shows the influence of *Ormond* and *Arthur Mervyn.* Her own testimony is direct, for the imaginary narrator who describes the plague which at the end of the twenty-first century destroys the human race tells us:

---

[9] Peacock, T. L., *Memoir of Percy Bysshe Shelley, Works,* ed. by H. Cole (1875), Vol. III, pp. 409–410.
[10] *Letters of Mary W. Shelley,* Int. by Henry H. Harper (The Bibliophile Society, Boston, MDCDXVIII), pp. 11–12.

While every mind was full of dismay at its effects, a craving for excitement had led us to peruse DeFoe's account, and the masterly delineations of the author of *Arthur Mervyn*.[11]

The approach of Lionel Verney to London, and the description of the hospital, are in the manner of Brown.

Brown's immediate influence upon American fiction was not marked. It is possible that his insistence upon American themes may have animated such visitors as John Davis, an Englishman who insisted upon the fact that "The United States is the country of my literary birth." Davis came to New York in 1798,[12] and proceeded to turn his wanderings in America, which appear to have been extensive, into narrative which can be called fiction only through courtesy. In *The Farmer of New Jersey* (1800), a domestic tale laid in New Jersey and Georgia, written with such haste that he forgets the names of his characters and has to publish a list of corrections, he introduces the Pocahontas story through one of the characters. In 1805 he developed this theme in *Captain Smith and the Princess Pocahontas*, expanded with revisions into *The First Settlers of Virginia* (1805). These are little more than rearrangements of Captain John Smith's *General History of Virginia*, with a desperate attempt to create a love story between Smith and Pocahontas. Davis was intensely interested in the Indians, and in his *Walter Kennedy* (1805) he takes his hero through the southwestern tribes, even marrying him to Oosnoqua of the Kaskaskias tribe, at the end. The various editions of Davis's books attest their popularity, but their realism rather than any constructive ability must account for it.

Certainly an absurd production like *The Asylum; or, Alonzo and Melissa* (1811) [13] by Isaac Mitchell (c. 1759–1812) stems from Mrs. Radcliffe and not from Brown. This love story of a young Yale student with the daughter of a cruel father is laid partly in a Gothic castle mysteriously located near Long Island Sound. The shrouded figures in Melissa's bedroom, her seeming death, Alonzo's foreign trip where he meets Franklin, and their final marriage are told in an older manner. Equally as unaffected by Brown's firm grasp of his material was Samuel

---

[11] *The Last Man*, by the author of *Frankenstein*, Vol. II, p. 208.

[12] See his "A Voyage from Bristol to New York," *Monthly Magazine*, III (1800), 167–172.

[13] Published first over his own signature as "Alonzo and Melissa," in *The Political Barometer*, a weekly paper of Poughkeepsie, New York, in 1804. A pirated version was published in 1811 by Daniel Jackson, Jr. and was reprinted at late as 1876. See article by D. S. Rankin in *Dictionary of American Biography*, Vol. XIV.

Woodworth's *The Champions of Freedom, or, The Mysterious Chief* (1816), a romance purporting to deal with the events of the War of 1812, with a backward glance at the Revolution. George Washington Willoughby, "a child of nature," is subjected to as many dangers from the opposite sex as the heroine of the seduction romance, but his escapes from a brothel and the battlefield do not make him quite immune. When a married flirt pursued him to the army, Woodworth remarks:

> I have never asserted that my hero was more than a man. Sophia conquered. Let fastidious virtue close the volume. I write nothing but the truth.

Somewhat better is *Laura* by "a Lady of Philadelphia" (1809), and here the description of the yellow fever in Philadelphia is reminiscent of Brown and has some reality. *Kelroy* (1812), by "a Lady of Pennsylvania," stands out even more definitely from its contemporaries. It has no seduction to its discredit, and the character of Mrs. Hammond, the mother who deliberately spends her capital in two years in order to marry her daughters advantageously, then wrecks Emily's happiness because of her hatred for her intended son-in-law, Kelroy, is a real person. The book has been attributed to Rebecca Rush, daughter of the famous physician of that day.

Brown's influence upon Poe was definite, as a comparison of the fifteenth chapter of *Edgar Huntly* with "The Pit and the Pendulum" will indicate. Hawthorne's tribute in "The Hall of Fantasy" is sufficient evidence of his study of his predecessor in the novel of human conscience. Through the nature of Poe and Hawthorne, the influence of Brown was principally of a general character. But his very existence was an inspiration to the American novelist. Without any strong love interest in his fiction, with a scorn for the sentimental excursions into the sensual with which he was surrounded, he proved that an artist could depict with insight and sympathy a human soul under temptation to commit crime or bending under the load of crime already committed. Under his touch the abnormal took on dignity. Wieland's defence at the trial while he is still insane, Clara Pleyel's fear that she herself is going insane, are not unworthy of the two greater artists who succeeded him in the treatment of such themes.

CHAPTER III

WASHINGTON IRVING AND OTHER PIONEERS

A LITERARY form rarely develops without a long period of preparation; the modern short story was centuries in the making. The impulse to tell a brief tale in narrative form is one of the most primitive impulses. But in the story, as it comes down through centuries in varied forms—myth, folk tale, fable, saga, romance or legend, rarely is character the intrinsic artistic element except with a genius such as Chaucer. Character comes at last to its own in the full flowering of the drama and in the development of the true novel. Following Sir Thomas Overbury's vignettes, less of character than of professions, Addison and Steele had, in the essay, realized its value when set against pictorial background, and Clarendon likewise in his portraits framed to illuminate the interpretation of history. But in the prose tale it would be difficult to prove its conscious recognition until, in brief compass, character and dramatic situation are made an artistic unity with appropriate setting in a new mode called the "short story." In a real sense, the modern short story grew out of the marriage of the prose tale and the character essay; in the work of Franklin, Hopkinson, and Brockden Brown the ancestors of "Rip Van Winkle" are to be found in America.

The fusion of these two impulses is to be found therefore in the work of Washington Irving. Born in New York City, April 3, 1783, in a provincial town devoted to commercial pursuits, he grew up with a dislike for business and a fondness for the theatre, and, in his wide reading, a devotion to romance. His early visits to England, France, and Italy as well as his travels in later life developed in him that keen dramatic sense and that understanding of the universal impulses in literature which made him eventually a world artist. He was a traveler who profited by what he saw. Unlike Emerson, he never "carried ruins to ruins," but like Scott, external objects struck his imagination with sounds that resounded often years later when their echoes had mingled with his own creative notes.

It was to be expected, of course, that the absorption of the character essay and the objective tale should not be immediate and complete, and both are found in *The Sketch Book* (1819). *The Sketch Book* was published first in separate parts. "The Wife," which appeared in the first installment with "Rip Van Winkle," and "The Pride of the Village," which came a little later, both illustrate the gradual evolution of the short story of character. "The Pride of the Village" begins with the narrator's interest in the simplicity of the inhabitants: he sees a funeral, asks the story of the dead girl, and it is told him. At this point, the short story really begins; but Irving has prefaced it with ten pages of description of *his* feelings in the midst of such surroundings. This subjective quality had to be subtracted from the form before the short story could develop, just as the objective tale could not grow into the short story until the author ceased to be a showman directing mere types and began to create characters in imagined situations and permit them to work out their own destinies. In other words, he had to dramatize them. That we lost through unfortunate conditions of the theatre a master playwright in Washington Irving is proved not only by his collaboration with John Howard Payne in successful plays like *Charles II* and *Richelieu* but also by his creation in Rip Van Winkle of a dramatic character which has lasted since 1828 on the American stage. Irving did not, it is true, write a play about Rip Van Winkle, but that it is the character and not the play which has accounted for its success hardly needs establishment.

Irving recognized that he was doing something new. In a letter to Henry Brevoort, from Paris, in 1824, he said:

For my part, I consider a story merely as a frame on which to stretch my materials. It is the play of thought, and sentiment, and language; the weaving in of characters, lightly yet expressively delineated; the familiar and faithful exhibition of scenes in common life; and the half-concealed vein of humor that is often playing through the whole,—these are among what I aim at, and upon which I felicitate myself in proportion as I think I succeed. I have preferred adopting the mode of sketches and short tales rather than long works, because I choose to take a line of writing peculiar to myself, rather than fall into the manner or school of any other writer; and there is a constant activity of thought and a nicety of execution required in writings of the kind, more than the world appears to imagine. It is comparatively easy to swell a story to any size when you have once the scheme and the characters in your mind; the mere interest of the story, too, carries the reader on through pages and pages of careless writing, and the author may often be dull for half a volume at a time, if he has some striking scene at the end of it; but in these short writings every page must have its merit.[1]

Among Irving's many narratives, those which are clearly short stories of character are comparatively easy to select. "Rip Van Winkle" and "The Legend of Sleepy Hollow" in *The Sketch Book*; "Dolph Heyliger" and "Annette Delarbre" in *Bracebridge Hall*; "The Story of the Young Italian," "Buckthorne; or, The Young Man of Great Expectations," and "Wolfert Webber" in *The Tales of a Traveller*. In the last book, the tales of banditti do not result in the creation of characters, but Irving, who had been in Italy in 1804 and 1805, represents the Italian in a much more accurate way than any English or American writer before him. He found out at first hand that the Latin race is not composed entirely of assassins and realized the difference between the facts and the conventional British picture of the Italian. Such idealistic romance of German extraction as "The Spectre Bridegroom" did not advance the art of fiction. When he used the method of the German romanticists, as well as their material, he did his less important work. But when, as in "Rip Van Winkle" or "The Legend of Sleepy Hollow," he simply took suggestions from German folk tales and wove them into a story of his own land in which the character owes nothing to Germany, he was doing something radically different.

Irving made no secret of his having used a German source for the sleep of Rip Van Winkle. In fact he states that he had found it in three folk tales. Perhaps the tale of "Peter Klaus" did provide some material, as has often been pointed out.[2] But Irving's Rip is no shepherd, stumbling upon a group of knights who play at bowls, and the similarities, even the recognition of his daughter, are superficial. For Peter Klaus never becomes a fictional human character. He remains a peg on which to hang a prose tale of the old fashioned sort.

It is the same story when we come to "The Legend of Sleepy Hollow." The incident of an apparently headless horseman who throws his head at his rival in love may have been derived from the *Volksmärchen* of J. A. Musaeus [3] in which the *Legenden von Rübezhal* con-

[1] P. M. Irving, *Life and Letters of Washington Irving*, Vol. II, p. 35.

[2] J. B. Thompson, "The Genesis of the Rip Van Winkle Legend," *Harpers Mag.*, LXVII (Sept., 1883), 617–622.

Henry O. Pochmann, "Irving's German Sources in the Sketch Book," *Studies in Philology*, XXVII (July, 1930), 477–507.

[3] See Pochmann, pp. 500–504.

tain a version of the story, but it is not this situation that makes "The Legend of Sleepy Hollow" a short story in the modern sense. It is the character of Ichabod Crane, the Yankee schoolmaster, his mixture of shrewdness, credulity, self-assertiveness and cowardice, which fix him in our memory. Ichabod Crane is American, not German, and the setting, too, even to the birds, is native.

Not only in the creation of the short story was Irving a pioneer. His work marks a progress in the American romance, so great as to be not merely a development, but a new species. The inconsistencies, the incongruities of which even Brown was guilty, give place to a completeness of structure and a professional surety of touch. Irving's romances, even when we know, through constant rereading, just what is to happen, charm us by the grace of their form and the solvent of a humor which is his alone. The Celtic flame, which came from his Scottish mother, shines in that lightness of touch, that blitheness of fancy which made the *History of New York* in 1809 mark an epoch in our literature. It is ostensibly history, but what keeps it alive is the fictional touch and the delightful incongruity. Wouter Van Twiller, who "was exactly five feet six inches in height and six feet five inches in circumference" is a real character, but he is a fictional character. Dietrich Knickerbocker, the supposed author of the *History*, is himself an invention who has baptized a whole section of the country with his name.

It is not easy nor would it be very profitable to separate the fiction from the history in his English or Spanish romances. While *Bracebridge Hall* and *The Alhambra* remain unsurpassed in their description of a foreign civilization, a criticism that has too long taken them for granted must be reminded what new things they were in English literature. No Englishman has yet written a book about America which approaches *Bracebridge Hall*. No Spaniard has understood our civilization as Irving did theirs. This power came from his genius for sympathy. He was looking for what was important, not for what was futile or banal; he took facts from life, legend, or history and fused them through the glow of his imagination into imperishable pictures. *The Conquest of Granada* (1829) is based upon fact, for Irving never shirked labor in order to be accurate. *The Alhambra* (1832) is romance, as are also *The Legends of the Conquest of Spain*. *The Alhambra* is a collection of episodes and has of course the beautiful but imprisoned maiden, the desperate lover, the lute tinkling in the moonlight, and the other stock figures of romance.

But there are also characters—such as Pedrogil, the water-carrier—who are as real as they well can be. Irving is never for a moment the mere teller of idealistic romance. At the very beginning of *The Alhambra,* in the sketch called "The Balcony" he conjures up the conventional picture of the beautiful girl being forced into a convent with her despairing lover hovering on the outskirts of the procession, and then reveals the truth that she is going in quite willingly. Romantic as his material was, Irving often used the method of the realist in his fiction; when this combination occurs, we have his masterpieces.

In any study of the growth of realism in American, or indeed in English fiction, the man who combined the severe training of the scholarly historian with the clear eye of the humorist must take his place as a pioneer. His great power as a narrative artist is seen when we compare such a recital of events as we find in *Astoria* with a recent novel, *I, James Lewis,* based upon Irving's work. His dramatic recital of events in *Astoria* is more interesting than the novel. When to this ability as a storyteller is added Irving's sense of the picturesque, his qualifications as a writer of fiction become apparent. In 1805, while in Florence, he even thought seriously of becoming a painter and studied for a brief time with Washington Allston. Though he gave up this project for lack of technical skill, the quick recognition of form and color shows clearly in his fiction. It was under the pen name of "Geoffrey Crayon" that *The Sketch Book* first appeared.

Leaving aside his authentic histories and biographies, his narrative work consists almost entirely of collections of short stories and sketches. He knew instinctively where his strength lay, and while he collected these fragments into organic wholes, we remember the short stories best. But above all, we remember those creations which owe their inception to his own fancy. The industrious scholarship which has searched for sources in German or Spanish legend is summed up by his latest biographer,[4] and the result is nearly always the same. Irving, like all the great adaptors, took what he chose and made it his own. Much more definite a list may be made of the specific instances in which he has inspired those who followed him. Some, like Dickens, openly acknowledged Irving's influence. Dickens writes of his own desire "to write a series of papers descriptive of the places and people I see, introducing

---

[4] See "Supplementary Studies," Vol. II, pp. 263–325, in Williams, Stanley T., *The Life of Washington Irving* (1935).

local tales, traditions and legends, something after the plan of Washington Irving's *Alhambra*." [5] Few lovers of the great British novelist recognize how the delight in those festivals, like Christmas, which reanimate the heart, the gusto for adventure, the sympathy for human weakness, all implicit in the nature of Charles Dickens, were deepened by his study of Irving.

The influence of "Dolph Heyliger" upon *The House of the Seven Gables* is clear. But the mere roll of American names who reveal their debt to him is enough. Longfellow, Poe, Kennedy, Willis, Curtis, Taylor, Bret Harte—practically every writer of short stories or sketches learned something from him in the technique of his art, either consciously or unconsciously. His wide recognition abroad began almost immediately and continued while the interest in romance survived.[6] In Spain alone forty-two translations of eight different works appeared. In French one hundred and thirteen translations were issued and in German sixty-one, including in both cases reprints. The *Sketch Book* was translated into fifteen languages.

But of even more importance was his creation in Rip Van Winkle of the individual in protest against the small town which insists upon his living according to its standards instead of his own. This lover of his own way, even if it leads to tragedy or merely to ostracism, lives in Sydney Carton and Huck Finn, permeates Harte's stories and survives in Penrod and in many other favorites of fiction. I have indicated elsewhere how it has reappeared on the stage. Any attempt to derive Rip from Irving himself, however, must be a failure. The man who devoted himself for years to the brave attempt to stave off his firm's inevitable bankruptcy, the diplomat who represented his country with distinction, the historian whose accurate researches still excite the admiration of those who have followed him, was not that kind of rebel. What created Rip was Irving's love of liberty, not of weakness, a love which enabled him at his death in 1859 to look back upon a career in which he had borne with dignity and urbanity the priority which his achievement as a pioneer in letters had brought to him.

Allied in friendship and literary method to Irving, James Kirke Paulding (1778–1860) was more distinctly a novelist. His *Diverting*

---

[5] Letter of Dickens to Forster, July, 1839, in John Forster's *Life of Charles Dickens*, Bk. II, Chap. VI.

[6] See Ferguson, John de Lancey, *American Literature in Spain* (1916). Also Williams' *Life*.

History of John Bull and Brother Jonathan (1812), a satire after the manner of Hopkinson's *Pretty Story*, is of interest in the persistence of that type. Paulding pays his respects not only to Great Britain, but also to travelers like Hall, Mrs. Trollope, and Fanny Wright (under assumed or real names), with not so much urbanity as Willis did later, but with some vigor. He concludes "that Squire Bull and Brother Jonathan were too much alike ever to be right down good friends." There are some shrewd observations on American weaknesses, also; especially the readiness to read anything that is written about us by foreigners. His attack on "Peter Porcupine" brings out the point that Jonathan's tenants "always pay well for seeing themselves handsomely abused in black and white."

Pauiding's short fiction consists largely of stories of situation, frequently, as in *The Book of St. Nicholas* (1836), dealing with supernatural occurrences which are, however, explainable by natural means or are even explained in detail, as in "The Ghost." In "The Dumb Girl" in *The Tales of the Good Woman* (1829) he approaches the short story of character, but the other stories of this collection partake of the nature of moral tales.

His first novel, *Koningsmarke; or, Old Times in the New World* [7] (1823) is a story of the Swedish settlements on the Delaware. The main character is Koningsmarke, a young man who comes to the settlement of Elsingburgh from Finland and who falls in love with a daughter of Heer Peter Piper, the governor of the colony. There is also a curious Negro woman called Bombie of the Frizzled Head, evidently a parody on Norna of the Fitful Head in Scott's *Pirate*. The Indians take the town of Elsingburgh and carry away Koningsmarke and Christina, the heroine, into captivity. Koningsmarke is about to be executed, having refused to marry an Indian woman who had selected him to take the place of her son who had been killed, when he is saved by Shadrach Moneypenny, a Philadelphia Quaker. The later use of a similar episode in *The Deerslayer* is interesting.

In *Koningsmarke*, Paulding indulges in some amusing satire on the writers of romance.

The farther we advance in our history, the more do we perceive the advantages of extempore writing. It is wonderful, with what a charming rapidity the thoughts flow, and the pen moves, when thus disembarrassed of all care for the

[7] First issued as *Koningsmarke, the Long Finne*.

past, all solicitude for the future. Incidents are invented or borrowed at pleasure, and put together with a degree of ease that is perfectly inconceivable by a plodding author, who thinks before he speaks, and stultifies himself with long cogitations as to probability, congruity, and all that sort of thing, which we despise, as appertaining to our ancient and irreconcilable enemy, common sense.

The best of Paulding's novels, *The Dutchman's Fireside* (1831), was written in part, according to the author "many years ago," and was inspired by Mrs. Anne Grant's *Memoirs of an American Lady*. It is a romance of the Dutch settlers, beginning during the French and Indian War, and is laid near Albany. Sybrandt Nestbrook, the hero, a shy and awkward boy, is quite well drawn and is not the usual hero of romance. He has a series of thrilling adventures among the Indians and saves Catalina Vancour, the heroine, from one of them. A vivid description of the defeat of Abercrombie before Ticonderoga forms the climax of the second volume and again anticipates Cooper, this time in *Satanstoe*. *The Dutchman's Fireside* was translated into French and Dutch. *Westward Ho* (1832) is a romance of Kentucky, centering in the household of Cuthbert Dangerfield, a Virginia planter, who seeks to recoup his lost fortunes in the West. Bushfield, one of the characters who is kin to Natty Bumppo, is the most interesting. Rainsford, the hero, who belongs to a race with a hereditary taint of madness, links the romance to an older school. Paulding evidently let his romances lie fallow, for his introduction to *The Old Continental; or, The Price of Liberty* (1846) states that it was written "several years before." The story deals with the sacrifices made by people in the humbler walks of life during the Revolution and the details are quite realistic. It is laid in Westchester County, New York, and in New York City. The hero suffers so much that the accumulated miseries become almost unbearable, but he is finally rewarded after he captures Major André. Paulding's last novel, *The Puritan and His Daughter* (1849), was an attack upon intolerance. In his picture of the Puritan, Harold Habingdon, who dominates his daughter, Miriam, completely and prevents her marriage with Langley Tyringham, the son of his neighbor and enemy, the Cavalier Hugh Tyringham, Paulding drew a fairly good portrait. The scene shifts from England and the war between Charles I and Cromwell, to Virginia and thence to New England. The Indian attack in Virginia and the persecution for witchcraft in New England are described with vigor. The regicide Goffe is once more brought in to save the village from the Indians.

But Paulding was working in an outworn fashion and in one with which he was never quite in sympathy. The amusing satire of the romance of his own day, which begins the second volume, is still worth reading.

Paulding has therefore to his credit, novels of Colonial life, of the Revolution, and of the frontier. He never reaches the sweep of Cooper, partly because of his basic love of realism and his propensity to satire. But his stories like Irving's have a mellow charm which makes them readable and they are usually unspoiled by didacticism. That he was never heartily a romanticist is illustrated in his contributions to the collection of short stories, *Tales of Glauber Spa* (1832). These were "Childe Roeliff's Pilgrimage" whose characters are carried from New York to Montreal; and "Selim," an Oriental tale. But both are satirical, either of contemporary or of exotic customs. This collection, edited by Bryant, represents the experimental stage in which the American short story still found itself. Of Bryant's own contributions, "The Skeleton's Cave" was romance of situation, and "Medfield" a story of the supernatural; Miss Sedgwick's "Le Bossu" was historical romance. It was an age of romance, and romance must not be written with the author's tongue in his cheek.

Like Paulding, but for different reasons, John Neal (1793–1876) belongs to the earlier nineteenth century romance. Although he wrote historical romances, when Cooper had made them fashionable, he had begun before Cooper to issue those powerful, if at times formless fictions, which in spite of their incoherence contain flashes of insight into character amounting almost to genius. He is, above all, representative of the romance of passion, stemming from Rousseau through Byron, and influenced also by Brockden Brown. His first story, *Keep Cool* (1817), is immature and wandering, with an attack on duelling and a defence of the Indians. *Logan* (1822), a novel of Colonial and Indian life, is better. Logan is a half-breed, whose son Harold's faculty of appearing in strange places, including the bedside of Elvira, the Governor's wife, is only one of several mysterious elements. Harold's vision in the forest, when he thinks he sees Logan, is, however, not bad, and the publishers even felt called upon to testify that it was original since the manuscript had been in their hands before *The Pirate* was published. But Neal is not a follower of Scott. His characters are intense and almost supernaturally energetic, and when they become involved in the activities of the Revolution, as in *Seventy Six* (1823), the story becomes at times quite thrilling, especially in the description of the crossing of the Delaware River and the attack at Trenton. The passionate element is always uppermost, however, and the scene in which Ellen almost succumbs to John Oadley, although she is in love with Chester and he with Clara, is as realistic as an insight into vicarious passion can make it. *Randolph* (1823) is an epistolary novel in which Neal succeeds in preserving the mystery surrounding his central character, Molton, somewhat after the manner of Brown, whose achievement in letters he criticizes with discrimination through Molton's words. In fact, Neal's judgments concerning recent British authors form one of the most interesting features of *Randolph*. He shows that he is not deceived by Byron's great reputation, though he is influenced by him. His objection to Greek temples for banking houses and his insistence upon suitability in architecture point far ahead to the principles of Louis Sullivan and Frank Lloyd Wright. In many ways Neal was a pioneer. In *Errata* (1823), for example, he attempted "that kind of colloquial manner which is natural to the impassioned and adventurous: varied and abrupt."

In 1823 Neal went to England and contributed to a number of English periodicals. Especially in *Brother Jonathan* (1825) he presented American characters for foreign consumption. The cupidity of the Yankee, the vulgarity of manners and customs in New York City are emphasized, and the sordid side of the Revolution is brought in with a realism that is early. *Rachel Dyer* (1828) is a story of witchcraft in New England about 1693, concerned largely with the trials of Martha Corey, Rachel Dyer, and the hero, George Burroughs. Neal includes a lengthy defence of his forefathers and the book fails as a novel because of the argumentative quality. *Authorship* (1830), laid in England, has some fine moments, especially the passage in which Holmes, the hero, tells Mary Edwards how love after marriage becomes something more than passion and describes the way memory adds to love. Neal shows through the heroine's criticisms of Holmes' writings how he recognized his own shortcomings:

"You have more than enough. First then, husband your resources better. Remember that everything ceases to astonish—to excite—to move—by repetition. Suffering—torture—death—anything may become familiar and tamed of its horrors by repetition. Don't launch your thunder at butterflies and gnats. Don't make your heroes go raving mad for a cause, an offence, which five rational words would remove or explain. One ceases to sympathize in such gratuitous and self-inflicted misery . . ."

The Down-Easters (1833) is a wild tale, beginning with some shrewd caricaturing of Yankee types, but plunging through three layers of narrators to tell a story of passion, revenge, and insanity. *Charcoal Sketches* (1838), essays and short stories, are not significant.

How definitely he belongs to the earlier periods of our fiction was proved by the novel in which he broke his long silence in 1859. *True Womanhood* is marked by the same incoherence of plot and dialogue, the same attempt at suspense by constant insistence upon mysteries which his invention was not able to establish. The story of Julia Parry, placed in a position in which she had either to lie or apparently to testify against her uncle and protector, might have been interesting if Neal had not interlarded it with interminable theological discussions. The great wave of Evangelicalism of the 'fifties is well described, but it belongs outside of the domain of fiction.

Neal is important in his attempt at realism, in his substitution of the active passionate woman, who desires love and is frank about it, in place of the simpering heroine in constant danger of seduction. His characters are, however, too often types, and his attempt at natural language, while praiseworthy, often results in sheer incoherence as must any attempt to reproduce exactly the conversation of men.

While Neal was testing his strength against English standards, another pioneer, Timothy Flint (1780–1840), was exploring the West. A Harvard graduate and a clergyman, he knew the regions bordering upon the Mississippi River through his own experiences, reflected in his *Recollections of the Last Ten Years* (1826), a readable account of his travels through Ohio, Illinois, Kentucky, Louisiana, Arkansas and Missouri. He misses the charm of New Orleans and in fact is blind to the merits of any civilization but his own, but he tries to be fair. In the course of his explorations, he was gathering material for his novels, the first of which, *Francis Berrian, or, The Mexican Patriot* (1826), is a contrast between American and Spanish ideals and practices. The story concerns Francis Berrian, a New England Puritan who takes a leading part in the Mexican Revolution of 1822, marries the beautiful Doña Martha Miguela d'Alvaro, and settles comfortably down in New England with Wilhelmina De Benvelt, a refugee, who also loves him, in the family. Berrian is a hero of the romantic-sentimental type. But the description of the Southwest is accurate, and there is a vigor and ease of narrative which holds the reader sufficiently.

Flint should have confined himself to the material he knew, for in *The Life and Adventures of Arthur Clenning* (1828) he let his fancy fly and produced one of the most absurd books ever written. The novel is laid principally upon an island near New Holland, upon which Arthur Clenning and Augusta Wellman, an English girl, are cast away. Augusta calmly tells her preserver that "he must never forget that the barriers which had formerly interposed between them, still existed," and that he must keep in the outer apartment! Their self-marriage, conducted according to the strict proprieties even to the extent of a witness in a Negress whom they have rescued apparently for the purpose, is delightful. So is their final settlement in Illinois, from which Augusta refuses to depart even when she finds herself heiress, having become a one-hundred percent Illinoisan. *George Mason, the Young Backwoodsman,* is a boy's book. More important is *The Shoshonee Valley* (1830), laid on the south side of the Oregon River. William Weldon, a New England mariner, and his Chinese wife, Yensi, decide to abandon civilization and live among the Indians. Jessy, their daughter, is made the center of a novel in which the international quality is certainly evident, for she is beloved by Areskoui, and Nelesho, rival chieftains, by Jules Landino, a Portuguese, and by Frederic Belden, a Philadelphian! After her abduction, insanity and suicide, nearly all the characters meet a bloody death. *The Shoshonee Valley* remains an interesting revelation of the confused and shifting racial standards of the early Far West, and has some claim to reality, even if, like *Francis Berrian*, it shows clearly the influence of Châteaubriand.

Among the novelists whose work was confined to the 'twenties, James McHenry (1785–1845) deserves mention if only for his versatility. His first novel, *The Wilderness; or Braddock's Times, A Tale of the West* (1823), is a romance of the region near Ft. Duquesne. McHenry took real names for his settlers, and since he had lived in Pittsburgh, he knew the region. The most startling feature of the book, however, is the treatment of Washington, who falls in love with the heroine, Maria Mackintosh, saves her in the disguise of an Indian chief from DeVilliers, the French commander, after Braddock's defeat, and then nobly rescues his chief rival from the stake. *The Spectre of the Forest* (1823), introduces the character of the regicide,[8] Goffe—afterwards used by Barker, Cooper, and Hawthorne—as a mysterious being who watches over a child, George Parnell, whom he sends to England to recover his paternal estate. George returns in time to save his beloved from an accusation of witchcraft, and there is some vigor in the description of the witch trials and the intolerance of the Puritans. McHenry's frontier fiction has not the veracity of Flint's or Hall's, but his Irish stories, especially *The Hearts of Steel* (1825), reveal a knowledge of the conditions in Ulster about 1750, consequent upon its treatment by Great Britain. McHenry was an ardent Presbyterian and an even more ardent sympathizer with Ireland, where he seems to have been born, and he portrays well the long memories of a dispossessed family and the fidelity of their clan.

The two historical novels of Mrs. Eliza Lanesford Foster Cushing must also be mentioned, since she was the daughter of Mrs. Hannah Foster, the author of *The Coquette,* and illustrates in one family the change from the novel of seduction to that of the Revolution. *Saratoga* (1824), and *Yorktown* (1826), are indeed not uninteresting. Catherine Courtland, the heroine of the first, is a relief after the sentimental "females," for she knows her own mind at least. There is some power, too, in the establishment of a sense of mystery in *Yorktown* concerning the relations of the characters. The war hardly enters, however, into either novel.

The early years of the nineteenth century saw the creation of the short story, the development of the historical romance, the romance of passion and of the frontier. Some of these were inspired by Irving, but already the influence of Cooper was at work.

---

[8] Walter Scott had introduced the regicide under the name of Richard Whalley in *Peveril of the Peak* (1822), Vol. I, Chapter 14.

CHAPTER IV

JAMES FENIMORE COOPER

COOPER's achievement is best realized when we return to him after an attempt to read the subjective and morbid analyses of the trivial which pass today under the name of "naturalism." It is like going from a darkened and stuffy chamber into the open air. Against the vivid pictures of nature which he unfolds stand great figures, intensely individual, dominant personalities, created by his imagination, and answering to the supreme test of the novelist's art, that of spiritual importance.

No one can understand Cooper's fiction unless he recognizes the close relation between his selection of characters and his social and political philosophy. He was above everything else a patrician, and because he was a patrician, he was a Democrat. The underlying distinction between the two kinds of political thinking which has separated our two great political parties since the foundation of the Republic, no matter what their names may have been, shines clearly not only in his novels but in his *American Democrat* and in his *Gleanings from Europe*. He belonged to the Democratic party because to him the individual leader, the head of the clan, or the tribe, was the important unit. His democracy was of the Jeffersonian kind, going back to the old theory of "the King and the Commons" against the middle class, against the oligarchy which shuns individual responsibility but depends upon certain institutions for its strength. For the institutional type of thinking, crystallized in American politics into the Federalist or the Whig parties, he had no liking. To him it meant impersonality, the tyranny of the tribe over the individual by subdual to superficial rules of conduct rather than obedience to the profounder laws of human nature. In *Homeward Bound* he puts the case vigorously against the oligarchy which ruled England at the time of the American Revolution. To him, the best organization of society was that in which he had grown up, the rule of a beneficent landlord like his father, who treated his tenants fairly, but who insisted upon his own rights. He drew his ideal picture of such a political and social organization in *The Crater* (1847), in which the hero who discovers an island in the Pacific rules it for a time absolutely.

His upbringing as well as his ancestry shows clearly in his novels. Born in Burlington, New Jersey, September 15, 1789, he was taken the next year by his father, William Cooper, to his estate on the shores of Otsego Lake, at the headwaters of the Susquehanna River, about one hundred and fifty miles from New York City. Here he came in contact with a frontier life and saw a few Indians, though not of the romantic type. The strongest influence upon him was the feudal organization of a society, mixed in its elements, over which his father ruled by virtue of his ownership of land and his official position as Judge of the County Court. Cooper was ingrained with the sense of the social and economic position of the landholder, and the responsibilities which it brings. Land is the great reality, and commercial wealth which may disappear gives no corresponding right to social significance. Marmaduke Temple in *The Pioneers*, Edward Effingham in *Home as Found*, Cornelius Little-page in *Satanstoe* represent the pride and the serenity of the landholder. From the same source springs the deep sense of wrong which Oliver Effingham in *The Pioneers* feels against the man who, he believes, has robbed him of his inheritance.

Cooper's career at Yale, from which he was dismissed in 1806 for some infraction of the rules, seems to have affected him little. A deep impression was made, however, by his naval experience, either on the merchant ship *The Sterling* or in the United States Navy, which he entered in 1808. His first duty led him to Lake Ontario, and his later expedition to Niagara gave him material for *The Pathfinder*. But Cooper felt keenly the inaction of the navy in time of peace, and in 1811, after his marriage with Susan DeLancey, he resigned from the service. He married into a family which had been Tory landholders, and his life as a country gentleman, either in Westchester or at Cooperstown, simply strengthened his opinions and ultimately gave him the leisure to write. His whaling interests led him to Sag Harbor and years later gave him material for *The Sea Lions*.

The story has often been told of the circumstances which led Cooper to write his first novel. He was reading aloud a novel of English life to Mrs. Cooper and closed the book, stating that he could write a better one. Challenged by his wife to do it, he wrote *Precaution*, published in November, 1820. Various guesses have been made at his model, but internal evidence points to Jane Austen's *Pride and Prejudice*. The Moseley family could easily be drawn after the Bennets, and the opening scenes, with the advent of the new family, the Jarvises, remind us of the opening of *Pride and Prejudice*. The love story of Emily Moseley and the Earl of Pendennys, which may indicate that Thackeray was one of *Precaution's* few readers, had decided similarities to the love affair of Elizabeth Bennet and Darcy. But if Cooper followed Jane Austen, rather than Mrs. Opie,[1] or any other of the novelists of English social life of the time, he followed her at a distance. It was not his proper medium, although certain of the characters, especially the terrible Aunt Wilson, remain in the memory. *Precaution* is of importance only because it proved to Cooper that he could write. For his first great novel he turned fortunately to material with which he was familiar. Westchester County, which the armies had crossed many times during the Revolution, he knew thoroughly; for his central character he turned to the story of a spy of whose sacrifices in the cause of the Colonies John Jay had told him some years before.

Efforts to find the actual prototype of Harvey Birch have failed.[2] Cooper denied that he had any particular person in mind and indeed, in the preface to *The Spy* (1821), written in 1831 and revised in 1849, he states clearly that he never knew the name of the individual, and had only the general facts of the employment of the spy, his masquerade as a British agent, his consequent persecution by his own countrymen, and his refusal to accept payment for his services.

Cooper created Harvey Birch in accordance with his theory of the fictional treatment of history. He put this theory very clearly in the preface to *The Pioneers:*

There was a constant temptation to delineate that which he had known, rather than that which he might have imagined. This rigid adhesion to truth, an indispensable requisite in history and travels, destroys the charm of fiction.

From the outlines Jay gave him, Cooper created a real man, one unlike the conventional heroes of romance. Birch is cool, shrewd, and courageous, uneducated, and without a trace of external glamour. In him Cooper visualized the soul of the average American who serves his

---

[1] According to his daughter, they had been reading one of Mrs. Opie's romances. *Correspondence of Cooper*, Vol. I, p. 38.

[2] Tremaine McDowell, "The Identity of Harvey Birch," *American Literature*, II (May, 1930), 111–120.

country without display, but with a patriotism deep if inarticulate. By making Birch a peddler, Cooper not only provided an excuse for his movements and made natural his visits to the Wharton family, but he imbued him with a real or apparent love of money which made his later refusal of all payment by Washington dramatic in its contrast. It was this element of moral contrast which made *The Spy* successful, just as it later made the fortune of Bret Harte. Cooper at the beginning of his career showed his ability to prepare for a striking scene by giving to his hero, in the earlier stages of the novel, qualities which intensify the later effects.

The Wharton family, with their divided sympathies, were drawn with complete understanding on Cooper's part of the philosophy of both Whig and Tory in the Revolution. His associations through his marriage with Susan DeLancey were Tory, but more important, his personal sympathy with the landholder and the rule of the head of the clan enabled him to paint the British officer, even of American birth, without descending to caricature. He knew also that the Revolution had been fought by a determined minority, against the active opposition of those whose loyalty or moneyed interest tied them to England, and in spite of the inertia of a great number of the inhabitants. Cooper not only loved his own country but was indeed in love with it. Yet his liberality is shown nowhere more clearly than in his picture of the times, and he does not hesitate to portray in the most vivid color of scorn the "skinners" or mercenary irregulars who, under the cloak of patriotic motives, plundered the inhabitants of the disputed ground of Westchester. He uses these miscreants for the purpose of heightening the portrait of Harvey Birch, whose stoical conduct while suffering at their hands leads to some of the best passages in the book. The officers on both sides are drawn with some skill, and the "females," as Cooper and, incidentally, nearly everyone else in his day insisted on calling them, provide one of his best portraits in Betty Flanagan. Washington is pictured with sufficient clarity to make him alive; how well Cooper drew him can be appreciated only in comparison with the many absurd attempts at the portrait of the "Father of his Country" in fiction, poetry and drama that were inspired by the success of *The Spy*.

The Spy was not, as is often the case in romantic fiction, the product of a few brief weeks. Cooper tells us in the preface that "so little was expected from the publication of an original work of this description, at the time it was written, that the first volume of *The Spy* was actually printed several months, before the author felt a sufficient inducement to write a line of the second." He felt little confidence in the reception which the work of a native author might receive, and his doubt was shared by his publisher. "To set his mind at rest," remarked Cooper, "the last chapter was actually written, printed, and paged, several weeks before the chapters which precede it were even thought of."

Cooper had underestimated both his powers and his audience. He had hit upon the work for which he was suited, and which, luckily for him, was then supremely popular. For the idealistic treatment of romantic material what is needed is a selection of a few simple elemental passions and motives, made real by being placed in the souls of live people, and made interesting by the imagination that can marshal striking events into dramatic scenes. No minute characterization is needed—everything is put on with a brush. But that does not mean that it is easy to write great romantic novels. If it were, more great ones would have been written. Their authors must have a driving force of belief in mankind's essential dignity, and that, after all, he is only a little lower than the angels. No one who despairs of his race can write romance, and Cooper never lost his faith in the Republic. The book became popular almost at once, and by March 1, 1822, a dramatization by C. P. Clinch began a long career at the Park Theatre, New York. In 1822 a translation into French was only the beginning of its translation into practically all cultivated tongues.

In 1823 Cooper created in *The Pioneers* the novel of the frontier. For the lay figures of Imlay and others who had preceded him, he substituted real characters, and he introduced at least two figures of permanent importance in fiction. Natty Bumppo, or Hawkeye, or Leatherstocking, is presented as an old man, who links, through his devotion to his master, Major Effingham, the colonial British tradition with the new life in the outskirts of civilization after the Revolution. Natty is the symbol of the pioneer spirit of America, and yet he is real. He is dignified, brave, elemental. His speech at his trial for resisting arrest is fine, and his answer, "Here," when Judge Marmaduke Temple speaks to him, is worthy of record, since it is used later in the greatest scene of *The Prairie*. Chingachgook, the last of the Mohicans, is the second great figure. He is the only Indian in the book, and he is contrasted vigorously with the whites. His stoicism and fidelity are shown in the first of the long series of death scenes, of which Cooper is a master. Both Natty and Chingachgook are, however, preliminary sketches for the later novels in which they appear. Cooper showed here his ability at the keeping of a secret; his dramatic revelation of the existence of Major Effingham, long concealed by his grandson, Oliver, and by Natty, is well done. Cooper had the skill to reveal Oliver's secret while apparently concealing it, so as to deceive the reader into thinking he was discovering something while in reality he was being taken only partially into the confidence of the author. Elizabeth Temple is one of the better heroines of Cooper. She is brave and self-respecting and does not, like her friend Louisa Grant, faint away in dangerous moments. Cooper rejected indignantly the suggestion that he drew her from his sister, but Marmaduke Temple was probably inspired by his father, and *The Pioneers* is based, of course, upon Cooper's own experiences at Otsego Lake. The story opens in 1793, and the description of the locality is like that of a painter. The weaknesses of *The Pioneers* are the interruptions to relate conversations of minor characters, and the arguments, direct and implied, concerning the preservation of game, forests, and fish. What Cooper says is quite correct, of course. His comparison between wasteful slaughter by the whites and Natty Bumppo's saner methods, which he had learned from the Indians, comes again to light in the pages of Willa Cather.

It would seem as though Cooper in these first great years surveyed the fields of romance and took two of them for his own. *The Pilot* (1823) was prompted by the publication of Scott's *Pirate*, as Cooper has indicated, but most of the latter is laid on shore, while the finest scenes of the former draw their inspiration from Cooper's vivid description of human beings struggling and conquering the element he knew so well. *The Pilot* was not read on account of the love stories of Lieutenant Griffith and Cecelia Howard and of Lieutenant Richard Barnstable and Katherine Plowden. While Katherine is not badly drawn, the love scenes are hopeless, and Cecelia is almost the feeblest of his women. She is excelled in absurdity, however, by Alice Dunscombe, whose set speech delivered in rotund periods while the sailors of the *Ariel* and the English soldiers suspend their hostilities in wonder is almost the crowning offence of Cooper's career. But as soon as he leaves the English countryside, of which he knew nothing, and takes us to the deck of the American frigate or her little consort, he becomes a master of narrative.

The passage of the frigate through the Devil's Grip or her later escape through the same rocky shallows established him as one of the few novelists who understand the difference between writing a story of the sea and putting the ocean into a narrative. As the central character he drew the mysterious figure of the pilot, John Paul Jones, although his full name never appears. His dramatic arrival occurs just at the proper moment to reveal, in the imminent danger of the frigate and the schooner, the power of the expert seaman over apparent destruction. Yet it is not to be denied that these moments in *The Pilot* are comparatively brief and that the figure of the Pilot as compared with Harvey Birch or Hawkeye remains a melodramatic shadow.

Cooper's contribution to the novel can best be appreciated if we consider chronology only in the development of the three fields of fiction in which he is eminent and in two of which he is supreme. His novels will be classified according to their chief interest, for in several there is present more than one of these elements.

The novels of the frontier and of Indian life contain, in all probability, his greatest creations. *The Pioneers* was followed in 1826 by *The Last of the Mohicans*. Here we have Hawkeye in his prime and Cooper's best drawn Indians, Uncas and Chingachgook. Here too we have all the paraphernalia of the romanticist—the splendor and the horror of war, the bold soldier in Heywood, the timid maiden in Alice, and the intrepidity of the brave woman in Cora. To these, however, he has added something new in fiction, the terror of the forest and the Indian trail. Somehow or other we read his pages with breathless interest in the characters, not so much for the sake of them as for some reason still deeper, some innate sympathy with human hope and fear itself. We are afraid that Uncas will not arrive in time to save Cora from the Huron. We follow breathlessly while he chases Magua, who is bearing Cora away, and then, when Uncas has thrown himself down the precipice to her rescue and the tomahawk has sunk into him and the knife into Cora, we awake as it were from a spell which a great novelist has cast upon us, and even read with interest the arrangements for their respective funerals. We were more interested in the success of the main movement of the story than in the lives or fortunes of the hero or heroine. It is, in other words, more of a disappointment than a sorrow that we feel at the tragic ending of the book.

Yet notwithstanding these limitations, there is marvelous writing in

The Last of the Mohicans. The thirtieth chapter is magnificent—the race pride of the Delawares and the Hurons is finely contrasted in the description of the great self-restraint of Uncas, who allows Cora to go with Magua because she is the Huron's prisoner, who has been loaned to the Delawares, while Alice and the others, who have escaped from the Hurons and sought refuge with the Delawares, are legitimately kept by them. This is worked out by a master in the creation of suspense. It leaves Cora still in danger and causes a rivalry between the tribes which results in one of the best battles in the series.

In *The Prairie* (1827), the figure of Hawkeye as an old man becomes ennobled with the shadow of approaching union with those elements of nature of which he is the symbol. He is set against the background of the Far West, of the Prairie. Ninety years have only dimmed, not destroyed, his faculties. He has become a trapper, though his rifle, Killdeer, still is with him and Hector, a toothless hound, is his companion. As before, he acts promptly but surely in saving his companions. Dangers are thick, as usual, and are well described, notably the rush of the buffaloes, when Hawkeye cleaves them by his skill into two parties, or again the prairie fire, when he saves his charges by burning a portion of the prairie, which leaves them a space to breathe. There are some fine scenes, in which Cooper seems to be a pioneer. That in which the Pawnee chief, Hard Heart, imprisoned among the Sioux, hears the approach of his people before the others, has been the prototype of many occasions, in fiction or drama, where the human being, with his faculties keyed beyond the normal by danger, has borne to him the welcome notes of succor.

The crowning glory of *The Prairie* is the death scene of the old hunter. Surrounded by the Pawnee chieftains, he sits awaiting death without fear. Middleton and Paul Hover come to find him and receive his last messages. These are in perfect keeping with his sense of values. He sends to Oliver Effingham, the descendant of his old master, his precious rifle, and he leaves his traps to his adopted son, the Pawnee Hard Heart. Then comes the answer to the call from the spirit world:

> The trapper had remained nearly motionless for an hour. His eyes alone had occasionally opened and shut. When opened, his gaze seemed fastened on the clouds which hung around the western horizon, reflecting the bright colors, and giving form and loveliness to the glorious tints of an American sunset. The hour—the calm beauty of the season—the occasion, all conspired to fill the

spectators with solemn awe. Suddenly, while musing on the remarkable position in which he was placed, Middleton felt the hand which he held grasp his own with incredible power, and the old man, supported on either side by his friends, rose upright to his feet. For a moment he looked about him, as if to invite all in presence to listen (the lingering remnant of human frailty), and then, with a fine military elevation of the head, and with a voice that might be heard in every part of that numerous assembly, he pronounced the word—

"Here!"

The similarity to the famous scene in Thackeray's *The Newcomes*, when Colonel Newcome says "Adsum" for the last time, is apparent. The slow decay of mental power, the gentle, simple nature of the two men, the natural man and the natural gentleman, the position of the scene in the last chapter of each book, prove beyond question the inspiration. The methods are that of the idealist and that of the realist—but in loftiness of conception, in a touch of imaginative power which bridges the chasm of death, the original scene of Cooper remains unsurpassed even by Thackeray's tender and appealing imitation.

In *The Pathfinder* (1840), Cooper tried the dangerous experiment of reviving a hero who has died in a singularly effective manner. He succeeded admirably, for he gave Natty, through his one love story, an added human quality. *The Pathfinder*, like *The Pioneers*, is not primarily an Indian story. In fact the Indians, Chingachgook, Arrowhead, the Tuscarora traitor, and his wife June, come into the story as distinctly minor characters. It is really a story of the water, for most of the action takes place on Lake Ontario, which Cooper had helped to bisect while in the navy. The youthful hero, Jasper Western, is the master of the *Scud*, the cutter on which the British expedition to the Thousand Islands takes place, and some of the most striking incidents, such as the storm which brings the *Scud* back to the fort at Oswego, while the weather and the French ship *Montcalm* forbid the *Scud* to enter the harbor, are laid on the lake. One of the best characters is Charles Cap, the sailor, who represents the British seaman in his obstinate moods, contemptuous of the Colonials, and his attempted handling of the *Scud*, which almost wrecks the boat, is vivid and dramatic. Mabel Dunham, the daughter of Sergeant Dunham, is fair, though not one of Cooper's best women. The renunciation by the Pathfinder of his hope of winning Mabel Dunham is noteworthy because it runs counter to the method of the sentimental novel of the period. According to the rules of this form of romance, the two young lovers should have given up their hopes because of the promise Mabel had made to the Pathfinder and to her father. Two lives would have been sacrificed for one. But long before Howells had pricked the bubble of this illogical idealism in *Silas Lapham*, Cooper had in *The Pathfinder* solved the problem in the rational way. He made the decision arise from the quality which distinguishes Natty, his innate reasonableness and common sense. The fighting, as usual, is well described.

The Deerslayer (1841), the last of the Leatherstocking Series to be written, is deservedly considered as one of the best. Deerslayer as a young man is more interesting than Natty Bumppo of *The Pioneers* or *The Pathfinder*, and rivals the picture of Hawkeye in *The Last of the Mohicans*. In *The Deerslayer* he wins his name of "Hawkeye" by killing his first "Mingo," through his dexterity in shooting quickly over his shoulder at the treacherous savage who has parted apparently in a friendly way from him, but who is about to kill him. In this book he wins his famous rifle "Killdeer" by gift from Judith Hutter or Hovey, who is really nameless, as the old squatter, Tom Hutter, was not her father. Little is made of the "chest" and its mystery of the parentage of Judith and Hetty. Their mother evidently was betrayed or abandoned and married Hutter to cover her disgrace. Hawkeye's relations with them are not badly painted. His truth and inherent decency prevent Judith's fascination from obtaining any hold upon him, and Hurry Harry's statements about her relations with the British officers also keep him from respecting her. It is this quality of self-respect which is one of Hawkeye's greatest attractions. The character of Hetty, the girl who is not quite normal, is one of Cooper's best women. Judith is not bad, either. Neither is the "sweet type" of which he is so fond. Her proposal of marriage to Deerslayer is not improbable, and the way he meets it and she accepts his decision is more true to human nature than some of Cooper's critics imagine.

Deerslayer is drawn with a poet's vision, which is keen in such moments as that in which he sees the lake for the first time:

Deerslayer made no answer; but he stood leaning on his rifle, gazing at the view which so much delighted him. . . . It was the air of deep repose—the solitudes, that spoke of scenes and forests untouched by the hands of man—the reign of nature, in a word, that gave so much pure delight to one of his habits and turn of mind. Still, he felt, though it was unconsciously, like a poet also. If he found a pleasure in studying this large and, to him, unusual opening into the mysteries and forms of the woods, as one is gratified in getting broader views of any subject that has long occupied his thoughts, he was not insensible to the innate loveliness of such a landscape neither, but felt a portion of that soothing of the spirit which is a common attendant of a scene so thoroughly pervaded by the holy calm of nature.

The return of Deerslayer to keep his parole is a good motive and not improbable. The torture scene is effective though a bit long drawn out, and the final touch of contrast in the steady approach of the British troops with their favorite weapon, the bayonet, is good art. The scenes on the lake, the "castle," and the "ark," give Cooper his chance to use his favorite arena, the water. It may be noted that in the later books of the Leatherstocking Series he combined his two great backgrounds, while in the first three he made use of the land alone.

In the Preface to *The Deerslayer* Cooper defends his Indians:

It has been objected to these books that they give a more favorable picture of the red man than he deserves. The writer apprehends that much of this objection arises from the habits of those who have made it. One of his critics, on the appearance of the first work in which Indian character was portrayed, objected that its "characters were Indians of the school of Heckewelder, rather than of the school of nature." These words quite probably contain the substance of the true answer to the objection. Heckewelder was an ardent, benevolent missionary, bent on the good of the red man, and seeing in him one who had the soul, reason, and characteristics of a fellow-being. The critic is understood to have been a very distinguished agent of the government, one very familiar with Indians, as they are seen at the councils to treat for the sale of their lands, where little or none of their domestic qualities come in play, and where, indeed, their evil passions are known to have the fullest scope. As just would it be to draw conclusions of the general state of American society from the scenes of the capital, as to suppose that the negotiating of one of these treaties is a fair picture of Indian life.

It is the privilege of all writers of fiction, more particularly when their works aspire to the elevation of romances, to present the *beau-idéal* of their characters to the reader. This it is which constitutes poetry, and to suppose that the red man is to be represented only in the squalid misery or in the degraded moral state that certainly more or less belongs to his condition, is, we apprehend, taking a very narrow view of an author's privileges. Such criticism would have deprived the world of even Homer.

The Leatherstocking Series should not be read in the order of composition, but we should rather trace through *The Deerslayer, The Last of the Mohicans, The Pathfinder, The Pioneers* and *The Prairie* the career of Cooper's greatest character. It is to him, even more than to the Indians, that the permanent quality of the series is due. They furnish some of the contrasts and the incidents, but he is both a real man and the epitome of the spirit of the pioneer who established the outposts of our civilization.

Cooper interrupted the Leatherstocking Series to write *The Wept of Wish-ton-Wish* (1829), a story of Connecticut in the late seventeenth century, in which Goffe, the regicide, appears to lead the villagers against the Indian attack. The most interesting character, however, is Conanchet, the son of Miantonimoh, chieftain of the Narragansetts. His struggle between his hatred of the whites and his personal devotion to Ruth Heathcote, who has befriended him, is well portrayed, and his death at the hands of Uncas, the Mohican chieftain, is in accord with the facts as given in John Winthrop's *Journal*. Cooper, however, used his right as a novelist to bring Conanchet back to his death on account of his plighted word to return after seeing his wife and child. In *Wyandotté* (1843), Cooper drew a more realistic picture of an Indian whose dual nature provides a moral contrast. As Wyandotté, he is a chieftain who saves Major Robert Willoughby and Maud Meredith, through gratitude. As "Nick" the degenerate Indian, he kills Captain Willoughby on account of beatings he has received from him. In either case he never forgets a friend or an enemy. *Wyandotté* is laid at the outbreak of the Revolution in what was later Tryon County, New York. As in *Lionel Lincoln*, the hero and his father are both officers in the British army. Maud Meredith, or Willoughby, as she is first called, is one of Cooper's best drawn women.

Cooper's trilogy, *Satanstoe* (1845), *The Chainbearer* (1845), and *The Redskins* (1846), belong partly to the fiction of the frontier and partly to the historical romance. About one third of *Satanstoe* and nearly all of *The Chainbearer* are laid in that region of New York centering at Albany with which Cooper was familiar. The inspiration of this trilogy was the desire of Cooper to serve the interests of the "patroons" or large landholders of New York State who were defending their inherited tenures against the desire of their tenants to own rather than to rent their land. This anti-rent agitation roused Cooper almost to fury, for all his instincts were those of the landholder, whose whole philosophy of life rests upon the sanctity of his title to what he considers the only form of property that conveys distinction. Cooper believed that a series of novels which would depict the hardships of the pioneers who had won their estates amid the perils of Indian attack and the lawlessness of the squatters, would convince his readers that the descendants of Cornelius Littlepage and Herman Mordaunt should be permitted to enjoy the fruits of their ancestors' foresight and courage. Naturally, the earliest of the series, *Satanstoe*, which centers around 1757, and in which the arguments concerning the anti-rent agitation hardly appear, is the best. It is indeed one of his great stories, though its best scenes, such as the rescue of Anneke Mordaunt by Corny Littlepage from the ice dam on the Hudson, and the attack of Abercrombie upon Ticonderoga are not, strictly speaking, scenes of the frontier. Critics of *Satanstoe* have not realized the art with which Cooper preserves, in the language of Corny Littlepage, who tells the story, just enough of the flavor of the eighteenth century to add to the reality of the picture. Anneke Mordaunt is one of his best women. The poise of this motherless young gentlewoman of old New York, who steers a straight course between the addresses of Colonel Bulstrode, the likable British officer, and those of Corny Littlepage, whom she loves and marries, is especially appealing. Susquesus, the Onandago, is one of Cooper's most successful pictures of Indian nature. He carries on through the three books, and the striking scene in which, as a man over one hundred years of age, he receives the Indians of his own scattered tribe, provides the one redeeming episode of *The Redskins*. This novel, laid in Cooper's own day, is almost unreadable, for the propaganda destroys it, but *The Chainbearer*, supposedly told by Mordaunt Littlepage, grandson of Cornelius, has some very good moments. Here the enemies of the Littlepages are not so much the Indians as the squatters, and the picture of the "Thousand-acres," as one family is called, provides a realistic portrait of the lower class of pioneers rather far in advance of its time. These are not the heroic type so often found in fiction, but the rough, even sordid, variety of which so many of the frontiersmen were examples.

The Oak Openings (1848), the last story of the frontier, is laid in Michigan at the outbreak of the War of 1812. The war is, however, merely the background for the flight of the Warings, led by Ben Boden, the bee hunter, in their efforts to escape the Indians. The novel is by no means one of Cooper's poorest, although the conversion of Scalping Peter, the tribeless chief, while almost too rapid for belief, is also too long drawn out for interest.

Cooper's Indians speak a language which was based upon his actual experiences in listening to speakers from different tribes, of which he tells us in more than one place. But whether correct or not, the speech of Uncas in which he explains why Chingachgook and he were wanderers on the face of the earth is supremely fitting:

"Once we slept where we could hear the salt lake speak in its anger. Then we were rulers and Sagamores over the land. But when a pale-face was seen on every brook, we followed the deer back to the river of our nation. The Delawares were gone. Few warriors of them all stayed to drink of the stream they loved. Then said my fathers, 'Here will we hunt. The waters of the river go into the salt lake. If we go toward the setting sun, we shall find streams that run into the great lakes of sweet water; there would a Mohican die, like fishes of the sea, in the clear springs. When the Manitto is ready, and shall say "come," we will follow the river to the sea, and take our own again.' Such, Delawares, is the belief of the children of the Turtle. Our eyes are on the rising, and not toward the setting sun. We know whence he comes, but we know not whither he goes. It is enough."

Those who harp upon Cooper's prolixity seem to forget his economy in other respects. Sufferers who have labored through hundreds of pages of recent fiction dealing with morbid analyses of the effects of mixed blood, should note how Cooper, having once mentioned the taint of Negro blood in Cora's mother, permits the reader to see for himself the attraction which this infusion of another and darker strain kindles in both Uncas and Magua.

The second great field of fiction which Cooper made his own produced no characters to rank with Leatherstocking. Yet among his eleven sea stories are several of his finest creations. In 1827 *The Red Rover* gave us another of those picturesque figures, in Captain Heidegger, which are a tribute to the perennial interest in the gentlemanly pirate. Cooper states in his preface that the incidents are imaginary, since America is poor in legend and tradition of the sea. The Red Rover, who has been made a pirate through his temerity in attacking an English naval officer who had insulted the Colonies, is a mysterious being, a copy in a way of the Pilot, and an example of that moral contrast which has its general appeal. His visit to the captain of the British man of war and his later victory over her are the high moments of the book. Harry Ark, or Wilder, or deLacey, is only one among many of Cooper's heroes whose parentage is settled in the last few pages.

Cooper continued in *The Water Witch* (1830) to lay the scene of his story in Colonial times. The most striking character, the so-called "Skimmer of the Seas," is again a "free trader," under which euphemistic name piracy was conducted in those days. His mistress, who poses in male attire, is a conventional character, just as "Roderick" was in *The Red Rover,* and the most faithfully drawn character is that of Alderman VanBeverout, through whom Cooper satirizes the commercial class for which he had so little admiration. The best scenes are those of the chase of the Skimmer's brigantine by the British man of war *Coquette,* and the striking rescue of the latter by the Skimmer when attacked by the French boats. This note of "blood is thicker than water" was struck more than once by Cooper and was usually effective.

In 1838 Cooper used the sea story to satirize social conditions in America and England of his own time, in *Homeward Bound.* The voyage from Portsmouth to New York is of interest now to the social historian, for the conversation of Edward and John Effingham, Americans of breeding, Edward's daughter Eve, Paul Powis, and the real and false Sir George Templetons gives us Cooper's opinions in copious doses. They are, from the point of view of fiction, only an interruption to the story, which has all the interest of the chase, even if the supposed reason for the pursuit of the *Montauk* by the British corvette *Foam* is mistaken. The landing on the coast of Africa, and the attack on the ship by the natives, is the best portion of the book. But no lover of Cooper would place either *Homeward Bound* or *Home as Found* (1838), its sequel, among his important work.

The Two Admirals (1842) is, however, certainly one of his great novels, and in some portions, notably the description of the battle of the French and English fleets, it remains unsurpassed in the language. Cooper, as often, is long in getting under way, and the lengthy account of the estate of Sir Wycherly Wychecombe and its final inheritance by his namesake from Virginia, who returns after many years to claim his rightful place, is of interest only as revealing a situation which may have given Thackeray an idea for *The Virginians.* But once launched on the sea, the story rises to epic grandeur. For the first time, in American fiction at least, Cooper marshalled the forces of two great fleets and, with the skill in word painting which has placed him among the first artists in the world, he brings us among the thunders of conflict, the agony of the dying and the cheers of the victors as though we were standing on the very deck of the *Plantagenet,* the flagship of Sir Gervaise Oakes, the British admiral. Intermingled with the conflict, and shaping its course, the storm that rules the waters and flings them into the guns of the men of war provides a background against which Cooper guides the ships with a surety that convinces even the most ignorant reader of his command of the technique of naval war. His long study of naval history had made him a master of the records of conflict on the ocean, but he was too great a novelist to depend for interest merely upon the accuracy of his knowledge. While we watch Admiral Oakes bringing his ships into their positions, we share his suspense, his deepening anxiety concerning the actions of his lifelong friend and subordinate, Admiral Bluewater, whose ships should long before have come to his help in the unequal contest. Cooper knew that suspense in the mind of a character, arising from his anxiety concerning the decision of another, is one of the strongest motives of fiction. He therefore laid the scene of his story in 1745, when Charles Edward, the young Pretender, had landed in Scotland. He made Bluewater a Jacobite, and he gave to him the difficult choice of being loyal to his friend and his duty or of being true to his allegiance to his rightful prince. There are few more thrilling moments in fiction than those in which Bluewater in the *Caesar* dashes in to the rescue of Oakes, who, caught between two fires, is replying to the broadsides of the French men of war. Bluewater receives a mortal wound while boarding *LePluton,* and his hesitation is forgotten.

The Two Admirals closes with one of Cooper's most effective scenes. Years after the battle, Sir Gervaise Oakes, whose mind has faltered, is brought into Westminster Abbey to pay his annual visit to the monument to Admiral Bluewater. He is staring vacantly at the figure, when a new party of visitors enters the chapel. Among them is Sir Wycherly Wychecombe, who had been with him in the great fight, and the sight of a strange yet remembered face kindles his memory into action. He springs to his feet and lives over again the supreme moment of his life. Then death claims him, as the admiral murmurs his old friend's name.

The dramatic quality of this scene proves once more that Cooper was not straying from his province when he attempted to write a play, even if the unfortunate conditions of the American theatre prevented the success of his one drama, *Upside Down; or, Philosophy in Petticoats,* which reached the stage of Burton's Chambers Street Theatre, New York, in

1850. But many years later Conan Doyle took from this scene in *The Two Admirals* the idea which became in his hands the one-act play of *Waterloo*, long a vehicle for Henry Irving. The many dramatizations of Cooper's novels by other hands, which include *The Spy*, *The Pilot*, *The Red Rover*, *The Water Witch*, *The Last of the Mohicans*, *The Pioneers*, *The Deerslayer*, *The Wept of Wish-ton-Wish*, and *The Bravo*, often in several versions, establish his claim to dramatic quality.

Perhaps Cooper realized his own ability in the narration of pursuit and the description of the sea-fight for they form the great attraction of *The Wing-and-Wing* (1842), deservedly one of his own favorites. It is laid in the Mediterranean in 1798–1799, a sea which, as he remarks truly, "has been the scene of more ruthless violence perhaps than any other portion of the globe." Certainly the adventures of Captain Raoul Yvard, of the French privateer *Feu Follet*, in avoiding the British ship *Proserpine*, his love story with Ghita Caraccioli, his capture and escape through the help of Ithuel Bolt, and his ultimate death form a more connected plot than is usual with Cooper. Ithuel Bolt is one of his best drawn characters. A native of New Hampshire, he has been impressed by the British, and he hates them bitterly. A mixture of shrewdness, honesty and chicanery, courage and common sense, he remains vividly in the memory. Nelson and Lady Hamilton appear in the background, but without distinction.

Cooper returned to his favorite New York for the beginning of his next sea story, *Afloat and Ashore* (1844). It is one of his very best. To anyone who remembers the fragrance of a boy and girl friendship, the story of Miles Wallingford and Lucy Hardinge must have a strong appeal. Starting in 1797 with the running away to sea of Miles and Rupert Hardinge, the character of the former is established through the hairbreadth escapes, wrecks, rescues, and voyages both in the Atlantic and Pacific. The capture of the *Crisis* by the Indians in the northwest and her recapture are done with Cooper's instinctive knowledge of the proper amount of detail. He should have brought the novel to a close, for the sequel, or second series of *Afloat and Ashore*, sometimes called *Miles Wallingford* (1844), repeats too often the incidents of the first. The interest of the love story wanes also. Yet Lucy Hardinge remains one of Cooper's real women. She blushes too much, it is true, but she can look a man in the face, and she really grows through the four volumes from girlhood to womanhood.

The Crater (1847) is one of Cooper's feeblest, for the story is submerged in social and political discussion. *Jack Tier* [3] (1848) is much better. While the possibility of "Jack Tier," in reality the wife of Stephen Spike, the captain of the *Molly Swash*, following her husband in the disguise of a sailor, is not great, she is one of the figures of Cooper who is remembered. Cooper's liberal attitude toward Mexico, for the novel is laid at the time of the Mexican War, is noteworthy, and the mysterious movements of Spike, who is bringing weapons to sell to the enemies of his country, are vividly described. *The Sea Lions* (1849) has some merit in the description of the contest between the rival captains for the possession of the seal island in the Antarctic regions. The character of Deacon Pratt, drawn from Cooper's own acquaintance with the natives of Sag Harbor, has the interest of caricature at least, and neither *The Sea Lions* nor *Jack Tier* deserves the neglect which has befallen it.

In the third field, that of the historical novel, Cooper's supremacy is not nearly so definite as in the fiction of the frontier or of the sea. He never surpassed *The Spy*, for he created no character in his other historical novels equal to Harvey Birch. In *Lionel Lincoln* (1825), laid at the beginning of the Revolution in Massachusetts, Cooper made the initial mistake of selecting for his hero an officer in the British army, and proceeded with a romance of crime, for which he had no especial ability. The mystery concerning the mad Sir Lionel, the father of the hero, is revealed in a confusing manner, and the misleading statements hinder the progress of the story without keeping up the suspense. There is a vivid description of the fight at Lexington and at Bunker Hill, and Cooper uses skilfully the secrecy incident upon the intrenchment of Dorchester Heights to cover Lionel Lincoln's escape from the American army. He knew, too, how to stimulate interest in a scene by describing the interest of those watching it, well illustrated by the account of the actions of the people in Boston while the preparations were being made for the attack on Breed's Hill. But the conversations in *Lionel Lincoln* are stilted, and the melodrama becomes at times unbearable.

It is a great mistake, however, and one frequently made, to dismiss Cooper's historical sense as inadequate. No one who has read *Satanstoe*, *The Chainbearer* and *The Redskins* should fail to see how Cooper is

---

[3] Printed as "The Islets of the Gulf; or, Rose Budd," *Graham's Magazine*, November, 1846–March, 1848.

best in the earliest of the three and weakest as he approaches his own time. In *Satanstoe* he puts us down in New York City in the middle of the eighteenth century, and his atmosphere, especially that of the theatre and of social life, is established in a masterly way. It is only when his thesis submerges the history that he begins to fail. It must be remembered, too, that twenty-four of his novels, about eighty per cent, are historical, and while another interest may be the prevailing one, the picture of a past civilization forms an unquestioned element in the greatness of *The Last of the Mohicans, The Red Rover, The Wept of Wish-ton-Wish, The Bravo, The Pathfinder, The Deerslayer, The Two Admirals, Wing-and-Wing,* and *Afloat and Ashore.* Like all historical novelists, Cooper was at his best when he was in sympathy with his material. When he dealt with the past of his beloved New York State in *The Spy, Satanstoe, The Deerslayer, The Last of the Mohicans, The Pathfinder, Afloat and Ashore,* or with the glories of the American or British navy in *The Pilot* or *The Two Admirals;* or when he sought and found a picturesque setting with which he could make himself familiar, as in *Wing-and-Wing,* or *The Bravo,* then he could make the past glow with color and life. But when, as in *Mercedes of Castile* (1840), he dealt with a civilization of which he knew little, he made an inevitable failure. The only interest of *Mercedes* lies in the voyage of Columbus, and that springs from Cooper's knowledge of the sea.

His skill and his limitations as an historical novelist are illustrated by the three books which came after he had been in Europe for five years and which have in their inception a certain unity. Cooper's European experiences made him even more sure of the advantages of democracy, and he conceived the idea of making these advantages patent by exposing the evils of oligarchy. He began with *The Bravo* (1831), laid in Venice during the decline in power of the republic. His hero, Jacopo Frontoni, is a concrete example of the evils of secret government by an oligarchy, not responsible to the people. His revolt and execution are only two of many striking incidents which portray the mystery and the espionage of Venetian life of that time. The race of the gondolas, the escapes, captures and recaptures, the outcries and sudden impulsive movements of crowds are done in Cooper's best manner. But *The Heidenmauer* (1832) is one of his distinct failures. It is laid in the Palatinate at the time when Luther's doctrines were becoming active. The pictures of the opposing forces of the nobility and the monastic orders are both conventional, and there is no character who comes alive. There are no great scenes to make up for this lack; the burning of the monastery is the nearest approach to one. *The Headsman* (1833), a story of Switzerland in the beginning of the eighteenth century, is much better. Here he was attacking the small-town mind, one of his most cherished enemies, and he depicts vividly the tragedy of Balthazar, the headsman of Berne, who loathes his office, but is compelled by tradition and public opinion to follow in the steps of his ancestors. The horror of his reputed son, Sigismund, at the thought of succeeding his father, and the grim joke which makes Melchior de Willading object to Sigismund, who is in reality the son of the Prince of Genoa, reveals the artificiality of rank. Cooper took the opportunity to give us splendid descriptions of Lake Leman and the snow storm on the mountains. The characters are quite as well drawn as those in *The Bravo*, especially Marguerite, Balthazar's wife, who, in two scenes, that of Balthazar's trial for murder and that of her daughter's wedding, rises almost to first rank through the brevity of her tragic utterance.

Cooper, like Scott and Stevenson, never bothered about anachronisms. In the Introduction to *Lionel Lincoln* he remarks:

> In this tale there are one or two anachronisms . . . as they are believed to be quite in character, connected with circumstances much more probable than facts, and to possess all the harmony of poetic coloring, the author is utterly unable to discover the reason they are not true.

In following the instinct of a romantic story-teller, he was quite correct. His anachronisms, notwithstanding Mark Twain's amusing sketch, are not usually noticeable, and his successful historical novels are justly scornful of dates.

The fourth group, in which his social and political theories run riot, contain his most lamentable failures, such as *The Monikins* (1835), *Home as Found* (1838), *The Redskins*, and his last story, *The Ways of the Hour* (1850). But even in this vicious attack on trial by jury, Cooper could not completely fail. The scene in which Mildred Millington, an insane woman accused of murder, by sheer power of will and cleverness tricks the star witness for the prosecution into confession of perjury, might make any modern writer of detective stories green with envy. Cooper's familiarity with legal processes, won through his many libel suits against the Whig newspapers of New York, gives a verisimilitude to this trial scene in *The Ways of the Hour*.

When Cooper closed his vigorous struggle against the powers of Whiggery, oligarchy and mediocrity, on September 14, 1851, Poe had just died and *The Scarlet Letter* had just been written. With the quarrels and criticisms which disturbed his life and which are now forgotten, we have little to do. He had the social courage to love his own country best, and he never hesitated to criticize her when he thought it would be for her good. Consequently he had his detractors at home and abroad. We are concerned with his contribution to literature. Like all great writers of romance, he is easy to parody, and the discovery of his faults requires no critical dexterity. Prolixity, diffuseness, lack of logic, the weakness of his "females," all these have been mentioned so often that they hardly need repetition. His greatest fault, the endowing of his characters with rotund, oratorical periods, becomes more glaring, of course, as the generations who finished their sentences disappear, conversation becomes interjectional, and sentences of more than three words are looked upon with suspicion.

He repeats his plots frequently. So often does a character have some mystery concerning his parentage that we begin to suspect even the most orthodox couples and the most impeccable orphans. The significant fact remains, however, that while this motive appears in eleven of his novels, it is only the trained critic who objects to it. So fertile is he in changing the circumstances that his readers can easily disregard it. For, after all, one does not read Cooper for plot, if by plot we understand a relationship of characters and story working out logically to a destined end. We read him for the narration of stirring events and the description of striking scenes. The sea and the forest are his great backgrounds, not mute, but living forces, playing their parts in the fortunes of the characters. Nature is neither subordinated into a mere interpretative function of man's thoughts, nor is it ever overpowering. Cooper's characters view Nature with appreciation and reverence, but do not apologize for their existence nor sentimentalize natural objects into their own life stories. It simply forms an adequate background for their actions. When conflict comes, they control it. To his great characters the secrets of the forest are open; the gloom of the impenetrable thickets speaks a message to Hawkeye and to Chingachgook which spells safety to them and their charges. The tempest or the rocks that menace the lives of their pursuers mean safety to the Pilot or the Red Rover. Never does Cooper make the mistake of his dreary imitators who subordinate their human characters to the waves. For that way boredom lies.

This supremacy of his characters over their surroundings is not accidental. It springs from his conception of art, which was to write about those things which are important, those scenes which are thrilling, those souls which have in them some flavor of nobility. In his great books he held fast to this conception, springing from his own nature. For it was the innate nobility of Cooper which led to his idealization of the "noble savage." He deals nearly always with chieftains, and his conception of Indian life as a feudal organization makes for literary success. The really magnificent scene when Uncas is revealed to the Delawares by the token of the turtle on his breast, and the voice of the young chieftain rekindles the power of memory in the old chieftain Tamerund, until he recognizes the grandson of his friend the older Uncas, is inspired by Cooper's understanding of the dramatic urge of the call of a lost leader. This particular tribe of the Delawares had fallen in the eyes of the others by their neutrality in the French and Indian war and by the tradition that they are "women." Uncas, a chieftain of the Mohicans, another tribe of the once great confederacy of the Lenni-Lenape, brings them back once more to their own self-respect through his ringing appeal to save Cora by their attack upon the Hurons. The union of the personal and the tribal instincts into one powerful motive sweeps them into victory.

His finest sea stories deal with admirals and captains, commanders all. The Pilot, the Red Rover, Sir Gervaise Oakes, Admiral Bluewater, know how to make themselves obeyed. In the lower ranks, the characters we remember best, like Long Tom Coffin, Neb Clawbonny, Ithuel Bolt, are distinguished by their loyalty to their leader. Loyalty, Cooper knew, is an appealing theme, and in *The Spy* he made it his own. But there had to be something in Cooper which created the glow of patriotism in which the soul of Harvey Birch was forged.

Balzac's tribute to Cooper has often been quoted, but his very praise, "If Cooper had succeeded in the painting of character to the same extent that he did in the painting of the phenomena of nature, he would have uttered the last word of our art," has led by implication to a belittling of Cooper's creation of character. Even discriminating critics, apparently afraid to credit too much to an American, have taken refuge in qualified apology. But in reality there is no need. Already in this discussion the reality of his great characters has been established as well as their secure position in the portrait gallery of American fiction. Leatherstocking and Uncas and Chingachgook have passed beyond, into the portrait gallery of the world, but what a longer list of Indians remains—Magua, Susquesus, Conanchet, Wyandotté and others—individualized, shaded into good and evil. How much more real are his young sea captains, Harry Wilder, Miles Wallingford, Raoul Yvard, or his young colonials like Corny Littlepage, than the young heroes of *Waverley* or *The Antiquary*. Even his women, feeble as they often are, have among them notable creations. Judith and Hetty Hutter, Elizabeth Temple, Maud Willoughby, Anneke Mordaunt, Lucy Hardinge, Katherine Plowden, Cora Munro—they are all real and all different. Cooper's worst women are imitations of the conventional romantic heroine of British fiction, like Alice Dunscombe; his best have that quality of independence, of initiative, which the very circumstances of American life developed, especially on the frontier.

One reason that Cooper's characters stand out so sharply is that some of the greatest scenes are those in which an individual fights against great odds for his life. Bound to the stake, or alone on the quarterdeck, or shut up in the blockhouse, his heroes struggle with the Indians, or with the elements, in that effort at self-preservation which is one of the most certain motives to win sympathy. Cooper instinctively chose not only this motive, but others, such as patriotism, loyalty, family affection, tribal feeling, which appeal to the largest number of readers. If he had been able to treat the motive of love with the same skill—but Balzac has appropriated the most fitting phrase.

It was partly because Cooper treated universal motives that his novels were soon translated into nearly all cultivated tongues. In 1833, Morse, the painter and inventor, wrote to a friend that Cooper's works "are published as soon as he produces them in thirty-four different places in Europe. They have been seen by American travellers in the languages of Turkey and Persia, in Constantinople, in Egypt, at Jerusalem, at Ispahan." [4]

Cooper's fame came rather from the appeal to the reader than from critical favor. His controversial writings hurt him in France and England, and it soon became difficult for his work to be judged objectively

[4] Lounsbury, T. R., *James Fenimore Cooper*, p. 77.

there. But the impressive lists of translations into German, French, Italian and Spanish prove that he became in every sense a world artist.[5] His influence upon foreign writers is not so easy to estimate. Goethe certainly was affected by *The Pioneers* in his *Novelle* (1827) and German novelists like "Charles Sealsfield," Friedrich Struberg, and Baldwin Möllhausen, who actually lived in America, developed a school of frontier fiction directly to be attributed to Cooper's work.

Cooper's influence upon his own countrymen belongs to a later chapter. When he died, the romantic idealistic wave had long been on the ebb. But for thirty years his tireless imagination had delighted the reading world by taking them into every continent and every sea in the distinguished company of the children of his fancy. With a creative instinct as sure as the Killdeer of Hawkeye or the compass of the Pilot, he left to others the morbid, the sentimental and the banal. He could not have done this if he had not possessed that quality which made him equally at home in the forests of New York or the drawing rooms of Paris, that self-respect without which no artist long endures.

[5] See especially R. E. Spiller and P. C. Blackburn, *A Descriptive Bibliography of the Writings of James Fenimore Cooper* (1934); Barba, P. A., "Cooper in Germany," *Ger. Amer. Annals*, Jan.–Feb., 1914; Morris, G. D., *Fenimore Cooper et Edgar Poe, d'après la critique française du dix neuvième siècle* (Paris, 1912); Ferguson, J. deL., *American Literature in Spain* (New York, 1916), pp. 32–54 and 208–213.

CHAPTER V

EDGAR ALLAN POE AND THE ESTABLISHMENT OF THE SHORT STORY

THE years 1829 to 1832 are landmarks in the history of the short story. At that time appeared almost simultaneously, in France and America, two artists in each country who, while not inventing the short story, modified it so that it henceforth became a definite and well recognized form. Each added qualities of his own, but in general the gain came in unity of effect and in variety of material.

Prosper Mérimée and Balzac antedate Hawthorne and Poe so slightly that there can be little question of influence. In 1829 six stories of Mérimée appeared, "Mateo Falcone," "The Vision of Charles XI," "The Taking of the Redoubt," "Tamango," "Federigo," and "The Pearl of Toledo." The first of these is distinctly a story of character, but a careful study of the remainder indicates that the short story in France grew not out of the essay but out of the tale. Balzac's first stories, "The Executioner (El Verdugo)," "Adieu," "Sarrazine," "A Passion in the Desert" and "An Episode under the Terror," came in 1830. These are stories of situation, sometimes of a horrible nature. Between their work and that of Poe there is some similarity, but it is rather in tone than in plot. There is little kinship between the Frenchmen and Hawthorne, in either plot or tone so far as this early work is concerned. Hawthorne, like Balzac, began in 1830, in *The Salem Gazette,* with "The Hollow of the Three Hills," while Poe's first short story, "Metzengerstein," did not appear until 1832, in the *Philadelphia Saturday Courier.* Yet, since Hawthorne's first great novel was written during the year after Poe's death, it is best to treat the younger artist first.

His romanticism, like that of the Frenchmen, was wholehearted in its assertion of the writer's freedom to seek his themes anywhere. Yet among the many critical stupidities which have obscured the contribution of Poe to American fiction is the assumption of his exotic quality. It is not hard to disprove this error so far as his fiction is concerned. Three of his stories, "The Gold Bug," "The Oblong Box," and "The Balloon-Hoax," are laid wholly or partly near Charleston; "A Tale of the Ragged Mountains" takes place near Charlottesville, Virginia; "Landor's Cottage" is distinctly said to be near New York City and, while "The Domain of Arnheim" and "The Landscape Garden" are not located, their owner, Mr. Ellison, is clearly an American. "The Sphinx," "Mellonta Tauta," "X-ing a Paragrab" and "The Strange Case of M. Valdemar" are probably connected with New York City. "The Elk" is definitely laid on the Wissahickon Creek in Philadelphia. *Arthur Gordon Pym* starts near New Bedford, Connecticut, and *The Journal of Julius Rodman* is an account of pioneering in the West. As has been shown [1] Poe was constantly concerned in his stories and essays with native material.

But of even more importance is Poe's relation to the major impulse of American life of his day. He was born in 1809, six years after Jefferson bought Louisiana, and he died in 1849, when Polk had carried our territory to the Pacific. In that period of material expansion Poe was exploring in poetry and fiction the limits of the human soul. The intrepidity of the pioneer who faced death daily, the restlessness which led him to abandon a field as soon as it was conquered, are matched by the daring of the artist who "dreamed dreams no mortal ever dared to dream before" and who ventured even into those studies of insanity where he lived among beings whose emotional torments were reflections of the unceasing terror of his own life.

It is not the place in this survey to discuss the details of that life. Most of the problems have arisen from the deliberate perversion of facts by his biographers, beginning with himself, or by the invention of theories concerning his nature which reveal not his impotency but that of his critics. There is no mystery about the real Poe, the hard working man of letters, proud as a demon, yet, in order to make a living, descending to many of the tricks he despised.

It is this duality in Poe that must always be borne in mind, and which he has revealed to us in "The Imp of the Perverse." As his friend Willis said, "He wrote with fastidious difficulty, and in a style too much above the popular level to be well paid." Yet no service is done to Poe or to

---

[1] Campbell, Killis, "The Backgrounds of Poe," in *The Mind of Poe and Other Studies* (Cambridge, 1933). See also the present writer's *The Soul of America* (Philadelphia, 1932).

criticism that does not attempt to separate his great stories from his trivial ones, which dire necessity made him publish. Above all, generalities are most dangerous concerning Poe, and in consequence he has had more generalities written about him than any other American author of his day.

The most helpful classification of Poe's sixty-eight short stories divides them into four main groups: the Arabesque, the Grotesque, the Ratiocinative and the Descriptive. In 1840 Poe published his *Tales of the Grotesque and Arabesque,* terms which he may have derived from an article by Walter Scott,[2] but which he used so frequently in his fiction and criticism that he made them his own. In a letter [3] written to T. W. White, April 30, 1835, he describes the kind of story most in demand by periodicals of the time. Their nature, he says, consists "in the ludicrous heightened into the grotesque, the fearful colored into the horrible, the witty exaggerated into the burlesque, and the singular heightened into the strange and the mystical."

The first and third of these qualities he incorporated into the Grotesque stories. They are twenty-two in number:

"The Duc de l'Omelette" (1832), "A Tale of Jerusalem" (1832), "Loss of Breath" (1832), "Bon-Bon" (1832), "Lionizing" (1835), "Four Beasts in One" (1836), "Mystification" (1837), "How to Write a Blackwood Article" (1838), "A Predicament" (1838), "The Devil in the Belfry" (1839), "The Man That Was Used Up" (1839), "Why the Little Frenchman Wears His Hand in a Sling" (1840), "The Business Man" (1840), "Never Bet the Devil Your Head" (1841), "Three Sundays in a Week" (1841), "Diddling Considered as One of the Exact Sciences" (1843), "The Spectacles" (1844), "The Balloon-Hoax" (1844), "The Angel of the Odd" (1844), "The Literary Life of Thingum-Bob, Esq." (1844), "The System of Dr. Tarr and Prof. Fether" (1845), "X-ing a Paragrab" (1849). The final titles are given here, several stories appearing with other titles in periodicals at these dates.

It will be noticed at once that no one of the great stories of Poe is included in this list, and that fifteen of the twenty-two were written by 1841. Four of the five stories of 1832 are Grotesques.[4] In short, they

---

[2] "On the Supernatural in Fictitious Composition," *Foreign Quarterly Review,* I (July, 1827), 60–98.

[3] See Napier Wilt, "Poe's Attitude Toward his Tales: A New Document," *Modern Philology,* XXV (August, 1927), 101–105.

[4] For the original forms see the reprints in *Edgar Allan Poe and the Philadelphia Saturday Courier,* edited by J. G. Varner (1933).

were written primarily to sell, and he did not treat the material seriously. Although he rewrote "A Decided Loss" as "Loss of Breath" and "A Bargain Lost" as "Bon-Bon" before he republished them, there is little improvement in the new versions. While they are often amusing, there is no genial humor, only a sardonic satire. Yet even these stories have been imitated by French realists like Eugène Mouton, whose "Crapaud Blanc" or "Le Squellette homogène" are distinctly in Poe's grotesque manner.

It is quite a different art which created the Arabesques. Within the thirty-six tales included in this group occur some of the very greatest short stories in the literature of the world. They are the products either of Poe's inspired imagination or of his fertile fancy, and while irony appears in a few cases, like "King Pest," he never loses, in the Arabesques, respect for his material. That material is selected with care on account of its strangeness, its appeal to the faculty of wonder. But if the material is romantic, the background and setting are usually painted with realistic detail. It has perhaps not been sufficiently recognized how wide was his experience of places. Through his early life in Richmond, his brief stay in Boston, his army service near Charleston, his dark days in Baltimore, his brighter years in Philadelphia and his struggles against disaster in New York, he became acquainted with the principal cities of the East. His years at Charlottesville as well as his army service gave him an opportunity to see rural landscape, while, of course, his boyhood in Scotland and England widened his horizon.

A chronological arrangement of the Arabesques,

"Metzengerstein" (1832), "Manuscript Found in a Bottle" (1833), "The Assignation" (1834), "Berenice" (1835), "Morella" (1835), "The Unparalleled Adventure of One Hans Pfaall" (1835), "King Pest" (1835), "Shadow—A Parable" (1835), "Silence—A Fable" (1838), "Ligeia" (1838), "The Fall of the House of Usher" (1839), "William Wilson" (1839), "The Conversation of Eiros and Charmion" (1839), "The Man of the Crowd" (1840), "A Descent into the Maelstrom" (1841), "The Island of the Fay" (1841), "The Colloquy of Monos and Una" (1841), "Eleonora" (1842), "The Oval Portrait" (1842), "The Masque of the Red Death" (1842), "The Pit and the Pendulum" (1843), "The Tell-Tale Heart" (1843), "The Black Cat" (1843), "A Tale of the Ragged Mountains" (1844), "The Premature Burial" (1844), "Mesmeric Revelation" (1844), "The Thousand and Second Tale of Scheherazade" (1845), "The Power of Words" (1845), "Some Words with a Mummy" (1845),

"The Imp of the Perverse" (1845), "The Facts in the Case of M. Valdemar" (1845), "The Sphinx" (1846), "The Cask of Amontillado" (1846), "Mellonta Tauta" (1849), "Hop Frog" (1849), "Von Kempelen and His Discovery" (1849),

reveals strikingly that the most significant period of Poe's fiction lay from 1835 to 1843. Nearly two thirds of the Arabesques deal with death, suggested, feared, described, or discussed. The death of a beautiful woman, the favorite theme of his poetry, appears again in several forms, in "Berenice," "Morella," "Ligeia," "Eleonora," and "The Oval Portrait." Sometimes death stalks through the story personified, as in "The Masque of the Red Death"; sometimes he fills us with awe by the shadow of his coming, as in "Shadow" or "The Fall of the House of Usher"; sometimes he is linked in our memory with a dreadful spectacle as in "Metzengerstein." Often the threat of death is used to establish a mood of terror, as in "The Premature Burial" or "The Pit and the Pendulum." Sometimes death is linked with the motive of revenge, as in "Hop Frog" or "The Cask of Amontillado." Twice we are led into the after life, in "The Colloquy of Monos and Una" and "The Conversation of Eiros and Charmion." Usually it is the death of the body, but in "William Wilson" it is the death of the spirit. Death is nearly always triumphant, but in Poe's own favorite, "Ligeia," the human will to live triumphs, if only for a moment, over the universal enemy.

Allied to the death motive, the theme of the supernatural is established in twenty-two of the Arabesques. In most of these the effect produced is that of terror. A short story is best adapted to produce this effect, for terror is dependent upon apprehension and shock and therefore, strictly speaking, it should not form the basis of a novel. When it is used as the motive of a longer work, the shocks, in order not to fail in appeal, must rise constantly in their intensity, and consequently they tend to become more and more startling till the effect degenerates by reason of excessive improbability. Poe realized this, and in his longest prose tale, *The Narrative of Arthur Gordon Pym*, the supernatural is not made the basis of the story but is brought in only at the end. At least five phases of the supernatural are found represented in his short stories. The description of the spirit world and of the relations of human beings with it appears in such stories as "Eleonora," "The Colloquy of Monos and Una," and "Shadow"; the denial of a natural law is developed in "Ligeia" or "Berenice." "William Wilson," "Metzengerstein" and "The Masque of the Red Death" are allegorical. The exaggeration of some natural law or process till it passes beyond the limits of reason is the basis of "Silence" or "The Tell-Tale Heart," and the abnormal connection between the seat of life and some external agency appears in "The Oval Portrait."

Classification, of course, is useful chiefly as a means of calling attention to variety; and this classification of the supernatural stories can hardly lay claim to the quality of complete exclusiveness. In his short story work, Poe used many and various methods. Generalizations, therefore, are dangerous, for often in the treatment of a single theme he is found to differ radically. "Eleonora" and "Berenice," for example, both deal with sorrow at the death of a beautiful woman, the theme which Poe declared to be the supreme topic of art. The effect of the former is to produce the sensation of beauty of the most ethereal kind—the supernatural element is introduced by suggestion, the message from the spirit world comes like an immaterial sigh from the spirit of his departed love. Delicacy, abstraction, atmosphere, are the notes most prominent. In "Berenice" the sensation most definite is that of horror; the means are material, the supernatural element is brought in with a shock not only to the credulity but also to the good taste of the reader, as Poe himself understood.

For the explanation of this difference in treatment we must turn to a sentence in "Eleonora" itself:

The question is not yet settled, whether much that is glorious, whether all that is profound—does not spring from disease of thought—from moods of mind exalted at the expense of the general intellect.

When the mood is spiritual, as in "Eleonora," the effect is artistic, when the mood is simply horrible and revolting, as in "Berenice," the thought becomes diseased, and the intellect, being subverted to the mood, has no restraining influence. This accounts for the wildness, the undue emotional or moody emphasis in many of Poe's stories, as well as for those lapses from artistic sanity, such as "The Facts in the Case of M. Valdemar," where the supernatural is degraded and the art becomes almost mechanical. But this temporary suspension of the laws of the general intellect has given rise to some of Poe's finest effects. With the sure instinct of the artist, he selected for treatment the most profound impulse in man's nature, that of self-preservation, but he went beyond the preservation of mere physical life and attacked the citadel of spiritual being, the integrity of human identity. Poe knew how often history records the sacrifice by suicide of physical life in order to avert madness, by which identity is lost. In the very first sentence of "The Tell-Tale Heart":

"True, nervous,—very, very dreadfully nervous I had been and am; but why will you say that I am mad?"

he strikes the note in its most obvious form. Not so obvious, perhaps, is the reason for his interest in the abnormal. But with the record of his dead brother and his living sister before his eyes, and with his own lesion of the brain, he must have lived in constant terror of losing his mental control. When the terror could no longer be borne, he sought oblivion in drink from the consciousness of his own identity. In one sense, it was avoiding insanity by a milder form of insanity.

Is it any wonder, considering the human instinct to deal with those matters which are forbidden, that he should combine this problem of identity with his favorite theme, the loss of a beautiful woman, in those studies, "Morella," "Ligeia," "Eleonora," in which the problem is solved for good or evil by the persistence of individuality in another form? In "Morella" the hero tells us "the notion of that identity *which at death is or is not lost for ever*—was to me, at all times, a consideration of intense interest." Morella, the dead wife, lives again in her child, until at the daughter's baptism the husband utters her mother's name, when she dies. In "Ligeia" the first wife returns and not only takes the form of Rowena, the second, who has died in her turn, but changes the physical appearance of Rowena to her own. These changes in "Morella" and "Ligeia" are wrought in a mood of terror, but in "Eleonora" the voice of the woman who has died comes like a benediction to the lover who has taken Ermengarde in her place, and the transfer of identity is made in peace.

In "The Fall of the House of Usher" the identity is first established between Roderick Usher and the house itself—then his fear of the decay of the building deepens into a fear of the termination of the family, a loss of racial identity. "The Haunted Palace," inserted in the story, continues in verse the theme of the ruin of the intellect through the symbolism of the decay of the house. Then the narrator notices the similarity between the twin brother and sister and the "sympathies of a scarcely intelligible nature" which had existed between them. Here is again a form of identity which the sister's premature interment apparently destroys, but which triumphs when her spirit calls Roderick Usher to her from the other world.

Poe next carried this theme of identity into that other world. In "The Colloquy of Monos and Una" the senses lose their identity. "The taste and the smell were inextricably confounded, and became one sentiment, abnormal and intense." Sight became sound—"sound sweet or discordant as the matters presenting themselves at my side were light or dark in shade." A sixth sense, that of duration, usurps the place of the others, till the body of Una comes to the grave, when "the light of enduring Love" for a moment illumines the place. But finally all individual entity is lost in that of time and place. In "Mesmeric Revelation," on the other hand, Poe reveals through the utterance of a man in a mesmeric trance the attitude of one who believes in the preservation of identity even after death. The mysticism of Poe did not lead to the absorption of the individual in God. That to him would be "an action of God returning upon itself—a purposeless and futile action. Man is a creature. Creatures are thoughts of God. It is the nature of thought to be irrevocable." Poe's conception of the relations of man to his Creator does not lose sight of the dignity which the freedom of the human will secures. Divine volition could have had its way completely, and does have it, in the inorganic life; but in organic life it permits, by the very complexity which produces violations of law, the possibility of pain. Pain is real and necessary to happiness. "Positive pleasure is a mere idea. To be happy at any one point we must have suffered at the same. . . . The pain of the primitive life of Earth is the sole basis of the bliss of the ultimate life in Heaven." Thus in 1844 Poe expressed the idea of relativity in human happiness. It was not, of course, original with him, but he put it forcibly, and it is to be noticed that there is no railing of the individual at his Creator for the inevitable pain of this life. In this Poe was ahead of his time, and he points forward in his fiction to that glorification of the individual's responsibility which was to flower in drama in Moody and O'Neill.

In contrast to the stories which dwell upon the different forms in which identity is preserved, "William Wilson" presents a study of the terrible effects of the separation of moral and physical identity. The namesake whom William Wilson meets at school is given reality by a gradual development of the struggle in Wilson's soul between admira-

tion and dislike for his schoolmate. How closely Poe follows in this concrete relationship the more subtle ebb and flow in the power of the conscience over human action, the story alone can reveal. The low voice of
the second William Wilson, his willingness to forego public triumphs
over his namesake if only *he* is conscious of them, his dramatic appearance only at crucial moments in Wilson's path of evil, his concealment
of his countenance until the climax of the story when Wilson, maddened
.by drink, plunges his sword through the bosom of his victim—all are
planned with the art that conceals art, to produce the destined effect.
That effect is best expressed in Poe's own words:

Not a thread in all his raiment—not a line in all the marked and singular linea-
ments of his face which was not, even in the most absolute identity, mine own.
    It was Wilson: but he spoke no longer in a whisper, and I could have fancied
that I myself was speaking while he said:
    "You have conquered, and I yield. Yet henceforward art thou also dead—
dead to the World, to Heaven, and to Hope! In me didst thou exist—and in
my death, see by this image, which is thine own, how utterly thou hast murdered thyself."

It is the supreme triumph of the moral over the sensual life of the individual, the triumph of the principle of identity, which has been defied
and takes its own revenge.
    This group of stories, unified through Poe's brilliant presentation of
the dark mysteries that through all time have accompanied those who
search beneath the superficial to analyze the sources of life, are the greatest of his fictions. As the Arabesques are the finest of his stories, so this
series of excursions in the "ultimate dim Thule" are his supreme achievement in that division of his work. Their excellence is due not only to
their originality, either of conception or combination of ideas, but also to
the clarity with which he described states of mind which passed the
limits of ordinary comprehension. The best way to appreciate his greatness is to compare him to the triteness or cloudiness of his contemporary,
Bronson Alcott, who was also dealing with problems of the unknown.
To Poe the name "transcendentalist" was a red rag, and although he remained blind to the greatest exponents of the school, he is to be forgiven,
for he knew instinctively that, for the purposes of fiction at least, he was
on the right track.
    For the supernatural, to be effective, must be at least momentarily
believed. A sensation, or at least a belief in the possibility of the elements

out of which a sensation is composed, is a powerful adjunct to the appeal of a short story of this nature. Mere belief is not enough, however, for we may believe in the possibility of events and yet remain passive on account of our lack of interest in the sensations. To vitalize the sensations there must be an emotion in the reader which is best secured by a concrete symbol upon which the emotion may center. That is why the figure of the pestilence in "The Masque of the Red Death," or the form of the dead wife in "Ligeia" is so powerful; why the voices of the dead multitude in "Shadow" produce so great an effect; why even the teeth of Berenice, horrible as they are, fasten emotion to sensation and fix them both in memory.

Another group of the Arabesques consists of Poe's excursions into the domain of science. Contemporary interest led him into a study of the effects of hypnotism in "The Facts in the Case of M. Valdemar," one of his failures to distinguish the point at which horror changes to mere repulsion. "Some Words with a Mummy" reflects his interest in galvanism; "Hans Pfaall" is on the border line between the Arabesque and the Grotesque, a half-serious attempt to match himself with those who had written about journeys to the moon. But Poe, like other writers of the nineteenth century, preferred to satirize the dogmatic claims of science, and this group of the Arabesques rarely rises to the height of "The Descent into the Maelstrom," where the interest indeed lies rather in the establishment of the mood than in the accuracy of the details.

Yet the relations of Poe to his imitators in the field of the scientific romance would furnish material for a volume. In order to estimate it properly, it would be necessary not only to compare his work with that of his imitators, especially Jules Verne in France, but also to trace back the path of possible mutual sources in the romantic school of the late eighteenth century in England. There seems to be, however, a decided difference between Poe's scientific romance and that of the French school. It has not perhaps been observed that Poe was both preceded and followed by writers of scientific romance who were concerned largely with establishing probability by means of detailed accounts of facts; while Poe spent his chief strength upon those imaginative flights such as the ending of *Arthur Gordon Pym*. If one traces, for example, the romantic accounts of voyages to the moon of which Cyrano de Bergerac and Voltaire and Lamartine had given examples, it is to be noticed that the imagination is hardly kept in check at all by objective reality. With

Defoe, on the contrary, the reality of objective detail is of importance, and the art of Defoe is spent largely in the endeavor to secure probability. Poe was concerned with probability, of course, but his methods included a much wider knowledge of modern science than Defoe, and emphasis has been laid by recent writers [5] upon his contribution in this direction. Poe's logic and clarity have impressed French critics, however, so greatly that they have, relatively speaking, underestimated the importance of his imaginative contribution. It is really not the accuracy of his scientific details for which he is to be most commended. Poe, as a matter of fact, hardly took them seriously. In "Hans Pfaall," for example, he introduces humorous and grotesque elements and really negatives the whole scientific atmosphere of his story by bringing the return messenger from the moon to the earth without any explanation whatever. Were he living now, he would take great satisfaction in knowing that the dirigible balloon R-34 came over in 1919 in exactly the number of hours in which he had brought his own balloon over the Atlantic Ocean. But Poe knew himself that the marvelous passage at the end of *Arthur Gordon Pym* was greater than the pseudo-scientific romance that he had created.

The methods by which Jules Verne made use of Poe's ideas illustrates to a certain degree the return of the impulse of the scientific romance upon itself. Like Defoe he is largely concerned with the establishing of probability. In his "Un Drame dans les Airs" a madman takes charge of a balloon, it is true, but he reasons lucidly in his conduct of it. In his *Cinq Semaines en Ballon* all the realistic details are given. Most interesting, perhaps, is his sequel to *Arthur Gordon Pym, Le Sphinx des Glaces*. He continues the story by reviving some of the survivors, follows the path of Pym, but, when they get to the island Tsalal, Verne departs from his model. There is no white terror, and when they approach the isle the supernatural elements do not appear. Verne dismisses them by concluding that Pym had hallucinations, and that the great white figure was a magnetic mountain with the form of a sphinx. This is only one of the instances in literature in which realism has attempted to destroy through its efforts at probability a great romantic creation. If any other evidence were needed to prove that Verne wore his pseudo-science with a solemn air, it is his derivation of the dramatic climax of

[5] Lemonnier, L., "Edgar Poe et le Roman scientifique français," *La Grande Revue*, XXXIV (August, 1930), 214–223.

his *Tour du Monde en quatre-vingts Jours,* from Poe's "Three Sundays in a Week"; or his story of "Docteur Ox" from a combination of "The Devil in the Belfry" and "Eiros and Charmion." Poe would not have mixed those two notes.

There are six Ratiocinative stories, two of which, "The Oblong Box" and "Thou Art the Man," are really burlesques of the detective story and might perhaps be classed among the Grotesques. But the four great tales, "The Murders in the Rue Morgue" (1841), "The Mystery of Marie Rogêt" (1842), "The Gold Bug" (1843), and "The Purloined Letter" (1844), are masterpieces of their kind. They were not the first stories of ratiocination, and Poe had evidently read Voltaire and some of the similar tales that appeared in *Blackwood's Magazine.* But Poe differs from these earlier writers and from the hosts of his imitators in several ways. The great mass of detective stories fail because there really is no problem; the efforts of the writers are devoted to throwing dust in the eyes of the reader and persuading him there is some mystery concerning a crime, for which, however, there is usually no motive. The result is mere irritation. But Poe always provides a problem, and there is never any attempt to deceive. On the contrary, Poe identifies the reader with the gradual unfolding of the solution until he secures that coöperation between writer and reader which means success. Poe brought to this work not only a keen analytical mind and mathematical powers of a high order, but also imagination, and it is this combination which he places before us in "The Purloined Letter." Here Dupin, the analyst, is at his best, even more truly a character than in "The Murders in the Rue Morgue." Here again Poe differs from his successors. Dupin is a real person; his imitations are mere names. In "The Purloined Letter" we are made aware through the appeal for help by the Prefect that a letter has been stolen from "an exalted personage," and that the thief, the Minister D——, is known but is protected by the danger which the disclosure of the letter would create; the problem is to secure the return of the letter secretly. Poe therefore apparently gives up at once the most interesting feature of such a search, the discovery of the robber. He also discards with scorn the mechanical methods of search in which Conan Doyle and others revel. The Prefect has examined D——'s house thoroughly, and the letter has not been found on the premises or upon his person. Thus "The Purloined Letter" starts where the usual story ends. Dupin proceeds to study the character of D——. D—— is a mathematician, also a poet, therefore he is dangerous, for he will evidently not hide the letter in any usual place. Dupin visits D——'s lodgings, sees a half-torn letter carelessly left in a rack, and decides that D—— has chosen to protect his theft by leaving it where the police, whose limitations are implied, would leave it undisturbed. Here a lesser artist would have ended the story. But Dupin does not take the letter at once. He observes it carefully, returns the next day with a facsimile, arranges for a disturbance in the street, and, while D——'s attention is engaged, substitutes the false for the real letter. Here, at the very end, Poe provides a motive for Dupin's interest beyond that of the mere detective. D—— has been using his power over a woman for political blackmail. Not knowing that his power has left him, he will again try to persecute her and will be defied and ruined. Dupin even writes a message to D—— in the false letter, for he hates him for injuries to himself as well as for his unprincipled conduct. We thus have human characters and motives, and a problem solved by the identification of the detective not only with the mental but also with the imaginative processes of the criminal.

Much the same methods had been used in "The Murders in the Rue Morgue" to prove that the assassin was *not* human, while in "Marie Rogêt" the analysis was more external, since Poe was working upon the details of a real murder and was not able to exercise his imagination to the same degree. In "The Gold Bug" the solution is obtained through the unraveling of a cryptogram, purely an intellectual exercise, in which Poe was unusually skilled. In the first paragraph of "The Murders in the Rue Morgue," as it appeared in the original manuscript, in *Graham's Magazine* and in the 1843 edition, he speaks of the possibility of the existence of a distinct organ devoted to analysis. That he omitted this paragraph in the revised version which appeared in the collection of his tales published in 1845, may indicate that he felt he had overestimated the importance of the analytical faculty. In any event, the fact that Poe wrote so few ratiocinative stories has been frequently commented upon. He was the first great artist in the field, and he gave an impetus to the writing of such tales in France and England hardly to be overestimated. The answer to the apparent paradox is to his credit. He knew that while he was first in this field, the field itself was not of large importance. Others could go on and write detective stories if they wished. But no one else could write the Arabesques.

The Descriptive stories, "The Landscape Garden" (1842), its expanded form "The Domain of Arnheim" (1847), "The Elk" (1844), and "Landor's Cottage" (1849), are interesting mainly through their revelation of Poe's love of natural beauty and his early recognition of the possibility of a profession which should not only restore but also improve nature. There is little or no attempt to establish any relation between human beings and inanimate nature. It remains a spectacle, or, as Poe says of Landor's cottage, "Its marvellous *effect* lay altogether in its artistic arrangement *as a picture.*"

Of the two longer narratives of Poe, *The Narrative of Arthur Gordon Pym* (1837–1838) becomes important only after he leaves his sources, Irving's *Astoria*, Benjamin Morell's *Narrative of Four Voyages to the South Seas and the Pacific*, and the *Address* of J. N. Reynolds,[6] made in the House of Representatives in 1836. The details of Pym's voyage as a stowaway grow more horrible until they become tiresome, but we are rewarded at the end by the powerful description of the imaginary region into which the boat of the voyagers drifts on to destruction. *The Journal of Julius Rodman* is a rewriting of earlier accounts of explorations in the West and Northwest, based upon Irving's *Astoria* and *Captain Bonneville* and upon the *History of the Expedition under the Command of Captains Lewis and Clark.*[7] There is, however, no imaginative flight comparable to the ending of *Arthur Gordon Pym*. Poe contented himself with modifying and rearranging details with an eye to the picturesque, but the fictional elements are unimportant.

After all, these two narratives are most significant in their evidence that the long story was not his province. His conception both of the poem and the story included brevity as its first requisite. The oft quoted passage from his review of Hawthorne's short stories [8] makes clear Poe's standards for this literary form which he did so much to establish:

> Were I called upon, however, to designate that class of composition which, next to such a poem as I have suggested, should best fulfil the demands and serve the purposes of ambitious genius, should offer it the most advantageous field of exertion, and afford it the fairest opportunity of display, I should speak

---

[6] See Woodberry's *Life*, Vol. I, pp. 191–193; and R. L. Rhea, *University of Texas Studies in English*, X (1930), 135–146.

[7] For detailed comparisons of *The Journal of Julius Rodman* and its sources, see articles by P. P. Crawford and H. A. Turner, *University of Texas Studies in English*, XII (1932), 158–170, and X (1930), 147–157. See also Woodberry's *Life*.

[8] Poe reviewed *Twice Told Tales* in *Graham's Magazine*, April–May, 1842. He revised this criticism, including *Mosses from an Old Manse*, for *Godey's Lady's Book*, November, 1847, from which the quotation is made.

at once of the brief prose tale. . . . The ordinary novel is objectionable, from its length, for reasons analogous to those which render length objectionable in the poem. As the novel cannot be read at one sitting, it cannot avail itself of the immense benefit of *totality*. Worldly interests, intervening during the pauses of perusal, modify, counteract and annul the impressions intended. But simple cessation in reading would, of itself, be sufficient to destroy the true unity. In the brief tale, however, the author is enabled to carry out his full design without interruption. During the hour of perusal, the soul of the reader is at the writer's control.

A skillful artist has constructed a tale. He has not fashioned his thoughts to accommodate his incidents, but having deliberately conceived a certain *single effect* to be wrought, he then invents such incidents, he then combines such events, and discusses them in such tone as may best serve him in establishing this preconceived effect. If his very first sentence tend not to the outbringing of this effect, then in his very first step has he committed a blunder. In the whole composition there should be no word written of which the tendency, direct or indirect, is not to the one pre-established design. And by such means, with such care and skill, a picture is at length painted which leaves in the mind of him who contemplates it with a kindred art, a sense of the fullest satisfaction. The idea of the tale, its thesis, has been presented unblemished, because undisturbed—an end absolutely demanded, yet, in the novel, altogether unattainable.

Poe carried out this theory of the short story in his own work. It will be noticed that he does not mention the revelation of character as important; it is the effect he is after, and his tales are primarily short stories of effect. That his characters are often types is true, but that is because they live in an atmosphere of the abnormal or the wonderful. To criticize them as unreal is easy, but one should establish first the meaning of "reality." For Poe's purposes they are part of the general effect; to have placed an ordinary person of common sense, engrossed with the task of earning his own living, into "Ligeia" or "The Fall of the House of Usher" would have been simply to misunderstand the meaning of art. For characters who are engaged in testing the limits of human endurance, in looking back to the shadows of preëxistence or forward to those of the future life, a large leisure and unlimited opportunities are essential.

But those who say that Poe has created no characters have failed utterly to recognize that vibrant sensitive nature who creates characters and then steps in among them, giving them, through the reflection of his thought and feeling, such life as they possess. The poet who sees the last fairy in "The Island of the Fay," the lover of Eleonora or of Ligeia, the tortured soul of William Wilson, even the friend of Roderick Usher who passes with him through scenes of terror, is a human being. He is a lonely soul, but he is not to be pitied for he is his own best companion and therefore he has solved the problem of living. The nature lover who could write "In truth, the man who would behold aright the glory of God upon earth must in solitude behold that glory" was in one of his most sincere moods. Tradition in Philadelphia still tells of the solitary man who walked upon the shores of the Wissahickon Creek and lay for hours drinking in the beauty of the landscape. Here again the danger of generalities is great. While we can identify Poe with some of his heroes, there are others who are as remote as can be from the "quiet, unobtrusive, thoughtful scholar" whom George R. Graham knew. Poe could dramatize crime, or diseased mental states, but it is not necessary to believe that he was a hereditary hypochondriac because he makes Julius Rodman one, more especially since in the description of Rodman he was following, at times verbally, the description of Merriwether Lewis as given by President Jefferson!

To produce his effect, Poe made use of every form of material that lay at hand.[9] From English and American magazines, of which he was an omnivorous reader, and from encyclopedias, he culled incidents, ideas, and situations, and with the high courage of the great adaptors, made them his own. One of the most interesting parallels with an American novelist lies in the similarity between "The Pit and the Pendulum" and the fifteenth chapter of Brockden Brown's *Edgar Huntly*. Huntly comes to life after his fall into the pit in much the same way as the sufferer in Poe's story, and he believes he is the victim of a tyrant who has shut him in a dungeon. His hunger becomes so great that he contemplates killing himself with a tomahawk, with its obvious resemblance to the blade of a great pendulum. The torment of the thirst caused by the panther Huntly kills and eats may have given rise to the effect of the highly seasoned meat upon the anonymous narrator in "The Pit and the Pendulum." The most interesting similarity, however, arises from the method of producing terror in both victims because their attempts at escape are blocked by darkness and their unfamiliarity with the surroundings, in brief, by depriving them of their usual experiences. Some of Poe's best

---

[9] For the best résumé of the many articles in which the sources of Poe's stories have been treated see Killis Campbell, "The Origins of Poe," in his *The Mind of Poe and Other Studies* (Cambridge, 1933).

effects are secured by similar negations of various kinds. "There is no quiet there, nor silence" in the land in which "Silence" is laid. "Ligeia" begins, "I cannot for my soul remember how, when, or even precisely where, I first became acquainted with the lady Ligeia." It is not a mere trick. The exquisite description of the changes which the death of Eleonora makes in the Valley of the Many Colored Grass is built upon the same principle. He could have learned this lesson from Brown without going to any foreign source.

In fact the efforts to derive Poe from English or Continental literature have not been very successful. For the best way to arrive at an appreciation of his genius is to compare, for example, "William Wilson" with its Spanish and German parallels. The basic idea of a double personality has long been common property. Poe may have been prompted to write his story by a brief account of a proposed drama by Lord Byron, recorded by Washington Irving,[10] which was to have dealt with a double who died by the sword thrust of the hero and revealed himself as the conscience of his destroyer. Poe probably read the *Knickerbocker* and certainly read *The Gift*, for he had a story in the same number; the speculations concerning his use of a play of Calderón which gave Byron, through Shelley, the idea of his drama, should have been settled by Woodberry's note.[11]

What Poe used were general suggestions, but he lifted the story, through the methods already outlined, into a much higher spiritual plane, and, by laying its scene amid the recollections of his own school days at Stoke Newington, he endowed it with reality.

Even less did he take, if he took anything at all, from Ernest T. A. Hoffmann's "Elixiere des Teufels," for the apparent resemblances [12] can be accounted for more easily by reference to Irving's account, and the final victory of the monk over his insane double is completely different from the catastrophe in "William Wilson." Poe may have read in translation Hoffmann's collection of tales, *Die Serapionsbrüder* (1819–

---

[10] *Knickerbocker Magazine*, VI (August, 1835), 142–144. Also in *The Gift* for 1835. Found conveniently in *An Unwritten Drama of Lord Byron*, edited by T. O. Mabbott (Metuchen, 1925).

[11] *Life*, Vol. I, p. 232n. Woodberry, starting with Irving's suggestion that the idea was inspired by a play called the *Embozada*, identifies the original as *El Purgatorio de San Patricio*, in which Un Hombre Embozado, or the muffled figure, is a character. There is no evidence that Poe saw the Spanish play.

[12] See Palmer Cobb, *The Influence of E. T. A. Hoffmann on the Tales of Edgar Allan Poe* (Chapel Hill, 1908).

1821), stories which were supposed to have been read before a club, just as Poe's projected *Tales of the Folio Club* were presumed to be read. But surely that idea might occur to anyone. Very little actual similarity in the stories is to be found. We might believe that the cleft in the House of Usher had been suggested by a similar appearance in Hoffmann's "Das Majorat," if it had not been for the fact that Scott mentions this occurrence in his article on the supernatural, which Poe probably saw. The closest parallel is that between Hoffmann's "Doge und Dogaressa" and Poe's "The Assignation." But here again the climax is quite different. Poe himself denied the influence in the preface to his *Tales of the Grotesque and Arabesque:* "If in many of my productions terror has been the thesis, I maintain that terror is not of Germany but of the soul." This sentence might, of course, be taken as evidence to the contrary,[13] had it not been for Poe's mention of some of the English stories from which he had received ideas in his "How to Write a Blackwood Article." Evidently he felt that the difference between "The Man in the Bell"[14] and "The Pit and the Pendulum" would be as obvious as their similarities, or he would not have given the source-hunters such a good lead. He would certainly have been amazed at the suggestion that "Silence" is derived from "Monos and Daimonos,"[15] apparently on the ground that a character in each sits on a rock and is fond of solitude. "Monos and Daimonos" is a rambling narrative—"Silence" is a brief piece of imaginative prose.

He may indeed have seen "Monos and Daimonos," for in the same issue of *The New Monthly Magazine* appeared a tale "Frogère," which illustrates the methods by which Poe built up a story. "Hop-Frog," that powerful and gruesome story of Poe, relates the revenge of a court jester whom the king has forced to drink wine, which the jester loathes, and whose love, Trippeta, has been grossly insulted by the king when she pleads for him. The jester waits his chance, until the king commands him to design a costume for him and his courtiers at a masquerade. Hop-Frog dresses them as orang-outangs, covered with tar and flax, chains them together and, by a clever device, drags them up through the ceiling, setting fire himself to the king's coat and escaping through the

---

[13] When "Metzengerstein" appeared first in *The Saturday Courier*, it had no subtitle. When it was reprinted in *The Southern Literary Messenger*, it was called "a tale in imitation of the German," possibly to make it more attractive.

[14] *Blackwood's Magazine*, X (November, 1821), 373-375.

[15] *New Monthly Magazine and Literary Journal*, XXVIII (1830), 387-392.

roof. The source of this story is usually given [16] as Lord Berners' translation of Froissart. But Froissart's narrative simply provides the background of a masquerade in which King Charles VI and five courtiers are dressed as satyrs, and, through an accident, the coats of the courtiers are set on fire. The king is not injured. As Professor Campbell has shown, Poe could have read an excerpt from Froissart's tale in *The Broadway Journal* [17] and a comparison of the excerpt with the original tale [18] proves that he need not have read that original at all. But what makes "Hop-Frog" such a great story is the way Poe breathes into the crippled jester the incarnate spirit of revenge. There is no jester and no revenge in Froissart. Did Poe then take from "Frogère," [19] a story of a jester at the court of the Emperor Paul of Russia, who is made the victim of a cruel jest by the Emperor and who in revenge is a party to the Emperor's death, the suggestion for "Hop-Frog"? The titles indicate it. But if so, Poe has changed the nature of the jest completely. The point to be stressed is that Poe created that portion of the story which is important, that the mere names become characters, a human motive of revenge is not merely indicated, but made the climax of the story. It seems therefore almost a critical stupidity to speak of the "sources" at all. By a curious coincidence, Hawthorne in his *American Note-Books* in 1838 speaks of the same historic incident.

Of more importance in "How to Write a Blackwood Article" is his remark that "Sensations are the great thing. Should you ever be drowned or hung, be sure and make a note of your sensations—they will be worth to you ten guineas a sheet." The recommendations he made to the hypothetical author not only satirize the staccato style of John Neal, but also reveal Poe's own system of creating an atmosphere of learning from a ready reference book of allusions. Who can criticize him for his many secondhand references when he has so disarmingly revealed the machinery by which the grotesque stories—and even some of the weaker arabesques—were made up to sell?

It is much more profitable, in a survey of fiction, to observe his methods than the reputed sources of his material. Poe first among Ameri-

---

[16] Woodberry: *Life of Poe*, Vol. II, p. 295.

[17] I (February, 1845), 71.

[18] *The Chronicles of Froissart*, translated out of French by Sir John Bourchier, Lord Berners. Cap. CXXXVIII, Vol. VI, pp. 96–100, Ed. (London, 1903).

[19] *New Monthly Magazine and Literary Journal*, XXVIII (1830), 491–496. By a curious chance, the story is signed "Px."

can writers of fiction understood how to begin at the beginning. The subjective, essay-like introductions of Irving, the introductory devices like "Mine Host" in Hawthorne's "Legends of the Province House" vanish. One has not read ten words in "The Fall of the House of Usher" before the tone of terror is established. In "The Tell-Tale Heart" the first words strike the keynote of the desired effect. The climax is equally well handled. In his very first story, the wild ride of the Prince Metzengerstein into the flames has the directness, the vigor, the economy of the reader's attention, that Poe gave to the short story:

> The career of the horseman was indisputably on his own part uncontrollable. The agony of his countenance, the convulsive struggle of his frame gave evidence of superhuman exertion; but no sound, save a solitary shriek, escaped from his lacerated lips, which were bitten through and through in the intensity of terror.

He was to carry the art of the climax to even greater heights in the sudden fall of the Shadow at the feet of the seven assembled guests, in the resurrection of Ligeia, in the living death of William Wilson. In brief, he was carrying out his own theory of the short story, and in doing this he was meeting the standard set by the most exacting critic of his time.

The strongest influence of Poe shows naturally in those phases of his work which were most easily imitated. The difference between Poe's methods in the ratiocinative story and those of his imitators has already been indicated. Of the Arabesques, the story of the supernatural and the pseudoscientific story found their most artistic expression in the work of Fitz-James O'Brien (1828–1862). This Irish-American, who came to this country in 1852, may rightly be treated here not only because of his death on the battlefield in defence of the Union, but also since his short stories seem to have begun with his residence in New York. O'Brien's work was uneven, and he experimented in the popular types of farce like "Belladonna" (1854), which seems to have been the first of the many stories he published in *Harper's Magazine,* or the sketches of social life like "The Beauty" or "A Drawing Room Drama," which give every evidence of haste.

His greatest talent lay in the treatment of the supernatural. "What Was It?", published in *Harper's* for March, 1859, for sheer originality of conception rivals the best fiction of its kind. It belongs to that phase of the supernatural in which the effect is produced by the failure of one or more of the senses to react when brought into contact with a phenomenon. This brings it within the larger class which results from the denial of some natural law, and it is one of the most effective as it is one of the most natural of devices. The originality of O'Brien's conception rests in his choice of the sense that is to fail to act.

The ghosts with which our literature is stocked usually fall into one group, those which can be seen but which fail to appeal to any other of the senses. Their authors have probably reasoned that the effect of terror was greater on account of this lack of appeal. They failed, however, to realize that the belief in the possibility of the appearance was weakened by the failure of each added sense to operate and that the supernatural is most effective when as many as possible of the senses may act except the most powerful, that of sight. O'Brien may have reasoned this out or he may have arrived at the result by the sheer force of genius, but in any case he arrived at the result. In the story "What Was It?", after preparing the way by a discussion of the most effective methods of producing terror, he tells of the mysterious something which drops on the chest of the hero while he lies in bed awaiting sleep. After a frightful struggle, he subdues the "thing" and is horrified to find after he turns on the light that he can see nothing, although he holds his captive in his grasp. He can *hear* the rapid breathing, and *feel* the writhing of the strange being, but to the eyes of the inmates of the house who have been awakened by his cries, he is holding nothing. He proves to them that he is not insane by dropping the monster on the bed, where it makes the impression of a small human being. The visitor finally dies of starvation, as no food can be found which it will eat. The effectiveness of the story is truly remarkable. The methods are those of Poe; the opening sentences being strikingly like the beginning of "The Black Cat," but the conception is O'Brien's. It was used long afterwards by Maupassant in "Le Horla," but in unity of construction and in realism of detail the Irish-American surpassed the great Frenchman.

Equally original is the conception, in "The Diamond Lens" (1858), of a microscopist who grinds a diamond into the most powerful lens in the world. Through this he sees in a drop of water a beautiful form with whom he falls in love. The utter hopelessness of his emotions when he realizes that the drop must evaporate and that she can never know him, lifts the story beyond the mere cleverness of pseudoscientific supernaturalism, for it indicates without comment the helplessness of man before the inexorable laws of Nature. "The Wondersmith," in which a set of mannikins who are endowed with fiendish attributes turn on their creator and his allies and kill them, is another artistic success, and again O'Brien anticipated such recent dramatic treatments of the theme as the robots of *R. U. R.* O'Brien has the courage not to explain his supernatural effects, and indeed in his best stories an explanation would ruin the effect.

In the year 1832, when Poe's first short story appeared, James Hall (1793–1868) published his *Legends of the West*. Born in Philadelphia, a pioneer, a soldier, a lawyer, and an editor, he knew the country from his birthplace to the Mississippi and beyond it. In his work we see the survival of that combination of the tale and the character sketch out of which the short story grew. With more understanding and sympathy than Timothy Flint, and with far greater sense of form, he wrote of the various types that made up the frontier, including the faith doctor, the backwoodsman, the hunter, the settler and the Indian, noting the singular phraseology of the people, their originality and their figures of speech.

His description of the French settlers—at Carondelet in Louisiana—is sympathetic in its contrast between the easy rule of the French and the oppressive rule of the English. At times Hall goes back to the eighteenth century, as in "Michel de Coucy," a story of Illinois near the Mississippi (Prairie de Rocher), about 1750, an amusing tale of French and Spanish jealousy. His humor is delightful; his descriptive power, especially of the prairies, is illustrated by a story like "The Emigrants." One of the most interesting tales is the vindication in "The Indian Hater" of Monson, whose wife, mother, and children had been destroyed by the Indians, and who devoted himself to revenge.

The second volume, *The Soldier's Bride and Other Tales* (1833), does not equal *The Legends of the West*, since it is made up of romantic tales or essay-like descriptions of places or eccentric characters. The supernatural is fairly well done in "Pete Featherton," laid in Kentucky. *The Tales of the Border* (1835) contains much better characterization. In this volume, he developed again the motive of revenge in "The Pioneer," a well written character story of a circuit rider who tells how his father and mother were killed by Indians and his sister carried off, and how for years he had devoted himself to revenge. Then, meeting his sister as the apparently contented wife of an Indian and mother of two children, he had had a revulsion of feeling and had determined to undo some of his own career of passion and revenge. In "The French Village" published first in his magazine, *The Western Souvenir*, in 1829, Hall draws a contrast between the contented life of the inhabitants under French rule and their disappearance before American "progress." His skill in character drawing is shown too in the picture of Pierre, the French barber in "The Dark Maid of Illinois," who thinks the prairie fire is a sign from Heaven on account of his marriage to the daughter of the chief of the Illini. Even better is "The New Moon," a story of the marriage of New Moon, a daughter of the chief of the Omawhaws, to Bolingbroke, a white trader, who is a cold-blooded creature and weds her simply to gain advantage in the business he is conducting.

The best stories in these early volumes were collected in 1846 under the title of *The Wilderness and the War Path*. Hall added two fine studies of Indian nature in "The Black Steed," in which the qualities of courage, persistence and wariness are made vividly alive in the person of the hero, and "The Red Sky of the Morning," a description of the hardships of the Indians in the Chippewa region on Lake Superior. His Indians are a fair compromise between the idealized portrait of the noble red man and the bloodthirsty savages of Bird, who may indeed have taken a hint from Hall for his character of Nick of the Woods. Hall's one novel, *Harpe's Head* (1833), is laid in Virginia and Kentucky at the end of the eighteenth century. "Harpe," the ruffian, is a sinister figure and remains in the memory. So does "Hark Short," the queer boy of North Carolina origin, who lives a lonely existence, unable to take advantage of the offers of those he has assisted, such as Colonel Hendrickson, whom he saves from the Indians. He is a remarkable picture of a human being who has grown up without kindness and is purely animal in his nature.

Hall does not hesitate to depict the unattractive side of the frontier, especially the violence of the outlaws. But his most striking quality, that of liberality, kept him from the wild exaggerations that disfigure Simms' border romances with purely typical figures. He left the first authentic picture of the West that our early short story produced, and he showed the capacity of the form in dealing with the varied incidents and characters of the frontier. For many years his fiction was the source and the model for later writers, just as his historical and descriptive writings, such as his *Sketches of History, Life, and Manners in the*

West (1835), or its revision, *The Romance of Western History; or, Sketches of History, Life and Manners in the West* (1857), have furnished later historians with a vivid and authoritative account of the settlement of the region he knew so well.

Even more realistic were the sketches which Caroline M. Kirkland (1801–1864) published in 1839 under the pen name of Mrs. Mary Clavers as *A New Home—Who'll Follow?; or Glimpses of Western Life*. So real indeed are they that they lie on the border line of fiction and the essay, and stem from *Our Village,* by Miss Mitford, herself perhaps inspired by Irving. The voyage to Michigan, the purchase of lots in what becomes "Montacute," the selling of swamps and the suffering from fever and ague antedate Dickens' *Martin Chuzzlewit* and later American realistic pictures of the frontier. The Montacute Female Beneficent Society, with Mrs. Campaspe Nippers at its head, is acutely described as "the hotbed from which springs every root of bitterness among the petticoated denizens of Montacute." Long before Sinclair Lewis, Mrs. Kirkland drew a picture of the tyranny of opinion in a small Western town.

Another writer of short stories, whose vitality has secured them a place in any survey of fiction, was Augustus Baldwin Longstreet (1790–1870). Born in Augusta, Georgia, he reproduced life in that state in his *Georgia Scenes* (1835), with a veracity and a humor that provide a startling contrast with most of the idealistic fiction of the day. *Georgia Scenes,* like Hall's stories, are partly tales and partly descriptive essays. Their importance lies in the faithful picture of life in Georgia, at periods from 1809 to 1835. It is no romantic plantation life; it is a lower middle-class frontier—cruel, rough, vigorous, and bearing evidence of the truth of its portrayal on every page. Longstreet showed his ability to plan a climax in such a story as "Georgia Theatrics," in which a traveler (and the reader) is horrified at overhearing the agonized cries of a boy apparently having his eyes gouged out by another, only to find that he has been listening to a rehearsal for a real contest. The effect of this sketch is increased when we read in "The Fight" of the brutality of personal conflict in Georgia at that time. Again, in "The Dance," a middle-aged man indulges in sentimental memories concerning his hostess, whom he had known twenty years before, only to find she has entirely forgotten him. There is delicious irony in "The Horse Swap," in which a trader congratulates himself on having disposed of a horse with a sore back, only to find his new nag to be blind and deaf. The best known is "The Militia Company Drill," describing the complete lack of unity and discipline of Captain Clodpole's band. According to the preface, this sketch was contributed by a friend,[20] but in any event, it is the undoubted source for Thomas Hardy's famous scene in *The Trumpet Major*. It was a free life that Longstreet represented, before the Evangelical repression of dancing and card-playing had become established. So true indeed was his picture that later, when he had become a Methodist clergyman and a college president, he is said to have endeavored to suppress the sketches. But they remain to delight readers who love human nature, even in the raw, and in the development of fiction they pointed the way in which Mark Twain and Bret Harte were to find success.

The short story in America was to take many forms, but one quality which Poe, Hawthorne, O'Brien, Hall, Mrs. Kirkland and Longstreet illustrate in different ways, remained characteristic. Whether idealistic or realistic in their methods, they were pioneers in their close scrutiny of new forms of life or in their imaginative reach into uncharted regions. To varying degrees they owe debts to the first great pioneer, Irving, but in any event they established upon firm foundations the literary form in which America retained so long its unquestioned supremacy.

[20] F. L. Pattee, in *American Literature Since 1870*, p. 298, attributes this sketch to Oliver Hillhouse Prince.

CHAPTER VI

THE DEVELOPMENT OF IDEALISTIC ROMANCE

To anyone who views our fiction in proper perspective, the fourth decade of the nineteenth century is of especial significance. It is not only that Hawthorne and Poe then began their work, but also because of the large number of writers of romance who, under the stimulus of Irving and Cooper, selected from life and history those themes and motives which seemed to them important and who created characters of heroic size and incidents which revealed new fields of discovery and exploration. Most frequently it was the history of their own country which they searched for material. The novelists of the 'eighties, who are usually credited with the literary discovery of America, had their prototypes not only in Irving and Cooper but also in many others who painted with skill and sympathy the struggles of the Colonists, the tragedy of the Indian's hopeless contest for his land, the heroic sacrifices of the Revolution, and the establishment of the Republic. While the playwrights were placing upon the stage over one hundred and fifty plays dealing with American history, the novelists were also responding to that natural demand for the romance of their own past, of which any nation worth the name has felt the impulse.

It would seem as though the celebration of the fiftieth anniversary of the ending of the Revolution in 1783 must have had a specific influence upon American romance. The appearance of *The Linwoods, The Hawks of Hawk-Hollow, Horse-Shoe Robinson* and *The Partisan* in 1835 was not accidental. Indeed Kennedy himself recognized this impulse in his preface to *Horse-Shoe Robinson*.

In a time of national expansion, it was natural too that Cooper's description of the frontier should be emulated by others. These topics were capable of being treated in bold strokes upon a large and sometimes too crowded a canvas, but it was an age crowded with events and the fiction was representative of it. There was also a scrutiny of social and international relations, and here again Cooper had shown the way.

Never dying, the moral and ethical novel persisted, and since this period saw the great waves of social and evangelical reform, it was only natural that fiction should have its share in the movement. Naturally it was the weakest from the artistic point of view. In such a period, while the cardinal principle of romance, the freedom in choice of material, forbade the novelists from limiting their scenes to the United States, the novels laid in Mexico and other parts of the New World were prompted by their intimate connection with native material.

At first glance Catherine Maria Sedgwick (1789–1867) seems to belong to the earlier generation, since her first novel, *A New England Tale,* appeared in 1822. It was begun as a Unitarian tract, and throughout her long and busy life the interests of Catherine Sedgwick were moral and social. But the influence of Cooper is as clear as that of Maria Edgeworth and she continued to write fiction until 1857. A liberal New England woman, educated at the boarding school kept by the father of John Howard Payne, she loved the theatre and even permitted her heroines to dance, but Edward Erskine, in *A New England Tale,* is condemned for card-playing, and when he adds duelling to this crime, he loses the heroine, Jane Elton, who is entirely too good to be true and who finds her haven in the love of a middle-aged Quaker, Mr. Lloyd. The best character is that of Aunt Wilson, a domineering hypocrite. *A New England Tale* was popular enough to call for a new edition in 1852 and was dramatized, though there is no evidence that it was put on the stage. *Redwood* (1824) is another moral tale, with some reality in the description of social customs in New England in the early part of the nineteenth century. The contrasted characters of the half-sisters, Ellen and Caroline Redwood, is noteworthy, since Miss Sedgwick makes Ellen, though angelic, not quite a prig, and permits Caroline, who is not at all an angel, to be more beautiful than the heroine. *Redwood* was translated into French, German, Italian, and Swedish, and was reprinted in England. But it is not as well done as *Hope Leslie* (1827), a story of Colonial and Indian life in the early seventeenth century, mainly in Connecticut. Although Hope Leslie, who has a genius for self-sacrifice, is the central character, one remembers more clearly her sister, Faith, who has been captured by the Pequods, marries one of them and refuses to return to white civilization when she has the opportunity. Magawisca, the Pequod girl who saves the hero, Everell Fletcher, by the loss of her arm, and Sir Philip Gardiner, that mysterious cavalier who appears so often in fiction as an apparent friend but a real foe to the Puritan oligarchy, are quite well drawn.

Miss Sedgwick wrote with a firm belief in the importance of the Puritan civilization but was not blind to its shortcomings. Any New England woman who could sum up the distinction between the Philadelphian and the Bostonian of her own day by remarking of the former that "they do not seem afraid to speak, lest they should commit themselves for life" had a gift for satire. This she reveals in *Clarence, a Tale of Our Own Times* (1830), laid in and near New York City, where Miss Sedgwick spent a good deal of her time. Gertrude Clarence is a sensible girl who saves her friend Emilie Layton from running away with an adventurer, and may possibly be the original of the character of "Gertrude" in Mrs. Mowatt's *Fashion*. Miss Sedgwick could write trenchant sentences such as that describing the scene between Emilie Layton and her lover after he had saved her. "It was one of those few blissful moments of life, that borrows nothing from memory and asks nothing from hope." Few novelists of the 'thirties could resist the temptation to treat the Revolution, but the interest of *The Linwoods* (1835) lies in the picture of the social life in New York City during the last two years of the contest rather than in the movement of armies. The division between friends, the efforts of the Tories to maintain their social connections with England, the confusion in New York City as the time for Clinton's departure approached, are touched with reality. The tragic story of Bessie Lee, who loses her mind for love of Jasper Meredith and searches for him from Connecticut to New York, is told with some power.

Miss Sedgwick wrote several stories for young people which need not detain us, but her last novel, *Married or Single* (1857), revealed again her knowledge of feminine nature. Grace Herbert, the girl of established position, without wealth, who "mistakes impulses for inspiration" and is dissatisfied with her life without doing anything about it, is one of her best portraits. The description of the way a man makes a girl care for him and then passes on his way unconscious is also veracious. Miss Sedgwick states in the introduction that the novel was written to show that a woman could have a place in the world without being married, but nearly all the girls get married just the same! The early introduction of spiritualism is worthy of note, and the seance is well described. The wave of theological sociology which swept over the country in the 'fifties is reflected through the novel, making the picture of life important to the social historian.

Miss Sedgwick's shorter fiction, especially in "Le Bossu," a story of the revolt of Pepin, the illegitimate son of Charlemagne, and "The White Scarf," a romance of the days of Charles VI of France, revealed her ability to depict life in scenes unfamiliar to her. She showed too in the first, through her understanding of the willingness of Blanche, the legendary beloved of Pepin, to prefer a life of religious devotion to marriage with any man except the one she truly loved, that breadth of view which is one of her most attractive qualities. When she wrote a seduction story of her own day, like "Fanny McDermott," she revealed her understanding of the value of reticence much better than Mrs. Rowson and her school.

Another Unitarian, and a more pronounced reformer, Lydia Maria Francis Child (1802–1880), belongs also to the school of Scott and Cooper. This daughter of Convers Francis had an active career as an abolitionist and, while her writings on that subject are more truly literature than the usual tract, it was because of an imaginative touch which made her a novelist. In *Hobomok* (1824), she drew a fairly accurate picture of the Salem Colony about 1630, and perhaps her abolition sentiment led her to picture the marriage of Hobomok with Mary Conant as only partially unhappy. Hobomok's withdrawal to the Iroquois upon the return of Mary's absent lover points forward to the Enoch Arden story, just as the wooing of Sally Oldham by proxy and her hint to John Collier that he had better be speaking for himself anticipates Longfellow's use of similar historical facts. *The Rebels* (1825) is a novel laid at the beginning of the Revolution in Boston, but it is largely a series of stilted love stories, secret marriages and grasping executors. Much more readable is her novel of Greek life, *Philothea* (1836). The heroine, who is the granddaughter of Anaxagoras, remains an ideal creation and suffers as a fictional character from Mrs. Child's tendency to convey, through her, moral doctrines that smack rather of New England than Athens, but Philothea's devotion to Paralus, the son of Pericles, after he has lost his memory, lingers long after Mrs. Child's heroines of American life are forgotten. She knew something of Greek life and was probably held rather by her sense of gentility than by ignorance from making her descriptions of the banquet hall of Pericles and Aspasia more realistic. Her distinction between

static and dynamic art is still worth reading; and she illustrates again
the principle that freedom in the choice of locality and material is the
most priceless gift of the romantic period. Certainly when she returned
in 1867 to her propaganda and produced an abolition novel, *A Romance
of the Republic*, laid in New Orleans, Boston, Europe and points north
and south, she fell below her earlier standards.

Free from propaganda, but still tinged at times with the Puritan desire for reform, Daniel Pierce Thompson (1795–1868) wrote one
story that deserves to live. His first novel, *May Martin* (1835), is a
book for boys, amateurish and stilted, and with a reformation of the
villain which is distressing. *The Green Mountain Boys* (1839) is much
better. This novel deals with the troubles between New York and New
Hampshire as colonies in connection with the so-called New Hampshire
grants. Then the Revolution comes on and the same pioneers who defended their rights against the aggressors of the colonial government of
New York now take up arms for the independence of their native
country. Ethan Allen is brought in early in the book and leads the
attack on Ticonderoga, then he is captured and disappears until the end
of the story. The best parts of the book are the realistic descriptions
of the fighting and the colloquial dialogue of the pioneers.

Locke Amsden (1847) is hardly a novel, for the slight thread of
story is used to carry Thompson's theories of education and scientific
study. *The Rangers, or The Tory's Daughter* (1851) is a conventional
romance beginning in 1775 in the Green Mountains, and *Gaut Gurley*
(1857), a story based on the illicit trade between the United States and
Canada from 1807 to 1815, borders on the dime novel. Thompson's
later stories even his competent biographer does not attempt to defend.

The attraction of romance tempted three American historians, all
New Englanders, into the field of fiction. Richard Hildreth (1807–
1865) was the first to publish his abolition novel, *The Slave; or Memoirs
of Archy Moore* (1836), which was reprinted for over twenty years
and appeared in French at least five times. It is told ostensibly by a
"white slave," the son of a Virginia planter, and is, of course, largely
made up of his sufferings and escapes which ultimately lead him to the
command of a British privateer in the War of 1812. While Hildreth
drew the usual idealized portrait of the octoroon, he did not hesitate to
represent the casual standards of the slave by uniting Archy to Cassie,

the daughter of Archy's white father by another slave woman. His pictures of the poorer whites and of the stretches of wilderness which a mistaken system of economy had brought on the South have some reality. But the general tone is that of romantic propaganda. It is worth noting that one of the leading slave characters is called "Thomas" and has an emotional piety which may possibly have had its effect upon Mrs. Stowe.

Among the novelists who described the New England scene, John Lothrop Motley (1814–1877) does not deserve the obscurity into which his far greater reputation as an historian has thrown him. *Morton's Hope; or, The Memoirs of a Provincial* (1839) is written with a vein of humor which relieves the stilted conversation. It is the first American novel which represents accurately the life at a German university, the adventures of Morton at Göttingen being true to conditions even a century later. *Merrymount, a Romance of the Massachusetts Colony* (1849) was written some years before its publication. The picture of Thomas Morton's colony at Merrymount and of Sir Christopher Gardiner, who has ambitious schemes for securing a stronghold in New England, are drawn with that Puritan prejudice which made his histories of less permanent value than those of Prescott or Parkman. It adds vigor, however, to his romance, but like Simms his machinery is too complicated and collapses at the end of the story. Francis Parkman also wrote a novel, *Vassal Morton* (1856), laid about 1845 and dealing with the adventures of a Harvard graduate who studies races and peoples and is imprisoned in Austria for years. There is little construction, but his interpretation of the political issues of the time is still worth reading.

The figure of Sir Christopher Gardiner was apparently a fascinating one to this school of romance, for he reappears not as the villain but as the centre of interest in *The White Chief Among the Red Men; or, The Knight of the Golden Mellice* (1859), by John Turvill Adams (1805–1882). Adams gives a fairer picture not only of Sir Christopher but also of seventeenth century New England than Motley. Winthrop, Endicott, Dudley come to reality in his pages and the instinctive sympathy of one gentleman for another, despite their difference of creed, makes the relations of Winthrop and Gardiner refreshing. The Indian Sassacus, chief of the Pequods, is quite well drawn. Adams' earlier novel, *The Lost Hunter* (1856), laid in Connecticut early in the nineteenth century, shows clearly the influence of Brockden Brown in the character James Armstrong, who attempts to sacrifice his daughter Faith in a fit of madness.

Easily the first in quality of this group of novelists, Robert Montgomery Bird (1806–1854) has only recently begun to come into his own. Born in Delaware, he lived during his creative period in Philadelphia. The publication of his plays, long kept from print by the selfishness of Edwin Forrest, who made a fortune from *The Gladiator* and *The Broker of Bogota*, has revealed him as a dramatist of distinction. When Forrest's refusal to keep his oral contract with him turned Bird's attention from the drama to the novel, his great interest in Mexico led him to write *Calavar; or, The Knight of the Conquest* (1834) and its sequel, *The Infidel; or, The Fall of Mexico* (1835). Nine years before Prescott published his *Conquest of Mexico*, Bird made the philosophy of conquest concrete in a vivid picture of Cortéz, doing justice to the combination of faith and avarice, of ruthless cruelty and dauntless courage, which made the Spanish character fit material for romance. Bird knew the rules of romance, and there is a hero in both novels who carries the love interest, but the intricate plots are not as interesting as the descriptions of conflict, and the handling of masses of men. *The Hawks of Hawk-Hollow* (1835) is laid in and near the Water Gap in Pennsylvania in 1782. The atmosphere of romance is well established through the decaying fortunes of the Gilbert family, Tories whose estates have been sequestered, and who in desperation have become outlaws. Oran Gilbert's devotion to Hyland, his younger brother, since they are the last of the race, their constant danger and the poetic justice of the death of Colonel Falconer, who has been the agent of their ruin, are woven into a novel in which the element of suspense is maintained through that dramatic sense which had enabled Bird to write the first play in the English language to be performed one thousand times within the life of its author.

In *Sheppard Lee* (1836) Bird tried the hazardous experiment of tracing the transmigration of the soul in contemporary times. Sheppard Lee is a farmer of New Jersey, who, having lost his property, is searching for buried treasure. He falls in a trance and being taken for a ghost, wishes that he might be a prosperous Philadelphia merchant whose dead body he finds. Beginning with this wish, which instantly results in his becoming Squire Higginson, alive, he becomes in turn a young Philadelphia buck, a rich miser, a Quaker philanthropist, a Negro slave, and a young Virginia planter. In each case he is driven to change his body on account of distress or danger only to find he has incurred worse trouble by so doing. He finally returns to his own shape and discovers that, according to his sister and brother-in-law, he has never left his farm. Bird uses his material cleverly to satirize conditions of the time. His picture of the social adventurer in Philadelphia is delightful, though he deftly refuses to paint "some dozen or two of such fanciful pictures as are found in novels of fashionable life, though never in fashionable life itself." Most interesting, considering Bird's Whig sympathies, is his description of the life of the slave in Virginia. He is the happy-go-lucky creature, half child and half adult, who was owned by an indulgent master, and who found his joy in freedom from responsibility. The effect of the abolition tract upon the slaves, their insurrection, and the murder of their master and his family, must have been interesting reading in 1836. Realism has hardly gone farther than the scene in which the oldest daughter hurls her young sister to death and then follows her in order to save them both from outrage. In *Sheppard Lee* Bird showed his ability at painting real life, and the way he reflects the various changes by alterations in the language and even the mental processes of the characters, secures that probability for an impossible situation which spells success in romance.

Bird's most popular novel, *Nick of the Woods* (1837), created a striking character, Nathan Slaughter, whose family have been killed by the Indians, and who devotes his life to revenge. James Hall had treated such a theme two years before in "The Pioneer," but Bird added greatly to the interest by giving him a dual nature. As Nathan the Quaker he manifests a horror of blood, while as the "Jibbenainosay" he kills his foes, leaving his mark upon each one. Bird keeps this duality a secret until quite late in the romance. The Indians are neither individualized nor idealized. They are painted as bloodthirsty, treacherous, and cruel, and Bird in the introduction argues in favor of the realistic treatment of them. This novel meets more frequently than is usually the case with romance the acid test of character portrayal. The conception of "Nick of the Woods," a man under the influence of one powerful passion, whose earlier injury in the head makes it possible to attribute some of his actions to disordered mental states, is an original one. The novel ran through many editions, being reprinted within this century, here and in London, and, like practically all Bird's work, being translated into German. *Peter Pilgrim; or, A Rambler's Recollections* (1838), is a collection of shorter sketches whose main interest lies in the realistic picture of a Mississippi River steamboat, which shows conclusively that many of the spectacular features which Mark Twain later described were already old-fashioned in 1838. *The Adventures of Robin Day* (1839) is a picaresque novel laid in Philadelphia, in Florida and on the seas, but is hardly up to the standard of the early novels. Neither is *Ipsico Poe*, a narrative of the eighteenth century in Virginia, which was not finished by Dr. Bird but was completed by his son, Reverend Frederick M. Bird, and published in 1889 as *The Belated Revenge*. Bird turned to journalism for support, his creative energies worn out by the struggle against unfortunate conditions for the man of letters in America.

Like Bird, a Philadelphian, Richard Penn Smith (1779–1854), the author of *The Forsaken* (1831), owes perhaps to his training as a playwright his ability to write a novel in which events are plentiful and suspense is preserved. The Revolution is, as usual, the background, and the description of the Michianza is vivid. The striking scene in which Miriam Gray, who has been convicted of the murder of her child, is rescued by her betrayer, Paul Gordon, bears a remarkable similarity to the famous episode, written years afterward, in *Adam Bede*. In 1836 Smith wrote in novel form *The Actress of Padua*, from Victor Hugo's *Angelo, Tyran de Padoue*, later making a play of it. His introduction proves again the similarity of impulse in the French and American schools of romance, and of particular interest are his cogent reasons for turning aside from the drama to the novel.

Charles Fenno Hoffman (1806–1884) of New York turned aside from poetry to write *Greyslaer* (1840), a story laid in the Mohawk region of New York during the Revolution. Greyslaer is a Whig, and the usual contest between the patriots and the Tories ensues. The novel is often said to have been based upon the Beauchampe-Sharpe murder in Kentucky, but in reality Greyslaer's attempt to murder Bradshaw is based on his forcible abduction and not on his seduction of Alida. *Greyslaer* ran through several editions.

Among the better romances of the Revolution laid in the Middle States is *Standish the Puritan* (1850), by "Eldred Grayson," the pen-name of Robert Hare (1781–1858), a professor of chemistry at the

University of Pennsylvania. The hero comes from Connecticut, but the action takes place chiefly in New York City. The mingled motives of the financiers who profited by the necessities of the colonies, even to forgery, are vividly pilloried, and the attitude of the British toward the Tories whom they secretly despise is well portrayed. Most interesting of the later representatives of this group is *The Quaker Soldier; or, The British in Philadelphia* (1858), by John Richter Jones. The hero, Charles Hazlewood, like Hugh Wynne much later, is a fighting Quaker who returns from remarkable foreign travel, extending even to Persia, to take part in the Battle of Germantown and to help avert the dangers of the Conway Cabal against Washington. By 1858 the realistic movement was beginning to have its effect and the characters are not mere types. The prophecy that some day the United States would find it possible to throw 300,000 soldiers into Germany or Italy indicates Jones' understanding of our capacity.

An unusual story, *Printz Hall* (1839), written apparently by Lemuel Sawyer, deals with the early Swedish settlements on the Delaware and their conflict with Peter Stuyvesant. A curious dwarf, Argal, is the center of a religious cult, of which a group of Finns are the principal representatives. There is considerable power in the description of their rites and the relation of Argal to the heroine is established with skill.

The danger of generalization is well illustrated by the development of fiction in the South. John Pendleton Kennedy (1795–1870), a native of Baltimore, seems in his first novel, *Swallow Barn; or, A Sojourn in the Old Dominion* (1832), to be a lineal successor of Irving. In the preface, Kennedy states that he has had great difficulty in preventing himself from writing a novel, and this charming leisurely description of life in Virginia about 1829 bears clear evidence of the share the essay had in the foundations of early fiction. Yet although we may dismiss the persistent tradition that Kennedy wrote the sixth chapter of *The Virginians,* we know that he furnished Thackeray with material. Kennedy's work points forward as well as backward. *Swallow Barn* has little plot, but the characters of Frank Meriwether and his family are skilfully established. The humorous fancy which created the despair of their neighbor, Mr. Tracy, when the success of his lawsuit over the disputed land left him without an occupation, proved Kennedy's possession of the comic spirit. In *Horse-Shoe Robinson; A Tale of the Tory Ascendancy* (1835), Kennedy adapted one aspect of the picaresque romance to the disturbed and doubtful conditions of the Revolution in 1780. Through the adventures of Major Arthur Butler and his gigantic sergeant, "Horse-Shoe" Robinson, he provided that unfailing combination, a gallant gentleman and a devoted follower whose common sense and physical power solves situations fraught with danger. Kennedy knew well how desperate was the struggle on the patriots' side to hold Virginia and the Carolinas at this period of the war, and through concrete illustrations, like Philip Lindsay, the father of the heroine, he drew pictures of the indifference and hostility of the wealthier classes to the struggle for independence. The Battle of King's Mountain, won by the mountaineers, is vividly pictured, and Kennedy's rescue of Major Butler shows how he could combine the interest of battle and the heroine's devotion to her lover, in the vivid and inspiring climax to a novel which surpasses in merit two of its contemporaries of 1835, *The Linwoods* and *The Partisan;* rivals another, *Hawks of Hawk-Hollow;* and even contests with *The Spy* and *Hugh Wynne* for a leading place among our novels of the Revolution. *Rob of the Bowl* (1838) is noteworthy for being the first and for many years the only novel of any importance which dealt with early colonial days in Maryland. Its general theme is best expressed in Kennedy's own words, "as a native of the state he feels a prompt sensibility to the fame of her Catholic founders, and though differing from them in his faith, cherishes the remembrance of their noble endeavors to establish religious freedom." Kennedy's liberality of mind, which made him, much later, take such a broad view of the relations of State and Union in the *Letters of Paul Ambrose on the Great Rebellion,* is one of his most attractive qualities. But the very fact that he wrote *Rob of the Bowl* to depict the conflict of Catholic and Protestant in Maryland in 1681, makes it necessary for him to insert so much history that the fictional quality of the book is somewhat hurt. The characters, from Lord Baltimore down to the pirate chief, are types, and even the mysterious figure of the cripple, Rob, hardly becomes alive. Kennedy turned away from literature to law and politics, and his *Quodlibet* (1840), sometimes referred to as a novel, is a political satire on the Democratic party in fictional form. It was a campaign document, and need not detain us. Yet *Horse-Shoe Robinson* and *Rob of the Bowl* were reprinted in 1928 and 1929, and the translation of all three of Kennedy's novels into German and their many editions in this country prove their vitality.

The intersectional novel had an early example in *The Kentuckian in New York* (1834), by William Alexander Caruthers (1800–1846), a Virginian by birth and a physician who published his romances anonymously. The Kentuckian, Montgomery Damon, evidently suggested by Paulding's play *The Lion of the West*, really has little to do with the story, which consists largely of the efforts of Victor Chevillère, a Virginian, to win the hand of Frances St. Clair, of New York, and to solve the mystery which surrounds her and makes her refuse him. Caruthers may have recognized the fact that he tells a narrative better than he conducts conversation, for Frances' story, told in writing, is refreshingly direct. Caruthers' views on duelling and on slavery, both of which he disapproves, are interesting. Yet he sees also the hopelessness of freeing the slaves suddenly when they form a majority of the inhabitants. He recognizes, too, the difference between the Southern and Northern aristocracy—how the latter is less secure because of the many gradations which cause the leaders in the North to insist upon their position while in the South, where there is a wider gulf, there is no such insistence.

The Cavaliers of Virginia, or, The Recluse of Jamestown, an Historical Romance of the Old Dominion (1834–1835) is a story laid in Jamestown a short time after the restoration of Charles II. Caruthers draws vividly the three-cornered struggle between the forces of tyranny, led by Governor Berkeley, the Roundhead element, still strong, and the Cavalier liberals under Nathaniel Bacon, who is the hero. Caruthers calls attention to the Virginia Revolution of 1676, which was led by Bacon against Berkeley in consequence of the latter's refusal to provide sufficient defence against the Indians, as a forerunner of the American Revolution. There is a vivid description of the attack on the Governor's house by the Roundheads, and of the battle between the Indians and Bacon. The victory of Bacon over Berkeley, his marriage to Virginia, and the death of the recluse end the story. The similarity of the situation in which the recluse leads the troops of Bacon in the fight to that of the story of Goffe the Regicide in New England is, of course, apparent.

The Knights of the Horseshoe (1845) was written probably at the same time as his earlier books. It is an historical account of Governor Spotswood's career about 1714, beginning with the burial of his half-brother, General Elliott, who had been executed for his loyalty to the Stuarts, and ending with Spotswood's expedition which discovered what is now West Virginia. Spotswood is fairly real, and the hero, Francis Lee, who has been attainted for his attempt to rescue Elliott, is also real for a romantic character. The Indians are depicted realistically, so far as their bloodthirsty quality is concerned. Caruthers' romances are quite readable; his style, except for the conversations, is natural and easy, and his two historical novels picture the early life of Virginia in an authentic manner.

The novel of the future had a peculiar example in *The Partisan Leader, A Tale of the Future,* by Edward William Sidney, a pen-name for Nathaniel Beverley Tucker (1784–1851). This novel was first published in 1835 with "1856" upon the title page. It was written by Professor Tucker for circulation in the Southern States but was suppressed and reissued in 1861. Professor Tucker's object was to call the attention of the Southern people to the necessity of maintaining their liberties, which he claimed were in immediate danger of being suppressed by the United States government. He pictures Van Buren as having kept the President's chair by fraud for several terms and as being in possession in 1849. In the meantime several of the Southern States had made commercial treaties with Great Britain after having seceded. The novel is hardly a well shaped piece of fiction, since the plot is rather incoherently managed. Its main interest lies in its representation of the States' rights position, taken as early as 1836, and the picture of brothers fighting against brothers as later turned out to be the case.

The most consistently professional novelist of this group was another Southerner, William Gilmore Simms (1806–1876). Born in Charleston, South Carolina, the son of an Irish merchant with a taste for adventure who left the scanty education of his child to his grandmother, Simms grew up in an atmosphere which provided him little but obstacles to overcome. The lack of opportunity for regular training, the rigid organization of a society which remained politely unaware of the achievements of their foremost man of letters, even his initial success at the bar, could not prevent him from the attempt, hazardous at that time anywhere in the United States, to devote himself to writing fiction and poetry. In the case of Simms, strict chronology is of less consequence than a study of the different species of his fiction. His first novel, *Martin Faber* (1833), was a romance of crime, a powerful if uneven book. It is the self-analysis of Martin Faber, who is about to be executed for the murder of Emily Andrews whom he has seduced. Faber's attribution of his crime to fate, a determinism which may go back to Calvinism, is consistently carried through the novel. Faber's love for William Harding, his exact opposite, his confession of the murder, Harding's impulse to confess in turn the circumstances of Faber's crime, Faber's ingenuity in turning this confession to Harding's social discredit, and Harding's ultimate revenge by the disclosure of the murdered girl's skeleton, are handled with a skill which for a first book is not inconsiderable. Certain scenes, such as that in which Faber bears the body of Emily to the cave and feels the life of his unborn child whom he is also murdering, are not unworthy, in their conception, of the much greater artist whose work was beginning in New England. Indeed, like Hawthorne, he seems to have read Brockden Brown, for the solitary walks of Faber and his self-analysis indicate a kinship to *Wieland* and *Edgar Huntly*.

After excursions into other fields of fiction, Simms returned, in *Confession; or, The Blind Heart* (1841), to the domestic novel of crime and self-analysis, of which *Martin Faber* was an early example. Edward Clifford tells his own story, of his childhood when his uncle and aunt treated him cruelly, of his love for his cousin Julia, of their marriage and happiness, then of the attempt of his best friend, William Edgerton, to seduce Julia, her repulsion of him, their journey to Alabama to avoid Edgerton, and the discovery on Clifford's part of Edgerton's pursuit. He challenges Edgerton, and Edgerton commits suicide. Clifford's insane jealousy is well portrayed. His self-torture, his twisting of even the most innocent actions of Julia reveal a morbidly sensitive nature. His determination to throw them together and test them, especially her, over and over again, is natural enough. Her failure to tell him of Edgerton's actions gives him some color of excuse; the devilish letters and other actions of her mother, who hates him, goad him on and lead him to poison Julia. Then, too late, he reads her letter, which proves her innocence. His impulse to give himself up, although the doctor's diagnosis of apoplexy saves him from suspicion, is checked by Kingsley, his friend, on the ground that he must *live* and atone for his crime.

The novel is carried on in one tone—a bit monotonous, but still powerful. One reason it is better than many others of Simms' novels lies in the absence of conversation; the characters of Edward Clifford, his uncle and aunt are quite real. Simms' prophecy of what will happen in Texas is worth noting and his defence of duelling as improving the standards of conduct is significant in view of the many fictional condemnations of the institution.

In *Castle Dismal; or, The Bachelor's Christmas, A Domestic Legend* (1844), Simms established the effect of crimes through a powerful story of the supernatural. It is told by a Ned Clifton, a visitor to a country place in South Carolina. He is put to bed in the haunted chamber, and Simms depicts with skill the effect of *chill* which precedes the ghosts, a woman and an older man. Clifton follows the woman into the woods and finds her in the arms of a younger man, with the older man watching them. On the third night, he sees the husband spring a trap by which a huge tree falls on the lover; then the woman rushes by him back to the house. This scene is in Simms' best manner. The next day Clifton goes on a deer hunt and gets lost. He meets an old man, William Potter, a Methodist preacher, who reminds him of the husband. The fourth night he dreams that the woman returns, after fleeing from her husband, wringing water from her hair. Clifton tells Potter of the dream, and Potter makes public confession in the pulpit the next Sunday and dies. Simms' use of the supernatural elements to keep up the suspense is masterly. The conversation is better than usual and the way in which things Clifton hears in the daytime come into his nightly visions will be recognized by any competent dreamer as authentic.

This combination of the supernatural with the story of crime is represented often in Simms' shorter narratives. The earlier ones included in *Carl Werner* (1838), being based largely on "monkish legends," are not as effective as those published in 1845 in *The Wigwam and the Cabin*. "Grayling, or Murder Will Out" is a well constructed supernatural story in which the appearance of a murdered man leads James Grayling, a boy, to the discovery and apprehension of his assassin by the heightening of mental and emotional processes which may account for his supposed vision of his murdered friend, the Major. "The Giant's Coffin" contains a strong climax in which an epileptic buries alive a man he hates; in his efforts to escape from his living grave, the victim cuts off his left hand which was caught and crushed in the fall of the rocky lid of the "coffin," only to drown ultimately by the rising of the river. It is a gruesome but powerful scene.

Those who imagine that realism began after the Civil War should read Simms' comment in "Grayling": "Our story-tellers are so resolute to deal in the real, the actual only, that they venture on no subjects the details of which are not equally vulgar and susceptible of proof.", and also his remark in "The Last Wager": "For, what is fiction, but the nice adaptation, by an artist, of certain ordinary occurrences in life, to a natural and probable conclusion?" Those who insist upon "romantic periods" or "realistic periods" will be puzzled by this apparent contradiction, but those who realize how each artist makes use of differing methods, even at times in the same novel, will not be surprised.

Of Simms' historical novels, the largest group are devoted to the Revolution. In seven novels, from 1835 to 1856, he painted, with a vigorous if at times a hurried pen, pictures of the last period of the war in South Carolina, when the skill of Nathaniel Greene and the daring of the partisan leaders, Marion, Sumter, and Lee, recovered the territory which the capture of Charleston and Gates' defeat at Camden had apparently left helpless before the victorious army of Cornwallis and Rawdon. *The Partisan* (1835) begins in 1780 when many of the Whigs had been momentarily driven into submission or neutrality. The hero, Major Singleton, is a representative of the younger, as Colonel Walton is of the older, group of patriots, who belong to the patrician landholders. Gates' defeat at Camden is described with the skill Simms usually showed when fighting was to be portrayed, and while there is little fighting under Marion's leadership, the life in his camp in the swamps is vividly drawn. Simms attempts to lighten the story with humor through a character, Lieutenant Porgy, who appears in several of the novels, but humor is not Simms' forte. As Poe remarked, "Porgy is a most insufferable bore." [1] Much better drawn is the Tory spy, Blonay, the half-breed son of an Indian and a witch, who takes an even greater share of attention in the sequel, *Mellichampe* (1836). The way in which this disfigured being, ignorant and half-savage, tracks Lieutenant Humphries, whose troop had trampled Blonay's mother to death, and the mixture of greed and of a queer sense of gratitude toward Janet Berkeley, the heroine of *Mellichampe*, makes Blonay unforgettable. His stoical conduct when Humphries finds him in the hollow tree and closes all avenues of escape from starvation to him might have led to a great scene, but Simms needed Blonay to save Ernest Mellichampe, the hero. So he made Humphries repent of his action against all probability and release the spy, who fell later by the bullets of his em-

---

[1] *Southern Literary Messenger*, January, 1836.

ployers, the British. It was this inability, except in a few cases, to carry a character or a motive through to its logical end, which prevented Simms from being a great novelist. This is illustrated in one of the best of the novels of the Revolution, *Katharine Walton* (1851), in which he returned to the characters of *The Partisan,* shortly after the rescue of Colonel Walton by Robert Singleton. He began well; the introduction of Singleton into the Walton home while Colonel Balfour and Colonel Craven were taking possession, his cool bearing while he pretends to be a loyalist captain, Furness, whom he has captured and whose letters he has taken, leads to scenes of suspense and danger for Singleton and Katharine, in which Simms as usual shone. But the weakness of *Katharine Walton* does not lie, as is usually stated, in his inability to represent the social life of Charleston after Katharine has been taken there. The interplay of Whig and Tory society is used suitably enough to provide occasions for carrying on the plot, for the conveying of information from Singleton to Kate and to Major Proctor, the British officer whose career is being sacrificed to the ambitions of Balfour and the hatred of Major Vaughn, his rival. The scenes in the city are a welcome relief from the rather tiresome descriptions of Porgy and his gastronomic feats. But the change of the chief interest from Singleton to the British officer Proctor midway in the book is unfortunate, first because Singleton is more interesting and second because Proctor's escape and desertion of the British cause after he kills Vaughn do not form a climax by which an American can be thrilled as he is, for example, by the rescue of Walton in *The Partisan.* Walton's execution at the end of *Katharine Walton* is tragic, but the book seems hurried; the last paragraph, in which Simms steps into the novel to defend his historical accuracy, is unforgivable. The central characters are all spirited people, however, and so was Simms. His real or presumed inability to enter into the feelings of the patrician of that time seems beside the point. Katharine Walton acts like a gentlewoman, even if she talks, like all Simms' characters, in a stilted fashion.

Simms might plead the examples of Scott and Cooper in his inability to endow with life the characters who carry the love interest. In *The Kinsmen* (1841), revised in 1854 as *The Scout,* the two half-brothers, Clarence and Edward Conway, Whig and Tory, rivals for the love of Flora Middleton, are much less real than Jack Bannister, the patriot scout, who watches over the other characters and ties the story together.

The burial of Mary Clarkson, Edward Conway's mistress, who had followed him disguised as a member of his Tory troop, the "Black Riders of the Congaree," and had been given her death blow by Bannister in ignorance of her real nature, is a striking scene. The remorse of her father, who had driven her from home, and of the scout, who had loved her as a girl, adds to the pathos of her lot, and the imminence of the danger of both men from the Tories and British provides that suspense which makes us keep on reading the novel despite the melodrama of the brotherly feud.

More interesting than *The Scout, Woodcraft* (1856), first published as *The Sword and the Distaff* (1853), pictures the conditions in Charleston and its neighborhood at the close of the Revolution. Mrs. Everleigh, the widow whose negroes have been stolen by the British, is as refreshing in her direct and natural language as Simms' usual heroines are unnatural, probably because she is fighting for her rights. Most interesting is the realistic description of the economic and social results of the Revolution, the thin line that divided plenty from ruin, and the portrayal of a class of citizens like Lieutenant Porgy who returned to a small plantation to find literally nothing on which to live. The triumphant entrance of Greene into Charleston and his refusal to permit Marion and the other partisans to parade with the regular troops because of their shabbiness and unruly nature sheds a new light upon one aspect of the Revolution.

In *The Forayers* (1855) and its sequel *Eutaw* (1856), Simms repeated the formula of his romances of the Revolution, in the strife of Whig and Tory, and again, as was natural, the evil or abnormal characters are best portrayed. The lovers, Sinclair and St. Julien, and the heroines, Carrie Sinclair and Bertha Travis, remain mere names. But the old Tory father, Colonel Sinclair, the double traitor Captain Travis, and, best of all, the half-mad girl, Nellie Floyd, who dogs the steps of Inglehardt's Tory band to persuade her brother to leave them, are the actors we remember. The battle of Eutaw is pictured with the skill Simms always showed in the description of conflict. In 1867 Simms returned to historical romance, in *Joscelyn, a Tale of the Revolution*, laid in Georgia at the beginning of the struggle, and representing the struggle of Whig and Tory and the strife that divided families.

But it was in his romance of colonial and Indian life that Simms wrote his best novel, *The Yemassee* (1835); and, from the inevitable com-

parison with Cooper, Simms emerges without apology. The chieftain of
the Indians, Sanutee, who foresees the destruction of his race before the
ruthless progress of the English settlers, is a notable figure. Betrayed
by some of his chiefs, among them his own son Occonestoga, who have
agreed to sell their lands to the English, he drives them into exile but
dies in the battle between the English and the Yemassee. Unsurpassed
even by Cooper is the scene of the degradation of Occonestoga, who lies
bound awaiting the moment when the arrow, the totem of the Yemassee,
shall be cut out of his shoulder and he shall be doomed not only to
banishment but to external exile from the happy hunting grounds of
the tribe. Matiwan, his mother, asks permission to say good-bye to him
and then kills him, believing that if he dies with the totem still untouched, she will see him in eternity.

In 1859 Simms returned to colonial life in *The Cassique of Kiawah*,
a romance of South Carolina, centering about Charleston in 1684. It
has few of the merits of *The Yemassee*, being a love story, with Simms'
usual unhappy vocabulary in scenes of passion or tenderness, and with
an absurd climax in which Harry Berkeley and Zuleime are dismissed
by the author, unhappily married, and discontented rather than tragic.
The picture of the life in colonial South Carolina is fairly vivid, especially the corruption of the governor, who takes bribes from the smug-
glers while pretending to act against them. The few Indians, who attack
the Cassique's home, are not individualized.   •

Considering the success of *The Yemassee*, many have wondered why
Simms made the Indian so infrequently the major theme of his novels.
They have neglected his shorter narratives, for four stories in *Carl
Werner* and six in *The Wigwam and the Cabin* deal with Indian characters. None rises to the level of *The Yemassee*, but there is a directness
and a sense of climax in "The Arm-Chair of Tustenuggee," depicting the
supernatural actions of a tree which covers the limbs of the Indian who
sits upon it; in "Oakatibbé," the tale of an Indian chief who returns to
his execution rather than break his word; in "Jocassee," a vigorous account of the warfare between two tribes of the Cherokees; and in "Lucas
de Ayllon," a semi-historical narrative of the revenge of Combahee, the
queen of the Muscaghees, a kindred tribe to the Yemassee, upon the
Spaniards who had killed her husband. "Caloya" too is of special interest
in its contrast of the Indian and the negro.

Simms' excursions into Spanish history, *Pelayo; a Story of the Goth*

(1838) and its sequel *Count Julian* (1845), are filled with conventional figures of early Spanish history centering around the seizure of King Witiza's throne by Roderick, the last Gothic king before the invasion of the Moors, and the treachery of Count Julian in revenge for his ill treatment. Simms knew little about Spanish character, early or late, though he read industriously, and *Vasconselos* (1854), which belongs evidently to an earlier period of composition, while based on some research, is far inferior to Bird's romance of Mexico, so far as an understanding of the mingled motives which animated the Spanish conquerors is concerned. De Soto is a caricature and Philip de Vasconselos, the Portuguese hero, is conventional. The relations of Olivia de Alvaro and her uncle are revolting rather than tragic, and the few bright spots are the tourneys and the battles. The Indians do not approach the level of those in *The Yemassee,* and the novel gives an impression of haste and carelessness. Nor is *The Damsel of Darien* (1839), of which Balboa is the hero, any better, although Simms took his history from Irving's *Companions of Columbus.*

Simms did his poorest work in the "border romances," although he was familiar with the localities of which he speaks, many of which he had visited with his father as a young man. There was apparently good material, but as Simms used it, it was really suitable only for background and for single episodes. In his first novel of this kind, *Guy Rivers* (1834), we forget the romantic hero and even the melodramatic villain who gives the title to the story. We remember only the vividly realistic scene in which the Yankee peddler is brutally treated by the people of the village. But isolated scenes do not make a novel. Simms conceived as his central motive for *Guy Rivers,* and for *Richard Hurdis; or, the Avenger of Blood, a Tale of Alabama* (1838), *Border Beagles, A Tale of Mississippi* (1840), and *Helen Halsey; or, The Swamp State of Conelachita* (1845), a romantic hero, usually a patrician from another section, in conflict with a band of robbers. The robbers he drew from the "Murrell gang," about whom he had heard at first hand from Virgil Stewart, who had captured Murrell. Yet the stories are sheer melodrama, for the characters talk in a language certainly never spoken by human beings. Even more serious is a fault not peculiar to Simms, but rather to romance. He can establish a sense of danger to Hurdis in a confederacy which spreads all over the South, and which Hurdis is defying apparently to his certain death; yet the confederacy collapses at one cavalry charge. A reader has the sense of irritation that comes in fiction when his apprehension has been awakened unjustifiably. Simms has been criticized unjustly, however, for the way his heroes are convicted, upon the slightest evidence, of murder, for he knew that justice was administered in that way on the frontier. Perhaps, after all, the material was not so good for fiction, for when life is illogical a novelist must treat it as Bret Harte knew how to do, but as Simms did not. He should have found his heroes among the men of the frontier and not built them upon a pattern created by Walter Scott.

In 1842 he wrote *Beauchampe; or, The Kentucky Tragedy, A Tale of Passion*. It was based upon the killing of Solomon P. Sharp by Jereboam Beauchamp, in Frankfort in 1825. Sharp had seduced Anne Cooke some years before Beauchamp married her and she demanded revenge upon her betrayer. Simms began the novel in its first form with the early history of "Margaret Cooper" in the village of Charlemont, her rejection of her lover, William Hinkley, and her seduction by Sharpe, under the name of Alfred Stevens and in the disguise of a clergyman. Her child dies and she leaves Charlemont forever. This portion of *Beauchampe* was renamed *Charlemont* and published, with quite a few revisions, in 1856, as a separate novel.[2] The second part of *Beauchampe* dealt with the meeting of young Orville Beauchampe and Anne Cooke, who has removed to Bowling Green, near Frankfort, her refusal and her later agreement to marry him, her confession before marriage of her relations with Stevens, and the appearance of Stevens under the name of Sharpe at their home. Beauchampe challenges Sharpe, who refuses to fight him and is consequently stabbed by Beauchampe. Simms follows closely the events of the trial, the verdict of guilty, the suicide of wife and husband in prison, and the dragging of the expiring

---

[2] Since every printed discussion of *Beauchampe* known to the writer speaks of *Charlemont* as a sequel to it, and the date of the latter is given as 1856, the facts should be given if only to relieve Simms from the charge of having deliberately returned to the theme after a lapse of fourteen years. The confusion has arisen from the rarity of the 1842 edition of *Beauchampe*. It is in two volumes. Volume I and pp. 1–57 of Volume II make up what is now known as *Charlemont*. The 1856 edition of *Charlemont* adds a new chapter (XXXVIII) and concludes, "The Chronicle of 'Charlemont' will find its fitting sequel in that of 'Beauchampe'—known proverbially as 'The Kentucky Tragedy.'" This is not, of course, in the 1842 edition.

Chapter VII of Volume II of the 1842 *Beauchampe* begins what is now known as *Beauchampe*, but up to page 57 the revised version gives new matter, and there are additions distributed through the text. Two pages are added. Simms was therefore entirely correct in calling *Beauchampe* a sequel to *Charlemont*.

Beauchampe to the scaffold. Here the novel in its first form ends, but in 1856 the second part was published separately as *Beauchampe, a Sequel to Charlemont*, and Simms not only revised it but added some gratuitous information concerning the minor characters. The novel is one of Simms' poorest, but it is of interest to note that some of the most melodramatic language, such as the vow of vengeance Margaret takes, is not in the edition of 1842. All his additions, in fact, weaken the story. Simms' critical taste was at fault also in the use of the real names of the characters and in the laying of the scene in Frankfort. Poe in *Politian* and Charlotte Barnes in *Octavia Bragaldi* had shown him in their dramatic treatments of the same story that it had better be laid in Rome in the seventeenth or in Milan in the fifteenth century. And when John Savage dramatized *Beauchampe* as *Sybil* in 1858, he changed the names, even though he kept the scene in Kentucky. Simms did not neglect Louisiana in the Southwestern stories, but *Marie de Bernière* (1853) is an absurd tale with no understanding of the charm of Creole life.

Toward the end of his career Simms printed in periodicals a number of romances which seem not to have been reprinted in book form. Among these is *Joscelyn*, which has already been mentioned. Two others are *Voltmeier; or the Mountain Men* (1869), laid in Spartanburg, South Carolina, about 1830, and *The Cub of the Panther, a Mountain Legend* (1869), laid in North Carolina and founded upon a folk ballad half a century old. They are "border romances" of a different kind, better written than *Richard Hurdis* or *Beauchampe*, but they were too late for one fashion and too early for another. Yet it is satisfactory to see the talent of the old romancer flash up again in the final battle in *Joscelyn*, and in the scene in *The Cub of the Panther* in which Michael Baynam kills the beast who is about to slay the woman he loves as she lies unconscious in the mountain snow. Even better is his portrayal of Dunbar's growing consciousness of guilt in *Joscelyn*. It was in this portrayal of human beings torn by the pangs of conscience that Simms might have done great work, but stern necessity and popular approval of his weaker romances led him into other fields.

As might have been expected, the novel of social relations, following Cooper at a distance, was written usually in New York. The performance was certainly not upon the level of the best of the historical romance. Theodore Sedgwick Fay (1807–1898), who had the advantage of European travel, produced in 1835 *Norman Leslie*, which has an international quality of a superficial sort, but which Poe justly criticized. *Sydney Clifton* (1839) is worth reading, however, if only to see how absurd Gothic romance can be when laid in New York and London. *The Countess Ida* (1840) is much better; it is one of the few American novels laid in Berlin, which Fay knew well. Fay attacks duelling vigorously in this novel, and his next, *Hoboken* (1843), is based upon the evils which spring from this practice for which the shores of New Jersey seemed to be the favorite location. The moral urge of Fay's novels would have spoiled them if his curious conversation had not done so.

Far better was the work of Fay's friend, Nathaniel Parker Willis (1806–1867). He had a more intimate acquaintance than Fay with social life both here and abroad, but, more important, he had that keen sense of social values which owing to our very lack of rigid distinctions has been developed to such a high degree in the United States. In such shorter stories as are included in *Life, Here and There; or Sketches of Society and Adventure* (1850) Willis depicted with a realistic pen the anatomy of love controlled by social inhibitions. In his picture of the poet who is sought after as a lion and as a lover by various women in England, but is treated by only one as a possible husband, he struck that note of the resentment of the artist against those who accept him merely as a celebrity and not as a human being, which was made the motive of his novel *Paul Fane* (1857). Here the contrast was international, for it is the attitude of Mildred Ashley, an English visitor to Boston, which for the first time implies that the young painter is an inferior. Willis drew very well the effect of such treatment upon an impressionable mind, conscious of artistic ability; the determination of Fane to conquer recognition as a person as well as an artist from the class to which Mildred Ashley belongs leads him to Italy and to England. Willis indicates through Paul Fane the material basis of social distinction in Europe and the less definite connection between wealth and such distinction in the United States, owing to the rapid rise and fall of fortunes. Willis was still affected by the idealistic manner, and Paul Fane's triumph over Mildred Ashley is hardly credible. But his fiction keeps its interest as one of the earliest expressions of that pride of craft of which Willis is a comforting example.

The novel hardly rose to the level of the drama in this field. Certainly Mrs. Mowatt's *The Fortune Hunter* (1842), although it was translated into German, is not in the same class as her play *Fashion*, which has proved its worth so often on the contemporary stage. She wrote her fiction too hastily, usually under the pen name of "Helen Berkeley," sometimes writing several articles for the same magazine under different names.

A curious development of the novel, prompted partly by the desire to mix morality and fiction and make the latter respectable, is illustrated by the work of William Ware (1797–1852), a Unitarian clergyman, who wrote three novels which had wide circulation. *Letters of Lucius M. Piso from Palmyra, to his Friend Marcus Curtius at Rome* (1837), later known as *Zenobia*, is a well written story, told through a Roman who comes to Palmyra about 270 A. D. The conflict of Rome with the East is fairly well established, and the philosophy can be skipped. In *Probus* (1838), later called *Aurelian*, the Unitarian flavor became more apparent and in *Julian* (1841) absurdity triumphs in the author's amiable domestic picture of the "brothers" and "sisters" of Christ created by Ware in order to emphasize His human to the exclusion of His divine nature. The novels of Ware are a fine example of the evil effects of propaganda, for when he is dealing with real history, as in his picture of the political and social conditions of Cæsarea and Herod's ambitions to be King of Judea, he rises at times almost to epic qualities of narrative, and his style is far above that of the average novelist of his day.

Whether Joseph Holt Ingraham (1809–1860) was fired by the success of Ware is now only conjectural, but he abandoned the field of American historical romances in which he had perpetrated such absurdities as *La Fitte; the Pirate of the Gulf* (1836) and had written better romances like *Burton; or, The Sieges*, whose hero was Aaron Burr. In 1855 he produced in *The Prince of the House of David* one of the most widely read books of its day. It is told by letters from Adina, a Jewish maiden, visiting in Jerusalem, to her father in Cairo, and gives the events leading up to the Crucifixion and Resurrection. The author, who was an Episcopal clergyman, wrote his books, he says, to convert liberal Jews to Christianity, but he keeps the propaganda in the introductions, where he also repudiates the many publications attributed to him,[3] but of which he was innocent. His later novels, *The Pillar of Fire*

[3] The Library of Congress contains twenty novels, dating from 1845 to 1850, attributed to Ingraham. They deal with the Revolution, the sea, the evils of city life, the days of Montezuma, even the days of Charles II in England. They are of interest simply as representing the constant imitation of prevailing modes of romance.

(1859), centering upon the career of Moses, and *The Throne of David* (1860), "an attempt to illustrate the grandeur of Hebraic history," to use Ingraham's own words, are too cluttered up with confused archæology to be readable today, although indeed all three of Ingraham's later novels have been reprinted within recent years.

The union of the historical and moral impulses in Ware and Ingraham were parallelled during the 'fifties by the combination of the picaresque and moral motives in such popular successes as *The Wide Wide World* (1850) of Susan Warner, and the many stories of Augusta Evans Wilson (1838–1909), of which *Beulah* (1859) and *St. Elmo* (1866) are the chief. The plots are the same—a virtuous adventuress, often a child, travels around a large or small area, accumulating moral experiences. The type had existed ever since Mrs. Rowson's day, and is based upon the profound statement given in *Resignation, An American Novel* (1825), "by a Lady," that "the world is a dangerous place for virtue." The appeal of such books is a matter of more significance to the social historian than to the literary critic, but it is founded upon the longing cherished by thousands of girls who lived a humdrum life for similar adventures. Mrs. Wilson's books added another element, probably derived from *Jane Eyre*. In her novels the heroine converts to morality a fascinating Byronic character, dark, dissipated, and dangerous. The struggles of Beulah and of Edna Earl in *St. Elmo* are nearer realism, and Mrs. Wilson, at least, knew what realism was, if she did not practice it. To this group of moral picaresques belongs also *The Lamplighter* (1854), by Maria S. Cummins, still worth reading, and her *Mabel Vaughan* (1857) which is not. It is a persistent type, often winning great popularity, as in the later work of E. P. Roe.

In the history of fiction, chronology, while important, is less significant than the development of the type. John Esten Cooke (1830–1886), although he published novels as late as 1885, belongs distinctly to the romantic impulse of which Bird, Kennedy and Simms were the chief representatives. He was born in Winchester, Virginia, and spent his early years in that valley region where English, Irish and German strains were mingled. This civilization is reflected in his first published novel, for which he wisely laid aside for later serial publication his earlier romances of European life in order to write about what he knew. *Leather Stocking and Silk* (1854) is a story of Virginia at the beginning of the nineteenth century. The plot is weak and the conversations are interminable, but the book is important historically because it represents the comfortable middle class of foreign extraction of which little is said in Southern romance. The mountaineers are brought in also, picturesque in their dances and merrymaking, and Hunter John Myers was drawn from a real person.

That Cooke's second published novel, *The Virginia Comedians* (1854), is his best, was due to the fact that it was inspired by his love for the past of Virginia and his interest in the theatre. He had known Kate Bateman, then just at the threshold of her successful career on the stage, as a child, and seeing her again in Richmond he built upon her vivid personality the character of Beatrice Hallam, the young actress who is the heroine of *The Virginia Comedians* in 1763. With cheerful disregard of facts he made her the daughter of Lewis Hallam, the first manager of the American Company, who in 1763 was dead, and while there was a "Miss Hallam" in the company, which really did open in Williamsburg in 1752, we know little about her. But Cooke knew that what is needed in romance is not facts but color, contrast and life, and these he gave in full measure. He created a picture of the social life of Colonial Virginia, its careless enjoyment, its irresponsibility, and its charm. He secures contrast through the hero-villain, Champ Effingham, whose pursuit of Beatrice Hallam as the proper prey of any gentleman represents accurately enough the attitude of the patrician, South or North, to the theatre of the eighteenth century. The scene at the Governor's Ball, to which Champ takes her against her will, is masterly. The discovery that she is not Hallam's daughter, but that of a good Virginian, is necessary before she can be married to Charles Waters, and her death is more dramatic than logical. That the struggle in the mind of Beatrice Hallam against the charm of Effingham would have puzzled an actress of the eighteenth century may be quite true, but Cooke is hardly to be criticized, for he gave us a situation that rarely fails to appeal. As usual, he put too much into his novel, the book falls apart in the middle, and the approach of the Revolution is hardly worked into the lengthy plot. It was dramatized, however, in 1856 with some success, by C. W. Tayleure. *The Last of the Foresters* (1856) returns to the Valley of Virginia, but it is simply a conventional love story with the usual long lost child, the portrait and the mark on the arm that restore him to his father. The efforts at humor are best treated with silence. *Henry St. John* (1857) is a sequel to *The Virginia Comedians*, and is concerned with the opening of the Revolution in Virginia. There is a love story, of course, between the hero and Bonnybell Vane, but the significance of the book lies in its contrast of Whig and Tory, the picture of the stupidity of such men as Governor Dunmore and the consequent change in the sentiment of the landholding class. For the reflected glamour which came from the crown of England they decided to substitute an independence which retained them the supremacy in days to come. Cooke has drawn well the part which social organization played before and during the Revolution.

Cooke was one of the most prolific of the Southern group, but much of his work was fugitive periodical writing. In 1858 he published, in the *Southern Literary Messenger, Greenway Court*, which was not put into book form until 1868, as *Fairfax; or The Master of Greenway Court*. It is a story of the Shenandoah Valley in 1748 and thereafter, with Lord Fairfax and George Washington as the principal historical figures, and belongs distinctly to his earliest period. Washington is introduced as a young surveyor, and provided with an early love story. The best part of the novel deals with the love of a half-breed, "Yellow Serpent" for Bertha Argal, who is really insane. The way in which his passion appeals to her although she does not love him, and the clever use she makes of it to rescue her companions are quite effectively pictured.

Cooke fought in the Civil War as a staff officer of General Stuart, and in 1866 he began his series of romances of the war with *Surry of Eagle's Nest*. Through the eyes of an imaginary aide to General Stonewall Jackson, whose duties naturally gave him opportunity for rapid movement, Cooke painted a remarkable picture of the war in Virginia up to the Battle of Chancellorsville in 1863. His talent for endowing historical characters with personal life bring Stonewall Jackson, "Jeb" Stuart, Turner Ashby, Pelham, and other Confederate leaders vividly into a struggle in which they live bravely and many die gloriously. Colonel Surry's duties give him opportunity also to visit his beloved, May Beverley, who is engaged to another man for most of the book. But neither she nor any of the other women are more than names. Even Violet Grafton, who rides through both lines to bring word to the Southern army, and is the heroine of a complicated romance, centering around a "strong silent man," Captain Mordaunt, does not come alive. We turn with relief from this episode, with its inevitable child lost in infancy, to the forced marches, the iron will of Stonewall Jackson, the rattle of Stuart's cavalry, the gallantry of the army which was fighting for the "lost cause" before it was lost. The calm critic, especially if his ancestry was on the other side of the struggle, cannot help smiling at the inevitable flight of the Union cavalry in every skirmish, and Cooke's figures concerning the relative numbers of the forces engaged would make any impartial historian gasp. But even in the extraordinary interview between McClellan and Surry, in which the former calmly discusses his plans with a captured prisoner, the attitude of McClellan toward the South is quite fairly represented, and a more accurate estimate of McClellan's abilities is given than would have appeared in a Northern novel in 1866. It is this sense of reality in the general atmosphere and in vivid scenes such as the death of Jackson which made *Surry* one of the best pictures of the Civil War in American fiction. It was superior to *Hilt to Hilt* (1869), in which Cooke continued the memoirs of Colonel Surry, but laid the scene among the partisan or guerrilla bands of the Shenandoah Valley, bringing his own home into the story. He claims that he is telling only facts, but certainly the climax, in which Captain St. Leger Landon, bound and about to be executed, leaps upon his enemy and seizes his throat in his teeth, has rarely been exceeded in the annals of melodrama. There are no great historic figures here to lift the story into permanent interest.

In *Mohun; or The Last Days of Lee and his Paladins*, (1869) Cooke continued to tell his story through the eyes of Surry, and again used his own experiences in the Civil War. General Stuart is once more a heroic figure. There is a complicated family quarrel and the Union and Confederate secret services are confusing rather than dramatic elements. But nowhere in fiction are we given as realistic a picture of the closing days of the war in Richmond. The wealthy blockade runners who have made money out of their countrymen's dire necessities, the confusion which brought to the surface elements not usually mentioned, are depicted together with the chivalric picture of the "lost cause." The apparent security of Richmond and at the same time the conviction on the part of those best informed that the end was near are also clearly indicated.

The Heir of Gaymount (1870), while not significant in its character drawing, and clearly, in its story of buried treasure found by a cryptogram, an imitation of "The Gold Bug," has a certain interest because of its reflection of Cooke's own experiences after the Civil War. The hero,

Edmund Carteret, faced with ruin, rejects the old easy going methods of agriculture which had impoverished the South, and represents the spirit which through variation of crops pointed to the future. Unfortunately Cooke was ahead of his time here, and his methods of telling the story were still the old ones. It was published first in *The Old Guard* in 1870, the magazine to which Simms was a contributor and which was devoted to the Democratic crusade for white supremacy in the South. The uneven quality of Cooke's work can be seen in a comparison of *Out of the Foam* (1871), one of the most absurd of his stories, laid in England during a war with France, probably the Napoleonic era, with *Her Majesty the Queen* (1873), a romance of the days of Charles I, which is quite readable. To be sure, it is a Cavalier of Virginia of 1860 whom he is describing, and not a Cavalier of England in the 1640's. But there are some strong scenes, notably that in which Charles I reveals his feelings before the portrait of Strafford. *Doctor VanDyke* (1872), a story of Williamsburg laid in 1772, is a mystery tale of no especial value. *Canolles; or, The Fortunes of a Partisan of '81* (1877), while not equal to Cooke's best stories, is unique in the romances dealing with the Revolution. The hero, Hartley Canolles Cartaret, refuses to accept a commission from the United States and fights as an independent captain of Rangers, owing allegiance only to Virginia. The reason he gives, his father's refusal to follow the Colonial cause to its logical conclusion in separation from England, with consequent ostracism, may seem fantastic, but to anyone familiar with the progress of opinion in the early days of the Revolution, Canolles is not impossible. In a sense, also, he was the symbol of the State pride which caused the Confederacy, set against the background of the Revolution. In 1880 Cooke tried to imitate *The Virginia Comedians* with a story of contrasts between the gentry of the Piedmont region in Virginia and the members of a circus troupe playing there in the late 'seventies. But he was not able to throw the romantic glamour about Mignon and her supposed father, the "Left Hander," with which he had invested the Hallam Company. There are some good touches, however, especially the description of the writer who is forgotten.

Fanchette (1883), a novel of life in Washington and on the eastern shore of Maryland about 1880, is an entertaining story, with some character drawing but with a heroine of mysterious parentage as usual, who without much reason sends the man she loves away because she does not recognize that fact. In 1885 Cooke joined the procession of those who had treated the Smith-Pocahontas story in a romantic version of *The General History of Virginia,* supposed to have been written by Amos Todkill, one of the adventurers. It is couched in an attempt at seventeenth-century language and is mainly concerned with an imaginary love story between Smith and Pocahontas. *My Lady Pokahontas* is neither history nor fiction and is artificial and dull. Cooke must have had little sense of humor, for when he takes Pokahontas to England he draws an amazing scene at the Globe Theatre in which Shakespeare and Smith converse and in which the playwright acknowledges that he has drawn Miranda from Pokahontas! Cooke's last long novel, *The Maurice Mystery* (1885), another story of the Piedmont country, is a long drawn out attempt on the part of a son, Haworth Dacis, to relieve his father's memory of the stain of murder. Cooke had no great ability in the creation of mysteries, although he was fond of them. He belonged to a school of writing which believed that suspense could be secured by postponing the explanation and by putting up straw men to be knocked down. He does not, however, deserve the comparative neglect which has befallen him, for he was a born story-teller; that he came belated into a period in which his methods no longer prevailed was his misfortune.

An historian of fiction can only record but cannot discuss the hundreds of novels which the prolific writers of the 'forties and 'fifties produced. Among the favorite themes was the Revolution, about one third of the romances being devoted to this conflict. The frontier, especially the life of the desperado, was also a frequent theme, particularly in the Southwest. The revelation of the evils of city life [4] was a constant inspiration to a host of novelists whose work varied from a respectable production like *Clinton Bradshaw* (1835) by Frederick W. Thomas, through the sensational novels of George Lippard, to even lower depths of deliberate appeal to scandal. They are only of significance as an indication of the growing popularity of fiction and the ever present love of the unusual which, whatever the literary fashion, keeps romance perennial.

[4] See Dunlap, George A., *The City in the American Novel* (Philadelphia, 1934).

NATHANIEL HAWTHORNE, THE ROMANCE OF THE MORAL LIFE

NATHANIEL HAWTHORNE marks the artistic culmination of the romance in America before the Civil War. Born in Salem in 1804, he began to write short stories while at Bowdoin College, and the *Seven Tales of My Native Land*, which he destroyed in disgust at their reception by a dilatory publisher, were in existence in 1825. Yet the 'thirties and the 'forties, the two decades in which the influence of Cooper stimulated the romance of history, the frontier and the sea,. found Hawthorne slowly maturing in his own special field, the romance of the moral life. He did not publish *The Scarlet Letter* until Poe was dead and Cooper had only one year more to live. By 1850 the romantic idealistic novel was apparently on the wane; and the great novels of Hawthorne came not in response to a popular demand, but in quiet neglect of any artistic direction but that of his own genius. Like Poe, he knew that his function was to write; that his sacrifices were fewer than those of his great rival was due only to his possession of a small income and the more successful effort of his friends, like Bancroft and Pierce, to provide employment for him in the public service. From the point of view of his establishment in fiction, however, his positions as Weigher in the Boston Custom House, from 1839 to 1841, as Surveyor of the Port at Salem from 1846 to 1849, and as Consul at Liverpool from 1853 to 1857 were interruptions which only the necessity for providing for his family justified. That these were serious interruptions, the chronological list of his writings will show at a glance. During 1837 and again in 1838 fourteen of his short stories appeared, while only three were published in 1839, one in 1840, and none in 1841. During his surveyorship at Salem, although he wrote a few stories, practically nothing except the essay "Main Street" appeared, and during his consulate nothing at all. Bitter as he felt at his dismissal by the Whigs in 1849, Sophia Hawthorne was right in welcoming him with the assurance, "Oh, then you can write your book!" and the publication of *The Scarlet Letter* (1850), *The House of the Seven Gables* (1851), and *The Blithedale Romance* (1852) justified the confidence of the woman who was in so many ways his protector and advisor. What is surprising, however, is not so much the interruption, for Hawthorne always took his duties seriously. It is rather the lack of inspiration from his surroundings, considering that his father was a sea-captain and the sea should have been in his blood. He felt the urge himself, for he notes in his journal: [1]

On board my salt vessels and colliers there are many things happening, many pictures which in future years, when I am again busy at the loom of fiction, I could weave in; but my fancy is rendered so torpid by my ungenial way of life that I cannot sketch off the scenes and portraits that interest me, and I am forced to trust them to my memory, with the hope of recalling them at some more favorable period.

But his official duties and his creative work remained things apart.

How restless Hawthorne was during these enforced periods of idleness can be understood only by the reading of the *Note-Books* and by his letters. But his long struggle for recognition was even more galling to him and was further embittered by the self-distrust which his own high critical standard fostered. He tried to destroy the copies of his first novel, *Fanshawe* (1828), a story of an abortive attempt at abduction laid in a college town, for which Brunswick, the site of Bowdoin College, is probably the model. *Fanshawe* is not a very important production. It is young and a bit solemn and the characters are mere types, but considering its relative excellence in 1828, there was no adequate reason for its destruction. He turned then definitely to the short story, probably seeing no other outlet than the periodicals and gift books of that pusillanimous age of American publishing.

His short stories are not, as in Poe's case, his supreme achievement in fiction. They are often preparatory treatments of themes used with far greater effect in his novels. Indeed, with the exception of *Fanshawe* (1828), Hawthorne's career is sharply divided chronologically between his creation of the two forms.

Hawthorne's short stories do not lend themselves to classification as profitably as do those of Poe. There is not the same variety of type and yet more than one interest is frequently combined in a single story. A

[1] *American Note-Books*, Riverside Edition, May 30, 1840, p. 220.

comparison of his earlier and later stories, however, reveals certain changes which may account for Hawthorne's abandonment of the form after the success of *The Scarlet Letter*. In any analysis of the stories now included in *Twice Told Tales* (1837–1842), *Mosses from an Old Manse* (1846), *The Snow Image and Other Twice Told Tales* (1851), and *Tales, Sketches and Other Papers*, first collected in 1883, it must be remembered that these dates do not represent accurately the time of the first publication of the individual stories.[2]

Of the eighty-three examples [3] of Hawthorne's shorter fiction so collected, twenty-nine (more than one-third) are obviously essays. They are of great interest, however, since their very inclusion shows that Hawthorne's short story grew out of the combination of the tale and the character sketch, and the tendency to write essays increased in the later years.

Hawthorne was at his best both in the short story and the novel when he dealt with the analysis of the effect of sin upon the heart, and when he threw around this tragedy the atmosphere of the supernatural and laid the scene within the past of New England which he loved so much, he produced his masterpieces. He did not always combine these three elements in his short stories, but the earliest published, "The Hollow of the Three Hills" (1830), is an example of the combination. It is a revelation of the character of a woman who comes to a witch to have revealed to her the evil fates of her parents, her husband, and her child, for which she has been responsible. The story ends with the words of the withered crone, "Here has been a sweet hour's sport!" It has unity also and, while Hawthorne did not always maintain that unity, it remained a quality of "My Kinsman, Major Molineaux," "The Wives of the Dead," and "The Gentle Boy," all in *The Token* for 1832.

In 1835 "The Gray Champion" personified the spirit of Puritanism in the recall of the regicide, Goffe, to defy the power of a king whose father he had condemned to death. "Young Goodman Brown" (1835) portrayed the horror of a young husband who believes his wife has been tainted by the moral leprosy of witchcraft by which he had himself been tempted. In the same year, in "The White Old Maid," Hawthorne

---

[2] See *A Bibliography of Nathaniel Hawthorne*, compiled by Nina C. Browne (Boston, New York, 1905), for dates of periodical publication.

[3] From *Tales and Sketches* only four, "The Antique Ring," "Graves and Goblins," "An Old Woman's Tale," and "Alice Doane's Appeal," are included. The remainder are definitely descriptions of travel or biographical sketches.

drew a contrast between the natures of two women, loving the same man, who is lying dead before them under a dark shadow of crime, which lengthens into the marvellous climax of reparation.

The sardonic satire of "The Devil in Manuscript" (1835), in which Hawthorne reveals his discouragement at the lack of appreciation by the publishers of his day for anything but schoolbooks and novels, is more than justified. What would have happened if his friend Horatio Bridge had not provided the necessary funds to publish *Twice Told Tales*, it is unpleasant to contemplate. The book gave him some reputation, helped by his classmate Longfellow's graceful tribute in the *North American Review*, and the years 1837 and 1838, as already indicated, were unusually rich in achievement. "Howe's Masquerade," "Edward Randolph's Portrait," "Lady Eleanore's Mantle" in 1838, and "Old Esther Dudley" (1839), grouped together as *Legends of the Province House*, touched the colonial life of Massachusetts with dignity and fused the warring elements of Tory grandeur and the new patriotism of the Revolution into a picture which glows with a light, sombre yet thrilling, in which human pride and human agony are revealed in imperishable colors. This was the height of his achievement in the short story. He wrote a few fine allegories, like "The Hall of Fantasy" (1843), "The Celestial Railroad" (1843), or "The Great Stone Face" (1850), a few vivid studies of the supernatural like "The Birthmark" (1843), "The Artist of the Beautiful" (1844), "Rappaccini's Daughter" (1844), and "The Snow Image" (1850). But the story of Colonial history faded into essay, the allegories became more plentiful, the moralizing tendency triumphed over the imaginative, in short Hawthorne's sense of "the story in it" grew less keen. It was time for him to work upon a larger canvas. That he was able to do so, makes him a greater figure in our fiction than Poe.

The firm assured tone of *The Scarlet Letter* (1850), its unity, the distinction of its style, were the fruit of his long preparation. The novel moves forward artistically, relentlessly, to its destined end. Hawthorne has scorned to win our interest by the salacious details of adultery; that is over before the story begins. If ever illicit passion was given dignity in fiction, it is in *The Scarlet Letter*, for Hester's sacrifice, not only her shielding of Arthur Dimmesdale, but her quiet pursuit of her daily duty, ennobles even her relations with the minister. She alone thought of others—Dimmesdale and Chillingworth thought only of themselves and found unhappiness. She worked for the ill and the needy, and in time her disgrace became her distinction. It never became her glory, for in the Puritan atmosphere that would have been impossible, but she was granted the greatest reward Hawthorne permits to his characters, the securing of their own self-respect.

The impression that is strongest in rereading *The Scarlet Letter* is its modern, its timeless quality. The central situation is as old as human life, but Hawthorne gave a new and an American setting to it. The book appeared in the same year as *Alton Locke,* two years before *Bleak House* or *Henry Esmond,* ten years before *The Mill on the Floss,* yet it seems to belong to a newer generation. All the critical disquisitions upon the correspondence of the American of the nineteenth century and the Englishman of the eighteenth, or of our national immaturity, vanish before this one book. America had lived fast in the life of the spirit, and while Hawthorne was not distinctly a development of his surroundings, he was a product of them.

The characters are few, as usual with Hawthorne—they are at first glance types of the passions and emotions that Hawthorne is studying. What is it that makes them so real, what almost persuades us that they are actual flesh and blood? It is because they are born of great passions and emotions, love, hate, and revenge, the love that has swept aside all barriers of restraint, the hate for the deepest wrong one man can do to another, the revenge which is shown after all to be without avail. The great moral lesson of *The Scarlet Letter* is all the more effective because it is not stated. It is the futility of human punishment for crime. The penalty imposed upon Hester Prynne by society has no effect. "The Scarlet Letter had not done its office." She was redeemed not by society's remedy, but by her own character. The self-inflicted punishment by Arthur Dimmesdale is likewise to no purpose. His mortification of the flesh, his veiled attempts at confession give him no relief, because he will not share the guilt with Hester. The punishment of one individual by another is also shown to be futile, for when Roger Chillingworth has driven Dimmesdale into confession and death, he not only feels that his victim has escaped him but also that his whole life has been built upon his revenge and its remnants are useless to him. The novel seems to be the incarnation of the voice of God saying "Vengeance is mine!" But we do not think about the moral purpose; what strikes us rather is the wonderful art that conceals the art. It has the quality, rare in romance, of holding our interest although we know the story—it approaches the highest conception of all—that in which the artist, knowing his audience is fully aware of his story, spends his force and craft upon the manner of his telling.

The House of the Seven Gables has not the power of *The Scarlet Letter,* but it is a triumph again of Hawthorne's method of insight. What more unpromising material can be imagined than an old house, peopled by an ugly old maid, without friends, an invalid convict, a simple country girl, and a rather shadowy photographer? Yet Hawthorne invested these few figures with a deep and growing interest, not so much by their actions or conversations, as by the vivid narrative and descriptive touches, by the way he brings us into the inmost souls of the characters. He makes us see them, not by the process of dissection, but by making them transparent to our eyes. Above all, he charms us by the beauty which he has the power to draw from all things, human or inanimate, because he has put it there. When he has taken a suggestion from another writer, as he probably did from Irving's "Dolph Heyliger," with its picture of old Dame Heyliger's reluctance in opening a shop and descending from the proud position of her forefathers, he has added qualities peculiarly his own. The moral of *The House of the Seven Gables* is clear enough. Evil will come out of evil, through many generations, but again it is not obtruded upon us.

The Blithedale Romance had its origin obviously in Hawthorne's experiences in the Brook Farm community from 1841 to 1842. He had never taken the community seriously, and it becomes merely a background for the reaction of emotions and passions of the four main characters: Hollingsworth, the earnest reformer of sinners; Coverdale, the reformer who is not so sure of his aim; Zenobia, the passionate, richly colored woman; and Priscilla, typical of purity. Hawthorne, of course, denied that he drew the characters from any definite persons, but certain traits of Margaret Fuller are easily discerned in Zenobia and of Theodore Parker in Hollingsworth. Miles Coverdale is the nearest approach to Hawthorne we have in his fiction. A careful reading of the *American Note-Books* reveals how closely Coverdale's relations to Blithedale parallel Hawthorne's to Brook Farm, even to such minor details as the heavy cold he took and the survey of the back buildings of the house in which Coverdale discovered Zenobia and Priscilla.[4] No

---

[4] *American Note-Books,* May 7, 1850, pp. 377–378.

critic of Hawthorne can be blind to the vagueness of the plot, or to the labored conversations of the characters. They are not as real as those of *The Scarlet Letter* or *The House of the Seven Gables*. What remains from the book is a clear impression of Coverdale's (and of course Hawthorne's) opinion of professional reformers, especially those who concentrate upon a single aim. But that is a theme for comedy, and *The Blithedale Romance* is not a comedy.

The Marble Faun (1860), while it has so much Roman background that it is often used as a guide book, owes its greatness not to this fact but to its study of the effect of crime upon the consciences of Donatello, of Hilda, and of Miriam. Indeed the spell of Italy never fell upon Hawthorne as it did upon Longfellow or Lowell, and even Donatello is not so much Italian as primitive. Italy remains as a background; any such understanding of Italian character as Marion Crawford or Edith Wharton were to represent in fiction was beyond the novelist who remained a Puritan at heart. His constant apologies for his sparse sympathy with Italy are indeed a bit pathetic. Yet he avoided the usual mistake of English and American novelists of representing the Italian as a complicated assassin; Donatello is a simple natural human being. The mystery of Miriam's sin and her relations with her pursuer whom Donatello murders is wisely kept, and the hint of its foundation in the tragedy of Beatrice Cenci is sufficiently clear to an adult mind, which does not need the explicit explanation of sexual irregularity. Probably the finest scene in the book is that in which Hilda is driven to the confessional by an overpowering desire to share her knowledge of the guilt of Donatello and Miriam. Hawthorne's use of the Catholic church is due, however, not so much to his understanding of its spiritual aspects, as to his realization of its dramatic possibilities; he seems unaware that Donatello would, long before Hilda, have found a similar refuge and consolation. Hawthorne's avoidance of this escape for Donatello may of course have been deliberate, for the gradual change in the faun's nature from a mere happy boy to a mature man through the working of remorse takes time and is the chief motive of the novel. It removes Donatello, however, from Italy to Hawthorne's country, the domain of the moral life. Perhaps there was some significance in the choice of the title *Transformation*, under which the novel was first published in England, for it is the subtitle of Brockden Brown's *Wieland* and may reflect the influence of that close student of moral values.

Hawthorne's methods of composition as well as his treatment of the supernatural are illustrated in a striking manner by his four unfinished romances. About the beginning of 1855 Hawthorne conceived the idea of an English romance, based on the return of an American heir to an English estate. In August he visited Smithell's Hall in Bolton le Moors, which boasted a legend concerning a bloody footstep, and from that time on, the idea of a bloody footstep upon the threshold of the hall, having some connection with the missing heir, becomes part of the projected romance of England. In the first form in which the romance was outlined, to which the title of *The Ancestral Footstep* has been given, it is not clear just what the cause of the footstep is. Hawthorne at different times states different ideas he is working out—for the romance is simply a collection of preparatory sketches—but it is always the result of a quarrel between two brothers who love the same woman. Sometimes the guilty party makes the footstep, sometimes the innocent one. Usually the second brother makes it, flies to America, and gives rise to the family from which the claimant descends. In *Doctor Grimshawe's Secret* we have the almost complete form of a romance based on the same general idea—that of a claimant returning from America to the home of his ancestors. There is here also a bloody footstep—with varying explanations; one that it was made by a Saxon thane who fought against a Norman baron on his own threshold, one that it was made by a fugitive who was slain there in the Wars of the Roses, and again that it was made by a Puritan, who had trodden in the blood of King Charles I and had been expelled by his family in consequence.

Hawthorne was not satisfied with *Dr. Grimshawe's Secret*, for the ending, in which Ned Redclyffe goes to England to reclaim his inheritance, is not conclusive, since he is not the heir, but has been taught to believe he is, as part of Dr. Grimshawe's revenge upon a family who have mistreated him. Yet there are portions of the book which are unexcelled in Hawthorne's fiction. In Chapter XI there is a remarkable description of a man living for years in a room shut in from the light of day because of his fear of the revenge which may be taken upon him for a crime. The fiendish nature of his attendant who pretends to protect him and who really feeds his constant terror by artful suggestions is unforgettable.

In *Septimius Felton* the main thread of the other stories is made secondary. The romance of the bloody footstep becomes a legend told by one of the characters, Sybil Dacy, of a scientist in England who had discovered the elixir of eternal life and who needed the life of a being dear to him to give as a recompense to Nature for his life, which she is to spare. He kills a young girl, and his footstep is bloody as he carries her into the hall. There is a vague reference to an English estate, made by a doctor who has some resemblance to Dr. Grimshawe. The main theme becomes that of the drink which is to give immortal life. Felton brews an elixir from a recipe which he takes from an English soldier, whom he kills at the battle of Concord. When he finally distills the elixir, it is shattered by Sybil Dacy to save Felton's life. It is really a poison, of which she dies.

In *The Dolliver Romance*, which was to have been the final form, and of which only three chapters exist, the bloody footstep and the American claimant shrink to a mere mention. The story of the elixir of life becomes the main theme and is carried on by totally different characters, an old apothecary and a little girl. Hawthorne's course in this series of romances is typical. It is a progress from the theme which must be treated realistically to that which can be treated idealistically—from a local theme to a universal one, and it remains a matter of regret that Hawthorne's conception of the great theme of immortal life remained uncompleted. For it had been in his mind at least since 1833, when it is mentioned in the sketch of Sir William Pepperell; it is the main theme of "Dr. Heidegger's Experiment" in 1837, and is referred to in "A Virtuoso's Collection" in 1842, in "The Birthmark" and "The Hall of Fantasy" in 1843, and in "A Select Party" in 1844. It was essentially the kind of supernatural motive, delicate and spiritual, that appealed to Hawthorne, and he was only following his natural bent when he abandoned the bloody footprint and substituted the elixir of eternal life.

It was the melodramatic aspect of the bloody footprint rather than its concreteness, however, which determined Hawthorne to abandon it. He knew as well as Poe that the supernatural needs the help of the concrete image in its establishment. It is this grip of the concrete that accounts for the longing we have to know what is behind the Minister's Black Veil, which explains the hold that the mystery of "The Birthmark" has upon our sympathies, and which accounts in large measure for the appeal of the supreme creation of our romance, *The Scarlet Letter*. Many and various are the thoughts the letter suggests, the sidelights it throws upon human nature, the ways in which it links the supernatural to the natural. Hawthorne suggests delicately the effect it had upon Hester Prynne, upon Arthur Dimmesdale, and upon the people, and then in the following passage describes a dramatic relation between the sinner, the effect of the sin, and the symbol of the sin, unsurpassed in English literature:

But that first object of which Pearl seemed to become aware was—shall we say it?—the scarlet letter on Hester's bosom. One day as her mother stooped over the cradle, the infant's eyes had been caught by the glimmering of the golden embroidery about the letter; and, putting up her little hand, she grasped at it, smiling, not doubtfully, but with a decided gleam that gave her face the look of a much older child. Then, gasping for breath, did Hester Prynne clutch the fatal token, instinctively endeavoring to tear it away; so infinite was the torture inflicted by the intelligent touch of Pearl's baby hand. Again, as if her mother's agonized gesture were meant only to make sport for her, did little Pearl look into her eyes and smile!

As usual, Hawthorne without mentioning it provides a possible natural explanation. The first color a child notices is red, the second yellow, so that the action of Pearl may have been a normal one. But Hawthorne has suggested a mystic influence in which we may prefer to believe. We surrender to his mood more easily because in Hawthorne there is no degradation of the supernatural, no forcible dragging of it over the line which separates it from the actual. Instead that line is made impalpable, the reader is brought into an atmosphere of twilight in which all things may happen, natural or supernatural. Once he surrenders himself to this atmosphere, all else follows naturally enough. He is not constantly reminded by bizarre or grotesque effects that he is in another land—the great though invisible effort of Hawthorne is to make him forget for a time that intellectual surrender. The world into which he has gone has laws of its own and they are not violated, with perhaps the single exception, in *The Scarlet Letter*, of the appearance of the symbol "A" in the sky. This is unlike Hawthorne and like Poe, for the laws of the undiscovered country in which Hawthorne rules are that no incident shall be introduced which could not be explained if the reader cares to lose the sense of the beautiful in the intellectual comfort of the prosaic.

Hawthorne had the idea of the *Scarlet Letter* for some time in his mind. He probably found his original inspiration in John Winthrop's *Journal*, in the description of the punishment of Mary Latham; and in "Endicott and the Red Cross" (1837) he had spoken of "a young woman, with no mean share of beauty, whose doom it was to wear the letter A on the breast of her gown . . . sporting with her infamy, the lost and desperate creature had embroidered the fatal token in scarlet cloth, with golden thread and the nicest art of needlework." Hawthorne's own account of the finding of the Scarlet Letter in the Custom House of Salem may be looked upon as fanciful.

Hawthorne evades the responsibility for the supernatural at times by introducing it as a tradition. One of the most interesting examples, which shows also his thorough knowledge of New England's past, lies in an incident in *The House of the Seven Gables*. Colonel Pyncheon has been instrumental in having an old man, Matthew Maule, persecuted as a wizard, and has taken some property which belonged to Maule. Maule curses him on the scaffold, telling him that "God will give him blood to drink." Of the death of Colonel Pyncheon, Hawthorne writes:

There is a tradition, only worth alluding to, as lending a tinge of superstitious awe to a scene gloomy enough without it, that a voice spoke loudly among the guests, the tones of which were those of old Matthew Maule, the executed wizard, saying "God hath given him blood to drink."

Again, as in the case of the *Scarlet Letter*, Hawthorne derived his inspiration from Colonial history. In Robert Calef's *More Wonders of the Invisible World*, published in 1700 as a reply to Cotton Mather's *Wonders of the Invisible World*, a record is given of the trial of Sarah Good, on June 30, 1692, one of those accused of having converse with the devil. Calef tells us that one of the magistrates, Noyes, urged her to confess, saying she was a witch. She replied:

"You are a liar,—I am no more a witch than you are a wizard, and if you take away my life, God will give you blood to drink."

Hawthorne's use of this incident is a phase of the supernatural which may be called thoroughly American, based as it is on a study of native material and treated with that modern avoidance of responsibility which emphasizes the emotional appeal of the supernatural and refers to the mood of the reader all questions of belief. The fact that Judge Hathorne, the novelist's ancestor, was one of the magistrates who presided at this trial makes the incident even more interesting. It only emphasizes, however, the essentially native quality of Hawthorne's genius. He was the logical outcome of the Puritan's interest in the supernatural, and it is to the Puritan that we must look for the beginnings of the supernatural in American literature.

Hawthorne takes plenty of time for his introduction of the abnormal. In "Old Esther Dudley" the possible supernatural appearances in the old house at midnight are prepared for by her custom of walking, late at night, to see that all is safe. In "Howe's Masquerade" the progress of the ghostly procession of the former governors of Massachusetts is smoothed by the fact that the guests at the fancy dress ball are already in the costume of bygone days. Poe rarely establishes the atmosphere so carefully as this, though he does so in one of his greatest short stories, "The Masque of the Red Death." He usually plunges at once into the abnormal, as in "The Tell Tale Heart" or "The Black Cat." This abruptness comes not from lack of art, of course, but from Poe's determination to begin at the beginning. Comparisons between the methods of the two greatest of our artists in the supernatural have been made perhaps sufficiently, but it is to be noticed that Hawthorne employed four of the five phases of the supernatural that were manifest in Poe. The contact with the spirit world is treated in "The Gray Champion" or "Howe's Masquerade"; the denial or reversal of a natural law is described in "Dr. Heidegger's Experiment"; the supernatural allegory is developed in "The Bosom Serpent" or "The Minister's Black Veil"; the abnormal connection of physical and mental traits is the theme of "The Birthmark" or "Rappaccini's Daughter." The exaggeration of some natural law or process until it passes into the supernatural seems not to have been used by Hawthorne.

Hawthorne's interest in the supernatural was not the only inheritance he received from his Puritan ancestors. The famous Puritan conscience, so trying to itself and to its neighbors, is the motive force of all his novels and of many of his short stories. It shows less directly in the perfection of his style. Sometimes when an impulse ceases to be a motive of life it becomes a motive of art, and the keen critical sense which led him to suppress *Fanshawe*, to abandon *The Ancestral Footstep, Dr. Grimshawe's Secret*, and *Septimius Felton* was a manifestation of the artistic conscience, as powerful in his case as in that of his ancestors, who took the responsibility of shedding blood upon their souls in order to preserve the Puritan theocracy. While he never hesitates to criticize his ancestors, we can easily see that he sympathized with their impatience with the eccentricities of Anne Hutchinson or the Quakers. In "The Gentle Boy" he makes clear that it was Catherine's business to look after her child and not preach to the unwilling hearers of New England. In "The Maypole of Merry Mount," while he pictures Endicott as intolerant, he shows his lack of sympathy with Thomas Morton and his revellers. After his Brook Farm experience, he had little interest in reformers or objectors of any kind; in politics he was a regular Democrat, and his article in the *Atlantic Monthly* in 1862, "Chiefly upon War Matters," shows his sane and well-balanced attitude toward national questions. The Civil War did not affect his fiction. He was devoted to the Union,[5] but it was to the whole Union and not simply New England.

This devotion sprang from his essentially native quality. In that most absurd *Life of Hawthorne* by Henry James, a lament is sounded concerning the lack of romantic material surrounding Hawthorne. But for his type of romance, historical background is not the essential. He knew American Colonial history as few knew it, but his concern was not with its glamour, but with its tragedy. The very paucity of romantic material stimulated a novelist who more than any of his rivals in romance was able to substitute imagination for experience. The subtle weaving into the plot of *The House of the Seven Gables* of the relation between Holgrave's hypnotic power and the witchcraft of his ancestor Matthew Maule, is an example of the motives which no experience could have suggested. It was that insight into character, revealed in such remarkable scenes as the interview between Hester and Arthur in the forest, or in the first meeting of Phoebe Pyncheon with the Judge (when her refusal to kiss him brings a flash of his real nature into his eyes), that show Hawthorne's understanding of human characters who conceal themselves behind spiritual repression or a mask of apparent rectitude.

That Hawthorne was aware of the dangers of too much analysis is shown by Coverdale's words in *The Blithedale Romance:*

"It is not, I apprehend, a healthy kind of mental occupation, to devote ourselves too exclusively to the study of individual men and women."

And yet he defends himself implicitly in another passage in the same book:

[Zenobia] should have been able to appreciate that quality of the intellect and the heart which impelled me (often against my own will, and to the detri-

---

[5] See *Life of Franklin Pierce*, esp. p. 415, in Riverside Edition of *Tales, Sketches and Other Papers*.

ment of my own comfort) to live in other lives, and to endeavor—by generous sympathies, by delicate intuitions, by taking note of things too slight for record, and by bringing my human spirit into manifold accordance with the companions whom God assigned me—to learn the secret which was hidden even from themselves.

Hawthorne, like Poe, was deeply interested in problems of identity. To him, it was man's most priceless possession. His praise of Holgrave in *The House of the Seven Gables* for having never, among all his changes of occupation, violated the innermost man is followed by the scene in which Holgrave refuses to use his hypnotic power to obtain an influence over Phoebe. How strong such a temptation might be Hawthorne knew instinctively, and he praises Holgrave in the significant words: "Let us, therefore,—concede to the daguerrotypist the rare and high quality of reverence for another's individuality." Hypnotism was indeed horrible to Hawthorne. In *The Blithedale Romance* Coverdale describes with loathing the "mystic sensuality of this singular age" and adds:

"It is unutterable, the horror and disgust with which I listened, and saw that, if these things were to be believed, the individual soul was virtually annihilated, and all that is sweet and pure in our present life debased, and that the idea of man's eternal responsibility was made ridiculous, and immortality rendered at once impossible and not worth acceptance. But I would have perished on the spot sooner than believe it."

In the light of these utterances Hawthorne's own feeling is probably represented in Arthur Dimmesdale's cry to Hester:

"We are not, Hester, the worst sinners in the world. There is one worse than the polluted priest! That old man's revenge has been blacker than my sin. He has violated, in cold blood, the sanctity of a human heart."

This is the unpardonable sin, in Hawthorne's code. The strong sense of the dignity of the individual will, even if it leads to sin, is shown also in *The Marble Faun* and in several of the short stories. The great scene on the scaffold when Arthur Dimmesdale, Hester Prynne, and Pearl stand together takes its significance from the fact that it is the triumph of identity, of the three souls welded together by a great passion. It has been prepared for throughout the book by the identification of Pearl and the Scarlet Letter, represented concretely by the crimson tunic with gold embroidery with which Hester has clothed her. Chillingsworth's search for the letter "A" on the breast of the minister, and his attempt to solve the problem of the relation between the minister's physical and spiritual illness also paves the way for this scene. He pays the penalty for his attempt to break down the minister's protecting wall of silence, just as the scientist in "The Birthmark" who had tried to disturb the identity Nature had given to his wife paid the extreme penalty of becoming the murderer of the woman he loved.

Hawthorne's own life was one long struggle to preserve his identity from causes that called him, from literary movements that would have engulfed him, even from friendships that he perhaps longed for. After Brook Farm, he made no more excursions into community life, and in *The Blithedale Romance* he warns us through Coverdale against men like Hollingsworth who have not only lost their own identity in the mistiness of a philanthropic theory, but are dangerous to anyone, especially to a woman, who becomes their friend. He resented, too, like Cooper, the tyranny of the small town. "Rome," says Kenyon in *The Marble Faun,* "is not like one of our New England villages, where we need the permission of each individual neighbor for every act that we do, every word that we utter, and every friend that we make or keep."

And yet the picture that has been drawn of Hawthorne as a remote and frosty soul is refuted first by such authentic tributes as the sentence with which his daughter's biography of her father closes, upon the start of his last journey with Franklin Pierce:

Like the snow image of an unbending but an old, old man, he stood for a moment gazing at me. My mother sobbed, as she walked behind him to the carriage. We have missed him in the sunshine, in the storm, in the twilight, ever since.[6]

Even more striking is that passage in Emerson's *Journals* for May 24, 1864, describing Hawthorne's funeral. "Clarke in the church said that Hawthorne had done more justice than any other to the shades of life, shown a sympathy with the crime in our nature, and, like Jesus, was the friend of sinners."

It is quite true that the great novels of Hawthorne deal with adultery, murder, and suicide, that his finest short stories represent souls tortured by remorse for the betrayal of their native land, or the murder of their

[6] Rose Hawthorne Lathrop, *Memories of Hawthorne* (1897), p. 480.

beloved. The sin itself is almost never portrayed; it is the after effect of sin. Frequently the crime is reflected in a picture, as in "Edward Randolph's Portrait," or "Prophetic Pictures," for it is necessary in order to provide the opportunity for remorse or revenge that some time elapse. There is never any mystery about the commission of the crime; suspense comes from the gradual development of the altered destiny of those, guilty or innocent, whom the sin affects. It has come usually from love, fulfilled or thwarted, for Hawthorne knew that the masterpieces of fiction are concerned with the emotions. In the *American Note-Books*, October 4, 1840, he says:

Indeed we are but shadows; we are not endowed with real life, and all that seems most real about us is but the thinnest substance of a dream—till the heart be touched. That touch creates us—then we begin to be,—thereby we are beings of reality and inheritors of eternity.

For the sinner, as Clarke truly said, Hawthorne had deep sympathy. His understanding for Hester's sufferings, for Donatello's remorse, for Zenobia's thwarted passion, for the sinners in "The Minister's Black Veil," in "The White Old Maid," in "Young Goodman Brown," in "Roger Malvin's Burial," in his very first story, "The Hollow of the Three Hills," is complete.

This sympathetic treatment of sin is not only humanity; it is also fine art. Not the first novelist, of course, to know this, Hawthorne secured his best effects by drawing characters who are noble, like Hester Prynne, but who have had moments when their strength or weakness has broken divine or human law. If they had been all bad, there would have been no moral contrast and therefore no such interest. Contrast is the life of fiction, and the vast majority of human beings, who are neither all bad nor all good, will reward the novelist who provides them with characters who are more lofty of moral stature than themselves, but who venture into crimes beyond their daring.

Although the romance has never ceased to be written in America, the passing of Hawthorne marks an epoch in its development. In his work, like the elixir of Septimius Felton, we see the essence of romance, a distillation freed from accidents and improbabilities. It is freed, too, almost from reality, being laid in that abstract moral existence in which the ideals of his imagination fused with the power of their compelling beauty the incidents of his fancy into those profound truths in whose presence mere facts become impertinent. Further than this in quality it could not go, and in any event, the current of idealistic romance was on the ebb, and the reaction to the realistic treatment of familiar life had already begun.

CHAPTER VIII

HERMAN MELVILLE AND THE EXOTIC ROMANCE

THE exotic romance found its chief representative in this period in the work of a strange genius whose proper position in the history of our fiction has suffered perhaps quite as much from the extravagant claims of admirers as from the neglect which at times was his portion. Melville has always been read, but from 1870 to 1890 his novels were reprinted in England rather than in the United States, and his most glowing tributes have come from John Masefield and other British critics who have accorded him that discriminating enthusiasm reserved by them for Americans who venture into fields of literary achievement uncharted by British writers. Much has recently been made of his life, but in reality Melville is interesting because of his books, and all that is vital in his career can be found there—disguised, of course, for the purposes of fiction. That career was a disappointment, not a tragedy. Born in New York City, August 1, 1819, of good stock, Melville had the courage to break away from a mercantile environment and to embark on a great adventure in the South Seas. He enjoyed it, and he wrote about it. For a brief time he was even famous, and then he awoke to the chilling fact that the re-telling of this adventure could not support his family, and that of the products of his own imagination, the world seemed to have no especial need. So for the last thirty years of his life he took refuge in the Customs Service and was silent so far as the publication of any important fiction is concerned. When he died in New York, September 28, 1891, he was obscure, and it is one of those grim commentaries on the rewards of literature that his death caused a revival of interest in his work. He had been unable, like Hawthorne, who was for a time his neighbor, and to whom he dedicated *Moby Dick*, to evolve great romance from the store of his own brooding, nor could he adopt the other course, chosen by a later romancer who also had his great experience, of leaving his family and continuing, at a distance, to rework into a variety of shapes the old material. For if Melville lacked the imagination of Hawthorne, he lacked even more the artistry of form which distinguished Bret Harte.

Typee: a Peep at Polynesian Life (1846) was the first fruit of adventure among the Typee Indians in the Marquesas Group of islands, where Melville had spent four months in 1842, after his escape from the whaler *Acushnet*. The entertaining narrative deals with his discovery of the valley of the Typees, a cannibal tribe in the interior of Nukuheva, and of his life there till his fear of being eaten leads to his escape. The Typees are depicted as children of nature, but they are not the "noble savages" of an earlier literature. They are bloodthirsty and cruel, but are also generous and hospitable. The most striking characters are Fayaway, the maiden who becomes his consort, Kory-Kory, Melville's special attendant, and Marheyo, Kory-Kory's father. Melville's descriptive ability is revealed not only in such charming pictures as Fayaway's standing in the boat with arms outstretched and her "tappa" waving like a sail in the breeze, but also in his description of the Typee valley, as he first sees it, curving away on both sides from the precipice where he lies. Certainly Blackmore must have read *Typee* before he wrote his famous description of the Doone Valley in *Lorna Doone*.

Omoo: a Narrative of Adventures in the South Seas (1847) is a description of Tahiti, to which Melville went in the *Julia*, which had carried him away from Nukaheva. There had been a mutiny and Melville was among those placed in confinement on the island, although he was afterward released. The description of the islanders is somewhat more prosaic than in *Typee*, and there are many criticisms of the devastating effects of civilization, which brought a storm of attack upon Melville from the Evangelical missionary societies. *Omoo* is not so interesting as *Typee*, though Doctor Long Ghost, Melville's companion, is a well-drawn character.

Typee and *Omoo*, when read in comparison with the latest descriptions of the South Seas, illustrate the slight hold that any travel books except the greatest have upon posterity. The interest which carried *Typee* and *Omoo* was partly novelty—others had written of the South Seas, but only in a formal style, and it remained for Melville to create characters like Fayaway and Kory-Kory and place them in a setting new and strange. But novelty alone was not sufficient—the books were believed to be records of fact, and even today their chief interest lies in the fidelity of Melville to the actual situation in the Marquesas and in Tahiti. In other words their value is ethnological rather than literary;

when that is said, the reason for the thirty years of silence has been given. If any proof were needed, it is to be found in the total oblivion of his next book, *Mardi* (1849), which is frankly romance and which is an incoherent account of the pursuit of a South Sea Cytherea, named Yillah, a white woman who has been brought up by the native priests for sacrifice. *Typee* and *Omoo* will outlast the sentimentalizing of the exotic in such books as those of Frederick O'Brien, for Melville wrote more simply and in general more sincerely and never bores the reader with painful insistence upon his virtue under temptation.

In *Redburn* (1849) Melville begins with an account of his experiences on the *Highlander*, the ship on which he made his first voyage in 1837 to Liverpool, and then recounts his adventures in England and his return. Notwithstanding Masefield's enthusiasm for *Redburn*, it is dull reading. Dana had done better with *Two Years Before the Mast*, because he had more selective power. *Redburn* is realistic, but misery is piled upon misery to such a degree that one ceases to sympathize with the author, especially when he abandons his chum, Harry Bolton, in a strange country upon their arrival in America. Having paid his respects to the atrocities of the merchant service, Melville painted a picture of an American man-of-war in *White Jacket* (1850). This is probably an accurate account of his life on the *United States*, which lasted from August, 1843 to October, 1844. When compared with a recently discovered journal of a sailor on this ship, Melville's account is seen to be much less accurate than was formerly supposed. Again Melville is a critic of the navy and dislikes both the discipline and the brutality. *White Jacket* is still worth reading, but there is little drama except the accounts of flogging, which he gives in great detail and from which he was saved only by the interposition of one of the officers. Few characters except Jack Chase, the captain of the foretop, remain after the book is closed.

It was in one book only that Melville rose to sustained greatness in fiction. *Moby Dick; or, The Whale* (1851) is a conception of the human soul possessed by a consuming desire for revenge upon the greatest of the animals, a theme which goes back to the fundamental passions of the race in its struggles for existence. Captain Ahab of Nantucket, whose leg has been cut off by Moby Dick, the White Whale, starts out to be revenged upon him. The story is told by Ishmael, one of the sailors who ships with Ahab. Through his eyes we see the implacable captain, who is a concrete example of the strength, courage, and indomitable will out of which heroes of fiction are made, with a touch of madness that is fitting to the theme. One has to wade through much that is forbidding; the confused introductory chapters and the tiresome lectures on the structure and classification of whales illustrate again Melville's besetting weaknesses, his lack of a sense of proportion and his inability to distinguish fact from fiction. But when the long journey through the Sea of Japan and the South Seas is over and the White Whale turns on its pursuers and rends them, there is painted an unforgettable scene in which the fury of man goes down, defeated by the fury of the great beast, driven to bay in its own chosen battleground. In this book Melville planned the climax with skill. He prepares us for the struggle by descriptions of several captures of whales, so at the climax we are familiar with the methods of attack. It is a pity that he did not more often plan so carefully, for the book is so episodic that even the great passion of Ahab cannot make of it an artistic unit. Melville seems to have been deliberate in this seeming carelessness, for in Chapter LXXXII he says, "There are some enterprises in which a careful disorderliness is the true method," but intention does not always make for righteousness in literature. Even more irritating is the chronic disorderliness of style on the part of a man who could write such magnificent English as "Bethink thee of the albatross; whence came those clouds of spiritual wonderment and pale dread, in which that white phantom sails in all imaginations? Not Coleridge first threw that spell, but God's great unflattering laureate, Nature."

A greater contrast than that which exists between *Moby Dick* and Melville's next book, *Pierre; or, The Ambiguities* (1852), can hardly be imagined. It is laid in a rural district not made very definite, and is an extraordinary mixture of imagination, triviality, eccentricity, emotion and futility. Pierre Glendinning is a young writer, son of a wealthy widow, and happily engaged to be married to Lucy Tartan. He meets an extraordinary young woman, Isabel, who informs him by letter that she is the daughter of his father by some illegitimate union that is not made clear, and her account of her early life includes a trip across the ocean and incarceration in a madhouse. Pierre decides that, inasmuch as he cannot inform his mother of the existence of this girl on account of his father's memory, he will calmly announce to the world that he has married her, in order that he may thereby devote himself to her care. The mere fact that he will break Lucy's heart and his mother's by this amiable idea does not seem to worry him. Isabel falls in with his plans, having indeed none of her own, and they proceed to the city. His mother promptly disinherits him, and he has a hard time in making a living in the city to which they go. Lucy writes him that she has determined to come and live with them, and she soon becomes a member of about the maddest household that has appeared in American fiction, until murder and suicide end them all. The book holds one's attention at times though the sheer power of Melville's riotous imagination and the sinister suggestion concerning the relations of Isabel and Pierre. The usual explanation for *Pierre* is that it was written by Melville as an attack upon the world, which already had failed to appreciate him, and his picture of Pierre's difficulties with publishers lends support to this interpretation. *Pierre* can hardly be taken seriously, however, on account of its total lack of construction. Could it be a satire or even a burlesque upon the theme often treated in Poe, the love of a man for a near relative with a more or less supernatural relationship? If this is true, it would be one of the ghastliest satires that was ever written. It may even be the prose amplification of the theme of *Ulalume*, the struggle in a man's nature between the spiritual and physical aspects of love, made concrete by two women who love him.

Melville returned to sanity with *Israel Potter* (1854–1855), a story of the Revolution based upon the career of the real Israel Potter, whose biography had been published in 1824. It is not in any sense noteworthy, partly because of Melville's continued railing at life, but more especially because of the absurdity of the pictures of historical characters, like George III and Benjamin Franklin. John Paul Jones is portrayed with more skill, but the fight of the *Bonhomme Richard* has been better done by lesser men. The intention of the book is definitely satiric. Potter, who fought at Bunker Hill, returns after forty years' exile and poverty to find the incipient monument celebrated, but he cannot secure a pension.

In *The Confidence Man: his Masquerade* (1857) satire overwhelmed completely the fictional impulse. It is not a novel, for there is no plot, and the characters are mere names. Upon a Mississippi steamboat, the *Fidèle*, plying from St. Louis to New Orleans, Melville introduces a number of frauds who practice upon the credulity of the passengers. A negro cripple, a solicitor for a bogus charity, a quack who sells panaceas, a vendor of stock in the Black Rapids Coal Company, a cosmopolitan, and a philanthropist indulge in tedious conversations with their victims or each other, upon confidence, originality in literature, or psychology, which Melville classes with palmistry, phrenology and "physiognomy." Some of these sharpers are in collusion with each other, others are plying their trades independently, but none of them elicit the faintest spark of interest. Satire upon life generally is sprinkled through the book, but there is little edge to it. Unconsciously Melville satirizes his own weakness by relating through one of the characters the narrative of the Indian hater of James Hall. For a brief moment the book becomes alive, under the inspiration of a born story-teller, then it relapses into tedium. *The Confidence Man* is the dullest of Melville's books, for the people in it are not mad, as the English biographer of Melville calls them; they are much worse—they are stupid.

Melville struggled on in spite of discouragement, writing for *Putnam's Magazine* and *Harper's Magazine* stories and sketches of very uneven merit. Some, like "The Lightning Rod Man," "Happy Failure," and "Jimmy Rose," are pathetic attempts. But in two instances he rose almost to the height of *Moby Dick. Benito Cereno,* printed in *Putnam's Magazine,* October to December, 1855, is a masterpiece. In this novelette narrating the mutiny of the negro slaves on board the *St. Dominick,* a Chilean merchant ship, Melville took the actual facts as given in *A Narrative of Voyages and Travels in the Northern and Southern Hemispheres,* by Amasa Delano (1817), and while following closely the original,[1] created out of a series of legal depositions a tale of terror which ante-dates the methods of Conrad by many years. What makes the story significant is the creation of suspense and the menace of a nameless danger. Captain Delano boards the *St. Dominick* to help a ship in distress. The haggard appearance of Captain Benito Cereno, his involved story of officers and men lost by scurvy and fever, the apparent devotion of Babo, the negro servant, who never leaves him, the strange figures of the negroes mutely sharpening their hatchets, the apparent but abortive efforts of the few white men left to speak to Delano, all deepen his apprehension. The test of such a story is the effect upon the reader, of course, and so real is the atmosphere Melville creates, that each time Delano sends his boat back to his own ship without him we feel a strong

---

[1] For the original depositions, see Harold H. Scudder, "Melville's *Benito Cereno* and Captain Delano's Voyages," *Publications Modern Language Association,* XLIII (June, 1928), 502–532.

desire, as though he were living, to warn him to go with it. It is the picture of one man, of our own race, alone amid the hostile strangers who are waiting to strike, that appeals so strongly. Melville wisely chose to believe the real Captain Delano's statement that he was alone, while other depositions declare one of his mates was with him. The dramatic leap of Benito into Delano's boat, and the capture of the *St. Dominick* by the Americans, are followed by a long deposition of Benito which breaks the spell, although in the final conversation between the two captains the tone of the story is resumed. It is to be questioned whether the picture of Benito, watched like a hawk by Babo, so that he cannot reveal to Delano the mutiny, would not have flashed retrospectively upon us with more effect if a brief explanation had been substituted for the long deposition. But rarely if ever has a novelist used so effectively the situation in which the sea makes a hopeless prisoner of the captain, who in normal times is the supreme dictator of life or death. Only Melville does it twice in the same story, for Benito and Delano are both surrounded by human beings whose only hope of freedom lies in mutiny and murder.

Next in merit to *Benito Cereno* was the series of short narratives and descriptions included under the title of *The Encantadas; or, Enchanted Isles*. To these barren islands of the Pacific, Melville gives the interest of utter desolation, of the absence of human beings, of rocky coasts where "the chief sound of life is a hiss." His sardonic descriptions of the turtles which have "the crowning curse of straightforwardness in a belittered world" are among the vivid touches. The best story is that of a woman, Hunilla, a half-breed Spanish Indian from Payta in Peru, whose husband and brother had gone with her to Norfolk Isles to gather tortoise oil, expecting to be called for by the French ship that had brought them. The men were drowned in their boat, and her husband Felipe's corpse came ashore. How can artistic repression go further than the paragraph after her rescue?

She but showed us her soul's lid, and the strange ciphers thereon engraved; all within, with pride's timidity, was withheld. Yet was there one exception. Holding out her small olive hand before our captain, she said in mild and slowest Spanish, "Señor, I buried him;" then paused, struggled as against the writhed coilings of a snake, and cringing suddenly, leaped up, repeating in impassioned pain, "I buried him, my life, my soul!"

The history of a long loneliness broken by a hint of another danger beside which loneliness was happiness is all recorded with an art rare in Melville's work and rare indeed anywhere.

The other stories which were published together with these two as *Piazza Tales* (1856) are not so important, except "The Bell Tower," a story of a bell-maker who attempts to create a figure which will take the place of a human bell-ringer and is killed by his own creation.

After thirty years of inactivity in fiction, Melville wrote *Billy Budd, Foretopman* between November, 1888 and April, 1891. It was found in his desk after his death, which occurred September 28, 1891. It is a straightforward story of contrasted crime and innocence, laid on the English man-of-war *Indomitable* in 1797, shortly after the mutiny of the *Nore*. *Billy Budd*, impressed by the man-of-war, is a handsome, good natured, popular seaman. Gradually he becomes aware of the apparently baseless enmity of John Claggart, the master-at-arms. Claggart is morbidly jealous of Budd's superb physical beauty and is an example of the depravity of nature which seeks to destroy what it hates. He accuses Budd of conspiracy to mutiny and, when both men are brought to Captain Vere's cabin, Budd is so outraged that he strikes Claggart and kills him. Melville analyzes well the struggle in Captain Vere's mind between his belief in Budd's innocence of conspiracy and his determination that the code of the navy shall be preserved by his execution for murder. The captain's character, in fact, is the best drawn and is established through the description of his last interview with Billy Budd and the skill with which he prevents any disturbance on the part of the sailors, who are horror struck at the execution of one of their favorites. The novelette is sheer tragedy; it is written with a clarity unsmirched by any of Melville's earlier turgid style, and may rank just below *Benito Cereno* and *The Encantadas*. It is one of the most curious instances of reviving power in our literature.

While it is true that Melville's greatest work is laid upon the ocean, it is not the sea itself which claims our interest; it is the effect of the sea in limiting the passions of human beings to the confines of a ship, which makes for intensity of danger, or it is the sea as background for the titanic struggle of Captain Ahab and the Whale. It was not Melville's fault that he came, a romanticist as to material, an idealist by method, when the vogue of that kind of romance was passing. But it was his fault, as a penetrating critic of his own day pointed out,[2] that he was born to create and resolved to anatomize; that he was born to see and insisted upon speculating. But romance dies only for a time, and Melville's best work is now secure from the neglect which embittered his life. One sentence in *Moby Dick* explains, however, the periodic necessity for his "revivals." "Heaven keep me," he says, "from ever completing anything." But in art it is those things that have been worked out into the serene balance of completeness that need no resurrection.

Inspired perhaps by *Typee* and *Omoo*, Dr. William Starbuck Mayo (1812–1895), laid his exotic romances in Africa. In *Kaloolah* (1849), the hero, Jonathan Romer, is from Nantucket and, since one of his family had had his leg crushed by a whale, the influence so far as Melville is concerned may have been mutual. Romer has a bewildering series of adventures among slavers and buys a girl, Kaloolah, and her brothers, who are natives of Framazugda, where they are members of a white race which had settled there hundreds, or perhaps thousands, of years before. After losing her, he finally reaches her country, which Mayo uses to satirize, by implication, conditions in the United States. Social precedence is established by a simple method. "For example, when a lady wishes to assume a certain position, the question is submitted to her friends, it being understood that if they will vote for her, her enemies will make no objection." Mayo has a lively style and holds our interest. His picture of the sea and the life on the ships is rather idealized, but on the other hand he stoutly maintains that the picture of "Jack's" mental and moral degradation after a flogging are purely mythical, thus squarely contradicting Melville.

Mayo knew the fascination that a romance of a primitive but civilized race can exert, and in *The Berber* (1850) his hero, Caspin el Subah, is pictured as a chieftain of a tribe which were descended from the earliest Arian Christians. His love story with Juanita, a Spanish maiden, is only one of three similar episodes, and anyone who is interested in the persistence of conventions in the midst of romance in 1850 may find research material in the arrangement of the various marriages. Mayo's shorter sketches, *Romance Dust* (1851), are romantic stories of adventure, mostly laid in Morocco, Portugal, or on the sea. They are interesting but add nothing to his contributions in the novel. Nor is his later story,

[2] *Putnam's Monthly Magazine*, IX (April, 1857), 384–393.

Never Again (1873), beginning in Baden and transferring to New York City, of equal significance with his exotic romances. Mayo, however, had a gift for social satire, and his analysis of the power and the limitations of money in American social organization is quite correct. He was the most important of the followers of Melville and had been in the localities he describes.

CHAPTER IX

THE TRANSITION TO REALISM

WHILE the idealistic treatment of romantic material was still popular in the 'fifties, there were already signs of a reaction to a more realistic portrayal of familiar life. The pioneers in this movement can hardly be distinguished at first glance from their contemporaries who were still pursuing the older methods, for often the material seemed to be the same. This critical obscurity has been due to the careless use of terms like "romantic method," and the failure to see that no matter what his material is, a novelist may begin by drawing types and end by drawing real people, and that the progress of American fiction lies in this direction and not in an abandonment of romantic scenes and incidents, which are perennial.

The first of this transition group to publish illustrates well this change in method. Harriet Beecher Stowe (1811–1896) began, so far as her novels are concerned, with an idealistic treatment of the Negro. Her New England birth and education, the proselyting zeal she inherited from her father, which led him to Cincinnati in 1826, the stern necessity of providing for her family, all brought about that reformatory urge so typical of the Beechers, which had to have expression. She had been writing for publication since 1833, and had won a prize for a short story in Hall's *Western Monthly Magazine* in that year but it was not till 1851, after her removal to Brunswick, Maine, that the agitation concerning the Fugitive Slave Law brought about *Uncle Tom's Cabin*. She had helped fugitive slaves across Ohio and had seen a Kentucky slave plantation, but most of her information came from hearsay or reading. Unconsciously following the methods of melodrama, she wrote the death scene of Uncle Tom first and built up the story to it. Published first in *The National Era*, an abolition paper, beginning June 5, 1851, it attracted little attention, but when issued in book form in 1852,[1] it

---

[1] A title page, filed for purposes of copyright, May 12, 1851, shows that contrary to the usual statements, Mrs. Stowe was contemplating book publication even before the story began to run as a serial.

soon sold by the hundred thousand, and as Lincoln truly remarked, it was one of the most potent forces in bringing on the War. Viewed critically now, it seems poor art. The characters are, from nearly all points of view, either black or white. Uncle Tom, Eva, Topsy, Eliza, are by any critical standard, absurdities, and if Legree and Loker seem overdrawn to us now, it can be imagined how the South looked upon them in 1852. To analyze the plot or characters is unnecessary, however, for if any other proof were needed, the long life of the dramatic version by George Aiken has established the theatrical quality of its figures and its incidents. Yet when a novel has become an historical landmark and when a sophisticated audience is thrilled by the play when well presented after half a century,[2] it is necessary to inquire the reason for its great human appeal. This lies in Mrs. Stowe's choice of one of the most dramatic of all themes, the spectacle of one human being under the absolute power of another. Two elements are necessary in order to secure that dramatic interest to the greatest degree. The two human beings must be as much alike, mentally, morally, and spiritually, as possible, in order to make the situation tragic, and the cruelty must be intense. Mrs. Stowe was forced, therefore, to select individuals from the white race that were much lower than the average and choose slaves that were much higher. She was also obliged to put the cruelty on with a brush. This she did, consciously or not, and the result was success.[3] After her visit to England as the guest of the friends of emancipation there, Mrs. Stowe returned to write *Dred; a Tale of the Great Dismal Swamp* (1856), in which she treated the theme of the tragedy consequent upon mixed blood. Here propaganda and interminable theological discussion overwhelmed the plot, and Mrs. Stowe committed the unpardonable error of continuing the novel after the heroine, Nina Gordon, had died.

Turning in 1859 to New England life, which she knew better than slavery, she produced her best novel, *The Minister's Wooing*, a story laid some time after the Revolution. Aaron Burr is brought in as a dangerous but fascinating person, but the interest of the book lies not in its history but in the study of human beings like Mary Scudder, in the

[2] The Players Club of New York presented the Aiken version as its revival in 1933, with a remarkable cast, headed by Otis Skinner as Uncle Tom. It proved to be the most successful revival in the long list of the Club's productions and was taken on tour.

[3] In 1853 a German translation was issued by Jewett, the original publisher, which may have had something to do with the Unionist attitude of the Germans in the Middle West.

throes of intense spiritual struggle. If her agony at the thought of her sailor lover, lost forever because he was not a member of her church, seems now unnatural, it was then stark reality, and was based on the experience of Mrs. Stowe's sister. The clergyman, Samuel Hopkins, is also a real person; not only was his sermon against the slave trade drawn from her own father's stock, but it is embedded in narrative which proved Mrs. Stowe's right to be called a master. She could not help the didactic tone which is never absent from her stories. She came from the ministerial class, she married into it, and the generations who had pondered over motives natural and supernatural speak in some of the finest passages in the book. The novelist who could write the passage beginning "There is a ladder to heaven, whose base God has placed in human affections, tender instincts, symbolic feelings, sacraments of love, through which the soul rises higher and higher, refining as she goes, till she outgrows the human, and changes as she rises, into the image of the divine," knew how to write English. Her analysis of the connection between loyalty to God and loyalty to the king, illuminating, as it does, the development of religious thought in a democracy, has reappeared in several modern histories of American thought, without credit to her. Life was serious with her, and in such a passage as "How strange this external habit of living! One thinks how to stick in a pin and how to tie a string,— one busies one's self with folding robes and putting away napkins, the day after some stroke that has cut the inner life in two, with the heart's blood dropping quietly at every step" we see the original perhaps of Emily Dickinson's poem, beginning

> The bustle in a house
> The morning after death.

Even in this novel she could not forget the Negro, and she paints her idealized picture in Candace, the serving woman who demolishes the arguments for the eternal damnation of the non-elect with an effective eloquence.

In 1861, after her third visit to Europe, she wrote her historical novel of Italian life, *Agnes of Sorrento*, which after its appearance in *The Cornhill Magazine* and *The Atlantic* was published in 1862. It is filled with the conventional Italian figures which bear no relation to actuality, and it marks no progress. Much better was *The Pearl of Orr's Island*, which was in her mind in 1852, but which was not published until 1862;

it is a good example of her virtues and defects as a novelist. At times it is exquisite in its depiction of the spiritual intensity of Mara Pennel, the little girl whose parents die and leave her to be brought up by her grandparents. The boy and girl life of Mara and "Moses," who is rescued from drowning and who is of Spanish descent, is real; her complete absorption in him, while it makes her ideal rather than real, is also artistically done. She is, of course, too much of an angel, but her visions of eternal life while she waits for the inevitable approach of death by tuberculosis are not only absolutely true to life, under such circumstances, but are also written in a style for which Mrs. Stowe need make no apology. In every land or race where faith has been deep, such men and women have lived, and New England produced many of them. Some of the characters, like Captain Kittridge, the unregenerate old salt; his daughter Sally, a foil in her vitality and coquetry to Mara; the old maid Aunt Roxy Toothacre, are very real and true to life on this island in Casco Bay. Mrs. Stowe did not seem to be aware, however, that the few words she puts into Captain Kittridge's mouth about Mara are more effective than the pages of preaching in which she steps into the novel herself. When the Captain says to Moses: "She only stopped a few days in our world, like the robins when they's goin' south: but there'll be a good many first and last that'll get into the kingdom for love of her. . . . I tell ye, Moses, ye' ought to get into heaven, if no one else does. I expect you are pretty well known among the angels by this time.", Mrs. Stowe is an artist. It is a pity she did not know when to stop.

Old Town Folks (1869) divides the honors, however, with The Minister's Wooing in Mrs. Stowe's work. This story, laid in New England about 1790, is rambling in construction, but there are many characters that are real. Horace Holyoke, who tells the story, is not so vivid, but Tina Percival, whom every male character loves, her husband Ellery Davenport, probably drawn again from Aaron Burr, Aunt Lois, the managing woman, "Grandma" Debby Kittery and Sam Lawson, the village ne'er-do-well, are among the best portraits she has drawn. The domestic scenes are real, and the spiritualistic visions of Horace are based on her husband, Calvin Stowe's own experiences.[4] Mrs. Stowe went out of her field in a social satire, Pink and White Tyranny (1871). There

---

[4] Fired probably by the success of Aiken's play, Mrs. Stowe dramatized Old Town Folks in 1869, but I cannot find evidence of its production.

is a fair revelation of a selfish woman's ability to ruin her husband's life, but Mrs. Stowe did not understand that a novelist cannot create society in its more exclusive forms by simply stating that her characters belong to it. In the same year she continued the career of Sam Lawson in his *Fireside Stories,* and published *My Wife and I,* an essay-like piece of fiction whose purpose seemed to be to prove a woman's right to a career. It is interesting simply for the opinions Mrs. Stowe expresses, such as, "For my part, I always said that one must have a strong conviction for a cause if he could stand the things its friends say for it, or read a weekly paper devoted to it." But neither it nor *We and Our Neighbors* (1875) are important fiction. In her last novel, *Poganuc People* (1878), she returned to New England life of the past, laying the scene in a country town in Connecticut about 1818. Nothing much happens to the heroine, Dolly Cushing, either at home or in Boston, but the picture of life is based upon Mrs. Stowe's own memory as a child.

Mrs. Stowe's position in our fiction will probably be determined by a book which is far from being her best work. But just because she was one of the greatest social and moral forces of her time, she could hardly hope to be one of its greatest artists. When the moral teacher was colored by the instinct for the supernatural and held in check by the power of an objective artist, New England gave us a Hawthorne; when the moral teacher overshadowed even the supernatural, and the artist remained subjective, New England produced Mrs. Stowe.

A novelist not usually given his proper place in the transition was John Townsend Trowbridge (1827–1916). Born in Monroe County, New York, he lived on a farm until he was seventeen and then, after teaching school in Illinois, went to New York and later to Boston, where he published under the name of "Paul Creyton." After several stories for boys, he wrote in *Neighbor Jackwood* (1857) a powerful anti-slavery novel, which he dramatized and which was acted at the Boston Museum in the same year. The main theme is the pursuit, capture and rescue of Camille, the octoroon slave, from Mobile, and her treatment by the people in a village in the Green Mountains. Camille is a type, but the New England characters are real, from Neighbor Jackwood, who befriends her, to Enos Crumlett, who betrays her to the slave hunters for money. In Grandmother Rigglesty, Trowbridge painted an almost perfect picture of ill-natured old age, which he emphasized even more in the play. *Coupon Bonds* (1865), a novelette which appeared first in the

Atlantic for September and October (1865), supplied a remarkably faithful picture of meanness in "Pa" and "Ma" Ducklow, whose adopted son Reuben has gone to the war without their help being given to his wife and children but who are endeavoring to profit by their investments in United States securities. There is a fine picture of the New England woman too, in Miss Beswick, who speaks her mind with definiteness and acerbity and who shames the Ducklows into an approach to decency. Tad, the second adopted son, who takes the bonds to cover his kite, is a real boy, before Aldrich or Mark Twain had given us their more extended treatments. Trowbridge had a profound contempt for the small-town mind; in his short story, "The Man Who Stole a Meeting House," he depicted the way in which a selfish, determined man can take advantage of the deadly inertia of such a community. Trowbridge chose to write fiction for young people, which imposed limitations to powers of observation of a high order. It is not within the scope of this survey to deal except occasionally with this branch of fiction, but to anyone whose reading began about the time when Trowbridge and Louisa Alcott were publishing their serials about boys and girls in the early days of *St. Nicholas*, it must seem that something fine and moreover very real was being recorded.

The novels of Oliver Wendell Holmes (1809–1894), while not of course his major achievement, belong distinctly to this period of transition. His contribution to the growth of realism lay in the scientific analysis of character and in the original use of heredity for the purposes of fiction. In *Elsie Venner*, which ran in the *Atlantic* from January, 1860 to April, 1861 as *The Professor's Story*, the old conventional relationship of a lost child with its presumed ancestors, without which the older romance could hardly have proceeded, gave way to a heredity of a far subtler nature. Elsie Venner's mother had been bitten by a snake before the birth of the child and Elsie has in consequence both a fascination and a repulsion for those who know her. This conception Dr. Holmes insists [5] was purely imaginary, and yet he received "the most startling confirmation of the possibility of the existence of a character like that which he had drawn as a purely imaginative conception" while the story was in progress. This is the scientist's and not the novelist's point of view, of course, and so was his attempt "to test the doctrine of 'original sin' and human responsibility for the disordered volition coming under

[5] Preface to *Elsie Venner*, p. viii, Riverside Edition.

that technical denomination." Fortunately this load of purpose did not crush his inspiration. Dr. Holmes was also careful to state that his story was well under way before *The Marble Faun* was known to him. But though the novels are contemporaneous, they belong to a different species. The mingling of human and animal natures in Donatello and in Elsie are so different that Holmes need not have been disturbed. His motive may have been a moral one, but he deals with it from the scientific-moral, not the romantic-moral, point of view. There is an atmosphere of clear daylight in his stories: he looks at life with the rationalistic inquiring gaze of the New Englander who has inherited the independence of Miles Standish but not the conscience of Cotton Mather.

The scene of *Elsie Venner* is a New England village, Pigwacket Centre, and the hero, Bernard Langdon, is a young medical student who is teaching school for the time being. Elsie loves him and tells him so, but he does not love her, although in a dramatic scene she has saved his life by overpowering the charm of the rattlesnake that is about to kill him. Through her consequent illness the poisonous nature passes out of her, but her life goes with it, and this similarity to "The Birthmark" may have caused Holmes' statement in his preface.

His next novel, *The Guardian Angel* (1867), is laid in Oxbow Village from 1859 to 1865. The heroine, Myrtle Hazard, is a compound of inherited tendencies from four different women among her ancestors. One had died for her faith, one had been accused of witchcraft, one had been a famous beauty, and one had had Indian blood in her. Myrtle is torn between the various elements in her nature, that of Judith Pride, the beauty, being the strongest. She becomes a nurse during the Civil War, and the hero, Clement Lindsay, as well as the villain, Murray Bradshaw, also enter the service, but the war is not an important element. The Guardian Angel of the village, Myles Gridley, is an elderly teacher who straightens out the complications, too numerous to mention; but it is the way Holmes tells the story rather than the plot that still makes the novel worth reading. It is much better than *A Mortal Antipathy* (1885), in which the plot becomes almost absurd. Maurice Kirkwood, a young engineer, has been injured when a small child by being dropped from the arms of a young aunt; as a result, he has acquired a mortal antipathy to any young woman. As he is engaged in his profession of engineering near the Corinna Institute for Young Ladies, he is given a large oppor-

tunity to exercise this antipathy, until he is cured of it by the stroke oar
of the Institute crew, who saves him from burning up in a fire. Certainly
Dr. Holmes' sense of humor must have deserted him when he wrote
this novel, but it belongs, in any event, to a much later period. His
achievement in the progress of realism lay not only in the scientific flavor
of his fiction but also in the natural, easy style in which every sentence
has a meaning. Like all realists of this time, however, he felt called upon
to explain and prepare for any unusual event, and the wires are sometimes too apparent. But he had to his credit at least one novel, *Elsie
Venner*, which belongs in the front rank of English fiction in the nineteenth century.

The work of John William DeForest (1826–1906), perhaps the
most truly a realist of the novelists who began to write in the early 'fifties,
has not been accorded its proper significance, except by William Dean
Howells, and his novels are now difficult to obtain. Yet a comparison of
his fiction with *Beulah* or *St. Elmo* or *The Wide, Wide World* will reveal at once how, side by side with these romantic-idealistic products, an
artist who saw clearly and who could paint relentlessly the portraits of
real men and women, was beginning to write. DeForest was born in
Humphreysville, Connecticut, and began his career as an historian, his
History of the Indians of Connecticut (1851) being based on careful
research, for which his early ill-health and sufficient means gave him
opportunity. His study of Colonial life resulted in his first novel, *Witch-
ing Times*,[6] a story of the tragedy and a bit of the comedy of the witchcraft delusion in Salem, beginning in 1691. DeForest secures the reader's
sympathy for Henry More, who fights the delusion and is executed for
witchcraft. The fictional characters, like his daughter Rachel, who is also
condemned and who is saved by her husband, Mark Stanton, are real
enough. The historical figures are imbued, too, with motives that are
sufficiently mixed to prevent their becoming mere types. Elder Noyse
[*sic*] is driven to extreme lengths by his passion for Rachel. Elder Parris
is a brutal tyrant who has to excite his parishioners in order to hold his
position. Cotton Mather is only half-deluded, but uses the delusion as
a means to further his place in the clerical oligarchy that ruled New England. Judge Hawthorne [*sic*] is contrasted with the clerical persecutors
by a calmer and more liberal attitude. There is a vivid picture of the
pressing to death of Giles Corey, with his cry of "More weight! more

---

[6] *Putnam's Magazine*, December, 1856–September, 1857.

weight!" in order to shorten his suffering. More's own trial is dramatic. The novel is too long, and DeForest's efforts to compare the intolerance of 1691 with that of 1857 interrupt the narrative, but the style is distinguished. It was a promising commencement. *Seacliff; or, The Mystery of the Westervelts* (1859), laid in Connecticut in his own time, although not one of his best novels, showed that power of drawing women realistically which marks DeForest out from most of his contemporaries. Ellen Westervelt's confession of her complicity in a plot to influence her uncle to alter his will in her favor, and her agony of soul when she finds she is suspected of infidelity to her husband, are powerfully done; her subsequent insanity and suicide are logical and dramatic.

When the Civil War broke out, DeForest recruited a company, the Twelfth Connecticut volunteers, of which he became captain. He fought through the war, and in 1867 he wrote the first realistic novel of that conflict in *Miss Ravenel's Conversion from Secession to Loyalty*. Henry Morford (1823–1881) in his *Shoulder Straps* (1863), *The Coward* (1863), and *The Days of Shoddy* (1864) had anticipated DeForest in the exposure of corruption and inefficiency in the army and the contractors that supplied it. But while there are spirited descriptions of Bull Run and Malvern Hill, Morford's characters belong to the older idealistic manner. They are of interest, however, to the social historian in their representation of the confusion of that time. There was considerable activity on the Confederate side also, which found its best representative in John Esten Cooke. There is also an unusual denunciation of war and an effective picture of the poor white who has remained true to the Confederacy in Sidney Lanier's *Tiger Lilies* (1867). To what lengths the minor romancers were carried is illustrated in an extraordinary novel, *The Aide-de-Camp* (1863) by James D. McCabe, Jr., in which a Confederate officer surveys through a secret door the proceedings of the Cabinet while Lincoln and his associates are deciding upon the relief of Fort Sumter! Such fiction written apparently in sincerity, makes clear how hopeless any compromise could have been, after Lincoln had once been elected. Among the other Civil War novels, *Sunnybank* (1866) by "Marion Harland" is interesting as an example of the Unionist point of view in a Virginia woman. Marion Harland, or Mrs. Mary Virginia Terhune, as she was in real life, made some approach to realism in the description of the Federal raids in a Virginia plantation, and the persecution of a loyal family by the Confederate authorities. Her characters, however, are merely types and her many novels need no analysis here.

There is little of the glamour in *Miss Ravenel's Conversion* that Cooke gave us in *Surry of Eagle's Nest;* it is war in its sordid reality, with no attempt to conceal the inefficiency and corruption that prevented so long the success of the Union forces. The political appointments of cowards, who were first promoted and then allowed quietly to resign, the nepotism which kept efficient officers in subordinate positions, are made concrete by vitriolic portraits of men whom DeForest knew and of whom he speaks freely in his letters home during his service.[7] Even more striking are his pictures of the fatalism or the cowardice of soldiers before the battle.[8] Long before Stephen Crane's *Red Badge of Courage,* DeForest had pictured the real feelings of the troops with a more authentic knowledge and with fewer journalistic touches. One very good scene is the final mustering out of the company by Captain Colburne, the hero of the novel, after three years fighting, when he finds that through death or transfer, he is the only one left of the original volunteers. But DeForest's characters form even a better claim to distinction in this novel. Lily Ravenel, who begins with a devotion to the South based on impulse and inheritance, grows, partly through her love for Colburne, into a realization of the great principle of Union. DeForest revealed again in her and in Mrs. LaRue, an adventuress, his knowledge of feminine nature. Any realist of today might be proud of his analysis of the emotions of a girl who has just received a proposal of marriage, or of the deliberate plans which Mrs. LaRue makes for an illicit affair with Colburne, or of her more successful efforts with Colonel Carter, himself a brilliant picture of that moral contrast between good and evil in one man's nature which always makes for interest. Mrs. LaRue is an accurate picture of the Creole, before Cable, but she is not so picturesque as she is real.

DeForest's short stories, which he wrote from 1860 for *Harper's* and *The Galaxy* but which became frequent in the *Atlantic* during 1868 and 1869, are not of equal importance with his novels. They usually deal

---

[7] Now in possession of his son, Effingham DeForest.

[8] See his article "The First Time Under Fire," *Harper's Magazine,* September, 1864. This and other descriptive sketches, appearing in *Harper's* during 1865 were based on an unpublished manuscript, *A Volunteer's Adventure.* For a detailed account of his Civil War experiences, see the forthcoming biography, *John William DeForest, Pioneer Realist and Soldier,* by Anne D. Jenovese.

with pretension and humbug, such as the delightful satire on insistent philanthropy and universal suffrage, "The City of Brass," [9] or else with the supernatural. In these stories, however, his analysis of feminine character, found in "The Taillefer Bell Ringings," [10] is of more significance than the mystery. We never learn what caused the bells to ring, but we do learn to know the widow, Mrs. Taillefer, of New Orleans. This city is the scene of one of the best of the stories, "A Gentleman of An Old School." [11] "The Brigade Commander" is a vivid story of the war.[12] "The Lauson Tragedy," [13] a murder mystery, is hardly more than a short story, and is to be remembered only for the small town's judgment of an innocent man because he has been to Germany and drinks beer.

Although DeForest was never west of the Mississippi River, he wrote in *Overland* (1870–1871) [14] an exciting story, laid about 1850–1852, beginning in Santa Fé and taking its characters across the deserts to California. There is a great deal of vivid description in the book, and DeForest establishes the sense of wildness and remoteness, as the party marches through the desert, surrounded by Indians, or as Thurstane, the hero, and his companions whirl down the San Juan or Colorado Rivers with precipices on each side. The interest is in part that of the moving picture of today. But DeForest's analysis of the way an army officer thinks and acts, the way he refrains from converting into a hero Texas Smith, the desperado whom the Spaniard Coronado has hired to murder Thurstane, but makes him go through with his sordid bargain, point to the realistic strain in his work that gives DeForest such relative importance.

In *Kate Beaumont* (1872) DeForest reflected his knowledge of life in South Carolina, which he had learned in his first visit during 1855 and again during his service in command of a district of the Freedman's Bureau from 1866 to 1868. He drew a vivid picture of a family feud

---

[9] *Atlantic Monthly*, October, 1869.

[10] *Atlantic Monthly*, August, 1869.

[11] *Atlantic Monthly*, May, 1868.

[12] *New York Times*, November 22, 1874, reprinted in *Stories by American Authors*, in which collection other stories by DeForest may be found. There is a story, "Fate Ferguston," in *The Galaxy*, January, 1867, signed "J. W." which is by DeForest. It is laid in the military district of Anderson, the far westernmost civil district of South Carolina, where DeForest was a military commandant in 1866. It is told so realistically that one is uncertain whether it is fiction or actual happening.

[13] *Atlantic Monthly*, April and May, 1870.

[14] *Galaxy*, August 1870–July 1871.

between the Beaumonts and the McAllisters, which interferes with the love story of Kate Beaumont and Frank McAllister, whose years of European study have made him cosmopolitan and who looks upon the feud as an anachronism. There are a number of vivid characterizations: Peyton Beaumont, Kate's father, a fire-eater whose irrational but natural love for his children lifts him into dignity; his sensible father-in-law, old Colonel Kershaw, who tries to heal the breach and is killed by Bentley Armitage, a handsome drunken brute whose wife, Nelly Beaumont, is the most interesting of the women. Spirited, patrician to her finger tips, enduring insults from her husband at which her pride revolts but which her pride also conceals for years, her clutch at her sister's sympathy, and her brave efforts to secure Kate's happiness with McAllister, make her fully worthy of the high place Howells gave her in his *Heroines of Fiction* when he placed her with his other favorites such as Hypatia, Maggie Tulliver and Bathsheba Everdene.[15] She belonged to a civilization where a combination of a high sense of personal honor, of quick temper and irrational conduct, of the taking of law into one's own hands, sprang from the social constitution of the plantation, whose owner had had so long the power of life and death over a subject race. There are some delightful touches, too, in the minor characters, such as Vincent Beaumont, who has studied medicine at Pennsylvania, but who refuses to practise, except upon his own slaves.

The Wetherell Affair (1873) is far inferior, because it was another excursion into the field of the murder mystery, for which DeForest was not fitted. But in *Honest John Vane* (1875) he wrote one of the best political novels in our fiction. It is a satire upon the corruption in Washington in Grant's administration. But DeForest does not simply criticize, he shows the effect of that vicious epoch upon a man who tries to be honest, and who is kept honest largely because he is expected to be. Vane is no hero; he has temptations caused by his wife's extravagance and he accepts stock from the railroad interests. But his frankness saves him when the inevitable exposure comes, and the mixture of weakness, shrewdness, and desire to live up to his reputation make him very human. The situation in Congress in which Vane is at first completely neglected, the interrelation of social and financial interests, the influence of Senator Ironman's passion for Mrs. Vane are depicted with directness

---

[15] See "The Heroine of *Kate Beaumont*," in *Heroines of Fiction*, Vol. II, pp. 152–163.

and knowledge, and the conversation between Vane and Dorman, the cynical lobbyist, is delightful.

As a companion piece to *Honest John Vane*, DeForest drew in *Playing the Mischief* (1875) a remarkable picture of a woman lobbyist, Mrs. Josephine Murray, a young widow who comes to Washington during Grant's administration to push a claim for damages to a barn belonging to her husband's father which had been destroyed during the War of 1812. Everyone is charmed by her, including George Hollowbread, an elderly Congressman whom she meets on the train down; Sykes Drummond, the member from her district; and Edgar Bradford, whom she had known before her marriage to Augustus Murray, and whom she really loves in her own inconstant way. We are not only told she is clever, however; her doings and sayings prove it. Her reception of Hollowbread's proposal, for example, which binds him but not her, is masterly, and she thinks quickly in nearly every emergency. Yet she can cast everything upon one die, if her emotions get the best of her, as this scene with Bradford proves:

"Listen to me!" she commanded, imperiously, while a tear of humiliation ˙rolled down her cheek. "I have something to tell you. I am ashamed to say it. But it is your fault. You drive me to it by your treatment of me. Besides, we are old friends, as you say; we can talk as men and women can not generally talk to each other; we act and hold hands and kiss like old friends, don't we? Why not say what we think, then? I think—I think—". And here she faltered, her mouth twitching pitiably, and her eyes avoiding him for an instant. "I think that you treat me very badly," she resumed, with an effort which turned her pale. "You treat me badly in kissing me when you mean nothing by it. I let you do it, to be sure. But why? It is because I hope that each kiss will be followed by a word; because I hope you are going to tell me that you love me, and want me—want me to be your wife. If I had thought you never meant to tell me that, I never would have let you touch your lips to me— never—never!"

This is realism, and for 1876 it is quite advanced. Bradford does not accept her love, either, in the way in which a hero of romance would have accepted it. Josie loses Bradford by her ruthlessness and deception, by the way she plays one admirer against another, becoming, in fact, engaged to Hollowbread and Drummond at the same time. The scene of Drummond's proposal, when he dominates her by the force of his passion, is also realistic for 1876. The way she gets rid of both of them, when her claim is finally passed, and the final scene, in which Josie vanishes into a splendid party at the house of an eminent financier, Allchin, who will probably pluck her of the $100,000 she has secured from the government, are both delightful.

The picture of Congress during the 'seventies, when the national treasury was being looted by claim agents of every description, is extremely well done. The way Josie's bill is switched from one committee to another at the last minute, by the professional lobbyist, Pike, whom she ultimately refuses to pay, in a very amusing scene, is quite in keeping with facts. The varying shades of dishonesty, from Hollowbread's reluctant action because of his infatuation, through Drummond's open dishonesty, and Pike's brazen bribery, are also realistic.

DeForest's blistering denunciation of the political generals who were capitalizing their Civil War records makes interesting reading now:

We may be allowed, perhaps, to devote one brief passage to the career of this brassy being [General Bangs] as a soldier. . . . Never but twice had he been under fire, and then only by dint of blundering—a blundering promptly rectified. Never had he devised a campaign, and never overlooked a field of victory. His real battles were carried on in his tent, or oftener in superb quarters in the midst of cities, surrounded by a staff of newspaper correspondents. These . heroes of the pen did for him all the fighting that he directed or knew how to direct. They did it on paper, and under his dictation. They wrote out his strategy and his tactics, and forwarded them for prompt publication. They put him at the head of columns on columns of print. No other general in history has won so many battles which were never fought, or which were fought under the management of others.

It seems hardly credible that the author of *Playing the Mischief* could have written *Justine's Lovers* (1878), in which Washington is once more the principal scene. The self-analysis of a girl struggling against sudden poverty provides a few good moments, but they are very few.

Irene the Missionary (1879) is a story laid in Syria, where DeForest had traveled in the 'fifties. The love story is natural and convincing. Irene is a Puritan, daughter of a clergyman, going out to Syria to teach in the mission at Beirut, with Mr. and Mrs. Payson. She is beautiful, and the three men whom she attracts—Hubertsen DeVries, of Albany, rich and an archæologist; Dr. Macklin, the medical missionary, sincere but not so cultivated; and Brassey, the consul, vulgar but a good poker player—all make love after their own fashion. She loves DeVries, but he is from another world, and his own hesitation to make a definite step toward marriage is not unnatural. DeForest again shows his knowledge of feminine nature, in Mrs. Payson's frank interest in making a match first with Macklin, then with DeVries. For 1879 Mrs. Payson is quite outspoken, when Macklin speaks to her of his love for Irene:

"So I have been waiting and watching,—watching for some sign of liking on her part, some indication which could lead me to hope, to feel tolerably sure of success."

"Waiting for her to speak first?" giggled Mrs. Payson. She could not look upon it as a hazardous or terrible thing to make an offer of marriage. Her simple belief was that most women were glad to get them, and exceedingly likely to accept them. She herself had had but one, and had received it with a throb of great gladness, and had not hesitated a moment to say yes.

The Bloody Chasm (1881) is a story of the reconciliation of North and South, immediately after the War. Silas Mather, a New Englander, had married a Beaufort and been treated rather badly by her family. He has been successful at making money. After his wife's death, he comes down to Charleston, to hunt up her niece, Virginia. There is a good picture of the poverty of South Carolina at that time and the Southern types—the proud bitter one in Virginia, her aunt who had not much brain but a good deal of training, and whose sole standard is to "act like a Beaufort," and the Negroes, Aunt Chloe and Uncle Phil—are well presented. The explanation of the decline of the Beauforts deserves quotation in full, but one line must suffice. "Colonel Beaufort, for instance, when he came to the estate, found himself with three hundred thousand dollars in property and two hundred thousand in debts. He seemed to think, sir, that that made five hundred thousand dollars, and he proceeded to live accordingly."

After a long silence DeForest, probably stimulated by the wave of historical romances, wrote a novel of the Revolution, *A Lover's Revolt* (1898), laid in and near Boston. The plot is not important, but the description of the battles of Lexington and of Bunker Hill showed that DeForest's earlier skill in the description of military movements had not deserted him. The picture of Prescott is fine, and the jealousy of the Colonial militia which forbade any real concert of the American forces is authentic.

In attempting to explain the lack of popularity which DeForest experienced, Howells was correct when he said:

A certain scornful bluntness in dealing with the disguises in which women's natures reveal themselves is perhaps at the root of that dislike which most women have felt for his fiction, and which in a nation of women readers has prevented it from ever winning a merited popularity. . . . Finer, not stronger workmen succeeded him, and a delicate realism, more responsive to the claims and appeals of the feminine over-soul, replaced his inexorable veracity.[16]

It is easy to criticize DeForest for a certain lack of construction, a tendency to draw his stories out too far, but he wrote of what he knew, and the author of *Miss Ravenel, Kate Beaumont, Honest John Vane*, and *Playing the Mischief* painted pictures of our national life which no nation should willingly permit to remain in obscurity.

In sharp contrast to DeForest's long career, the life of Theodore Winthrop (1828–1861) was brief, but it contained high promise of ability in fiction. Born in New Haven, he graduated from Yale College in 1848, traveled in Europe and in the Far West and practised law in St. Louis. Joining the army on April 19, 1861, he was killed at Great Bethel on June 10.[17] Most of his work was published posthumously. His first novel, *Cecil Dreeme* (1861), ran to its fifteenth edition by 1863. Laid in New York City at the time of writing, the plot is somewhat melodramatic. Clara Denham, who had apparently drowned herself three days before her proposed marriage with Densdeth, lives as a man, "Cecil Dreeme," in a studio near Washington Square. Her adventures are well told, although the conversations are in the older manner. Winthrop showed in his first story the ability to draw distinctions such as are found in his description of Clara:

It was a face that forbade all formal criticism. No passport face. Other women one names beautiful for a feature, a smile or a dimple—that link between a feature and a smile. . . . Grace she had . . . perhaps a more subtle charm than beauty. Beauty is passive; grace is active. Beauty reveals the nature; grace interprets it.

The best of Winthrop's novels, *John Brent* (1862), is a story of the West. Through the eyes of his friend Richard Wade, John Brent is pictured as a virile energetic character, spending his life in having new experiences, which lead him back to the East, upon a remarkable horse, Don Fulano. Their meeting with Ellen Clitheroe in the Mormon cara-

---

[16] Howells, W. D., *Heroines of Fiction*, pp. 153 and 162.
[17] For a vivid description of Winthrop's death, see Rebecca Harding Davis, *Bits of Gossip* (1904).

van, her abduction by Murker and Larrup, and the chase to her rescue are told in a vivid narrative, with its climax in the dramatic scene in which Don Fulano tramples Murker to death after Brent has been shot. Brent's search after Ellen in England introduces another interesting character, Padiham, the mechanic who is looking after Ellen and her father. The picture of the West is correct, with more reality and less melodrama than Bret Harte, although some of the characters, like Sizzum, the leader of the Mormons, are still in the idealistic tradition. The analysis of the nature of a gentleman is an example of Winthrop's insight and power of expression. There was the soul of a poet in Winthrop, which was revealed most clearly in *The Canoe and the Saddle* (1863), a vivid account of his travels in the Northwest from Port Townsend to the Dalles, based upon Winthrop's own wanderings about 1850. His glowing pictures of the scenery and their effect upon him culminate in the description of the mountains. "And, studying the light and the majesty of Tacoma," he writes, "there passed from it and entered into my being, to dwell there evermore by the side of many such, a thought and an image of solemn beauty, which I could thenceforth evoke whenever in the world I must have peace or die." Winthrop's skill in narrative is shown in the short tale, "Hamitchou's Legend," of an Indian chief who has adventures strikingly similar to Rip Van Winkle's and his descriptive power is revealed in the picture of the mission of the Atinams. The Puritan New Englander had learned by his experiences in the West:

And in all that period while I was so near to Nature, the great lessons of the wilderness deepened into my heart day by day, the hedges of conventionalism withered away from my horizon, and all the pedantries of scholastic thought perished out of my mind forever.

Edwin Brothertoft (1862), a romance of the Revolution laid outside New York City, is not on the level of his other work. But Winthrop had already shown an understanding of the channels through which moral earnestness passes into beauty, which lifts his prose at times to the level of a nineteenth-century Jonathan Edwards.

Bayard Taylor (1825–1878), like Dr. Holmes, was a poet, which is probably the reason that his fiction reached an imaginative level which entitles some of it to a permanent place in our literary history. His novels were written between 1863 and 1870, after his many years of wandering had borne fruit in his volumes of travel and of verse, and after his diplomatic career as Secretary of Legation at St. Petersburg seemed to be closed.

He had already written short stories dealing not very successfully with spiritualism,[18] then did much better work in "Friend Eli's Daughter," in the *Atlantic* for 1862, a quiet, spiritual revelation of the depth of feeling among the Quakers with whom he had been brought up in Chester County, Pennsylvania. In the preface of *Hannah Thurston* (1863), his first novel, he said, "I do not, therefore, rest the interest of the book on its slender plot, but on the fidelity with which it represents certain types of character and phases of society." When a novel is written primarily to do those things and only secondarily to reveal character, it is not likely to rise to greatness. The scene of *Hannah Thurston* is Ptolemy, New York, the time 1852–1853, when reformatory projects of all kinds were rampant. Taylor was a cosmopolitan and a devout lover of personal liberty. Knowing this, it is easy to understand why Temperance Reformers, Graham Bread Advocates, Woman's Righters, Abolitionists, Spiritualists, Vegetarians, and organizers of communities are the subjects of his keen ridicule.

The love story of Hannah Thurston, a Quaker and an Abolitionist, is rather thin, but any enemy of the small-town mind can still enjoy Taylor's thrusts at it, and the social historian will find the book a source of rich material. Taylor had a sense of the dramatic at all times; the scene in which Mrs. Merryfield, who has left her husband for a socialistic community, is brought back to him by the feeling that their children are waiting for them both in the next life anticipates the striking climax of Ibsen's *The Wild Duck*.

In *John Godfrey's Fortunes* (1864), Taylor wrote a better novel, though still dwelling upon his background, this time literary life in New York City in the 'forties which he knew well. Though there is unquestioned influence of *David Copperfield*, especially in the character of Alexander Penrose who is another Steerforth, the main situations and characters reflect his own hard struggles to earn a living after his return in 1846 from his first trip abroad. The literary soirées, the vanity of the poetasters, the almost total absence of the "real people"—all are depicted with the skill of a man who had built great hopes of a career as a poet but who never had the leisure to do his best. There is still a trace

[18] See "The Confessions of a Medium," *Atlantic Monthly*, December, 1860; "The Haunted Shanty," *Atlantic Monthly*, July, 1861.

of the idealistic method in Taylor, but realism triumphs in such a scene as that in which John Godfrey, despairing of winning Isabel Haworth, asks Jane Berry, a girl who had been betrayed but whom he had befriended, to become his mistress. The sentimental heroine would have reproached in eloquent terms the man who had helped her to build a new life of self-respect and who now threatened to destroy it. Jane simply tells him she is willing if he loves her, but if not, she will not consent, for his sake as well as her own. She knows he does not love her, and her very adoration of him gives her a strength to save them both. If her distinction seems fine drawn to a generation which looks upon *Ann Vickers* as a masterpiece, it is because they and not Bayard Taylor are unconscious of the meaning of reality.

The Story of Kennett (1866) is Taylor's best novel. Laid in his own home town of Kennett Square, about 1796, the characters were drawn from real people, although only one, "Sandy Flash," the highwayman, appears under his own name. Here Taylor ceased to be a satirist; he was in love with his material, yet he was even more concerned with his characters than with the background he knew so well, and he produced a masterpiece. The book was fused into unity by the strong, emotional but inarticulate character of Mary Potter. Years before, when a bound girl, she had, partly through her desire to rise, agreed to a secret marriage with Alfred Barton, the younger son of Squire Barton whom everyone dreaded and none loved. To her weak husband she had given a promise never to reveal their marriage till his father's death, which seemed imminent. But to everyone's disappointment the old man lives on, and Mary Potter keeps her word, even when her son Gilbert is born and has to grow up with a shadow upon him. Mary Potter is no mere type of the Magdalen of fiction. Through the steel in her nature, she conquers a place even in that limited community, and when at Squire Barton's funeral the thunderstruck neighbors see her move up in deep black and take her place at her husband's side, the reader can feel the pent up emotions of a great character who has paid, through twenty-five years, the price of folly, and has won at last, not love, but self-respect. Gilbert Potter, Sandy Flash, his woman, Deb Smith, Betsy Lavender, the village seamstress and general helper, all are extremely well drawn. How dramatic many of the scenes are, and how strong a hold upon the locality the novel has taken was proved by the crowds who attended the pageant adapted from it by John T. Hall and produced at the Longwood Open Air Theatre in 1933. So great was its popularity that it had to be repeated several times, and at least half of the audiences were made up of farmer's families to whom every element of the story, after nearly seventy years, bore the test of reality.

In *Joseph and His Friend* (1870), also a story of rural life in Pennsylvania, with some scenes in Philadelphia, Taylor did not rise to the level of *The Story of Kennett*. The central situation, that of a boy of twenty-two being tricked into a marriage with a woman of thirty, is not an appealing one, for the reader is rather irritated than grieved by his action, so sympathy does not follow him closely at first. Yet the story becomes interesting by its revelation of the complications and deep passions which may arise in a quiet neighborhood, and Joseph's longing for a broader life than his limited horizon can give him probably is based on Taylor's own experiences.

Taylor published in 1872 the best of his short stories, which had been appearing in the *Atlantic* from 1860 to 1871, under the title of *Beauty and the Beast and Tales of Home*. In it are mingled romantic-idealistic tales of old Russia, like "Beauty and the Beast"; amusing satires on transcendentalism and advocates of woman suffrage; and quiet, spiritual studies of the lives of the farmers, sometimes Quakers, of his native State. The best, such as "The Strange Friend," "Jacob Flint's Journey," "Twin-Love," and "Friend Eli's Daughter," represent the deeper currents in the lives of simple, natural people, and herein lay Taylor's contribution, in the short story, to realism. He was concerned also with the problem of identity in "Twin-Love" or in "Can a Life Hide Itself," and even better in a story published in 1874 in the *Atlantic,* "Who Was She?" In this he created an original situation in which a woman conceals her identity from a man who has become interested in her through finding her notebook in the woods, and tests him, through their frequent meetings in social gatherings, until she proves conclusively that she in her real person does not attract him and then, still incognito, she puts an end to their correspondence. The way in which Taylor reveals through the man's own words in telling the story how the woman longed to have him come up to her own standard and had found him wanting, proves his mastery of character drawing. His knowledge of life, in many aspects, was the great source of Taylor's strength, and his constant search for the nobility of human nature enables him to portray with fidelity the reaction even of narrow lives to the highest impulses. When the neighboring farmers, usually inarticulate, in "The Strange Friend" express their sympathy for the alien people who have lost their eldest son, he simply says: "The better qualities of human nature always develop a temporary good breeding," and it is all explained.

New England introspection, with a glance back at the methods of Emily Brontë, and an approach to realism in the revelation of feminine character, make the novels of Elizabeth Barstow Stoddard (1823–1902) take a place in the transition of the 'sixties. *The Morgesons* (1862), laid in "Surrey," a New England village, is told by the heroine, Cassandra Morgeson, a girl who spends considerable time in trying to understand herself. Her sister Veronica is a bit abnormal, and the two brothers whom they marry are types rather than real men. But there is a certain power in the book; the relations of the two girls after their mother is found dead in her chair are well drawn. The contrast between castes in New England, which is an essential part of *The Morgesons*, is also touched in *Two Men* (1865). Jason Waters, a house carpenter, marries Sarah Parke, whose father is much richer, but Jason, like Luke Morgeson, conquers a position through sheer ability. Jason is well drawn as the dependable man who takes care of the rest while they indulge in emotional reactions. Mrs. Stoddard skilfully depicts the situation, often occurring in real life, in which Sarah marries Jason while being in love with her cousin, Osmond Luce, who is a wanderer. The other characters are types, including an octoroon whose threatened marriage with Sarah's son brings on her death. *Temple House* (1867) is also laid in a New England village and is concerned with the interrelations of a family of which Argus Gates is the center. He returns after a long absence, and the story is largely his attempt to preserve his independence of action while assuming financial responsibility for his brother's wife and daughter and for a young Spaniard whom he has saved from drowning. Even his love for Virginia Brande is to him a threat against his freedom until he is forced to defend her, through certain complications, and ends by marrying her. Argus Gates is the best of Mrs. Stoddard's male characters; he is an advance over the self-sacrificing heroes of an older type, for, while he helps others, he determines to preserve as much freedom as possible from the most insistent of obligations, that incurred by a benefactor. Mrs. Stoddard's contribution to the portrayal of the intense self-restrained New England characters, running a bit to seed but still preserving their individualities, is significant. She points forward to Miss Jewett and Mrs. Freeman, with not so much charm as the former nor with the relentlessness of the latter.

Although she produced no important novel, Rose Terry Cooke (1827–1892) illustrates the transition which the 'sixties brought to the short story. Born in the suburbs of Hartford, Connecticut, she was precocious in her writing, but her early work, which found its way into *Graham's* and *Harper's*, was in the romantic-idealistic fashion of the time. In the early days of the *Atlantic*, she began to touch New England character with more surety. The fidelity of the woman who waits for the sailor whom she had refused to marry is portrayed with sympathy in "Eben Jackson." [19] The belated romance of a woman's life is touched with tenderness in "Miss Lucinda." [20] There is still too much attempt at fine writing, even in a story like "The Sphinx's Children," [21] in which she sketches the careers of the world's leaders who have succeeded through their ruthlessness. But the realistic trend suited her tendency toward truth, and she steadily grew better. "A Woman" [22] is a moving story of the effect of the Civil War upon an apparently superficial nature, which the tragedy of Bull Run lifts into dignity. "Freedom Wheeler's Controversy with Providence" [23] is a powerful story of the desire of a hard man to have a son with his own name. The lot of his wife is depicted with a grim fidelity to fact which even Mrs. Freeman was not to surpass; here is the deadly monotony of a toil-worn existence: "her sole variety of a weekday being when one kind of pie gave place to another." She drew well the life of a New England farmer's wife, "the life that sent them to early graves, to madhouses, to suicide; the life that is so beautiful in the poet's numbers, so terrible in its stony, bloomless, oppressive reality." She wove the spell of loneliness in the unmarried women, and the hard lot if they are married to the stern, inarticulate men. Mrs. Cooke had, too, the saving grace of humor. There is a delightful picture in "Amandar" [24] of the self-sufficiency of a woman who has killed her children by overfeeding and who calmly attributes their early deaths to other causes. Mrs. Cooke knew the secret of elicit-

[19] *Atlantic Monthly*, March, 1858.
[20] *Atlantic Monthly*, August, 1861.
[21] *Atlantic Monthly*, June, 1860.
[22] *Atlantic Monthly*, December, 1862.
[23] *Atlantic Monthly*, August, 1877.
[24] *Harper's Magazine*, September, 1880.

ing sympathy, especially for characters who do not ask it. In "Miss Beulah's Bonnet," it is not because a woman whose bonnet has been ruined gives up for economy's sake her one great solace of church-going and yet keeps her word to give her niece the fifteen dollars she has promised her for her honeymoon that we respect her. It is rather because she never thinks of doing otherwise. There is too much of a tendency to draw a moral lesson at times, but the tang of Mrs. Cooke's comments nearly always save the day. Of "laudamy and calamy," the two universal drugs of the day, she remarks, "they certainly slew their thousands and to the accompaniment of the jawbones of more than one ass." The best of her short stories are to be found in the collections *Somebody's Neighbors* (1881), *Root-Bound and Other Sketches* (1885), and *The Sphinx's Children* (1886), but the magazines must be consulted for others. *Happy Dodd* (1878), her first long story, is simply a religious tract; and *Steadfast* (1889), a novel of Connecticut laid about 1748, while better, is not so important as her short fiction. Here she is a pioneer who could moreover progress into even greater reality as the taste for truth became apparent.

Like DeForest, Rebecca Harding Davis is significant in her revelation of woman's nature, in her long period of production, and in the variety of her scenes. Like him, too, she has suffered from a lack of appreciation of her great significance in the development of realism. Born June 24, 1831, at Washington, Pennsylvania, where she was educated, she knew life in the Gulf States, in Wheeling, West Virginia, and in Philadelphia, where she went after her marriage in 1863 to L. Clarke Davis (one of the editors of the *Philadelphia Inquirer* and later of the *Public Ledger*), and where she lived until her death in 1910. But she also visited North Carolina and Kentucky, was familiar with the New Jersey scene, and always wrote of what she knew.

Her first significant contribution to realism was a short story, "Life in the Iron Mills," published in the *Atlantic Monthly* in April, 1861. It is uncompromising in its grim picture of the iron worker, Hugh Wolfe, and of "Deb" who loves him. His longing to be a sculptor, the recognition by a distinguished artist of the merit of his statue, made of the refuse of the shop, his struggle with himself when Deb steals money from the artist and gives it to Hugh to escape from the life he hates, are powerfully drawn. His arrest and condemnation to nineteen years' imprisonment, and his suicide, complete the story with a restraint which secures the sympathy of the reader by the writer's scorn for the methods which are usually used to arouse it.

Next came a novel, *Margret Howth* (1862), which is laid in and near a milling town, settled by New England and Pennsylvania people. It comes near to being a great novel—marred by too much preaching at the end; but the characters are vividly etched against a background of real life that could have been depicted only by an artist who saw clearly and was filled with human sympathy. The book was called "A Story of Today" when it ran anonymously through the *Atlantic*, October, 1861 to March, 1862. Rebecca Harding's own words show that she chose her method deliberately:

My story is very crude and homely, as I said,—only a rough sketch of one or two of those people whom you see every day, and call "dregs," sometimes,— a dull, plain bit of prose, such as you might pick for yourself out of any of these warehouses or back-streets. I expect you to call it stale and plebeian, for I know the glimpses of life it pleases you best to find; idyls delicately tinted; passion-veined hearts, cut bare for curious eyes; prophetic utterances, concrete and clear; or some word of pathos or fun from the old friends who have endenizened themselves in everybody's home. You want something, in fact, to lift you out of this crowded, tobacco-stained commonplace, to kindle and chafe and glow in you. I want you to dig into this commonplace, this vulgar American life, and see what is in it. Sometimes I think it has a new and awful significance that we do not see.

The story centers around the mill owned by Dr. Knowles, a ruthless philanthropist, who sells it to Stephen Holmes in order that he may carry on his plans for the bettering of slum conditions. He determines to have as his helper Margret Howth, a girl who loves Holmes and who is supporting her father and mother by clerical work at the mill. Holmes has apparently given her up, partly through her own sacrifice, in order that he may progress. Margret is no idealized heroine:

Nature had made the woman in a freak of rare sincerity. There were no reflected lights about her; no gloss on her skin, no glitter in her eyes; no varnish on her soul. . . . She tried desperately, I say, to clutch the far, uncertain hope at the end, to make happiness out of it, to give it to her silent gnawing heart to feed on. She thrust out of sight all possible life that might have called her true self into being, and clung to this present shallow duty and shallow reward. Pitiful and vain so to cling! It is the way of women. As if any human soul could bury that which might have been, in that which is!

The contrast between Margret's personal sorrow and the life of the quadroon cripple, Lois Yare, is well drawn. Lois is a huckster, with a cheerful soul, who has just welcomed back her worthless father, Joe Yare, from prison, where he is in imminent danger of returning if Holmes betrays him. Rebecca Harding had an ability to bring a spiritual value out of realism which is very rare:

> She had no self-poised artist sense, this Lois,—knew nothing of Nature's laws, as you do. Yet sometimes, watching the dun sea of the prairie rise and fall in the crimson light of early morning, or, in the farms, breathing the blue air trembling up to heaven exultant with the life of bird and forest, she forgot the poor vile thing she was, some coarse weight fell off, and something within, not the sickly Lois of the mill, went out, free, like an exile dreaming of home.

The author knew she was doing something different. Her description of the romantic-idealistic novel proves this:

> That was the time for holding up virtue and vice; no trouble then in seeing which were sheep and which were goats! A person could write a story with a moral to it, then, I should hope! People that were born in those days had no fancy for going through the world with half-and-half characters, such as we put up with; so Nature turned out complete specimens of each class, with all the appendages of dress, fortune, *et cetera*, chording decently. . . . Of course I do not mean that these times are gone: they are alive (in a modern fashion) in many places in the world; some of my friends have described them in prose and verse. I only mean to say that I never was there; I was born unlucky. I am willing to do my best, but I live in the commonplace.

The theme of the moral contrast grew in her work before Bret Harte. The way Knowles tries to strip Margret of every personal affection so that she will dedicate herself to this work of his is excellent.

There are eloquent passages describing the "waiting pause while the States stood still, and from the peoples came the first awful murmurs of the storm that was to shake the earth." This was in 1860, just after the election, and before Christmas. But the war is not the theme of the book. She brings it back to the personal love of Holmes and Margret, who wins him after all, and for whom he gives up the heiress who would have made his path easy. This part is dragged out too much, but the main portion of the book, up to the death of Lois, is one of the best that the period produced. It actually throbs with the sense of pity for the oppressed, for those whose lot is hard, and with a faith that is triumphant over all the apparent brutality of life.

For the next five years Mrs. Davis devoted herself to short stories, most of which appeared in the *Atlantic Monthly*. They are of uneven merit, but in "John Lamar," [25] and "David Gaunt" [26] she drew realistic pictures of the Civil War in the mountain region of what is now West Virginia. There is no glory of war, but rather its cruelty manifested by the poisoning of wells and the burning of the houses of the noncombatants by both sides. In "John Lamar" she recreates the confusion of emotions in the Negro slave, Ben, until the hopelessness of his future situation, South or North, and the words of an abolitionist soldier, fire him to murder his master, Lamar, who is about to escape from the Union prison. True to life, also, is the lack of enthusiasm with which the clergyman, David Gaunt, joins the Union forces, or Joe Schofield dies in trying to reach the Confederate camp at Blue's Gap to warn them of the Union attack, not because of patriotism but in order to revenge himself upon the force that has killed his son. It is a fine study of the way the Civil War remained a personal matter in a disputed border country. The attitude of the regular army soldier, Douglas Palmer, who has already become a professional, is well established. So is the character of "Dode" Schofield, "the only creature in the United States who thought she came into the world to learn and not to teach." In Mrs. Davis's next story, "Paul Blecker," [27] the analysis of the women's characters is made more prominent than the picture of war, for she represents them as restless, a bit morbid, but determined to control their own lives. Yet her short stories of the war are the first to picture it correctly, ante-dating DeForest's novel by five years. Long afterward in her autobiography [28] she speaks even more frankly of that time:

I had just come up from the border where I had seen the actual war; the filthy spewings of it; the political jobbery in Union and Confederate camps; the malignant personal hatreds wearing patriotic masks, and glutted by burning homes and outraged women; the chances in it, well improved on both sides, for brutish men to grow more brutish, and for honorable gentlemen to degenerate into thieves and sots. War may be an armed angel with a mission, but she has the personal habits of the slums. This would-be seer [Alcott] who was talking of it, and the real seer [Emerson] who listened, knew no more of war as it was, than I had done in my cherry-tree when I dreamed of bannered legions of crusaders debouching in the misty fields.

[25] *Atlantic Monthly*, April, 1862.
[26] *Atlantic Monthly*, September and October, 1862.
[27] *Atlantic Monthly*, May and June, 1863.
[28] *Bits of Gossip* (1904).

One of the best of the short fiction is "The Wife's Story," [29] a power-ful narrative revealing the processes of a woman's mind, not quite normal. She is from Concord, where she had known Margaret Fuller, and has a soul-torturing conscience which analyzes all emotions; and she is contrasted with her husband's family, the Mannings, who come from the Middle West, strong physically and robust mentally. It is the contrast which Moody drew years later in *The Great Divide*. Her stories of the sea on the New Jersey coast, "Out of the Sea" [30] and "The High Tide of December," [31] are well worth reading if only for her description of the stormy coast around Barnegat.

In 1867 [32] she returned to the novel with *Waiting for the Verdict* which, if it had not been overloaded with propaganda, would have been a great one, and which, even as it is, ranks with the best of this period. The characters are finely drawn. Rosslyn Burley, the illegitimate daugh-ter of James Strebling, a Kentucky landowner, and Margaret Burley, is a finished portrait, as is her grandfather, Joe Burley the carter, who has brought her up. Garrick Randolph, the scholar gentleman, Rosslyn's husband, who sells his faithful Negro slave, Hugh, to keep a secret concerning his inheritance, gives Mrs. Davis an opportunity to portray the loyalty and the hopelessness of the Negro. The most vivid char-acter, however, is that of Hugh's son, "Sap" at first, and Dr. John Broderip later. He becomes a famous surgeon in Philadelphia, without anyone suspecting his Negro blood. His decision to tell the woman he loves of this taint, and the repulsion Margaret Conrad feels for him, are very well done, even if his determination to tell his secret and devote himself to his race, with its climax in his leading his colored regiment into Richmond, is a bit too spectacular! One of the best passages is the scene in Broderip's hospital. Nathan, his brother, has come to him for treatment. Broderip knows that he need only make a slight cut, and his secret is safe.

Broderip stood up, the steel probe in his hand. His wife, waiting for his strong arm, for the tenderness and passion gathered and barred within his breast in his solitary life . . . all the world of goodness, and culture, and beauty into which he had fought his way during these years, waited, it seemed to him, with her, on that side of the thin, glass barrier. On this side, what? With the few black

---

[29] *Atlantic Monthly*, July, 1864.
[30] *Atlantic Monthly*, May, 1865.
[31] *Atlantic Monthly*, January, 1866.
[32] *Galaxy*, March–December, 1867, published 1868.

drops that made him kin to this creature, looking up at him with a brute's intelligence in his eyes—the fortunes of his race. There was no middle ground. Let him acknowledge the mulatto as his brother, and he stood alone, shut out from every human relation with the world to which he belonged. . . . . After a long while the surgeon's hands began to move about Nathan again gently, and the sallow face, when it bent over him, was transfigured with the strength and nobility of a great thought. A touch at the bottom of the maelstrom will send the doomed man to the upper life again; and that chance word of poor Nat's had struck Broderip's soul out of its murderous depths into the free light and air. He put his hand on the mulatto's broad, melancholy forehead and held it there a moment. Nat smiled humbly, when he took it off, at this remarkable token of the great man's kindness. He never knew what that touch meant to him.

It is a pity Mrs. Davis turned the novel into an appeal so definitely to the nation—for the Negro—waiting for its verdict, but she knew both sides and saw the problem clearly, even in 1867—much better than Tourgée—and realized the handicaps of the Negro and the Northern attitude of hostility to him. The reality of her fiction can best be appreciated when it is compared to Epes Sargent's *Peculiar* (1864) an absurd story in which a Negro is endowed with angelic qualities which enable him to check a white man in the very moment of his revenge by a few well-turned speeches.

Mrs. Davis's contribution to realism is seen in a novelette, "A Pearl of Great Price," [33] a fine study of a woman, Bertha Müller, who is a representative of real religion among a set of people who make theology important. Somehow Mrs. Davis makes her in her great sacrifice, without self-pity, a notable figure. *Dallas Galbraith* (1868), is a good study of an inarticulate boy who suffers for another's crime. The plot is at times melodramatic, especially in the scenes which prove his innocence, but the characters of Dallas and of his grandmother, dominating her property in West Virginia, and all her family, are excellent. *Natasqua,* a long short story,[34] laid on the New Jersey coast, begins well but runs into a conventional mould at the end. *Kitty's Choice* (1873) [35] contains a realistic study of the development of a girl from a pretty pleasant creature to a determined woman who rises to the emergency when she learns

---

[33] *Lippincott's Magazine,* December 1868–January 1869. Reprinted in *Short Stories for Spare Moments,* Second Series, 1869.
[34] *Scribner's Monthly,* November, 1870 to January, 1871. Published, 1896.
[35] *Lippincott's Magazine,* April to July, 1873, as "Berrytown."

that the wife of the man she loves is still alive, an eater of opium, and who continues to direct his life after his wife's death.

Even better is *Earthen Pitchers*,[36] beginning with the delightfully satiric picture of the Saturday evenings at Jenny Derby's in Philadelphia, where everything is "copy," even the pictures having been borrowed for advertising purposes. Jenny's love for Niel Goddard, the artist; the way his love for Audrey Swenson is killed by the shock to his vanity; the scene at Lewes, in which Jenny, following them to the seashore, walks into the quicksand—all remain vividly in the memory.

The best of her fiction of the 'seventies, however, was *John Andross* (1874), a story of character as affected by political corruption, the Whiskey Ring, and corporation lobbying in Pennsylvania. It begins in the coal and iron region near Lock Haven, and moves into Philadelphia and Harrisburg. John Andross, a charming but easily swayed young man, is the center of the book. He is ruined by his passion for Anna Maddox, a remarkable picture of the vampire—a pretty, apparently innocent girl, who sways not only John Andross, but also Clay Braddock, a more serious type, and Ware, a newspaper man, whom she marries secretly. She is also attractive to Houston Laird, a capitalist who has a hold on Andross, through his knowledge of a forgery by Andross's father. As a contrast to Anna, Isabel Latimer, the slower but more substantial woman who is engaged to Braddock, is also well done. The background of corruption is not over stressed, and the description of the iron furnace is realistic, especially the scene in which Andross, after escaping from Laird's influence, decides to return to it for the sake of winning Anna and Laird watches Andross's face by the light of the furnace and knows Andross is his once more. Mrs. Davis's ability to depict Braddock's passion for Anna and love for Isabel at the same time is remarkable. The drowning of Andross in saving Anna has a fine touch of realism in her insisting upon her husband and his companion attending to *her* and leaving Isabel helpless to save Andross. A bit too much Evangelicalism and a looseness of structure, but also passionate devotion to the right, animate the book. The way Houston Laird works, not merely bribing quietly, but also putting upright men like Colonel Latimer in office as a smoke screen, or letting Andross think he is playing straight in the legislature until the time comes when he needs his aid most, shows her knowledge of practical politics. *A Law*

[36] *Scribner's Magazine*, November, 1873 to April, 1874.

Unto Herself (1878), laid in the suburbs of Philadelphia and on the seacoast near Tuckerton, New Jersey, is hardly up to Mrs. Davis's standard.

That the strength of Mrs. Davis lay in her character drawing was shown in the skilful pen pictures, very brief, which she published in *Scribner's Monthly* in 1874 and 1875. "The Doctor's Wife," well poised, without beauty, but who "did not carry her little luxuries with the uneasy vanity of a workman in his Sunday shirt"; "The Best Fellow in the World," the optimist "who had honor but no honesty"; "The Pepper-Pot Woman," who had lived with two men without being married, but who had brought up five children not her own; and "The Rose of Carolina," a realistic picture of the Southern woman, "quite sure of her footing both socially and in her opinions; she stands at ease even in her little ignorances, without conceit or anxiety." "Dolly" is a picture of a young Moravian girl; in this sketch and in "The Poetess of Clap City," Mrs. Davis draws the picture of a competent woman who makes life suit her, rather than wait for it to be shaped by others to her needs.

Only one of these did she reprint in her *Silhouettes of American Life* (1892), a collection of short stories published in magazines during the 'seventies and 'eighties. She treated a variety of places and themes in these two decades, always with a decided realism. "Marcia" is a vivid picture of a Southern girl who comes to Philadelphia to write,[37] and is hopelessly ignorant, even of grammar. Several deal with the South. "Walhalla,"[38] laid among the German Swiss in South Carolina, is a study in content with nature. Hans is "the only man in America who took time to look at the world he lived in." "Tirar y Soult"[39] is a story of the heroism of a little Creole who gives to a Northern visitor the horse which means safety from the morass. "At the Station" is laid in North Carolina;[40] and Mrs. Davis begins it with the sentence: "Nothing could well be more commonplace or ignoble than the corner of the world in which Miss Dilly now spent her life," yet this middle-aged woman is one of the rare spirits to whom locality means nothing.

In "Mademoiselle Joan,"[41] Mrs. Davis wrote a fine story of the supernatural, laid in a Canadian village on the Saguenay. The struggle

[37] *Harper's Magazine*, November, 1876.
[38] *Scribner's Monthly*, May, 1880.
[39] *Scribner's Monthly*, December, 1888.
[40] *Scribner's Monthly*, December, 1888.
[41] *Atlantic Monthly*, September, 1886.

of the spirit of Joan, whose sister, La Veuve Badleigh, has married a widower, Labidie, to protect the children from the nameless evil their stepmother will bring upon them, is related with a realism that makes the supernatural effective.

"Across the Gulf" [42] is in her best manner. The contrast between the clergyman, the Reverend William Imlay, and the actors with whom a train wreck brings him into intimate contact, gave Mrs. Davis an opportunity to describe the real condition "backstage" as it broke upon the vision of a person who still looked upon the profession as lost souls. The quiet way the young actress puts him out of her life is very effective, and the ability of Mrs. Davis to limn a portrait in a sentence was still with her. Mrs. Imlay, the clergyman's mother, is "a neat compact package of fulfilled duties," who wonders what the actress on the boat is thinking. "It was the very question she had asked about the sea-lion in the Park, yesterday." "Kent Hampden" (1892) is a boy's story, laid mostly in Wheeling about 1824. It is unusual in her work, for it is laid in the past.

Doctor Warrick's Daughters (1896) is a fine study of two contrasted women, Mildred and Anne Warrick, daughters of Dr. and Mrs. Warrick, who live in Luxborough, Pennsylvania, a small town not far from Philadelphia. The prologue, which deals with the death of their mother, Sarah, is striking. She hears from the oculist that she must die soon:

Coming into the street, she saw workmen busy everywhere removing the flags and decorations from the houses. Black streamers hung from many windows; groups of excited men stood talking on the street; some of them wore crape on their arms, and they spoke low as if in the presence of the dead.

She stopped, bewildered. Had they heard—that it was only a month?

"What has happened?" she asked some one hurrying by.

"Lincoln was murdered last night!" the woman said. "Why, where have you been not to know it?"

"Is that all?" said Sarah.

Frances Waldeaux (1897) is the story of a mother's love for her son, George, and of his marriage to a coarse woman, Lisa, who is the daughter of a Russian prince and Pauline Felix, and who traps him on board ship, going to Europe. Frances Waldeaux is apparently light and cheerful. She is really a woman of great ability, whose husband had been worthless, and she writes a joke column to support her son. The Euro-

---

[42] *Lippincott's Magazine*, July, 1881.

pean scenes in Vannes and in Munich are correct enough, but they are only background, and the end is conventional. But Mrs. Davis's insight is shown in the remark of Lucy Dunbar, who has loved George but who is considering marriage with a prince and fortune-hunter, "Mind you, I don't accuse anybody, but when the needle has once touched the magnet it answers to its call ever after."

The faults of Rebecca Harding Davis are clear to anyone who reads her critically. She repeats her plots, which are her weakest elements; there are improbabilities in her best stories, but she was a master in character drawing. No one in American fiction before her had painted with such skill two individuals: first, the woman of moderate means, working and directing her household and shaping the lives of those around her without demand or display; and second, the apparently light and dependent woman, who grips the lives of the men who love her relentlessly and brings them to ruin. She must have known one or both of these women; perhaps she was the first. It is our misfortune that some of her best work lies unreprinted in the pages of the magazines, and that she told the truth too uncompromisingly before it had become the fashion to do so.

Among those who began to write fiction in the 'fifties, Josiah Gilbert Holland (1819–1881) illustrates clearly the survival of the moral tone. He was an essayist of wide popularity, and a poet, but the moving impulse of such poems as *Bitter Sweet* was narrative and moral. His first novel, *The Bay Path* (1857), dealt with the theological intolerance of a Connecticut community from 1638 to 1652. It was slow in movement and, while accurate in its interpretation of the social and religious atmosphere of the time, it created no memorable characters. *Miss Gilbert's Career* (1860), laid in a Connecticut industrial town, has reality in its setting, and in the handicaps of an unknown novelist. The characters are still types, however. Between the writing of these novels and his later fiction, he had become, in 1870, the first editor of *Scribner's Monthly* and his three novels that followed were all published in that magazine. He had traveled widely; as a result, the new monthly laid stress upon travel articles and fiction that tended toward romance.

Arthur Bonnicastle (1873) is a story of an imaginative boy, growing up in a New England town; at least the beginning is probably autobiographical. His college life at Yale is told in terms of his moral development, and he acts under the temptations which beset him in New

York City in a natural way. He is human, yet not altogether real, and perhaps the best character is that of old Mrs. Sanderson, who dominates everyone in her household until the end. *The Story of Sevenoaks* (1875) is a better novel, for the plot is more thoroughly worked out. Robert Belcher, the mill-owner of Sevenoaks, a town not clearly localized, but placed according to Holland "in Maine, or New Hampshire, or Vermont, or New York," is the central figure. He is a type, of course, just as Mulberry Sellers was, but he represented truly the unscrupulous, ruthless money-maker of the gilded age. Beginning with his theft of the patents of the inventor, Paul Benedict, he founds his fortune upon his ability to defy or mould public opinion by his skill in leading men apparently to their advantage but really to his own. His financial operations in the oil fields of Pennsylvania and later, after he goes to New York City, in the purchase and ruin of a railroad are real, even if they seem now an old story. From the point of view of fiction, the best claim of the book to notice is the way in which Belcher meets defeat at the hands of a woman, Mrs. Dillingham, whom he tries to make the instrument of his schemes against Paul Benedict. She has been leading him on, for her own amusement, but his coarseness and lack of understanding of any nature finer than his own turns her into an enemy even before she discovers in Paul Benedict her own brother, long estranged from her. Belcher's final catastrophe, brought on by his forgery of Benedict's transfer of his patent rights, and the gradual breaking down of his character through his dissipation, are also well portrayed. He comes near to being a great portrait of a moral failure, and if Holland had not stopped so often to preach, the effect would have been greatly strengthened.

Nicholas Minturn (1876) is a study of a young man of wealth who desires to be of service to mankind. He not only has to learn the real social and economic conditions in New York City in order to draw the line between actual poverty and fraud but also has to combat the inertia of poor and rich and the futility of those who make economic betterment a social playground. It is easy to smile at Holland's enthusiasms, but Minturn's attempt to reform the fraudulent beggars by providing jobs suited to their actual capacities is perhaps as near a solution as has been reached. His criticism of the disorganization caused by charitable over-organization is keen, and his remedies are in part being adopted today. It is interesting to read his comment in 1876 that if an announcement were made that $100,000,000 would be available for relief in a single season in New York, it would develop enough pauperism to absorb it!

Holland's novels will remain important documents to the social and economic historian. As fiction they suffer from too much preaching, which has led to the impression that he was a clergyman. He did have an ability to draw characters, and he had studied Dickens carefully and learned to a certain degree how to incarnate hypocrisy and dishonesty as in Benson, the banker of *Nicholas Minturn*, or Belcher, the promoter of *Sevenoaks*. His literary method places him in the transition period, but his editorship of *Scribner's Monthly* makes him one of the forces which led to the newer impulses of the 'seventies. His merit can best be appreciated when he is compared with such a novelist as the Reverend E. P. Roe who began in 1873 to pour forth a series of absurd productions which sold widely and preached plentifully the special form of sentimental Evangelicalism to which Roe belonged. The closing scenes of *Barriers Burned Away* (1873) in which the hero converts the heroine to his own way of thinking on the shore of Lake Superior while the roaring blasts of the Chicago fire compel them to dip themselves into the lake at intervals, are so bad that the critical judgment which confuses Holland's work with Roe's is unfortunate. His popularity emphasizes the service of the better novelists of this transition in raising the taste of the audience above the stilted conversation and the nauseating pietism of the type of fiction Roe represented.

Although she was a contemporary of Howells and James, Elizabeth Stuart Phelps Ward (1844–1911) ante-dated them in the first publication of her fiction, and that she belongs to the period of transition to realism is evident from her tribute to the effect the stories of Rebecca Harding Davis had upon her. Indeed the significant changes which took place in her own work illustrate clearly that transition. She won her first fame through her description of the life after death as viewed by her own form of belief, evolved through an inheritance of clerical tradition, influenced by liberal ideas and by the growing concern with spiritualism. She presents, therefore, an interesting example of the New England mind, exploring fields of romance of a new kind, and yet led through her hatred of injustice into a realistic picture of the sufferings of the unhappy.

Born in Andover, Massachusetts, the daughter of the Reverend

Austin Phelps, Professor of Rhetoric at Andover, and of Elizabeth Stuart, whose religious books were extremely popular, she grew up in an atmosphere of letters. Her first story was printed in *The Youth's Companion* in 1857. If she wrote "Tenty Scran," published anonymously in November, 1860, in the *Atlantic Monthly*, she was one of the earliest of the realists.[43] This quiet story of Content Scranton, who takes up her life as a sewing woman after a disappointment in love and who refuses to marry her lover when he returns, shattered in health, to find her at forty mistress of herself, is told with an art that seems too consummate for a girl of sixteen. There is a maturity in "Tenty Scran's" acceptance of sorrow and a clear-sightedness in her judgment of Ned Parker that mark it out distinctly from the sentimental tale of its day or indeed from Miss Phelps' Sunday-school books like *Mercy Glidden* (1865). It is much better too than the early short stories that followed it, such as "A Sacrifice Consumed," [44] a tale of the woman who has lost a lover in the Civil War, or "What Did She See With?" [45] an account of a maid who has the power to see in a trance things that are lost, and even identifies at a great distance an erring woman who had disappeared years before. This story is significant, however, because of the realistic picture of the occult phenomena. The best of her early stories was "The Tenth of January," [46] a vivid narrative based upon an actual occurrence in the Pemberton Mills, at Lawrence, Massachusetts. Mrs. Ward tells in her *Chapters from a Life* how she studied the locality and questioned eye witnesses who had seen the building crash with hundreds of employees under the ruins and who had taken part in the struggle to save the victims until the fire added its horror and put an end to rescue. She creates characters to make the tragedy and the heroism personal and concrete, especially Asenath Martyn, the cripple

---

[43] The story is attributed to her in the *Atlantic Monthly Index* and a recent letter from Mr. Ellery Sedgwick, editor of the *Atlantic Monthly*, confirms the statement. Yet Mrs. Ward states definitely in her *Chapters from a Life* (p. 78) that "the first story of mine which appeared in the *Atlantic* was a fictitious narrative of certain psychical phenomena occurring in Connecticut," evidently referring to "What Did She See With?" (*Atlantic Monthly*, August, 1866). Since she speaks of the deep impression it made upon her to be represented in that magazine, it seems incredible that she should have forgotten the publication of a story in its pages at the age of sixteen. Moreover, she states also (p. 75) that she published in *Harper's Magazine* in 1864 "A Sacrifice Consumed," and only later wrote for the *Atlantic Monthly*.

[44] *Harper's Magazine*, January, 1864.

[45] *Atlantic Monthly*, August, 1866. Published as "What Was the Matter?" in *Men, Women, and Ghosts* (1869).

[46] *Atlantic Monthly*, March, 1868.

who gives up her chance of safety to the girl who has supplanted her in her lover's heart. By this means she leads up to the climax:

But above the crackle and the roar a woman's voice rang out like a bell:—
"We're going home, to die no more."
A child's notes quavered in the chorus. From sealed and unseen graves, white young lips swelled the glad refrain,—
"We're going, going home."
The crawling smoke turned yellow, turned red. Voice after voice broke and hushed utterly. One only sang on like silver. It flung defiance down at death. It chimed into the lurid sky without a tremor. For one stood beside her in the furnace, and his form was like unto the form of the Son of God. Their eyes met. Why should not Asenath sing?
"Senath!" cried the old man out upon the burning bricks; he was scorched now, from his gray hair to his patched boots.
The answer came triumphantly,—
"To die no more, no more, no more!"

The stark simplicity with which she made live again this sublime moment in which the faith and courage of New England nature looked unmoved on the face of death brought her recognition from Whittier and others and encouraged her to go on. The story was published in her first collection, *Men, Women, and Ghosts* (1869).

In 1864 she had already begun her first novel, *The Gates Ajar*, which took two years to write and which awaited publication until 1868. It was written in the hope of helping the women whose dead had fallen in the Civil War. It is the journal of Mary Cabot, a New England girl whose brother, Royal, has been killed in the Civil War and who is inconsolable until her aunt Winifred Forceythe comes to visit her and brings her little daughter, Faith. Mrs. Forceythe is a widow, and the book is simply a series of conversations in which she proves to Mary that she will see Roy in the future life. Strictly speaking, it is hardly a novel, for the death of Mrs. Forceythe is the only event of importance, and it is hard to see now why the book had such a great vogue. By 1884 it had passed through fifty-six editions in America. It sold over 100,000 copies in England and it was translated into French, German, Dutch and Italian. It is easy to see how it appealed to thousands of American women who longed to be convinced that they would see those they had lost in the war, but the foreign appreciation must have rested on something more universal, the demand of human beings for some surety of the continuity of life itself.

The Gates Ajar has an importance in our literature as one more development of the Puritan interest in the supernatural. Hawthorne and Poe had wisely avoided a description of the future life in their fiction, but Elizabeth Phelps went back to a more primitive and polemical impulse which stems from the Mathers. The Unitarian chill was passing over New England religious feeling when she was born, but she belonged by inheritance to the orthodox wing, so that her work may be looked upon in one sense as a reaction. It was based on emotion that liked to be analyzed, emotion with the New England consciousness of itself. It was also a protest against the traditional orthodox idea of Heaven, that of the residence of an overwhelming Divinity which would swallow up earthly affections; and a more human idea is presented of a place "with mountains and trees" where individuality was to be preserved. There she should have stopped, for in her other discussions of the future life—*Beyond the Gates* (1883), *The Gates Between* (1887), and *Within the Gates* (1901)—she attempted to go into detail, and from the point of view of fiction, that way madness lies. *Beyond the Gates* is the dream of a woman who thinks she dies and goes to Heaven. *The Gates Between* is the account of the adventures in the other world of a Dr. Esmerald Thorne, an unspiritual person who is accidentally killed, and *Within the Gates* is a dramatized form of the same story. Of course the difficulty with all these books lies in the fact that the difference between time and eternity makes impossible the same relations as those that existed on earth, and consequently a realistic description of the future life creates absurdities at once.

Just as *The Gates Ajar* was an argument against the conventional Evangelical picture of Heaven, so Mrs. Ward's second novel, *Hedged In* (1870), was a protest against the moral and social standards of this world. It illustrates very well the way the idealistic method was giving place gradually to realism. The character of "Nixy" Trent, who has "gone wrong" and who fights a bitter battle against the hypocrisy of the narrow-minded, changes too radically to be convincing. But when she brings her baby into the world amid the foulness of Thicket Street in the 'forties, into a room filled with steam from the wash tub and surrounded by drunkenness and disease, realism could hardly go further. Nixy Trent at the beginning is real in her nature; she leaves her child on a doorstep without much of a qualm, and it is only later that the ethical purpose of Mrs. Ward proved too much for the artist in her.

But *Hedged In* was only a preparation for *The Silent Partner* (1871), one of her best stories, with scenes that are unsurpassed of their kind in English fiction except in the pages of Charles Dickens. Into it she put her earnest passion for justice for the women and girls who worked in the factories. Perhaps she hoped to do for them what Mrs. Stowe had done for the Negro. But perhaps because she declined to sentimentalize her characters and treated even the mill-owners fairly, the book had no such great popularity. Yet Sip Garth, the worker in the cotton mill at Five Forks, and her deaf and dumb degenerate sister, Catty, are remarkable portraits. Only slightly less real is Perley Kelso, who owns part of the mill and who is kept from improving conditions by her male partners and has to content herself with being a silent partner and palliating evils she might have prevented. The tragedy of Catty, who, because of her prenatal conditions hears nothing but the great wheels of the mill, reaches its climax in the scene when Sip has to tell her that she is going blind:

She sat down on the edge of the bed with Catty as soon as they were alone. She had dried her eyes to bear it now. Catty must understand. She was quite determined to have it over. She set her lips together, and knotted her knuckles tightly.

The light was out, but a shaft of wan moonlight from the kitchen windows struck into the closet bedroom, and lay across the floor and across the patch counterpane. Catty sat in it. She was unusually quiet, and her face indicated some alarm or uneasiness, when Sip held up her trembling hand in the strip of light to command her close attention, and touched her eyes. Catty put out her supple fingers and groped, poor thing, after Sip's silent words. Walled up and walled in now from that long mystery which we call life, except at the groping, lithe, magnetic fingers, she was an ugly girl.

Sip looked at her for a minute fiercely.

"I should like to know what God means!" she said. But she did not say it to Catty. She would not speak to Catty till she had wiped her dry lips to wipe the words off. Whatever He meant, Catty should not hear the words.

She tried, instead, to tell her very gently, and quite as if He meant a gentle thing by Catty, how it was.

In the strip of unreal light, the two hands, the groping hand and the trembling hand, interchanging unreal, soundless words, seemed to hang with a pitiful significance. One might have thought, to see them, how the mystery of suffering and the mystery of love grope and tremble forever after one another, with no speech nor language but a sign.

"There's something I've got to tell you, dear," said the trembling hand.

"For love's sake?" asked the hand that groped.

"For love's sake," said the trembling hand.

"Yes," nodded Catty, with content.

"A long time ago," said Sip; "before we went to Waltham, Catty, when you picked the wool—"

"And hurt my hands," said Catty, scowling.

"Something went wrong," said the trembling hand, "with your poor eyes, Catty. O your poor, poor eyes, my dear! All that you had left,—the dear eyes that saw me and loved me, and that I taught to understand so much, and to be so happy for love's sake! The poor eyes that I tried to keep at home, and safe, and would have died for, if they need never, never have looked upon an evil thing! The dear eyes, Catty, that I would have hunted the world over, if I could, to find pretty things for, and pleasant things and good things, and that I never had anything for but such a miserable little room that they got so tired of! The poor dear eyes!"

The shrunken and disfigured eyes, that had been such wandering, wicked eyes, turned and strained painfully in the half-light. Sip had said some of this with her stiff lips, but the trembling hand had made it for the most part plain to the groping hand. Catty herself sat and trembled suddenly.

When should she see the supper-table plain again? the groping hand made out to ask. And the picture by the china-closet? And the flies upon the window-pane?

"Never!" said the trembling hand.

But when should she see Sip's face again without the blur?

"Never! O Catty, never again!"

The trembling hand caught the groping hand to sting it with quick kisses. Sip could not, would not, see what the poor hand might say. She held it up in the streak of light. God might see. She held it up, and pulled Catty down upon her knees, with her face in the patch counterpane.

It is the method, of course, she had learned from Dickens; the illumination of details by human sympathy, even to the repetition which drives the picture home. She did not learn from him, however, to lighten the misery with humor, or the novel would have made even a greater impression through contrast. But the gallant lonely fight of Sip Garth to protect the one human being she has left makes her a memorable creation.

In 1877 *The Story of Avis* dealt powerfully, if a bit morbidly, with the love story of Avis Dobell, a painter, and Philip Ostrander, a brilliant but morally unstable college teacher. The struggle between the artist and those normal relations of life which interfere with her career differs from the theme so often treated by James, since it is expressed in terms of a woman's feelings amid the insistent claims of domesticity.

Avis is a real person in her first dismay at the domestic difficulties, for Miss Phelps, like nearly all the women novelists of the 'seventies, makes the babies cry all night. There are too many of these details, but when Avis is faced with an important crisis like that in which the woman to whom Philip had been engaged calls upon her, she meets the situation with quiet dignity. When she has to tell Philip, driven by illness back from Europe, that their little boy is dead, or has to face their future with the glamour of passion gone and the dying man depending on her tenderness as well as her courage for his very living, she again meets the emergency. Just as quietly she faces the failure of her power to paint. But unlike Roderick Hudson, her nature deepens instead of narrows under misfortune. Philip Ostrander's decline is quite as much due to his intellectual inconstancy as to his lack of moral fiber, and while he is not so well drawn as Howells' picture of Bartley Hubbard, that was hardly to be expected from Elizabeth Phelps' fierce belief at that time that this was indeed "a man's world." "God may have been in a just mood, but he was not in a merciful one, when knowing that they were to be in the same world with men, he made women," is her summing up of the situation. Her own life at Andover made it possible for her to write the remarkable passage in which she describes the ideal teacher. It is worth many a course in "Education."

Her seriousness so far as her own sex is concerned led her to treat, in *Dr. Zay* (1882), the career of a woman physician which forms a sharp contrast to Howells' *Dr. Breen's Practice*. It is not of great importance. Nor were her much more ambitious attempts at historical novels, written in collaboration with Herbert D. Ward, whom she married in 1888, remarkable achievements. *The Master of the Magicians* (1890), is a readable story of Babylon at the time of Nebuchadrezzar, in which Daniel is the hero. The figures are conventional types, however, rather than real people, and the descriptions of Babylonian life are essays rather than fiction. Compared with Crawford's *Zoroaster*, on a kindred theme, it has little of the spell of the East. *Come Forth* (1891), a story of Christ in his human relations with Lazarus, Mary, Martha, and other biblical figures is somewhat better, but the historical romance was not Mrs. Ward's forte. She tells us in her autobiography that the books were largely her husband's creation.

Out of her summers at Gloucester, Massachusetts, came the inspiration for her finest work. She tells eloquently in her autobiography how she began to understand the nature of the fishermen and their temptations and to appreciate the inarticulate heroism of men who brave danger and of women who live in the constant shadow of fear. Some effective short stories, approaching novelettes, first grew out of these experiences. *The Madonna of the Tubs* [47] depicted the grief of a wife whose husband has quarrelled with her on the eve of the voyage in which he is supposed to be lost. This character, based on Mrs. Ward's laundress, is one of her best studies of married loyalty and human misunderstanding. If she permitted a happy ending to this narrative, *Jack the Fisherman* [48] ran into tragedy. The struggle of this sailor, who inherits a taste for alcohol, against which he fights but which leads him finally to murder and suicide, is drawn with knowledge and sympathy.

But these were only preparation for her masterpiece, *A Singular Life* (1894). In this novel she made a daring attempt at the creation of a character who should parallel in modern times the life and passion of Christ. The dangers of such a plan are obvious. But the artistic skill and the deep sincerity of Mrs. Ward surmounted them. Through the rejection of Emanuel Bayard by his own orthodox New England church and his establishment of an independent chapel at Windover, a thin disguise for Gloucester, not only is he removed from the limitations of creed, but he is made the representative of the spiritualized, the distilled essence of Christianity. This widened the appeal of the book, and the manly nature of Emanuel, developed through individual acts of kindness and understanding, each of which creates a new character, made it secure. Job Slip, the drunkard, and Lena, the prostitute, whom he saves at the risk of his life and of his reputation, are of course figures that might have been looked for from a disciple of Dickens. Jane Granite, who adores Bayard at a distance, and Ben Trawl, her lover, who hates him not only for that reason but also because Ben is the son of the saloon-keeper, real as they are, might also have been expected. But the triumph of Mrs. Ward lay in the love story of Bayard and Helen Carruth, the daughter of the professor of theology at Bayard's seminary. Helen is not the usual romantic heroine. Bayard has revolted against the rigid creed of the seminary; Helen has never taken its intricacies very seriously, and yet she is a product of the culture of which the theology of an older New England was a part. Her sense of humor,

[47] *Harper's Magazine*, December, 1885. In book form, 1887.
[48] *Century Magazine*, June, 1887. In book form, 1887.

rather rare among Mrs. Ward's heroines, is keen, and it makes more
attractive her womanly sympathy and natural reticence and self-respect
in the trying situation created by Bayard's poverty and consequent inability to tell her of his love. Unlike some other heroines of fiction, she
does not understand everything at once. As Mrs. Ward so well puts
the case:

> The position of a man who may not love a woman and must not invite her
> to marry him—or, to put it a little differently, who must not love and cannot
> marry—is one which it seems to be asking too much of women to understand.
> At all events they seldom or never do. The withdrawals, the feints, the veils
> and chills and silences, by which a woman in a similar position protects herself,
> may be as transparent as golden mist to him whom she evades; but the sturdy
> retreat of a masculine conscience from a too tender or too tempting situation
> is as opaque as a gravestone to the feminine perception.

Mrs. Ward knew that the inner struggle between love and duty is
more dramatic and intense than any conflict with external forces. Even
when Bayard tells Helen of his passion for her, how well this feeling
is expressed:

> But she faltered, and her courage forsook her when she looked up into his
> face. All the anguish of the man that the woman cannot share, and may not
> understand, started out in visible lines and signs upon his features; all the
> solemn responsibility for her, for himself, and for the unknown consequences
> of their sacred passion; the solitary burden, which it is his to wear in the name
> of love, and which presses hardest upon him whose spirit is higher and stronger
> than mere human joy.

When Mrs. Ward is dealing with events, she can be brief and telling.
The marriage, the dedication of the new building at which Bayard is
struck down by a stone thrown by Ben Trawl, the capture of the fugitive
under water by Lena, the death of Bayard, are recounted with power
and economy. It is tragedy, but tragedy that exalts, for the victory remains with Bayard in the love of his people, symbolized by the flags
of the fishing fleet, fluttering at half mast over all the waters within
the sight of Windover. *A Singular Life* is one of the foremost of American novels because it is based on life itself, built up through Mrs. Ward's
own experiences in her valiant efforts to fight the evils of a rough seafaring town. But it would have failed if she had been content to paint
merely the sordid side of that life. There must be something that rises

out of misery to make great literature, and she was able to place against its setting one of the most exquisite love stories in American fiction.

Mrs. Ward's later novels did not approach the standard of *A Singular Life*. She was too much concerned with propaganda against vivisection in *Trixy* (1904) or with the consequences of insomnia, in *Walled In* (1907), reflecting her own suffering. The best of the later novelettes was *The Man in the Case* (1906), a touching story of a girl's sacrifice to save her brother, an escaped convict.

The short stories of Mrs. Ward are found most conveniently in the collections *Men, Women, and Ghosts* (1869), *Sealed Orders* (1879), *Fourteen to One* (1891), *The Oath of Allegiance and Other Stories* (1909), and *The Empty House and Other Stories* (1910). The first group of her novels, those suggested by a spiritual interest or that of the supernatural, of which *A Singular Life* is the finest example, is represented by such stories as "Since I Died," "The Presence," "His Soul to Keep," or "The Joy Giver." The second group, those written to improve moral, social, or economic conditions, of which *The Silent Partner* is the representative novel, contains some of her best short stories, such as "The Tenth of January," "The Lady of Shalott," and "Jack the Fisherman." A large number of the short stories deal with the relations of men and women, usually married or engaged, in which the course of love does not run smoothly. In her novel *The Story of Avis* this arose from the clashing of emotions and interests, but in her short stories it often comes from the misunderstandings which arise from the inevitable readjustments of married life. "The Empty House," for example, represents with marked realism the situation caused by the separation of husband and wife during the summer. Often, perhaps too often, the long waiting of a wife for a husband thought dead or of a woman for her lover is retold. One of the most appealing, "The Oath of Allegiance," tells of the agony of a girl whose lover goes to the Civil War without speaking of marriage and is killed. Her feeling that she could have stood the grief if she had only been given the most precious gift to a woman, that of knowing she is loved by the man she has chosen, is told without sentimentality, and her pride and joy when the yellow, stained letter he had written to her is finally found years afterward is told with the restraint which marked Mrs. Ward's better stories. The Civil War and the sea are the elements which often separate her characters, and the stories like "The Madonna of the Tubs" or "Annie Laurie" owe their effectiveness to her own experience or observation. Quite a number of the stories deal with self-sacrifice: "Shut In," "A Brave Deed," "Sealed Orders," and best of all, "The Chief Operator," the story of a girl who stays at her post to warn the families in the valley of the coming flood till it is too late for her own escape.

With the exception of the two historical novels, her stories deal with American life. She has described the life in a New England milling town in *The Silent Partner*; in a New England fishing village in *A Singular Life*, "The Madonna of the Tubs," or "Jack the Fisherman"; and in a college town in *The Story of Avis*, *Walled In*, and *Donald Marcy* (1893). The atmosphere in these places is well caught, the milling town best probably, for of the really masculine life of college she does not show any great knowledge. With a very few exceptions, her fiction is limited to New England. When she lays the scene in Virginia, as in "The Bell of St. Basil's," the chief character, the president of a college deserted by all but himself, is really a New England Puritan. This provincialism is her strength as well as her limitation. It affects her theory of fiction as given in her chapter "Art for Truth's Sake," in her *Chapters from a Life*. No artist, she says, is complete "who refuses to portray life exactly as it is." But she differs from Howells in his criticism of the fiction of New England "because it was her instinct and her conscience to be true to an ideal life rather than to life itself." To Mrs. Ward, "moral character is to human life what air is to the natural world;—it is elemental." Thus her people are often incarnate moral or unmoral forces, and tend to become types, as in the series of novels beginning with *The Gates Ajar*. In *The Silent Partner*, the terrible fidelity to actual details saves the story from abstraction; and the sheer beauty of conception lifts *A Singular Life* into that realm of truth which is above mere facts.

Mrs. Ward understood the New England character thoroughly. She has represented it on its hard, unyielding side—in the story of "Long, Long Ago" in which Rachel Frost, living across the street from her clerical fiancé who is dying, cannot go to him on account of public opinion. The great inheritance for her people is that of the intellect; the great tragedy occurs when the children cannot go to college. The affectionate, half-respectful, half-protecting attitude of the New England congregation toward their minister, which took the place of the awe and worship of an earlier time, is often represented. In one of her best stories, "His Father's Heart," it is joined effectively to her favorite theme of self-sacrifice.

Perhaps the most serious criticism of Mrs. Ward lies in a certain monotony of subject and tone. While she had such a high opinion of the human relations of this world as to carry them, sublimated, over into the next, her people in this world are too often far from happy. Cripples, mental and physical, abound, and the novels might almost be called studies in human suffering. Her own insomnia crops up in *Walled In*, and the shadow of suffering might be said to hang over her fiction. The best is the brightest, for though Bayard does suffer from an incurable disease, still the love story is such a glorious one that one cannot help placing him among the happy of this earth. Mrs. Ward needs no excuse for representing life as full of care and unhappiness. But simply from the point of view of contrast, so essential in art, she might have tried more often to throw a charm over suffering as Dickens did. But here again her inheritance revealed itself. The Puritan took his misery seriously; it was a thing to ponder over. He did not put on a bright face and forget it; he bore it bravely but he bore it always with him; he tasted it now and then to make sure it was still at the boiling point. He did not make sport of it—anything so intimately associated with himself was not to be treated lightly. In its unpleasant forms this quality is trying. But when it flowers into the self-respect which is the parent of courtesy, as in "A Chariot of Fire," one of her later and better short stories, it justifies itself completely. This self-respect manifests itself, also, in the serene unconsciousness on the part of Mrs. Ward's characters of any social cleavage that could make them uneasy. They are gentle folk, usually in modest circumstances, but of the shifting social values of the post-Civil War period they are blissfully unaware. To the social historian of the future they will therefore be an interesting study. But it is not primarily for that reason that Mrs. Ward is important. With an artistic sincerity, a narrative ability of a high order, and a descriptive power at times rising to greatness, she combined a sense of moral values which give weight and substance to her fiction.

In the development of realism, Lowell's editorship of the *Atlantic Monthly* was a potent factor. He provided opportunities for practically every one of this group of writers, with an unerring instinct for the best in contemporary American fiction. After he ceased to be editor, his influence continued until, under Howells, the supremacy of the *Atlantic* became an established fact. In its pages is found fiction of a high quality which has not been reprinted, or has been allowed to go out of print. *Malbone: An Oldport Romance* (1869) by Thomas Wentworth Higginson (1823–1911), is an early example of the novel that deals with Americans of breeding without the bias of satire. The portrait of Philip Malbone, who "with a personal refinement that almost amounted to purity, was constantly drifting into loves more profoundly perilous than if they had belonged to a grosser man," who was "no more capable of unkindness than of constancy," is a remarkable picture of an individual as well as of a type.

These pioneers of realism were all endowed with imagination as well as acute powers of observation. Holmes, Trowbridge, Taylor, DeForest, Holland, and Mrs. Ward began as poets, and the rest either wrote verse or had a great love for and appreciation of it. They were all, however, concerned with the life of their time, and they subjected it to earnest scrutiny. Their major contributions were the revelation of fictional possibilities in people who had been presumed to be inarticulate, or those whom economic or social oppression had submerged. A love of justice and a deep sympathy for the unhappy animated them all, and their satire was directed against the active corruption or the hopeless drifting of the time. It is not without significance that no adequate treatment of the two, DeForest and Mrs. Davis, who maintained the satiric attitude longest, has appeared in any history of our literature. And yet these two to the historian should be the most interesting, for they are the most uncompromising of the realists who prepared the way for what was to come.

CHAPTER X

THE FICTION OF FANTASY

WHILE the trend toward the realistic treatment of familiar life was taking place, there still persisted the perennial impulse toward romance. It took the form largely of the choice of material and often made use of realistic methods, but its distinguishing quality lay in the unusual plots, the product of powerful imagination, and the courage with which a fantasy, woven out of strange characters, whose whims are often delightful, was established in terms of reality.

Edward Everett Hale (1822–1909) was distinctly a writer of the transition. As early as 1842 he wrote for the *Boston Miscellany*, in the company of Hawthorne and Lowell, and in his first collected volume of short stories, *If, Yes and Perhaps* (1868), he reprinted such an amusing story as "The South American Editor" from that early time. Even at the beginning, he had developed his recipe, to take an impossible situation and make it appear probable by simplicity and directness which for the moment convince his readers. For example, in "A Piece of Possible History" (1857), Homer and David are brought together. In September, 1859, he published in the *Atlantic* "My Double and How He Undid Me," a delicious piece of fooling, in which a popular minister hires an Irish farmer who looks exactly like him to attend functions in his place and provides him with a series of clichés like "Very well, thank you, and *you?*" or "I agree in general with my friend on the other side of the room" which carry him along safely for a while and end of course in amusing disaster when Dennis loses his head at a great meeting and mixes his replies. It is a keen satire on social and public life where no one wants to listen but rather to talk. "The Children of the Public" (1863) is rather more dramatic, for a man and a girl, meeting on a boat and having nothing, win a lottery prize, with amazing results.

In the *Atlantic* for December, 1863, appeared the story that made him famous, "The Man Without a Country." It was inspired by patriotism. Hale created an army officer, Philip Nolan, who had been concerned with the treachery of Aaron Burr, and who, when asked at his trial if he wished to say anything to show that he had always been faithful to the United States, cried out "Damn the United States. I wish I may never hear of the United States again." He is sentenced to be sent on one cruise after another on a government vessel with instructions to the officers that no one is to permit him to hear the name of his country. The way in which his longing for home becomes a tragedy, and especially the fine touch by which the red tape of the army and navy keeps him from being pardoned when no one is really interested in maintaining his exile, established Hale as a short story writer of the first rank. Even at the end when the supposed narrator of the tale breaks orders and lets Nolan, on his death bed, hear the name of his country, the restrained tone of the story keeps it from sentimentality. There was a real Philip Nolan, who was killed in Texas in 1801, but it was not his history that inspired Hale but a remark of Vallandigham of Ohio that he did not wish to live in a country that tolerated the actions of Lincoln's administration.

Hale was a clergyman and while his work is remarkably free from a theological tinge, he was at times an implicit teacher. In *Sybaris and Other Homes* (1869), which had appeared in part in the *Atlantic,* he satirized contemporary conditions by depicting an ideal condition of society in "Sybaris" on the site of the ancient city. It is fantastic sociology, made to approach reality by plausible details. But the extraordinary solution for marital difficulties by requiring every man of thirty and every woman of twenty-five to be married or go into exile, points forward to Stockton rather than to Bellamy. Sometimes, as in the novelette *Ten Times One is Ten* (1870), the purpose is a bit too evident, yet while the impulse which prompted this account of the influence which a dead man had upon the lives of his friends, was more ethical than artistic, it is hardly fair criticism to dismiss the book because it proved so powerful that clubs were formed in many places to carry out its principles. It proves however from its form that Hale was essentially a short story writer, though he attempted longer fiction. For example, *In His Name* (1874) a story of the Waldenses in the twelfth century has only one central incident, the ride to save the life of a young girl, Felicie Waldo, who has been poisoned inadvertently by her mother. In order to make a novelette, other matters are introduced including imaginary history. *The Fortunes of Rachel* (1884), an account of an English girl who, left an orphan by the death of her parents, arrived finally at Washington as the wife of a Supreme Court justice, is interesting as showing an improvement over *The Wide, Wide World* and its like. But it proved also that the treatment of real life without a touch of fantasy was not Hale's forte. His other novelettes, including a sequel to "The Man Without a Country" under the title of *Philip Nolan's Friends* (1876) in which he traced the real Philip Nolan to his death in Texas and wrote a romance ending with the American ownership of New Orleans, need not detain us. He tried to write historical romance in *East and West* (1892), a story of the settlement of the Ohio about 1789–1790. But it has no distinction. Perhaps an explanation of their lack of merit may be found in his Introduction to the first volume of the complete edition of his works in 1898. "Five or six times," he says, "I have extended the short story." But that is not the way great novels are written.

It was fancy of a gentle kind which inspired the *Reveries of a Bachelor,* by Donald Grant Mitchell (1822–1908), which began in September, 1849, in *The Southern Literary Messenger* as by "Ik Marvel," and appeared complete in 1850. Together with *Dream Life,* (1851) they represent the border line between fiction and essay. Mitchell had begun with fiction [1] but it was the revelation of his own personality that made the books interesting. When he attempted more definite fiction as in his novel of *Dr. Johns* (1866), he told a leisurely story of New England life from the 'twenties to the 'forties, centering around the character of a clergyman, drawn probably from his father. What makes *Dr. Johns* appealing is Mitchell's liberality. The contrast of the two Frenchwomen, Adèle and her mother, and their standards of thought and belief with the rigid tenets of the Connecticut village is portrayed by a man whom travel had broadened. The return of Reuben Johns, the minister's son, through the influence of Catholicism, to a liberalized form of Congregationalism, is a concrete instance of Mitchell's philosophy, which was to find good in everything. He was one of the late flowers of the Puritan plant that had borne its share of strength and was softening into grace and delicacy.

Like Mitchell's fiction, fanciful and subjective, *Prue and I* (1857), by George William Curtis (1824–1892), was more tonic in its tone. The New York bank clerk who lives contentedly upon his visions, who knows that the people whose lives he watches are not more happy but only

---

[1] "Frank Upton," *Knickerbocker Magazine*, June, 1842.

more active, has solved the problem of life, at least in one way. In *Trumps* (1861), Curtis presented a broader picture of urban life in New York, with some penetrating satire of the social, political, and economic organization of a large city in the 'thirties. There is a certain reality in the evil characters like Abel Newt, whose charm and intelligence fall a prey to his ruthless selfishness and his love of liquor, and the methods by which his sister Fanny secures her husband are startlingly natural for 1861. But most of the good characters are ideal types, and the influence of Dickens is apparent.

Hale, Mitchell, and Curtis had other interests besides fiction, but Harriet Prescott (1835–1920), or as she became in 1865, Harriet Prescott Spofford, devoted herself to it throughout a career which began in 1859 with "In a Cellar," [2] and terminated with a volume of short stories, *The Elder's People*, in 1920. Born in Calais, Maine, and brought up in Newburyport, Massachusetts, where Thomas Wentworth Higginson encouraged her, she spun her best stories out of her imagination, which took her over times and countries she knew only by wide reading, among which Poe and Charles Reade are the most easily traceable influences. But in her best work, there is an individual quality which placed her in the very first rank. What made "In a Cellar" a fine short story was not the pursuit of the diamond, for she had no great ability at a detective story, but it was the glowing style, the conversations, cryptic and allusive, and the description of the gem itself, evidence of a remarkable knowledge for a girl of twenty-four. She showed already an ability to project herself into an imaginary atmosphere, for in this story of Paris, where she had never been, she established the background so well that Lowell thought it was a translation. In 1860 appeared anonymously her first novel, *Sir Rohan's Ghost*. The plot is reminiscent of Poe, for Sir Rohan's ghost is the memory of a woman whom he had wronged, tired of, and tried to kill, but who has left a daughter with whom he fell in love. But the flashes of insight into the relations of the soul and the body, superbly reproduced in language, stand out in bold relief against the trivialities of some of the fiction of that day.

"It is a singular thing, this joy," said he. "It makes me tremble; it seems unnatural. I have heard of people of great faith as suddenly feeling their spirituality wonderfully increased, and of others who experienced unaccountable

[2] *Atlantic Monthly*, February, 1859.

mirthfulness, or happiness, or strength. But Death or some great suffering always supervened," he added with a shudder.

"I wonder why," said Miriam.

"Perhaps the soul," said St. Denys, "always goes a little faster than life, a little beyond the fact; and so, having beat out and reached its mortal bars, surges back and flows with a double current over the mood of the hour."

Or a passage which has a note of prophecy of the marvels of the radio:

Frequently, while at his work, he had a perception of certain harmonious properties of the universe, and more particularly of those particles composing the atmosphere, which seemed to emit one vast gentle accord as they moved interfluently among themselves. So perfect and integral must this harmony be, Sir Rohan reasoned, that unless when disturbed by some extraneous or adverse influence it is imperceptible to mortal ears; and thus, whenever heard by him, he knew that the vibrations were audible only by means of this dissonant and divulsive presence, as hostile, it appeared, to the kind forces of nature as to him. At the time when his eyes felt these cold finger-tips, he became aware also of this outer harmony throbbing in long rhythmical waves of finest sound, as if drawn from silver wires, by a low, hot wind. This was unapproachable, almost infinite; on all sides of him he heard a chord produced perhaps millions of cycles away, but on its bosom and overtopping it like the foam on a long sea-swell, the atoms of air immediately in contact with himself seemed each to drop a golden note of full music down, till a distinct melody, bursting with tune and modulated by this grand spheric accompaniment, panted along the hot summer noon.

In 1860, Harriet Prescott published one of the most powerful short stories in the language, "The Amber Gods." [3] The story is told by Georgione Willoughby, born of a race of sea captains, one of whom had brought the necklace of curious amber figures from India. They act as a charm against the love of Rose, a painter whom she desires to win, so she puts them by. His passion for her is only infatuation, for he really loves her sister, Lucy, who unwittingly wears the beads that keep him from her. The last paragraphs are magnificent in their courage— the reader is compelled to believe if only for a moment in the communication from another world:

"So I passed out of the room, down the staircase. The servants below did not see me, but the hounds crouched and whined. I paused before the great ebony clock; again the fountain broke, and it chimed the half-hour; it was half past one; another quarter, and the next time its ponderous silver ham-

[3] *Atlantic Monthly,* January and February, 1860.

mers woke the house, it would be two. Half past one? Why, then, did not the hands move? Why cling fixed on a point five minutes before the first quarter struck? To and fro, soundless and purposeless, swung the long pendulum. And, ah! what was this thing I had become? I had done with time. Not for me the hands moved on their recurrent circle any more.

"I must have died at ten minutes past one."

Quite as remarkable was "Circumstance," [4] a story of a woman in colonial days in New England, who, returning from the bedside of a sick neighbor, is seized by the "Indian Devil," a species of wildcat, which carries her to a tree and prepares to devour her. In her desperation she chants a hymn and finds that the music charms him. Then begins the long vigil in which she fights for her life with her voice, until her husband comes to her aid. The suspense in this story is kept up by skilful means, and the sustaining power of the New England faith has hardly ever been so well portrayed.[5] While the conception is romantic, the details are told with a realism that haunts one long afterward. Miss Prescott was not unaffected by the tendency of the time, and "The South Breaker," and "Knitting Sale Socks," [6] are based on real knowledge. The descriptions are vivid; the sea is a living thing as it tears the boats apart on the South Breaker. Those who think the "stream of consciousness" story is a modern invention should read Harriet Prescott's fiction. Then, as now, it sometimes led to incoherence, but in such a story as "The Strathsays," [7] it presents a powerful picture of the relations of a mother and her daughters, told through the eyes of the youngest, whose face has been burned accidentally and who finds only horror where she should have found sympathy.

Azarian, an Episode (1864) is a prose poem, written with distinction, but with ideal characters, especially Azarian, one of those marvelous men whom women create. Ruth Yetton, whom he loves and leaves, is much better, both in her gallant effort to protect her father and in her relations with Azarian. *Azarian* can best be judged as a romance of feeling, in its great superiority to the sentimental romance of the 'fifties or to Neal's romance of passion.

---

[4] *Atlantic Monthly*, May, 1860.

[5] The story is based on a real incident which happened to her maternal grandmother, Mrs. Sarah Hitchings, of Calais, Maine; see *Harriet Prescott Spofford*, by Elizabeth K. Halbeisen (1935), p. 12.

[6] *Atlantic Monthly*, May and June, 1862; and February, 1861.

[7] *Atlantic Monthly*, January, 1863.

Mrs. Spofford did not often concern herself with questions of the day, but one of her best stories, "Down the River," [8] has for its central character a young Negro slave girl, Salome or Flor, "who worshipped the great dark earth, imparted to it her confidence, asked of it her boons; . . . the dust of which she was made was what she could best comprehend." The ideal method naturally led the author to attribute ideas to Flor to which such a girl would have been a stranger, but Flor's loyalty to her young mistress, her dim notions about freedom, her flight to avoid betraying the hiding place of the runaway slave who has befriended her, and her voyage down the river are clothed in that pictorial language of which Mrs. Spofford was a master. When she tried to imagine war itself, as in "Ray," [9] or a Confederate prison, as in "Out of Prison," [10] she failed. Her acquaintance with the South probably came through her correspondence with Colonel Higginson.

When Mrs. Spofford dealt with passion she was uneven but sometimes she scored a decided success. In a novelette, *The Rim*,[11] laid in the South, she is writing in an older fashion, with the dark and forceful hero to which we had become accustomed. She almost succeeds in "D'Outre Mort" [12] in her attempt to depict the soul after death. But in "Rougegorge" [13] she matched her strength with Poe, and not unworthily. Rougegorge, a French nobleman, hears his friend, St. Marc, has killed himself for love of Ayacinthe de Valentinois, and he determines on revenging him. He marries Ayacinthe who has grown to love him and is prepared to give him her life completely. But he avoids her and tells her on their wedding night he is doing it out of revenge. She pretends to accept their life on his terms, and charms him so that he in turn falls in love with her, and then she repels him. But before that she had planned an original vengeance. The room in which she had passed her wedding night without him she fills with flowers, especially the hyacinth. Then she reminds him that it was *his*, and she leaves it for another. He sleeps in it and is gradually poisoned by the flowers. The conversations are very natural, which is not always the case in her romances. It was a theme for a romanticist, as Henry James' treatment of a somewhat

[8] *Atlantic Monthly*, October, 1865.
[9] *Atlantic Monthly*, January, 1864.
[10] *Harper's Magazine*, July, 1865.
[11] *Atlantic Monthly*, May, June, July, 1864.
[12] *Galaxy*, November, 1866.
[13] *Lippincott's Magazine*, May, 1869.

similar plot in "Osborne's Revenge" in 1868 proved, for her story is superior to his.

In her novelette, *A Thief in the Night* (1872), a study of passionate love, it is again the form rather than the matter which attracts. When Catherine is contrasting the two men who love her, after she studies her handsome husband, Beaudesfords, "she raised her glance and Gaston stood surveying her with his darkening eyes,—the plain face with its scar, its ruggedness, its gloom, and the other went out of her mind like a star in the night."

The dates of the volumes of Mrs. Spofford's collected stories are misleading, for *The Scarlet Poppy and Other Stories* (1894) contains in general later stories than those in *Old Madame and Other Tragedies* (1900). In the latter the best is "Her Story," [14] a very powerful appeal of a woman who is in an insane asylum, who has lost her husband's love through a younger woman. The ending is worthy of the author of "The Amber Gods."

And so, you see, if I were a clod, if I had no memory, no desires, if I had never been happy before, I might be happy now. I am confident the doctor thinks me well. But he has no orders to let me go. Sometimes it is so wearisome. And it might be worse if lately I had not been allowed a new service. And that is to try to make a woman smile who came here a year ago. She is a little woman, swarthy as a Malay, but her hair, that grows as rapidly as a fungus grows in the night, is whiter than leprosy: her eyebrows are so long and white that they veil and blanch her dark dim eyes; and she has no front teeth. A stone from a falling spire struck her from her horse, they say. The blow battered her and beat out reason and beauty. Her mind is dead: she remembers nothing, knows nothing; but she follows me about like a dog: she seems to want to do something for me, to propitiate me. All she ever says is to beg me to do her no harm. She will not go to sleep without my hand in hers. Sometimes, after long effort, I think there is a gleam of intelligence, but the doctor says there was once too much intelligence, and her case is hopeless.

Hopeless, poor thing!—that is an awful word: I could not wish it said for my worst enemy.

In spite of these ten years I cannot feel that it has yet been said for me.

If I am strange just now, it is only the excitement of seeing you, only the habit of the strange sights and sounds here. I should be calm and well enough at home. I sit and picture to myself that some time Spencer will come for me —will take me to my girls, my fireside, my music. I shall hear his voice, I shall rest in his arms, I shall be blest again. For, oh, Elizabeth, I do forgive him all!

[14] *Lippincott's Magazine*, December, 1872.

Or, if he will not dare to trust himself at first, I picture to myself how he will send another—some old friend who knew me before my trouble—who will see me and judge, and carry back report that I am all I used to be—some friend who will open the gates of heaven to me, or close the gates of hell upon me—who will hold my life and my fate.

If—oh if it should be you, Elizabeth!

In "Ordronnaux" [15] there is a passage that is one of her flashes of insight into the relation of sound and color:

For since color, as well as sound, is the result of vibration, all that is necessary may be to combine the initial of light and sound, which it would seem that electricity could do in some attachment to the present musical instrument; so that the strings, for instance, should produce the vibration requisite to render the violet rays, the brass the brilliant yellows, the wood the deep rich reds.

The stories of the 'eighties show her in a new rôle, that of a satirist; the influence of the story of familiar life in checking her fancy was not happy, because she did not go all the way. The improbabilities irritate rather than stimulate, but occasionally as in the description of the flood in "Mrs. Claxton's Skeleton" [16] she rises to a height. The conversations are more natural, too, and the style as ever is distinguished.

In the later 'nineties, Mrs. Spofford published several novelettes that are remarkable at times in their revelation of women in emotional moods. The struggle is well portrayed in *A Master Spirit* (1896) between Domina's longing to surrender herself to the passion of Gratian which will take her to the opera stage and her desire for the spiritual peace which her love for a blind clergyman offers her. Mrs. Spofford uses again the spell of Domina's singing to bring peace to a mad girl and to "Madonna," the old opera singer who is trying to change her life. A similar theme is developed even more artistically in *The Maid He Married* (1899) [17] where there is a remarkable description of the way the emotional moods of a girl, torn between her older simple life and that of a luxurious existence which is promised her, are swayed by the music of the symphony to which she is listening. Another scene, in which she sings all night with a little boy in her arms fighting an unsuccessful battle with death, takes us back to "Circumstance" and

[15] *Scribner's Monthly,* September and October, 1874.

[16] *Harper's Magazine,* March, 1883.

[17] Written originally as "At the Symphony," *Harper's Bazaar,* January 10, 1891; revised and issued as "The Maid He Married" in the *Bazaar,* November 11 to December 2, 1893.

proves that while the terror is not so keen, the skill of Mrs. Spofford was not by any means in abeyance.

In *An Inheritance* (1897), there is a fine study of the life of Nancy Donner, who had been married by Dr. Donner for her money, who finds this out and goes quietly about her life, never letting him know she knows, until the sterling quality of her nature wins first his respect and then his affection.

In 1906 Mrs. Spofford gathered into a volume, *Old Washington,* five romantic pictures of life in the Capitol shortly after the Civil War. The stoic courage of the Southern women who were hoping for an appointment in a government department or pressing a claim for damages is portrayed with sympathy and some skill, but without the power of her earlier romance. The best are "A Little Old Woman," and "A Thanksgiving Breakfast," dating from the 'nineties in their creation.

The Making of a Fortune (1911), a novelette, has too much romantic glare to be of importance. But during the first two decades of the twentieth century she wrote stories of New England character which, in their collected form, were called *The Elder's People* (1920). Elder Perry and Miss Mahala are the principals, and of course the comparison with Mrs. Deland's *Dr. Lavendar's People* is inevitable. But Mrs. Spofford's stories have sufficient originality and difference of locality to let them be judged on their own merits which are high. The dialect is veracious, and the descriptions are at times exquisite.

Mrs. Spofford wrote in her long career two hundred and seventy-five short stories.[18] She could not always be at her best, but she reflects in her career some of the most important phases of the short story. No one has better portrayed the relations of sound and color, the influence of glorious music upon the fates of human beings. Few except Poe and Hawthorne have established so well the mystic relation of gems and flowers upon their characters, and we have to go back to Cooper and Melville for her equals in describing the moods of the sea. The artist who wrote "The Amber Gods" in 1860 and published *The Elder's People* in 1920, swinging the complete circle between romantic idealism and classic realism, remains a remarkable phenomenon in our literature.

With the work of Thomas Bailey Aldrich (1836–1907) we come to a novelist who just as clearly looks toward the newer fictional impulse

[18] According to the authoritative critical biography by Elizabeth Halbeisen.

as Hale or Mrs. Stowe reflected the older. His art contemplates rather than probes for hidden meanings; it is concerned definitely more with the manner of expression than with the matter. The deep earnestness which characterized both Mrs. Stowe and Mrs. Davis, on which Taylor insisted in his characters, and with which Mrs. Spofford's work is so imbued, this earnestness of motive gives place in Aldrich to an originality of fancy, a delightful inconsequence, and a deftness in narration and description. There is, too, a certain aloofness from his characters, which impresses the reader as though he were too well bred to intrude upon their privacy so far as to search their inner natures to the utmost. It springs, however, from the objective quality of his art, a quality he shares with his great master, Hawthorne.

His first novel, *Daisy's Necklace* (1857), is called by him a burlesque, and as he remarks in the Epilogue is a curious mixture of Dickens, Hood, and Charles Reade, and he might have added, of Longfellow and Poe. But even in this immature story of a young man's love and struggle in lower New York City, there are flashes of poetic fancy.

He also contributed short stories to *The Knickerbocker* in 1857 and 1858, but of the stories published in his first volume, *Out of His Head; A Romance* (1862), only one has been included in his own selection for his completed works. *Out of His Head* [19] is a novelette, written by Paul Lynde, who is in an insane asylum, and who does queer things, including self-accusation of a murder really committed by someone else. Aldrich's phrase-making ability was already evident—"Grief is one of the quiet colors that wash." The other stories in this first volume, with the exception of "Père Antoine's Date-Palm," are unimportant. This is a charming story; the central situation, that of a palm tree growing out of the grave of a girl, the child of Père Antoine's friend and the woman he loved, being touched tenderly without sentimentality and with that humor which never deserted Aldrich. His experiences as a war-correspondent and his editorial work, which took him to Boston in 1865, but more particularly his devotion to poetry, interrupted his work in fiction. In 1867, however, he published "A Struggle for Life" in the *Atlantic*, and his manner was established. This story was a good analysis of the feelings of a man shut up by accident in a tomb, who divides one candle in four pieces to preserve him from hunger and resolutely, as he thinks, lives a day and a night upon it. When he is rescued, he has been only

[19] *Knickerbocker Magazine*, October, 1858.

one hour and twenty minutes in the tomb. Aldrich was not satisfied with this surprise; he provides another at the end of the tale, by showing the incident, which has been told about a certain young man with gray hair and dimmed eyes, to have been entirely imaginary, and the sympathy which has been elicited for him is unjustified. This ability to create and maintain suspense was due to Aldrich's dramatic power, of which his acted plays, *Mercedes* and *Judith of Bethulia*, only begin to indicate the extent. In April, 1873, the appearance of "Marjorie Daw" in the *Atlantic* marked an important moment in the American short story. The art with which the portrait of this girl is built up by the letter of one young man to another, until she seems to him and to the reader to live and breathe, only to find that she exists in the imagination of Delaney, is a triumph for the realistic treatment of romantic material. Marjorie Daw, who never existed, even in the story, is more real than almost any other heroine of her time. Delicately Aldrich shows how this girl, created by Delaney to amuse his bedridden friend in New York, can be more actual than a real person. This note of surprise is kept up in the stories of the 'seventies, like "Miss Mehetabel's Son" or "Madame Olympe Zambriski," which were published in 1873 as *Marjorie Daw and Other People*. An appealing story, "The Little Violinist," written in 1874, represented Aldrich on a more serious side. It was the prose treatment of facts which formed the inspiration also for Austin Dobson's "The Child Musician."

Like all artists of importance, Aldrich declines to be neatly classified. While he was developing the short story of fantasy, of which "Marjorie Daw" is a shining example, he wrote in *The Story of a Bad Boy* (1869) [20] a realistic picture of life in Portsmouth, New Hampshire, where he had been sent to school under his grandfather's care while his parents remained in New Orleans. Remembering Miles Wallingford in *Afloat and Ashore* or Corny Littlepage in *Satanstoe*, or Tad Ducklow in *Coupon Bonds*, it would be incorrect to say that Tom Bailey was the first real boy in American fiction. But Cooper's boys quickly grow up and Tad Ducklow is after all only a sketch. Five years before *Tom Sawyer* was published, Aldrich had written the first complete narrative in which the American boy was presented as a human being with that combination of pluck, mischief, chivalry, inarticulate ideality, clan

[20] Running through *Our Young Folks*, beginning January, 1869, it was published in 1870.

loyalty and calf love, of which any normal healthy boy is composed. The many super-boys who shot Indians, or the virtuous youths of the Sunday-school type who had paraded through our fiction make Tom Bailey only the more remarkable. Aldrich was in love with his material; the fight, the firing of the town cannon, the attempted running away to sea, are told with that delightful touch which makes the book one that no boy can ever be too old to cherish. While Aldrich lightened nearly every scene with humor, he knew that to be a funny man at all times is a mistake, and probably the best chapter is that in which little Binny Wallace is carried out to sea, never to return. The character of Binny Wallace, over-sensitive and frail, is extremely well done. So, too, are Ben, the returned sailor, and Grandfather Nutter. Best of all is the way Aldrich represents the conversation of boys. The preparations for Tom's battle with Conway the bully, who has been making Binny's life miserable, will illustrate this:

"Then the thing must go on," said Adams, with dignity. "Rodgers, as I understand it, is your second, Conway? Bailey, come here. What's the row about?"

"He was thrashing Binny Wallace."

"No, I wasn't," interrupted Conway; "but I was going to, because he knows who put Meeks's mortar over our door. And I know well enough who did it; it was that sneaking little mulatter!"—pointing at me.

"Oh, by George!" I cried, reddening at the insult.

"Cool is the word," said Adams, as he bound a handkerchief round my head and carefully tucked away the long straggling locks that offered a tempting advantage to the enemy. "Who ever heard of a fellow with such a head of hair going into action!" muttered Phil, twitching the handkerchief to ascertain if it were securely tied. He then loosened my gallowses (braces), and buckled them tightly above my hips. "Now, then, bantam, never say die!"

And then, after the victory:

. . . I could stand very little, and see not at all (having pommelled the school-pump for the last twenty seconds), when Conway retired from the field. As Phil Adams stepped up to shake hands with me, he received a telling blow in the stomach; for all the fight was not out of me yet, and I mistook him for a new adversary.

Convinced of my error, I accepted his congratulations, with those of the other boys, blandly and blindly. I remember that Binny Wallace wanted to give me his silver pencil case. The gentle soul had stood throughout the contest with his face turned to the fence, suffering untold agony.

A good wash at the pump, and a cold key applied to my eye, refreshed me amazingly. Escorted by two or three of the schoolfellows, I walked home through the pleasant autumn twilight, battered but triumphant. As I went along, my cap cocked on one side to keep the chilly air from my eye, I felt that I was not only following my nose, but following it so closely, that I was in some danger of treading on it. I seemed to have nose enough for the whole party. My left cheek, also, was puffed out like a dumpling. I could not help saying to myself, "If *this* is victory, how about that other fellow?"

Prudence Palfrey (1874) is called a "Rivermouth Romance" by Aldrich; it is essentially romantic, belonging to that form of novel in which unusual events occur in a life normally placid. The New England town is stirred by the coming of two outsiders—John Dent, the nephew of Ralph Dent, the guardian of Prudence, and James Dillingham, an attractive young clergyman who takes the place of old Parson Wibird Hawkins, largely at Ralph Dent's instance. Both love Prudence, and there is a certain amount of reality in the description of the jealousy Ralph Dent feels for his nephew when he finds that John has fallen in love with his ward and in his refusal to permit him any longer to stay in his house. But after this the plot becomes not impossible, but worse, improbable. That a gambler and a cutthroat should try to become a clergyman, with the daily risk of detection, is hard to swallow, but that he should expect to make his permanent home in Rivermouth, the town to which John Dent, whom he has robbed, will naturally return, is too much. One reads *Prudence Palfrey*, however, for the charm of its style and for flashes of description; for example, when Prudence, after Dillingham's first sermon; remarks of him, "He is very handsome, and seems to be unconscious that he is conscious of it."

The Queen of Sheba (1877) is planned in the age-long fashion of romance. As Aldrich says in the introductory pages concerning Edward Lynde's excursion:

> He had simply ridden off into the rosy June weather, with no settled destination, no care for tomorrow, and as independent as a bird of the tourist's ordinary requirements.

Lynde's meeting with the escaped lunatics from the asylum, especially with the young girl who tells him she is the Queen of Sheba and also that he is her husband, is fantastic, of course, but it leads to his being placed in one of the most tragic positions possible. For when he meets Ruth Denham three years later in Geneva, perfectly sane, and falls in love with her, he is torn between his belief that she is not the same woman and his fear that she is. The conventions of the 'seventies make it difficult for him to solve the mystery; but her identification and the explanation of her temporary insanity are a bit long drawn out, even for that time. The characters seem less real now than in *Prudence Palfrey* or *The Stillwater Tragedy*, but they talk as people did in the 'seventies, and Aldrich's remarks about them as well as his word pictures of scenery, both in New Hampshire and Switzerland, are, as usual, delightful. The poet in Aldrich shone through his fiction, as it had done in Longfellow's *Hyperion*, and it gave us the glowing picture of the sunrise over the town of Stillwater which opens *The Stillwater Tragedy* (1880). This novel is often called a murder mystery, but its significance does not lie in this, for no one would have been convicted on the evidence that threatens Richard Shackford. Neither are the troubles consequent upon the conflict between Slocum and his union laborers very profoundly handled. The characters of Richard Shackford and Margaret Slocum, and their love story, give the book its distinction. Margaret is much more true than Daisy Miller, for Daisy is a caricature. Girls like Margaret Slocum have rarely come into American fiction; yet America was and still is full of them.

How much of Aldrich there is in the novel *The Second Son* (1888), in which he collaborated with Mrs. M. O. W. Oliphant, it is difficult to say. There is no fantasy in this story of the three brothers, sons of the Squire of Melcombe; it is interesting mainly because it represents Aldrich writing about an English scene with his usual distinction of style, and his customary ironical touch.

Among the best of Aldrich's later short stories are "Two Bites at a Cherry," [21] a clever study of the emotions of a man who had been refused by a woman fifteen years before, who hears of her husband's death and then, when he meets her in Naples, feels that he is still in love with her. When he tells her so, he finds to his dismay that she has married again. The natural way in which their earlier relations prevents him from having to use her married name is only one of the instances of Aldrich's art as a story-teller. It is shown, too, in "Her Dying Words," [22] in the analysis of the feelings of two lovers on a wreck in the ocean. These stories of the 'eighties and early 'nineties were col-

[21] *Atlantic Monthly*, January, 1886.
[22] *Scribner's Monthly*, August, 1893.

lected in *Two Bites at a Cherry, with Other Tales* (1893). His last
collection, *A Sea Turn and Other Matters* (1902), showed no diminu-
tion of power. His ironic touch deepened somewhat in "Shaw's Folly,"
an amusing story of a wealthy man who tries to found a model tenement and is victimized by his tenants. The realistic treatment of romantic material persisted in "An Untold Story," a brief sketch in two
parts laid in Buda Pesth. In the first we see a young girl throw herself
into the Danube; in the second, we see the same woman, rich and im-
perious, sitting in a carriage with a man who is recognized by the
narrator as one who had hurriedly come upon the scene just after the
girl had been rescued in the earlier episode. Aldrich knew how the
story that leaves much to the imagination is the most powerful of all.
The apparently effortless ease with which the prose of Aldrich flows
on has prevented a full appreciation of his services to American fiction.
To have created Tom Bailey and Marjorie Daw should be enough to
establish him securely. But an even greater claim lies in that unerring
instinct which led him to choose the right words, full of life and color,
so that each sentence becomes in itself an achievement.

Much more prolific in fiction than Aldrich, Francis Richard Stockton (1834–1902) was also less even in merit. In consequence there has
been no unanimity in critical appraisal of one of the most gifted and
most original writers of fantastic romance. Born and educated in Philadelphia, of mingled English, French, and Irish ancestry, he became,
after his graduation from the Central High School, a wood engraver,
but even before he left that profession he wrote fiction. "Kate," an
anonymous short story in the *Southern Literary Messenger* for December, 1859, has already a note of the poetic, although the scene is
modern, and *A Story of Champaigne*, a serial which appeared in the
same magazine in 1861,[23] signed "F.R.S.," is a romance of France in
the days of Louis XIV. There is no historical interest; Stockton simply
followed his natural bent in choosing time and place in which he might
lead his hero through remarkable adventures in company with a dwarf,
Tiberius, without considering probability. It would seem as though the
novelette were a satire upon the romantic novel, for Tiberius, having
secured access to a lawyer's office which contains a will he desires to
destroy, solves the problem by burning up all the counsellor's papers in
order to save himself the trouble of searching for the will!

[23] January, February, April, and May.

These and other early stories [24] reveal Stockton experimenting with the romance of familiar life and the frankly impossible tale of ghosts and fairies, both tinged with humor. For a time he devoted himself to fairy stories for boys and girls, collected from the *Riverside Magazine* as *Ting-a-ling* (1870). During the 'sixties and 'seventies, Stockton was associated in an editorial capacity with *Hearth and Home* and *St. Nicholas*, but after 1880 he devoted himself entirely to his creative work.

Stockton's choice of the fantastic was deliberate. In "The Pilgrims' Packets" [25] he prefaces a charming tale of a fairy who loved an abbot and was exorcised for her pains, by a remark of the supposed author, "The Materialists and Realists of Literature will have none of me. They object to my machinery and send me to the children. But I have nothing for children. There is a moral purpose running through my story—a purpose for maturest minds."

Stockton began *Rudder Grange* as a short story in *Scribner's Monthly* for November, 1874. A young married pair take a canal boat for a house, and Stockton established in this and the succeeding installments that illusion of reality which permitted the most unlikely happenings without straining the readers' credulity. The success of this illusion depended partly on the apparently effortless style which is deliberately stripped of ornament, and partly upon the characters. The narrator is a real person; so is Euphemia, his wife. But the introduction of Pomona, the maid, in the second installment marked the creation of one of those humorous beings which make incongruity a living art. Her remarkable rendition of dime novels aloud, a trait borrowed from the real Pomona, an orphan of fourteen who was employed by the Stocktons, provide some delightful moments, like that in which the new dog, having chased the rest of the family to the roof, rushes at Pomona, who has just arrived at the new suburban home. Calmly she proceeds:

"Do you know, ma'am," said she to Euphemia, "that if I had come here yesterday, that dog would have had my life's blood."

"And why don't he have it to-day?" said Euphemia, who, with myself, was utterly amazed at the behavior of the dog.

"Because I know more to-day than I did yesterday," answered Pomona. "It is only this afternoon that I read something, as I was coming here on the cars. This is it," . . .

---

[24] "Mahala's Drive," *Lippincott's Magazine*, November, 1868; "The Fairy and the Ghost," *Lippincott's Magazine*, January, 1870.
[25] *Scribner's Monthly*, January, 1873.

Standing there with one book still under her arm, the newspaper half un-wrapped from it, hanging down and flapping in the breeze, she opened the other volume at the scissors-place, turned back a page or two, and began to read as follows:

" 'Lord Edward slowly san-ter-ed up the bro-ad anc-es-tral walk, when sudden-ly from out a cop-se, there sprang a fur-i-ous hound. The marsh-man, con-ce-al-ed in a tree expected to see the life's blood of the young nob-leman stain the path. But no, Lord Edward did not stop nor turn his head. With a smile, he strode stead-i-ly on. Well he knew that if by be-traying no em-otion, he could show the dog that he was walking where he had a right, the bru-te would re-cog-nize that right and let him pass un-sca-thed. Thus in this mo-ment of peril his nob-le courage saved him. The hound, abashed, returned to his cov-ert, and Lord Edward pass-ed on.

" 'Foi-led again,' mutter-ed the marsh-man.' "

Fittingly the dog is called "Lord Edward," and he and Pomona pro-tect their master and mistress or take care of the new house during the camping out excursion, a satire on anyone who leaves a comfortable house for the pleasures of mosquitoes and life in the open air. The wed-ding trip of Pomona and Jonas which ends in a lunatic asylum is an-other original episode. In fact the book is simply a collection of episodes, one of which, "Our Tavern," in its first form in the *Century* for Au-gust, 1878, had no connection with *Rudder Grange*, which appeared in book form in 1879. So popular was it that Stockton took his characters to Florida and to Europe in three stories which appeared in the *Century* in 1882 and 1883 and were published with others in *The Rudder Grang-ers Abroad* (1891). They are amusing but hardly up to the level of the earlier book. In *Pomona's Travels* (1894), a series of letters which she writes to Euphemia from England and Scotland, there is some searching analysis of English manners and social classifications from the point of view of Pomona's frank scrutiny. Any traveler will sympathize with Pomona's remark concerning her disappointment in visiting the scenes of romantic fiction. "I must say I liked the story better before I saw the country where the things happened. The mind of man is capable of soarings which nature weakens at when she sees what she is called upon to do."

Stockton's short stories, which he wrote continuously throughout his career, deal with many themes. The most famous, "The Lady or the Tiger?" appeared in the *Century* for November, 1882, and made a pro-found impression. It was not only the ending which left it undecided whether the princess had signaled to her lover in the arena to choose the door behind which stood death or the door which concealed another woman whom he would be forced to marry; it was rather because the problem was not merely one of situation but one which depended upon the character of the princess. She is nameless, yet she remains one of the vivid personalities in fiction, for she represents not only the universal qualities of womanhood but also the uncertainty of feminine impulse. In a brief story, where not a word is wasted, Stockton combined the fundamental motives of love, hate, and the preservation of life. So many letters were written to Stockton begging him for the solution that he replied in an article [26] in which he parried all inquiries, but revealed the fact that Robert Browning had decided "that *such* a princess, under *such* circumstances, would direct her lover to the tiger's door." Browning's recognition that the point at issue is the character of the princess is of interest.

In the volume of which this was the title story, *The Lady or the Tiger? and Other Stories* (1884), a clever tale, "His Wife's Deceased Sister" (1884), reflected Stockton's difficulty in reaching again the level of popular approval he had set for himself. "Our Story" (1883) has another form of surprise. Two young writers, a man and a woman, are collaborating and are rescued by a mysterious stranger from a compromising situation resulting from their efforts at privacy. He devotes himself to them and, just as he is leaving the pension, he confesses that he too is a writer. The story concludes, "Our story was never finished. His was. This is it." The sudden change from the subjective to the objective points of view makes the reader go back over the tale and review it in a different light. In this volume appear also stories of the Negro and of the supernatural. "The Transferred Ghost" [27] is precious fooling. Stockton's ghosts usually take the form of a human being; they are not wraiths, but they have a spectral quality. The best thing about them is the natural conversation in which they indulge. The ghost of Mr. John Hinckman, who is not dead, converses amiably with his nephew:

"Yes, I am his ghost," my companion replied, "and yet I have no right to be. And this is what makes me so uneasy, and so much afraid of him. It is a

---

[26] "How I Wrote 'The Lady or the Tiger?' and What Came of the Writing of It," *Ladies' Home Journal*, November, 1893, pp. 1–2.
[27] *Century Magazine*, May, 1882.

strange story, and, I truly believe, without precedent. Two years and a half ago, John Hinckman was dangerously ill in this very room. At one time he was so far gone that he was really believed to be dead. It was in consequence of too precipitate a report in regard to this matter that I was, at that time, appointed to be his ghost. Imagine my surprise and horror, sir, when, after I had accepted the position and assumed its responsibilities, that old man revived, became convalescent, and eventually regained his usual health. My situation was now one of extreme delicacy and embarrassment. I had no power to return to my original unembodiment, and I had no right to be the ghost of a man who was not dead. I was advised by my friends to quietly maintain my position, and was assured that, as John Hinckman was an elderly man, it could not be long before I could rightfully assume the position for which I had been selected. But I tell you, sir," he continued, with animation, "the old fellow seems as vigorous as ever, and I have no idea how much longer this annoying state of things will continue. I spend my time trying to get out of that old man's way. I must not leave this house, and he seems to follow me everywhere. I tell you, sir, he haunts me."

Stockton was deluged with requests to solve the problem stated in "The Lady or the Tiger?" and replied by a sequel, "The Discourager of Hesitancy" (1885). A delegation of strangers who come to the King's court to ask the solution are told the story of a prince who had come to the same court to marry and who is compelled to wed blindfold and to choose among forty damsels the wife he has just wedded. One slightly smiles and one frowns. When he pauses, the Discourager of Hesitancy, armed with a sharp scimitar, who has attended him since his arrival, whispers "I am here!" and the prince guesses correctly. But the reader has now two answers to guess instead of one.

The finest efforts of Stockton in the short story, however, came in those masterpieces of pure fancy, written in some cases for *St. Nicholas,* but appealing even more to adults than to children. The best of them are included in *The Bee Man of Orn and Other Fanciful Tales* (1887). Laid nowhere in particular, but usually in a past time, they apparently are bound by no laws of possibility; but in reality they are remarkable comments upon human strength and weakness. The Bee Man,[28] who is happy in his poverty, is stirred to unrest by a Junior Sorcerer, who sends him out to find the being from whom he has been transformed. After amusing adventures, he saves a baby from being eaten by a dragon, and as a result feels that he has been the baby and is changed to its form.

[28] First appeared in *St. Nicholas,* November, 1883, as "The Bee Man and His Original Form."

Years later the Junior Sorcerer, now promoted to be a Senior Sorcerer, finds the Bee Man just as he had seen him in the first place, before he had been disturbed and sent on a career of self-analysis. The underlying philosophy of the basic changelessness of nature and of life is established through a whimsical inconsequence of events, all of which really obey immutable laws. "Prince Hassak's March" [29] is a satire on the ruthless progress through other people's rights.

"The Griffin and the Minor Canon," [30] written in England and suggested by the Chester Cathedral, is a searching indictment of the cowardice and selfishness of the herd. When the Griffin comes to see his own image sculptured on the Cathedral, everyone is afraid to meet him but the Minor Canon, whose courage is equalled only by his charity and self-sacrifice. But instead of being grateful to him, the people blame him for bringing the Griffin and demand that he go to the "dreadful wilds" from which the Griffin has come, hoping the Griffin will seek him there. But the Griffin remains, taking the Minor Canon's place in his school and among the poor and the rich, with remarkable effects in diminishing the numbers of the unemployed. As the Equinox, the only time the Griffin eats, approaches, he finds out through the anxiety of the people where the Minor Canon has gone. He is furious and he goes after him. Then comes a touch which no one but Stockton would have thought of:

"Do you know," said the monster, when he had finished, "that I have had, and still have, a great liking for you?"

"I am very glad to hear it," said the Minor Canon, with his usual politeness. . . .

"I am not at all sure that you would be," said the Griffin, "if you thoroughly understood the state of the case, but we will not consider that now. If some things were different, other things would be otherwise. I have been so enraged by discovering the manner in which you have been treated that I have determined that you shall at last enjoy the rewards and honors to which you are entitled. Lie down and have a good sleep, and then I will take you back to the town."

The people load the Minor Canon with honors, and still fear the Griffin. But as Stockton concludes:

But they need never have been afraid of the Griffin. The autumnal equinox day came around, and the monster ate nothing. If he could not have the

[29] *St. Nicholas*, December, 1883.
[30] *St. Nicholas*, October, 1885.

Minor Canon, he did not care for anything. So, lying down, with his eyes fixed upon the great stone griffin, he gradually declined and died. It was a good thing for some of the people of the town that they did not know this.

"Old Pipes and the Dryad" [31] is a poetic fancy of a piper, seventy years of age, who is kissed by a Dryad he has liberated and becomes thirty years younger. "The Queen's Museum" [32] is a delightful satire on absolute rule and upon any attempt to direct human interest by force. In "The Battle of the Third Cousins" [33] Stockton pokes fun at the assumptions of medical science through Selim, the old guardian of one of the rivals for a throne, who on any emergency simply increases the number of chews to each mouthful, and who tells the Princess that he is a germ doctor.

"Then I suppose," said the Princess, "you know how to cure the diseases?"
"You must not expect too much," answered the old man. "It ought to be a great satisfaction to us to know what sort of germ is at the bottom of our woes."

Stockton was at his very best in the middle 'eighties. *The Late Mrs. Null*, written in 1885 but published in 1886, was laid in the South, which Stockton knew well, since both his mother and his wife were Virginians. For charm of dialogue, for whimsicality, for revelation of the Southern Negro, the novel is a masterpiece. There really is no "Mrs. Null." The young girl, Annie Peyton, who assumes this name, as an amateur detective, is the niece of an extraordinary person, Mrs. Keswick, who has driven her husband to suicide, broken off the engagement of her nephew, Junius Keswick, to Roberta March, and made it impossible for Annie to live with her. Stockton establishes Mrs. Keswick's character deftly through the conversation between Junius, who has come to visit her, and Old Uncle Isham:

Uncle Isham stood on the ground, his feet close to the bottom step; his hat was in his hand, and his upturned face wore an expression of earnestness which seemed to set uncomfortably upon it. "Mahs' Junius," said he, "dar ain't no acciden' come to ole miss; she's done gone cos she wanted to, an' she ain't come back cos she didn't want to. Dat's ole miss, right fru."
"I suppose," said the young man, "that as she went away on foot she must

[31] *St. Nicholas*, June, 1885.
[32] *St. Nicholas*, September, 1884.
[33] *St. Nicholas*, September, 1885.

be staying with some of the neighbors. If we were to make inquiries, it certainly would not be difficult to find out where she is."

"Mahs' Junius," said Uncle Isham, his black eyes shining brighter and brighter as he spoke, "dar's cullud people, an' white folks too, in dis yere county who'd put on der bes' clothes an' black der shoes, an' skip off wid alacrousness, to do de wus kin' o' sin, dat dey knowed fur sartin would send 'em down to de deepes' an' hottes' gullies ob de lower regions, but nuffin in dis worl' could make one o' dem people go 'quirin' 'bout ole miss when she didn't want to be 'quired about."

Equally as good is the scene in which Aunt Patsy, the "two-hundred year old Negress," girds herself up to go and tell her "Ole Miss" what she thinks of her. The way in which the emotions of the lovers grow and change is very natural. Lawrence Croft's passage from his temperate affection for Roberta, made up of circumstances, to his real love for Annie Peyton is a skilful picture of a situation that often happens in real life.

In its first form *The Casting Away of Mrs. Lecks and Mrs. Aleshine* (1886) consisted of three installments in the *Century*, beginning in August, 1886, but so great was the desire for a sequel that *The Dusantes* was published in 1888, and the two have now become one novel. These two plain middle-aged women from Meadowville, Pennsylvania, are entitled to places in any portrait gallery of American fiction. Their very names, slight alterations of Lex, law, and Allshine, reflection, indicate their varying natures. In their courage, when shipwrecked in the Pacific Ocean, they paddle bravely behind Craig in their life preservers, to the deserted island of the Dusantes; in their industry, and insistence upon paying their board to the absent owners, they are the embodiment of a certain kind of American woman who had not been in fiction before. They are not mere caricatures; they are real individuals. We laugh with them almost as often as we laugh at them, and we share their scorn of the selfish missionary, Mr. Enderton, who is a caricature, and enter into their natural curiosity to know who the absent owners of the island may be. Of course the book may also be considered as a satire on all stories of island castaways. The application of the common-sense methods of Mrs. Lecks and Mrs. Aleshine to such a situation produces humor through the inevitable incongruity which results. One remarkable quality is the way in which Stockton differentiates the two women. This is done largely by their conversation; while Mrs. Lecks is the natural leader, there is a steady pertinacity about Mrs. Aleshine which makes her no mere shadow of her friend. Long after the book has been read, the pictures of the three leading characters bobbing up and down in the Pacific Ocean, eating the sausage and the bread which the foresight of the women has kept from the water, or the slide down the mountain after the Dusantes have been met, remain to delight us. Through the novel, like a motif, runs the ginger jar in which Mrs. Lecks has put the board money and which brings the Dusantes, father, adopted mother, and daughter, across the Pacific and the continent to return it to her, only to meet her refusal to accept it.

Stockton was not unvaryingly at the level of *Mrs. Null* or *The Casting Away of Mrs. Lecks and Mrs. Aleshine*. *The Hundredth Man* (1887) is almost bare of the fancy which made these stories memorable. Perhaps Stockton was being affected by the realistic atmosphere of the period, but if so it was a mistake. *The Hundredth Man* is too cluttered with details about a restaurant, and Horace Stratford's search for the unusual man is not essentially interesting. *Ardis Claverden* (1890), laid in Virginia, has more charm, especially in the minor characters, of whom Dr. Lester, the forty-year-old lover of Ardis, who quietly watches over her without speaking of his affection, is almost in Stockton's best manner. *The House of Martha* (1891) and *Squirrel Inn* (1891), a novelette from which the real Squirrel Inn took its name, have some amusing situations, but this group of novels, while they are distinctly readable, do not seem to possess the special qualities which mark Stockton out from his contemporaries.

There was another field, however, in which he made a distinct contribution. Stockton early revealed his ability to imagine situations in which the ordinary laws of Nature are placed in abeyance. His treatment of the supernatural in "The Transferred Ghost" was definitely humorous. So was "Amos Kilbright" (1888), an amusing story of a materialized spirit from 1785 who is unmaterialized by a German psychologist on his wedding day and finally brought back to earth in time to be married.

In *A Vizier of the Two Horned Alexander* (1899), Mr. Crowder insists that he has lived through several centuries, and some clever incongruities result. But more significant because less definitely burlesque were his stories of inventions which he presented with a disarming air of probability. Often the intention is entirely humorous, as in "A Tale of

Negative Gravity" (1884), in which the inventor of a machine that neutralizes the law of gravity gets rid of it on account of the trouble it causes. Sometimes, however, there is a more serious note amounting to prophecy. In *The Great War Syndicate* (1889) Stockton imagines a war between Great Britain and the United States, in which a syndicate takes over the control of operations by America. A motor bomb known as "The Peace Compellor" is invented, of such a tremendous destructive power that after one example of its efficiency Great Britain collapses. Through this apparently humorous story Stockton pointed in 1889 the way not only to some of the methods suggested during the Great War but to the ultimate fate of the world if the inventive capacity for destruction is not curbed. In *The Great Stone of Sardis* (1897) he places the operations of a scientist, Roland Clews, in 1947. Clews sends an expedition to discover the North Pole by means of a submarine under the ice, connected by a telegraphic cable with this country. Clews also invents a projectile automatically penetrating for a tremendous distance anything it hits. By an accident this goes down into the earth and Clews, following it, finds that the earth is an immense diamond. He clogs up the hole, to prevent anyone else having the terrific sensations he experiences when he is exposed to the diamond rays. Long before modern thought was beginning to question seriously whether physical science had not dangerously outstripped in its discoveries the capacity of social science to adjust these discoveries to human safety and rational progress, Stockton had, like Poe and Jules Verne, anticipated in his imagination the actual discoveries of chemists and physicists.

He is, of course, not polemical; his concern is to write a good story. Who but he could have placed an ice mine, the relic of a glacier, in a country place in New Jersey, in "My Terminal Moraine" (1892); or in "The Water Devil," (1891) built up a fine study of fear on the part of a ship's crew when their vessel is apparently in the clutch of a sea monster, really the loose end of a broken cable which has made connection with "stored electricity" in the hold? Stockton was very fond of sea stories. He does not bother the reader with technical descriptions; the sea is usually a place of escape where strange things may happen. They are nearly always humorous—the voice of Mary Phillips on her wreck sounding across the Bay of Bengal to Rockwell on his deserted ship, "Don't you remember me? I lived on Forty-second Street," makes stories like "Derelict" amusing studies of incongruity. One of the best of the short stories is "The Remarkable Wreck of the Thomas Hyke" (1884), in which a ship stands straight up with her stern in the air.

Among the novels, *The Adventures of Captain Horn* (1895) is a good yarn of shipwrecked people on the coast of Peru. Nearly all of Stockton's people, incidentally, are shipwrecked. The marriage of Captain Horn and Edna Markham by the old Negro, Cheditafa, who has been a priest in his own country, is one of those absurdities whose elaborate explanation it must have greatly pleased Stockton to write. Its sequel, *Mrs. Cliff's Yacht* (1896), is not nearly so good, and *The Merry Chanter* (1890), an account of a cruise along the New England coast, is a bit too placid. There is more vigor in *Kate Bonnet* (1902), a novel of piracy in the early seventeenth century, in which probability is completely thrown to the winds. The book must have been intended as a satire upon the piratical romance, and looked upon from that point of view it is a success, for the pirates, including the famous Blackbeard, are as absurd as anyone could desire.

The best of the later novels of Stockton are *The Associate Hermits* (1899), a clever satire on the cult of individuality; *A Bicycle of Cathay* (1900), a picaresque romance in which Stockton indicates skilfully how a number of girls may become interested in a passing young man while each of them retains a deeper interest in other men; and *The Captain's Toll Gate*, published posthumously in 1903, which has more plot than is usual in his later periods. The pursuit of the Captain by Maria Part, an old maid, is completely real.

In Stockton's last collection of short stories, *John Gayther's Garden* (1902), also posthumous, he provided a certain unity by having the tales told by a group of people in a country house. Among the visitors are Pomona and Jonas, and in the story Jonas contributes, "The Foreign Prince and the Hermit's Daughter," Stockton almost recaptures the flavor of his prime. "The Vice Consort" is a good study of feminine psychology, in which six women ask Margaret Temple to be their successor because they think she is not too attractive. The sea, science, and the supernatural all have their representatives; it would seem that Stockton had endeavored to preserve these characteristic notes in his final volume.

In *John Gayther's Garden*, Pomona makes a remark which is significant in view of the differing quality of Stockton's long list of novels and stories. She says, "There's two ways of ending a story. One is to wind it up, and the other is to let it run down." In the realm of pure fancy, where Stockton was most at home, he shaped his fiction, long or short, into artistic unity, often with a dramatic climax, and produced short stories like "The Griffin and the Minor Canon," or "The Lady or the Tiger?" or longer ones like *The Casting Away of Mrs. Lecks and Mrs. Aleshine*. In another division of his fiction, especially that written after 1889, he too often permitted the realistic details to overwhelm that imaginative faculty in which he was hardly surpassed. These novels do not exactly "run down," but they amble gently along and, while they often delight with their shrewd comments, they do not create permanent characterizations. Yet at his best, Stockton has supremely the quality of permanence. A new edition in 1933 of *Mrs. Lecks and Mrs. Aleshine* reveals the constant demand for that remarkable story. With the vivid and poetic fancy of "The Griffin and the Minor Canon," of "The Bee Man of Orn," or "The Lady or the Tiger?" time has nothing to do. They belong in the serene land of enchantment where only those may enter who have not left youth behind.

CHAPTER XI

BRET HARTE AND THE FICTION OF MORAL CONTRAST

LIKE all great artists Bret Harte declines to be neatly classified; and the generalizations which have been made concerning both his work and his character are often misleading. Born in Albany in 1836, the year in which one of his masters in fiction was publishing *Sketches by Boz*, his mixed ancestry accounts partly for his attitude toward life. His grandfather was a Jew who separated from his Christian wife and reared later a Jewish family who remained in ignorance of his first marriage. Bret Harte's father, Henry Harte, was a teacher of Greek, a man of culture and of literary aspirations which came to nothing, and a convert to Catholicism. With a Jewish grandfather, a Catholic father, and an Episcopalian mother, it is perhaps not to be wondered at that Bret Harte became a tolerant sceptic, and that the moral outlook of his characters was at times confused. His regular education was finished at thirteen, yet he was an omnivorous reader, and a precocious writer of verse.

His emigration to the West seems to have been due to his mother's second marriage quite as much as to his own desire, and from the time he arrived in Oakland, California, a boy of seventeen, until he left the West in 1871, he remained an observer of a spectacle into which he never became completely absorbed. He saw, it is true, many aspects of that life. He worked as a drug clerk and an express messenger, taught school, mined for gold, and in 1858, became job printer and assistant editor of the *Northern Californian*, at Uniontown, on the sea coast in Humboldt County.

If his sketch published about forty years later, "How I Went to the Mines," is autobiographical, he had from the first that imperturbable, fatalistic, and observant attitude toward even the smallest details which was one element of his success. Returning to San Francisco in 1860, he continued in that training school, the printing office, which developed so many of the writers of fiction of the time, writing for *The Golden Era* and the *Californian*. It was to the *Californian*, a paper established partly through his efforts in 1864, that he contributed several of his *Condensed Novels*, parodies of famous novelists. They are of significance since in nearly every case it was romantic-idealistic fiction that he burlesqued.

He had already been writing original fiction, his first clearly identified story, "My Metamorphosis," appearing in *The Golden Era*, April 29, 1860. It has none of the characteristics of his important work, and is laid in England and Florence without any sense of locality. But its interest lies in his use of the same situation in one of his latest stories, "A Vision of the Fountain," where he reveals by the title, the influence of Hawthorne's "The Vision of the Fountain," in *Twice Told Tales*.

The first of the early stories to show a germ of his later manner was "The Man of No Account," published in *The Era* for October, 1860. It is only a sketch, but there is the contrast of the apparent uselessness and the real worth of David Fagg, and it is laid in the California scene. Perhaps a recognition of these qualities made it the earliest of his stories to be included by him in his final selection for his collected writings. In these early stories, however, he was experimenting; that he did not quite realize his own strength is shown by his omission of "M'liss," which had appeared first in *The Era* in December, 1860, as "The Work on Red Mountain," from his first collected volume, *Condensed Novels and Other Papers* (1867). He had revised and lengthened "M'liss" for *The Era* in 1863, without satisfaction to himself, and he included it only in 1870 after he had established his method. Yet in its vivid contrast between Melissa Smith and the more respectable elements of "Smith's Pocket" lay a literary nugget of more value than any gold which M'liss's drunken father had ever found. Harte's sympathy with the girl who hates to be dragooned into uniformity was to create later some of his most striking characters. Perhaps his own critical taste saw the theatrical quality of the story, for it was dramatized by Clay Greene and others into one of the most successful and one of the most violent melodramas of its day.

That he looked to the East for approval is shown by the appearance of "The Legend of Monte del Diablo" in the *Atlantic* for October, 1863. It is a story laid about 1770, concerning the struggle between a Jesuit missionary and the Devil, with a vision of the mining days to come. He was learning to write at a good school, for the graceful ironic touch of

Irving is reflected in it. But in their haste to dismiss this story for that reason, critics of Bret Harte have not noticed that two of the elements of his later success were implicit in it, both of them stemming from Irving. First, his humor, and second, his sense of the value of contrast, not only between the two most definite spiritual adversaries, the Church and the Devil, but also between the old Spanish civilization and the gold rush. Harte included this story in his first volume and also two similar tales, "The Adventure of Padre Vincentio" [1] and "The Legend of Devil's Point"; [2] two satirical attacks upon the methods of speculators in "The Devil and the Broker" [3] and "The Ogress of Silver Land"; [4] a slight sketch, "The Ruins of San Francisco"; [5] and "A Night at Wingdam," [6] a description of a hotel in the interior of California. These sketches are of interest as proving that it was not alone the California scene that mattered. Some other element had to be added before he achieved his great manner.

In the *Overland Monthly* for August, 1868, of which Harte was editor, appeared "The Luck of Roaring Camp." The love of children which had been revealed in "M'liss," the delightful irony, the sense of the value of vivid contrasts, the qualities of unity and compression which he had gradually been acquiring, are all seen in this fine short story. He was working too with material which responded exactly to such treatment. The striking contrast of the innocent child and the rough mining camp is accentuated in almost every paragraph. "Deaths were by no means uncommon in Roaring Camp, but a birth was a new thing." The selection of Stumpy, "the putative head of two families" as the nurse, the rapid sketch of the miners, beginning, "The greatest scamp had a Raphael face, with a profusion of blond hair; Oakhurst, a gambler, had the melancholy air and intellectual abstractions of a Hamlet"; the procession which passes around the dead mother and the new baby, Stumpy's extraordinary christening, "according to the laws of the United States

---

[1] *The Californian,* April 15, 1865. Where the periodical date is of interest, either in the establishment of chronology or in the representation of Harte's diversified avenues of publication, it is given; in other cases, the date of the volume in which the story first appears.

[2] *The Californian,* June 25, 1864.

[3] *The Californian,* November 26, 1864.

[4] *The Californian,* August 13, 1864.

[5] *The Californian,* April 15, 1865.

[6] *Golden Era,* November 18, 1860.

and the State of California, so help me God," the drowning of Kentuck with "the Luck" in his arms, are vivid contrasts.

Next came a masterpiece, "The Outcasts of Poker Flat," in *The Overland Monthly* for January, 1869. Harte did not make the short story American and modern as he claimed.[7] Irving had made it American, and Hawthorne and Poe had made it modern; but there is an immediate establishment of both character and situation, told in a cool detached ironic manner, which captivates the reader at once:

As Mr. John Oakhurst, gambler, stepped into the main street of Poker Flat on the morning of the 23d of November, 1850, he was conscious of a change in its moral atmosphere since the preceding night. Two or three men, conversing earnestly together, ceased as he approached, and exchanged significant glances. There was a Sabbath lull in the air, which, in a settlement unused to Sabbath influences, looked ominous.

Mr. Oakhurst's calm, handsome face betrayed small concern in these indications. Whether he was conscious of any predisposing cause was another question. "I reckon they're after somebody," he reflected; "likely it's me." He returned to his pocket the handkerchief with which he had been whipping away the red dust of Poker Flat from his neat boots, and quietly discharged his mind of any further conjecture.

In point of fact, Poker Flat was "after somebody." It had lately suffered the loss of several thousand dollars, two valuable horses, and a prominent citizen. It was experiencing a spasm of virtuous reaction, quite as lawless and ungovernable as any of the acts that had provoked it. A secret committee had determined to rid the town of all improper persons. This was done permanently in regard to two men who were then hanging from the boughs of a sycamore in the gulch, and temporarily in the banishment of certain other objectionable characters. I regret to say that some of these were ladies. It is but due to the sex, however, to state that their impropriety was professional, and it was only in such easily established standards of evil that Poker Flat ventured to sit in judgment.

Mr. Oakhurst was right in supposing that he was included in this category. A few of the committee had urged hanging him as a possible example and a sure method of reimbursing themselves from his pockets of the sums he had won from them. "It's agin justice," said Jim Wheeler, "to let this yer young man from Roaring Camp—an entire stranger—carry away our money." But a crude sentiment of equity residing in the breasts of those who had been fortunate enough to win from Mr. Oakhurst overruled this narrower local prejudice.

---

[7] See his article, "The Rise of the Short Story," *Cornhill Magazine*, July, 1899.

The prose tale had come far from its beginning in "There was a man"! Not a physical feature of Oakhurst is described, yet we know him at once in those essentials that make him important. With the same marvelous economy of the reader's attention, the standards of life in Poker Flat are established. Where in fiction has more been said in felicitous English than is expressed in the last quoted sentence? This irony, never bitter, however blasting it may be, pervades the story. The contrast of the four outcasts, Mother Shipton, the Duchess, Uncle Billy and Oakhurst, with the two young innocent people, Tom Simson and Piney, who are eloping, is delightful. But the greater effect comes from the contrasts within the characters—the harlot who starves herself without heroics to save Piney; the efforts of the Duchess to keep Piney from knowing her real nature, and best of all, the gambler who keeps up the spirits of the little group, shut in by the snow, and gives up the one chance of safety to Tom, "the Innocent," and yet who kills himself when hope is lost. Within four thousand words, a tragedy involving six lives is told, swiftly, inevitably, with the surety of great art.

The best of the stories included in the epoch-making volume of 1870 contain this moral contrast. "Miggles," [8] who keeps "Jim," her former lover, when he becomes paralytic, refrains from marrying him because it would be "playing it rather low down on Jim, to take advantage of his being so helpless." "The Idyll of Red Gulch," [9] in which one of Harte's favorite themes, the attraction of a girl of refinement for a rough and even drunken giant, is run through to tragedy, is remarkable for the way "Miss Mary" is revealed to us by the reactions of Sandy Morton and his abandoned mistress, Tommy's mother. In "Brown of Calaveras" [10] Harte created Jack Hamlin, another gambler, who became one of his most popular characters. He is much like John Oakhurst, and begins his fictional life with a sacrifice, giving up his plan to abscond with his friend's wife and going away alone. "Tennessee's Partner" [11] is another of the great stories, a tale of the constant but inarticulate devotion of one man to another.

It is a mistake, however, to speak of Harte's later work as if he had one great moment before he left California in 1871. His work is uneven

[8] *Overland Monthly*, June, 1869.
[9] *Overland Monthly*, December, 1869.
[10] *Overland Monthly*, March, 1870.
[11] *Overland Monthly*, October, 1869.

and he drops often into sheer melodrama, but when he was inspired by the motive he knew best how to treat, that of the moral contrast, he remained a master.

In "Mrs. Skaggs' Husbands" (1873) the relations of Johnson, the drunkard, to the boy Tommy, who takes care of him, are admirably pictured, and in the description of the river where Johnson apparently meets his death, there is magnificent writing, even if the ending is weak. Bret Harte's love for children shows in "How Santa Claus Came to Simpson's Bar," [12] and the fifty-mile ride of Dick Bullen to bring a few Christmas presents to a little boy is undoubtedly made more interesting by Dick's previous potations. Indeed, in "A Passage in the Life of John Oakhurst" (1875), occurs one of Harte's best studies of a married flirt and some of his most blistering satire of hypocrisy. In "Wan Lee, the Pagan" [13] the loyalty of a Chinese boy, a thief, to a little girl and his death at the hands of a mob reveal Bret Harte in his search for redeeming qualities in apparently unpromising elements in California life.

Certainly "A Blue Grass Penelope," [14] "The Heritage of Dedlow Marsh," [15] "Colonel Starbottle's Client" (1892), "The Conspiracy of Mrs. Bunker," [16] "Salomy Jane's Kiss" (1898)—which was dramatized successfully by Paul Armstrong, "The Bell Ringer of Angel's," [17] "A Protegée of Jack Hamlin's" (1894), "The Judgment of Bolinas Plain," [18]—the basis of Bret Harte's only successful play, "Sue"—and "Jack Hamlin's Convalescence" (1902), would have made the reputation of a lesser artist.

Nor is it correct to say that his longer short stories, or his novelettes, are necessarily of an inferior quality. There is not the unity in these which characterizes "The Outcasts," but some are significant for other reasons. *Thankful Blossom* (1877) is a fine story of the Revolution; *Jeff Briggs' Love Story* [19] is a striking contrast between the Western lover and a girl from the East. *Maruja* [20] is another contrast, almost as successful, between a girl of Spanish descent and her American lover.

[12] *Atlantic Monthly*, March, 1872.
[13] *Scribner's Monthly*, September, 1874.
[14] *New York Sun*, June 29–July 6, 1884.
[15] *Harper's Weekly*, June 29, 1889.
[16] *The Idler*, February to July, 1892.
[17] *Harper's Weekly*, November, 1893.
[18] *Pall Mall Magazine*, January, 1895.
[19] *London Daily Chronicle*, 1880.
[20] *Harper's Weekly*, June–July, 1885.

In *Snow Bound at Eagle's* [21] the effect of the climate upon John Hale, an Eastern man, and upon two Eastern women, is a powerful study. Even such a wildly romantic tale as *The Crusade of The Excelsior* [22] has some well drawn characters, among them Perkins, the professional revolutionist. In *A Millionaire of Rough and Ready* (1887) there is a remarkable description of a man being struck with paralysis just after finding gold.

Kate Howard, the heroine of *A Ward of the Golden Gate* (1890), who realizes that she is not the proper person to bring up her daughter and makes her the ward of the city of San Francisco, is well drawn, as is also Colonel Pendleton. *A Sappho of Green Springs* [23] reveals the delicacy of feeling of Jack Hamlin who, starting to search for the mysterious poetess who has sent verses in to the editor of *The Excelsior* describing "the second twilight of the ferns" and other aspects of Nature in her reticent moods, abandons the search at the author's request. *Sally Dows* [24] is a charming story of a Georgia girl of a practical nature, much more real than the usual Southern girl of romance. In the description of the battle which opens the story and the fight with the blood hounds, Harte is in his element.

In two of the novelettes, Bret Harte shows his ability at drawing international contrasts. In *A Phyllis of the Sierras* (1888) he drew a contrast between the Englishman of a well-established family, represented by Francis Mainwaring, and the Western civilization of two types, the rougher in Minty Sharpe and the more cultivated in James Bradley and his family. Bret Harte knew both kinds of Westerners, and his comparison between them and the English is fairer than that of Henry James. He drew in James Bradley the well-poised American of good ancestry who is at home in the company at Oldenhurst, the English country house. Bret Harte reveals his understanding of British nature without any undue love for it or any desire to satirize it. In *The Ancestors of Peter Atherly* (1897), he drew a man who had Indian blood in his veins and who was supposed to be descended from an English noble family. Again we have the international contrast, and we have the final sacrifice when he gives himself up to the Indians in order to save an English girl and her sister who have been recaptured. Bret Harte indi-

---

[21] *New York Sun,* Christmas Issue, 1885.
[22] *Harper's Weekly,* January–May, 1887.
[23] *Lippincott's Magazine,* May, 1890.
[24] *English Illustrated Magazine,* October, 1892–March, 1893.

cates here quite well that the stoical qualities in Peter Atherly may have been derived either from his British ancestry or from his aboriginal inheritance.

Bret Harte wrote only one long novel, *Gabriel Conroy*.[25] While it cannot be said to have been completely successful, it hardly deserves the general condemnation under which it has fallen. Harte did not have the constructive ability for a novel, and the plot becomes at times confused, but the character of Gabriel Conroy is not by any means his worst creation, and the opening scene describing the castaways in the snow is in his very best manner. He showed, too, in three novelettes which really comprise one complete story, *A Waif of the Plains* (1890), *Susy, a Story of the Plains* (1893), and *Clarence, a Novel* (1895), that he could sustain the development of character. Clarence is developed from a boy, through circumstances, to a cool, determined man, showing at times the traits of his father, Hamilton Brant, the desperado, always keeping up to the standard of conduct he had set for himself as a boy. *Susy*, too, is well done, and the opening scene in which the two children are lost in the open desert country is epic in its quality.

It is his method then, even more than his material, which secured Harte's success. It would be idle, of course, to deny that much of the interest in his fiction comes from the romantic life which California of the 'fifties presented. It was not primitive but elemental, for a civilization in which the Oxford graduate or the sophisticated Eastern man rubbed shoulders with the man from Pike County, Missouri, or the Southern fire-eater, like Colonel Starbottle, provided vigorous action and colorful scenes of which Harte took full advantage. It gave him, too, the right to attribute to some of his characters subtler shades of emotion than a merely primitive form of life could have developed. Amusements were of a definite character, and the saloon and the gaming table were born of the very uncertainties of the life. The opportunities for rapid fortune attracted persons like John Oakhurst, Jack Hamlin, and Kate Howard. Even the professions were filled by men like Colonel Starbottle, who knew little law but could sway a jury by his eloquence and could shoot straight.

The absence for a certain time and in certain places of the usual safeguards of law and order developed a wider and more elemental justice, swifter and more dramatic, and therefore more fruitful to the writer of

[25] *Scribner's Monthly*, November, 1875–August, 1876.

fiction. The cheapness of life which might be ended by a pistol shot or by an earthquake gave Harte an opportunity to depict men whose indifference to danger became almost medieval. As a background to this life, and in sharp contrast to it, was the picturesque Spanish civilization, with three centuries behind it. Harte used this material, however, mainly as a foil to the American. He rarely, except in stories like "The Passing of Enriquez," made use of the Spaniard in his heroic phases.

Because of its nature, this life in California presented vivid contrasts, moral, social, and racial. It is to this quality, therefore, rather than to its locality that its availability as material for fiction was due. When we catalogue the characters that through their excellence come first to our minds—John Oakhurst, Jack Hamlin, Colonel Starbottle, Kate Howard, Sandy Morton, Kentuck, M'liss, Miggles, Wan Lee, Joseph Corbin—it will be seen how few are Californians. They are rather citizens of a country that is the land of Bret Harte. They are not like the Pennsylvania Quakers of Taylor, the New Englanders of Mrs. Cooke, the mountaineers of Mrs. Davis, or later the Creoles of Cable, indigenous to the soil. They are not like Hawkeye, the epitome of an earlier romantic scene, for while Hawkeye is great because he is so truly an expression of the forces of nature and the frontier, Harte's best characters are rebels and outlaws, defying even the loose laws of the community in which they live. He was never in love with his material as Irving was with his Hudson, or Mrs. Stowe with her New England. One of his greatest assets, his objective quality, may be due to the fact that he remained always an Easterner. He was never absorbed by the West, by the frontier. His cool detached attitude resulted in his supreme success and yet set a limitation to it. It made it easy, almost inevitable, that he should leave the West and later his native country. That he did not deepen in his art after he went to Germany as commercial agent, in 1878, or during his continued expatriation in Scotland and England, is not surprising. Life there provided sharp contrasts, but they were not for him. When he dealt with Scottish characters, as in "Young Robin Gray," [26] or with German life in "The Indiscretion of Elsbeth" (1896), he wrote charming stories which added little to his reputation. But they would have added greatly to the reputation of others. His two most striking gifts were his power of observation and his vivid imagination. Obviously, only the second of these could be exercised at a distance from

[26] *Good Words*, February, 1894.

his material, and while practical necessities kept him abroad,[27] it was on the whole not to the advantage of his art. It is idle to speculate on what his achievement might have been if he had sought in the life of the East the moral contrasts he drew so well in the West. There were many that lay close at hand.

In any event, his accomplishment was a great one. In his pages the appealing characters and vivid incidents paint in bold relief the East and the West, the North and the South, the American and the Spaniard, the Occidental and the Oriental, the English and the American. Strength of body and of mind brings out in contrast the helplessness of a child, depicted with a sympathy turned especially toward those upon whose shoulders fall too early the responsibilities of life. Above all other forms of tyranny, Harte hated, like Irving and Hawthorne, the tyranny of the small-town mind, and he struck back at his critics vigorously when he wrote in the Introduction to his poetical works:

He has been repeatedly cautioned, kindly and unkindly, intelligently and unintelligently, against his alleged tendency to confuse recognised standards of morality by extenuating lives of recklessness, and often criminality, with a single solitary virtue. He might easily show that he has never written a sermon, that he has never moralised or commented upon the actions of his heroes, that he has never voiced a creed or obtrusively demonstrated an ethical opinion. . . . But . . . he will, without claiming to be a religious man or a moralist, but simply as an artist, reverently and humbly conform to the rules laid down by a Great Poet who created the parable of the "Prodigal Son" and the "Good Samaritan," whose works have lasted eighteen hundred years, and will remain when the present writer and his generation are forgotten.

Finally, despite all his theatricality and the touching up of his situations, he helped on the cause of realism by his probing beneath the surface for the more profound causes of human conduct. When he speaks of Clarence Brant's tolerance for Susy's vagaries, he quietly observes: "He did not dream that his capacity for patience was only the slow wasting of his love." Again he remarks, "Clarence Brant was a modest man, but the egotism of modesty is more fatal than that of pretension for it has the haunting consciousness of superior virtue." Those who have solemnly repeated the critical cliché that Bret Harte is unmoral because he could draw unmoral characters with skill, might read with profit the

[27] See his explanation in letters to his wife, especially those from Glasgow, August 17, 1885, and from London, November 28, 1887, in *The Letters of Bret Harte*, ed. by Geoffrey Bret Harte (1926).

sentence in *The First Family of Tasajara*,[28] "The step from passive to active wrong doing is not only easy, it is often a relief: it is that return to sincerity which we all require." In spite of his delightful irony concerning the relations of men and women, he could indicate well the dawn of real love, with an understanding of the byways of the approach to love which again reveals him as a keen and sympathetic observer. The description of the relations of Eleanor Keene and James Hurlstone in *The Crusade of the Excelsior* is a fine example of this delicacy of treatment.

Above all Harte was essentially an artist in words and in phrases. In his prose as well as his verse he wrote magnificent English. It was just because he was a poet that his work in fiction was translated rapidly into the principal continental tongues. Even *Gabriel Conroy* passed through several editions in Germany. He remains a world artist not merely because of his depiction of the gold rush of California, but because he discovered that other, richer vein, the sympathy which even the most puritanical feel for the sinner who leads them vicariously into the paths of adventure which they have shunned, but of which they love to read in the pages of fiction.

His influence upon later fiction, both in America and in England, has been marked. Just as Irving taught Dickens, and Dickens taught Bret Harte, to portray the human beings in which good and evil are mingled in dramatic contrasts, so Harte taught nearly every American writer of short stories and many like Kipling in England, some of the essential lessons of his art. But again, just as Poe must be distinguished from his imitators in the detective story, so Harte must not be blamed for the confused moral sentimentality of his weaker followers. His harlots were often generous or courageous or broadly tolerant, but they never slipped on purity and impurity like the season's costumes. His gamblers might be brave or tender-hearted or chivalric to a woman, but they remained gamblers and conducted their main business with a cold eye and a steady hand. The keen humor which shoots a steady gleam through his best stories, was responsible not only for their qualities of entertainment, but it preserved in him that sense of proportion which was one of his great gifts to the development of the short story.

[28] *Macmillan's Magazine*, August–December, 1891.

CHAPTER XII

MARK TWAIN AND THE ROMANCE OF YOUTH

THERE has hardly ever been seen in literature so striking a contrast as that which exists between two writers of fiction who made their reputations at the same time and who even collaborated in the description of Western life. They were both lovers of the rebel and the individual, and both protested in their lives and writings against the tyranny of uniformity and convention. Yet any comparison that is not superficial reveals at once their essential differences. Mark Twain, unlike Bret Harte, was the product of the Middle Western frontier; he fitted into the Far Western frontier easily and became a part of it. His enthusiasm, his hatred of wrongs, and his larger variety of invention, mark him as distinct from Harte, who simply avoided what he disliked and who led no crusades. Mark Twain learned much, however, from his rival in their brief companionship in the art of expression, and it is interesting to note that when they wrote the play, *Ah Sin*, together, it is hard to distinguish, from the manuscript, between their respective portions. Yet in their published works, Bret Harte and Mark Twain reveal no marked similarities of style.

It is not easy nor would it be profitable to draw the line sharply between those writings of Mark Twain which have sufficient plot and character drawing to be called fiction and those works which are so purely humorous, so definitely dependent upon descriptions of travel or relations of bizarre events, that they fall outside that category. His *Autobiography* has revealed how closely he sticks to facts in his fiction and this very fidelity prevents at times the illusion which imagination creates from facts, and which is the life of the novel or the short story. The two most striking qualities of his humor, his exaggeration and his creation of incongruity, tend to prevent unity, and are the causes of the disjointedness of thought and the lack of a basic plan which prevent the fusion of the whole work into a great novel. It is easy to rule *The Innocents Abroad*, *A Tramp Abroad*, *Following the Equator* and the miscellaneous sketches like "Cannibalism in the Cars" from consideration. The most significant critical fact that arises from such a clearing of the ground is that Mark Twain's most important work remains. The European travel books were amusing, but the *nil admirari* attitude which was fresh in 1869 has lost much of its savor now. It is quite another matter with those personal narratives like *Roughing It* or *Life on the Mississippi*.

They are based upon a varied and eventful life. Samuel Langhorne Clemens (1835–1910) grew up in the easy-going, slave-holding Missouri town of Hannibal. His father, who died in 1847, was a Virginian, and had, like Hawkins in *The Gilded Age*, taken up a large section of land in Tennessee. Clemens was educated largely in the printing offices of the *Missouri Courier* and the *Hannibal Journal*, for which he wrote verse as well as prose. In June, 1853, he started on a tour of observation which began in St. Louis and included New York, Philadelphia, Washington, Cincinnati, and New Orleans, working at his printing trade, and writing humorous sketches. In 1857, being disappointed in his project to go to South America, he became a pilot on the Mississippi River. This piloting life on the Mississippi left a deep impression upon him. Most of *Life on the Mississippi* is autobiographical. The voyage had another consequence owing to the explosion which resulted in the death of Henry Clemens through an overdose of morphine given to him accidentally by Samuel. His best biographer, Paine, says of the occurrence, "He never really looked young again. Gray hairs had come and they did not disappear. His face took on the serious, pathetic look which from that time it always had in repose. At twenty-three, he looked thirty. At thirty, he looked nearer forty." While on the river he met an older pilot, Isaiah Sellers, who wrote articles for the New Orleans' *Picayune* and signed them "Mark Twain," from the custom of heaving the lead. Clemens imitated the rather pompous style of Sellers in a burlesque account of a trip supposed to be made by a steamer with a Chinese captain in 1763. It was published in the New Orleans *True Delta* in 1859, and, according to Clemens, it affected Sellers so deeply that he never wrote afterwards. Clemens regretted the matter and seems to have taken the name later on as a form of reparation.[1]

The appointment of his brother Orion as territorial secretary of Nevada gave Samuel Clemens the opportunity of seeing the silver mining

---

[1] *Life on the Mississippi*, Chapter L.

at its height and led to his connection with *The Enterprise* of Virginia City. Leaving Nevada on account of a projected duel, he went to California, and later became associated with Bret Harte on the *Californian;* and he claims that he heard the story of the jumping frog while taking momentary shelter from the rain in a mining camp. The story was published in the *Californian* and was sent East in 1864, at the suggestion of Artemus Ward, where it was published in the *Saturday Press.* Mark Twain himself calls attention to a Greek form of the same story in his article *The Private History of the Jumping Frog Story.*

His literary career as distinguished from his life as a journalist began with *The Celebrated Jumping Frog of Calaveras County and Other Sketches* (1867). His first trip around the world which resulted in *The Innocents Abroad,* started in June, 1867, but the book itself was not published until 1869. In 1870 he married Olivia Langdon of Elmira, New York, to his great good fortune. Far from restraining his creative power, as has sometimes been suggested, she saved him by her criticism from those lapses into bad taste of which the notorious speech at the Whittier dinner was an example, and from which he himself would have been the greatest sufferer. Mark Twain's critical sense was not strong and it was again his good fortune to meet with a restraining influence in Howells and Aldrich, and in a group of men and women of culture at Hartford, Connecticut, where he spent the years from 1871 to 1891. His later tours in Europe and his publishing ventures do not concern us except as the assumption of the debts of the firm of which he was a silent partner place him with Walter Scott among those writers of fiction who made gallant and successful attempts to pay the obligations of others by their own endeavors.

Mark Twain's career had to an unusual degree an effect upon his fiction. It was not only that he used his own adventures as a basis, but his interests, his sympathies, even his prejudices colored the selection of his material. This subjective quality is a source of the vitality of his best work and of the extravagance and even dullness of his worst. This uneven achievement is seen in his first important work, *Roughing It* (1872). Much of *Roughing It* is fiction, in the sense that it is not historically true. It has, to be sure, no unity, except through the character of the narrator, but it is a vivid picture of life in Nevada and in California, told by an amused and tolerant critic, who has created, as the teller of the story, a being whom he calls "I." If he had given this person a fictitious name, we should not hesitate to class *Roughing It* with *Robinson Crusoe* as romance. For even the narrator does not pretend to vouch for the accuracy of his stories about silver miners, desperadoes, Mormons, road agents, and card sharps. There is an exaggeration, at times excessive, but there are also scenes such as the conversation between "Scotty" and the minister which are superlatively funny. When one is searching for quotable humorous passages, it is to *Roughing It* that he returns most often.

In 1873 Mark Twain and Charles Dudley Warner wrote what they hoped to be the great American novel in *The Gilded Age*. Beginning about 1845, it is the prose epic of the age that prepared for the great expansion and corruption of the post Civil War period and extends into that period itself. Going back to his own experience, Mark Twain brings Squire Hawkins and his family from Tennessee to Missouri, adopting Laura van Brunt, who becomes one of the heroines. Her deception by George Selby and her subsequent murder of Selby, her trial and acquittal are truly melodramatic, and the canvas becomes confused by the introduction of too many characters. Clay, for example, another orphan who has been adopted by Squire Hawkins, was created apparently to support the family. In a book of this kind they might just as well have been supported by the authors. But in addition to the lobbying at Washington in which Laura leads a project to sell the Tennessee land which the Squire had preëmpted and which runs like a central motive through the book, another plot was added, for which Warner was responsible. Ruth Bolton, a Philadelphia Quaker, her father and mother, Henry Brierly and Philip Stirling, who eventually marries Ruth and who makes money in Pennsylvania coal lands, are the principal characters. The two younger men are joined to the main plot through Colonel Sellers and Laura, who meet them when they come to the West on a preliminary survey for a railroad. Colonel Sellers is the best drawn character, the arch optimist who is always about to make his fortune but never does, and who becomes the epitome of the better side of the age's humbug. Mark Twain claimed that he drew him from his mother's cousin, James Lampton, who was constantly saying "There's millions in it!" But the character was probably a joint contribution. Warner had lived with a Mr. and Mrs. Philip Price near Philadelphia when as a young man he was studying law at the University of Pennsylvania. Mr. Price, who was the original of Mr. Bolton in the novel, was engaged in a coal-mining project in Illinois which sent as its representative to that State, a Philadelphia engineer, Escol (not Eschol) Sellers in 1854. The project failed, as did several other schemes with which Escol Sellers was connected, often because he was ahead of his day. Warner either knew or had heard of the real Escol Sellers, the name of the character as it was first projected, not, as Mark Twain says in his *Autobiography*, a Western farmer "in a cheap and humble way," but a member of a well-established Philadelphia family. According to his family, Escol was constantly irritated by newspaper references to him as the original Colonel Sellers. Curiously enough, he was born in Mulberry Court, Philadelphia, which again through Warner, may have given him his second and final name. There are so many errors in the account of the creation of Colonel Sellers in the *Autobiography* that it seems evident that Warner should have a share in the credit for one of the most vivid figures in American fiction. On the stage, John T. Raymond made Mulberry Sellers, as he had been renamed, a popular figure. The play was originally written by Gilbert S. Densmore, a newspaper man in San Francisco, but Mark Twain was able to preserve the dramatic rights and the resultant compromise was partly his work. The manuscript of the play reveals a melodrama, leading to the trial of Laura, who is saved by Colonel Sellers' appeal to the jury. The wealth of material in *The Gilded Age* makes it more interesting as a social study than as a novel. Outside of Colonel Sellers, the characters rarely seem to do anything of their own initiative; they are moved about and their actions are determined for them. The illusion is not by any means complete; one thinks of them constantly as characters in a book. At times, they are introduced and dismissed publicly by the authors. There is none of that sense of the finished and carefully constructed work of art which forbids the introduction of any element that does not tend to the conclusion.

The explanation of this deficiency is found in Mark Twain's own words in the beginning of a long story, *Those Extraordinary Twins:*

A man who is not born with the novel-writing gift has a troublesome time of it when he tries to build a novel. I know this from experience. He has no clear idea of his story; in fact he has no story. He merely has some people in his mind, and an incident or two, also a locality. He knows these people, he knows the selected locality, and he trusts that he can plunge those people into those incidents with interesting results. So he goes to work. To write a novel? No—that is a thought which comes later; in the beginning he is only proposing to tell a little tale; a very little tale; a six-page tale. But as it is a tale which he is not acquainted with, and can only find out what it is by listening as it goes along telling itself, it is more than apt to go on and on and on till it spreads itself into a book. I know about this, because it has happened to me so many times.

And I have noticed another thing: that as the short tale grows into the long tale, the original intention (or motif) is apt to get abolished and find itself superseded by a quite different one.

In 1876 came *Tom Sawyer*. It was drawn in part from Mark Twain's own life. Tom, he tells us, was the compound of three boys, but there was, in Tom, Mark Twain's own love of adventure, which prompts him to become a pirate and which leads him into nearly all the interesting incidents of the book. It is Tom's desire to go just a little farther than the rest of the party which leads him to become lost with Becky Thatcher in the cave. Huckleberry Finn, Twain insisted, was drawn from actual life and was the son of the town drunkard of Hannibal; and Becky Thatcher was Laura Hawkins, his first sweetheart. It will be noticed that he had already used her real name for the heroine of *The Gilded Age*. Sid was his elder brother. *Tom Sawyer* does not break so definitely as Aldrich's *The Story of a Bad Boy* with the older type of boys' books in which incidents of buried treasure and of pirate life figure so prominently. *Tom Sawyer* rather grows out of the older material through Mark Twain's satire of it and through the humor which makes of it a new thing. Coloring the life he knew in Hannibal, was his reading of romances like the Robin Hood ballads; and the effect of the darkness of the cave, the slow dwindling of the candles, the sense of the passage of time, is strongly reminiscent of Aldrich's *A Struggle for Life*. Tom's first outline of his projected search for buried treasure, his description of the hieroglyphics and the dead tree with the limbs sticking out show unmistakable traces of "The Gold Bug." Mark Twain naturally made use of stories of Indian life and incidents derived from Negro tales. The very first trick Tom plays on Aunt Polly is given in Schoolcraft's legends of Manabozho, the Indian deity.

The originality of Mark Twain comes not so much, then, from the selection of his incidents, but it arises rather from his knowledge of human nature, which adds to these incidents elements that either kindle the memory of boyhood or, in any event, charm the readers by their revelations of human weaknesses. Tom's cleverness in persuading his friends to whitewash the fence for him might be merely amusing, but because it is a revelation of the methods by which, on a larger scale, competitors of many industries were making fortunes out of their fellow countrymen during that period, it takes on a larger significance. Tom's purchase of a reputation for learning by his deft bartering of the Sunday school tickets contains also, in epitome, a description of the methods by which railway systems were refinanced from solvency to insolvency. But the great strength of *Tom Sawyer* is the way in which Mark Twain preserves the boy attitude throughout. Tom Sawyer is not all heroic. He is willing to let Muff Potter be hanged at first, out of terror of Injun Joe and out of regard for his own oath. He is not above deceit, but he will not lie outright, where a lie will materially benefit him. He has a longing for adventure, and he insists on carrying his adventures out. Howells calls attention to the fact that Tom Sawyer has standards of respectability which are unknown to Huck Finn, who is never confused with him. Huck Finn looks up to Tom and is even willing to be educated in order that he may become a member of the robber band which Tom will organize. *Tom Sawyer* too belongs in that class of fiction which can be enjoyed by both children and adults, and he lives in a select company with Tom Brown of Rugby and Tom Bailey of Portsmouth.

The Prince and the Pauper (1882) has been deservedly not only one of the most popular of Mark Twain's books, but also one which has met the severer standards of criticism. It is the best constructed of his fictional narratives, with the greatest unity in its plot and with that combination of romantic selection of material and realistic presentation of detail which makes usually for success. Once the basic impossibility of the central situation is forgotten, the lesser improbabilities are explained or, better, prepared for with a skill which Mark Twain did not always exhibit. His success in this instance illustrates the truth of the old principle of story-telling: "Prefer probable impossibilities to improbable possibilities." In real life Tom Canty would have betrayed himself in a hundred ways which even the excellent excuse of mental aberration would not have covered. Mark Twain's invention of the King's command to the supposed prince to refrain further from denying his identity was a master stroke, for at once it did away with the chief source of the danger of discovery and it secured the sympathy of the reader for the little outcast, who otherwise would have been acting a lie of his own will. Such an act of the King would have been in keeping with Henry's character

and with the state of politics at that time. The supporters of the Princess
Mary were alert and were in constant danger of their lives. Their leader,
the Duke of Norfolk, was in prison and under sentence of death. If such
a substitution as the story is based upon had really taken place, it would
have been to the interest of the Protector's party to conceal it in order
to secure the accession of Edward VI. But Mark Twain, with the genius
of a great story-teller, did not dwell too much upon the facts of history.
It mattered little to him that Edward VI was only nine years old at the
time of Henry's death. The boy Prince was a picturesque figure, and he
would do. It is not indicated in the romance just how old Edward is,
though his language, his strength of character and his ability with the
cudgels are those of a boy at least sixteen. Perhaps some of the kingly
qualities of another Edward may have unconsciously affected Mark
Twain's picture of Edward VI, for it was to a romance of the days of
Edward the First that he owed the original inspiration of the story. It
was in the summer of 1877 that he, according to Mr. Paine's biography,
"picked up from among the books at the farm a little juvenile volume,
an English story of the thirteenth century, by Charlotte M. Yonge, entitled *The Prince and the Page*." It was a story of Edward I and his
cousins, Richard and Henry de Montfort; in part it told of the submerged personality of the latter, picturing him as having dwelt in disguise as a blind beggar for a period of years. It was a story of a sort and
with a setting that Mark Twain loved, and as he read there came a cor-
relative idea. Not only would he disguise a prince as a beggar, but a
beggar as a prince. He would have them change places in the world, and
each learn the burdens of the other's life. For the cruel punishments
which he describes with such indignation he drew information from
J. Hammond Trumbull's *The True Blue Laws of Connecticut and New
Haven* (1876), which attempted to show the comparative mildness of the
laws of New England as compared with those of the mother country.

But for the main theme of his story he had no need for source or
reference. It was a compound of his two most striking qualities, his unquenchable love of youth and his constant hatred of injustice. It was because these two impulses gave birth to *The Prince and the Pauper*, just
as they did to the *Joan of Arc*, that these books take their places in the list
of Mark Twain's great contributions. Their European setting was a detail, for the foreign background was usually to him a hindrance, not a
help, but Tom Canty's dreams and the mimic court he held among his

chums stand him in good stead when he has the real robes of the prince placed upon him; it is to be noticed that after the substitution the pauper acts much more like a Prince than the Prince acts like a pauper. This was of course only to be expected, for it was to the interest of Tom Canty to obey the king's orders and it was to the Prince's interest to impress anyone he could with his royal character. Yet we cannot help but feel that it was the intention of Mark Twain to show in this and in other ways the essential likeness of all ranks, no matter what their origin; to preach, in other words, the great lesson of democracy. Just as Cooper showed the advantages of the democratic organization of society by painting the evils of oligarchy in *The Headsman* or *The Bravo,* so Mark Twain, by revealing the accidental nature of the differences between Edward Tudor and Tom Canty, shows the inconsistencies of monarchical rule. It was a stroke of genius, too, to release the Prince from the sordid life of Offal Court and send him on his wanderings. It gave Tom time to play the Prince, but it served also another purpose. It provided Mark Twain an opportunity to depict the rogue life of the sixteenth century, which he has done in a manner that excites the admiration even of the trained historian. Sometimes he keeps almost to the letter of his original, *The English Rogue,* as in the description of the artificial sore or "clune" which Hugo grafted on the Prince's leg. Sometimes he expands a brief incident into two chapters, as in the conviction of the Prince for stealing the pig, and the device by which Hendon secures his liberty. Here he improves upon the original and incidentally turns the judge's action from an act of injustice to one of generous dealing. It was not only for the education of the Prince that these wanderings were invented. Through the fictional description of the punishments for beggary in the days of Henry VIII, Mark Twain was voicing his constant protest against the unjust treatment of one human being by another. King Edward's first actions are the undoing of wrongs of which Prince Edward had learned by personal suffering. Mark Twain would have enjoyed nothing so much as the power to redress wrongs with a royal flourish. A dramatic version of the story by Abby Sage Richardson, arranged for the stage by David Belasco, was produced by Daniel Frohman, with Elsie Leslie in the double rôle of Tom Canty and the Prince, at the Park Theatre, Philadelphia, December 24, 1889. It was a success, and after a New York season it was produced in England. It was revived in 1920 by William Faversham.

In *Life on the Mississippi* (1883), Mark Twain returned to one of his great sources of inspiration, the river he knew so well. It is fiction only in the sense that *Roughing It* is fiction, and it has the disadvantage of breaking into two parts. The earlier portion, which describes his "learning the river" is the better. Mark Twain, who had lived on or near the Mississippi when a boy, now approaches the great stream almost as an adversary to be conquered, but as an adversary who is also a friend. There is a poet speaking in the first part of *Life on the Mississippi* who disappears in the later portion when the traveler returns twenty-one years later to recapture a spell that lives only in the memory.

The Adventures of Huckleberry Finn (1884) is generally preferred to *Tom Sawyer*, probably because the autobiographical method preserves that illusion of reality which is the life of fiction. The remarks which Mark Twain made about Tom Sawyer are out of place in this scheme, and while they were an element in the delightful humor of the earlier book, they interrupted its unity as a piece of fiction. But unity was never Mark Twain's strong point, and *Huckleberry Finn* appeared first in episodic installments in *The Century* in 1884. Tom was a product, too, of the romances he had read; Huck is a picaresque vagabond in whom there is much of Mark Twain's longing for adventure. It must be confessed that the "king" and the "duke" become a bit tiresome and the scheme by which Huck is made to represent Tom is over-elaborate and drags needlessly on. But *Huckleberry Finn* remains one of Mark Twain's great books, and it does not need the introduction of a character named "Brother Penrod" in the forty-first chapter to prove how Booth Tarkington was influenced by Mark Twain in the creation of his adolescent types.

A Connecticut Yankee in King Arthur's Court (1889) falls far below *Huckleberry Finn* in its quality. It is a satire, degenerating into burlesque, of the court of King Arthur, by the device of placing a Yankee in that court and letting him meet conditions through the application of modern methods. There are no characters, and the humor becomes farcical at once. There is no veracity, either, in the abuses the Yankee seeks to rectify, as there was in *The Prince and the Pauper*. For Mark Twain has transferred economic and social tyranny of much later centuries to the sixth century, of which he obviously knew almost nothing. We cannot become excited about tyranny which Mark Twain has created in order to attack it, and the book must be judged not as fiction but as humor.

Here it falls below his best work for another reason. The basic humor arises from the incongruity of a Yankee appearing at King Arthur's Court. But this is a theme for a short narrative. A reader fails to be amused by incongruity when he can expect nothing but incongruity, for one of its essential elements is that of surprise. The further adventures of Colonel Sellers were given in *The American Claimant* (1892). It is an amusing extravaganza, in which the Colonel, settled in Washington as a claim agent, becomes by the death of a relative a claimant to the title and estates of the Earl of Rossmore. The characters, including the visiting son of the Earl, are caricatures. Mark Twain's sequels, with the exception of *Huckleberry Finn*, were not successful. *Tom Sawyer Abroad* (1894) and *Tom Sawyer Detective* (1896) were disappointments.

Pudd'nhead Wilson (1894) is a rambling narrative laid in "Dawson's Landing" and St. Louis, about 1830. There are possibilities in the plot and characters which are not realized in the execution. Pudd'nhead Wilson receives his name because he is too clever for the small town and it is not until he proves Tom Driscoll the murderer of his uncle, by means of the finger prints Wilson has been collecting for years, that he is recognized. But he really never becomes a living person till the final scene; he is only the outline of one. Roxy, the light Negress who puts her child in the place of her master's, is too close to racial reality and not sufficiently individualized to become the center of interest as she should be. For to her belongs the most striking situation in the book, when her worthless child, known as Tom Driscoll, who has grown up mean and dishonest, accepts the offer of his freed mother to permit him to sell her into slavery to save him from the consequences of his thievery. Here Mark Twain created a situation out of which a great novelist might have taken advantage. But the recital is tame, not because it is brief, for obviously brevity is in keeping with tragedy, but because Tom Driscoll's feelings are analyzed instead of Roxy's, and no one is interested in Tom. Tom is irritating because he is so inconsistently drawn. At times he is clever; at times stupid. He kills his uncle when he is discovered robbing him, calmly puts on a disguise and departs for St. Louis, acting with the resolution of a professional criminal. Yet at the trial of Count Luigi for the murder of the Judge, Tom collapses weakly when Pudd'nhead Wilson makes his charge against him. His conversation, too, is stilted and bookish. The failure of *Pudd'nhead Wilson* arose, in all probability, from the fact that Mark Twain wrote first the story of the Italian twins, then superimposed the other characters upon them, to such an extent that the twins may be easily omitted from any analysis of the story. That he recognized this weakness has already been shown.

When *Personal Recollections of Joan of Arc* ran through *Harper's Magazine* in 1895, it was published anonymously, since Mark Twain wished it to be judged as a serious account of a character in which he had been interested from the early days in Hannibal. Here, as in *The Prince and the Pauper*, he worked hard in acquainting himself with the facts of her life, her trial, and the rehabilitation of her character—ordered by the Pope about twenty-five years after her death. But *Joan of Arc* is not a history. It is fiction, told through the eyes of her supposed secretary, the Sieur Louis de Conte. This device gives life to the narrative and makes possible a sympathetic interpretation not only of Joan's actions but also of her thoughts and motives. The early portion, dealing with Joan's life at Domremy, is especially well done, and the battles are portrayed with the vigor of a man who could always take pleasure in a fight. The trial drags at times, partly because Mark Twain spends so much time denouncing the judges, but as a whole Joan of Arc emerges as a Norman peasant, the inspiration of a mingled Latin and Celtic race which would follow a leader to the death. There is not much of the humor which is so characteristic of the earlier books; what there is, is provided by imaginary characters like Noël and the Paladin.

Mark Twain's sketches are seldom short stories in the proper sense. They were usually written definitely as contributions to humor and were often models of their kind. But certain of his short stories rise into real importance not on account of their humorous expression but because of their basic ideas, which reveal inventive qualities of a high c. der. "The Man that Corrupted Hadleyburg" (1899) is a powerful arraignment of the self-righteous small town, which prides itself on being honest. But a stranger who has been insulted by Hadleyburg decides upon an unique revenge, the corruption of the town's leading citizens. He leaves with a Mr. Richards a bag which he states contains gold coin, and which is to be given to the citizen of the town who has done the stranger a service some time before. He is to be identified by the remark he made to the stranger when the service was rendered, and this sentence is enclosed in a sealed envelope. After a few days, nineteen of the leading citizens receive a note telling them what the sentence is, that it was said to a man named Goodson, who is dead, and that the writer, who overheard the remark, knows that the donor would be glad if the gold came to the recipient. The poison begins to work. The way in which even Richards, who is honest, begins to wonder whether he may not have made the remark, is a remarkable, if sardonic, study of human weakness and cupidity. The dramatic meeting at which the Rev. Mr. Burgess reads out the slips of paper, on which each citizen has written the words he knows he has not said, thereby exposing himself to ridicule, is portrayed in Mark Twain's best manner. Here the story should have stopped, for the author's pursuit of Richards until his character disintegrates and he dies is an anticlimax. To the same order of fiction belongs "The $30,000 Bequest" (1904), in which a man writes to a relative that he is leaving him a bequest of $30,000 on condition that he must not inquire concerning it and must not even attend the funeral of his benefactor. The recipient changes his whole manner of living, gives up his efforts to progress normally, and ruins himself by speculation, only to find that his supposed benefactor has not left any money and has revenged himself in this way for ills of his own. These stories reveal Mark Twain as a realist, probing beneath the surface of life for the evil in human nature.

In lighter vein, "Is He Living or Is He Dead" (1893) relates the means by which three young French artists build up a reputation for François Millet by pretending he is dead and selling his paintings as those of a master. The similarity of a recent successful play, *Prenez Garde à la Peinture,* by René Fauchois, adapted by Sidney Howard as *The Late Christopher Bean,* is another illustration of the influence of Mark Twain upon later writers.

Certain qualities in Mark Twain lifted him out of the category of the professional humorists who flourished during his early period, men like Artemus Ward, Josh Billings, or Bill Nye, who are now practically forgotten. Mark Twain never allowed himself to be taken merely as a "funny man." Although he said in *Following the Equator,* "I have never been able to tell lies anybody would doubt or a truth anybody would believe," yet his sincere love of justice and his wide sympathy forced recognition of other phases of his work than his fun-making and saved him from being considered merely as a joker. He never descended to bad spelling and eccentricities to attract attention, and while he sacrificed immediate laughter, he won thereby an universal appeal. This quality of Mark Twain has carried his work abroad and made him a world artist.

But it was, after all, his ability to create character and his gift of narrative which distinguished him most clearly from the other humorists. While it is impossible to accept his statement in the *Literary Essays* that "the humorous story is American, the comic story is English and the witty story is French," his definition of the humorous story as one that "may be spun out to great length and may wander about as much as it pleases, and arrive nowhere in particular" is illuminating in its explanation of his strength and his weakness as a writer of fiction. Like Bret Harte he is best in his episodes, and it is through them that he built up the characters of Tom Sawyer, Huck Finn, Colonel Sellers, Tom Canty, Joan of Arc, those by which he will be best remembered. All but Colonel Sellers were under eighteen years of age.

He helped the cause of realism by his faithful representation of a civilization in Missouri which he knew; but, notwithstanding his denunciations of Scott and Cooper, he was really at home in a land of romance, and he could lead his readers into it best through the heart of a boy, whether that boy dreamt on the banks of the Mississippi of the mighty river flowing past him, or had visions in his den in Offal Court of the splendors of a princely castle. His wife's name for him, "Youth," reveals her thorough understanding of his nature. It was not because he failed to mature, however, but because he never grew old, that Mark Twain's fiction retains its vitality and makes its perennial appeal.

When he died in 1910 he left as definite an impression as any American writer of his generation. But the spontaneous and almost world-wide tributes during his centenary in 1935 were paid not so much to the novelist as to the great humorist who had added so largely to the joy of mankind.

CHAPTER XIII

WILLIAM DEAN HOWELLS AND THE ESTABLISHMENT OF REALISM

In the work of William Dean Howells, realism came into its own. His creative achievement was so preëminent for a quarter of a century that he became in a sense a standard rather than a competitor. As Clyde Fitch truly said, "It was the Howells Age." For while others were discussing the qualities that should belong to "the great American novel," he had quietly written it, and he had supplemented his creative achievement by a criticism that rivalled that of Poe in analysis and that of Lowell in constructive quality. As assistant editor and editor of *The Atlantic Monthly* from 1866 to 1881, and later from "The Editor's Study" and the "Easy Chair" in *Harper's Magazine,* he led a never ceasing crusade for truth to life in all forms of art. His cardinal virtues of simplicity and naturalness were reflected also in his farce-comedies which, acted by thousands of his countrymen, taught them good manners through their reproduction of conversation written by a playwright who might, under more favorable circumstances in the theatre, have become one of the foremost dramatists of his day.

His life was as sane and progressive as it was distinctly American. Born March 1, 1837, he came of pioneer stock that had transplanted its Welsh inheritance first to New York, then to Ohio. But it was to the East that he turned for inspiration. Primitive as the life of Ohio was— he has painted a vivid picture of it in *The Leatherwood God*—there was little of the wild or remote about it. It was for him and his parents a life of struggle, though the struggle was not for material prosperity, but for the opportunity for mental and spiritual progress.

As we learn from *My Year in a Log Cabin* (1893) and "The Country Printer" in *Impressions and Experiences* (1896), his education was largely that of his father's editorial room and printing-shop. Just as Emerson, Lowell, Hawthorne, Longfellow and Holmes were college-bred as a matter of course, so Howells, Mark Twain, Bret Harte, Gilder and others of their generation were practical printers. This practical knowledge of printing, helped him to secure the assistant editorship of *The Atlantic Monthly* in 1866, after he had returned from Italy.

The other great influence upon his early years was his wide reading. He has given a pleasant picture of the literary interest in Columbus in *My Literary Friends and Acquaintance* (1900) and in *Years of My Youth* (1916), and those who knew the serene poise and wide interests of one of the most truly cultivated men of his time can easily visualize him as a boy in the Ohio town, with its keen interest in the older civilizations and its pride in having at least one contributor to *The Atlantic Monthly*. It is seldom that we are privileged to follow so closely the influences that have shaped the tastes and achievements of a great novelist, but in the case of Howells the record has been provided by his autobiographical volumes. Not only in the books already mentioned, but also in *My Literary Passions* (1895) and in *Heroines of Fiction* (1901) we can see how the boy and the man selected the poets and novelists that fostered the innate preference for the truth and for the real presentation of it which remained his constant quality. Beginning with Goldsmith and Irving, continuing through Pope, Chaucer, Longfellow, and Tennyson, through Dickens, Thackeray, Eliot, and Trollope, he followed, aware that he was "of the Academy," until he had beaten out a way for himself to a manner that was his own.

The many speculations concerning the influence of the French and Russian novelists upon Howells may be set at rest by his own testimony to the present writer; expressed with that nice distinction in the choice of words which was so characteristic of him:

Harry James introduced me to Flaubert and Balzac, and then I read Turgenev and Tolstoy for myself; but I had already grown into my realistic method, and I was authorized rather than inspired by the Frenchmen.

It was this very rational way of taking life that prevented him from being a great poet, though it was as a poet that he first published. While *Venetian Life, Italian Journeys,* and *Tuscan Cities* are charming, to him the Bridge of Sighs was a "pathetic swindle" and Italy was a surface rather than a mine. His Venetian consulate was, however, invaluable to him. It gave him breadth of vision, it opened to him the international point of view, and it confirmed him in his estimate of American men and women.

His real life as a man of letters began in 1866, when he went to Boston as assistant editor of *The Atlantic Monthly*. The literary supremacy of Boston at that time was unquestioned. Besides *The Atlantic Monthly*, there were *The North American Review* under Lowell, *Every Saturday* under Aldrich, *Our Young Folks* under J. T. Trowbridge and Lucy Larcom. These dominated the magazine world of America, and into the circle which their editors drew around them Howells fitted easily. "My home is still among them," he wrote years afterward, "on this side and on that side of the line between the living and the dead which invisibly passes through all the streets of the cities of men."

How Howells came into fiction is illustrated in the essay-like story, "A Romance of Real Life." [1] He scrutinizes the material and the characters as he creates them: especially the second mate who represents himself as hunting his family upon his return from a two years' voyage to China, only to find his wife and baby dead. In a perfectly natural way, the teller of the story helps him and finds out for himself that the mate had really been imprisoned for bigamy and that his children wanted nothing to do with him. It is of course a deft attack on the romantic-idealistic story, and the crash of the picture drawn by the mate when his daughter tells the real facts is an argument for realism. This story also shows how Howells passed from the essay to the short story, for "A Romance of Real Life" is included in *Suburban Sketches* (1871), of which the remainder are descriptive essays.

Howells' first novel too grew naturally out of his descriptions of travel. *Their Wedding Journey* (1871) introduces two of his best drawn characters, Basil and Isabella March, on their wedding trip from Boston to New York, then, by way of Albany, to Niagara, Montreal, and Quebec. There is little plot; it is a record of impressions, in which Howells expresses his opinions on American and foreign civilizations, and in which he pays his respects to Irving, as they pass through scenes "that Irving has made part of the common dream land." Basil March is an honest, whimsical insurance broker, who, in order to be married, has given up a hope of becoming a writer. He is not too enthusiastic, yet he is interested in life in a healthy way—a man who will be brave in a crisis, but who is willing to let trifles drift and who refuses to become excited in the situations in which Isabella becomes flurried. He is the typical cultivated American without wealth. When he comes in contact

[1] *Atlantic Monthly*, March, 1870.

with French or English civilization, he is not overwhelmed nor does
he take the *nil admirari* attitude of Mark Twain. Isabella, his comple-
ment, affords Howells an opportunity to make some very keen observations on feminine character. If she is not so distinct as Basil, it is
not because she is colorless, but because she is more variable, more impulsive, and therefore less consistent.

During their journey the Marches meet Colonel Ellison, his wife
Fanny, and his cousin Kitty Ellison, from Erie Creek, New York, who
become the central characters of *A Chance Acquaintance* (1873). They
are contrasted with Miles Arbuton, a Bostonian who is made up of circumstances and tradition and has little personality. The love story between Kitty and Miles is not very thrilling, nor is it intended to be,
and their separation is no tragedy. Howells was still feeling for a
method in fiction, and he made use of his Italian experiences in *A Foregone Conclusion* (1875). This is a disappointing book; Florida Vervain
is rather colorless, and the priest who falls in love with her, Don Ippolito, is unreal. Henry Ferris, the American consul who is also a
painter, is well drawn, especially in his contempt for what he does not
understand, but the novel as a whole is a failure.

Much better was a story in the *Atlantic, Private Theatricals*,[2] which,
for some reason, Howells did not reprint. It contains a remarkable picture of a charming young widow, Rosabel Farrell, who is continually dramatizing every friend and every situation. She breaks up,
apparently with deliberation, a great friendship between two men, Gilbert and Easton, who have been comrades in the Civil War; becomes
engaged to Easton, without really loving him; lets Gilbert, who has
fallen in love with her also, see that she cares for him; and distributes
unhappiness to several other persons who are part of the background of
a New England farm during the summer season. Yet in the supreme
moment, she has the courage to tell Easton that she does not love him,
although she will marry him as she has promised, in a scene which is
memorable for its delicacy and reality. In this novel Howells showed
his ability at conversation which reveals more than it says. The last
interview between Mrs. Farrell and Mrs. Gilbert, the sister-in-law of
her fiancé, is superb in its flashes of revelation of character. The desperate need Mrs. Farrell has of counsel in her dilemma when she
recognizes that she loves Gilbert, and the appeal she makes to Mrs.

[2] November, 1875 to May, 1876. Published for the first time in 1921 as *Mrs. Farrell*.

Gilbert to send him away, are expressed in an unusual conversation in which the woman who has brought on a bad situation finds it too much for her. The final chapter, which sends Mrs. Farrell on the stage to make only a partial success, is another piece of shrewd analysis of feminine character. Among all the heroines of Howells, she remains an individual, one of the most real of his creations, an active not, as usual, a passive force.

The Lady of the Aroostook (1879) is the story of Lydia Blood, a Maine girl, who visits her aunt in Venice, and who by an accident becomes the only woman on the boat which gives the book its title. Here the contrast is between the Americans and the English, and Howells was on surer ground than in *A Foregone Conclusion*. Perhaps only those who have been privileged to attend a joint function of the English and American colonies on foreign soil can appreciate to the full Howells' description:

> The former oratory of the Palazzo Grinzelli, which served as the English chapel, was filled with travelers of both the English-speaking nationalities, as distinguishable by their dress as by their face. Lydia's aunt affected the English style, but some instinctive elegance betrayed her, and every English-woman there knew and hated her for an American, though she was a precisian in her liturgy, instant in all the responses and genuflexions.

The interest in the two novels laid in Italy, rested upon the American characters. Howells probably recognized this fact, for he returned to American soil and based his next novel, *The Undiscovered Country* (1880), upon a subject just then much in vogue, that of spiritualism. The characters of Dr. Boynton, half dupe and half charlatan, his daughter Egeria, whom he mesmerizes and through whom he conducts the seances, her lover Edward Ford, who exposes the tricks, are well drawn. The sordid quality of the atmosphere is accurately depicted, and indeed, while Howells' reasonable realistic attitude toward the supernatural prevents the creation of illusion, it makes his study important as a criticism of a recurrent phenomenon. Of the spiritualism of the 'seventies, he says truly that it failed through a materialistic basis; it gave no stimulus toward the conduct of life; it simply tried to show that there is a future life without any important deductions from that fact. *A Fearful Responsibility* (1881), a novelette dealing again with Americans in Italy, and *Dr. Breen's Practice* (1881), an amusing picture of a young woman physician, contained some discriminating pictures of the uncertainties and the subtler undercurrents of certainty in feminine nature, but they were still tentative in their artistic purpose. Yet a comparison with Elizabeth Stuart Phelps' novel of *Dr. Zay* (1883), or with Charles Reade's *A Woman Hater* (1877), shows the greater reality of Howells' treatment of the character of a woman physician.

With *A Modern Instance* (1882), Howells passed into his artistic maturity, commencing that series of remarkable studies of American character which established him as the foremost novelist since Hawthorne. He chose first the smart, young, unscrupulous newspaper man, Bartley Hubbard, an example of the newer generation that was pushing aside the journalist with a feeling for literature, like Evans in *A Woman's Reason,* and also displacing the less able if not less shifty variety which Dickens had portrayed in Jefferson Brick. Howells traced Hubbard's rise from an obscure New England town to his success in Boston and his failure on account of his inherent dishonesty. Bartley Hubbard is a type, but not merely of a class: he is a distinct personality. He has good points, among them his treatment of his jealous and foolish wife, Marcia, who has run away from her parents, Squire Gaylord and his wife, to marry Bartley. He has industry and ability; but from the time when he violates a confidence for the sake of a good story, his disintegration begins. There is no reformation; the events go on to the sordid end in a western city. *A Modern Instance* is a novel which at first tries the reader somewhat with detail, but finally the details blur and the purpose of the book becomes distinct. It is the story of average life, all the more terrible in its lesson because no lesson is preached. Bartley Hubbard is no villain—his weakness and selfishness might have been counterbalanced by his energy and industry and by his flashes of courage, had it not been for his lack of standards. He simply could not play fair, and he could not see why he was not playing fair. There are many notable passages; one of the finest leads to the last speech of Judge Gaylord, who in his old age has gone to the distant city where Bartley has fled. There Bartley has instituted divorce proceedings against Marcia. Ever since the marriage of his daughter, the squire has longed to tell his son-in-law his opinion of him; in defending her case, he rises to the opportunity, paying for it, however, with his life.

Howells' next novel, *A Woman's Reason* (1883), is a subtle study of feminine nature, of class feeling, and of social values in Boston.

Helen Harkness, suddenly left penniless by the death of her father, an apparently wealthy merchant, cannot adjust herself to conditions for which she has not been prepared. She can be honest, in returning a few thousands which do not belong to her, but she has nothing which the world wishes to purchase. Howells rather avoids than solves the problem by bringing her lover back to her at the end of the novel. There is some delightful satire, especially of Marion Butler, a friend of Helen, who "was very English in dress and had the effect of feeling as if she looked very English," and there is an international contrast in Lord Rainford, who falls in love with Helen but whom she does not marry. The novel has not, however, the breadth of *A Modern Instance,* and it seems now like a breathing space before Howells approached his masterpiece.

The Rise of Silas Lapham (1884) surpasses all other novels dealing with the American self-made man, because it is not a satire, but a well-rounded portrait. Silas Lapham is a plain New Englander, who has succeeded in his paint business and who has frozen out without compunction a partner, Rogers, who had proved incompetent. He is vulgar, too, in his bragging of the qualities of his paint, and his taste is remarkable, to say the least. But there is potential greatness in "the Colonel," as his wife and daughters call him, and this greatness arises from fundamental qualities, while his lack of culture is due largely to lack of opportunity. The man who had been recognized by his comrades as the best one to lead them across the river in the face of the enemy, the man who had made the "Persis brand" of paint the best paint on the market, rises in the hour of temptation to moral heights unreached even by his wife, who had been his conscience. It is an imaginative quality, which is hinted at only in the beginning and that finds its expression in his somewhat tiresome pursuit of the ideal paint, which, combined with his Puritan conscience, wins out in the end. The temptation that Rogers places before him is made as strong as possible. Lapham's competitors are pressing him, and he has lost money in speculation, when Rogers proposes to him that a milling property which Lapham has taken over from his former partner for a bad debt should be sold to an English syndicate, who are planning to establish a community there. Silas knows that a railroad needs the milling property and that, owing to its control of the situation, the road will force any owner to sell at a ruinous sacrifice. He declines to sell without informing the English agents of the situation, but when he finds that they are willing, for the sake of their commission, to risk their clients' money, he refuses to agree. Then Rogers makes his last appeal to Mrs. Lapham, that Silas has now the chance to repair the wrong he had done to him years before, and he begs Silas to sell the property to him and ask no questions. Here Mrs. Lapham, who cannot see beyond the personal question, deserts her husband, and he faces the problem alone. It may be objected that few men would have hesitated, but the history of American business has justified Howells in his conclusion of the episode. Lapham indulges in no heroics about it; he shows the same reserved feeling that he could not do otherwise that animated the hero of chivalry. The very large-ness of his success provides him with a substitute for the "noblesse oblige" of an earlier civilization. He had been at the top of his world and he could not stoop to do a mean thing. It was his habit of self-reliance, too, developed by the very fact of his material rise through his own efforts, that enables him to see his way through the cloud of sophistry in which even his wife is lost, and to decide that he cannot regain his fortune at the expense of his self-respect. It is a question whether in any other civilization than ours, a stage-driver would have developed this kind of self-reliance.

In the love story between Tom Corey and Penelope Lapham, Howells showed his knowledge of social values as well as his uncom-promising realism. Here his satire is directed at the romantic novel in which a suitor loves one sister while everyone, including the other sister, believes he is in love with the latter, which had so often been the means of exacting the useless self-sacrifice of two people to prevent one's being unhappy. Howells was not given to love stories. "The whole business of love and love making and marrying," he says, "is painted by the novelists in a monstrous disproportion to the other relations of life." But he showed in this novel that he could describe the tragedy that arises from Irene's mistake and could make his characters solve the situation to the ultimate happiness of Tom and Penelope. There are remarkable scenes in *Silas Lapham*. The dinner at the Coreys' in which Lapham gets drunk; the interview between him and Tom the next morning at the office; Penelope's refusal of Tom's offer of marriage and her final impulsive caress are memorable. But Howells does not seek "scenes" for it.

It was in this novel that the supreme quality of Howells' art began to reveal itself. Its very essence is moderation. It divests itself of all mere devices of ornament, and proceeds not by the selection of striking scenes, but by the insight into human character. Rogers, the arch tempter of Silas Lapham, has despaired of success, and in revenge writes to Mrs. Lapham that her husband is having an illicit affair with his secretary. She worries about it, then visits his office, and discovers his absolute innocence.

That night she showed him the anonymous scrawl which had kindled her fury against him. He turned it listlessly over in his hand. "I guess I know who it's from," he said, giving it back to her, "and I guess you do too, Persis."
"But how—how could he—"
"Mebbe he believed it," said Lapham, with patience that cut her more keenly that any reproach. "You did."

The human quality of Silas Lapham, of his daughters Penelope and Irene, of Tom Corey and his father, was shown decidedly in the artistic success of the dramatization of the novel, and its production by the Theatre Guild in New York in the autumn of 1919. Mr. Hackett's impersonation of Silas was a triumph, and as one watched the 'seventies coming to life again upon that stage, the union of what Tom Corey and Penelope Lapham represented seemed to say all that was needed to be said about the past and the future of the Republic.

To this gallery of fictional portraiture Howells next added, in the charming story of *Indian Summer* (1885), the figure of Lina Bowen. This quiet yet spirited heroine of Howells' is confronted with almost as difficult a problem in the affections as Lapham had experienced in his business relations. Lina Bowen, a widow residing in Florence, has to watch the growing fascination of her young charge, Imogene Graham, for Theodore Colville, a man of forty, who, flattered by the affection of Imogene, responds to the appeal of youth while he is really not in love with her. Mrs. Bowen not only recognizes that she has begun to care for Colville, but also that he really loves her, with the maturer passion which is even less able to recognize its growth than the more insistent desire of a younger man. Fettered by her responsibility as Imogene's guardian, she has to remain an almost helpless spectator of an affair which would mean unhappiness for both of her friends and for herself. The development of her nature under this trial until the intervention of a younger suitor for Imogene solves the problem is one of Howells' signal achievements. With that rare critical ability to distinguish his best work, he always selected *Indian Summer* as second only to *Silas Lapham*.

The Minister's Charge; or, The Apprenticeship of Lemuel Barker (1887) is a study of the responsibility of all of us for the lives that surround us. Lemuel Barker, who comes from a small town to Boston to make his way as a writer, is a real person. He has no great ability; when he presents himself at the home of Mr. Sewell, the Unitarian clergyman, and expects the latter to arrange his career for him, even the most unsympathetic reader can visualize Mr. Sewell's dismay. Lemuel Barker is taken through many adventures and returns at last to his home town without the fame of which he dreamed. There are episodes which are so real that they must stir the conscience in nearly all of us, such as the way Sewell gets rid of Barker one night when he comes in his distress to seek the minister's help, and Sewell, who is busy with his sermon for the next day, is in despair when he thinks of the tiresome interview ahead of him. But *The Minister's Charge* is not one of the great books, for Howells made the mistake of treating a tiresome hero seriously. For comedy Lemuel Barker would have been fine material. Howells next proved his versatility by the brilliant social comedy of *April Hopes* (1888). Seldom does he make the love story of youth his main theme, but the contrasted temperaments of Dan Mavering, fickle and superficial, yet generous and sensible, and Alice Pasmer, with more depth, yet too intense for her own happiness or that of anyone else, provides an opportunity for the breaking and renewal of an engagement which ends in a marriage that will probably not be happy ever afterwards. There is delightful social satire in *April Hopes;* the description of the way rumor spreads concerning the broken engagement is almost perfect of its kind. Yet Howells never lets the background submerge the two central characters. In *Annie Kilburn* (1888) Howells returned to New England town life. The three elements in such a town —the older, solid inhabitants, of which Annie Kilburn, a girl of thirty-one, is representative; the "summer people," satirized cleverly in Mrs. Munger; and the laboring class—present a complex social problem which Howells makes no attempt to solve. The delightful situation in which Mrs. Munger proposes to give a dramatic performance for the benefit of the needy, followed by an entertainment from which they would be excluded, is sketched with Howells' usual skill. He emphasizes the necessity of justice rather than charity to those who work without much margin, and he has little mercy for those who make the necessities of others a social playground. There are many well-drawn characters in *Annie Kilburn:* Peck, the orthodox clergyman; Putney, the lawyer who drinks too much but who routs the manufacturer, Gerrish, when the latter is trying to take away Peck's pulpit because he is too independent; and Dr. Morrell, the amiable onlooker, who marries Annie in the end.

The change in Howells' residence to New York City was reflected in 1889 in *A Hazard of New Fortunes.* Basil and Isabella March come to New York, where he is to edit a magazine. Dreyfoos, the vulgar parvenu, who owns the paper, his wife, his son Conrad, and his daughters are etched with skill, as are also Lindau, a German revolutionary, Fulkerson, the business manager, and Beaton, an artist. Beaton is one of the best drawn painters in modern fiction. The unreliability of his nature, his hesitation between his love for his art and his desire for wealth, his self-pity at his own growing moral and artistic degradation are admirably portrayed. March meets a moral crisis when Dreyfoos wishes him to break with Lindau, who is too much of an anarchist to suit a member of the "shoddy aristocracy." March wins quietly and Dreyfoos, after his son is killed in a labor riot, sells the paper to him and Fulkerson. Basil March develops steadily in the novel and Howells rose to the presentation of a metropolitan life of more complexity than had been portrayed previously in his fiction.

In *The Shadow of a Dream* (1890) March represents the realist's position of common sense against the morbid influence of a dream. He tries to persuade Hermia Faulkner, a widow who wishes to marry the Reverend James Nevill, that she must not sacrifice their happiness because her husband had had a recurrent dream in which his funeral took place at the same time as their wedding. The art with which the actual telling of the dream to the reader is postponed, thereby keeping up the suspense, is the most noteworthy element in this novelette. *An Imperative Duty* (1892), a study of the race problem, is one of the weakest of all Howells' novels. His picture of the Negro and his arguments for miscegenation are best forgotten.

There is a keenness in the analysis of the defaulter Northwick, in *The Quality of Mercy* (1892), which atones somewhat for the looseness of plot. The many departures of trusted financial officials for Canada at that time probably suggested to Howells that he portray the state of mind of such a man. Northwick's flight is the climax of long years of defalcation and clever manipulation of his books; his determination to depart with about forty thousand dollars still in his hands as treasurer and to retrieve his fortunes and repay all he owes is not improbable. The most realistic touch comes with his failure to do anything with this money, and his final return and death are logical also. It is another ironic picture of the futility of the man without character but so much interested was Howells in his central figure that he failed to make his daughters or any other characters memorable. The scene is Hatboro, but it is not painted with the same fidelity as in *Annie Kilburn*.

The World of Chance (1893) is an important document in Howells' development; for through the career of the young writer, Shelley Ray, he reaffirms his belief in the principles of realism. The part chance plays in the lives of everyone is the theme of the book. Ray comes to New York with his novel, *A Modern Romeo;* Howells depicts with satirical accuracy the way the hopes, fears, and enthusiasms of the creator of fiction die before the passive resistance of the publishing houses toward an unknown author. The final acceptance of the novel by Brandreth, the publisher who had first refused it, on account of his irritation at his failure to secure the work of the best-known novelists; the way the book hung fire; the favorable review in a leading journal due to the absence of the regular reviewer; and the accident which brought *A Modern Romeo* to the notice of his substitute—all these and other incidents connected with the fate of a book are told with a delightful humor that still showed no sign of decline. For Howells was writing of things which he knew intimately, and his own early struggles were probably reflected in Ray's efforts to become established. Howells does not content himself with a mere recital of facts, however. His conclusion is "Nothing, then, that seemed chance was really chance. It was the operation of a law so large that we caught a glimpse of its vast orbit once or twice in a lifetime. It was Providence." It is this ability of Howells to evolve a truth out of facts which marked him out from the many mere photographers who have followed him. His treatment of the love episode between Ray and Peace Denton is masterly in its realism. The great affection he feels for her, in which there is no glamour of passion, and his qualified proposal to her, which she rejects and which leaves him with a sense of mingled regret and relief, will strike a responsive chord in nearly any man's memory. The inconclusive ending of the love story may have prevented *The World of Chance* from being one of Howells' most popular novels, but Howells was quite right when he said, "People expected love to begin mysteriously but they did not like it to end so: though life itself began mysteriously and ended so." Ray is much more appealing than Bartley Hubbard or Lemuel Barker, and yet he is just as real. There is a decided falling off in *The Coast of Bohemia* (1893), in which Howells brings a girl to New York to study painting. The people are not inherently interesting; they seem typical rather than real. Perhaps the introduction to the Biographical Edition reveals the reason. Howells deliberately studied an atmosphere of which he knew comparatively little, while in *The World of Chance* he was familiar with every step of Ray's progress.

In 1894 the leader of the realistic movement became in *A Traveler from Altruria* an idealist, and presented a treatise on social conditions under the guise of a novel. All the characters are abstractions, beginning with the visitor, Mr. Homos, and including the various types, the banker, the clergyman, the lawyer, the doctor, the professor of political economy, and the retired manufacturer, with whom he converses about his country, Altruria, which is delightfully vague in its geography. The main body of the novel consists of the satire of America through the answers to the traveller's questions concerning the United States. Howells' satire is, of course, keen, but as fiction the book does not rank with his important work. After a slight novelette, *The Day of Their Wedding*, Howells wrote one of his best stories in *The Landlord at Lion's Head* (1897). The central character, Jeff Durgin, a boy who grows up in the mountains of New England where his family keep a hotel, and who is sent to Harvard, remains as one of Howells' living portraits. He is fundamentally selfish, curiously true at times and at others fickle, unafraid of anything, and with a certain charm which leads people to like him while he is with them and to criticize him when the spell is broken. Harvard does little for him; he remains at heart primitive and he returns at last to his own place. One of the best episodes is his flirtation with Bessie Lynde, a Boston girl who is slightly passé but to whom he is an experience which relieves the boredom of her existence. She is quite a match for him in a sentimental adventure in which neither is damaged. Jeff Durgin is one who demands that life give him what he desires, and he usually gets it. Howells drew in this story some of his striking antitheses. "Society," he observes, "is interested in a man's future, not his past, as it is interested in a woman's past, not her future." The Marches lighten with their conversation the slight novel *An Open-eyed Conspiracy* (1897), laid at Saratoga. To any lover of the theatre, *The Story of a Play* (1898) is a fascinating account of the difficulties a playwright faces in the production of his work. Howells was on familiar ground, for his experience with Lawrence Barrett in writing *A Counterfeit Presentment* and *Yorick's Love* had acquainted him with the temperamental nature of the actor. Launcelot Godolphin, the actor-manager who takes Maxwell's play and at first succeeds in it, is a splendid reproduction of a romantic stage personage. He has the patronizing attitude toward a playwright that was characteristic of the time, but Maxwell also has to contend with his wife's jealousy of the leading actress, not only as a woman, but as the stage interpreter of the love story which is based upon her own. It is a delightful turn in the plot which appeases Mrs. Maxwell's jealousy through Godolphin's realization that the actress is stealing the applause from him, so that her presence is no longer required in the cast.

Ragged Lady (1899), although it has a charming heroine, is not important. More significant because it suggests a contrast with Howells' first novel is *Their Silver Wedding Journey* (1899), which takes the Marches to Europe, principally to Germany. Some of the characters they meet on shipboard are well drawn, particularly Burnamy, a young newspaper man, and General Triscoe, the expatriated American. The novel represents the educated American's view of Europe, appreciative but feeling the essentially more human aspect of life in the United States. The Americans are not brought into contact with the European social organization; Europe remains scenery to them. So it does in *The Kentons* (1902), in which an Ohio family go abroad to cure Ellen Kenton of an infatuation. Curiously enough, Howells states that the Kentons had never been abroad, although he had taken them there in a short story "At The Sign of the Savage" in 1881.

Letters Home (1903) is a narrative told by means of letters written by a number of people who have come to New York City from Boston, from rural New York, and from Iowa, but the story is not one of his important productions.

In *The Son of Royal Langbrith* (1904) Howells' art rose once more to its higher level. It is a story of the after effects of a man's crimes and of the way in which circumstances conspire to prevent the discovery of his misdeeds. When the novel opens Royal Langbrith has been dead for nineteen years. His son James has been brought up by his mother to idealize his father's memory, and with a recognition of the value of illusion, Mrs. Langbrith protects her husband's memory from the desire of Dr. Anther to reveal him as the scoundrel he had really been. The preparations James Langbrith makes for the memorial to his father are delightfully ironic. Perhaps best of all is the way in which Dr. Anther's love for Mrs. Langbrith keeps him from telling the secret and the gradual fading away of his desire to enlighten James Langbrith. Realism could hardly go farther than the scene in which John Langbrith, Royal's brother, who has belonged to the conspiracy of silence concerning Royal's character for nearly twenty years, and has even conducted the business, finally blurts out the truth. He meets James on a train and, his nervous dyspepsia having been incautiously exposed to a luncheon on the Boston and Maine railroad, his physical suffering makes it impossible for him to bear the continued eulogy of his brother from his nephew's lips. Even then, when the inherent honesty of James Langbrith makes him wish to let the community know of his father's real character, he is persuaded by his fiancée not to do so, and Royal Langbrith remains a symbol of respectability in his grave. Between this novel and Howells' last significant work came a slight novelette, *Miss Bellard's Inspiration* (1905); a somewhat better story, *Fennel and Rue* (1908); and a sequel to *A Traveler from Altruria*, *Through the Eye of the Needle* (1907), in which Altruria is described by letters from an American woman who has married Mr. Homos. Through a servant Howells puts his finger on the weakness of the communistic scheme of Altruria. "Everybody wants to have something of his own, and the trouble seems to come from that."

In his last novel, *The Leatherwood God* (1916), Howells returned to the traditions of his early life in Ohio to represent with success the reactions of a comparatively primitive society to a religious impostor, Joseph Dylks, whose career he derived from the narrative of Judge Taneyhill. The story is laid in the 'thirties, when emotional life was a relief from the hard conditions of the frontier, and Dylks has little difficulty in mounting by degrees from the rank of a prophet to that of a deity, until the necessity of performing a miracle brings him to his end. He is defeated by the rougher elements of unbelief and the sceptic

Squire Braile, who is a delightfully sarcastic person. The novel is made concrete by Dylks' discovery that among the women of Leatherwood Creek there is his wife, who had believed him dead and had married again. The strange influence he had over her and his son, and even over his brother-in-law, who distrusts him, is well indicated. *The Leatherwood God* is important not only in its revelation of Howells' unimpaired strength at the end of his career in fiction, but as his only excursion into the past. His posthumous novel, *The Vacation of the Kelwyns* (1920), had been written about 1900, and is laid in a rural district in New Hampshire during a summer in the 'seventies. The contrast between Professor Kelwyn's family and the owners of the house they rent is amusing, and there is some power in the character drawing, especially in that of Parthenope Brooke, a forthright young woman. Most interesting, however, are the passages in which he satirizes the novels on which Parthenope had been reared, which "inculcated a varying doctrine of eager conscience, romanticized actuality, painful devotion, and bullied adoration, with auroral gleams of religious sentimentality."

Howells' short stories are relatively less important than his novels. They are distributed through his career, two being printed with *A Fearful Responsibility* in 1881, but the best belong to the later period. In the stories included in *A Pair of Patient Lovers* (1901), the methods are the same as in his novels. Moral questions are propounded, especially those involving the responsibility of human beings for the difficulties of others. The relentless pressure of circumstances by which a woman dominates the life of another is the theme of the title story, and perhaps the best, "A Circle in the Water," shows how a criminal whose dishonesty has imperilled the career of Basil March and shadowed that of his own daughter, is forgiven by all he had wronged, through that liberality which flowed from Howells' own nature to that of his characters.

Questionable Shapes (1903) and *Between the Dark and the Daylight* (1907) are in general stories of the supernatural. Howells makes the mistake of discussing it, often through a psychologist, Wanhope, and the sceptical attitude of the latter is obviously not the right one to establish the belief, at least temporarily, in the supernatural, which is essential to its artistic presentation. Yet there are fine passages such as the description in "The Angel of the Lord," of Ormond's reconciliation to the idea of death, and it is interesting to note Howells' reference to

Longfellow's "Two Angels," written on the occasion of Mrs. Lowell's death.

That the art of Howells was conscious makes it the more significant. He always knew what he was doing. In his first novel he outlined his theory of fiction and he repeated more than once the description of what he believed to be the proper material for treatment:

It was in all respects an ordinary carful of human beings, and it was perhaps the more worthy to be studied on that account. As in literature the true artist will shun the use even of real events if they are of an improbable character, so the sincere observer of man will not desire to look upon his heroic or occasional phases, but will seek him in his habitual moods of vacancy and tiresomeness. To me, at any rate, he is at such times very precious; and I never perceive him to be so much a man and a brother as when I feel the pressure of his vast, natural, unaffected dullness. Then I am able to enter confidently into his life and inhabit there, to think his shallow and feeble thoughts, to be moved by his dumb, stupid desires, to be dimly illumined by his stinted inspirations, to share his foolish prejudices, to practice his obtuse selfishness. Yes, it is a very amusing world, if you do not refuse to be amused; and our friends were very willing to be entertained.[3]

Twenty years later he made Shelley Ray, in *The World of Chance*, think aloud:

If he had made a book which appealed to the feeling and knowledge of the great, simply conditioned, sound hearted, common schooled American mass whom the Simpsons represented, he had made his fortune. He put aside that other question, which from time to time presses upon every artist, whether he would rather please the few who despise the judgment of the many, or the many who have no taste, but somehow have in their keeping the touchstone by which a work of art proves itself a human interest and not merely a polite pleasure.

This is the democratic theory of art. One may agree with it or not, but it is at least intelligible, and he had some great models in English fiction to urge in justification. Defoe, Richardson, Dickens, and George Eliot held similar theories, and it was the author of *Amos Barton* who said:

Depend upon it, you would gain unspeakably if you would learn with me to see some of the poetry and the pathos, the tragedy and the comedy, lying in the experience of a human soul that looks out through dull grey eyes, and that speaks in a voice of quite ordinary tones.

[3] *Their Wedding Journey*, pp. 86–87.

This democratic theory of art permitted Howells a wide range not only in his choice of individual types of character, but also in his portrayal of American life in its general social contrasts. He deals with life in many aspects, the Coreys, Bellinghams, and Hilarys illustrating the patrician caste of Boston, the Marches the people of breeding but not of wealth, and the newly rich being represented in the Laphams and the Dreyfooses. He treats less frequently the comfortably established provincials of the stripe of Annie Kilburn or the Gaylords, touching here and there the poorer classes, such as the Durgins, but dealing only rarely and then for but a short time with the lowest economic strata, as in the beginning of *The Minister's Charge*.

Howells' attitude toward the patrician is unabashed, tolerant, and slightly amused. In the passage at arms between the Laphams and the Coreys, he has described cleverly the clash between people in trade and the descendants of people in trade, and he represents Corey himself as seeing the weakness of his caste. Howells has admirably revealed the difficulty which a woman of that class finds in facing certain actualities of life in *A Woman's Reason*. One of his subtlest studies, the character of Bessie Lynde in *The Landlord at Lion's Head*, is drawn from this group. But one feels that Howells' real interest does not lie in this direction. There are certain elements in the life of those whose social position is secure and whose material wealth makes repose of mind easy, and leisure an active and not a passive mood, which Howells does not develop at all.

What he was interested in was the middle class, for the same reason perhaps that Dickens chose to portray them, because they represent their feelings more openly and therefore provide more appropriate material for fiction. He realized, however, the vast contrasts within this broad class; he has described some of them cleverly in *Annie Kilburn*.

In the process of that expansion from a New England village to an American town of which Putney spoke, Hatboro' had suffered one kind of deterioration which Annie could not help noticing. She remembered a distinctly intellectual life, which might still exist in its elements, but which certainly no longer had as definite expression. There used to be houses in which people, maiden aunts and hale grandmothers, took a keen interest in literature, and read the new books and discussed them, some time after they had ceased to be new in the publishing centres, but whilst they were still not old. But now the grandmothers had died out, and the maiden aunts had faded in, and she could not find just such houses anywhere in Hatboro'. The decay of the Unitarians as a sect perhaps had something to do with the literary lapse of the place: their highly intellectualised belief had favoured taste in a direction where the more ritualistic and emotional religions did not promote it; and it is certain that they were no longer the leading people.

It would have been hard to say just who these leading people were. The old political and juristic pre-eminence which the lawyers had once enjoyed was a tradition; the learned professions yielded in distinction to the growing manufacturers; the situation might be summed up in the fact that Colonel Marvin of the shoe interest and Mr. Wilmington now filled the place once held by Judge Kilburn and Squire Putney. The social life in private houses had undoubtedly shrunk; but it had expanded in the direction of church sociables, and it had become much more ecclesiastical in every way, without becoming more religious. As formerly, some people were acceptable, and some were not; but it was, as everywhere else, more a question of money; there was an aristocracy and a commonalty, but there was a confusion and a more ready convertibility in the materials of each.

The realistic writer who describes contemporary life must become a satirist to a certain extent. Howells chose for his keenest satire the class which rose into financial prominence after the Civil War, owing to the commercial expansion caused by the discoveries of new wants, the increase in manufactures due to a decline in the shipping industries, and the general readjustment of conditions which came after the conflict. Many large fortunes, too, had been made in contracts during the war, and the "shoddy aristocracy," as it was often called, was a choice subject for satire. It will be an interesting period for the social historian, when we get far enough away from it to view it correctly. To many it still seems a vast desert of crudity, bad taste, and political corruption; a day of the breaking down of old traditions, of quick making of fortunes, of consequent vulgarity and pretence. It was an inevitable result of conditions of the war, however. The great Southern landholding families and the great Northern merchant princes both saw their possessions swept away, one by the war, the other by the tariff. The social standards they had helped to make and preserve were also swept away in part. With the unsettling of traditions, the disturbance of artistic ideals of all kinds set in, and this was unfavorable to literature, as it was to painting and to architecture.

It was less disturbing to literature, for the satirist had his field provided for him, and there can be no question of the ability of Howells as a satirist. His books are full of clever epigrams, hitting our weaknesses, our self-deceptions, our compromises with our consciences, our relations with other men and other women. Some of his most interesting remarks are concerned with the relations of men and women. Thus in speaking of an elderly man, Rufus Kilburn, he remarks:

Till he began to break, after they went abroad, he had his own way in everything; but as men grow old or infirm they fall into subjection to their womenkind; their rude wills yield in the suppler insistence of the feminine purpose; they take the colour of the feminine moods and emotions; the cycle of life completes itself where it began, in helpless dependence upon the sex; and Rufus Kilburn did not escape the common lot.

The style of Howells, however, is not only well fitted to be a satiric vehicle. It has also a sustained power which cannot be well illustrated by quotation, but which by its clarity, its force, and its finish keeps the reader always interested. A passage from *April Hopes* will at least indicate this quality:

It has been the experience of every one to have some alien concern come into his life and torment him with more anxiety than any affair of his own. This is, perhaps, a hint from the infinite sympathy which feels for us all that none of us can hope to free himself from the troubles of others, that we are each bound to each by ties which, for the most part, we cannot perceive, but which, at the moment their stress comes, we cannot break.

It was not satire alone, therefore, that secured Howells his audience. It was his really deep insight into certain phases of human character, his careful study of human emotions, of human purposes and motives, his kindly, tolerant attitude toward mankind, the probability of his events and characters, and the art with which his plot, slight as it often is, works out logically and inevitably to the destined end. He never made use of the easy "God out of the car," he even avoided the use of striking situations which he might have employed, he resolutely determined to represent the human comedy as it is; and as a result his novels form a contribution to our literature and to the study of our national life which it is difficult to over-estimate.

On the occasion of his seventy-fifth birthday in 1912, at the dinner given to celebrate his unique position in American letters, a letter [4] was read from Henry James, in which his great friend and rival analyzed brilliantly the contribution of Howells. Among many other things he said:

[4] *The Letters of Henry James*, ed. by Percy Lubbock (1920), Vol. II, pp. 221–226.

The *real* affair of the American case and character, as it met your view and brushed your sensibility, that was what inspired and attached you, and, heedless of foolish flurries from other quarters, of all wild or weak slashings of the air and wavings in the void, you gave yourself to it with an incorruptible faith.

A little further on he added:

However, these things take us far, and what I wished mainly to put on record is my sense of that unfailing, testifying truth in you which will keep you from ever being neglected. The critical intelligence—if any such fitful and discredited light may still be conceived as within our sphere—has not at all begun to render you its tribute. The more inquiringly and perceivingly it shall still be projected upon the American life we used to know, the more it shall be moved by the analytic and historic spirit, the more indispensable, the more a vessel of light, will you be found.

He had his reward not only in the approval of his countrymen and the gratitude which many a young apostle of realism felt for the man who was never too busy to help a comrade less fortunate than himself. Recognition from abroad came also. As early as 1879 Turgenev had appreciated his genius,[5] generously speaking of his writings as "superior to those of anyone now living," and Taine's discriminating criticism of *Silas Lapham*, "c'est le meilleur roman écrit par un Américain, le plus semblable à ceux de Balzac," [6] was written in connection with its translation into French in 1888. By that time he had secured his position abroad as a world artist, which remained unshaken at his death in 1920.

It was not only in his fiction but also in his criticism that he led the fight for truth in art and, even more important, that he revealed the limitations of the realistic method. It was just because he was so familiar with the great French and Russian novelists that he could avoid the pitfalls into which they might have led him. It was our good fortune that to him realism meant the treatment of real life in its most important aspects, that he never lost the sense of the significant in order to avoid the charge of treating the obvious, and that he resolutely set his face against the celebration of the sordid holes and corners of life in the false idea that this was realism. He ran cheerfully the risk of being called "bourgeois" and "parochial," knowing that he shared the danger with some other great masters of English fiction, and he carried the war

---

[5] See letter from President Hayes, *Life in Letters of William Dean Howells*, Vol. I, p. 280.
[6] *Ibid.*, Vol. I, p. 412.

into Africa in that passage in *Criticism and Fiction* which should be a bugle-call to all those who refuse to acknowledge that the introduction of the methods of comparative anatomy and experimental pathology into literature is a notable achievement:

English and American readers require of a novelist whom they respect unquestionable proof of his seriousness, if he proposes to deal with certain phases of life; they require a sort of scientific decorum. He can no longer expect to be received on the ground of entertainment only; he assumes a higher function, something like that of a physician or a priest, and they expect him to be bound by laws as sacred as those of such professions; they hold him solemnly pledged not to betray them or abuse their confidence. If he will accept the conditions, they give him their confidence, and he may then treat to his greater honor, and not at all to his disadvantage, of such experiences, such relations of men and women as George Eliot treats in *Adam Bede,* in *Daniel Deronda,* in *Romola,* in almost all her books; such as Hawthorne treats in *The Scarlet Letter;* such as Dickens treats in *David Copperfield;* such as Thackeray treats in *Pendennis,* and glances at in every one of his fictions; such as most of the masters of English fiction have at some time treated more or less openly. It is quite false or quite mistaken to suppose that our novels have left untouched these most important realities of life. They have only not made them their stock in trade; they have kept a true perspective in regard to them; they have relegated them in their pictures of life to the space and place they occupy in life itself, as we know it in England and America.

It is perhaps after all for this exquisite sense of proportion, for his unfaltering recognition of fundamental values both in life and in literature that Howells will ultimately be remembered.

CHAPTER XIV

HENRY JAMES AND THE FICTION OF INTERNATIONAL RELATIONS

It was perhaps a happy accident that the two leaders of the realistic movement in American fiction should have chosen such different material. While Howells, with deeper insight into American life, was preoccupied with the opportunities that life afforded, Henry James chose deliberately the contrasts between American and foreign civilizations as a means of providing characters for which those racial distinctions would form an illuminating background. It is only fair, therefore, to judge him in terms of his success in interpreting characters and situations not only in and for themselves, but also as true or false to the national traits of the races he selects. The novelist who deals with international contrasts must keep himself constantly in touch with the various elements in his complicated and difficult task. Not only knowledge but also sympathy, which depends upon knowledge even if it does not always follow it, is essential to preserve that balance of understanding without which an international contrast loses reason for existence.

At first glance, the education and experience of Henry James seem to have been designed to give him the varied outlook needed for his later effort. Born in New York City in 1843, his education was deeply affected by the theory of his father, Henry James, Senior, that life in its reality was to be found across the sea. His son has made it clear that the fortune left by the founder of the family, William James, an Irishman, who came to this country shortly after the Revolution, permitted his descendants to live in an atmosphere ignorant of business. Any atmosphere of which Henry James, Senior, was the determining factor must have been stimulating, and the novelist as a child met Bryant, Willis, Curtis, Ripley, and other writers. He was fond of the theatre and his first compositions seem to have been dramatic. From the age of twelve he was taken from one school to another, in Geneva, Paris, Bonn, and other places. In 1860, while living at Newport, he met John La

Farge, who introduced him to Balzac and Mérimée and during the years 1862 and 1863, while registered at the Harvard Law School, he listened to Lowell's lectures on literature. It was an education which unfitted him for sympathy with the expanding economic conditions in the United States, and the political corruption of the 'sixties and 'seventies horrified a nature which had no love of combat and no crusading spirit. He was unable to see the wide contrasts in the social organization of his native country, and he sought refuge in a civilization where values were established through long usage, where changes in social and financial status, being more difficult of accomplishment, presented opportunities for tragedy and comedy that were absent in the more fluid life in the United States.

Upon a closer scrutiny, however, the experience of Henry James is revealed as much narrower than is generally supposed. He felt this keenly, for, as he writes to his brother William in 1903:

I have practically never travelled at all—having never been economically able to; I've only gone, for short periods, a few times—so much fewer than I've wanted—to Italy: never anywhere else that I've seen every one about me here (who is, or was, anyone) perpetually making for. These visions I've had, one by one, all to give up—Spain, Greece, Sicily, any glimpse of the East, or in fact of anything; even to the extent of rummaging about in France; even to the extent of trudging about, a little, in Switzerland. Counting out my few dips into Italy, there has been no time at which *any* "abroad" was financially convenient or possible.[1]

After 1869, except for occasional visits, he made his home in London or at Rye, in Sussex, and his point of view became increasingly that of an expatriate until his pathetic gesture in becoming a British subject in 1916 was only a concrete expression of an alienation from his native scene and an absorption into English life which had become as complete as such a process can ever be. It was in fact only England that he came to know well, so far as social life was concerned. Much as he loved Italy, he writes to Grace Morton in 1874, "I have been nearly a year in Italy and have hardly spoken to an Italian creature save washerwomen and waiters."[2]

His life in Paris during 1875 and 1876 encountered, too, the closed

[1] *Letters of Henry James*, Vol. I, pp. 417–418.
[2] *Ibid.*, Vol. I, p. 36.

atmosphere of France. While he met Flaubert and through him Edmund de Goncourt, Daudet, de Maupassant, and Zola, they apparently gave him little. "I have seen almost nothing of the literary fraternity," he writes Howells in May, 1876, "and there are fifty reasons why I should not become intimate with them. I don't like their wares, and they don't like any others." [3] And he tells William James in July, "I have got nothing important out of Paris nor am likely to." [4] Of the social life of Paris he apparently saw at this time practically nothing. The international contrasts in the fiction of Henry James which are based on real knowledge must be limited, then, to those between America and England. How effective these were can only be judged by a review of his work.

Henry James began his fiction with "The Story of a Year," in the *Atlantic Monthly* for March, 1865. During his entire career he continued to write short stories and novelettes, and, owing to his growing habit of drawing out a theme to its ultimate limits, it would not be profitable to attempt to differentiate between these two types. They can more easily be disinguished from his novels, yet they can best be treated not as a distinct product but rather in groups as they occur throughout his career. "The Story of a Year" is of no intrinsic importance, being the account of a rather shallow girl whose lover goes to the Civil War and who is untrue to her engagement. From 1865 to 1875 James published twenty-four short stories, of which only six were included in *A Passionate Pilgrim and Other Tales* (1875), his first book. During these years he was experimenting with varying success in the treatment of native and foreign material. The study of character after the manner of Hawthorne is represented in "The Romance of Certain Old Clothes," [5] a clear and well balanced contrast between two sisters who become the wives of the same man, and the supernatural revenge of the first wife upon her successor for violating her property is all the more effective for not being explained. The effect of the supernatural as a background to an impending family doom is not badly established in "De Grey," [6] laid in New York City in 1820. "De Grey" belongs also to another group of these early stories, those in which a change in the relations of characters is brought about by a sorrow caused by loss or

[3] *Letters of Henry James*, Vol. I, p. 49.
[4] *Letters of Henry James*, Vol. I, p. 51.
[5] *Atlantic Monthly*, February, 1868.
[6] *Atlantic Monthly*, July, 1868.

death. Among the best of these are "Poor Richard," [7] the story of a young man who, through a lie, prevents the woman he loves from receiving the last visit of his rival before he goes to war, and "My Friend Bingham," [8] in which the accidental killing of the child of a young widow leads to George Bingham's marriage with her.

James was concerned from the beginning with the relations of an artist to his work, and one of his finest stories is "The Madonna of the Future," [9] a study of a painter who worships his ideal of a woman for twenty years, while she grows old and coarse, never understanding him. Already he was acquiring that mastery of prose style which enabled him to write:

> He took his hint, of course, and the young woman, possibly sat smiling before his canvas. But, meanwhile the painter's idea had taken wings. No lovely human outline could claim it to vulgar fact. He saw the fair form made perfect; he rose to the vision without tremor, without effort of wing; he communed with it face to face, and resolved into finer and lovelier truth the purity which completes it as the perfume completes the rose. That's what they call idealism; the word's vastly abused, but the thing is good.

James had not therefore by any means repudiated the romantic selection of material. In fact, *Gabrielle de Bergerac* [10] is laid in the period just before the French Revolution. But his analysis of the heroine's character and the fine phrasing are what interest the reader rather than the historic background.

The stories laid on foreign soil dealt at first with American characters. "Travelling Companions" [11] is noteworthy for the exquisite description of Leonardo's Last Supper, with which it opens, and because it is one of the few love stories which ends by a scene of acceptance, but Italy is only the background. In "A Passionate Pilgrim," [12] however, the American, Clement Searle, really comes into contrast with his English relations and does not suffer, even in his manners, in comparison with them. In fact, he comes off much better than the American, Scrope, does in "Adina," [13] when his ruthlessness results in his losing Adina, his fiancée, to the young Italian, Angelo Beati.

[7] *Atlantic Monthly*, June–August, 1867.
[8] *Atlantic Monthly*, March, 1867.
[9] *Atlantic Monthly*, March, 1873.
[10] *Atlantic Monthly*, July–September, 1869. Published in book form in 1918.
[11] *Atlantic Monthly*, November and December, 1870.
[12] *Atlantic Monthly*, March–April, 1871.
[13] *Scribner's Magazine*, May–June, 1874.

Perhaps the most interesting of these early international contrasts is *Madame de Mauves*.[14] Here Longmore, the American, falls in love with Madame de Mauves, an American who had married, when quite young, a Frenchman whom she idealized and who neglects her. Indeed, he lets Longmore know through his sister that he is not averse to the American's devotion to his wife, since it covers his own tracks. Madame de Mauves, however, appeals to Longmore not to bring his ideals down to the level of M. de Mauves, and he departs. The story ends in melodrama, but the contrast of the conscience of the American and the polish of the French, while a bit conventional, is successfully established.

Although Henry James considered *Roderick Hudson* his first novel, *Watch and Ward* (1871) [15] really takes that place. It is a clear, straightforward story, with no distinction of plot. Roger Lawrence, the central character, is a fairly rich, old young man, of temperate life, who is constantly being used by his friends. He is as unromantic as a hero could well be; it is significant that Henry James' first novel dealt with familiar material which was treated in a realistic manner. He had been developing steadily in his short stories toward this realism of treatment, and even when he dealt with the supernatural or the French Revolution he had demonstrated the possibility of combining romantic material with realism of character drawing. In *Watch and Ward*, Roger Lawrence brings up the little girl accidentally left to him, with tenderness and fidelity, which flower into love, only to find her preferring a younger man. He meets that situation with quiet courage and good sense that finally rescue her from an unfortunate infatuation and lead to his ultimate reward. Lawrence is a preliminary sketch for a more finished portrait in the character of Rowland Mallet in *Roderick Hudson* (1876). Rowland Mallet has also a generous nature and a long suffering patience, but what distinguishes him and Roger Lawrence from the usual hero of American fiction is his unlimited leisure. James' family fortunes and his long European sojourn as well as his reading of English and Continental fiction had unfitted him for the development of an American in terms of his business career. With an artist he could deal, however, and he drew in Roderick Hudson, the young sculptor whom Rowland finds in Northampton, Massachusetts, eating his heart

---

[14] *Galaxy*, February–March, 1874.
[15] *Atlantic Monthly*, August–December, 1871; published as a book in 1878.

out, and whom he takes to Rome, a remarkable picture of the temperamental genius. Roderick's selfishness and unstability wreck not only his own life but also those of his mother and Mary Garland, the New England Puritan to whom he is betrothed. Notwithstanding Roderick's genius, it is Rowland's character in which James is endeavoring to interest us. The other characters are seen through him, and some of the best passages contain our introductions to them through his eyes. It is his high opinion of Mary Garland which sustains her, for she is not so interesting as Christina Light, the girl of American parentage whose beauty inflames Roderick and brings on the ultimate tragedy. One of the best touches in the book is Christina's instinctive desire to justify her conduct to Rowland; it is as though his quiet moral force sent up a danger signal to her, while with Roderick the track was quite open. But the finest thing is the way in which Rowland meets the failure of his experiment in giving Roderick his opportunity, and his acceptance of the ironic situation in which Mrs. Hudson blames him for Roderick's failure and Mary Garland shows herself quite willing to sacrifice him on the fatal night when Roderick falls or throws himself over the cliff in the Alps. James, of course, was not the first to use in fiction the truth that human beings are rewarded or censured, not in terms of their conduct, but in terms of the love they have inspired in their judges. But he built upon this truth a real picture of life; if he took too long to establish his effects, the writing at the end is swift and sure. The international contrasts are not as yet important; the Prince Casamassima whom Christina Light is forced to marry is shadowy, and the Cavaliere, with his suggested paternity of Christina, savors of melodrama.

The international contrast became definite in *The American* (1877). It began, as James tells in his introduction to the New York Edition, with the conception of an American being wronged by an aristocratic society in another country, of his having his enemies in his power, and then of his relinquishing his revenge in disgust. James recognized that this situation was romantic, because to him the romantic meant "the unknown," but he did not seem to comprehend that in the choice of an American business man like Christopher Newman and of the French patricians like the Bellegardes he was deliberately venturing into fields which his lack of understanding and his inexperience alike made unfamiliar ground. Christopher Newman was his main concern, and he secures to a certain degree our sympathy and interest for him, in his

love for Madame de Cintré, in his independent and self-respecting attitude toward her mother, the Marquise de Bellegarde, and her brother
the Marquis, who accept him at first and then reject him. His love story
with Madame de Cintré, who leaves him to enter a Carmelite convent
in order to avoid her family's efforts to marry her to Lord Deepmere,
is irritating rather than tragic. Christopher Newman is not, however,
one of James' best characters. As a representative American who has
made a large fortune in business, he is, compared to Silas Lapham, a
shadowy figure; as a social contrast to the Bellegardes, he simply does
not exist. James, in order to provide a strong contrast, pitted Newman
against the most stubbornly exclusive society in Europe, all the more
insistent upon its social prestige because under the Second Empire that
was all that remained to it. But the Bellegardes are as unconvincing in
their rôle of French patricians as Christopher Newman is in his. When
James was writing *The American* in 1875 in Paris, he had not become
acquainted with the society of the Faubourg St. Germain; it was only
in 1907, when he visited Mrs. Wharton, that he came to know the older
French society. Recent French criticism [16] describes his picture of the
Faubourg St. Germain as a conventional one, drawn from reading
Stendhal, Balzac, Charles de Bernard, and Octave Feuillet. According
to this authority, he approaches the Faubourg with the "naïve défér-
ence oratoire que s'imposaient, en les nommant, les bourgeois français de
1850." In any event, the Marquise de Bellegarde is English, not French,
and her earlier murder of her husband in order to obtain control of her
daughter's destiny is prompted by personal, not racial, reasons. James
in his introduction to *The American*, written after he knew the Faubourg, shows that he realizes that the Bellegardes would not have acted
as he drew them; and indeed the lack of motivation in their treatment of
Newman, and Madame de Cintré's inconsistent conduct takes them out
of the category of importance.

In short, James presented an international contrast in which neither
the American nor the French characters were really representative of
the nations to which they belonged. The interest comes not from the
international quality but from the picture of a man fighting against
forces which he only partly understands, and which he is too proud to
meet upon their own level. Probably the best scene is the visit of Newman to the Duchess, who is said to be the leader of the set to which the

[16] See Marie-Reine Garnier, *Henry James et La France*, 1927.

Bellegardes belong, armed with the document which will ruin them. Gradually, while he talks to the Duchess and her other visitor, his inner nature begins to despise the anticipated revenge. The power to develop a moral crisis through the medium of social intercourse was James' great forte, and he already had begun to reveal it in *The American*. The novel was translated into German in 1877, but it was not till 1884 that a French version appeared. It was dramatized by James and the play had some success in England in 1891.

The Europeans (1878) has none of the virtues of *The American* and all its faults. Felix Young and his sister, the Baroness Münster, who visit their cousins in New England, are mere names. It was in *Daisy Miller* (1879) that James wrote his most popular story. This study of an American girl with youth and charm, who scandalizes Rome through her free and easy defiance of social conventions and dies of fever contracted through her midnight visit to the Colosseum with a young Italian, has provided Europeans with a convenient name for the species she is supposed to represent. For at least thirty years American girls were called "Daisy Millers" by Europeans. James states in his introduction that Daisy was drawn from a young girl he met in Rome in 1877. According to the family of Joaquin Miller, Daisy was suggested by the character of Mollie Wopsus in Miller's novel *One Fair Woman* (1876), and James wrote to the poet stating that he had named his heroine "Miller" in consequence. In the absence of any documentary evidence from Henry James, this story is of interest only because it is a partial explanation of the irritation which the character creates in the mind of a critic who prefers a well-rounded portrait to a caricature. There is a superficial resemblance between Daisy Miller and Mollie Wopsus, a Western girl who behaves with remarkable freedom in Rome. But whether James was inspired by the latter or not, the fact remains that Daisy Miller is a compound of two different types of American girl which he has confused. To anyone who lived in a European capital during the late nineteenth century, the unconventional American girl, usually a student of music or of painting, was very familiar. She could take care of herself, and if she shocked the European friends to whom her anxious relatives had confided her, she took their cold shoulders with indifference. But she did not possess the charm, the active innocence, and the personal daintiness with which James endowed Daisy Miller. There was another and a quite different type who had these qualities but who would not have acted like Daisy Miller because she would not have cared to be conspicuous. We need not in these days join the chorus of denunciation which fell upon Henry James for committing "an outrage on American girlhood." What he may be criticized for, as an apostle of realism, is the confusion of values which resulted in caricature. It is unfortunate that caricature so often makes a wider popular appeal than a well-rounded portrait. Bessie Alden, the heroine of *An International Episode* (1879), is much more truly representative of American girlhood than Daisy Miller, yet she has been relatively forgotten. Her conduct in the difficult situation in which she and her sister find themselves in London when they meet with indifference where their own earlier hospitality at Newport had given them a right to expect cordiality, makes her as consistent an American type as Daisy Miller was inconsistent.

In *Confidence* (1880) James returned to the study of Americans in Europe and wrote one of the cleverest and the most unified of his novelettes. Bernard Longueville is a remarkable study of the man who desires above all else to retain self-knowledge and self-control. When James remarks: "Bernard's sense of his own shrewdness—always tolerably acute—had never received such a bruise as this present perception that a great many things had been taking place in his clever mind without his clever mind suspecting them," the interesting series of relations developed between him and Angela Vivian, Gordon Wright, and Blanche Evers is explained in terms of the subconscious. Blanche Evers, "the light mockery of whose tone struck him as the echo of an unforgotten air," is one of his best pictures of an apparently frivolous but really able woman. *Washington Square* (1881), however, is a very dull book about dull people. James had begun to lose his sense of the American scene, and the book was evidently written for English readers, since he explains carefully how things are done "in New York." But the tepid love story of Catherine Sloper is incapable of exciting interest.

By 1880 Henry James' realistic method had become established, and he made it serve his purpose in his masterpiece, *The Portrait of a Lady* (1881). Around the character of Isabel Archer, an American girl whose personal charm, fineness of feeling, and profound capacity for inarticulate suffering make her the best of his heroines, he built up a story which is the record of her reactions. She is taken to England by her aunt, Mrs. Touchett, a striking portrait of a rich and ruthless old woman.

While she is in England her cousin, Ralph Touchett, an invalid with a sense of humor, and Lord Warburton, the Radical possessor of a large estate, fall in love with her. She is also pursued by her first lover, Caspar Goodwood. As usual, these men are at leisure, permanently or temporarily. She desires, however, to remain independent for a time; Ralph Touchett, unknown to her, secures a fortune for her through the bequest of his father. Having presented her with all the advantages of youth, charm, wealth, and friendship, James then introduces the sinister figures who are to wreck her happiness. Madame Merle, a visitor at Garden Court, the home of the Touchetts in England, introduces to her at Rome Gilbert Osmond, an expatriated American of slender means, a widower with a little girl, Pansy. Osmond is the weak spot in the book. He is said to be clever and charming, but nothing he says or does establishes this claim on the author's part. Osmond's conversation is at times banal, and while it is true that he is created for the purpose of his effect upon Isabel Archer, it was James' duty to endow him with those qualities which a young girl, in love with life and longing for beauty, would idealize into the man she could worship. There was the situation; James had skilfully led up to it, but he failed to provide the lover who should sweep Isabel off her feet. The result is that our opinion of Isabel's intelligence is lowered. A girl who could refuse real men like Caspar Goodwood and Lord Warburton and be blind to the tender chivalry of Ralph Touchett should have been given a man with some positive characteristics, if only for the sake of that climax of interest which the reader has a right to demand. It is not fatal for us to hate the leading character—it is dangerous for us to become irritated by her; and we become irritated with Isabel Archer just as we did in *Daniel Deronda* when Gwendolen Hareth took Grandcourt, who is somewhat the same type of refined brute as Osmond and may have suggested him. What saves the story is the development of Isabel Archer's nature under the shadow of disillusion. With a bravery that is infinitely touching, with a self-control that enables her to steer clearly through the rocks that surround her, and with a disarming courtesy which the highly bred of her nation know best how to preserve, she keeps her self-respect to the end. Her final rebellion, when she insists upon going to Ralph at his deathbed against Osmond's command, and her reaction to Goodwood's passionate plea to go away with him and end her misery, are all kept within the tone that James had established for her. So, too, in those remarkable scenes when she sees Osmond and Madame Merle together and the first suspicion of their earlier relations dawns upon her, or in the later interviews with Madame Merle when she repels the studied insolence of her husband's mistress, she completely justifies the title of the story. The characters of *The Portrait of a Lady* are, with the exception of Lord Warburton, Americans, and England and Italy provide scenic background only.

Among the best of the many short stories written during this period are "A Bundle of Letters" (1880), a clever series of descriptions of the guests at a pension in Paris, and "The Point of View" (1883), a series of letters describing America from Americans expatriated and otherwise, and from foreigners, in which it is interesting, in view of James' constant dread of vulgarity, to hear one of the Americans remark—"Vulgarity! a stupid, superficial question-begging accusation, which has become today the easiest refuge of mediocrity." *Lady Barberina* (1884) has an unusual situation arising from the marriage of Jackson Lemon, a rich young American, to Lady Barberina Canterville, one of a large family of girls. Her dislike of America and her return for a visit to England, from which she refuses to move, explain perhaps why the situation does not often arise in real life. In fact, Howells had only just before spoken of this plot as impossible!

Many of the short stories of this period were simply dull. Some of them like "Pandora" and "Georgina's Reasons" [17] were written for newspaper syndicates, a method of publication not especially suited to the art of Henry James.

The Bostonians (1886), which Henry James omitted with regret from his collected edition, is not one of his best. The treatment of "impressionism" or mesmerism, of which Verena Tarrant, a young girl, is the representative, is not so effective as Howells' earlier use of the theme in *The Undiscovered Country*. While there is some drama in the struggle between the love of Basil Ransom and the desire of Olive Chancellor, his neurotic cousin, for the control of Verena, the novel takes place in a vacuum of interest.

With *The Princess Casamassima* (1886) James turned to the Eng-

---

[17] In his admirable Bibliography, to which I wish to tender my acknowledgment, LeRoy Phillips states that the original dates of publication have not been established. "Pandora" was published Sunday, June 1, and June 8, 1884 in the New York *Sun* and the Philadelphia *Times*. "Georgina's Reasons" appeared in the same journals Sunday, July 20 and 27, and August 3, 1884.

lish scene and created a character, Hyacinth Robinson, the child of an English nobleman who had been killed by Hyacinth's mother, a French-woman. He grows up with a great longing to be a cultivated gentle-man, but knows he is an outsider and joins a group of anarchists. He is taken up by the Princess Casamassima, who is in England for purposes never clearly explained, and who is vaguer than she was in *Roderick Hudson*. The story ends in confusion. Hyacinth's suicide or murder may be due to a variety of causes, but the anarchists belong so decidedly in the realm of comic opera that it would be idle to speculate upon their relations to the death of the hero. It was not a fruitful period for Henry James. *The Reverberator* (1888), a novelette portraying some carica-tures of the flamboyant type of American travelers in the Dosson fam-ily and perhaps the most detestable of American journalists in Flack, had no material worthy of James' art. In the introduction to this novel-ette, which for some unaccountable reason he perpetuated in the New York Edition, he explains that he treats beings like Francie Dosson and Daisy Miller because the American business man is incomprehensible to him and the older woman nothing. The group of Americans he in-troduces in *A London Life* (1889) are little better. Laura Wing is too solemn for a heroine, and the only character one can be interested in for a moment is Wendover, the young American who is put in a false position by Lady Davenant's proposal to him that he marry Laura. "The Liar" (1888) stands out among the short stories of this time for its conception of the painter who takes his revenge upon the man who has won the woman the painter loves by painting him as he really is, a hopeless liar. The recognition by the wife as she and her husband view the picture alone in the studio, while the painter watches them unseen from above, and the return of the husband to destroy the painting, are well handled. Generally speaking, however, the short stories of this period are dull, and it would seem that James had to lie fallow for awhile between his greatest efforts.

In *The Tragic Muse* (1890), however, he redeemed himself. It is a study of the artist's life in contrast with the world, a theme in which James was at his best. The characters and scene are English, and by 1890 James had become well acquainted with the interrelations of social and artistic life in his adopted country. But the merit of *The Tragic Muse* lies in the fact that he left for a time the easier paths of caricature and depicted real people whom one remembers. With a directness unusual and refreshing, James introduces a group of English gentlefolk; Nick Dormer, who is marked for a political career, but who wishes to paint; his mother, Lady Agnes Dormer, whose income is much smaller than her ambitions and whose daughters, Grace and Biddy, are not marrying with that celerity which their uncertain circumstances demand; their cousin, Peter Sherringham, a rising diplomat, who loves the theatre; and, hovering in the background, his sister, Julia Dallow, a rich young widow, who is to be the good angel of all the Dormers if Nick will only appreciate her efforts to provide him with a seat in Parliament. Into this circle Miriam Rooth, a young English girl who wishes to become an actress, enters as a disturbing element. She is made known to us through the minds of the other characters for, as James tells us, "We have chosen, as it happens, for some of the great advantages it carries with it, the indirect vision." The difference between this method as used in *The Tragic Muse* and in some of the later novels lies in its success. Miriam Rooth becomes real not only through her struggles to succeed, but also through her effect upon Peter Sherringham, who is infatuated with her, and upon Nick Dormer, who looks upon her as a model to paint. Nick and Peter are more alive than James' American men just because they are developed in terms of their great interest in their professions. In Nick's case the struggle lies between a desire to create beauty and the lure of a career in politics with a rich wife and an adoring family whose fortunes he will have secured by his marriage. His choice is precipitated by Julia's visit to his studio while he is painting Miriam's portrait, but it is due primarily to "the two men in him, quite separate, whose leading figures had little in common."

The conflict in Peter is between his passion for Miriam and his love for his career, and here James spoils a good situation by the interminable final scene in which Peter begs her to marry him and leave the stage, on the very night of her triumph. The uneven quality of his art is revealed in the contrast between this orgy of long speeches and the deftly managed farewell of Miriam to Nick, whom she really prefers, or the exquisite interview between Biddy Dormer and Peter, when Biddy, who adores her cousin, bravely holds up for his inspection Nick's portrait of Miriam, thus submitting herself to the inevitable comparison between the brilliancy of Miriam's beauty and her own more modest charm. *The Tragic Muse* is huddled at the end, for James marries off Miriam to her actor-manager, Basil Dashwood, and rewards Biddy for her brave and inarticulate devotion with the remains of Peter's love. But notwithstanding these defects, the novel remains a rich canvas in which the British worship of property and position sets off like a dark background the concrete figures of those to whom the creation of beauty is the great concern.

From 1889 to 1894, James' devotion to fiction was interrupted by his efforts to write plays. His play-writing lies outside our present province, but it is significant that his only approach to success came from his dramatization of *The American. Guy Domville*, whose production was the occasion of a riot in the theatre which drove its sensitive author from the stage, illustrates how unsuited for drama was his method of developing a character through the effect of others upon him. *Guy Domville* is noteworthy also as one of the few efforts of James to place his scenes in the eighteenth century. But, at least in the script, James' characters are conventional and might just as well have lived in the nineteenth. During the interval between *The Tragic Muse* and *The Other House* (1896), James was also concerned with shorter fiction, often in the form of the "nouvelle." The most interesting group deals with writers and contain James' theories concerning fiction put in an even more significant fashion than in his definitely critical work. In *The Lesson of the Master* (1888–1892), Henry St. George, a prosperous writer who could, it is intimated, appeal to the select few but who prefers to make money, persuades his disciple to consecrate himself to art and leave a promising affair with Marian Fancourt, who on his return from the Continent he finds married to St. George. St. George becomes James' mouthpiece and will be referred to later, but the irony of the situation is itself appealing. Through "The Death of the Lion" (1895) and "The Next Time" (1896) come interesting revelations of James' attitudes. The struggle of a writer trying to do his best work, but prevented by the necessity of earning a living for his family, gives a note of tragedy to "The Next Time." "Sir Dominick Ferrand" (1893) [18] has an appealing hero, Peter Baron, a young man of fine and sensitive feeling, poor, struggling and lonely, "with the creative head without the creative hand." The most delightful perhaps is "The Coxon Fund" (1895), the story of an irresponsible genius, Frank Saltram, based partly on Coleridge, the object of the care of a group of adherents, one of whom tells the story. How much James packs into the description of Mrs. Saltram!

---

[18] In *The Cosmopolitan*, July-August, 1892, as "Jersey Villas."

"A deeply wronged, justly resentful, quite irreproachable and insufferable person. She often appeared at my chambers to talk over his lapses; for if as she declared, she had washed her hands of him, she had carefully preserved the water of this ablution, which she handed about for analysis."

"The Real Thing" (1893) has a fine contrast between the two reduced gentlefolk who are useless as models for a painter because they cannot be anything but themselves. It is in a sense a criticism of photographic realism in all art. To this period belongs also one of James' finest stories, *The Altar of the Dead* (1895), one of his few studies of pure affection. The character of Stransom is revealed in terms of the love he has borne for Mary Antrim, and for his other friends who are dead but who live in his memory. Through his visits to the church where he has had a candle perpetually lighted for each of these friends, he meets a woman who comes for a similar purpose. Their gradual approach to a deep understanding of the sanctity of their feeling, and their separation when she finds that the one friend he has not commemorated, Acton Hague, was her lover who had wronged her even more deeply than he had insulted Stransom, are told with the clarity and the sympathy with which an artist reveals a great emotion. It is a triumph too of a realist in the field of idealism. In his next novel, *The Other House* (1896), he ventured not so successfully into the field of passion, ruled by cleverness and with a curious limitation of emotion. The novel verges on the melodramatic, and indeed James made of it a three-act play which never saw the stage. Rose Armiger's passion for Tony Bream, which leads her to murder his little daughter who stands in the way of his second marriage, is so intense that it touches her with dignity. She is one of the most easily remembered of his heroines.

Henry James had always been impressed with the value of the supernatural as literary material. Under the influence of Hawthorne he had written "The Romance of Certain Old Clothes" in 1868. In 1891 he began a series of short stories with "Sir Edmund Orme," told by a young man who sees an apparition of a gentleman long dead who had been grievously wronged by the mother of the girl he loves. Sir Edmund is no wraith; he looks like a living being, and he is visible to the narrator only because the latter loves Charlotte Marden. Only one of the senses acts, that of sight, but at the end of the story, when Mrs. Marden dies, worn out by the fear from which she has suffered so many years—that her daughter will see Sir Edmund as she sees him—a voice sounds that may be a call from the other world. It may also be the voice of the dying woman, and again we see the method of Hawthorne, this time in the provision of an alternative natural explanation. "The Private Life" (1893), a story of two men who have double personalities, was not so successful. In "Owen Wingrave" (1893), the supernatural is used to test the courage of a man who has declined to enter the army. In "The Friend of the Friends" (1896),[19] there is a striking story of a man and a woman each of whom has had a vision of a parent who is at a long distance off at the time of death. By a series of accidents, told by the fiancée of the man, they never meet in real life, but on the night of the woman's death she appears to the man. So vivid is his vision that he insists it is real, but his fiancée breaks their engagement because she knows that the dead woman visits him. Some years later he kills himself, in response to her call from the other world.

These stories gain their main importance from their being preliminary studies for one of the greatest of all examples of supernatural fiction, *The Turn of the Screw* (1898). Inspired by an incident related to him by Archbishop Benson, James created a young governess faced with an appalling situation when her two charges, a boy of ten and girl of eight, seem to be summoned by the ghosts of the former steward, Peter Quint, and of the governess, Miss Jessel. These ghosts, like Sir Edmund Orme, are not wraiths; they appear like human beings and they present themselves on the tops of towers or across sheets of water, which, if the children were to come to them, would be places of danger. James' method of telling the story entirely through the consciousness of the governess is exactly suited to this theme, for the children deny that they see anything, and even the housekeeper, through whom she learns of the evil character of Peter Quint and Miss Jessel, believes in them only through her belief in the governess. The sympathy of the reader grows steadily for this gallant young woman, fighting for the souls and bodies of her charges, against the powers of evil, and the final scene, in which the boy dies in her arms, saved, she believes, from the malignant presence that stands looking through the window in broad daylight, is unforgettable. Fortunately, as James tells us,[20] he "ruled out subjective complications of her own" and while, like his great master, Hawthorne, he leaves the

---

[19] Printed first in *The Chap Book*, May 1, 1896, as "The Way It Came."
[20] See *Letters*, ed. Lubbock, Vol. I, p. 299.

way open for the explanation through the hallucination of the governess, he nowhere suggests it. James himself calls the story "a piece of ingenuity pure and simple, of cold artistic calculation," but he also makes clear how he has deliberately not explained the evil which Peter Quint and Miss Jessel have done to the children, nor the evil to which they are calling them. Like a true artist he knew that the success of the story depended upon the very absence of detail, how the reader left to himself would imagine more horror than any actual occurrence or peril presented by the author. It is this nameless terror, brooding over the story that makes it great. It draws freely upon that vicarious experience of evil which any person of imagination has at his disposal. To those without imagination, the story does not belong. And how wise James was in not making the evils specific has been proved by the many explanations with which the psychologists have enriched the history of human error. *The Turn of the Screw* is not simply a great story; it warns off the premises of art the pseudo-realists who plague us with the tiresome details of sexual evil, and who cannot read the sign post planted by one of the greatest realists in fiction.

James did not always trust so confidently the intelligence of his audience. Two years before *The Turn of the Screw* closed the first and greatest period of his achievement, he had begun in *The Spoils of Poynton* (1896–1897) [21] a series of novels in which a thin story was strung out to unnecessary lengths by a finely drawn analysis of motives not intrinsically worthy of the effort. The conflict between Mrs. Gereth and Mona Brigstock, her son's fiancée, over the furniture of Poynton, even as interpreted through Fleda Vetch's love for Owen Gereth, does not seem important. One of those curious lapses in James' standards baffles us at the very outset of this novel. Mrs. Gereth and Fleda meet at a house party at Mrs. Brigstock's home, and these two women, whose exquisite taste is the foundation of the story, found their friendship upon their ridicule, at their first meeting, of the furniture and the personal habits of the people whose hospitality they are enjoying! But the characters are hardly alive. James had become interested at this time almost exclusively in the manner of the telling—the story in it had become of less importance. This would not have mattered if the characters had been significant, but the central theme has not enough vitality to animate them.

[21] First published as "The Old Things," *Atlantic Monthly*, April–October, 1896.

What Maizie Knew (1897), is a study in the relations of certain English people without character or standards of conduct, as seen through the eyes of a little girl. The divorces, liaisons, and rearrangements of the adults, which transfer her from the custody of her parents to that of the second husband of her stepmother are not worth relating, and the only feeling of satisfaction which the novel gives lies in Maizie's final flight with her governess, Mrs. Wix, from as worthless a crew as James ever brought together. *The Awkward Age* (1899), is little better. It is a study of the system of English society which provides no place for the "young person." The set that surrounds Nanda Brookenham, a girl of eighteen, is presumably clever and corrupt, though the cleverness consists principally of saying darkly allusive things, and its corruption is not very convincing. There is a certain amusement to be obtained from watching Mrs. Brookenham and the "Duchess" spar for "Mitchy," a wealthy man, for their respective daughters, but even Nanda's plight in losing the man she loves because she "knows too much" does not rise to the dignity of tragedy. In this same period of involved indirectness, *The Sacred Fount* (1901) is an intellectual exercise rather than a novelette, in which the effort to find out which of a selected group of human beings at a house party in England is responsible for the sudden change in Gilbert Long is hardly worth while.

It is significant that when James rose once more to at least an approach to his earlier and higher level in *The Wings of the Dove* (1902), he should draw the inspiration for his central character from the recollection of a young cousin, in the earlier New York days. Mildred Theale, the American girl, doomed to an early death and determined to see and enjoy life to the utmost, is a tragic figure. James endows her with charm, some beauty, and with those rarest of all the elements of breeding, the unwillingness to hurt others and the charity that attributes to them motives higher than they possess. It is probably because the experience or the memory of so many Americans includes at least one girl who might have sat for Milly's portrait that the book makes its appeal. James nowhere makes clear the nature of Milly's disease, but that her health depends upon her will to live provides him a logical end for her, after she finds out that Densher, the young English journalist she loves, has been engaged to Kate Croy, her friend. The relations of Densher and Kate are irritating rather than tragic, and the calm way Kate proposes to Densher that he marry Milly and inherit her money, so that they will later be free to marry, relieves the reader from any further interest in her. After Milly "turns her face to the wall" the story flags, and finally passes out into confusion of motive and situation. That Kate Croy, who has planned such a cold-blooded scheme, should refuse to marry Densher because he has fallen in love with Milly's memory is absurd.

In a letter to Howells,[22] James states that the germ of *The Ambassadors* (1903) was suggested by his friend. This central idea is expressed by Lambert Strether, the American editor, who goes to France to rescue Chad Newsome, the young artist, from his entanglement with Madame de Vionnet. It is simply that everyone should live to the full, which Strether has not done. Certainly he seems peculiarly ineffective for the editor of a great magazine. There is a certain comedy in the advent of the various "ambassadors" who try to separate Chad from the liberal education he is receiving at the hands of Madame de Vionnet. But the lack of any really interesting characters and the involved and long drawn out approach to such few events as the novel contains make it less significant than *The Wings of the Dove,* which indeed it anticipated in the order of composition. In *The Golden Bowl* (1904), things have almost ceased to happen. The four central characters, Maggie Verver and her father Adam Verver, her husband the Roman Prince, and Charlotte Stant, who has presumably been the Prince's mistress and who marries Adam Verver, are involved in a series of complications which spring not so much from events as from their speculations concerning events. Outside of Maggie Verver, who is a competent American girl, and her father, a retired business man, the characters are faint. They spend so much time "beautifully wondering" that they do or say almost nothing, and since there is little effective international contrast, the impression is that of a theme drawn out intolerably thin. This thinness of plot and the involved style are to be found also in James' later short stories, included in *The Soft Side* (1900), *The Better Sort* (1903) and *The Finer Grain* (1910). Occasionally, as in "The Velvet Glove," the indignation of the artist at being treated as such a social impossibility that a woman of fashion can permit him to take liberties with her in return for his literary services, warms a story into life. It is, incidentally, the theme N. P. Willis had treated in *Paul Fane*. "The Bench of Desolation," also in *The Finer Grain*, has some appeal. But in these stories, as in *The Outcry* (1911), a novelette dealing with the sale of objects of art by Englishmen to rich Americans, the besetting sins of James' later manner are only too apparent.

After James' death in 1916, two unfinished novels were published. *The Ivory Tower* (1917) is unimportant except for the return of the novelist to his native scene, since the story is laid in Newport. But *The Sense of the Past*, begun in 1900 and laid aside until 1914, is one of the most interesting of his books. He returned in it to the supernatural, and he combined with this interest one rarely employed by him, that of the past. Ralph Pendrel, a young American, is in love with the ordered beauty of the survivals of the past, and when he falls heir to a house in London, his appreciation is keen. In the dusk of this stately mansion, Ralph sees the portrait of a young man, dating from about 1820, with his back to the observer. The imaginary interplay of sympathy between Ralph and the portrait, which seems to descend from its frame and to have Ralph's own countenance, is created with that magic of which few but Hawthorne and James had the secret. It is interesting that the very next chapter opens with an allusion to Hilda's confession in *The Marble Faun*. Ralph's impulse to confession takes the shape, however, of telling the American Ambassador that he has exchanged identities with the earlier Ralph Pendrel, who had come over to England about 1820, and the realism of James' method brings the Ambassador back with Ralph to the old house, in justifiable doubt as to his sanity. Then when Ralph steps into the house, he takes up the career of his earlier self, meets his cousin Molly Midmore, to whom he has become engaged by family arrangement, and James preserves rather cleverly Ralph's sense that he is *acting* the part of the earlier American. The fragment goes only as far as his meeting with Mrs. Midmore, Perry, her son, Sir Cantopher, who hopes to marry Nan, the younger sister, and Nan herself. In the Notes, which James had dictated, we learn that he was to develop a sense of horror on Ralph's part of being shut up in the past, a longing for his own time and a realization that Nan is the only one who understands him. James had intended to introduce the Ralph Pendrel of 1820, returning as a spirit to warn his counterpart that he was not to change from Molly to Nan, and these visits were to be as terrible to the hero as the visits of the ghosts in *The Turn of the Screw*. Nan is to let him know that she loved the Ralph of 1820 without return, and he is finally to be recalled by the influence of the modern girl whom he loves and who, sensing danger to him, comes over to London. There were great possibilities in this plot, which became the basis for one of the finest examples of contemporary drama, John L. Balderston's *Berkeley Square*. Balderston made several changes, notably in the transference of the time to the eighteenth century, but it remains a curious justification of James' belief in his own qualifications as a dramatist, that his last novel should have provided inspiration for a play both artistically and popularly successful.

Henry James is to a certain degree a paradox in the history of American fiction. His letters are studded with regret for the lack of popular appreciation of his work during his lifetime, and yet he has been the subject of more critical attention than any other novelist since the Civil War. These studies of the function and method of his art have multiplied not only because of his achievement but also because he knew so definitely what he was doing and because he has outlined his philosophy of composition so frequently. He expressed this conception of art strikingly through the character of Henry St. George in *The Lesson of the Master*, in his advice to a younger writer:

If you haven't a plan, if you *don't* mean to keep it up, surely you're within your rights; it's nobody's business, no one can force you, and not more than two or three people will notice you don't go straight. The others—*all* the rest, every blest soul in England, will think you do—will think you *are* keeping it up: upon my honour they will! I shall be one of the two or three who know better. Now the question is whether you can do it for two or three.

Or again St. George says:

". . . I've got everything in fact but the great thing."
"The great thing?" Paul kept echoing.
"The sense of having done the best—the sense which is the real life of the artist and the absence of which is his death, of having drawn from his intellectual instrument the finest music that nature had hidden in it, of having played it as it should be played. He either does that or he doesn't—and if he doesn't he isn't worth speaking of. Therefore, precisely, those who really know *don't* speak of him. He may still hear a great chatter, but what he hears most is the incorruptible silence of Fame. . . ."

This theory of art is in sharp contrast to the democratic theory of Howells and concerns both their material and their method. It is this sense of working for the few and for his own self-imposed standard, that accounts for the peculiarities of James' career. Beginning with a laudable independence of judgment as to what he should and what he should not do, his sense of the importance of the corrective judgment of the intelligent popular taste was gradually lost. There is a wholesome check upon an author's mannerisms in his constantly squaring up his work to the right kind of popular approbation. If an author deliberately disregards criticism and popular appreciation, he must set up some tribunal, some standard. He may say it is the "few," the "elect," but the very selection of the few is subjective, and it comes down finally to self-judgment. This leads to mannerisms and peculiarities, since they are perfectly right by the self-constituted standard, and in process of time become the standard itself. This is what happened to Henry James.

The indirectness of his method was deliberate. He was interested not so much in individuals as in the relations of individuals, of types, of nationalities. This made him proceed by revealing characters through other characters, or by showing the relations of two people through the conversation or even through the relations of others. This indirection was potential even in his early work, but it became definite in *The Princess Casamassima* in 1886.[23]

This indirectness is all the more remarkable since in one place at least James takes this view of the relations of the writer and reader:

. . . he has, that is, but one to think of—the benefit, whatever it may be, involved in his having cast a spell upon the simpler, the very simplest, forms of attention. That is all he is entitled to; he is entitled to nothing, he is bound to admit, that can come to him from the reader, as a result on the latter's part of any act of reflexion or discrimination.[24]

This seems a very modest demand upon the reader, but James makes much more than this. In fact toward the end of his career this desire for indirectness affected his language, and some of his works became rhetorical puzzles. It is worth noting that this lapse from clarity which began to show most definitely in *What Maizie Knew*, coincided with James' beginning to dictate to a stenographer. Compare such a sentence as this from "The Beast in the Jungle" (1903) with that quoted from "The Madonna of the Future" (1873):

That at last, at last, he certainly hadn't it, to speak of, or had it but in the scantiest measure—such soon enough, as things went with him, became the inference with which his old obsession had to reckon; and this it was not

[23] See James' analysis of the hero as reflector of the other characters, Introduction, New York Edition, pp. xiv–xxv.
[24] Introduction to *Portrait of a Lady*, New York Edition, p. xviii.

helped to do by the more and more confirmed appearance that the great vagueness casting the long shadow in which he had lived had, to attest itself, almost no margin left.

In discussing James' relation to American life, it must be remembered that after the first ten years he rarely treated his native scene and then with relatively little success. The study of conditions in this country after the war to which Howells made such important contributions finds no corresponding purpose or achievement in James. He fails entirely to present Americans in their professional or business relations, or to treat in any way the intellectual life of America, and consequently *The Bostonians* or *Washington Square* seem vague and bodiless. He has left the earnestness out of the American man, the quality by which he is most distinguished. James has of course made clear that he has not tried to deal with such phases of native material.

In his novels of international relations, there is no lack of American characters. He began with "A Passionate Pilgrim" an impressive list of narratives in which American manners, customs, modes of thought, standards of taste, and sense of honor are brought into contrast with European, principally English, standards. At first glance, it would seem that he has treated many and various American types, but on closer scrutiny, it becomes apparent that the men fall into three groups—the young man of leisure, like Longmore, Rowland Mallet, Bernard Longueville, or Jackson Lemon; the retired business man like Christopher Newman or Adam Verver; the artist, including the painter like Chad Newsome, the sculptor like Roderick Hudson, or the man of letters like Strether. Only in the third class does the man's work have any bearing upon his development. With the women, where this issue does not arise, there is more variety. The finest types, Isabel Archer, Bessie Alden or Milly Theale, are far removed from Daisy Miller or Francie Dosson. The serious, domestic woman, like Maggie Verver, is quite distinct from the brilliant but more unstable girl like Charlotte Stant or Angela Vivian; the frivolous Blanche Evers differs from the deplorable transplanted Americans like Selena Barrington. It is not unfair to say that the most easily remembered of all the Americans are the most outrageous caricatures like Daisy Miller, Francie Dosson, Selena Barrington, Mrs. Headway in "The Siege of London," or Flack the reporter in *The Reverberator*. What one misses in James' novels are a few Americans who are sure of themselves, men who have played some part in intellectual life or in public affairs, women of recognized experience in social leadership. There is much of the air of the great world in James, but the Americans do not contribute to it, for even the best of them are tinged with a certain looseness of standards or social uncertainty. That Mildred Theale, the product of several generations of good breeding in New York, should be embarrassed at an English dinner table is improbable, but that James should take the time to tell about it is inexcusable.

It cannot be said that in general James represented English life any more favorably than he did American. He furnishes his English characters with more social surety, but he endowed the characters of *The Awkward Age*, *What Maizie Knew*, or *A London Life* with more vagaries of moral conduct. Even in *The Tragic Muse* the scramble for Peter Sherringham on the part of the Dormer family is pitiable, and the English worship of money is emphasized quite as strongly as the American lack of manners.

In the search for reasons for James' lack of popular appeal, his general avoidance of strong emotions and passions must not be overlooked. As his great inspiration, Hawthorne, so well expressed it:

Indeed, we are but shadows: we are not endowed with real life, and all that seems most real about us is but the thinnest substance of a dream,—till the heart be touched. That touch creates us,—then we begin to be—thereby we are beings of reality and inheritors of eternity.[25]

Perhaps this avoidance of the emotions, this refuge in intellectual relations, comes from James' desire not to be too obvious, but as Mrs. Wharton has said, "In the effort to avoid the obvious, one frequently misses the significant." It is not only that his studies are monsters of coolness and proceed with too definite an intellectual program, but even when an emotional relation is in progress, as in *The Golden Bowl*, we are kept so much out of the confidence of the characters and their creator that we fail to understand even what they feel about each other. It is true we are constantly told what they *think* about each other, but it is a serious lack in a novel when the characters seem determined to conceal their own emotions.

Much of this lack of heart springs from the cool, critical, detached attitude of James toward life and toward his characters. He was one of

[25] *American Note-Books*, Riverside Edition, p. 223.

the most penetrating critics of his time, and his constant occupation with critical judgment hurt perhaps that spontaneity so necessary in the creation of emotional relations. Critical taste keeps out the unnecessary, but it is hardly good critical taste that takes the heart out of a novelist's characters. Such exquisite stories as *The Altar of the Dead* or the appealing approach to love-making which brings Biddy Dormer out of the pages of *The Tragic Muse* into vivid life are the exceptions which prove the general truth. That James recognized it is shown in the terrible fate of the man who had no heart in "The Beast in the Jungle."

Remembering how incomplete after all are his representations of Americans in Europe, Henry James is probably more important in the development of realism than in the international novel. His work proves conclusively that if realism is to mean anything definite, it must. be confined to the treatment rather than to the selection of material. James at first seems to have discarded the usual elements of romance, to have stripped life of its illusions and of its sentimentality. He analyzes it, discusses it, classifies it, retaining an interest in a special limited problem. "One must be narrow to penetrate," says Paul Muniment in *The Princess Casamassima*. Outside of the stories of the supernatural, the only element of romance which he allows himself is a mystery of motive which he creates deliberately. Beginning about 1896, the characters spend much of their time "wonderfully wondering" why the other characters are doing certain things. Sometimes the motives would be clear enough if left to themselves, but a certain mystery is thrown around them by the evident inability of the other characters to understand them. This is not a very attractive form of mystery, since it is an intellectual barrier to comprehension instead of a stimulus to interest like the other forms of romance, and it impedes the progress of the reader's understanding without furnishing the element of suspense which the mystery of Scott or of Hawthorne did furnish. The reader feels that it might be cleared up at once if the writer would only say what he meant, for it is directly to be traced to his obscurity, not to the dark and yet inevitable marshalling of events.

That this method was deliberate is proved by James' success when he chooses romantic material as in *The Turn of the Screw* or *The Sense of the Past*. He still preserves his realistic method and the great success of the first story lies in the way the realistic method keeps in check the romantic material and secures our belief in the visitors from the other world. To him the choice of material was of secondary importance; the method was what mattered.

When his limitations are noted, however, he remains a great artist who had inventive powers of a high order and standards which he maintained with a courage that excites our admiration, even if we feel that in some ways these standards were artificial. In his earlier period, James wrote English that has rarely been surpassed, and which any lover of the magnificent phrase must cherish. Notwithstanding the persistent efforts of a cult to which cleverness is the one god, his later books, with the exceptions already noted, will remain unread except by the few for whom he wrote them. For these intellectual puzzles there remains, to use his own vivid phrase, "the incorruptible silence of Fame."

CHAPTER XV

WEIR MITCHELL, PIONEER AND PATRICIAN

WHILE Weir Mitchell was not the first American to use the knowledge of the physician in the analysis of character, he was the first to combine in fiction the modern scientific spirit with the art of a great master of romance. Dr. Holmes had anticipated him in the realistic treatment of heredity, but Dr. Mitchell's achievement was far more varied and substantial. Like Holmes, he was a poet, and he therefore wrote with the clarity of those who choose the fitting word only after imagination has endowed the precision of the scientist with the corrective selection of the artist.

His long and varied career was a continuous preparation for his fiction. Born in Philadelphia in 1829, he wrote verse when he was a boy of twelve and told stories to amuse his friends. He was educated at the College of the University of Pennsylvania when Henry Reed was inspiring students there with a love of English literature, and his medical education was gained at Jefferson Medical College, where his father, Dr. John K. Mitchell, himself a poet, was a member of the staff. Weir Mitchell's career as a physician is of interest to us here mainly because he became the foremost specialist in nervous diseases in the United States, and in the practice of his profession learned how to read, beneath the surface, the complicated motives of human conduct. Early in the Civil War he was appointed acting assistant surgeon in the army, and his duties at Turner's Lane Hospital in Philadelphia gave him the inspiration for his first published short story in 1865 and his last novel in 1913, the year before his death.

The first story, "The Case of George Dedlow," was sent without his knowledge by his friend, Dr. W. H. Furness, to the *Atlantic Monthly*, where it appeared anonymously as the leading article in July, 1866. Dr. Mitchell wrote of war from a new point of view, that of an army surgeon who, changing to the infantry, had both arms and legs shot off at intervals, and the feelings, both physical and mental, of the patient are

analyzed with a scientific realism which is maintained until the end of
the story. Then Dedlow goes to a spiritualistic seance, and his legs appear from the spirit world to become reunited for, alas, but a moment
to his body. The satiric intention is clear, but Dr. Mitchell's account was
so realistic that several persons sent money for the supposed sufferer
and even went out to the "Stump Hospital" to see him. These mistaken
charities are not so surprising, for the story has to the very end the
veracity of a clinical report, touched with an imaginative quality which
lifts it above the mere recital of events. Already there was apparent a
faculty to dramatize and to project himself into the feelings and emotions of his characters which made him a great novelist. This same
dramatic quality appeared in "The Autobiography of a Quack," again
printed anonymously in the *Atlantic Monthly*, in October and November, 1867. It was a realistic account of the devices by which a dishonest and ignorant physician proceeds, and it gave a veracious picture
of the seamy side of life in Philadelphia and other large cities. Home-
opathy, spiritualism and other pet aversions of the orthodox physician
were treated in a humorous way, and the cold-blooded manner in which
the quack tells his story made it a successful piece of irony. Many years
later, in 1900, Dr. Mitchell expanded this short story into a novelette.

Among the early stories, which he continued to publish in the *Atlantic*, "Was He Dead?" (1870) is a striking instance of imaginative
treatment of science, in which a dead murderer is revived for a moment
to reveal the innocence of a man already executed for the crime. Phrases
like "The awful security of death" and "That curious respect which
genius, incapable of self-comprehension, has for talent, whose laws it can
see and admire" are an earnest of what was to come in *Characteristics*.
His ability to write conversation which reproduces the unfinished sentences of real life was shown in "Miss Helen" (1873), a charming
dream story laid at Newport, and his romantic "A Draft on the Bank of
Spain" (1872) [1] indicated another direction which his fiction was to
take. These early stories, either anonymous or signed "W.M.," prove
that his writing was not accidental but was probably checked by his professional duties. They strike a fresh note in the short story of the 'sixties
and 'seventies, however, and they led in a few years to his more important work.

His first historical novelette, *Thee and You*, appeared in *Lippincott's*

[1] *Lippincott's Magazine*, June, 1872.

for May and June, 1876, under the name of "Edward Kearsely," and was published in book form in 1880. *Thee and You* is laid in Philadelphia early in the century. The conflict of Quaker ideals and those of the world's people is the background, but the most interesting figure is that of Heinrich Schmidt, a German refugee, who loves Priscilla White hopelessly. When he finds out that she feels herself bound to a rascal, John Oldmixon, he forces a duel upon him and drives him from the city, although he is himself mortally wounded. The duel as told by young Shelburne, the only witness, is thrilling in its direct and vivid narrative. *Hephzibah Guinness* [2] (1880) is a novelette laid in Philadelphia in 1807. Hephzibah represents the intolerance and personal desire to order others' lives which characterized one element in the Quakers of that day. In order to keep young Marguerite Howard, her ward, within her own control and bring her up a member of the Society of Friends, she conceals the letters which Marguerite's father had written from France, which reveal the fact that the little girl is not his child. This concealment has tragic consequences, for there is a taint of insanity in the Howard family which threatens for a time to prevent the marriage of Marguerite. These novelettes are interesting as preliminary studies to *Hugh Wynne* and *The Red City*.

In his first long novel, *In War Time* (1885), Weir Mitchell chose as the background the effect of the Civil War as he had seen it in the hospitals and in the neighborhood of Philadelphia. But what made it important was the creation of character. Dr. Ezra Wendell is the first of those studies in the psychology of cowardice, which remain unrivalled in our fiction. He is a New England man, who has had to leave the army because he had abandoned his post and exposed a number of wounded men to death or capture, and he has come to Philadelphia to rebuild his career. He is no villain; he has ability and charm, but he has no stamina. Through his courtesy he wins as patients Colonel Morton and his eldest son, Edward, and through his charm, the love of Alice Westerley, a delightful woman. He loses her, however, through his fatal weakness, in a situation which demanded truth and moral courage. Called in some haste from Edward Morton's room, where his patient is suffering from a heart attack, Dr. Wendell gives too hasty a glance at the vials on the table and directs Arthur Morton, the younger brother, to give Edward the wrong medicine. Edward dies in consequence. When Wendell is

[2] *Lippincott's Magazine*, April, May, June, 1878.

recalled by Mrs. Morton, who believes that Arthur has made the mistake and is anxious only that her living son shall be spared a lifetime of regret, the physician lies, apparently to save Arthur but in reality to save himself, and assures them that the medicine was correct. Mrs. Morton, who knows this is not the fact, sends him a check for five thousand dollars, which Edward had promised to loan him, and he accepts it on account of his pressing financial difficulties. Although she does not know all the story, Alice Westerley believes this has been sent as a bribe and, while she has forgiven his earlier cowardice in the war, because that was remote to her, she cannot forgive the weakness of character of which she has herself been a witness. Wendell is not a mere type; he has flashes of courage and his final confession to Alice of his guilt is all the more tragic because it is useless. In fact, so real was he to Dr. Oliver Wendell Holmes that he protested to his friend against the choice of his own middle name for the character! Already in this first novel, Dr. Mitchell showed his ability in epigram. "Perhaps, could we hear all that is said behind our backs, existence would be nearly impossible except for the few, who would then make what was left of it intolerable."

Even better was *Roland Blake* (1886). Dr. Mitchell chose the name because Roland stood to him for chivalry and Blake for mysticism. This New Englander, a captain in the Intelligence Service of the Union Army, is ostensibly the hero of the novel, but the most original creations are Octopia and Robert Darnell. Captain Darnell, of the Confederate Secret Service, is a double traitor, selling his information to the Northern army, attempting to murder Blake, who has been sent to meet him, and descending later to blackmail and suicide. Vivid as he is, however, Octopia is a masterpiece. A nervous semi-invalid, she preys upon the affection and sympathy of her elderly cousin, Mrs. Wynne, and the latter's granddaughter, Olivia. Her hold upon them is based partly on her knowledge of the suicide of Arthur Wynne, Olivia's father, but is strengthened daily by the way she grips them in the tentacles of her insistent demands for sympathy with her suffering. Her very name, Octopia, is a stroke of genius, and in a few words Dr. Mitchell gives you a picture of her:

As Olivia seated herself, she saw her cousin's long hands rising and falling on the coverlet, and said, gently,—
"You are suffering, cousin; can I help you?"

To an experienced eye the movements would have seemed too regular to be the expression of pain.

"Yes, I suffer; I cannot bear these struggles with you, Olivia. You are like all young people; you have no real sympathy. When I am dead you will remember me and wish in vain you had done more to help a pain-broken woman. I don't want you to answer me; I cannot talk long, and I have something to say."

Olivia watched the sallow face, with its look of languid inaction, noticing for the first time, being a clever but undeveloped observer, that the lips spoke without the other features appearing to take any expressive interest in the thoughts thus uttered.

Octopia has the traditions and breeding of a gentlewoman and, like all real people, she has her own curious standards. She is willing to threaten Mrs. Wynne to gain the rich woman's consent to Darnell's suit for Olivia, but she "was never truly resolute to use implacably the weapon she carried. She had been selling her soul in fractions, but was irresolute as to completing the transaction." How natural, too, is her horror when Darnell, impatient at her failure, attempts to threaten Mrs. Wynne himself. Octopia's struggle to preserve her ideal of her brother's character is the redeeming trait in her which presents the moral contrast, so fruitful a motive in fiction and drama. What almost chills our blood in reading about Octopia is the realization that there are thousands of such women who are daily crushing the lives of those who are bound to them by a subtle and powerful force that almost creates a belief in the positive existence of evil. This clutch of the feminine neurotic, obsessed by her longing for power over others, has had brilliant treatments in contemporary drama, such as *The Silver Cord* and *Strange Interlude*, but Dr. Mitchell anticipated Sidney Howard and Eugene O'Neill in his revelation of the feminine struggle for possession and direction of human lives.

Roland Blake is a compound of practical good sense and of romantic impulses which lead him to follow Mrs. Wynne and Olivia when they fly to Cape May Courthouse to avoid Octopia. His desire to protect them from Darnell is akin to his rescue of the Confederate when the latter is wounded on the battlefield. Dr. Mitchell never saw actual war, but long before the time of Stephen Crane he had painted from his imagination the real feeling of the soldiers before a battle. He had heard, of course, of fighting at first hand. Three brothers were in the service and the two who escaped death were full of what they had seen. Several cousins fought on the Confederate side. He knew Grant and Sherman, and General "Baldy" Smith was a great friend. At his table General Dodge of South Carolina and other Confederate officers found the hospitality that knew no North or South.

Dr. Mitchell's love of the open air and his knowledge of woodcraft were represented in a dramatic story, *Far in the Forest* (1889), laid in the frontier districts of Northern Pennsylvania before the Civil War. There are a number of well-drawn characters. Bessy Preston has brought her husband, an opium-eater, to recover in the healthful atmosphere, but finds that he can secure whiskey just as well there and that there is just as much danger of injustice on the frontier as in the cities. The German baron, Riverius, who loves her and who is accused of murdering Miriam Richmond, provides a sharp contrast; Dr. Mitchell shows how Riverius' very superiority to the men who threaten to lynch him is his danger. One of the best studies is the blind man, Philetus Richmond, who is mentally unsound, and whose causeless jealousy of Riverius is another element in the plot. The salvation of Riverius by the remorse of Ance Vickers, the real murderer, who, with Mrs. Preston, sets the woods on fire, gave occasion to a fine description of the fury of such a conflagration. *Far in the Forest* had much more structure than another out-of-doors book, *When All the Woods are Green* (1894), based on the author's experiences in Canada, which has been a favorite, however, with devoted fishermen.

In 1892 Dr. Mitchell invented in *Characteristics* a form of fiction which, while sharing some qualities with *The Autocrat of the Breakfast Table*, is distinct in its essentials. The novel is told by Dr. Owen North and consists largely of conversations among a group of friends, of whom Vincent, a lawyer; Mrs. Vincent; Clayborne, an historian; St. Clair, a sculptor; and Alice Leigh, are the principal figures. Gradually these characters become distinct; the way in which Mrs. Vincent remains the center of the group, giving to each a deep and understanding sympathy, until she finally brings the love story of Owen North and Alice Leigh to its climax, is a tribute to those friendships between men and women that flower best perhaps in America. Dr. Mitchell's wide reading and clear insight into human strength and weakness show in the conversations or in the short stories which are told by the group. While the talk never grows heavy, Dr. Mitchell does not hesitate to be serious; through

Dr. North, one of the foremost scientists of his day, he expresses his belief in immortality:

"Once, by a death-bed in a hospital, I heard a surgeon say, as a man ceased to breathe, 'It has stopped; the engine has ceased to go.' His senior, an old man, replied, 'No; the engineer has left it.' I have ceased to reason about it. At every dead man's side I feel more and more that something, immaterial as the Being who willed the thing to live, has escaped me and my analysis."

Dr. North and His Friends (1900), the sequel to *Characteristics,* adds to the group two effective studies. Sybil Maywood, Clayborne's young cousin, is one of the earliest appearances in our fiction of the dual personality. Slightly deformed in body, but beautiful in feature, she attracts St. Clair, the sculptor. In her normal state she falls in love with him, but conquers her love when she realizes its hopelessness. In another state, however, she loves him still and writes letters to him which reveal her passion. In her normal life she is unaware of these events, but the subconscious strain proves almost too much for her frail physique. Xerxes Crofter, the financial pirate from the West whom Dr. North outwits and cures, is also well done. He shocks nearly all the group, and the scene in which they try to conceal their dislike for him, until Sibyl blurts out the reason for their distrust, is a remarkable study of social contrasts. St. Clair wreaks his dislike upon Crofter by making a bust of him which reveals his real nature. Crofter understands this method of attack and retaliates by purchasing, through a third person, St. Clair's statue of an Indian and presenting it to a cigar dealer to stand in front of his store. But Vincent's icy courtesy he does not understand. Of all the characters, Vincent, "whose manners have no accent," is probably the best picture of an American of breeding. His serenity, his poise, the illimitable quality of his reserves, and his innate sense of justice are presented in such quiet comments, as "Bad manners never die," or in his nice distinction between the traveling American and the traveling Englishman in *Characteristics.* He was drawn primarily from Dr. Mitchell's brother-in-law, John L. Cadwalader, but, like all the group, he was not simply a copy of one person, but a part of a composite picture of Dr. Mitchell's circle. Conversation has now become a lost art, but those who had the privilege of dropping in at Dr. Mitchell's on Saturday evenings, when, after nine o'clock, he was at home to his friends, and listening to what has been accurately described as "the best talk in

Philadelphia," know how *Characteristics* and *Dr. North* are records of something very fine that has gone perhaps forever, except in the pages of his books.

Between *Characteristics* and *Dr. North*, Dr. Mitchell had returned to the historical romance in *Hugh Wynne, Free Quaker* (1897). This novel, unquestionably the best fiction dealing with the Revolution, was written in about six weeks,[3] but Dr. Mitchell had been preparing for it through seven years' study. His own words in *Dr. North* best express his methods:

I said: "I have long desired to ask you something about the historical novel. How do you approach it?"

"To answer you I should have to lecture."

"Why not?" said Clayborne.

"Well, do not let me bore you. Suppose I have a story to tell and wish to evolve character amid the scenery and events of an historical episode. Suppose, for instance, the story to lie largely in a great city. For years I must study the topography, dress, manners, and family histories; must be able in mind to visit this or that house; know where to call, whom I shall see, the hours of meals, the diet, games, etc. I must know what people say on meeting and parting. Then I must read letters, diaries, and so on, to get the speech forms and to enable me, if it be autobiography, to command the written style of the day. Most men who write thus of another time try to give the effect of actuality by an excessive use of archaic forms. Only enough should be used to keep from time to time some touch of this past, and not so much as to distract incessantly by needless reminders. It is an art, and, like all good art effects, it escapes complete analysis.

"Then, as to the use of historical characters. These must naturally influence the fate of your puppets; they must never be themselves the most prominent personages of your story."

It was only natural that the greatest novel of the Revolution should come from a native of Philadelphia. There the great struggle had centered; there the nation was born; near by, at Valley Forge, the darkest hours of the conflict had been passed; there treason had been conceived; and we know now that when Sir William Howe left Philadelphia, the Revolution had been won. Philadelphia had suffered less change than any other Colonial city, and when Dr. Mitchell was born, it was surrounded by the atmosphere he needed. In the neighboring township of

[3] On the manuscript in the Library of the University of Pennsylvania is written, "Begun July 16—ended August 30, 1895. Revised by Oct. 7, 1895." Published first, *Century Magazine*, November, 1896–October, 1897.

Merion he found the name of his hero. One of Mrs. Mitchell's ancestors, Edward Wynne, had settled there in 1682, and the region even yet bears the family name.

When Dr. Mitchell wrote *Hugh Wynne*, he worked all day and part of the night, composing in that continued spell of inspiration in which historical romance should be written. Yet the manuscript reveals how careful was the revision, and there is no evidence of haste in the splendid sweep of the narrative. Again Dr. Mitchell's dramatic power, which is revealed in his poetry so often, enabled him to enter into the spirit of this descendant of hot-blooded Welsh squires, tempered by the discipline of the Society of Friends into a will of steel. Hugh tells his own story as a rule, but through the clever device which enables him at times to use the journal of his friend Jack Warder, we can learn much about the hero which he would not have told unless he had stepped out of his self-contained nature. We follow Hugh through his boyhood at the Academy and College of Philadelphia; through his eyes see his stern Quaker father, his Aunt Gainor—a delightfully impulsive woman—and his French mother, who dies young. Perhaps there is no task so hard for the author of the autobiographical novel as the description of a boy's love for his mother; but in *Hugh Wynne* exactly the right note is struck, even when the news of her death comes to him:

I have no mind to dwell on this sad calamity. I went to and fro, finding neither possibility of repose nor any consolation. I saw as I rode, or lay in my boat, that one dear face, its blue-eyed tenderness, its smile of love. I could never thus recall to sight any other of those who, in after-years, have left me; but this one face is here to-day as I write, forever smiling and forever young.

Dr. Mitchell knew well how to introduce a character. Captain Arthur Wynne, who is the evil genius of the story, meets Hugh first at the tavern when Hugh, drunk and gambling recklessly with the British officers, is sobered by the appearance of his mother and Jack Warder. With Arthur Wynne's insult to her and Hugh's blow which fells him, their relations are established and Hugh passes out of boyhood. The older romance would have painted Arthur Wynne merely as a villain, but Dr. Mitchell gave him, through his instant recovery of his self-control, an advantage which enables him to worm his way into the confidence of the family and to win Darthea Peniston's love. The rivalry between him and Hugh is only one of the many conflicts in which the reader is never at a loss to know on which side his sympathy lies. There is a vigorous description of the battle of Germantown, at which Hugh is captured, a realistic picture of the British prison at the Walnut Street jail, and, after Hugh's escape, a brilliant account of the Mischianza, the land and water spectacle in which Major André shone. Dr. Mitchell's sketch of André follows the usual romantic convention, but his analysis of Arnold's character is more keen. It is the modern student of psychology who made Hugh say:

I did not wonder that the Shippens did all they could to break off this strange love affair. They failed: for when a delicate minded, sensitive, well bred woman falls in love with a strong, coarse, passionate man, there is no more to be said except "Take her."

Another quality in *Hugh Wynne* that makes it unusual is the way Dr. Mitchell reveals the fact, often forgotten, that, even in war time, life goes on. He brings in the war frequently, but he never lets it submerge the characters. We see everything through the eyes of Hugh or Jack Warder; unlike Scott or Cooper, Mitchell could weave the bright thread of a charming love story through the dark background of war. Darthea Peniston is real—wayward, impulsive, but turning at last from her infatuation to a finer passion.

The great success of *Hugh Wynne* encouraged Dr. Mitchell to write *The Adventures of François* (1899), a novel laid before and during the French Revolution. It had been foreshadowed by "A Little More Burgundy" (1895), a short story in which a thief saves a noble family from the Terror. From the point of view of history, *François* shows clearly the thorough preparation Dr. Mitchell made, and, according to him, the story was partly a true one. In the realistic picture of the seamy side of a thief's life in Paris, the influence of Defoe is also shown. Dr. Mitchell was a great admirer of the first English realist and possessed an unusual collection of the rarer editions. François "had a great heart, but no conscience," and, as Mme. des Illes, whom he saved from the Jacobins, said: "He had many delicacies of character, but that of which nature meant to make a gentleman and a man of refinement, desertion and evil fortune made a thief and a reprobate."

The novel is truly picaresque and moves rapidly. From time to time the paths of François and the Marquis de Ste. Luce cross each other, and the relations of this pair of opposites is made more plausible by the instinctive sympathy of François with the patrician side of the dispute. He is little interested in the politics of the Revolution; his decisions are personal and he takes his place beside the Marquis at the head of the staircase in the latter's château, up which the Jacobin mob is about to rush, simply because Mme. Renée, the daughter of the Marquis, has been kind to him. The fight on the stairs is exhilarating and formed the best moment of the play which Langdon Mitchell made out of his father's novel. Through the prison, in the shadow of death, and finally out of the underground passages of Paris, François pursues his way, always cool and courageous, laughing at fate, a true "picaro."

Circumstance (1901) is laid in Philadelphia shortly after the Civil War. It is not historical romance, however, but is a study of characters as they are ruled and decided by circumstances. Nearly all the people in the book are hindered from pursuing a program they have chosen by situations they cannot control. Lucretia Hunter, the adventuress, who through skilful flattery wins the interest of Kitty Morrow, a featherhead, and through her becomes the attendant of her uncle, old John Fairthorne, is the best character. She is more forcible than Octopia Darnell, and she supplants Mary Fairthorne, John Fairthorne's other niece, because Mary is really too fine to use the methods Lucretia employs. Then, when Lucretia seems about to secure John Fairthorne, she in turn is defeated by the young doctor, Sidney Archer, who understands her, by the reappearance of her divorced husband, and by the dishonesty of her brother, Lionel Craig, whom she adores and protects. Dr. Mitchell drew on his own experiences, as usual. When Dr. Archer tells Lucretia that if Mr. Fairthorne leaves her more than $30,000 in his will, he will break it by testifying that Mr. Fairthorne was of unsound mind, Dr. Mitchell was telling an incident in which he played a similar part. "But," he once said with a smile, "I let the woman have only $10,000 in real life. It cost no one anything to increase the amount in the novel." He understood that an exact reproduction of events is not fiction.

There are too many characters in *Circumstance* for complete unity, but *Constance Trescot* (1905) is admirably constructed. It is the story of a New England woman who loves her husband passionately and too inclusively. This tendency is accentuated by the fact that they go to St. Ann, Missouri, soon after the Civil War to look after the affairs of her uncle; and her husband, Major Trescot, who has been wounded in the war, has to conduct a law suit which brings upon him popular dislike and the active enmity of Greyhurst, the opposing attorney. Constance at first helps him by her charm and impulsive sympathy, but her effect upon Greyhurst is not fortunate. Those who think they invented "sex appeal" should read the description of Constance when Greyhurst first calls upon the Trescots and the men have come to a complete disagreement:

> Greyhurst cooled instantly. He was in the presence of one of the rare women who, for good or ill, attract because of some inexplicable quality of sex. Incapable of analysis, it accounts for divorces and ruined households, even for suicides or murders. It may be faithful to a great passion, and be modified by character and education, and even by religion; but it is felt, whether the woman wishes it or not, and she who has it instinctively knows its power.

Her power is all the more effective because she uses it without apparent knowledge of it and in absolute indifference on her part to its effect. Here again, contemporary fiction might learn a lesson. When Greyhurst kills Trescot at the trial, Constance finds that the one interest she had in life is gone. She has been brought up without any religion; she has therefore no resource in her sorrow but to devote herself to revenge, for Greyhurst is released by a jury on the plea of self-defence. Brooding over her loss till she becomes obsessed with an *idée fixe*, she returns to St. Ann and first sends Greyhurst the telegram which Trescot had been about to show him when Greyhurst shot him. This takes away from Greyhurst the consolation he had been nursing, that Trescot had been intending to draw on him. Mrs. Trescot, knowing Greyhurst's sensitive, impressionable nature, begins to haunt him, taking every opportunity when she sees him in the streets of following about twenty paces behind him. The knowledge that this black gowned figure is there, or may be there, for she does not weaken the effect by too frequent repetition, drives him to the borders of sanity. She uses her wealth to frustrate certain real estate purchases Greyhurst desires to make; she breaks off the engagement with the woman he loves. Goaded beyond bearing, he kills himself in her presence. Then she finds her life empty again and, failing in her attempt to sacrifice her sister to her needs, she is left alone. The story was based on the career of a young school teacher whose husband was murdered before the war in a Southwestern town because he spoke against slavery, but the art of the story consists in the picture of the gradual disintegration of Constance Trescot's nature. As usual, Dr. Mitchell's skill is shown in what he omits, for in the process of her vengeance Constance Trescot never uses the admiration Greyhurst feels for her as a woman. Consequently her revenge has a cold implacable quality which makes her difficult to forget.

Dr. Mitchell returned to Philadelphia of the past in *The Red City* (1907), so called because of the prevailing color of the brick dwellings. The period was suggested by the historian John B. McMaster, and, as usual, diaries, especially that of Elizabeth Drinker, were used to give the local color. For a hero, Dr. Mitchell created a French emigré, René, Vicomte de Corval, who with his mother flies from the French Revolution after his father has been murdered. This choice was a happy one, since it gave the author an opportunity for social contrasts, and the irony of the Vicomtesse objecting to her son's marriage with Margaret Swanwick, the daughter of the Quaker gentlewoman with whom the almost penniless refugees are living, is delightful. Dr. Mitchell recreated Hugh Wynne and Aunt Gainor Wynne, and, for a protector and advisor of René, brought the German nobleman, masquerading under the name of Schmidt, from *Thee and You*. The conflict of the French and English sympathies during Washington's administration are woven into the story with Dr. Mitchell's usual skill. René's desire for revenge upon Carteaux, the Jacobin who had been responsible for the Vicomte's death, finds its opportunity when he comes to America as the secretary of "Citizen Genêt." The duel in which René is wounded, his later pursuit of Carteaux on the road to New York, the second duel in which Carteaux is shot, and the complications arising from the fact that Carteaux is the bearer of important dispatches, all tie into the fate of Randolph, the Secretary of State. The yellow fever epidemic of 1793 is touched briefly but realistically, for Dr. Mitchell knew what Brockden Brown did not, that misery is not in itself interesting and that its only excuse in fiction is the opportunity it gives for the development of character.

Dr. Mitchell never lost his interest in the short story, which he considered to be a separate form of art from the novel. His most significant contribution to this field was his volume *Little Stories* (1903), in some instances marvellous bits of compression. "A Consultation," in which one physician brings to another a complicated moral problem, is probably unique in fiction. The other short stories, while interesting, especially *A Diplomatic Adventure* (1906), almost a novelette in length, and its sequel contained in a volume, *The Guillotine Club and Other Stories* (1910), are not of the same significance as his longer fiction. But in any consideration of this phase of his work, the short stories told by the characters in *Characteristics* and in *Dr. North and His Friends* must not be forgotten. There is enough material given there simply as a by-product to make several volumes of short stories.

John Sherwood, Iron Master (1911), while not one of his best books, has several fine characters and dramatic situations. John Sherwood is a boy of real imaginative ability, who is forced into the iron business, develops into a hard man without much sympathy, and then is brought into contacts which open life to him in a new way. There is a remarkable study of insanity, also, in the character of the Reverend Benedict Norman, who believes his wife is unfaithful to him and who tries to kill her. When he is killed by a fall, his wife Helen refuses to take any of his property. Later, after his will is found, it is discovered that he has left his money to a hospital and has stated that he does so because he knows his wife is guilty with his friend Heath. Sherwood is faced with this situation since he finds the will. Heath, who is innocent, has just married Lucy Howard, one of Sherwood's best friends. Sherwood has grown to love Helen Norman. What shall he do? He finally decides to pay the amount left to the hospital as a donation and tell Helen he loves her. She burns the will with his consent. Dr. Mitchell provided, in this story, that opportunity for equity to triumph over law, which is always satisfactory—in life or fiction.

Dr. Mitchell's last novel showed no failing of his power. In *Westways* (1913), written at the age of eighty-four, he returned to the days of the Civil War but, unlike *Roland Blake*, the novel began before the war, on an estate of the Penhallows on the western slope of the Alleghenies. Dr. Mitchell felt that the fortunes of a family that had been for years the center of a community would be worth following. However, that portion of the story is not so interesting as the later part, in which both James and John Penhallow, uncle and nephew, take part in the War. There is a vivid description of Gettysburg, especially of the way the Pennsylvania troops in the center of the lines met the charge of Pickett's men and, after being hurled back, rallied and saved the day. Dr. Mitchell wrote from the point of view of a colonel of artillery, James Penhallow, who is shot in the head and suffers concussion of the brain which affects his mental state disastrously for a long time. Through John Penhallow's eyes the closing campaigns of Grant are described, also with vividness, and Roland Blake once more appears. The horrors of war, the dirt and torture from the flies and heat are not spared, but the grim exhilaration of war is there also. So, too, are the after effects, represented by the mental illness of James Penhallow, cured at last by a great surgeon who was probably drawn from Dr. Agnew.

Weir Mitchell's significance in American fiction becomes more apparent when we realize that before his time the abnormal had usually been treated idealistically, and that in Poe and Hawthorne the emotion had possessed the character and created a type. Even Holmes was transitional in this regard; but in characters like Octopia Darnell, Lucretia Hunter, and Constance Trescot, the woman is real, and the abnormal nature remains under artistic control. Much is due to the creative imagination, of course, but quite as much to the ability of Weir Mitchell to coin those phrases which remain in our memory by the royal right of insight. It is not only in the description of abnormal characters that these flashes of insight are given us. All the novels have them. They are studded with sentences or paragraphs which shine like facets of discrimination. Ezra Wendell, the surgeon of *In War Time*, "was possessed of none of that realistic, half-dramatic faculty, which in its highest developments and united with tenderness, constitutes the genius of sympathy." Roland Blake "had that fine honor which is to honesty as is the flower to the leaf." "Society is kept in existence by a series of moral credits." And from *Dr. North*—"In fact the brain in those who grow old wholesomely does not seem to age as does the rest of the human body, nor to feel as distinctly as do the locomotive mechanisms the exasperating vetoes of time." Who but Dr. Mitchell could have written "Moods are the climates of the mind"?

Just as Dr. Mitchell's fame as a physician diverted attention from his artistic work, so it happened that his greatest popularity arose from that field of fiction in which he was not a pioneer. Romance was in the air when *Hugh Wynne, Free Quaker*, appeared in 1896, but it rises clearly above its nearest rivals in the portrayal of American history, both in time and permanence. Literature is supposed to be a reflection of life, but it often leads and determines public ideas, and it is a question whether the great vogue of historical novels which revealed to Americans their splendid past may not have partly accounted for the national temper which brought on the Spanish War. The country was, as it were, feeling its oats.

It would be a mistake, however, to draw too sharp a distinction between the historical novels of Dr. Mitchell and those which for lack of a less abused term we may call the novels of character. *Hugh Wynne* surpasses all other stories of the Revolution just because its creator used in romance the methods which make *Roland Blake* and *Constance Trescot* such triumphs. Most romantic novels are concerned with deeds, not psychology, but the artists who wrote *Quentin Durward, The Spy,* or *Henry Esmond* knew that the touchstone of permanence is the creation of character. Hugh Wynne, his Aunt Gainor, Darthea Peniston, remain in the memory as few of the actors in romantic stories do. The repressions of the Quaker, overcome by the natural instincts of the patriot, result in a hero whose self-control is an element in the artistic development. For we feel that Hugh, the narrator, is understating his dangers and his emotions, and the reader is led unconsciously to intensify both. This identifies him with the writer and the consequent union carries him on.

In the historical novels Weir Mitchell used also the realistic method. Washington, Hamilton, Arnold, Dr. Rush and many others stand out as they never do even in the pages of history. Dr. Mitchell did not make a demigod of Washington; he painted him as he was, a Virginia hunting squire, who swore heartily, was not averse to a risqué story, but on the other hand was a character waiting only the opportunity to rise to greatness. Above all he drew him as a gentleman. Washington was a special study of Dr. Mitchell's, and *The Youth of Washington* (1904), told in the form of an imaginary autobiography, is a remarkable imaginative picture. Novelists have usually dismissed Washington at the close of the Revolution, but in *The Red City* Washington, the statesman, is described in one vivid scene in which he is more human than anywhere else in literature. First we hear him in his Cabinet meeting, settling the fate of Randolph, his Secretary of State, whom he believed to be disloyal. Then, freighted with care, he steps into the hall where the Vicomte de Courval is waiting with an important dispatch and where the Custis children and their friends are being taught dancing, and they run to meet him. The patience with which he attends to de Courval's message to Randolph, which the latter in his agitation had waved aside, and the courtesy with which he speaks to the group of little dancers reveal in a few moments the central fact of Washington's nature, that great self-control which made him, instead of a mere personality, a great character, which not even the psychoanalysts of contemporary biography have been able to tarnish.

Dr. Mitchell's critical judgment of his own work was unusually accurate. As he expressed it in a letter to me: "Of course *Hugh Wynne* is regarded as the book which is likely to have any continuous life—let us say, the immortality of a decade. But *François* is the book of my affections and the only novel with which I can find no fault is *Constance Trescot*."

If I were asked to express in one sentence the most essential quality in the life and work of Weir Mitchell, I think I should quote George Meredith's comment upon *Roland Blake*, which he had read three times. "It has about it," he said, "a kind of nobility." Throughout Dr. Mitchell's life, in war or peace, in the grave moments of decision such as those which fell to his lot as a director of a trust company in Philadelphia, betrayed by its most trusted officer, or in the lighter moments when he presided over the dinners of the Franklin Inn, he was always a gallant spirit. This quality he has imparted to his characters. Roland Blake, Hugh Wynne, Jack Warder, René de Courval, George Trescot, John Penhallow, Darthea Peniston, even François the thief, are patricians. They do not argue about the matter of caste like the Americans of Henry James, who saw his countrymen through a haze of social hopelessness. From whatever time or place they come, they are natural gentlefolk, sometimes a bit provincial, but much oftener they are Americans who have their secure standards, who have traveled and seen the best of other civilizations and remained content with their own inheritance of culture. More than any other of the Northern novelists of his generation, he made them his own. Howells was doing another great task, the representation of the class who had risen since the Civil War, and while Cable, Page, and Hopkinson Smith painted the Southern patrician, Dr. Mitchell's people were of a different species. Since then Mrs. Wharton has depicted this class supremely well once more, but with the difference that lies between New York and Philadelphia.

Like all men of spirit, Weir Mitchell had a large capacity for scorn. In his fiction and poetry this revealed itself in his artistic reticence, springing from the innate refinement of his soul. He knew death in its most horrible form; he knew life in its most terrible aspects. He had read human minds in the grim emptiness of decay or the frantic activity of the possessed. With his great narrative and descriptive power, he could have painted marvellous portraits of the human race in its moments of disgrace. But with a restraint which puts to shame those who, in the sacred name of realism, have prostituted their art and have exploited the base or banal in our national life, the great physiologist showed how well he knew the difference between pathology and literature. He never pays his readers the doubtful compliment of assuming that they are depraved. The scientist knew how bitter life can be, for in *Roland Blake* he said, "If memory were perfect, life would be unendurable." But the artist knew that the highest function of literature is to record those lofty moments which alone make endurable the rest of life. That he found those lofty moments in American life, of the past and the present, will, I believe, become Weir Mitchell's final claim to remembrance.

CHAPTER XVI

PLACE AND RACE IN AMERICAN FICTION

FROM the days of Brackenridge and Royall Tyler, American novelists have not been unaware of locality. During the period before the Civil War, they sought most often that glamour which the past lends to scenes and events. But after the war, which preserved the Union, it seemed as though fiction had a mission to portray all sections of the re-united country to each other and by interpreting the racial strains which made up the United States provide that understanding which would make possible the "more perfect union" of which the founders of the Republic had dreamed. It seems at first glance a paradox that the emphasis upon local color should tend toward a solidarity of feeling, but to those who realize that the strength of the Union depends upon the freedom of each section to govern its own local affairs, there is no paradox.

Nearly all the group whose work has been treated in the chapter dealing with the transition to realism had a keen interest in the places they described; it is a mistake to speak of Bret Harte as though he discovered something new in the fictional treatment of a locality. But it is true that the great success of Harte and Mark Twain stimulated several of the novelists who began to write in the 'seventies. Howells began with books of travel, but with him locality became second to character. Of the others who began in the 'sixties, Weir Mitchell dealt with Philadelphia of the past and present, and Mrs. Ward distinctly with New England. The magazines played their part, too, in the stimulation of interest in locality. Nearly every issue of *Scribner's Monthly* in the early 'seventies contains a leading article describing the States or sections, especially those of the South and the West. Edward King was especially active in this regard and his direct inspiration of the work of Cable is a matter of record. It would obviously be impossible even to chronicle all the fiction, especially the short stories, which from 1870 on capitalized this interest. But certain of the novelists rise above the rest on account of their fidelity to the life they described and the permanent quality of their art.

Priority of a year or so means little in such a classification, but Sarah Orne Jewett (1849–1909) seems to have been the first of this group to publish. Born in Berwick, Maine, she came of seafaring stock, but her father broke from this tradition and studied medicine. As a child, Sarah Jewett went with him on his visits and grew to know the country districts, as well as the seaports of Maine. The dwindling farms, the great pine forests stimulated the mind of an imaginative girl who read *Cranford* and *The Pearl of Orr's Island* and pondered over a departing glory which she only later knew was departing. She began with verse and children's stories, but in December, 1869, she had the felicity to see "Mr. Bruce" in the *Atlantic,* and without undue haste she continued, with Howells' encouragement, to write about the life she knew. "Mr. Bruce," a story of a girl who masquerades as a waitress in her father's house, has little of her later quality. The early stories were published as *Old Friends and New* (1879) and her rapid improvement is evident even in this first volume. In "Lady Ferry," a story of the effect made on a child by a woman who has outlived her own generation, Miss Jewett said, "One often hears of the influence of climate upon character: there is a strong influence of place: and the inanimate things which surround us indoors and out make us follow out in our lives their own silent characteristics." The best of these early stories are "Miss Sydney's Flowers," in which a self-centered woman finds the seeds of kindness grow in "the empty garden of her heart," and "A Lost Lover," a sad but a charming tale of the loss of an illusion. In the nine years between "Mr. Bruce" and "A Lost Lover," Miss Jewett had matured her style into that quiet distinction which is her great claim to remembrance. Some of the early stories like "A Shore House" and "Deephaven Cronies" were incorporated in her first novel, *Deephaven* (1877).

Strictly speaking, *Deephaven* is not a novel, but a series of connected episodes describing scenes and characters in this imaginary seaport of New England. It is based on Berwick, of course, but Miss Jewett never condescended to the merely photographic art. Through the eyes of a young girl visitor to Deephaven, she reveals the beauty of a civilization proud even in its decay, and uncompromising with progress. The delicate shades of social distinction, which are preserved by the patricians who represent them and by the commonalty who recognize them, are touched with humor and yet with sympathy. Perhaps the best chapter is "In Shadow," in which she describes the desolation of the cottage where the father and mother have died, and the children are being taken by the more or less unwilling charity of relatives and neighbors. Death, in its approach, its coming and its effects, is treated with absolute reality. There is a more definite plot in *A Country Doctor* (1884), and Miss Jewett's own childhood is reflected in the life of Anna Prince, who accompanies her guardian, Dr. Leslie, in his rounds and who becomes a physician. The opening of *A Country Doctor*, describing the desperate struggle of Nan's mother to reach her home at the farm with her little girl before she dies, is as fine a narrative as Miss Jewett ever wrote; her observation of life is frequently couched in memorable sentences like "Conformity is the inspiration of much second rate virtue." Her understanding of New England nature is shown in the remark of Dr. Ferris, a friend of Dr. Leslie, that "for intense self centred, smouldering volcanoes of humanity, New England cannot be matched the world over," and her understanding of the country people at a funeral is complete. "They pay homage to Death," she observes, "rather than to the dead." The novel contains a fine contrast between this country life and that in Dunport, on the coast, where Nan goes to visit her father's sister, long estranged, and takes her place to her aunt's surprise easily and naturally in the social life of the town. Less interesting are her struggles between love and her profession, and Miss Jewett's naïve remark that the superabundance of women proves that some should not marry savors rather of New England than of human nature. *A Country Doctor* is a better study of the woman physician, however, than Howells' *Dr. Breen's Practice* or Mrs. Ward's *Doctor Zay*, partly because we are spared the details of her medical experience, and the character drawing of Dr. Leslie and the Thacher relatives and neighbors is skilful.

In *A Marsh Island* (1885), Miss Jewett wrote a love story in which she was so desirous of depicting a man and a girl who were hesitating to acknowledge the growth of love that, with all her art, she never makes them quite alive. Dick Dale, the rich young painter who spends a summer in Farmer Owen's house on Marsh Island, is drawn back from his fancy for Doris Owen because of his sense of difference, and his hesitation is not unnatural. The conflict in Doris Owen lies between her love for Dan Lester, who has always worshipped her, and the fascination which the charm of Dale throws over her. But the conflict in either case is too delicate for passion, and the reality of the picture arises from the exquisite descriptions of the place and the careful arrangement of detail in the life of the farm. To Miss Jewett, nature is alive—its processes are intentional and the sun and the breeze and the waters of the marsh are more actual than the human beings. *A Marsh Island* is a prose poem of earth and water, but it is not a great novel.

Meanwhile she was steadily progressing in the art of the short story. *The Mate of the Daylight and Friends Ashore* (1883), it is true, marked no distinct advance, although "An Only Son" is a moving recital of the agony of a father who believes incorrectly that his son has robbed him of money belonging to the town, and who ages rapidly in the one day which elapses before the truth is known. But in *A White Heron and Other Stories* (1886), she rose to a very high level. "A White Heron" is perfect of its kind. The conflict in the heart of a little girl between her worship of the young ornithologist who is searching for the white heron and her love for the bird which she has seen from the top of the pine tree is expressed in the inevitable manner that distinguishes the artist:

No, she must keep silence! What is it that suddenly forbids her and makes her dumb? Has she been nine years growing and now, when the great world for the first time puts out a hand to her, must she thrust it aside for a bird's sake? The murmur of the pine's green branches is in her ears, she remembers how the white heron came flying through the golden air and how they watched the sea and the morning together, and Sylvia cannot speak; she cannot tell the heron's secret and give its life away.

And in "Marsh Rosemary" Miss Jewett tells in a few words of a tragedy which the great soul of a plain woman lifts into dignity. It is not only the plot, which is Enoch Arden reversed; it is the way Miss Jewett illuminates the dark passages of Ann Floyd's life with the light of her unbending courage. When Jerry Lane, her shiftless husband, is reported dead, he blooms into an ideal, and she is happy. Then the news is brought to her, by the one woman she dislikes most, that he is living, married again in a distant town. Ann's later journey to denounce him, the vision of his wife and baby and the warmth and comfort she sees through the window, her return without a word to her loneliness, are told with the same marvelous economy.

There is more variety than is generally appreciated in Miss Jewett's short stories. In *The King of Folly Island and Other People* (1888) we find next to the weird atmosphere of "The Landscape Chamber," in which she rivals Hawthorne, the realistic comedy of "Law Lane," in which Mrs. Powder, a delightful person, reconciles two warring families who have impoverished themselves for generations over a law suit by convincing Mrs. Barnet that she is dying and thereby wringing her consent to the marriage of her son and Ruth Crosby. In this story she states clearly "there are no new plots to the comedies and tragedies of life," and she took the situation from Shakespeare just as she took it from Hawthorne in "The Village Shop," but she made of it a new thing. Miss Jaffrey, with her sacrifice in keeping a shop, is not Hepzibah Pyncheon, even if her gallant struggle has a similar origin, and Miss Jewett no more hesitated to take such a suggestion than Hawthorne had hesitated to take it from Irving.

That this variety has its limits was shown in her comparative failure to treat French Canadian life in "Mère Pochette" in this volume, or Irish life in "The Last of the Bogans" in her next collection, *Strangers and Wayfarers* (1890). But when she is dealing with the tragedies which come to people of good blood who meet loss, she could treat the South in "The Mistress of Sydenham Plantation" almost as well as New England. After all, it is the same tragedy, for if we compare it to "The Town Poor," one of the most poignant stories of New England women who suffer bravely the final degradation of public charity, it is the high heart that makes both stories significant.

The past is always strong in Miss Jewett's stories. "A Native of Winby," published in the *Atlantic* in 1891 and becoming the title story for *A Native of Winby and Other Tales* (1893), is of especial importance since it tells of the return of a distinguished senator from the West to the little village in New England where he had been born, and the disappointment he feels at first at the lack of general recognition. Then he comes to the home of Mrs. Abby Hender, and the fragrance of a boy and girl friendship is waiting for him, without sentimentality to mar it. The man who has achieved much and the woman who has fought her own fight against trouble and her narrowing life meet on the common ground of the democracy of a childhood spent together. Abby's remark to her granddaughter at the end is characteristic: "I've always been lookin' forward to seein' him again, an' now it's all over." The strength of friendship also strikes the keynote of "Decoration Day," and the love of adventure in "The Flight of Betsey Lane," who journeys from the poorhouse to the Centennial Exposition at Philadelphia. One of the most charming of her stories is "A War Debt." It is laid in the South, but the central character, Tom Preston, is a New England man who goes down to return a silver cup which had been taken from the Bellamys during the War, and had been rescued by Tom's father. It is a study in courtesy, of the reaction of good breeding in one section to that of another. It appeared in *Harper's Magazine* for January, 1895, and in the same year was included in *The Life of Nancy*, which also contains "The Hiltons' Holiday," a fine study of relative values in the pursuit of happiness. There is delightful comedy in "The Only Rose," in which Mrs. Beckford tries to decide on which of her three husbands' graves she will lay a special tribute, and in "All My Sad Captains," in which the widow Lunn chooses among three of the elderly sea captains that Miss Jewett knew so well.

The note of hero worship and of the love of England are both illustrated in "The Queen's Twin," the title story of the collection of 1899. Abby Martin of Dunnet Landing, being born on the same day as Queen Victoria, builds her life upon this fact. Having an opportunity to go to England as cook on a vessel, she sees the Queen and declines to see anything else, refusing to spoil one great effect by the intrusion of lesser ones. There was no apparent decline in this later period, "Martha's Lady," a study in the power of devotion to illuminate a life being one of her best stories.

Indeed, her masterpiece came at this time. *The Country of the Pointed Firs* (1896) is one of the rare pieces of art which occur but seldom in a nation's literature. It is hardly a novel; it is a series of cameos, episodes in the life of Dunnet, a seafaring town of Maine. Seldom does an author repeat an earlier success, but Miss Jewett went far beyond *Deephaven* in unity and that complete fusion of character and situation which distinguishes *The Country of the Pointed Firs*. The principal characters, Mrs. Almira Todd, with whom the narrator lives during the summer, her mother, her brother William, and the shepherdess whom William marries, are portraits, not photographs. Drawn with the pencil of insight, colored by the genius of sympathy, retouched by the loving care of memory, and set in a background of sky and sea which Miss Jewett has made her own, they are triumphs of the art of fiction. Episodic as the chapters are, they glide into one another so smoothly that the joints are invisible. The shrewd, kindly nature of Almira Todd, with a tang of criticism for her neighbors and an insistence upon curing them with her herbs whether they will or not, is the moving spirit. But her mother and brother who live together on Green Island, especially the inarticulate William, whose forty years of courtship of Esther Hight, the shepherdess, is finally ended with her grim mother's death, are almost as finely etched. His annual trout fishing in Esther's country, where no fish are to be caught, is one of the most delightful episodes. The family reunion of the Bowdens, the conquest of old 'Lijah Tilley, the story of "poor Joanna" all fit into the picture. Out of the simplest happenings Miss Jewett created the importance that arises from the integrity of characters, who win their own self-respect from the forgetfulness of self, and whose shy kindnesses are masked by protective silence. Miss Jewett puts it all so well in the introduction to the Bowden reunion:

It is very rare in country life, where high days and holidays are few, that any occasion of general interest proves to be less than great. Such is the hidden fire of enthusiasm in the New England nature that, once given an outlet, it shines forth with almost volcanic light and heat. In quiet neighborhoods such inward force does not waste itself upon those petty excitements of every day that belong to cities, but when, at long intervals, the altars to patriotism, to friendship, to the ties of kindred, are reared in our familiar fields, then the fires glow, the flames come up as if from the inexhaustible burning heart of the earth; the primal fires break through the granite dust in which our souls are set.

Caught perhaps by the vogue of the historical romance, Miss Jewett wrote *The Tory Lover* (1901), in which the scenes are laid in Massachusetts, in England and on the sea. She worked hard and the atmosphere of colonial Berwick is caught accurately. The struggle in Lieutenant Wallingford's nature between his loyalty to the King and to his country reflects many a similar struggle during the Revolution. But Miss Jewett could not acquire the large manner, which the historical romance demands.[1]

The conventional judgment of Miss Jewett's fiction places her short stories on a higher plane than her novels. But the characters that make the deepest impression come from the longer narratives, for the obvious reason that she has had more time to establish them. As a matter of fact, her significance must be judged in terms of quality, not quantity. In both her short and her long narratives her achievement was to paint imperishably the decaying grandeur of New England, symbolized in the towns, once great seaports, which live on memories of former splen-

---

[1] See *Letters of Sarah Orne Jewett*, pp. 209–210, for account of the real Tory from whom she drew the character.

dor. As is natural, her characters are largely feminine, members of families whose men have died or gone away. In the cities they are content to live on quietly, existing on narrowed incomes, cheered by the homage of other women who cherish them as the representatives of a more virile civilization. In the country, they have a harder struggle with the menace of the poorhouse ever present. This harder aspect of life is not so often stressed as it was later, but Miss Jewett did not shirk its presentation. She felt, however, that misery or lack of breeding was not necessarily of supreme importance in fiction. As she says in the preface to *Deephaven* in the edition of 1893:

There will also exist that other class of country people who preserve the best traditions of culture and of manners, from some divine inborn instinct toward what is simplest and best and purest, who know the best because they themselves are of kin to it. Human nature is the same the world over, provincial and rustic influences must ever produce much the same effects upon character, and town life will ever have in its gift the spirit of the present, while it may take again from the quiet of the hills and fields and the conservatism of country hearts a gift from the spirit of the past.

She knew her strength and usually her limitations, although her stories of Irish characters in New England which became increasingly frequent in her later period prove only more clearly that her forte lay in the treatment of her own people and her own section. She was right, from the very beginning of her career, in refusing to imitate any changing fashion of literary method and in cultivating her own limpid and distinctive style. She had her literary gods, of course, and two sentences from Flaubert stood always on her desk. But her manner shows no appreciable influence from him or from anyone. A reading of her letters and a glance at her portrait taken after her honorary degree had made her "the first daughter of Bowdoin" reveal clearly the serene nature of which the ordered beauty of her style is the inevitable expression.

If novelists are to be classified in terms of their supreme achievement, Helen Hunt Jackson (1830–1885) belongs clearly to this group for she will be remembered for her one novel of the Far West. Yet it came at the end of her career, which began with poetry as early as 1865. In September, 1871, the "Saxe Holm Stories," which she never acknowledged but which are hers, began to appear in *Scribner's Monthly*, and two volumes of them were published in 1874 and 1878. They are love stories, sometimes quite powerful and sometimes sentimental, studies of those elements in life which interfere with the progress or duration of passion. Usually the situation dominates the characters, but in "Farmer Bassett's Romance" there is a realistic treatment of the farmer who is fascinated by a summer visitor and who is made to realize how unsuited a match between them would be. Mrs. Jackson had a preference for anonymity, for her first novels, *Mercy Philbrick's Choice* (1876) and *Hetty's Strange History* (1877), both appeared in the "No Name Series." The first is a fine study of a young widow's character, possibly reflecting the author's own experience after the sudden death of her first husband, Edward Hunt. It is laid in a New England village, and the prophecy that the intense individuality of that civilization will end in national apathy shows her understanding of her own section. The horror of a "sea captain's widow" earning her own living is worthy of Miss Jewett. *Hetty's Strange History* is not so important, and the picture of the Canadian province in which she hides herself is conventional.

In 1872 Helen Hunt had gone to California, had married again, and had become interested in the Indian question. The first fruit was her well-documented discussion of the treatment of the Indians in *A Century of Dishonor* (1881). Disappointed in the reception of this book, she determined to appeal through fiction. *Ramona* (1884) is romance, idealistic in treatment, inspired like *Uncle Tom's Cabin* by a woman's indignation at injustice. While it is laid in California at a time shortly after the Mexican War, it is hardly an historical novel. Mrs. Jackson placed it in the past in order to obtain the glow and color of the Spanish civilization before it had been swept away by the American invasion. The main characters are imaginary, and those based on real people were drawn from persons she met while in California. With the instinct of an imaginative artist, she treated freely scenes she visited in California, notably the Camulos Ranch, one of the few remaining examples of the *hacienda* existing in 1881. Some of the incidents of the novel, indeed, were based on events that had happened to the owners of that ranch, but the characters were her own. By making Ramona the child of a Scotchman and an Indian woman, she made more probable the girl's love for Alessandro, the Temecula Indian. Both are attractive fictional creations. Ramona lives by her devotion, courage, and generosity, and her quiet heroism in bearing the knowledge that her foster-mother, Señora Moreno, mistress of the ranch, dislikes her and protects her only through a sense of duty to the dead sister who has left her Ramona as a trust. Señora Moreno is extremely well drawn; a woman who not only ruled her household, but who appeared to do it through her son Felipe, the one being she loved, and who accomplished her ends implacably and fed her love of power with the lives of all around her. It is she who drives Ramona and Alessandro to leave the ranch secretly and take up the long wandering which brings Alessandro eventually to madness and death. Like Cooper's Uncas, he is a "noble savage," but there is reality in his foreboding sense of responsibility for Ramona's future and his brooding helplessness in the face of wrong that he cannot analyze or defy. It was to call attention to the oppression of his race that the novel was written, and yet Mrs. Jackson proved herself a novelist rather than a mere propagandist by using the details of oppression to develop and reveal character instead of describing misery simply for its own sake. She knew her facts and uses them skilfully, as in the murder of Alessandro, which parallels almost exactly an actual case, but she controls facts rather than permits them to control her. Her portraits of Father Salvierderra, the Franciscan friar, of Felipe Moreno, who loves Ramona hopelessly so long and who is finally rewarded, and that of "Aunt Ri," the pioneer from Tennessee, are admirable. In *Ramona*, too, Mrs. Jackson came into the maturity of her style. Quotable passages abound, such as the description of Father Salvierderra's morning song, or the growth of love in Ramona's heart.

Zeph (1885), published posthumously, is laid in Colorado and was uncompleted. It has some realism in its picture of an old maid's love story. Mrs. Jackson's later short stories, in which her interest in places led her to lay the scenes in Prince Edward's Island, the Saranac region in New York, and Lancaster County in Pennsylvania, were published in 1887 as *Between Whiles*. They are competently written but they do not rise to the level of *Ramona*, whose continued life after one hundred and thirty-five reprintings, was evidenced by an edition of 50,000 copies in 1935.

Usually a novelist's impulse to deal with the life of a locality was confined to one section, but Constance Fenimore Woolson dealt not only with the Northwest and the South but also with the European scene. She was born in Claremont, New Hampshire, in 1840, her mother, Hannah Cooper Pomeroy Woolson, being the niece of James Fenimore Cooper. She was educated in Cleveland, Ohio, and as a girl spent her summers at Mackinac Island in the straits between Lake Huron and

Lake Michigan. In 1858 she graduated from Madame Chegary's school in New York City, which was to appear in her novel *Anne,* and began her contributions to periodicals with a sketch, "The Happy Valley," in *Harper's* for July, 1870. This description of a German community on the Tuscarawas River in Ohio, which she used later in a short story, "Wilhemina," was her first article to be written and shows how like Howells she began with an interest in the scene, out of which characters later developed. In the same month her sketch, "The Fairy Island," a description of Mackinac Island, appeared in *Putnam's.* With this Lake region she was thoroughly familiar, and when she turned to it as material for fiction, after a few preliminary stories of a somewhat conventional character, it is interesting to see how the quality of her work improved. Even in a comparatively poor story, "One Versus Two," the writing becomes alive when the characters reach the Lake country.[2] From 1872 to 1878 she made the Lake country the background for twenty-three stories.[3]

Miss Woolson had the rare gift of self-criticism, and her selection for her first volume of stories, *Castle Nowhere; Lake Country Sketches* (1875), includes the most significant of her early work, although "A Flower of the Snow," [4] might easily have been included. How far she had come in three years may be seen by comparing this book with her first published volume, *The Old Stone House* (1873), a rather pietistic story for children. How strong Bret Harte's influence was upon her is seen in the story "Misery Landing," in which the hero, who has fled from a love he does not wish to pursue, tells in his diary his admiration for Harte, "who shows us the good in the heart of the outcast," and who makes the shrewd observation that "everywhere it is the cultivated people only who are taken with Bret." "The Lady of Little Fishing" shows even more clearly Harte's influence. The narrator, Mitchell, tells of the saintly woman who suddenly appeared among the rough hunters and trappers, thirty years before, and preached to them, so that they worshipped her. The relapse of the rough men when they discover their idol is simply a woman, is not badly done, and the fact that the narrator is the one she loved is concealed to make a dramatic ending. It is the "moral contrast" again. Some of the stories deal with Mackinac Island, some

[2] *Lippincott's,* August, 1872.
[3] See Kern, John D., *Constance Fenimore Woolson* (1934), for a complete analysis of these stories.
[4] *Galaxy,* January, 1874.

with the shores of Lake Superior, some with Ohio. Nearly always, however, the scenery is the background; the central character is an outsider who proves sometimes a disturbing influence or, as in "The Old Agency," in which she describes from real life the courtly French priest who forms such a contrast to his parishioners, he is a mystery and a benediction. Miss Woolson, like Bret Harte, remains an observer rather than a partaker of the life. But her descriptions of the marshes in "St. Clair Flats" or of the fog in "Castle Nowhere" are masterly.

On account of her mother's health, Miss Woolson was constantly traveling, and between 1873 and 1879 she spent her time largely in Florida and the Carolinas. The result came, as before, in the form of travel sketches, short stories, and novels. Between 1875 and 1879 she published fourteen short stories with a Southern background. The best of these are included in *Rodman the Keeper* (1880). She used first the Florida scene. "Miss Elisabetha," laid before the Civil War, is a tragic story of the efficient Northern woman who manages the life of her ward, "Doro," keeps him from his proper career and sees him sink into contented laziness. "The South Devil" is one of her finest achievements. The way she establishes the mystical relation between the great swamp and Carl, the young musician who hears the harmonies the swamp sings only to him, and who cannot keep away from it though it may mean death to him, reveals her great power of understanding the relations of place and human character. It is not only vivid descriptions of the "rank luxuriance of the heart of the swamp, a riot of intoxicating, steaming, swarming, fragrant, beautiful tropical life, without man to make or mar it. All the world was once so, before man was made." The swamp is active, living. When Mark goes into it to save his brother, "the matted water vines caught at his boat like hundreds of hands; the great lily leaves slowly sank and let the light boat glide over them." In "Sister St. Luke," a story of the boundless courage of a timid Spanish nun who saves two shipwrecked men from the tornado, Miss Woolson not only showed her knowledge of the seacoast of Florida, but also revealed the breadth of her understanding of races not her own. So in "Felipa," the passionate devotion of a little Minorcan girl to a man and a woman, themselves lovers, whom she adores in different ways, is rendered powerfully and objectively.

Next Miss Woolson turned to the mountain regions of Tennessee and western North Carolina. But in her first story of this region,

"Crowder's Cove," [5] the mountaineer, John Crowder, appears only as a "neutral" in the Civil War, and the main characters are a New England woman and a Southern girl of very different origin from the mountain people. Even in "Up in the Blue Ridge," which appeared in *Appleton's* for August, 1878, three months after Miss Murfree's first story had been published in the *Atlantic,* the mountaineers are described but are only the background. The conflict is between the Northern characters like Stephen Wainwright and John Royce, and the Southerner Richard Eliot, who, though he is associated with a gang of moonshiners, is distinctly one of the planter class. The story is really a study of the reactions of Wainwright, who risks his life to save Eliot, because of his interest in Honor Dooris, Eliot's cousin.

Much more significant than her stories of the mountaineers are Miss Woolson's sympathetic revelations of the conditions in Reconstruction days in the South. "Old Gardiston," laid in no very definite spot in the rice lands of the Carolinas, is a touching picture of a girl's proud resistance to her growing love for a Northern officer, made real by the description of brave economies a man could not have imagined. "In the Cotton Country," on the other hand, is a story of a woman's hopeless suffering from the effects of war, without any expectation of the future, a woman whose husband had been called away at the altar and whom she had never seen again. This picture of apathy, of courage only to endure, is as realistic as it well can be. It is to her credit also that while Negro rule was still being imposed upon the South with Federal bayonets, a Northern woman told through her fictional characters the truth. She made it even more evident in 1878 in "King David," a story of a New England teacher who goes South to educate the Negroes and fails hopelessly because of their shiftlessness and drunkenness. It is another Northerner, a liquor-seller and political organizer, who helps to defeat him, but King David's failure is inherent because he tries to treat the Negroes as his equals. The very title shows her skill in her implication of the magnitude of the problem. These, together with "Rodman the Keeper," a study in the isolation of a Northern officer who becomes the warden of a Union cemetery in a Southern community, are the best of the post-war stories.

Miss Woolson began her first novel, *Anne* (1882), on the island of Mackinac, which she knew so well, and the scenes of Anne's girlhood as

[5] *Appleton's Journal,* March 18, 1876.

she grows up, a strong, tender, brave nature, meeting the responsibilities of her young step-sister Tita and the boys, when her father's death leaves them to her, have been the favorite portions of the book. There are remarkable character portraits in Miss Lois, a New England Puritan who had come out to convert the Indians, and the two clergymen, Père Michaux and Dr. Gaston, who watch over Anne. It seems a pity that after establishing so well these characters and the atmosphere of an army post in the 'fifties, Miss Woolson should have taken Anne away to New York City, to the school she herself had attended, but after all she builds up by deft touches the girl's reaction to the social organization which meets her with the cruelty which is the lot of "the islander." Her life under the patronage of her wealthy aunt gives Miss Woolson ample opportunity for keen social satire, and there has hardly ever been written a better picture of an American girl of character and natural breeding thrown into unconscious rivalry with women of the world, first suffering defeat and finally accomplishing victory. Anne's relations with Helen Lorrington and their rivalry for the love of Heathcote are developed with that insight into the capacity of women for friendship, love, and hate in which the realist again shone. There is, of course, too much in the novel, especially at the end, where Helen's murderer is brought to confession by means hardly credible; but the novel created marked critical approval even in its serial form in *Harper's Magazine*.[6]

In *For the Major* (1883) Miss Woolson showed none of the faults but all the virtues of *Anne*. It is much shorter, and the tone is kept with a restrained power that is almost beyond praise. The people are Southerners with high standards of conduct, living in "Far Edgerley," a hill town on the eastern flank of "Chillawassee Mountain" in North Carolina. They are not mountaineers, however, but a little group of survivals from the past of the South. Major Scarborough Carroll; his second wife, Madam Marion Carroll; Sara, his daughter by his first wife; and "Scar," his little son by his second, live on the Farms. He has been a distinguished man, but he is beginning to fail. The skill with which Marion Carroll guards the Major from the townspeople, so that his mental faltering shall not be apparent, even more the way she keeps Sara from tiring her father by insistence on his preserving the high ideals which Sara has had from her childhood about him, is unusual. Gradually through the conversations of different characters we learn,

[6] See J. Henry Harper, *The House of Harper*, 484–487.

just as we do in real life, how Major Carroll has married Marion, a widow much younger than himself, how her first husband had fled, after a shooting affray, taking their boy away with him, and how she had heard of the pursuit and the drowning of both of them. Beginning with gratitude, her love for the Major has grown into a devotion that makes her an epic figure. How she conceals her real age, not from vanity but because of the Major's delight in her youth, how her blonde beauty lends itself to her brave artifices, above all how her unwavering watchfulness fights for the security and peace which her earlier life makes precious to her, is told with an art that no one of that day could surpass. Then into that security comes the disturbing element. Her eldest son, who is not dead, finds her and, under an assumed name, comes to Far Edgerley. She cannot acknowledge him, and here Sara plays her part, acting as go-between and almost killing her own chance of happiness with the young rector, Frederick Owen, so that her father will not suffer. There is a remarkable scene in which Marion Carroll waits until the Major is asleep to go to the death-bed of her son, which for quiet heroism is hard to surpass. Then when the Major's mind finally fails and he becomes like a child, Mrs. Carroll at once relaxes her vigilance of years, becomes overnight her real age, and tells her story to Owen. The passage in which she reveals to Owen her well-guarded secret, is an example of the art of fiction in which a great novelist pays a tribute to the imaginative power of her reader:

". . . And now I must come to my second reason for telling you. You remember I said that there were two. This is something which even Sara does not know—I would not give her any of that burden; she could not help me, and she had enough to bear. She could not help me; but now you can. It is something I want you to do for me. It could not be done before, it could not be done until the Major became as he is at present. No one now living knows; still, as you are to be one of us, I should like to have you do it for me."

And then she told him.

Miss Woolson scorns to spoil her effect by explanations. But when Owen marries the Major to Marion, the reader suddenly realizes that this is the last gesture of a great soul, who, having learned from her son that her first husband was alive at the time of her marriage to Major Carroll, does what she can to make herself in truth the wife of the man she has loved so dearly. All her life she has lived for others; this at least she can do for herself.

If *For the Major* reminds one of an etching in which one central figure stands out in exquisite proportions against a background whose very limitations present that figure to perfection, *East Angels* (1886) is a glowing canvas, rich with color, where the characters gain each in his own way in vividness from their contrast or association with the rich languor of the Florida landscape. The principal actors are from the North. Miss Woolson proceeds to build up slowly a strong moral contrast between two groups of characters, those who insist upon doing right even at the cost of happiness and those who demand their own happiness and sweep ruthlessly aside anyone in their way. Margaret Harold, married at seventeen to a charming, selfish husband who leaves her for a Frenchwoman shortly after their union, is one of those women who builds her life on self-sacrifice. Not only does she crush down the love she begins to feel for Evert Winthrop, but she does the harder thing—she bears quietly the implicit blame of the separation. Skilfully Miss Woolson shows how the others, led by Mrs. Rutherford, a professional invalid who succeeds in making the attentions she demands from Margaret seem like a favor to her, all expect Margaret to "do her duty." Even Evert Winthrop is deceived at first, but when Lance Harold returns to Margaret, leaves her again and once more comes back, an invalid, Margaret has to combat not only her own desire but also Winthrop's determined passion. To draw a character whose achievement lies in renunciation is not easy, for her very inarticulate acceptance of the path she has chosen forbids the expression of her deep feeling. Winthrop's final restraint and respect for her determination are not so credible, but, as he is drawn, they were at least possible.

Mrs. Thorne, the owner of East Angels, is another illustration of self-sacrifice. A New England school teacher who had married a Southern planter of English descent, she is described delightfully by her neighbor, Mrs. Carew:

". . . However, I ought to say that poor little Mistress Thorne has certainly done her very best to acquire our Southern ways; she has actually tried to make herself over, root, stem, and branch, from her original New England sharpness to our own softer temperament, though I always feel sure, at the same moment, that, in the core of the rock, the old sap burns still—like the soul under the ribs of death, you know; not that I mean that exactly (though she *is* thin), but simply that the leopard cannot change his spots, nor the zebra his stripes, nor," added the good lady—altering her tone to solemnity as she perceived that her language was becoming Biblical—"the wild *cony* her *young*. . . ."

Mrs. Thorne's desperate sense of duty, which makes her try to become a Southern woman, while she prays secretly during the Civil War for "her own people," leads to a remarkable scene on her death-bed when she confides to Margaret how she has loathed the life she has had to live. Opposed to these stern self-schooled people are not only Lance Harold and Mrs. Rutherford, who are drawn with malicious insight, but, more important, Garda Thorne, Mrs. Thorne's daughter. With a good deal of Spanish blood, her beauty, her utter selfishness and her rapidly changing emotional reactions make her very much alive. Miss Woolson does not draw any conclusions or preach any lesson; nor does she reward her good characters, like George Eliot, with the satisfaction of self-respect. They are unhappy, but they cannot do otherwise. Marriage, to Margaret Harold, is for better or worse, and divorce is out of the question.

There are some remarkable scenes, as usual, in *East Angels*. The landscape plays its part in the nightlong search of Winthrop and Margaret for Lance in the great swamp with its deadly poisonous sweetness. And how well Miss Woolson conveys her knowledge of woman's nature in the conversation between Margaret and Winthrop concerning Garda:

"We seem to have much the same idea of her," said Winthrop. "I shouldn't have thought it possible," he added.

"That we should agree in anything?" said Margaret, with a faint smile.

"No, not that; but a woman so seldom has the same idea of another woman that a man has. And—if you will allow me to say it—I think the man's idea often the more correct one, for a woman will betray (confide, if you like the term better) more of her inner nature, her real self, to a man, when she knows him well and likes him, than she ever will to any woman, no matter how well she may know and like her."

Margaret concurred in this.

"So you agree with me there too? Another surprise! What I have said is true enough, but women generally dispute it."

"What you have said is true, after a fashion," Margaret answered. "But the inner feelings you speak of, the real self, which a woman confides to the man she likes rather than to a woman, these are generally her ideal feelings, her ideal self; what she thinks she feels, or hopes to feel, rather than the actual feeling; what she wishes to be, rather than what she is. She may or may not attain her ideal; but in the mean time she is judged, by those of her own sex at least, according to her present qualities, what she has already attained; what she is practically, and every day."

In *Jupiter Lights* (1889), Miss Woolson combined the coast of Georgia and the Lake country, but as usual the characters dominate the scene. In Eve Bruce, a Northern woman who comes to Romney Island in the sounds south of Savannah, Miss Woolson depicted a strong-willed nature, impatient of the weaker but none the less tenacious Southern woman, her brother's widow. Her horror when she finds Cicely has re-married, her rescue of Cicely and her little nephew from the crazed dipsomaniac husband, her flight with them to Port aux Pins on Lake Superior, and her own ultimate love story make up a novel with more action than is usual with Miss Woolson, some of it, especially the final scenes in Italy, being too melodramatic. It is, however, a fine study of the havoc made by any woman who tries to manage another's life.

So far Miss Woolson had made a woman the central character of her novels, but in her last, *Horace Chase* (1894), she presented a study of the self-made man, thirty-seven years old, who marries a girl of nineteen, Ruth Franklin. The Franklins are from New York but live either in Asheville, North Carolina, or at St. Augustine because they have been left property there by an aunt who belonged to a North Carolina family. The situation is one of frequent occurrence in which a family without much energy depend upon a strong nature and at the same time secretly look down upon him as beneath their social stratum. Horace Chase dominates the novel, and his reception of Ruth's confession of her in-fatuation for a younger man, and her journey to her lover only to find he has forgotten her, is quite in keeping with a largeness of view which success has given Chase. But while there is good character analysis, es-pecially of the women, who care more for the son and brother than they do for each other, *Horace Chase* does not leave the same sense of artistic completeness as do the earlier novels.

Miss Woolson's later short stories were concerned largely with Euro-pean scenes. After her mother's death in 1879, she went to England and the Continent, staying most frequently in Italy. Her first short story written abroad, "Miss Grief," [7] is of special interest because the central character is a woman who dies of privation rather than change her

[7] *Lippincott's Magazine*, May, 1880.

powerful but crude drama to suit the critical judgment of a popular author. Curiously enough, it was not included in either of the two collections published after her death, *The Front Yard and Other Italian Stories* (1895) and *Dorothy and Other Italian Stories* (1896), for it is one of the best. The similarity of this theme to some of those used later by Henry James is also noteworthy, since it was in 1880, under his guidance, that she grew to know Florence, her favorite among Italian cities. In these later stories, the American characters are the most important; sometimes indeed they are the only ones. The European scene remains the background, but it is an integral part of the narrative. Sometimes, as in "The Street of the Hyacinth," [8] it is the belief that she can paint which brings an American girl to Rome, but it is her poise and courage under disappointment that lend distinction to the narrative. In "The Front Yard" [9] not only the scene but also the Italian characters form a contrast to the American. This is a fine study of a New England woman, Prudence Wilkins, who has married an Italian and who takes care of his family after his death, including a terrible old woman, the grandmother of his first wife. Living in Assisi, Prudence is oblivious to its meaning. To her life is not beauty but duty. The one thing she longs for is a "front yard" such as she had had in New Hampshire, but each time she saves up enough to start one, she makes a new sacrifice for her adopted family. Courage and fixity of purpose make the Americans in the later stories memorable. The way Mrs. Azubah Ash, an elderly woman, rises to command the situation after her son has killed his rival in "Neptune's Shore," [10] the clear grit of the fourteen-year-old lad in "A Transplanted Boy," [11] who plays a man's part, without heroics; both are revelations of a power that showed no sign of weakening.

When the social scene is important, her Americans are never the vague uncertain figures of Henry James. Even the expatriated Americans like Mrs. Churchill in "A Pink Villa" are real. But what distinguishes Miss Woolson's stories from the usual magazine fiction is the way she can fix a character with one brief sentence. "No vulgar affluence oppressed Isabella. She had six hundred dollars a year of her own and each dollar was well bred." Her art is a fine art; one returns to her fiction for the sheer joy in well-controlled creation. She knew her own limita-

[8] *Century Magazine*, May–June, 1882.
[9] *Harper's Magazine*, December, 1888.
[10] *Harper's Magazine*, October, 1888.
[11] *Harper's Magazine*, February, 1894.

tions as well as those of her characters. For the daring female of literature she had no respect, and she puts the case for her own manner brilliantly in one of her short stories, "At the Chateau of Corinne." In her
delicate and distinguished art, she and Miss Jewett represented at its
height that ability to guide with a firm hand the steeds of imagination
and introspection which carried the so-called feminine impulse in American fiction very far toward perfection. Henry James in his *Partial Portraits* chose to place her with George Eliot, Trollope, and Turgenev,
and his judgment was sounder than that which has apparently forgotten her. But at the time of her death (she fell or threw herself from
her window in Venice in 1894), she was recognized as one of the most
consummate artists in that great epoch of the novel.

The artistic quality of Miss Woolson is most quickly established by a
comparison of her work with that of Edward Eggleston (1837–1902),
who began to publish fiction at almost the same moment. Born in Vevay,
Indiana, on the bank of the Ohio River, he knew the backwoods life at
first hand and, to a great degree, educated himself. He returned from
Minnesota, where he had gone for his health at eighteen, and became a
Methodist circuit rider in Indiana. Giving up writing, at which he had
made some attempts, because he deemed it unfit for a minister, he was
led eventually by his natural ability to editorial positions in Illinois,
Brooklyn, and New York City.

Among his first short stories, most of which are sheer romance, "Hul-
dah the Help" [12] is noteworthy as being simple in plot and realistic in
treatment, with Dickens as a model. His first novel, *The Hoosier Schoolmaster* (1871), was a story of Indiana life, based upon the experiences of
his brother, George Cary Eggleston. Eggleston is usually credited with
being a pioneer in realism, but when *The Hoosier Schoolmaster* is compared with *Their Wedding Journey* or *Watch and Ward*, both also of
1871, or with *Margret Howth* of 1862, the mistake is evident. His material, that of the village life of Indiana in his own boyhood, is described
as he knew it. But the characters are all types, not real people. Ralph
Hartsook, the young schoolmaster, is the noble youth of romance who
conquers all difficulties; Hannah Thomson, the "hired girl" whom he
marries, is the long suffering saint who has almost no identity. Most of
the characters are sheer caricatures. The book has value as an historical
document; Eggleston minces no words in satirizing the meanness,

[12] *Scribner's Monthly*, December, 1870.

cowardice, and intolerance of a small community. But he tells us about it; the characters do not usually reveal themselves, for the morally good ones, at least, talk in exalted periods. Perhaps the most natural is "Bud" Means, the inarticulate giant, but even he is scarcely human, although he was based on a real character. The popularity of the book must have been due to its revelation of a phase of life that was not familiar, for it was translated into French by Madame Blanc for the *Revue des deux Mondes* and also into Danish, Dutch, and German.

Eggleston wrote next *The End of the World* (1872), a love story dealing with the expected ascension of the Millerites, which he had witnessed as a boy in Indiana, and *The Mystery of Metropolisville* (1873), laid in a border town in Minnesota. Here again the material only is of importance. There is a good description of a Minnesota boom town, and Plausby, the real estate operator, is a vivid caricature. There is not much construction, however, and some of the incidents, especially the drowning of Kate, the hero's sister, are quite melodramatic. *The Circuit Rider* (1874) is better. Here Eggleston's talent as an historian showed in his picture of the Methodist preacher during Madison's administration, as he went through the Middle West and Kentucky. The character of Morton Goodwin is heroic because of the physical difficulties he overcame, and because he was one of the civilizing influences of the West. Eggleston's comments are shrewd and often humorous, but the style is still unfinished.

By the time he published *Roxy* (1878) he had learned how to write. This is a strong and vivid picture of life in Southern Indiana about 1840, built upon his own experience. Roxy Adams, who has the crusading spirit that carried Methodism over the country and a great desire to go to Texas as a missionary with Mark Bonamy, her young husband, and who finds it is her mission to stay at home and save him, is a real character. Mark is also well drawn as an able, eloquent, passionate man, morally weak, whose affair with Nancy Kirtley, a descendant of the shiftless white class, is not unnatural. Roxy's visit to Nancy and her offer to take her husband's child that is coming are described in a manner that shows how far Eggleston had progressed in seven years. Roxy's return to her husband is also natural, since she was a strong character and he was a vivid personality. The novel is realistic in the true sense, and Eggleston's observation are even better than in *The Circuit Rider*. He lays the blame for the small-town mind properly:

The Puritan preachers, the brave cobblers and tinkers, whom the seventeenth century stuck in the stocks and prisonhouses, and the fervent Wesleyan village blacksmiths and Yorkshire farmers of the eighteenth century are yet masters of the nineteenth. To this day we take our most innocent amusements in a guilty and apologetic fashion, bowing to the venerable prejudice, and saying: "By your leave, sir."

Again, he remarks:

The faithful discharge of a duty disagreeable to others maketh the heart of the righteous to rejoice. . . . If there is one thing a woman cannot stand, it is bloodshed—unless it be upon a large scale.

In *The Graysons* (1887) the picture of life in Illinois when Abraham Lincoln was beginning to practise in that state is historically true; and the interest arises as usual from the description of the habits of the people. The Graysons are farmers in moderate circumstances, and Tom Grayson becomes the defendant in the famous trial in which Lincoln clears his client by leading the principal witness for the prosecution to swear that he saw the shooting by moonlight when there was no moon. The trial is managed skilfully, but it is hardly good fictional material, since Lincoln's device is so well known that there is little suspense. The description of the poor whites at Broad Run is very realistic, and they are not made picturesque. They are pictured as descendants of the debtor class who had come over from England years before and had remained shiftless and unprogressive.

Eggleston's last novel, *The Faith Doctor* (1891) is, next to *Roxy*, his best story. It is partly a social satire and partly a satire on faith-healing. His picture of the charlatan, Mrs. Frankland, the missionary to the "weary rich," is clever:

She did not think of her purpose nakedly; she was an artist in drapery, and her ideas never presented themselves in the nude; she was indeed quite incapable of seeing the bare truth; truth itself became visible to her only when it had on a wedding garment.

But the hero, Charley Millard, will attract the attention of any thoughtful critic. He is a remarkable picture of a man who has risen without any violent ambition, both in his banking career and social life, because people like him and because, while he is tactful and not too aggressive, he is at heart sound and true. In his liking for things that are fine and his quiet disregard of his own humble origin while never attempting to conceal it, he represents thousands of young American men who expect no great events in their lives and who need, like him, a great interest to spur them on. Such men are hard to draw, but Eggleston succeeded in making him real. Eggleston's short stories are relatively unimportant and his boys' books, like *The Hoosier Schoolboy* (1882), owe their interest to his material. That he wrote better books as he progressed and that he began to realize that crudity of material does not necessarily mean crudity of its artistic presentation marks his superiority over some of our contemporary novelists who have not learned that lesson.

While Miss Woolson had treated the French Canadian and the Spaniard, they had simply formed a background for the American of English descent. But in the stories of George W. Cable the older Creole civilization of Louisiana became the center of as picturesque a life as anyone except Bret Harte had discovered. With Harte, however, the color came from the new relations of different civilizations; with Cable it was inherent in the very life of these descendants of the first French and Spanish settlers of Louisiana.

Cable was born in New Orleans in 1844, of Virginian descent on his father's side, but through his mother of New England ancestry. He was of such diminutive stature that when his mother and sisters were exiled from New Orleans for refusing to take the oath of allegiance, they had no difficulty in securing permission for their "little brother" to accompany them. After fighting through the remainder of the War in the Confederate cavalry, he entered the cotton business with an occasional excursion into journalism. His desire to write was stimulated by the criticism of a group of friends who met in the evenings, and one of them, after a trip to California, urged Cable to go there for local color. "I told him," Cable replied, "that while he was away I had discovered in New Orleans a mine of literary material of which none of us had been aware." One of his stories came to the notice of Edward King, and "Sieur George" was published in *Scribner's Monthly* in October, 1873. It is a story of the lifelong sacrifice of a man who, in his propensity for gambling away in the lottery not only his own fortune but that of others, stems from Bret Harte. With " 'Tite Poulette," which is a preliminary study for *Madame Delphine*, it strikes the notes of loyalty and devotion. Together with the stories that followed, these were published in 1879 as *Old Creole Days*. Here the life of New Orleans in the early nineteenth century was reincarnated in its romantic phases. The family pride of the Creoles is made the theme of "Belles Demoiselles," with a dramatic touch by which the Count de Charleu-Marot and "Injun Charlie," descendants of a common ancestor, show each in his own way the strong sense of kinship. The old filibustering of the Caribbean Sea is the background for the "Café des Exiles," and one of the best, "Posson Jone'," draws a delightful contrast between Parson Jones, an American clergyman from West Florida and Jules St. Ange, an "elegant little heathen" of New Orleans. The confusion of moral values has rarely been used so artistically in the development of character based upon racial differences.

In his first novel, *The Grandissimes* (1880), Cable revealed both his strength and his weakness. The plot is not only involved, but is also presented in so indirect a manner as to cause unnecessary confusion. The feud of the Grandissime family with that of the DeGrapions could have been made clear in a few words, but Cable was so anxious to establish the atmosphere of Louisiana in 1803–1804 that he loads the novel with unnecessary detail. Yet the characters gradually shape themselves into clarity. Honoré Grandissime is a type hard to make interesting, the good man who is reasonable and sees both sides of such questions as those precipitated by the cession of Louisiana to the United States. Yet he is real; and Aurora DeGrapion-Nancanou, the charming Creole widow whom he loves, is much more living than the usual heroine of romance. Cable lost an opportunity of contrast with the American of the era by making his other hero, Joseph Frowenfeld, a German-American whose qualities are mostly Teutonic. Cable seems to have realized this, for he makes old Agricola Fusilier, the irreconcilable Creole, remark to Joseph, "You are not an American—you were merely born in America." When Cable treats slavery he arraigns it, calls it "a monument of the shame of two races," and through the tragedies of the colored Honoré Grandissime, of Palmyre, and especially of Bras Coupé, the African king, he produces some of his best effects. When Bras Coupé, who has been married to Palmyre to punish her and then prevented from seeing her, stalks into his master's sick room calling, "Bras-Coupé oulé so' femme!" (Bras Coupé wants his wife!) Cable was able to create a situation through which shines the royal quality of the huge slave who in his own day in Africa had had slaves of his own.

In his masterpiece, *Madame Delphine* (1881), a novelette, Cable again took the tragedy of mixed blood for his theme. The story is unfolded rapidly and deftly, the style is exquisite, and the character of Madame Delphine, the quadroon of 1821, is lifted into splendor by her sacrifice that strikes at the very roots of life, the love of a mother for her child. There have rarely been written in English more intensely dramatic scenes than that in which Madame Delphine, in order to make it possible for her daughter to marry her white lover, denies that Olive is her own child. What appeals especially in the novelette is the union of a mother's love with the power of the church to defeat a law which would separate a man and a woman who love each other. Cable uses expertly the dramatic qualities of the confessional, and when Madame Delphine, under the great emotional stress, dies after confessing her lie to Père Jerome, it seems an inevitable climax. The unpleasant theme of miscegenation is forgotten, for not Olive but her mother is the heroine.

In *Dr. Sevier* (1882) Cable left the field he had made his own to write of New Orleans of a later time and a less romantic situation. Beginning in 1856, the novel progresses into the Civil War, but the principal interest is the study of Dr. Sevier, a man of middle age, who acts as a guardian angel to two younger characters, John and Mary Richling, who represent the conflict between Southern and Northern ideals. Dr. Sevier is well drawn, proud, impetuous, generous with money but not in his judgments of others, and incapable of understanding the insecurity of the poor. It is one of Cable's best stories, but it has not the charm of his earlier fiction. That the charm came primarily from his Creole material was proved by *Bonaventure* (1888), a story of a Creole who was brought up among the Acadians, descendants of the exiles from Nova Scotia, who had remained unassimilated by the Creole civilization. In *Bonaventure* the life of the Acadians and the Creoles is treated on its idyllic rather than on its picturesque side. Bonaventure becomes a teacher among the Acadians at Grande Pointe, devoting his life to service. Cable hardly ever did anything finer than his character drawing of Bonaventure, of Zosephine, whom he first loves but who marries 'Thanase, of Claude St. Pierre, his young protegé, and of the American book agent, Tarbox, who is a vivid contrast to the simple peasant atmosphere of the Acadians. There is humor and there are word pictures of unusual quality, particularly the description of the outlaw who has killed 'Thanase and who has to watch helplessly the flood creeping up on him in his hiding place in the marshes. The episodic nature of Cable's fiction is shown in the original publication of this novel in the *Century*, where it appeared during 1887 and 1888 as three separate stories, "Carancro," "Grande Pointe," and "Au Large," each complete to a certain extent in itself.

In 1894 came a story of Reconstruction, *John Marsh, Southerner*, laid vaguely in "the state of Dixie." It has a reality which at times is impressive, though it is not quite up to the level of Page's *Red Rock*. The picture of the South after the war, groping to find a way out of conditions almost insolvable, is made the background for the development of two characters in particular, John Marsh and Barbara Garnet. John is a high strung, courageous boy who is quick to act in a situation calling for personal courage, but who can be misled in the somewhat intricate land deals with which the novel is concerned. Cable showed in one vivid incident early in John's life, when he is beaten by an ex-slave, that he could sympathize not only with the outrages to the Negro, but also with the horror of a white boy set in what seems to him incurable disgrace. Barbara is attractive and natural, and is one of the few romantic heroines who is remembered.

Throughout his career Cable continued to write short stories, none of which have the haunting glamour of *Old Creole Days*. The volume *Strange True Stories of Louisiana* (1889) is supposed to be based upon fact, but the effort to be faithful results in a bareness which perhaps comes from trying to treat with reality themes with which reality has nothing to do. Yet in his novelette *The Entomologist*,[13] published together with shorter stories, "The Taxidermist" and "The Solitary," as *Strong Hearts* (1899), there is some of his best descriptive writing. The description of the sea in "The Solitary" or the passage of the ruby throat in "The Taxidermist" are prose poems of high quality.

In 1901 Cable turned to the Civil War for what should have been a great novel; but *The Cavalier* is not one. Into it he put his own experiences with Forrest's scouts, and Forrest appears as Edgar Ferry-Durand, the dashing cavalry leader. Dick Smith, who tells the story, may have reflected some of Cable's own adventures or he may have been imaginary, but in any event the midnight raids, the skirmishes, and the escapes of Charlotte Oliver, the woman spy who loves Captain Ferry although she is married to a man she despises, are described by one who knew what he was writing about. Certain scenes are thrilling, and curi-

---

[13] *Scribner's Magazine*, January–March, 1899.

ously enough the best has to do with the death of a Union captain who begs Charlotte Oliver, his nurse, to sing "The Star Spangled Banner" for him. She conquers her reluctance and starts the song, when it is taken up by his captured force outside his window, who, in defiance of the leveled weapons of their guard, sing the chorus to the end. The scene may be open to criticism from the point of view of those who object to a reference to the flag in fiction as sentimental, but any American who can read it unmoved is to be pitied. The liberality of Cable, who had left the South for Northampton, Massachusetts, in 1885, showed his recognition of the valor of both sides and should have added to the interest of the book. But Cable made the mistake of telling a passionate love story through the eyes of another man, who in the autobiographical novel should be the chief character, but whose own love story hardly comes to life.

In 1908 Cable returned once more to the Civil War in *Kincaid's Battery*, laid principally in New Orleans, with excursions into Manassas and the conflict in the Southwest, and with its climax in Farragut's attack on the forts in Mobile Bay. While the descriptions of the war itself are clear and vivid, the novel suffers from that confusion of plot and of language which had been the weakness of *The Grandissimes* and which from now on became more and more apparent. The love stories are made intricate not by skill in the invention of plot, but by the blindness of the characters. Yet the account of the battle of Mobile Bay, when the ram *Tennessee*, with the day lost, turned back to fight the whole Union fleet, is one of the best prose descriptions of a naval conflict.

Between the two Civil War romances, Cable produced a far finer work than either, *Bylow Hill* (1902). The plot was presented to him in 1896 by Dr. Weir Mitchell, who did not care to use it, and while Cable made some changes, he followed fairly closely the real facts which had come to Dr. Mitchell in his practice. It is a story of the intense jealousy on the part of a young New England clergyman, Arthur Winslow, of his wife, a Southern girl, whom he believes to be guilty of adultery with one of his best friends. Going insane, he tries to kill her and she escapes. In the novel he dies, and she returns after a time; in real life she died, and the husband became cured. It is not so much the plot, although its directness probably kept Cable from his besetting sin of wandering, but it is the distinguished quality of the style and the character drawing that make it one of his best stories. There is also

an indefinable charm which arises from the atmosphere of refined comradeship of the group of friends before madness strikes its note of
tragedy. Cable's satirical power was still keen—witness his description
of Mrs. Morris, "who had always taken such care of her innocence
that her cultivation of the virtues had been only incidental," and who
"morally had more fat than fibre."

By 1914, when *Gideon's Band* appeared, the incoherence of Cable
spoiled a very good central idea. The rivalry of the Hayle and Courteney steamship lines on the Mississippi River in 1852, the presence on
Hugh Courteney's boat of Ramsey Hayle and her family, the outbreak
of cholera among the steerage passengers and the consequent terror of
the first cabin, all set against a background of slavery, formed a colorful
scene which Cable could create, but which he was no longer able to
interpret. At times it is practically impossible to know which character
is speaking. That Cable is perhaps after all a writer of novelettes and
short stories rather than a novelist is indicated by the way in which the
love story in *The Flower of the Chapdelaines* (1918) disappears entirely from the memory, while one of the manuscripts, whose discovery
and publication are the means of bringing the lovers together, remains.
This manuscript, called "The Island of the Holy Cross," is a powerful
narrative of a slave insurrection in the Danish West Indies. Cable's
last novel, *Lovers of Louisiana* (1918)—he died in 1925—was an attempt at a contrast between Southerners who are looking forward to
the New South, and the conservative Creoles who prefer the old. There
is too much preaching, and the characters remain abstract.

Cable will be remembered, I believe, almost exclusively for his
stories of Creole life. This is not fair to him, but it is a fact that when
a writer deals supremely well with one aspect of life, his other work
often receives less recognition than it deserves. His treatment of slavery,
for example, was broad-minded and much saner than that of Mrs. Stowe.
In his fiction, both races recognize the evils of slavery, even if they try
to cure the symptoms rather than the cause of the disease. Not writing
polemical tracts, he does not degrade his white characters nor does he
idealize to any marked degree his Negro characters. But slavery was
not his most significant theme. It was the picturesque life of the Creole
race before and after the cession of Louisiana. The very name is romantic, and their descent largely from adventurers of French and Spanish blood, of the development of customs and institutions so different

from ours, brought in the charm of the exotic. Their standards of life were more personal; life was cheaper and honor more dear. Within the race itself there were many contrasts, with a few strong characters ruling a large and unthrifty population, which enjoyed freedom from responsibility as their greatest blessing—a race living contentedly an unsanitary life with a shadow of dread in the yellow fever always hanging over them; a loyal, tender, revengeful race; in short, a Latin race affected by climate and by years of irresponsible power over a subject people. In a sense, it is an Old World survival in the New World—undemocratic in its political and social organization and therefore more romantic.

The fairness of Cable's attitude toward slavery may best be recognized when the novels of Albion W. Tourgée (1838–1905), once so popular, are read now when the political passions of Reconstruction times have cooled. A native of Ohio, he fought in the Civil War, studied law, and settled in Greensboro, North Carolina, in 1865, remaining in the South until 1879 and serving as judge and later as pension agent. His early novel, 'Toinette, and his novelettes, John Eax and Mamelon, though published first in 1882, had been written "about a decade earlier," according to Tourgée. There is some skill in the creation of a mystery in 'Toinette, which begins about 1858 and proceeds through the War, but the complications of the plot strain the reader's credulity and, with the novelettes, it seems to reflect an irritation on Tourgée's part against the planter class, which was probably caused by his attitude and consequent treatment while in the South. Figs and Thistles (1879), a story of Ohio, is better. It is usually said to be based on Garfield's early career, but it seems to parallel even more closely Tourgée's own political experiences. There is also a vivid description of the battle of Bull Run and the campaign around Chattanooga. Tourgée's most popular novel, A Fool's Errand (1879), is distinctly autobiographical, since Comfort Servosse, the hero, is a Michigan soldier who settles in "Dixie" and tries to solve some of the problems of Reconstruction. The interest of the book is more historical than artistic, and therefore its importance rests now on its accuracy. Tourgée's advocacy of a plan of reconstruction based on the obliteration of State lines, and the remaking of the South into Territories to be readmitted, shows his lack of understanding of the real situation. Yet he also seems to recognize the impossibility of the solution which was adopted by the Republican leaders. The novel was dramatized by Steele MacKaye in 1881 but did not succeed. *Bricks without Straw* (1880) is another propaganda novel, with too much argument for fine art, but with a certain skill in dramatizing situations. The character of Molly Ainslie, who goes South to teach the Negroes, is not badly drawn, but Tourgée was apparently unable to grasp the real reason of her social ostracism. Hensden Le Moyne, the relic of the old Whig Southerner, is also well drawn. The title indicates the hopelessness of the expectation on the part of the sympathizers with the Negro that he would progress without effective help on the part of the North, or a change of attitude on that of the South. If Tourgée could have realized that a faithful picture of the tragedies resulting from mixed blood like *Madame Delphine* was a better argument for the Negro than long-winded discussion, his novel *Pactolus Prime* (1890) might have been important, for the central character, a light Negro, who brings his little daughter up in Washington as the child of his former master, has some moments of appeal. Tourgée's short stories collected under the title of *With Gauge and Swallow, Attorneys* (1889), like his novels, contain some interesting legal incidents, but his historical romance, *Out of the Sunset Sea* (1893), told in the first person by an English lad who, after amazing adventures in Spain goes with Columbus on his first voyage, is as absurd as a total misconception of the character of Columbus could make it.

Just as the Californians objected to Bret Harte's stories, so Cable's treatment of the Creole was not satisfactory to that race. Grace Elizabeth King (1851–1932) seems to have been inspired to write her short stories by a feeling that justice had not been done to a people whose blood she shared. The note she struck most insistently was the romance of a decaying grandeur, akin in some ways to that of Miss Jewett but more dramatic because it came suddenly with the Civil War rather than through slower economic change. Her stories abound in vivid contrasts—between whites and Negroes, between splendor and poverty, and between French and American civilizations. Her women are especially well portrayed. She had been educated in the fashionable pension of the Mesdames Cenas, which appears as the Institute St. Denis in several of the stories. Her characters look to Paris rather than to the North for their fashions and their education.

Her earliest story, "Monsieur Motte," was published in the *Princeton Review* in 1886 and gave the title to her first collection in 1888. It is one of her best, for she knew how to build up the anticipation of a great moment in the heart of a young girl, who looks forward to seeing her mysterious uncle, Monsieur Motte, at her graduation, only to find that there is no such person but that Marcelite, the quadroon, has taken care of her. The pride of race and caste, which makes the orphan girl long for a family to which she may belong, intensifies the bitter tragedy of the discovery. In her next volume, *Tales of a Time and Place* (1892), there is a remarkable study of racial differences in "Madrilène, or the Festival of the Dead." How well Miss King knew the quadroon is shown in the paragraph in which Madame Lais, proprietress of one of the *chambres garnies,* tries to resist the stranger who comes to take from her Madrilène, the white girl whom Madame Lais has deceived into thinking she is a quadroon:

> She put forth her hands to take Madrilène from the stranger . . . Her lips were trembling, too, in spite of her efforts, and her face—quadroons do not get white; they blacken for pallors—black spots settled around Madame Lais's mouth, under her eyes, on her cheeks. In her assurance she was white: in her fear she was all negro.

"Bonne Maman" [14] is a fine study of the patrician who has hidden in a poor neighborhood from her relatives, and who has the pride that can stand want but not the middle ground of pity. The third volume, *Balcony Stories* (1893), contains among others four of distinction: "A Drama of Three," "A Crippled Hope," "Anne Marie and Jean Marie," and "The Little Convent Girl." The last is a heartbreaking story of a girl, put on a steamboat plying between Cincinnati and New Orleans, whose father has just died and who is going to her mother, whom she does not remember. Through deft touches Miss King endows the girl with delicacy, timidity, and gentility, so that the meeting with her quadroon mother is intensely tragic. *The Pleasant Ways of St. Médard* (1916), a series of episodes in the lives of a family whose head returns after the war to find his property gone, is not so effective. Miss King continued to write short stories, but turned her attention more definitely to history and biography. In 1924, however, she published *La Dame de Sainte Hermaine,* a charming novel of Louisiana in the eighteenth century. The central character, Marie St. Hermaine, is depicted skilfully through the devotion of four characters, of whom Bienville, the first

[14] *Harper's Magazine,* July, 1886.

governor of Louisiana, is the chief. Miss King presented here the inter-relations of France and her colony in Louisiana, a subject not usually touched in fiction.

In the work of Kate Chopin (1851–1904), it is not the glamour of the Creole past but the emotional life of a passionate people with which she is concerned. Her work is significant indeed not in terms of quantity but of quality. Her output was not large, but she carried the art of the short story to a height which even Cable did not surpass. The daughter of an Irish gentleman who had come to St. Louis in 1825 and of a mother who belonged to an old Creole family, Kate O'Flaherty inherited a temperament which made her brief, cameo-like stories something unusual in American fiction. She was married in 1870 to Oscar Chopin, a Creole on whose plantation at Cloutierville she learned to know the Creole and Acadian races in Louisiana. She began to write only after her husband's death and her return to St. Louis, her first story, "Wiser than a God," appearing in December, 1889, in *The Musical Journal of Philadelphia*.[15] This has no touch of her later quality, but in her novel *At Fault* (1890) there was more promise. It is the first novel to be laid in the Cane River section of central Louisiana. The best characters are the Creoles, especially the young widow, Thérèse Lafirme, who manages her plantation of four thousand acres. There is reality too in the story of the disintegration of Fanny Hosmer, wife of David Hosmer, of St. Louis, but it was not until she perfected her short story art that Kate Chopin rose to distinction. She rewrote, revised, and polished her stories, trying always for the brief deft expression which left so much to the imagination. In "A Very Fine Fiddle," in which old Cleophas, whose whole life is wrapt up in his music, refuses to play on anything but the old fiddle which in their dire poverty his little daughter has sold, it is the finality of the crisis wrought by the inexorable logic of the Latin race which challenges our admiration. The standards are Latin, too. There is a delightful picture of Hector Santien, the New Orleans gambler in "In and Out of Old Natchitoches," who watches over his young cousin when she comes to the city, but is never seen with her, lest it compromise her reputation. "Beyond the Bayou" is a powerful narrative of LaFolle, the Negress who, in order to save

---

[15] This and several other of her uncollected stories have been published as an appendix to the authoritative biography, *Kate Chopin*, by D. S. Rankin (Philadelphia, 1932).

the life of the little boy she loves, breaks through an *idée fixe* of long years that she dare not cross the bayou.

In December, 1893, Mrs. Chopin published in *Vogue* one of the greatest short stories in the language, *Désirée's Baby*. With a few adroit touches, she builds up a picture of Armand Aubigny, a Louisiana planter whose pride of race is so great that he overlooks the mystery concerning the birth of Désirée, whom he loves, for he has enough family for both of them. When their baby is a few months old, she wakens to the horror of the knowledge that it has Negro blood and turns in her agony to her husband, who sends her away with an incisive cruelty which in a few words makes a gulf open between them. Then with the baby in her arms:

. . . she walked across a deserted field, where the stubble bruised her tender feet, so delicately shod, and tore her thin gown to shreds. She disappeared among the reeds and willows that grew thick along the banks of the deep, sluggish bayou: and she did not come back again.

In his desire to cleanse his house of all that belonged to the woman who had brought this disgrace upon him, Armand burns up her belongings. Then comes the climax:

The last thing to go was a tiny bundle of letters; innocent little scribblings that Désirée had sent to him during the days of their espousal. There was the remnant of one back in the drawer from which he took them. But it was not Désirée's; it was part of an old letter from his mother to his father. He read it. She was thanking God for the blessing of her husband's love:—

"But, above all," she wrote, "night and day, I thank the good God for having so arranged our lives that our dear Armand will never know that his mother, who adores him, belongs to the race that is cursed with the brand of slavery."

Where in any fiction has a human being so blindly brought Nemesis upon himself? Where, except in the pages of Poe or of deMaupassant, which Mrs. Chopin frequently translated, has one sentence so shut the door of hope on a man's future? Pride of a more attractive nature is the inspiration for "A Gentleman of Bayou-Têche," wrought in a spirit of comedy. These stories, with many others, were published in 1894 as *Bayou Folk;* and she continued her studies of Creole and Acadian life, collected in 1897 in *A Night in Acadie*. Mrs. Chopin was never content simply to paint local color; it is always character or situation which dominates the story. There is an unusual understanding of a man's passion in "At Chênière Caminda," in the depiction of Antoine Bocaze's relief when the summer visitor whom he has been hopelessly worshipping at a distance dies, and the torturing thought that some other man may possess her is over. "After the Winter" is an exquisite study of the effect of resurgent memory. Her treatment of the Negro is just right in "A Dresden Lady in Dixie," in which an old Negro who has taken the blame of a theft to save a little Acadian girl dramatizes the event as a struggle between "De Sperrit" and "Satan" and eventually believes it himself. Even better is "Nég Créol," where the loyalty of the Negro who provides his former mistress with food in her poverty keeps him from attending her funeral, because he wishes to maintain among his associates the fiction that his family, the Boisdurés, are wealthy and prosperous. Not all of her best short stories were reprinted in book form. In "Lilacs" [16] there is another one of those endings which tells so much. The contrast between the life which Adrienne Farival lives in Paris and the peace of the convent in which every year she spends two weeks at lilac time, with the nuns who have taught her, is established with Mrs. Chopin's usual certainty. Then comes the discovery of her real life, her repulse at the convent door, and the Mother Superior's message that she must not be received—and the final sentence:

After a short while, a lay sister came out of the door with a broom and swept away the lilac blossoms which Adrienne had let fall upon the portico.

Mrs. Chopin's last novel, *The Awakening* (1899), caused a storm of unfavorable criticism. Mrs. Chopin, whose married life had been unusually happy and who, apparently for her children's sake or her husband's memory, never remarried, created in Edna Pontellier a woman who has been very impressionable in her girlhood in Kentucky and has married a Creole without really loving him. She becomes infatuated with a man younger than herself and, when he goes away, gives herself to an attractive roué, due to her disappointed sexual longing for Robert. When Robert returns, she confesses her passion for him and he leaves her, being too decent for the liaison she is ready to enter. She drowns herself. The reality of the book is striking, in its revelation of the shifting moods of a passionate woman, and it is told with admirable

[16] *New Orleans Times Democrat*, December 20, 1896, reprinted in D. S. Rankin's biography.

economy. But the basic fault lies in Edna's utter selfishness, which deprives her of sympathy. The standards are Continental rather than
Creole, and the novel belongs rather among studies of morbid psychology than local color.

Just as truly as Cable stood for Louisiana, Thomas Nelson Page
(1853–1922) was representative of the life of Virginia. Two governors
of the State were among his ancestors, his father fought in the Civil
War, and as a boy he saw it at first hand. Despite the consequent family
losses, he studied at Washington and Lee and the Law School of the
University of Virginia, and remained at the bar even after his success in
literature. He began his contributions to *Scribner's Monthly* with a
poem, "Uncle Gabe's White Folks," in 1876. It was the same note of
fidelity of a Negro to his master that he struck in his first short story,
"Marse Chan," written in 1880 though not published until April, 1884,
in *The Century*. From the point of view of literary effect, it was a good
idea to tell the story through a Negro's eyes. The episode of "de ole
marster" going in to the fire to save his slave who had done his bidding
and was in danger of his life is made more dramatic because of the narrator's complete absence of comment. To him, the "marster" had a right
to send his slave into danger, but that implied a duty to save him in turn,
even if it cost his owner his eyesight. Equally inevitable was the slave's
fidelity to the charge given him as a boy to look after his young master,
Channing, who had been placed in his arms as an infant.

"Meh Lady," a charming love story told again through the eyes of
an old Negro; a lighter vein touched in "Unc' Edinburg's Drowndin' ";
a vivid story of the supernatural in "No Haid Pawn"; and other stories
were published in 1887 as *In Ole Virginia*. The appeal of these is undoubtedly heightened by the dialect. The description of the marriage
between "Meh Lady" and the Northern colonel is in exactly the right
tone:

> "An' when de preacher git to dat part whar ax who give dis woman to de
> man, he sort o' wait an' he eye sort o' rove to me disconfused like he ax me ef
> I know; an' I don' know huccome 'twuz, but I think 'bout Marse Jeems an'
> Mistis when he ax me dat, an' Marse Phil, whar all dead, an' all de scufflin' we
> done been th'oo, an' how de chile ain' got no body to teck her part now 'sep jes'
> me; an' now, when he wait an' look at me dat way, an' ax me dat, I 'bleeged to
> speak up, I jes' step for'ard an' say:
> "   " 'Ole Billy.'

"An' jes' den de sun crawl roun' de winder shetter an' res' on her like it pourin' light all over her. . . ."

Page continued to write short stories throughout his career, of which the most distinctive were included in *Elsket and Other Stories* (1891), *The Burial of the Guns* (1894), and *Bred in the Bone* (1904). He did not limit his treatment of the motive of loyalty to the South, one of his best stories, "Elsket," being the recital of a Norse woman's fidelity.

Another theme which Page treated with distinction in "Little Darby," "Bred in the Bone" or "Run to Seed" is the persistence of hereditary characteristics. "Little Darby," is a story of a poor, illiterate boy, who not only saves the Confederate army at the risk of his life, but also lays himself open to the charge of being a deserter by coming home to aid his mother without waiting for a furlough. He is descended from a race that had once been of good English stock. The writing of this story is an illuminating illustration of Page's literary creed. In a letter to me sent in consequence of a printed criticism of his fiction, he explains the genesis of "Little Darby" and also of his earlier stories:

I have no doubt that your estimate of the comparative merits of my short stories and of my novels is absolutely correct and I have a secret fear that my earlier stories, those in dialect, are superior in their appeal to any that I have written since. If I find you selecting "Marse Chan" and "Meh Lady" in preference to "Edinburg's Drowndin'" and "Polly," I have no right to complain and it brings me to a reflection which I have always had: as to what is the secret of the success of the story or novel. Is it the theme or the art with which any theme, reasonably broad, is handled, or is it something growing out of the union of the two? Personally I have always estimated "Edinburg's Drowndin'" as possibly the broadest of my stories, at least as the one giving a reflection of the broadest current of the old Southern life, and so far as literary art is concerned, it seems to me at least on a par with the others. I think, therefore, it must be the unrelieved tragedy in "Marse Chan" or the fact that "Meh Lady" appealed to both sides, and was written to make this appeal, that has given them a prestige, if I may use so important a word, far beyond that of "Edinburg's Drowndin'" and "Ole 'Stracted." "Little Darby," "Run to Seed" and "Elsket," which you have signalized with the stamp of your imprimatur, I also think among the very best stories I have written. The first two of these appeal to me almost as much as the dialect stories. The first of these was written on precisely the same theme with "Marse Chan" and out of the consciousness that whereas the tragedy of "Marse Chan" was laid in the highest social rank, the incident which had given rise to it was based on a letter written by a poor girl, of much lower rank, to her lover, who like "Marse Chan" had found his death on the battlefield, and I felt somehow that it was due to that class that I should testify with whatever power I might possess, to their devotion to the South. If there is a difference it seems to me that it lies rather in the fact that readers estimate as more romantic a tragedy in the upper ranks of life than in the lower, whereas, we know that rank has nothing to do with it.

It will be noticed that even in the denial of the importance of caste there is an implicit recognition of it, and his celebration of personality and stamina is always that which derives from long-rooted ancestry. The "incident" of which Page speaks consisted of a letter found on the body of a Georgia soldier from a girl who told him of her love but added, "Don't come without a furlough; for if you don't come honorable, I won't marry you." "Marse Chan" simply receives a letter from the girl he loves—no such message is added—and it is only in "Little Darby" that it is made important. But as an example of literary conscience, Page's explanation has its evident interest.

The quality which makes these short stories great is the surety with which the effect is reached. Whether the chief note be that of loyalty or terror or the heritage of good blood, the appeal is swift and sure. No one can read "Marse Chan" or "Meh Lady" without a thrill as the old Negro tells in simple, unaffected language a story of devotion so deep and lasting that to it the gates of death are but an incident. It is a great tribute to the race that showed this devotion, but indirectly it proves a far greater one to the race that inspired it. This note of loyalty is the one that Page strikes best. In his stories we see this sentiment developed in many ways against a background perhaps the most picturesque in our native land, that of the South before the war. The relations of the planter and his slaves, in which one human being had power of life and death over others, and in which a sense of personal responsibility and personal dependence was often highly developed, formed a fruitful field for an artist like Page. He touched this civilization with a loving hand, extracting from it beauty, both from its mirth and its agony, and proving again, if it were necessary, that to describe a country or a race in literature one must love it.

Page's first novel, *On Newfound River* (1891), is a Montague-Capulet story of Virginia before the war, based on an event in his first wife's family. It is interesting but hardly on a level with his second. In 1898 Page wrote in *Red Rock* the best novel of the Reconstruction Era. This period covered the most impressionable years of his life, and the intolerable conditions, which are only now beginning to be fully recognized, burned into his memory and make the novel alive. It is all the more vivid because of his restraint. Had he chosen, he could have painted in lurid colors the misery in which brave people, who asked only to be let alone with their great problem, were plunged, through the ignorance and fanaticism of the ruling party in the national administration. But Page knew that for fictional effect the oppression must bear hard upon concrete individuals, and that they must meet it bravely and without self-pity. The best characters are Dr. Cary, the old-time Whig who had opposed secession but fought for the South when his State had entered the conflict; Blair Cary, his high-spirited daughter; and Captain Steve Allen, the center of the resistance to the measures of the civil and military rule from the North. Page knew, too, that the tyranny of the carpet-baggers must also be individualized, and Jonadab Leech is probably the most vivid of all the portraits. But on the other hand, the Northern characters like Ruth Welch, her father, Major Welch, and Captain Middleton, are treated with complete fairness. In fact, to Major Welch is given probably the best scene in the novel, in which he rises in the lawsuit instituted to recover the Red Rock estate from the treachery of the former overseer, Hiram Still, and refuses to defend his estate, which he has purchased in good faith, because he finds the sale is tainted with fraud. *Red Rock* has been criticized because Blair Cary and Ruth Welch are so much alike. But perhaps the greatest significance of the novel lies in Page's recognition that men and women of honor are pretty much the same in either section. Again his own words are of special interest:

It may interest you to know that when I first undertook to write "Red Rock," after having written a third or more of the novel I discovered that I had drifted into the production of a political tract. I bodily discarded what I had written, and going back beyond the War, in order to secure a background and a point of departure which would enable me to take a more serene path, I rewrote it entirely. I had discovered that the real facts in the Reconstruction period were so terrible that I was unable to describe them fully, without subjecting myself to the charge of gross exaggeration. The story of this period of National madness will doubtless be written sometime and if any man will steep himself as I did, myself, in such records as the "Ku Klux Reports" issued by the Government in 1872, and, "A Voice from South Carolina" published in Charleston by Dr. Leland in 1879; "The Prostrate State," and the news-papers of the reconstruction period I think that he will agree with me in feeling that we are too near the time to be able to present the facts with true art.

The Old Gentleman of the Black Stock (1897), while sheer romance, is based on a profound reality. The lonely old gentleman, Basil Miles, who brings together the young lovers who might have separated over a misunderstanding, is a symbol of the truth that a man who has lost the first place in the affections of a woman through his own selfishness faces an old age in which memory brings nothing but regret, and the consciousness that even friendship has its reservations in which someone else is more important. It is perhaps the recognition of this truth that made the book so widely read.

The main theme of *Gordon Keith* (1903) is the contrast of a Southern man of good stock with the Northern parvenu as represented in the society of New York City. The picture of the latter is not very convincing, and the representatives of the North are types rather than individuals. The best portions of the book deal with the wilder elements in a mining town in the South. Much better was the last novel to be published in Page's lifetime, *John Marvel, Assistant* (1909), even though the title is a poor one, for Henry Glave is the hero, not John Marvel. Glave is refreshing after the usual romantic hero. He is a young lawyer who leaves the South and starts afresh in a large Western city, probably Chicago. He is the mixture of honesty, courage, impulsiveness, sensitiveness, false pride, carelessness, keenness, and stupidity which make up a well-rounded character. The picture of Glave taking the poor family to their home in a cab and hoping no one will see him will strike a responsive chord in almost any reader. Eleanor Leigh, whom he loves, is also more real than most heroines, and the background of politics and social welfare shows that Page could work on a larger canvas than he had previously attempted.

In his later short stories, collected in 1913 as *The Land of the Spirit*, Page was inspired by the moral and spiritual awakening which he believed he saw in the early twentieth century. He made no attempt to preach, but by retelling of the incidents surrounding the birth of Christ, or by calling attention, in "The Stranger's Pew," to the inhospitable reception which Christ would receive in a modern church, or by reciting in "The Bigot," the evil effects of earlier intolerance, he tried to indicate a spirit of charity with less confusion of values than Bret Harte. That there were indications of such a spirit in the social legislation either attempted or achieved during this period is true. But that Page succeeded in transferring it to the pages of fiction is not so evident. The question whether it is good material for short stories is raised by the way in which "The Old Planters," a story of the personality of an old Confederate veteran and its effect upon a group of traveling men from the North, stands out as the best in the volume. In that field Page was at home.

His last novel, *The Red Riders* (1924), was not quite completed by him and was published posthumously by his brother, Rosewell Page. It is a story of South Carolina, before, during, and after the Civil War, and leads up to the successful attempt to rescue the State from the rule of the carpet-baggers and Negroes. It would be manifestly unfair to judge a novel which had not the benefit of the author's final revision, but while it has its fine moments, as in the sentence, "Lee's surrender was like the shifting of a cornerstone," it fails just where *Red Rock* succeeded, because Page interprets the conditions so often instead of permitting his characters to reveal them through their own words and actions. The pictures of Lincoln, Stanton, and Thaddeus Stevens are correct, but they give the impression of being the product of research, while in *Red Rock* he kept away largely from actual historical personages, and the story seems to spring from real experience.

It was also perhaps the interruption caused by his public career as Ambassador to Italy which made his later fiction less significant. He was an historian of the Old South as well as its novelist, and the future historian will have to depend on him for at least the social history of that section. Like Cooper, he was a democrat because he was essentially a patrician, but his democracy, with which he has delightfully imbued his characters, is quite a different kind from that of Howells. The latter really believed that all men are equal. Page's characters start with an inherited certainty of breeding which permits them to disregard artificial social restrictions and meet every man on the basis of his worth. They meet in one way perfectly Marion Crawford's definition of a gentleman, for they are always thinking how they may treat others with courtesy. But this courtesy and kindness of heart springs not from any recognition of equality, but from a duty which implies a protection that is in its essence a quiet conviction of superiority. It springs, of course, from centuries of power over others, white or black, and its chivalry is the chivalry of feudalism, not democracy. That makes it good material for fiction.

The association of Francis Hopkinson Smith (1838–1915) with Thomas Nelson Page has become inevitable, for both won their fame through the revelation of Southern character, and yet there are essential differences in their work. Smith was born in Baltimore, a great-grandson of Francis Hopkinson, and resembled his ancestor in his versatility. A constructing engineer, building the Race Rock lighthouse and the foundations for the Statue of Liberty, he also became a painter of distinction. In his diary, written in 1857–1858, kept during a trip made through Maryland, Pennsylvania, and Virginia, Smith showed already his ability at narration and description, his acute observation, and his wide interest in people of all kinds, which made him one of the best of companions. Together with the short stories found with this manuscript,[17] the diary makes clear that Smith's instinct for composition was not merely an outgrowth of his painting as is usually stated, but developed with it from his earliest years. It was, however, in connection with his sketches of travel that he wrote his "Church of San Pablo-Seville," with which his published writing may be said to begin. This was included in his *Well Worn Roads of Spain and Holland* (1886), followed by his *White Umbrella in Mexico* (1889). There was a certain fictional quality in these travel sketches; they differed from the usual books of their kind in making no attempt to relate facts but rather endeavoring to present an enthusiastic treatment of the picturesque in which the impressions of those who already knew Spain or Mexico were deepened and overlaid with Smith's own.

In 1891 Smith created in *Colonel Carter of Cartersville* the character of George Fairfax Carter, the Southern gentleman of optimistic nature, whose childlike trusting character, courtliness of manner, and belief in the goodness of everyone made a fictional type which may vie with Mulberry Sellers or John Oakhurst in its effectiveness. "The Colonel" is located in New York City, trying to finance a projected railroad which is to make Cartersville, the old family place in the South, a booming town. He is a Virginian first—anything else afterward—as Smith describes him:

What a frank, generous, tender-hearted fellow he is: happy as a boy; hospitable to the verge of beggary; enthusiastic as he is visionary; simple as he is genuine. A Virginian of good birth, fair education, and limited knowledge of the world and of men, proud of his ancestry, proud of his State, and proud of

---

[17] A full description of this manuscript, together with short stories written about the same time, will be found in the authoritative biography by Courtland Y. White, III, now in preparation.

himself; believing in states' rights, slavery, and the Confederacy; and away down in the bottom of his soul still clinging to the belief that the poor white trash of the earth includes about everybody outside of Fairfax County.

In this book Smith showed himself a master of character-drawing. The old Negro, Chad, drawn from his father's servant, Daddy Bill, who lived to be ninety-six years old; Aunt Nancy, who periodically returns the Colonel to solvency; Fitz, the broker; and the Major, who is Smith himself, all are real people. Even minor characters like Major Yancey and Judge Kerfoot, who come up from Cartersville to aid the Colonel in his preposterous duel with Klutchem, a broker who has insulted him, are clearly differentiated from Colonel Carter. Yancey is the undistinguished type, midway between the patrician and the poor white, which only rarely had come into fiction, but which Smith had already described in his first published short story, "Six Hours in Squantico." [18]

The plot of the novelette is not so important as the atmosphere, but Smith's skill was manifest in the way the courtesy of Colonel Carter disarms his creditors and his infinite capacity for friendship brings to him the fortune which his own efforts would have been powerless to secure. In 1903 Smith wrote a sequel to Colonel Carter of Cartersville, Colonel Carter's Christmas, in which the same characters appear. It has some of the charm of the original, but a note of sentimentality makes it less important. Smith's early short stories, included in A Day at Laguerre's, and Other Days (1892), were distinctly stories of atmosphere, whether in the Bronx or in Italy, Spain or Constantinople.

In his next two novels Smith used his experience as a constructing engineer. Tom Grogan (1896) contains a fine character study of an Irishwoman, Mary Grogan, who after her husband's death conducts his business as a contracting stevedore, fighting the union and the politicians who try to ruin her. There are delightful episodes, such as her breaking with her fist the plank behind the sullen countenance of her enemy and warning him that the next time she will not miss him. She is very appealing in her brave and cheerful acceptance of fate, coupled with her natural longing as a woman for the lost support and advice of Tom, her husband, whose death she conceals because she knows the disinclination of contractors to deal with a woman. The climax, in which she wins the legal right to trade under the firm name of "Tom Grogan," is managed skilfully. Caleb West, Master Diver (1898) has no

[18] Harper's Magazine, June, 1890.

such striking character, and the plot is the old one of the middle-aged husband, the young wife, and the younger lover. The central characters in both novels were drawn from real people, but Mary Grogan was a new figure in fiction while Caleb West was not.

The Fortunes of Oliver Horn (1902) was partly autobiographical. In the adventures of the young Southern painter, who goes from Kennedy Square in Baltimore in the late 'fifties to seek his fortune in New York City, Smith was telling of his own struggles. Richard Horn, Oliver's father, whose inventions succeed only at the end of the book, was drawn from his own father. Mrs. Horn was his mother. The atmosphere of Kennedy Square, laid in Baltimore, but really drawn from Pulaski Square in Savannah, Georgia, and that of the artists' studios in New York are extremely well presented. The book is too rambling in construction, but the characters of Oliver, Richard, Miss Lavinia Clendenning, a maiden lady, as well as the Negroes, are very real. Perhaps Smith is too much concerned with setting his characters off against the background, rather than allowing them to reveal themselves, as "Tom Grogan" does, but that, after all, is the fault of the romantic-idealistic novel in general.

Smith had his own theories about short story writing, which he gives in the Preface to a volume, *At Close Range* (1905), mostly in lighter vein, the product of his lecture tours.

At the same close range I try to search the secret places of the many minds and hearts which in my nomadic life cross my path. In these magnifyings and probings the unexpected is oft times revealed: tenderness hiding behind suspected cruelty; refinement under assumed coarseness; the joy of giving forcing its way through thick crusts of pretended avarice.

In *The Tides of Barnegat* (1906) Smith brought into fiction a phase of American life that had not been treated, except by Rebecca Harding Davis, and by her in a different way. He laid the story in that region of New Jersey where in 1850 there was a civilization now passed away. The decline of mining and milling industries had left even in the 'nineties deserted villages where once prosperous towns had flourished. In one of these he established a contrast between two sisters, Jane and Lucy Cobden, the first a woman who built up her life on sacrifice to the duty she had assumed when Lucy, carried away by a girl's infatuation for Barton Holt, had a son by him and was taken abroad by Jane to keep her father's name from disgrace. Barton was the son of one of those sea captains who still kept alive the memory of a prosperous commerce. Smith went to Barnegat Light, still in operation, and lived among the life-saving crew to gain the atmosphere for that portion of the story. He builds up the plot of *The Tides of Barnegat* with more unity than is usual with him. The way in which the effects of passion pass over Lucy and Barton, who have gone away, but keep Jane from marrying Doctor John Cavendish, whom she loves, and choke back the pride Captain Holt feels in his grandson Archie is grimly ironical. How well Smith puts the feeling of Jane when Lucy returns, a rich widow, and treats Archie as though he were nothing to her:

Jane looked at Lucy with searching eyes—looked as a man looks when someone he must not strike has thrown a glove in his face.

The title of the novel indicates how the effects of the lie Lucy has acted sweep in upon her. Smith never constructed a better climax. Her terror when she learns that Barton Holt is coming home to claim her and Archie leads to the powerful scene when Archie is drowned trying to save Barton from the wreck, and Captain Holt, over the dead bodies of his son and grandson, tells Lucy before them all just what she is. The storm and the wreck are described with the pictorial quality always at Smith's command.

The Romance of an Old Fashioned Gentleman (1907), a novelette beginning also in the 'fifties, but this time in Maryland, is a study of contrasted standards again. A painter, Adam Gregg, turns his back upon a love that would mean betrayal of trust and, years later, saves the son of the woman who had loved him from financial dishonesty by telling him the story. If Gregg's sacrifice, like that of Jane Cobden, has baffled some critics who like to speak of this school of romance as sentimental, there is no answer except to call attention to the fact that there are such people and to be thankful for it. *Peter* (1908) gave us a lovable character, a middle-aged bank teller in New York City, who watches over the other characters in a novel that has charm but is rather loose in construction. More interesting than the hero, John Breen, is Garry Minott, who is a well-etched portrait of hundreds of young men whose standards are gradually undermined by the conditions of a great city.

It was Smith's own opinion that *Kennedy Square* (1911) was his best novel and, while he was wrong, the reason he gave was theoretically correct. To him, everything in the novel happened logically as a result of a previous action of one of the characters and was never accidental. But while the setting is delightful in its picture of the 'forties in the old square he had treated in *Oliver Horn,* the central situation, while not accidental, is incredible, and consequently no logical sequence is possible. The main characters were drawn as before from his own family, but no art could make readers believe that a father could exile his son forever for defending the honor of a girl he loved, even if the offender was a guest. It makes no difference whether the event happened or not: probability and not possibility determines the material for fiction. Two novels were published posthumously. *Felix O'Day* (1915) is the story of the search of an Irish baronet in New York for the wife who has left him. It was not one of his best stories, and *Enoch Crane* (1916), while he planned it, contained only three chapters by him, the remainder being written by his son, F. Berkeley Smith.

Hopkinson Smith once told me that the models from whom he learned to write were Bret Harte in his early stories, Daudet in *Sappho* and DeAmicis in his account of Spain. From the first, he said, he learned unity and compression. What he really learned was the literary value of the moral contrast, for unity and compression were not Smith's striking traits. From Daudet he learned the necessity of a finished style, and this he did secure. From DeAmicis he learned that "an author may wear his heart on his sleeve without exciting derision, if he does it in the right way." Here Smith was not on such safe ground, for the most serious defect in his work arises from the habit of his characters of speaking out loud their deepest emotions when they would in all likelihood have concealed them. His versatility was an advantage and a handicap. His engineering training led him to plan his stories carefully, but his sense of the picturesque often caused him to interrupt the narrative for the sake of colorful descriptions, delightful in themselves, but bearing no necessary relation to the story. He was not a hasty writer, and his work was constantly revised. Perhaps it was again his painter's instinct which enabled him to depict so vividly characters like Colonel Carter, Aunt Nancy, Miss Lavinia, Lucy Cobden, Tom Grogan, and Garry Minott. His best characters come from his novels or novelettes, for he needed time to develop them. Among this group of writers he probably was the most cosmopolitan and treated scenes not only of the South but of New

York, New Jersey, and other points he visited, while his European settings have already been noted. He belongs, however, with those who made place and race a constant study and revealed them effectively. And Colonel Carter alone should secure his permanent place in the history of American fiction.

The stimulus of local color and primitive life was well illustrated in the career of Mary Noailles Murfree (1850–1922). Born near Murfreesboro, Tennessee, of Colonial stock, she grew up in Nashville and became acquainted with the mountaineers of the Cumberland Valley during summer vacations. Her earliest essay-like stories, "Flirts and Their Ways" [19] and "My Daughter's Admirers," [20] are trivial in nature and utterly unlike her later work. They appeared under the name of "R. Emmett Dembry," and when her first novel, *Beyond the Seas*, was written in 1876 she sent it under the same name to *Lippincott's*. It was not published, however, until 1886 under the title *Where the Battle Was Fought*, when it had been practically rewritten. It deals with the patrician group to which she belonged, and the battlefield of Murfreesboro enters into the lives of the characters, since they live in constant remembrance of what it had meant to them. The plot is somewhat melodramatic, but the picture of the higher provincial type in Tennessee has certain merit.

It was with her short stories of the Tennessee mountaineers that she made her reputation. In May, 1878, in the *Atlantic* appeared a short story, "The Dancin' Party at Harrison's Cove," signed "Charles Egbert Craddock," the first time she used the pen-name by which her work continued to be known. "Egbert Craddock" was the name of a character in this story in its first form, but before it was sent, she adopted the name and gave the character a new one.[21] This story shows Bret Harte's influence in the contrast between the "fighting parson," and a gentleman from the summer hotel who dominates the mountaineers and prevents a murder by the power of the memory of what he had done "at Shiloh." The fatalism of the Johns family, who know that their son will probably be killed if he goes to the dance but see no way to prevent it, is finely portrayed.

The succeeding stories, which were gathered together under the title

[19] *Lippincott's Magazine*, May, 1874.
[20] *Lippincott's Magazine*, July, 1875.
[21] For details of the early stories, I am indebted to Professors C. L. Lewis and E. W. Parks, both basing their statements upon the evidence of Miss Fanny N. D. Murfree.

In the Tennessee Mountains (1884), presented vividly the wildness and elemental quality of the region. The dialect is veracious and Miss Murfree brings out clearly the independence and the shiftlessness of the mountain men: their preference for a life in which they do as they please to a life in which they might make more money, but in which they would be confined by the standards of others. It is a life in which the men dominate, and they spend their time in much the same way as do the British gentry—in hunting and fishing. The heroic acts are usually those of the women; there is a delightfully ironic tale, "Drifting Down Lost Creek," in which Cynthia Ware saves the life of Evander Price, without his suspecting it, and is rewarded by seeing him marry another woman. The word painting is at times powerful, as in the description of the fire in "Over on the T'Other Mounting," and there is a successful establishment of the supernatural in "The 'Harnt' that Walks Chilhowee." The mountaineer's dislike of law is portrayed in "Electioneering on Big Injun Mounting," when the candidate for district attorney, who has been attacked by a drunken man, tells them that if he dies, he does not wish his assailant prosecuted. This wins him the election, for they recognize that his mountain instincts have come to the surface, when it is a *personal quarrel* and he wants no interference by the *law* in his own affairs.

Miss Murfree's work was uneven. Some of her books were juveniles and her fiction is best interpreted through the types of characters she treated. The mystic preacher, Hi Kelsey, who had been a violent man but had reformed after his wife's death, makes *The Prophet of the Great Smoky Mountains* (1885) important. Dorinda Cayce, who admires the parson because he is different, is also real. *In the "Stranger People's" Country* (1891) is a strong novel, with more real character development than some of the others, if a more leisurely movement. The main theme is the hopeless love of "Fee" Guthrie for "Litt" Pettingill. Fee is a very well-drawn character; he is simple, straightforward, yet not by any means a fool. "Litt" is an unusual character, an elfish, sprite-like being, who teases him and everyone, and who falls in love with the stranger, Shattuck, who has come to dig in the tombs of the "Little Stranger People" who, he thinks, may be Indians or children, but who are supposed by some to be aboriginal Aztecs. Guthrie is shot to death by the sheriff, and "Litt" waits for the stranger to come back, but in vain. Miss Murfree shows in this novel the native's lack of appreciation of

the beauties of the landscape—he has always seen it, he is concerned only
with the signs of rain, as it may affect his corn and his barley. The humor
is characteristic. "Litt" is talking to "Fee" Guthrie after the fight:

> She changed color. "War ennybody hurt?" she quavered.
>
> "Listen at the female 'oman!" he exclaimed, in exasperation, because of the
> contradictions of sentiment she presented. "Fairly dotes on the idee o' other
> folks a-fightin', an' yit can't abide the notion o' nobody gittin' hurt! The
> Guthries hev the name o' shootin' straight, Litt Pettingill, an' I'd be powerful
> 'shamed ef in twelve shots I done no damage. 'Tain't been my policy nor my
> practice ter waste lead an' powder."

In *The Juggler* (1897) is seen the effect of the romantic-idealistic
movement of the late 'nineties on a writer who had won fame through
her realistic portraits of actual people. Her labored explanations of the
reasons for her hero's disappearance after he had lost the funds of his
employers, show the writer who was caught between two fires. A romanticist would have given the incident without bothering further, a
classic realist of conviction would have invented a more probable story.
The novel, however, is better constructed than usual with her; the
effect of the juggler upon the people, who believe him possessed by
Satan, is well depicted.

Miss Murfree was inspired by the success of the historical romance
of the 'nineties to turn to the Cherokee country of the eighteenth century. Her historical novels, of which *A Spectre of Power* (1903) and
The Amulet (1906) are the best, suffer from the same difficulty as
The Juggler. The scenes are painted with accuracy, but she was too careful to explain motives when the action is really not sufficiently motivated.
There is a certain skill in the creation of an atmosphere of constant
danger, and the Indians' worship of their mystical amulet, a tourmaline,
is charmingly interpreted through the sympathy of Arabella Howard,
the heroine of the novel. But the historical romances of Miss Murfree
would never alone have secured her marked attention.

Toward the end of her career, Miss Murfree returned to her mountaineers in *The Ordeal* (1912), but they had become simply a background for a novelette dealing with the relations of a group of quite
different people from nearby cities, one of whom is murdered through a
mistake by the moonshiners. The main interest lies in the effort to rescue
a little boy who has been abducted by the murderers to prevent their
capture. If anything were needed to prove that the interest in her work

was due to the material of her earlier stories, this book would be sufficient. Her collection of short stories published in the same year, *The Raid of the Guerilla*, while treating the mountaineer more sympathetically, has not the charm and objectivity of the earlier stories. Her very earliest fiction, before she used the mountain people, and her later work raise the question whether she was not at heart a romantic idealist who for a short time achieved realism by the sheer potency of a primitive type.

Certainly the contrast between her fiction and that of John Fox, Jr. (1863–1919) would indicate this interpretation. The youngest and the least important of this group, Fox, was born at Stony Point, Kentucky, educated at Transylvania University, studied at Harvard, and worked for a time on the *New York Sun* and the *Times*. He became acquainted at first hand with the mountaineer of Kentucky through his association with a volunteer police force which eventually made the country more law-abiding. With the instinct of a journalist, Fox saw the potential contrasts between the mountaineers and the patricians of the "Bluegrass" country and he made this the basis for several novels and many short stories, only a few of which are of significance. Beginning with *A Mountain Europa* (1894) which was in the *Century* as early as 1892, the idyllic picture of a mountain girl set, pure and innocent, in the grim surroundings of the mountains, constantly reappears. Some validity is given to the picture of a feud in *A Cumberland Vendetta* (1895) because of Fox's own activity in the volunteer police force which finally established peace in the mountains. Twice Fox rose almost to the level of the others in this group. In *The Little Shepherd of Kingdom Come* (1903), his usual faults are evident; a reckless use of superlatives in speaking of Kentucky—"there love was as far from lust as heaven from hell," and the idealistic picture of the mountaineers' devotion to the Union, which was in reality largely a lack of interest in any war not of their own making. But the character of Chad Budford, the mountain boy who assumes responsibility early, is well drawn, and through him are vividly pictured the bitter struggle which divided Kentucky families, the social ostracism meted out to Union sympathizers on one side and on the other the harsh treatment of the adherents of the Confederacy by the Union forces. Fox is best in the idealistic romance; his historic sense is not so accurate. He calmly states that "the postbellum terrors of reconstruction were practically unknown in the State." However this may have been, his explanation that the closely knit ties of family accounted for this lack of persecution leaves out the significant fact that Kentucky had never seceded from the Union, and the partisan rage of Thaddeus Stevens could not operate in consequence.

The Trail of the Lonesome Pine (1908) is an interesting picture of the struggle between the mountain standards and the new industrial forces represented concretely by a young Kentucky engineer. Fox succeeds in his effort to show the inevitable result of such a contest, but some of his incidents such as the shooting of a mountaineer by one of his own clan to avoid his being hanged was done better by Bird in *Hawks of Hawk-Hollow* in 1835. *Crittenden* (1900) was based on Fox's own experiences as a Rough Rider and a newspaper correspondent in Cuba. It shares now the fate of all fiction which dealt with that conflict; while the picture of the fight at San Juan Hill is vivid, and the description of the effect of the Spanish War in its unification of national spirit is adequate, they are not enough to make a novel. Fox attempted to repeat his success in dealing with a mountain boy in *The Heart of the Hills* (1913) and almost succeeded, for there is something very appealing in Jason Hawn's lonely struggle to reach a level he only vaguely apprehends. But neither in this, nor in *The Kentuckians* (1909), where the conventional contrasts appeared, nor in *Erskine Dale, Pioneer*, an historical novel, did he capture the imagination as he had done with his two best known stories.

Fox dedicated *A Mountain Europa* to James Lane Allen, but just as truly as Allen must be differentiated from the other Southern writers of this generation, Fox belongs definitely to the impulse which prompted their work. Younger than Allen, his work belongs to an older fashion.

This group of writers pursued of course different methods and varied in the length of their careers. Miss Woolson, Eggleston, Mrs. Jackson, Mrs. Chopin, and Tourgée had finished their work by the end of the century or before it. Miss Jewett, Cable, Page, Smith, Miss King, Miss Murfree and Fox continued into the twentieth century. It is the usual commonplace of criticism to speak of this group as having done their only significant work in the beginning of their careers, but this is not by any means true. By its very nature, fiction which reveals for the first time a place or a race attracts attention by its novelty. But if the 'seventies gave us *Deephaven, Castle Nowhere, The Hoosier Schoolmaster, Roxy* and *Old Creole Days*, in the 'eighties came *A Country Doctor*,

The White Heron, Anne, For the Major, East Angels, Ramona, The Grandissimes, Madame Delphine, Bonaventure, In Ole Virginia, Monsieur Motte, In the Tennessee Mountains, and *The Prophet of the Great Smoky Mountains.* To the 'nineties belong *A Native of Winby, The Country of the Pointed Firs, The Front Yard and Other Stories, Red Rock, The Old Gentleman of the Black Stock, Balcony Stories, Bayou Folk, Colonel Carter, Tom Grogan, Elsket and Other Stories,* and *Bred in the Bone.* And the broader canvas on which Page and Smith were working still had to its credit in the twentieth century *John Marvel, Assistant* and *The Tides of Barnegat,* while *The Little Shepherd of Kingdom Come* is a survival of their earlier manner. It was an impulse, therefore, originating in the 'seventies and rising to its height in the 'eighties and 'nineties. It rediscovered to Americans the romance that lay around them. It was generally a brave world these men and women painted, shot through with loyalty and patriotism, with sacrifice for the sake of honor, with a pride of race that passes from memory to memory. When this life faded out of America, it left a void that has not been filled. But before it disappeared, it was interpreted by those who wrought with skill and sincerity. It is the fashion today to refer to it as a dream, but perhaps when we cease to be interested in prying into the purlieus of our national byways, we shall return for comfort to this record of what was at least a noble dream.

CHAPTER XVII

JOEL CHANDLER HARRIS AND THE
FICTION OF FOLKLORE

IN that dangerous but fascinating zone of fiction where animals are interpreted through the feelings of man, Joel Chandler Harris (1848-1908) found inspiration which made him one of the most significant figures of our literature. He was born near Eatonton, Georgia, of a family well known in the neighborhood. When his father, an Irishman who worked at times for the Harris family, deserted his mother shortly after the boy's birth, she resumed her maiden name. Joel Harris was educated in the printing room of a country newspaper and by wide reading in the extensive library of its proprietor. Newspaper work took him to Macon, to New Orleans, to Forsyth and Savannah, and finally in 1877 to Atlanta, Georgia, where he joined the staff of the *Atlanta Constitution*. From the early days on *The Countryman* he had written, and like Franklin he sent his contributions anonymously to his paper. While still on the staff of *The Countryman,* he became interested in Negro folklore and stored in his memory many elements he later used.

Like all great creations, the Uncle Remus stories were a growth. The name, which he probably took from a Negro gardener at Forsyth, first appeared in a sketch, "Uncle Remus's Politics," in the *Atlanta Constitution* on November 28, 1876, and it was not until three years later that Uncle Remus and "Brer Rabbit" became associated. The earlier sketches were humorous conversations in which Uncle Remus gave his opinions on various matters, from the church revival to temperance reform. In December, 1877, Harris read in *Lippincott's Magazine* "The Folk Lore of the Southern Negroes," by William Owens, which called his attention to its literary possibilities. Indeed the stories of the Tar Baby, of "Buh Wolf's" funeral, of the harnessing of "Buh Wolf" and of the race between the Rabbit and the Frog are given. In the Tar Baby story "Buh Wolf" is the deluded animal instead of "Brer Fox." A comparison of these stories with Harris's versions illustrates the difference between the material for literature and the result of imagination of a high order creating the product of art. The most significant change lies in the character of Brother Rabbit. "Buh Rabbit is foppish, vain, quick witted, though at times a great fool." That is not the "Brer Rabbit" of Harris. The stories gain immeasurably by being placed in the mouth of the old Negro, and his kindly relations with the little boy provide just the proper audience. The very effort to interpret the stories for a child calls forth some of the finest strokes of narration and description. The relation is also singularly fortunate since it reveals the nature of Uncle Remus himself, half child and half adult. He is a real Negro—a shrewd, kindly nature, superstitious, with a keen sense of humor, and with the proprietary attitude of the slave toward his white folks. Harris tells us in his Preface to the first collection that he tried to reveal the poetic as well as the humorous qualities of the Negro, to suggest "a curious exaltation of mind and temperament not to be defined by words."

The first of the stories appeared in *The Constitution* as "Negro Folklore. The Story of Mr. Rabbit and Mr. Fox, as Told by Uncle Remus" (July 20, 1879). This sketch which became afterwards the Introduction to the first published volume, attracted so much attention that he continued it in "Brer Rabbit, Brer Fox, and the Tar Baby" on November 16, although the escape of Brer Rabbit took place only in a third installment, "Showing How Brer Rabbit was Too Sharp for Brer Fox." [1]

The division of the original story into three parts shows again Harris's art in providing a climax which piques the curiosity of the little boy. It is to a certain degree a journalistic trick, but it is justified by its effect. Then followed the stories which are probably the closest rivals of the "Tar Baby"—"The Story of the Deluge," "The Awful Fate of Brer Wolf," "Mr. Rabbit Nibbles Up the Butter" and others, which were collected in 1880 under the title, *Uncle Remus, His Songs and His Sayings.* In the Introduction Harris tells us that "its intention is perfectly serious; and even if it were otherwise, it seems to me that a volume written wholly in dialect must have its solemn, not to say melancholy features . . . Each legend," he adds, "has its variants, but in every instance I have retained that particular version which seemed to me most characteristic, and have given it without embellishment and without exaggeration." But of course Harris did more than that. About the same time, Francis

---

[1] For the original forms of the stories, see most conveniently Wiggins, R. L., *The Life of Joel Chandler Harris* (1918).

James Child was preparing his monumental collection of the English and Scottish popular ballads. With the restraint of the scholar, he published for each ballad the variant forms, leaving to his readers the privilege of comparison. Harris, on the contrary, gathered the different versions from Negroes and other sources, passed them all through the fusing process of imagination, and the result, representing probably no one version, became literature.

In the first volume, which has been translated into twenty-seven foreign languages, Harris presented thirty-four of the most popular legends, which were comparatively well known. After that he found it more difficult to proceed. Negroes were reluctant to tell these stories to the white race, and only when he had gained their confidence by telling some himself was he able to stimulate them into narrative. In the second series, *Nights with Uncle Remus* (1883), he tells how he related to a group of train hands at a railway station "The Tar Baby" and "Brer Rabbit and the Mosquitoes," and then for two hours they vied with each other in telling stories they knew. This second series, some of which appeared first in the *Century* in 1883, is quite on the level with the first, and it is interesting to note that while the time of the first series is indicated as being after the Civil War, the second is placed in slavery days. Daddy Jack, an ancient Negro from the Coast, is introduced at times as a storyteller, but his dialect is more difficult to understand and his stories are less appealing than those of Uncle Remus.

Harris continued to publish collections of folklore stories, the best of them, in addition to the two first, being *Uncle Remus and His Friends* (1892) and *Told by Uncle Remus* (1905), and there was a posthumous volume, *Uncle Remus and the Little Boy* (1910). In the two last, the son of the first little boy is the audience. This little boy is old-fashioned and Uncle Remus and "Mis' Sally" try to educate him to some of the joys of childhood. There is also a series more definitely intended for children.[2]

Much discussion has raged over the origin of these folk-tales, since similar stories appear in the folklore of the American Indians both in North and South America. Harris believed that in this case the Indians borrowed them from the Negroes, since he was able to show in many in-

---

[2] *Little Mr. Thimblefinger* (1894), *Mr. Rabbit at Home* (1895), *The Story of Aaron* (1895), *Aaron in the Wildwoods* (1897) and *Plantation Pageants* (1899).

stances that the tales have variants among the Kaffir tribes of Africa.[3] They may of course go back to races ante-dating both the African and the American Indian. Certainly such a tale as "How the Tortoise Outran the Deer" has the stamp of universality as well as antiquity. Some of the stories reflect ancient European customs which may have had African counterparts. "Mr. Rabbit Nibbles Up the Butter," with its trial by fire of the accused robber, reminds a reader at once of medieval customs. There is, of course, the possibility of influence from American fiction of white origin. "A Ghost Story," in *Nights with Uncle Remus,* in which a man steals the dollars from the eyes of a dead woman who returns for them, has striking resemblance to Poe's "Berenice," which may indeed prove that Poe was influenced by a story told in his infancy by a Negro.

The attitude of Uncle Remus toward the stories forms one of their charms. He believes in them heartily. When the little boy asks him who "Miss Meadows" [4] is, he replies:

"Don't ax me, honey. She wuz in de tale, Miss Meadows en de gals wuz, en de tale I give you like hit wer' gun ter me."

Or again, [5] when the second little boy asks him:

"Did the man really and truly think that Brother Wolf was Brother Rabbit?"

"When you pin me down dat away," responded Uncle Remus, "I'm bleeze ter tell you dat I ain't too certain and sho' 'bout dat. De tale come down fum my great-granddaddy's great-granddaddy; it come on down ter my daddy and des es he gun it ter me, des dataway I done gun it ter you."

In "How Old Craney Crow Lost his Head," [6] after Uncle Remus has said that the swamp went to sleep, the little boy objects:

"Do you believe it, Uncle Remus? Mother says the stories are fables." Thus the little boy was imbued, without knowing it, with the modern spirit of scientific doubt.

"Does you speck I'd tell you a tale dat I don't believe? Why, I dunner how I'd put de words one atter de yuther. Whensomever you ain't believin' what

[3] See Introduction to *Nights with Uncle Remus* for an extended series of comparisons with the Kaffir folklore.

[4] "Mr. Rabbit Grossly Deceives Mr. Fox," in *Uncle Remus, His Songs and His Sayings.*

[5] "Brother Rabbit's Cradle," in *Told by Uncle Remus.*

[6] *Told by Uncle Remus.*

I'm a tellin', honey, des le' me know, an' I won't take de time and trouble fer ter tell it."

Throwing the responsibility for a story upon some other authority and then creating an implicit trust in the veracity of the source is an old device, of course, but it is a good one. Uncle Remus understood, too, how to avoid a point about which he was ignorant. When Brother Rabbit has been caught and held fast by the Tar Baby, and Brother Fox saunters up to capture him, the tale [7] concludes:

> Here Uncle Remus paused, and drew a two-pound yam out of the ashes.
> "Did the fox eat the rabbit?" asked the little boy to whom the story had been told.
> "Dat's all de fur de tale goes," replied the old man. "He mout, en den agin he moutent. Some say Jedge B'ar come 'long en losed 'im—some say he didn't. I hear Miss Sally callin'. You better run 'long."

The Uncle Remus stories were written, of course, for adults, and the solemn objections which have been made to the ethics of Brother Rabbit as corrupters of youth must have amused Harris. Harris claimed that weakness in its conflict with strength and mischief rather than dishonesty were celebrated in the stories. Certainly some of the exploits of Brother Rabbit partake of the curious moral distinctions of the Negro race. But in reality the great response which the stories received was due to our subconscious sympathy with any hero, human or beast, who matches mind against brute strength and wins. It may arise from dim racial memories of a day when the human race itself matched its brain against overmastering animal force that threatened to annihilate it, and triumphed by strategy not unlike that of Brother Rabbit.

There is little hint of a race question in these stories. The relations of Uncle Remus to his white owners or employers is affectionate and exacting, but it is that of an older child. Once in a while, as in the story "Why the Negro is Black," when Uncle Remus tells the boy that "time wuz wen we wuz all niggers tergedder," we have a touch of race pride, but it is not race animosity.

The fame of Harris as the creator of Uncle Remus and Brother Rabbit has obscured his significant work as a writer of seven volumes of short stories, two novels, and three novelettes dealing with Southern life. Here again his art deepened from the early journalistic sketches into literature

---

[7] "The Wonderful Tar-Baby Story," in *Uncle Remus, His Songs and His Sayings.*

of permanent value. "Mingo," which appeared in *Harper's* in 1882 and became the title story of his first collection, *Mingo and Other Sketches* (1884), strikes a different note from that of Cable, Page, or Smith. It is the contrast not of white and Negro, but of the patrician and the middle class. The resentment of Feratia Bivins, when Emily Wornum comes to visit her after the death of the daughter Emily has disowned because the girl had married Feratia's son, "seemed to represent the real or fancied wrongs of a class, and to spring from the pent-up rage of a century." In "At Teague Poteet's" Harris gives a less romanticized picture of the mountaineers than Miss Murfree's. His picture of the expedition of Federal troops to fraternize with the Union men in the mountains, only to return with bullet holes in them, represents exactly the attitude of most of the mountaineers who wished simply to be let alone. It was not their war.

It was in "Free Joe and the Rest of the World," appearing first in *The Century* for November, 1884, that Harris reached the summit of his art as a writer of short stories. This tragic picture of the free Negro of 1850, who because he was free was more helpless than any slave, is a masterly study of the individual who is at odds with the civilization of which he is a part. The whites disliked him because he was "the embodiment of that vague and mysterious danger that seemed to be forever lurking on the outskirts of slavery." The Negroes despised him because he belonged to no one. The very helplessness of Joe in the face of the cruelty of "Spite" Calderwood, owner of Joe's wife, Lucinda, who sells her away when he finds Joe is meeting her in the woods, is pictured objectively, as in all great art. It seems as though Harris knew instinctively what Eugene O'Neill long after discovered, that there is a nobility in the lowest lives if they be animated with one great emotion. In Joe it is his love for Lucinda, but there is no sentimentality about his relations with her, no self-pity when she does not come. He simply waits at their accustomed meeting-place, ignorant for weeks that she has been sold, waiting even after he suspects the truth. Then how quietly Harris ends the story:

Receiving no response, Mr. Staley went to Free Joe, and shook him by the shoulder; but the negro made no response. He was dead. His hat was off, his head was bent, and a smile was on his face. It was as if he had bowed and smiled when death stood before him, humble to the last. His clothes were ragged; his hands were rough and callous; his shoes were literally tied together with strings; he was shabby in the extreme. A passer-by glancing at him, could have no idea that such a humble creature had been summoned as a witness before the Lord God of Hosts.

There are no polemics concerning slavery, the story may be construed as a defence or an attack upon it. It is neither; it is a celebration of the unquenchable spark of hope which dignifies even the outcast.

It became the title story for *Free Joe and Other Sketches* (1887), in which Harris establishes contrasts between Northern and Southern characters. The Northern man who came South before the war appears in "Little Compton"; the Northern soldier who came during the war and remained, in "Aunt Fountain's Prisoner"; the Northern man who comes down in the 'seventies prospecting, in "Trouble at Lost Mountain"; and the Northern girl who visits the pine woods for her health, in "Azalia." In each case they are elements which change the current of events, but the Southern civilization remains the most interesting part of the picture. In "Azalia," there are two remarkable portraits of the Georgia "tackies," Mrs. Stucky and her son Bud. This race had settled in Georgia before the Revolution and had remained at the very bottom of civilization. Harris speaks of the "wonderful serenity" of Mrs. Stucky's face: "a pale, unhealthy-looking face, with sunken eyes, high cheekbones, and thin lips that seemed never to have troubled themselves to smile." Bud conceives a hopeless passion for the Northern visitor, Helen Eustis, never speaks to her, but communicates with the other characters almost entirely through his love of music. Bud's death-bed, in which his mother tries to keep him alive by the sheer force of her will, and his prayer to her to "let him go," leads to the visit of Helen to their hut after his death. She finds that Mrs. Stucky has built a little contrivance of boards around his footprint. So extreme was their poverty that this was the only memento that she possessed of her son.

In the next volume, *Balaam and his Master* (1891), the baleful effect of the system which gave power of life or death to a headstrong young man is revealed in the title story. There is a touching story of Negro fidelity in "Ananias" and a telling contrast between the old and new forces in the South in "The Old Bascom Place." *Tales of the Home Folks in Peace and War* (1898) strikes the earlier notes again; but in "A Belle of St. Valérien," there is a story of French Canadians, which reflects Harris's knowledge gained through his marriage with Esther La Rose, a Canadian girl. The keen sense of humor which shone through the Uncle Remus sketches was shown again in *The Chronicles of Aunt Minervy Ann* (1899), delightful comedies told by a Negress who was drawn from real life, and whose hot temper and vigorous vocabulary are provided with several opportunities for expression when she visits her husband who is sitting in the legislature.

Harris's ability to make his characters real was shown in a collection of stories, *On the Wing of Occasions* (1900), dealing with the Civil War, mainly through the adventures of Captain McCarthy, of the Confederate Secret Service, and "Texas Jack Omohundro." So vivid was Harris's account of the latter's association with Wilkes Booth that he received letters from friends of the real scout protesting that they could prove an alibi for him. In "The Kidnapping of President Lincoln," an imaginary account of the kidnapping of the President by "Billy Sanders," who became a favorite creation of Harris, there is a remarkable account of the effect of Lincoln's character upon his captors. So impressed are they that they voluntarily give up their advantage. While there is some extravaganza in the story, it represents with fidelity the attitude of many Southerners toward Lincoln after his death. The stories are all interesting and are on a higher level than those included in *The Making of a Statesman* (1902).

In the early days on the *Atlanta Constitution*, Harris was writing fiction and indeed printed a novel, *The Romance of Rockville*, which ran from April 16 to September 10, 1878. While it has not the finished style of his later work, it is a spirited story of Georgia life in 1848. Years afterward Harris used certain elements in the plot and even the names of some of the characters in his first published long novel, *Sister Jane, Her Friends and Acquaintances* (1896). William Wornum, the planter and school teacher, becomes William Wornum, the quiet lawyer, but both are men of forty, who hesitate to tell the girl they love of their affection because they believe they are too old. It is an idyllic picture of life in a Georgia town before the Civil War. There is no treatment of the Negro problem, but the relations of the poorer whites to their richer neighbors is illustrated in the story of Mandy Satterlee and her child. The life is more democratic than in Cable or Page; it is the life of a middle class, with no rigid line between them and the planter class in Virginia, with whom they intermarry. But there is a difference so far as fiction is concerned in that the contrasts are not so sharp.

The same atmosphere is portrayed in *Gabriel Tolliver* (1902), a novel which begins before the Civil War but deals mostly with the Reconstruction period. The evils of that time are depicted fairly, and the murder of the carpet-bagger, Hotchkiss, by a jealous Negro is made with some skill the basis of the charge against Gabriel Tolliver. But the rescue of Gabriel by Billy Sanders hardly comes up to Harris's usual standard and the love-making is not very thrilling. There are, however, some well-known characters: Gabriel himself, Nan Dorrington, Pulaski Tomlin, and several of the Negroes. Best of all is the picture of the town with its aroma of friendliness and universal acquaintance, of personal interest in human life, and sympathy with the joy and suffering of others.

Of the three novelettes, *On the Plantation* (1892) is partly fiction but mostly autobiography; it is one of the most interesting of his books. Harris's life as a boy, when he was learning his printer's trade with *The Countryman*, his adventures in coon-hunting, chasing Negroes, helping deserters to escape, and the arrival of Sherman's army are all told with the coloring of a vivid personality. *A Little Union Scout* (1904) was based on the career of a woman who was a Union spy, and had some flavor of originality in its method, for it is told by a Southern soldier who afterwards marries her. But neither it nor *Shadow Between His Shoulder Blades* (1909), another war story in which Mr. Sanders again appears, was on the level of his finest work.

Harris's fiction, outside of the Uncle Remus stories, belongs to a certain degree in the same category with that of Cable, Page, and Smith. There is the same sympathetic description of Southern life, going back at times to some distance. Speaking of a character in "The Colonel's Nigger Dog," he said:

> As a child she had imbibed the spirit of the Revolution, and everything she said and did was flavored with the energy and independence that gave our colonial society its special and most beautiful significance—the significance of candor and simplicity.

The description of Shady Dale in *Gabriel Tolliver*, however, makes clear a distinction between Harris and the rest of the Southern writers of his era. The feudalism which is at the basis of their life is not so marked in his. He speaks of the social life in Shady Dale as "homogeneous." In this word he reflects the differences in origin and traditions which distinguish Georgia from Louisiana or Virginia, but even more clearly, he reveals his own philosophy of life. In his democracy, he was more akin to Howells than to Page, for his broad sympathies, strengthened perhaps by his early history and the heredity from that shadowy father who gave him also his Celtic humor, led him to look upon human beings for themselves and not as members of a caste.

Harris was in no sense an apologist for slavery. He loved the past and he could not help seeing the absurdity of the attempts of Northern enthusiasts to advance the Negro faster than his abilities warranted. The creator of Uncle Remus knew the race as well as anyone; the picture of the young Negro in "Azalia," who believes that it is just as well to hold the book upside down because the lesson cannot spill out of it, is an example of his humorous approach. But Harris could paint the other side of the shield as well. In "Mom Bi" he tells the story of a Negress who, while devoted to her master, left him at once when made free, to find the child he had sold away from her. And in *On the Plantation*, he describes a real occurrence:

> In a corner of the fence, not far from the road, Joe found an old negro woman shivering and moaning. Near her lay an old negro man, his shoulders covered with an old ragged shawl.
> "Who is that lying there?" asked Joe.
> "It is my old man, suh."
> "What is the matter with him?"
> "He dead, suh! But bless God, he died free."

One of the most engaging qualities of Harris was his modesty, which led him to decline such honors as the honorary degree offered him in 1905 by the University of Pennsylvania, because he could not bring himself to appear in such a public way. In "The Late Mr. Watkins of Georgia" [8] he gives an amusing account of the war that raged among folklore societies "in seven different languages and thirteen different dialects" about the relations of the story of Mr. Watkins and an Indian legend, "A Sympathetic Vine." Source-hunting has hardly ever been so delightfully satirized. Though he had nothing of the academic about him, he was widely read; the influence of his favorites, Goldsmith, Montaigne, Sir Thomas Browne, Thackeray, and Hawthorne, is seen clearly in the easy distinction of his style, the wide range of his vocabulary, and his keen sense of the delicate gradations of meaning. Reread-

[8] *Tales of the Home Folks in Peace and War.*

ing him is a delight, even if the plot is known, because of the unfettered flow of narrative and the natural dialogue. How great progress he made in this matter of style can best be realized by comparing *A Romance of Rockville* with "Free Joe" or *Gabriel Tolliver*.

His command of dialogue is one of the elements of his success in the Uncle Remus stories. Here is real dialect, not the colloquial slang that often passes for it. Harris knew the difference. In a letter to E. L. Burlingame in 1898 he said truly: "The difference between real dialect and lingo is that the first is preservative while the latter is destructive of language. Judged by this standard the negro dialect is as perfect as any the world ever saw."

But style alone could not have produced "Brer Rabbit" and "Uncle Remus." It was the imagination of Harris, which shines in his poetry, and his great heart, broad enough to take into its comprehension and sympathy the patrician and the cracker, the town-dweller and the mountaineer, the white and the Negro, human beings and the lower animals. His deepest feeling was always for the weak in conflict with the ruthless. Fate had played him a cruel trick before he was born, but from the iron that entered into the soul of Mary Harris there came a finely tempered instrument of genius, provincial but not local, which has added an imperishable quality to world literature, and which could have been born only in America.

CHAPTER XVIII

FRANCIS MARION CRAWFORD AND THE COSMOPOLITAN NOVEL

THE mistaken theory that an American novelist must limit himself to the American scene was triumphantly refuted by Marion Crawford's achievement. Of all our novelists he was most truly cosmopolitan, not only by education and experience but also through his liberal habit of mind. Born in 1854 at Bagni du Lucca in Italy, the son of Thomas Crawford, the well-known American sculptor, he was by inheritance Irish on his father's side and, on his mother's, a descendant of the sister of General Francis Marion of Revolutionary fame. Julia Ward Howe was his mother's sister. His father and mother had met in Rome, and the reactions of Gloria Dalrymple in *Casa Braccio* to Roman society were probably suggested by Mrs. Crawford's experience in Rome in the 'forties. His education was begun in Italy, but he studied at St. Paul's School in New Hampshire from 1866 to 1869; his first appearance in print was in the school paper, *Horæ Scholastica,* December, 1868, with an essay on "Carpet-Baggers." More important, he came under the influence of his aunt, Julia Ward Howe, and her circle of friends, whose stimulating interest in all forms of art strengthened the inherited tendency of Crawford to create beauty. In 1870 he went to England to prepare for Cambridge University, where he spent only one year, transferring to the Polytechnicum at Karlsruhe in 1873 and returning to his mother's home in Rome, studying at the university there. Through these apparently desultory phases of his education, Crawford was mastering several languages, learning national characteristics and unconsciously preparing himself for his later career. In 1879 his interest in Sanskrit sent him to Bombay, where the collapse of the family fortunes led him to editorial work on the *Indian Herald* of Allahabad. In 1881 he came to America hoping for a college position as a teacher of comparative philology. Failing to secure this, he began to write magazine articles for the *Critic* and the *New York World,* re-

maining by reason of his vivid and charming personality the center of
interest to admiring relatives and friends. Like his characters, Crawford worked or played with vigor. Life was always an adventure, on
sea or land.

Like Cooper, he seems to have been started on his career by an accident. He happened to tell his uncle, Samuel Ward, and George Brett
of Macmillan's about a diamond merchant, Mr. Jacobs, whom he had
met in India, and they urged him to write the story for publication. In
about six weeks he wrote *Mr. Isaacs* (1882) and it was at once a popular
success. Curiously enough, a parody, *Dr. Jacobs,* which I remember
reading as a boy of seven, took the original name of the hero.

Crawford was to write better novels than *Mr. Isaacs,* but already his
mastery of language which his study of so many tongues had given him
was apparent. Through Paul Griggs, the American editor of an Anglo-
Indian newspaper, who in certain respects represents Crawford himself,
he tells the story of Abdul-Hafiz-ben-Isâk, a wealthy Persian diamond
merchant who is living in Simla, India. "Mr. Isaacs," unlike the usual
hero of romance, is alive. His charm, his intellectual power, his courage,
and his philosophical calm are Eastern, and he undergoes no violent
change. But his love for Katharine Westonhaugh, an English girl,
gives him a new conception of the relations of man and woman. He
has already three wives, "for the sake of respectability," but his passion for them has been incidental, and his progress from a sensual to a
spiritual conception of love is revealed delicately but definitely. Such a
situation was in itself a difficult one, and Crawford solved it by Katharine's death through jungle fever. Mr. Isaacs goes away with Ram Lal,
a mystic, to become one of his brotherhood. Crawford had not learned
his art completely as yet. The conversations are too long at times and
there is too much of philosophic discussion. But there is also plenty of
action, in the tiger hunt and the saving of Shere Ali by Isaacs, in which
Ram Lal brings down the mist which allows them to escape from
the trap laid by his enemies. The description of true marriage, which
Griggs gives to Isaacs early in the book, is an earnest of that power
which made Crawford one of the best portrayers of love in all those
phases which he felt it good art to depict. Thus at the beginning of his
career he realized that a good love story is of perennial appeal and he
proceeded to write some of the best that the English language possesses. Crawford returned to Italy, married, and by 1885 was settled at

Sorrento, where he worked and studied until his death in 1909. After 1892, when he made his first lecture tour in the United States, it was his custom to spend at least three months of the year working in New York City and giving occasional lectures. Unlike James, he never lost his American point of view and he retained his American citizenship to the end.

In any critical survey of Crawford's work, his own theory of the art of novel-writing must be considered. He expressed it definitely in his monograph, *The Novel—What It Is* (1893), but throughout many of his novels he also made his position clear. He was primarily the teller of a good story, and he used any method, realistic or idealistic, which suited him. Art should be free to choose its theme anywhere, but to him the photographic representation of life was anathema. As he says in *To Leeward:*

If men are only interesting for what they are, regardless of what they may be, a day of any one's actual experience must be a thousand times more interesting than all the fictions that ever were written. If art consists in the accurate presentation of detail, then the highest art is the petrifaction of nature, and the wax-works of an anatomical museum are more artistically beautiful than all the marbles of Phidias and Praxiteles. True art depends upon an a priori capacity for distinguishing the beautiful from the ugly, and the grand from the grotesque; and true knowledge of the world lies in the knowledge of good and evil, not confounding the noble with the ignoble under one smearing of mud, nor yet whitewashing the devil into an ill-gotten reputation for cleanliness.

He had also no interest in the novel with a purpose:

In art of all kinds the moral lesson is a mistake. It is one thing to exhibit an ideal worthy to be imitated, though inimitable in all its perfection, but so clearly noble as to appeal directly to the sympathetic string that hangs untuned in the dullest human heart; to make man brave without arrogance, woman pure without prudishness, love enduring yet earthly, not angelic, friendship sincere but not ridiculous. It is quite another matter to write a "guide to morality" or a "hand-book for practical sinners" and call either one a novel, no matter how much fiction it may contain.[1]

That he carried out these principles in his fiction no one can dispute.

In discussing the forty-five novels which Marion Crawford wrote in twenty-eight years, chronology must be subservient to a classification

[1] *The Novel*, pp. 19–20.

according to the time and place with which the novel is concerned. Seven were definitely historical; thirty-eight were written of periods either contemporary or shortly before his own day. The larger group may be reclassified according to the countries in which they are laid, for in this way a sense of his broad cosmopolitan view may best be obtained.

His most significant achievement, one in which he has not been surpassed by any writer in English, lay in the novels dealing with Italian life. This is not surprising, since he knew that life well in its social, political and economic phases. His large library dealing with Italy was collected to serve the great ambition of his life, never realized, of writing a definitive history of Italy. Preliminary studies like *Ave Roma Immortalis* and *The Rulers of the South* reveal the synthetic power of his mind and his grasp of the subject. His knowledge of Italian character is expressed in *Saracinesca:*

For, in spite of a vast number of writers of all nations who have attempted to describe Italian life, and who, from an imperfect acquaintance with the people, have fallen into the error of supposing them to live perpetually in a highly complicated state of mind, the foundation of the Italian character is simple—far more so than that of his hereditary antagonist, the northern European. It is enough to notice that the Italian habitually expresses what he feels, while it is the chief pride of Northern men that whatever they may feel they express nothing. The chief object of most Italians is to make life agreeable; the chief object of the Teutonic races is to make it profitable. Hence the Italian excels in the art of pleasing, and in pleasing by means of the arts; whereas the Northern man is pre-eminent in the faculty of producing wealth under any circumstances, and when he has amassed enough possessions to think of enjoying his leisure, has generally been under the necessity of employing Southern art as a means to that end.

Crawford's conversion to Catholicism, which took place in India, made it easier for him to understand the Italian nature and to appreciate the many shades of belief which permitted, for example, the Saracinesca family to remain good Catholics and still be political opponents of the Pope. Of the sixteen Italian stories, fourteen are laid wholly or partly in Rome. *A Roman Singer* (1884) is a charming novel of artistic life, with a striking character, Professor Cornello Grandi. It was based on years of acquaintance with the musical circles in Rome. *To Leeward* (1884) is not so successful because the central character, Leonora Carnethy, an English girl who marries Marcantonio, Marchese Carontoni, without loving him truly and who leaves him for Julius Batiscombe, an English man of letters, is so supremely selfish that even Crawford could not make her very interesting. But Marcantonio is a fine picture of an Italian, who goes mad under the stress of grief at his wife's unfaithfulness; while the ending is sheer melodrama, there are several passages which showed the promise of the power that was coming.

In 1887 Crawford's art reached a high level in *Marzio's Crucifix*. Here he created the character of a silversmith, in whom "the gifts of the artist, the tenacity of the workman and the small astuteness of the plebeian were mingled with an appearance of something which was not precisely ideality, but which might easily be fanaticism." Two strong passions control him, love for his art and hatred for his brother Paolo, a priest, who represents not only the religion Marzio has rejected but also those qualities of mind and soul which make Marzio feel his inferiority. When Don Paolo brings the commission from the Cardinal for a silver crucifix, Marzio accepts it, for his love of beauty has already led him to make a crucifix and he knows it is a masterpiece. Wrathful over his brother's interference to save Lucia, Marzio's daughter, from his parental tyranny, the silversmith plans his brother's murder. Then, while he is alone in his shop, peering down into the black depths underneath the house where the body might be concealed, the silver figure of the Christ falls from its position and, startled by the sound, Marzio feels the mood of murder pass from him. Gradually his desire for revenge is lost as the minute changes wrought by his chisel bring the crucifix to artistic perfection:

He laid the silver figure of the Christ straight before him upon the leathern pad, and looked intently at it, while his hands played idly with the tools upon the table. His deep-set, heavy eyes gazed fixedly at the wonderful face, with an expression which had not yet been there. There was no longer any smile upon his thin lips, and his dark emaciated features were restful and quiet, almost solemn in their repose.

"I am glad I did not do it," he said aloud after some minutes.

The climax of the novel comes when Marzio brings the crucifix to Paolo's bedside where his brother is lying injured and places it where the apparently dying man may see it. Paolo does not die, but the spirit of evil passes out of Marzio's soul. The unity of the novel, the perfect preservation of the tone, the art with which Crawford united the greatest symbol of Christianity and the love of beauty to bring peace to an unhappy heart, make it one of the finest novels in the language. Before he wrote it, he learned the art of the silversmith and could create the forms of which Marzio was the master. Marzio was drawn from Sor Pepé, Crawford's teacher. When it was crowned, together with *Zoroaster*, by the French Academy, it is noteworthy that Crawford was the first foreigner since Charles Dickens to be so honored.

Crawford's versatility was shown by his turning from the ideal conceptions and the humble surroundings of *Marzio's Crucifix* to the reality of Italian social life in the series of novels dealing with three generations of a patrician Italian family. In the first of these, *Saracinesca* (1887), he began with a comparison of the Europe of 1865 with that of 1885, and showed how complete was his understanding of the complex life of the Continent. While the story is laid in 1865, it brings in few historical characters. It is distinctly a love story, with a background of social life. The Prince Saracinesca and his son Giovanni represent the Roman nobles, conservative, courageous, generous, good lovers and haters, quick to strike back at those who injure them, and still feudal in their sense of responsibility to those who occupy their lands. Corona, Duchessa d'Astrardente, who has married an old roué to save her father from ruin, is as typical an Italian woman of high principle as Giovanni Saracinesca is a man, and when they discover their mutual love, they act according to their respective standards. To the critical judgments which refuse to believe that great passion can exalt as well as debase, Corona and Giovanni may seem ideal figures rather than real, but it is the criticisms rather than the characters which are untrue to human nature. There is certainly nothing ideal in Del Ferice, the spy who hangs on the skirts of society, or in Donna Tullia, who tries to prevent the marriage of Giovanni and Corona after the old Duca d'Astrardente dies. Crawford is especially happy in the conversation of plotters, in which one character dominates the other, and Del Ferice's scheme promises not only to revenge himself on Giovanni but also to secure Donna Tullia's property. It also serves to introduce the other Giovanni Saracinesca, who plays an important part in the sequel. The characters are practically all Italian, with the exception of the French painter, Anastase Gouache. Through him Crawford brings in quite naturally such distinctions as "The works of man are never so beautiful as when they are falling to decay; the works of God are most beautiful when they are young."

Sant' Ilario (1889) takes up the fortunes of the family about a year and a half after the conclusion of *Saracinesca*. The plot is exceedingly complicated and is at times melodramatic, but the characters steadily develop. Through her efforts to save Faustina Montevarchi, a young girl who loves Anastase Gouache, against the will of her family, Corona excites Giovanni's suspicion of her fidelity to him, and the deep love each bears the other turns for a time to jealousy and distrust. The most interesting new character is the other Giovanni Saracinesca, who had been an innkeeper but who was able to resume the title of the Marchese di San Giacinto, which had been allowed to lapse because of financial distress. Crawford was fond of heredity as a motive of romance, and this newcomer, huge in frame, slow of thought, but quick of action, becomes an integral part of the social structure, marrying another daughter of the Montevarchi and becoming involved in the claim for the estate of the Saracinesci, of whom he really represents the older branch. The book might be eptomized in the sentence "Blood will tell," and Crawford was running true to the instincts of the romanticist in using the motive.

The third member of the trilogy, *Don Orsino* (1892), treats of the new forces which made the Rome of 1887 differ from the Rome of twenty years before. Don Orsino, the eldest son of Giovanni and Corona, is a very real young Italian to whom the ways of his fathers do not appeal. He is bored by his idle life and enters into the speculative projects brought on by the expansion under the new Kingdom of Italy. Del Ferice, apparently friendly, really brings on his financial ruin by methods often used in the real estate business, and Don Orsino is only saved by the sacrifice of the mysterious Consuelo, Madame d' Aranjuez, who loves him but marries Del Ferice, conveniently widowed, who in consequence releases Don Orsino. What distinguishes Crawford's manipulation of events from the usual romance of the period is his courage in separating the hero and heroine, not by accident but by a recognition on her part that Don Orsino's passion for her was only an infatuation for a woman older than himself. Her sacrifice was a real one, but Consuelo's preference for a marriage with Del Ferice, with all his limitations, to the slow tragedy of a life tied to a man who would gradually cease to love her, has had many parallel instances in real life. In *Don Orsino* the intricate story of Consuelo's parentage savors of melodrama, but it is justified since it reveals a touching story of self-sacrifice on the part of Count Spicca, the melancholy duelist, who appears in all the Saracinesca stories. The older members of the family enter into the novel only slightly, but Don Orsino is no copy of them. His conversation individualizes him, as a man of a new era, restless, not content with leisure and the satisfaction of passion, but with character tempered by his experiences. Always an Italian, he seems like a man whom only an American novelist could have created or understood.

Corleone (1896), which takes the Saracinesca family to Sicily, involves Don Orsino in the complications of the Corleone, a noble family of evil reputation, and finally weds him to Vittoria Corleone. It is hardly up to the level of the other members of the series, though in Don Ippolito Saracinesca, the priest who keeps the secret of the confessional, Crawford added a striking character.

Less definitely associated with the Saracinesca group, but dealing with the same order of society, *Pietro Ghisleri* (1893) is one of his most fascinating stories. The plot is intricate, but it is the character drawing which makes the book important. Pietro Ghisleri is a complicated gentleman, who struggles out of the meshes of a liaison and ultimately wins the love of an English girl, Laura Carlyon, who is much more natural than Crawford's English characters usually are. Pietro, through his sensitiveness to his own defects and his high sense of honor in most directions, gains and keeps our sympathy. The description of the coming of second love to Pietro is in Crawford's best manner. Another remarkable character is that of Adele Savelli, Laura's half-sister, who does her best to ruin Laura by dexterously denying charges against her which Adele has herself invented. She is foiled by Pietro and San Giacinto in some excellent scenes, but not before she has done all the mischief of which such a creature is capable.

The first part of *Casa Braccio* (1895), dealing with the flight of Sister Maria Addolorata, some time in the 'forties, from her convent with Angus Dalrymple, a Scottish nobleman, is not so well done. But in the second part, which has to do with the fortunes of their daughter, Gloria Dalrymple, Crawford depicted a revenge of an unusual nature. Gloria has married an artist, Angelo Reanda, and, quarrelling with him, she goes to Paul Griggs, the American journalist who loves her, lives with him, and bears him a child. Then, tiring of him, she writes to her husband, begging him to take her back. He pays no attention to the letters. Finally, in despair, she commits suicide, telling Griggs she does it to save him from the burden of her support. He worships her memory till Angelo in turn dies and, as a parting malicious gift, sends him Gloria's letters. Griggs opens the package at the last note, in which she tells Angelo how she loathes her lover's very touch, and though each letter is like a dagger to him, he cannot refrain from reading them to the end.

Some of Crawford's later stories of Rome, like *Cecelia* (1902) or *A Lady of Rome* (1906), while interesting, were hardly up to his earlier standard. *The Heart of Rome* (1903) is well written and contains some of his shrewdest observations. The character of young Sabina Conti, who has inherited the courage if not the ruthlessness of her amusing mother, the Princess, is quite real, and is of more importance than the somewhat involved tale of the "lost water" of Rome. Still better was *The White Sister* (1909), in which he showed in his last year that he was still capable of inciting sympathy for human beings fighting against fate. Angela Chiarmonte enters the order of the White Sisters of Santa Giovanna d'Aza five years after her lover, Giovanni Severi, a young engineer officer, is reported dead in Africa. On his return she makes every effort to keep her vows, even when he brings her to his rooms by a false message, and she escapes only by an appeal to his better nature. It is only when, in the hospital, he refuses to allow the operation which will save him until she agrees to apply through Monsignor Saracinesca for an annulment of her vows, that she weakens. It is this struggle to keep her self-respect which made the story so appealing and has led to its dramatization on the stage and in the moving pictures. Usually such a situation is distressing, and in *Casa Braccio* Crawford himself had not succeeded with it, but it was the character of Sister Giovanni and the unpolemical way in which Crawford treated the situation that made a fine story. He does not judge the right or wrong of the matter: he is interested simply in the dramatic value of a conflict between human love and religious duty in its strongest and most concrete form. Of the Italian stories laid outside of Rome, *Corleone* has already been discussed. *Children of the King* (1892) is laid in Southern Italy, mostly in or near Sorrento. It has some good characters, especially Ruggiero and Sebastino, sailors who are by tradition descended from King Roger, and is more significant than *Taquisara* (1896), laid in Naples and concerned largely with the efforts of the Count and Countess Macomber to obtain their niece's estate.

Marion Crawford wrote seven novels in which the scene is laid in America, and one, *A Rose of Yesterday* (1896), in which the characters are American but the scene is Switzerland. His earliest effort in this field, *An American Politician* (1884), is hardly important. The hero,

John Harrington, is a reform politician in Boston. His struggles against the combination of railroad corruptionists and the Irish machine are conventional, and his final speech on the occasion of an election for President by the House of Representatives is absurd. Much better was *The Three Fates* (1892), for here Crawford was on familiar ground— the struggles of a young writer, George Wood, to gain recognition in New York. While Wood's career does not directly parallel Crawford's, the latter knew the intricate relations of publishing and newspaper criticism, and some of his shrewdest remarks about novel-writing are included in this book. The main plot, however, deals with Wood's love for three different women. He loves Constance Fearing sincerely; when she decides after a year's struggle with her too introspective nature that she does not care for him sufficiently to marry him, he is caught on the rebound by his cousin, Mamie Trimm, who has loved him since her childhood. This part of the book is the best. Mamie's mother, "Totty" Trimm, is as perfect a picture of a schemer as can well be imagined. Finding out by surreptitious examination of the strong box of Tom Craik, her own brother, that he intends to make George his heir, she lays siege to George by every artifice which her wealth places at her command. The scene in which she lets him know that Mamie loves him and combats the reviving influence of Constance Fearing, who begins to care for George too late, is as real as though it were out of the pages of Howells at his best. When Mamie finds out what her mother has done, and refuses to marry George, his relief is natural enough, but we are simply told that he finally loves Grace Fearing, a widow, and believes his passion hopeless. The ending is not convincing, but the revelation of the different ways in which a man may love or think he loves a woman, and the character portrayals of George Wood, Totty and Mamie Trimm make it the best of Crawford's novels dealing with American life.

Next best are *Katherine Lauderdale* (1894) and its sequel, The *Ralstons* (1895). They are studies of the reactions of the members of a wealthy New York family upon each other, and of the consequences of a secret marriage between Katherine Lauderdale and her cousin, Jack Ralston. The effect of money, both in the power it gives Robert Ralston, of the oldest generation, to determine consciously or unconsciously the actions of his family, and in the cruelty and avarice of his nephew, Alexander Lauderdale, is well portrayed. So, too, is the gradual development of resistance in Katherine Lauderdale to the tyranny of her father, Alexander. But Jack Ralston's willingness to tolerate for months after his marriage the arrangement which permits him only an occasional glimpse of his wife is inconceivable; the careful observance of the conventions of social life, even in the 'nineties, makes the characters run to types rather than individuals. There is some very good writing in both books, however, such as the death scene of Walter Crowdie, the epileptic painter, son of Paul Griggs, who comes into the novel himself. The reluctance of Emma Lauderdale, Katherine's mother, to give up the palm of beauty which she has held so long, even to her daughter, is also a very human trait and, as he usually does with the traits of his characters, Crawford makes use of this jealousy in the progress of the plot. The contrast, too, between Emma and her cousin, the elder Katherine Ralston, who, having had a son, is able to look upon her own life in a broader way, through her sympathy with him, reveals Crawford's ability to understand feminine nature. But the novels are too long drawn out and their excellences lie in episodes and scenes rather than in the characters. They are more clearly distinct, however, than those in *Marion Darche* (1893), where the episodes are more melodramatic, especially in the scene in which Marion sets herself on fire to permit her husband, a convicted criminal, to escape. *A Rose of Yesterday* (1896), laid in Lucerne, has a strong situation, in which a woman discovers that her husband has caused the arrest of their son's mental growth. But the story is hardly worked out. Crawford's Americans, in general, are written about for themselves and not in contrast with other races. Like Crawford himself they were usually spirited people, and, if he limited himself largely to persons of wealth or to professional writers or painters, he was only following his invariable custom of writing about the life he knew. Certainly if George Wood or Jack Ralston have not the significance of Silas Lapham, they are red-blooded realities compared to the Americans of *Washington Square* or *The Bostonians*. He must have recognized, however, that his talent lay in other fields than in the analysis of moral values and social standards of America, for after 1894 he did not return to the American scene but treated American characters as individuals in a cosmopolitan *milieu*.

Of the three modern novels in which the characters are all English, *A Tale of a Lonely Parish* (1886) is the only one of merit, and even it does not rank with his best. It is laid in a remote country parish in

Essex; the interest arises from the natural way in which crime comes in from the outside to disturb its serenity. The similarity of the plot to Anne Brontë's *Tenant of Wildfell Hall* is apparent, but there is a charm in the picture of the quiet of an English community which reflects Crawford's life while he was preparing for Cambridge. *Adam Johnstone's Son* (1895) is laid in Amalfi, though all the people in it are English, but neither it nor *The Undesirable Governess* (1910), a posthumous novel, a clever but extremely light story, need detain us. Crawford knew the English race, as he showed in *Paul Patoff*, but employed them best in contrast with others, or in his historical novels.

Much more significant were the two stories laid in Germany. *Greifenstein* (1889) is one of the very few novels written in English and laid at a German university which has any resemblance to reality. The hero, a young *korps-student* at "Schwarzburg University," acts in that period of freedom which elapses between the strict regimen of the gymnasium and the more serious business of life just as his prototypes do. Crawford's experience at Karlsruhe made him choose this hero from the most picturesque of the three classes of German university students—those who are there to enjoy life, those who are there to study, and those who apparently do neither.

Crawford proved in *A Cigarette Maker's Romance* (1890) that he could make out of apparently unpromising materials one of the most charming love stories in fiction. Although the scene is Munich, the characters are all Slavs who are employed in a small tobacco workroom. Each character, however, is etched in with the art which could discover spiritual nobility even in the most humble economic life, and in the very recognition of caste could obliterate its outlines under the influence of a great love. Count Boris Skariatine, an exile from Russia through a quarrel with his father, is employed by Fischelowitz, the tobacconist, to fill cigarettes. He is possessed by the recurrent hallucination that he receives letters from home recalling him to his rightful place. Every Wednesday he waits in his shabby room to receive the messengers that do not come, then on Thursday returns to work, forgetting whatever has happened and once more pursuing his normal life. Fischelowitz and some of the workers are mildly amused at the "mad Count," but Vjera, the young Polish girl who worships him, and the Cossack, masquerading as "Schmidt," watch over him. Every Tuesday, touched by her devotion, the Count tells Vjera he loves her and will take her to Russia, and then forgets all about the matter the next day. How details can become intensely dramatic when they are fused by the impulse of deep feeling Crawford proved in the desperate efforts of Vjera to secure for the Count the fifty marks which he tells her are absolutely necessary to save his honor. That this sum is needed to pay a debt to his employer which he has quixotically assumed makes no difference, and the sacrifice by Vjera of her one beauty, her red gold hair, which leaves her plain features unredeemed, gives her the charm with which sacrifice sometimes endows a woman in the eyes of the man she loves. Her devotion passes finally beyond the wall of illusion and, when the messengers do come to tell him that his father and brother are dead and he is to return to his estates, the love her passion has inspired remains with him. One of the most effective elements in the story is the quiet way in which Count Boris accepts the inheritance as a matter of course. It makes no change in him, since his profound courtesy and his simple dignity have remained with him through poverty and suffering. *A Cigarette Maker's Romance* is unimpeded in its movement, unified in time and place, and the tone is preserved with absolute fidelity.

Crawford was not so happy in his story of modern Constantinople and England, *Paul Patoff* (1887), although the study of insanity in Madame Patoff has some merit, and Paul Griggs reappears in an interesting rôle; nor in *The Witch of Prague* (1891), a fantastic tale of Bohemia in which hypnotism plays an important part. *With the Immortals* (1888) is of more interest, since he brings to a group of people near Amalfi the figures of Heine, Francis I, and others, and his knowledge of literature and history comes into play.

It will be noticed that in his Italian, American, English, and German stories, Crawford is not so much concerned with international contrasts as with the interrelations of people of one race. There is another group of novels, however, in which the international flavor is more apparent. *Mr. Isaacs* belonged to this class, and so did his second story, *Dr. Claudius* (1883). In the latter, the hero, a Swedish privatdocent at Heidelberg, is contrasted with English and American characters in a series of adventures which bring them across the ocean to Newport. Toward the end of his career Crawford wrote a triology which centers around the character of Margaret Donne, an English girl of American descent, who becomes an opera singer. *Fair Margaret* (1905), *The Prima Donna* (1908), and *The Diva's Ruby* (1908) are extremely readable books, but they do not add greatly to his reputation. Yet Margaret, Van Torp, the American millionaire, and Logotheti, the Greek, are vividly drawn.

It was in his historical novels that Crawford's wide cosmopolitan sympathy and his thorough knowledge of the past met to produce some creations of the first rank. His own views upon the historical romance may be found in *The Novel—What It Is*. There he remarks:

But in the case of the historical novel there is a very important provision which must never be forgotten under any circumstances. It must be good. . . . No author can make Julius Cæsar, Mary Stuart, or Louis XIV ridiculous; but no writer should forget that they can make a laughing stock of him in his book almost as easily as they could have done in real life. On the whole, therefore, the historical novel is always likely to prove more dangerous to the writer than to the reader, since, when it fails to be a great book, it will in all likelihood be an absurd one.

His first historical romance, *Zoroaster* (1885), a tale of Persia beginning about 550 B. C., is tragic in the unhappy outcome of the love story of Zoroaster, Persian soldier and scholar; Crawford paints with skill the movements of races and the contrasts of Persian and Jewish characters. The conquest of Babylon by Cyrus is especially well done. *Khaled* (1891), a tale of Arabia, is more fantastic. Khaled is a supernatural being who is to receive a soul when Zehowah, the Sultan's daughter, loves him. It is an unusual book, is said to have been Crawford's own favorite and it establishes the sense of the mystery of the East of which Crawford had given a modern treatment in *Mr. Isaacs*. The final scene, in which Khaled and Zehowah are alone, deserted by the guards and waiting for the attack of the Bedouins, is a fine illustration of the way peril may reveal the love of a woman which she has not confessed even to herself.

It was in *Via Crucis* (1898), however, that Crawford wrote his masterpiece. For this story of the Second Crusade he created the character of Gilbert Warde, a young English noble of Norman descent, of whom his stepfather's enmity and the war between King Stephen and the Empress Maud had made an exile. He is not, however, the usual marvelous and precocious boy of eighteen. The perfidy of his mother, whom he had worshipped and who had married his father's murderer, and the loss of his childhood's companion, Beatrix de Curboil, who as his stepfather's daughter was within the forbidden degrees of kindred, have matured him suddenly "through the destruction of his highest and most beautiful illusion and of his dearest and happiest hope." It is not only the rapid succession of events which take him to the court of France and later to the East that makes this a great book. It is rather the remarkable picture of the Norman character at its best. The quickness of mind and adaptability to circumstances which had made William the Conqueror master of the field of Hastings while the Saxon nobility died bravely and stupidly around Harold Godwin; the personal loyalty and self-respect; the patrician attitude which protected those dependent upon them but forbade familiarity; the religious enthusiasm that built the abbeys of England—all are there. But even more admirable are subtler touches like this:

But to the Englishman it was real, for he was under that strange melancholy which only Northmen know, and which is the most real suffering in all the world. It is a dim sadness that gathers like a cloud about strong men's souls, and they fear it, and sometimes kill themselves to escape from it into the outer darkness beyond; but sometimes it drives them to bad deeds and the shedding of innocent blood, and now and then the better sort of such men turn from the world and hide themselves in the abodes of sorrow and pain and prayer. The signs of it are that when it has no cause it seizes upon trifles to make them its reasons, and more often it torments young men than the old; and no woman nor southern person has ever known it, nor can even understand it. But it follows the northern blood from generation to generation, like retribution for an evil without a name done long ago by the northern race.[2]

Here is no fantasy of romance—here is reality, based upon Crawford's own periods of melancholy and the explanation, perhaps, of the curious melancholy of Abraham Lincoln at crucial moments of his life. The historical characters are vividly sketched, especially Queen Eleanor with her mixture of good and evil, the mother of Richard of the Lion Heart and of King John; and Henry Plantagenet, the boy who was to be King of England, already a man in his passion and ruthlessness. The Crusade is brought in sufficiently without tiresome details, and Crawford showed how great faith and courage were hampered by cupidity and jealousy. But even in his criticism of the weaknesses of the period, Marion Crawford shows his deep understanding and sympathy with the medieval spirit. Like Scott, he loved it; he was as free from the insularity that mars *The Cloister and the Hearth* or *Hereward the*

[2] *Via Crucis*, Chapter XIX.

Wake as he was from the undue sense of effort that made *Romola* "smell of the lamp." He brings in one paragraph in the fifth chapter of *Via Crucis* a description of education which might be studied with profit today, but one never feels that he is teaching.

In the Palace of the King [3] (1900), an historical romance of the time of Philip II of Spain, is hardly up to the standard of *Via Crucis*. It was planned first as a play for Viola Allen, then written as a novel, and later dramatized. This method of creation has resulted in remarkable unity, for all the events take place inside of a few hours, but it produces melodrama at times, especially in the scene in which Dolores de Mendoza defies the King. At other times, particularly in her love-making with Don John of Austria, she is more natural. The character of Inez, Dolores' blind sister, who also loves Don John, is an original one, and her blindness is used skilfully in the plot.

Almost on a level with *Via Crucis* is *Marietta* (1901), a story of Venice about 1470. The characters, as usual with Crawford, are mainly fictitious, but the sense of the period is kept marvelously. He prepared himself thoroughly, as usual, by going to Murano, where most of the novel is laid, and studying the processes of glass-blowing. His hero, Zorzi, a Dalmatian, is an apprentice to the glass-blower Angelo Beroviero; the devotion of the young artist to his craft is equaled only by his love for Marietta, Angelo's daughter. The power of the guild, the tenacity with which their secrets are kept, establish a natural obstacle to the progress of Zorzi's love and yet give him ultimately a means of winning his cherished desire. There are other excellent characterizations, among them the Greek pirate, Aristarchi.

In *Arethusa* (1907), a story of Constantinople in 1376, the ruthless cruelty of the struggle between the Emperor Johannes and his son Andronicus for the throne is merely the background for a charming love story between Carlo Zeno, a Venetian soldier, and Zoë, who calls herself "Arethusa," and who had been sold to him as a slave. While not equal to his best novels, *Arethusa* belongs in the second rank and is more probable than *Stradella* (1909), a tale of Venice in the seventeenth century. This is full of incident, but the many escapes of Ales-

---

[3] According to *My Cousin, Marion Crawford*, by Maud Howe Elliott (p. 278), he made his usual careful investigation of the Spanish background. But a letter from Crawford's widow, the present Mme. Tomasetti, states positively that he was never in Spain. If not, the novel is an extraordinary example of imaginative projection, since the atmosphere bears every evidence of reality.

sandro Stradella, a Sicilian musician, and Ortensia, his pupil and ultimately his wife, are difficult to swallow. Crawford apologizes for these
improbabilities at the climax of the novel by attributing the tale to a
manuscript account of a similar affair.

Marion Crawford possessed the two main requisites for the writing
of historical novels. First he had a wide knowledge of history, so that
whether the story is laid in England, France, Italy, Spain, Arabia or
Persia, the atmosphere has the illusion of verity. But this knowledge
would not have been sufficient without his vivid imagination. This
created living men and women under fictitious or historical names. It
was his imagination which could survey the gathered facts in a broad
vision and fuse them into those admirable descriptions of the movements of social progress or decay or those comparisons of racial characteristics which illuminate the pages of his romances. How much he can
pack into one sentence!

Mankind moves westward with the sun; men's thoughts turn back to the bright
East, the source of every faith that moves humanity; at first, for faith's sake,
men may retrace their migration to its source and give their own blood for
their holy places; and after them a generation will give its money for the honour of its God; but at the last, and surely, comes the time of memory's fading,
the winter of belief, the night of faith's day, wherein a delicately nurtured and
greedy race will give neither gold nor blood, but only a prayer or a smile for
the hope of a life to come.[4]

To the same category belong his comparisons between the Norman
and the Italian in *Via Crucis* and between the Persian and the Semite
in *Zoroaster*. Sometimes this contrast is touched with satire as in the
definition of a socialist in *Marzio's Crucifix*. I cannot quote it all, but
the remark that "In England a socialist is equal to a French conservative republican" is as true today as it was then.

Crawford's short stories are usually concerned with the supernatural
and were collected after his death under the title *Wandering Ghosts*
(1911). The best is "The Upper Berth" (1894), which marks the next
step in the progress made memorable by Fitz-James O'Brien's "What
Was It?". In this earlier story, the senses of touch and hearing acted,
but the ghost was invisible. In "The Upper Berth," the being which
enters the stateroom of the ocean liner can be felt and heard and smelt,
with a strong odor of the sea. It is seen only dimly and the horror is

[4] *Via Crucis*, Chapter XIII.

measured in terms of the fear which has led three men to suicide in that stateroom. As I said in discussing O'Brien's story, the supernatural is very effective when the sense of sight does not act but the other senses do. Crawford has added one sense to O'Brien's two, and the result is correspondingly powerful.

It is this imaginative quality which impresses us most in the work of Crawford, whether historical or modern. In his forty-five novels, he repeats himself very seldom. When a character appears more than once, he bears the same name, but he is rarely the hero. And what a gallery of portraits he has created! Mr. Isaacs, Marzio, the three Saracinesci, San Giacinto, Count Boris, Vjera, Pietro Ghisleri, Paul Griggs, Gilbert Warde, Queen Eleanor, Zorzi, Marietta, and many others. How well he can describe the effect of one individual upon another, as he does in the scene in which Philip II dominates all in his presence except his brother. He is concerned principally with human beings, although there are remarkable pictures of scenery of which the description of the Himalayas in *Mr. Isaacs* will serve as an example. Above everything else he knew how to describe the relations of men and women. Sometimes these are dramatic and profoundly moving, but often they are touched lightly, as in the advice of Totty Trimm to her daughter in *The Three Fates:*

". . . It is not true that if you run away men will follow you. They are far too lazy for that. You must come to them, but not too often. What they most want is amusement, and between their amusements, to be allowed to do exactly what their high and mighty intellects suggest to them, without comment. Never ask a man where he has been, what he has seen, nor what he has heard. If he has anything to tell, he will tell you, and if he has not you only humiliate him by discovering the emptiness of his thoughts. Always ask his opinion. If he has none himself, he knows somebody who has, no matter what the subject may be." [5]

As this passage will indicate, Crawford is a keen social satirist. He had the artist's love for his craft and he could send a shaft at the attitude of those who patronize art:

Among a set of people whose profession it is to do always, and in all things, precisely what their neighbors do, the man who makes his living by doing what other people cannot do, must always be a marked figure.[6]

He has given the best distinction between a gentleman and a snob:

[5] Chapter XVI.
[6] *Sant' Ilario,* Chapter XVII.

The snob thinks most of the treatment he receives from the world; the gentleman thinks first how he shall act courteously to others.[7]

Another of Crawford's virtues is his liberal attitude toward all forms of belief and opinion. In each he sought what was best, although he never hesitated to criticize what was weakest. This liberality came of course from his extensive knowledge. Before he wrote *The Witch of Prague* he lived in that city long enough to learn Bohemian. It was the sixteenth language he had acquired. The final impression that he leaves is that of the supreme entertainer. He is rarely dull. The man who wrote forty-five novels could not always be at his best. But his really great inventive power, his unflagging industry, his sense of "the story in it," his belief in hearty romance, his powerful imagination, his grasp of material, ancient or modern—all these, combined with a style clear, forcible, and unaffected, make him an artist who may rank with any novelist of his day.

Next to Crawford, Thomas Allibone Janvier (1849–1913) was the best interpreter of the Latin nature in the American fiction of the period. Born in Philadelphia of a stock that had descended from a French refugee of 1683, he understood instinctively the fictional qualities of French and Spanish types, and he obtained first-hand knowledge of them not only in New York City but also in his travels in New Mexico and Mexico in 1881 to 1884 and during his long stay in France during the 'nineties.

He wrote fiction as early as 1870 for *Lippincott's Magazine*, but "In Love with a Shadow" is mere fooling. His first important volume was *The Aztec Treasure House* (1890), a stirring novel of adventure told by an archæologist, Dr. Thomas Palgrave, of his search for the lost city of Culhuacan, accompanied by Fray Antonio, two American engineers, Pablo, a Mexican boy, and the remarkable donkey Sabio. Without spoiling the novel with symbolism, Janvier personifies in this expedition the three motives which had led to the earliest Spanish conquest—the spirit of discovery, the love of gold, and the desire to spread Christianity. The suspense is maintained with skill through the long journey, when, led by the mystic symbol of King Chaltzantzin, the adventurers pass through the cave of the dead, over the lake where an unknown race is buried beneath the water, until the lost city is finally found. Here they become

---

[7] *The Heart of Rome*, Chapter I.

involved in a revolution and, after many defeats, the voluntary martyr-dom of Fray Antonio leads to the safety of the rest. Janvier not only made the narrative thrilling, but he drew the characters well, and his descriptive power is at times of a high order.

In *Color Studies* (1885), his stories of Mexican life are prefaced by some charming treatments of artist life in Washington Square. Here the races mingle, and the contrasts help in the establishment of atmos-phere. The longest story, "A Mexican Campaign," proved that Janvier could tell a good love story with a light and urbane touch that allies him at times to a school of writing to be discussed later.

Janvier struck a more serious note in his *Stories of Old New Spain* (1891). In "Niñita," he painted well the contrast between the American, Grant, who has no serious intentions in his love-making, and the imme-diate attempt at vengeance on the part of Niñita's father and lover. He understood the different standards of honor between a race to whom life is not worth sacrificing for a love affair and the race that will not live with a stain on it while there is a chance that the enemy through whom the stain has been given may be destroyed. The exquisite story "The Legend of Padre José" is a prose poem, introduced sympathetically by Janvier:

In these simple, trustful minds, illuminating them with a light that brightens the dark places of weary lives, the old stories live on through the centuries; passing from lip to heart, from heart to lip, and so to heart again, yet gaining always a more mellow beauty with the passing years.

The novel *In the Sargasso Sea* (1898) is a fairly vivid narrative of an American who is lost at sea and wanders for a long time among the wrecks which have drifted into that curious region east of the main Gulf Stream and to the south of the branch which sweeps across the North Atlantic to the Azores. It has not the crisp quality, however, found in Janvier's tragic short stories. *In Great Waters* (1901), is laid in Holland, in Provence, near Duluth, and off the English coast.

Janvier's versatility was shown in his amusing satires of the social life of Philadelphians. He had published in 1891 a collection of stories, *The Uncle of an Angel*, in which he created the character of Dorothy Lee, a Philadelphia girl whose long residence in Europe had made her im-patient of the mental and social processes of the stodgy type of Phila-delphian, of which her uncle, Mr. Hutchinson Port, is an example. Port can still be seen at the windows of more than one Philadelphia club; Janvier used him again in "In the St. Peter's Set," published in *The Passing of Thomas and Other Stories* (1901). Here Dorothy Lee, now Mrs. Pennington Brown, shocks her uncle by forcing him to attend a dinner for some new people, the Ballingwoods, who have made money in leather. What makes the story a fine bit of social satire is Mrs. Ballingwood's frank revelation of their real origin and Janvier's ability to show deftly by the reception of it the difference between two kinds of Philadelphians—those that are the pride and those that are the despair of their fellow citizens.

There were stories of modern Provence in this volume, but the best of the fiction inspired by this region, which Janvier knew so well, was collected in 1912 under the title of *From the South of France*. There are charming love stories like "The Roses of Monsieur Alphonse" or the development of ironic situations such as "The Recrudescence of Madame Vic." "A Consolate Giantess" is a good illustration of Janvier's method. The situation in which three lion tamers have been eaten by the famished lion "Néron," and the promptness with which the widowed giantess has married the understudy is farcical, of course. But the naïveté of the widow as she tells her story is delicious:

"But in one way, Monsieur, my feeling toward our Néron is without painful complications: he is, and the thought endears him to me beyond expression, the substantial link that unites my happiness of the present with my happiness of the past. When I think of him in that way I cannot withhold from him my affections. Forgetting his misdirected energies, forgetting his impulsive errors, I remember only that that faithful animal is at once the incarnation and the sarcophagus of all—of all save my adored Félix—that I most have loved: of my adored Marius, of my adored Victor, of my adored Alexandre!"

After Janvier's death, a number of his stories, some of which date back to 1891, were collected under the title of *At the Casa Napoléon* (1914). They deal with the proprietors and guests of a little hotel on a side street near Fifth Avenue and are among his most finished products. The people, whether they are gamblers, adventurers, or honest troupers, are etched skilfully, and the clever use of the moral contrast proves if it were necessary that Bret Harte was one of the influences upon Janvier.

The careful student of French comedy in the original has probably noticed that to an American there is an added flavor caused by the apparent incongruity between the language, from which our vocabulary of social life has largely been derived, and the ideas, which in English would have been expressed in much more homely words. Some of this delightful incongruity Janvier has succeeded in transferring to his stories. He has also portrayed the thrift and the shrewdness of the French provincial, as few writers of English have done. In the Mexican stories, he accomplished even more. When two races dislike each other's views, it is difficult for them to come to an understanding; but when they dislike each other's virtues, complete sympathy is impossible. Yet a reading of Janvier's fiction would be for many the first step toward that understanding.

Other novelists followed or anticipated Crawford in the cosmopolitan tone of their fiction. Generally they tended toward romance, and among those who frankly aimed at the telling of a good story, without any undue effort at probability, Mrs. Frances Hodgson Burnett (1849–1924) was one of the most successful.

Born in England, she belongs to our fiction through her long residence here which began in 1865, and through her keen sense of the picturesque possibilities of certain phases of our life. *Louisiana* (1881) presented an appealing picture of a North Carolina farmer's daughter, placed in a difficult position by the whim of a visiting woman of fashion. How definitely cosmopolitan was Mrs. Burnett's theory of fiction may be seen from her comment on the fact that she had been accumulating material in her little village in East Tennessee from which she should draw as long as she lived. And she adds: "I do not mean that it was merely East Tennessee material, or character, or dialect; it was human material, which is the same, with shades of difference, in all regions of earth." [8] Early in her career she established her formula, the placing of an American in an English setting, with a consequent racial contrast. Even in her earliest novels, like *Haworth's* (1879), Stephen Murdoch, the young American, acts and talks like one, and Mrs. Burnett's constant visits to England and the Continent kept her sense of national characteristics alive. *A Fair Barbarian* (1881) was a clever portrait of a young American girl placed suddenly in a conservative British atmosphere. Almost from the beginning Mrs. Burnett provided material for drama either of her own or other's shaping. William Gillette and Augustus Thomas both turned to her fiction at the beginnings of their careers.

[8] *The Romantick Lady*, p. 37.

She always took her share in the dramatization, however, and later adapted her own novels independently. This theatrical quality was an element in the great popular success of her fiction, but the romantic glamour which she threw around her characters and the accidental nature of many of her events are now seen to be elements of weakness. The best of her novels laid in America, *Through One Administration,* will be discussed in a later treatment of the political novel; here she was writing about people she knew, with a more definitely realistic method. It is easy to criticize her greatest success, *Little Lord Fauntleroy* (1886) on the ground of sentimentality, but a reading of her biography by her son, Vivian, from whom the character was drawn, will reveal how intimately the love of Mrs. Burnett for her two boys entered into the book. The friendly, democratic child whom she transferred to fiction was a real creation which even the absurd trappings with which he was loaded in the stage version could not quite obscure.

Mrs. Burnett wrote too much, of course, but she was a born story-teller, and there remain several of her novels which should not be forgotten. *In Connection with the DeWilloughby Claim* (1899) made vivid her early life in Tennessee, for Tom deWilloughby who leaves his Tennessee home and becomes a store-keeper in North Carolina is a real person. Among her later books, *T. Tembarom* (1913) contained some of her best characters, especially the hero, born in Brooklyn, who inherits an English estate and who carried his independence and self-respect through many strange events. It is better organized than *The Shuttle* (1907), another cosmopolitan story, although *Tembarom* was an amplification of a minor character in that novel. Mrs. Burnett's power did not flag even toward the end, for her later ventures into the supernatural, *The Secret Garden* (1911) and *The White People* (1917) contain some of her most artistic effects.

James, Crawford, Janvier, and Mrs. Burnett were not, of course, the only American novelists who struck the cosmopolitan or international note. It seems best, however, to interpret the work of another group, who frequently made use of European characters, through the form rather than through the material of their fiction.

CHAPTER XIX

THE URBANE NOTE IN AMERICAN FICTION

It has not generally been recognized that parallel with the searching analysis of life and with the glamorous return to the past, there were written in the later years of the nineteenth century novels and short stories which have as their distinguishing trait an urbanity of tone, a breadth of view, which came often from travel and observation of other lands and a quiet certainty of standards, social and artistic. Henry James, Weir Mitchell, and Marion Crawford had of course possessed this urbanity, but there are other figures, less well remembered now, which deserve the critical attention of any lover of the fitting word. It is not with them a question of material; each wrote at times of home and of abroad. It is rather in the charm of creation, both of character and of phrase, that they excel. They usually wrote of the life of cities, just as the group it is the fashion to call realists wrote often of rural life, and the attrition of urban conditions had much to do with that polish of style and tolerance of view which make their work so charming. They were critics, too, of life—no novelist of worth can help being a critic—but their scrutiny was not relentless, although it was keen; it is wisdom rather than force that distinguishes them.

The oldest of this group belongs by chronology to an earlier generation. Charles Dudley Warner (1829–1900) had collaborated with Mark Twain in *The Gilded Age* (1873) and was most prolific in the essay, but in his trilogy of novels, *A Little Journey in the World* (1889), *The Golden House* (1894), and *That Fortune* (1899), he presented a picture of life in New York City which carries that conviction of reality characteristic of a wise and mellow scrutiny. In *A Little Journey* there is shown the spiritual disintegration of a girl of fine instincts, Margaret Debree, through her marriage with Rodney Henderson, who is laying the foundations for his great fortune. Warner's skill is shown in his avoidance of the theatric. There is no violent struggle; her love for her husband and the insistent clutch of luxury turn her life into spiritual insignificance. The pity of it is that she becomes reconciled to the ruthless and dubious methods of Henderson by that confusion of moral values which arise so easily in the mind of a woman whose love of beauty and whose charitable instincts make wealth a necessity to her. Margaret's death in childbirth is, Warner confessed, a concession to his reluctance to carry the tragedy on to its logical end. *A Little Journey* has many penetrating passages in which the restlessness of American life is portrayed. Such comments as: "Americans are born with a fear of not being busy." and "Life was a good deal like reading the dictionary and remembering none of the words." are too true to be pleasant. And how contemporary is his criticism of the "passionate and pantheistic novels" of the young women writers of that time who have now passed into oblivion. Warner pays his respects also to the analytical novelists:

I am more and more convinced that men and women act more upon impulse and less upon deep reflection and self-examination than the analytic novelists would have us believe, duly weighing motives and balancing considerations; and that men and women know themselves much less thoroughly than they suppose they do. There is a great deal of exaggeration, I am convinced, about the inward struggles and self-conflicts.

In *The Golden House* some very real characters are developed, especially Jack Delancy, the rich and idle young man who is ruined by one of Henderson's financial schemes; and his wife Edith, whose breeding and traditions hamper her in her attempt to save him from the clutches of Carmen, Henderson's second wife, who had been one of the leading characters in the first book. Through Father Damon, an Anglican rector of a parish in the slums, and Dr. Ruth Leigh, who cures the bodies but has little belief in the souls of her patients, Warner draws the conditions of the poor accurately, but rather as a contrast to the lives of the others than for themselves. Warner drew admirably the complexity of city life and its heartlessness, made concrete by a woman like Carmen, who drops Jack completely when it is convenient and burns up Henderson's latest will with the connivance of Mavick, a well drawn type of the ambitious diplomat. *That Fortune* carries Carmen and Mavick, who have married, into a conflict with the next generation in the persons of their daughter and Philip Burnett, who ultimately wins her, and brings the career of Carmen and Mavick to its logical conclusion. When Mavick loses the fortune which Henderson had built up, the essential artificiality of a distinction built solely upon money is made clear without any preaching. In the career of Philip Burnett, the young lawyer who leaves the profession for journalism

and fiction there is an echo of Warner's own career; in the ease with which
Carmen reconciles herself to the marriage once her fortune is lost is an
other indication of the superficial nature of her rise to social importance.
The trilogy forms a clear picture of the manners of the idle rich, of the
women who pursue "culture" and, as Warner remarks, come out of an
hour's lecture on Steele with the knowledge that he "was an author and
lived in the eighteenth century."

Warner never grows indignant over the evils he depicts. This is life,
good and bad, with self-sacrifice and complete selfishness, quiet courage
and helpless weakness rubbing elbows constantly. Between *The Gilded
Age* and *The Golden House* his friend Howells had shown him a new
manner; indeed, he refers to "Silas Lapham Paint" in his fictional travel
book, *Their Pilgrimage* (1886). He had not the structural power of
Howells; he never quite lost the essayist in his fiction, but his characters
are real and, while his satire is delightful, he never lets it submerge the
story.

Henry Cuyler Bunner (1855–1896) represents the fiction of fancy,
often humorous, rich in invention and delightful in phrasing, the work
of a poet in prose. New York is usually his scene, in the city or in the suburbs, for though he sometimes wrote of the regions "up state," where he
was born, his inspiration was distinctly urban. His long editorship of *Puck*,
with its natural consequence in much fugitive humorous writing, did not
lower his sense of values, and his stories, long and short, gained from his
journalistic experience point and emphasis. But they differed from journalism because he was not content merely to denote, and his connotations
are among the most delightful elements of his fiction. His first novel,
A Woman of Honor (1883), a story of artistic and social life in New York
City, was not so sure in tone or so individual in quality as his later work.
But he used rather effectively the situation in which an unmarried woman
saves the reputation of a married flirt, who has come to the studio of the
girl's lover, by appearing herself, to the surprise of all, and risking her
own future. Of course the model for this incident lay in Sardou's *Les
Pattes de Mouche*, but Bunner anticipated Bronson Howard and Oscar
Wilde in its use. It was only one result of his careful study of French fiction and drama, which showed clearly in his compression and mastery of
form, which, incidentally, Poe had taught the Frenchmen. Guy de Maupassant was his most definite model; later, in 1893, he published under
the title *Made in France* a number of short stories, not translations of de

Maupassant, for Bunner believed that a literal translation was an impossibility, but rather adaptations of the original situation in Bunner's own manner. Sometimes he kept the French scene, sometimes he transferred it to America, always with skill and the sense for an ironic situation. Yet the stories are interesting mainly as showing the inspiration for his method, for none of them equals the best of his original fiction.

The Midge (1886) is a novelette of rare delicacy and restraint. The plot is not new, but the relations of Evert Peters, a bachelor living on Washington Square, and the little girl he has promised her dying mother to befriend are developed with a skill which illumines Peters' middle age with the touch of youth and embues the childhood of "the Midge" with the fragrance of maternal solicitude. When the naval officer, Hathaway, comes into the picture and the young people love each other, Peters has to face not only the consciousnes of his own passion for "the Midge," but a keener temptation in the discovery of Hathaway's illicit relations with a South American woman whose family are blackmailing him into marriage. Peters' sacrifice becomes active, therefore, not merely passive, and is conducted without sentimentality. In *The Story of a New York House* (1887), Bunner traced two families, the Dolphs and the Van Ripers, up and down the financial and social ladder through three generations. The novelette has the very flavor of New York City, and the death of Jacob Dolph when the house which his father had built in 1807 is torn down comes as a natural climax.

Charming as his novelettes are, Bunner's best work was done in the short story. He began in 1879 in collaboration with Brander Matthews in "The Documents in the Case," in *Scribner's Monthly,* and after one volume, *In Partnership,* in which he and Matthews collected their joint efforts, he continued with a singular clarity and variety to cultivate his own distinctive vein. *Short Sixes* (1890), *Zadoc Pine* (1891), and *More Short Sixes* (1894) contain his most significant stories, and since they have been rearranged in later collections, they may be discussed as a whole. Bunner's ideal of life is that of the liberal; excess of any kind is distasteful to him. "As One Having Authority" is a powerful story in which the hysterical excesses of a Southern camp meeting of poor whites are brought under control by a chance visitor, the Episcopal Bishop Waldegrave of New York, who calms them not only by his assertion of the merciful nature of God, but also by the power of his personality. It is the experience, the poise which comes from the adult mind of the city, dispelling the confusion of the emotional adolescent. It is also the individual against the mob, and this note is again struck effectively in "Zadoc Pine," the story of a plain American from the Adirondacks who comes to a New Jersey suburban town and defies the labor unions to make him join them.

While Bunner can represent with success the triumph of social values over individuals as in "Natural Selection," he makes clear in some of the finest stories that delicacy and refinement are not limited by economic standards. "The Love Letters of Smith" is the record of an unusual courtship conducted by an illiterate lumberman who lives in the same tenement as a little seamstress, whom he woos by unobtrusive gifts of flowers and by a remarkable series of letters which he has taken from a book of correspondence. What distinguishes the story is the recognition on the man's part of the defences which such a woman would throw up against an unknown lover, and his patience and tenderness, which culminate in his postscript to his formal and conventional proposal: "If not understood, will you mary me?" The humor of Bunner touches human weaknesses without malice. "Hector" builds up a picture of the timid ladies who feel so secure while they have the large watch dog to whom they give the name of the Trojan hero. When the dog has puppies, her pride and their dismay may be imagined. It is not merely the situation, however; the whole philosophy of feminine dependence is implicit. Even more of a character study is contained in "What Mrs. Fortescue Did." A rich man, Filley, who has been left a little girl to look after, employs a distant cousin, Mrs. Filley, who lives in an old ladies' home, to visit and report on the child's welfare. She is illiterate, but she gets Mrs. Fortescue, a retired actress, to write the letters for her. When Mrs. Filley dies, Mrs. Fortescue continues the visits and reports till she is discovered. Her consequent interview with Mr. Filley is delicious, especially her dramatization of the situation at the school, where she has represented herself as Mrs. Filley, the "second wife" of Mr. Filley. Then he produces a note from the real Mrs. Filley, written just before she died:

"dere mr Filley i kno that fort escew woman is gone to kepon senden them re ports an nottel you ime dedd but iam Sara Filley."

"She sent that to me," said Mr. Filley, "by Dr. Butts, the house physician. and between us we managed to get a 'line' on you, Mrs. Fortescue; so that there's been a little duplicity on both sides."

Mrs. Fortescue looked at him with admiration mingled with respect; then she looked puzzled.

"But why, if you knew it all along, why did you—"

"Why did I let you go on?" repeated Mr. Filley. "Well, you've got to have the whole duplicity, I see." He went back to the drawer and took out another object. It was a faded photograph of a young lady with her hair done up in a net, and with a hat like a soap-dish standing straight up on her head.

"Twenty-five years ago," said Mr. Filley, "boy; three dollars a week in an architect's office; spent two-fifty of them, two weeks running, for flowers for that young lady when she played her first engagement in New Haven. Walked there. Paid the other fifty cents to get into the theatre. Lived on apples the rest of the week. Every boy does it. Never forgets it. Place always remains soft."

And, as Mrs. Fortescue sat and looked long and earnestly at the picture, a soft color came into her face that was born rather of memory than of her love for acting; and yet it wonderfully simulated youth and fresh beauty and a young joy in life.

Among the other first class stories are "Cutwater of Seneca"; "Mr. Wick's Aunt," in which Bunner's hatred of intolerance is turned on two self-appointed custodians of public morals; "The Two Churches of 'Quawket," in which a certain kind of clerical insincerity is cleverly described. Bunner's satire is never bitter, nor is it ever tinctured with mere propaganda. His urbanity arises from a wide knowledge of life and literature, from his contempt of the small-town mind, whether it exists in the small town or elsewhere. He was of the metropolis in every sense, and his frequent choice of New York City for his scene was not preoccupation with local color, but rather a denial of provinciality.

The sense of reserved power which is one of the attributes of urbanity shows clearly in the fiction of Arthur Sherburne Hardy (1847–1930). Born at Andover, Massachusetts, he was educated in part at Neuchâtel, Switzerland. Before he graduated from Phillips Andover, he had tried to enlist in the army, and his final education was at West Point. His army experience, his professorships of Mathematics at Grinnell and Dartmouth, his editorship of the *Cosmopolitan* after Howells, and his distinguished career as a diplomat in Persia, Greece, Roumania, Servia, Switzerland, and Spain, rounded out a career in every sense cosmopolitan. The clarity of style, the exquisite sense of proportion which mark his novels and short stories may have arisen in part from his scientific training and from the wide reading, especially in French, which shines in his pages not only in quotation but also in allusion. But his imagination, which was first expressed in his poem *Francesca of Rimini* (1878), was his chief source of power.

His first novel, *But Yet a Woman* (1883), revealed the maturity of an artist whose strength lay in the creation of characters whose fate is determined not by themselves alone nor only by circumstances, but by that combination of love, sacrifice, and the intervention of experience and wisdom which make up life as it is. The story is laid in France at the time of the abortive effort of the royalist party to restore "Henri Cinq" after the collapse of the Thiers ministry. But politics plays little part in the book. It is primarily a love story, in which a young surgeon, Roger Lande, is loved by two women, Stéphanie Milevski, a widow, and Rénée, her young niece, who has intended to enter a convent. What makes the book so charming is the sympathetic insight of Hardy into the growing love of Rénée and the quiet acceptance by Stéphanie of the situation. Father LeBlanc is a remarkable picture of a priest who, realizing that Rénée is not intended for convent life, moulds events so that Stéphanie takes Rénée a journey into Spain and brings about a realization on Rénée's part of her love for the young surgeon. Father LeBlanc's leaving Pliny's heroic story of Arria where Stéphanie will see it and have it translated aloud by Rénée; and his parting words to Roger Lande as the latter starts for Spain, "Say to Mademoiselle Rénée that M. Michel sent you, and to Madame Milevski, that it was I," are only two of the scenes in which he skilfully plays the part of Providence. Stéphanie, however, has the feeling that she is herself the means of bringing the lovers together, and her final entry into a convent is logical for a nature that must be devoted to a cause, political or religious. Hardy laid the novel in France partly because the contrasts he desired were between scepticism and a society homogeneous in its religion, and partly because he believed in the universality of art. As he makes Roger Lande say:

". . . And these accessories, of time, and place, and manners, they are only the frame of the picture; it is the vulgar eye that is attracted by them solely. How many times, as I have set out on my morning visits or entered the door of the Hôtel-Dieu St. Luc, I have wished that I had some poet with me, who should strip all that I was about to see of what was local and accidental, and write anew the story of human suffering and endurance. Besides the inheritance of suffering, transmitted from age to age, there is another,—the *capacity* to suffer. . . ."

After a few introductory chapters in which he drew a brief but tragic picture of the love of Schonberg, a philosopher, for Noël, a girl he meets at Dinant in Flanders, Hardy brought the scene of *The Wind of Destiny*

(1886) to native ground in Ashurst, a country place near a large city. The main story takes place shortly before the Civil War, when Schonberg's two adopted nieces, Seraphine and Elize Foy, are living near Jack and Gladys Temple and the latter's cousin, Rowan Ferguson. These characters belong to that stratum of American society which traveled, knew various civilizations and yet preserved unimpaired its own traditions, a class rarely met with in American fiction, before the Civil War, since it does not lend itself to social satire in the sense in which it was then known. But it is not only that in Hardy's novels we meet people of breeding: they are also people of intelligence. The tragic love story of Gladys Temple is the main motive of the novel, through which Hardy showed again his remarkable ability in revealing the moods of a woman. Gladys, failing to gain Rowan's love, marries Jack Temple on the rebound, is honest with her husband in telling him of her earlier passion, and finds after Rowan's return that marriage has only made her passion for her lover more intense. The novel sweeps on to its vivid climax. On the very night Rowan tells Seraphine of his love for her, Gladys goes to his studio and, wrought up to a high pitch of emotion, she falls before his door unconscious of the cold rain beating her into stupor. Rowan carries her to her home and does his best to save her from the consequences of her rashness and to keep his own path to Seraphine clear of a passion he has never shared. Hardy's art showed again in the way he reveals Jack Temple's understanding of the hopeless position in which the modern husband is placed in such a case. His visit to Rowan is brief and telling:

". . . You don't think I came here to talk, do you? All I want to say is this: if what has happened doesn't kill her, the sight of you, or me either, will. When are you going away?"

"You might have spared yourself any anxiety on that score," replied Rowan.

"Well, I thought so; but some people are always standing on their rights, you know."

. . . The slow, deliberate tones of his voice stirred Rowan's anger, but the haggard face confronting him checked its utterance.

"When the market drops," pursued Jack, "somebody's better off; but these damned random affairs, when everybody fails and nobody's to blame— Come, little girl," he said to Mabel, going out the door.

The description of the later suicide of Gladys showed Hardy, the poet, in a picture which has hardly had its equal till Edwin Arlington Robinson brought his heroine to another river in *Roman Bartholow*, with the same load upon her life. Rowan loses Seraphine and ends his life at Manassas. *The Wind of Destiny* is not only a novel of magnificent phrases; it is a powerful study of the hand of Fate shaping the lives of spirited people who, like Noël and Gladys, cannot live with a stain upon themselves, and end life without understanding the full effect upon those they leave behind. The New England strain in Hardy shows in Schonberg's philosophy: "Duty, and resignation, and the approval of self—there is nothing else." But the duty is to be carried out without apparent anxiety, "the foe to good looks and good manners." Hardy wrote a sequel to *The Wind of Destiny* in *His Daughter First* (1903), in which the main interest lies in the relation of Jack Temple to his daughter Mabel, who has grown up, and the way this relation affects his own love for Dolly Kensett. There is much of the same charm, but not so much power as in the earlier book. In 1889 Hardy had written in *Passe Rose* a brilliant historical romance of the time of Charlemagne, laid in Maestricht and Aix. The character of Passe Rose, a girl who had danced before Queen Hildegarde at the age of six and who is eminently able to take care of herself in her wanderings in search of her love, is the thread upon which the romance is hung. Hardy draws well the disturbed conditions of that time, the violence, the relentless way in which one human being would crush another, and yet the piety and mysticism which rose like a flame through it all.

Hardy's best short stories are to be found in *Diane and her Friends* (1914), published between 1908 and 1914 in various magazines. They deal with French characters, including a clever detective, M. Joly, but the most charming are those in which Diane baffles her foes or aids her friends. She fights always with a rapier, real or symbolic, as in "The Defense of Diane" or "The Ambassador," a charming story in which Diane tries to save her daughter, Anne, from M. de Balloy, a roué and gambler. M. Sade, her ambassador to the actress who is de Balloy's mistress, asks the woman to sign the following letter to Anne:

"Mademoiselle,—Monsieur de Balloy aspires to your hand. In exchange he offers you—what! A heart without honor. But black as is that heart, it is mine, and I will not surrender it to you."

"You wish me to sign that?" said a voice over his shoulder. "Oh, how little you understand us! Give me the pen."

She took his place and wrote in turn:—

"Mademoiselle,—Monsieur de Balloy aspires to your hand. The heart which he offers you I, who once believed in its promises, give you willingly. It is too black for even me."

When Mr. Sade sends these to Diane she thanks him; and the end of the story is delightful. His reply to her is in a single sentence: "Oh, woman, woman! not to tell me which note you made use of!"

Number 13, Rue du Bon Diable (1917), an unusual detective story in which M. Joly once more figures, is only a slight novelette. But in *Helen* (1916) Hardy's mastery of the European scene and his insight into international differences were again apparent. He draws the interesting situation in which Helen Lee, French on one side and American on the other, leaves the fostering care of her grandmother, Mrs. Lee, which has become a limitation, and seizes the opportunity which the bequest of her uncle, Hector de Chavigny, offers her to achieve the freedom of action for which she has longed. It seems at first a pity that Hardy drops out of his story the stern woman who:

. . . struggled awhile with the sense of loneliness, the enervating tide of self-pity, then faced conscience resolutely again. . . . Conscience answered that a love shared is never lost, that the abdication of self is not defeat, that she was reaping what she had sown, pain for pain and bitterness for bitterness,—the helpless bitterness of pride which sees too late.

Hardy uses Mrs. Lee only for contrast with Helen's maternal grandmother, Madame de Chavigny, who has nothing but love, long forbidden by her husband's discarding of their daughter after her marriage with an American. Hardy brings Helen into the diplomatic circle in Paris with the assured touch of one who knew the human side of diplomats; she manages adroitly her own love story with Jean de Trécour until she shatters French conventions by the passionate farewell at the Gare de Lyon whence Jean is to go to Corea. The contrast between the friendship of Helen for David Fearing, the executor of her uncle's will, who has loved her almost at first sight, and her first romantic passion for Jean leads naturally enough after the latter's death at Cairo to a more mature passion. These character contrasts are more delicately indicated than is usual in international stories, where time is often wasted by insistence on racial differences. Hardy knew that with people of breeding the fundamental instincts are not always clouded by difference of race. Helen's French grandmother understands her better than Mrs. Lee because she loves her more. To any American who has lived in Europe there is something very appealing in the way in which Mrs. Stuart, a type of American woman who is annoying by her assumption of a vast knowledge of the affairs of her acquaintances, devotes herself to Jean de Trécour, when he is dying in Cairo, from that combination of real sympathy and efficiency with which many an American woman has met a similar situation.

There is a constant temptation to quote Hardy. "Work is a great blessing. After evil came into the world, work was given as an antidote, not a punishment." "The young look into women's eyes to see their own reflections; the old, to see the woman." "In the love of every man there is something reminiscent of childhood—obedience; as in the love of every woman there is something prophetic of motherhood—sovereignty."

These are not merely purple passages. They illuminate the characters, and it is for the creation of characters—strong, vital, rarely bored or helpless, who, whether in modern life or the middle ages, in Europe or America, struggle for the control of their own destinies and, if they end in tragedy, meet their fate with dignity—that Hardy's place in any really critical survey of American fiction must remain secure.

Though it was by his delicacy of imagination that Henry Harland (1861-1905) ultimately won his place, he had two almost distinct manners which reflect his change of residence from America to Europe. Born in New York City, where he had a hard struggle to obtain the leisure to write, he began, under the pen name of "Sidney Luska," with stories of Jewish life, which his own extraction and experience made familiar to him. His first novel, *As It Was Written* (1885), is a grim and powerful story of the imagination, told by a Jewish musician, Ernest Neuman. Two weeks before the date set for his wedding to Veronika Pathzuol, he leaves her about midnight and, when he goes to see her the next morning, driven there by a fear of something evil, he finds her murdered by a knife thrust. Harland's description of Neuman's disturbed mind, his refusal to make any defence when he is accused of the murder, his trial and final acquittal for lack of motive are well done. The testimony which tells against him most is that of the janitor and his wife who swear that they saw him re-enter the house and that he had not left it at one o'clock when they closed it. The lack of any desire on Neuman's part to find the real murderer is at first hard to understand. He simply collapses, gives up his music, and becomes a waiter in a restaurant. Through a series of incidents Neuman comes into possession of a letter from his dead father forbidding him to marry since the women who have married into his race have proved faithless, and naming a friend, Nicholas Pathzuol, as the man with whom his own mother had been guilty. The effect of this charge and of the belief that Veronika Pathzuol was the daughter of this man brings on an emotional state in which Ernest composes a remarkable piece of music. As he transcribes it, he seems to be in the power of some force that drives him on faster than his mind can follow. Then he is amazed to discover that he has written, at the end, words instead of music. These words tell how he did return to Veronika, without knowing it, and killed her. The power of the book lies in its straightforward, direct establishment of a sense of occult or emotional force dominating Ernest Neuman, and of implacable Fate driving him on to doom. The message of his father, even though it has not yet been received, animates him and causes him to murder the woman he loves best. He is a study in duality, and his lack of desire to probe the matter of the death, which seems at first preposterous, really springs from the knowledge of his subconscious self that the testimony of the janitor is true while his normal self does not remember it. Harland does not condescend to explanations. He simply tells the story—without morbid introspection—and by the treatment of romantic material in a realistic way he produces that illusion in which the impossible becomes for the moment credible. Harland's other novels of German-Jewish life were not upon the same high level. *Mrs. Peixada* (1886), a melodramatic story of marital suffering and consequent murder, has even a note of comedy which leaves the impression that Harland was not treating his material seriously. *The Yoke of the Thorah* (1887) is somewhat better, and the picture of the family solidarity of the Jewish race and the intolerance on their part for the hero, who loves a Christian, is realistic. But there is no sympathy elicited for the central characters as there was for Ernest Neuman.

After 1889 Harland lived in Paris or London, where he and Aubrey Beardsley founded *The Yellow Book* in 1894. The change in his style began in 1889 with *A Latin Quarter Courtship*, a light but charming novelette telling of the love of a young American writer and a French girl. The conversations form the attraction of the book, and through them the characters, even the minor ones like the painter, Hiram Palmer, who has "the largest collection of Palmers in existence," emerge into reality. Through Palmer, Harland states his belief that "Art means truth, interpreted by the imagination" and it is his imagination which really links *As It Was Written* to *The Cardinal's Snuff-Box*. *Grandison Mather* (1889) his next novel, is transitional. There is a charm in the love story of Tom Gardiner and Rose Cartret, who meet in Rome; the story of their married life in New York City is romantic in several of its incidents and in their eternal hopefulness under discouragement. But the struggle of Tom to succeed as a writer is told realistically, especially the rejection of his first novel, its ultimate success, and Tom's disappointment at his first royalty. Harland's own career is represented in this struggle, for Tom publishes under a pen name, "Grandison Mather," just as Harland did, and Harland's own desperate efforts to establish himself by rising at two o'clock in the morning and writing till it was time to go to his monotonous clerical labors, are transferred to the novel. The completion of his work by Rose may reflect the devotion of his own talented wife who finished his last novel many years later.

Harland portrays well the difficulties of an educated young man, who has no profession, in finding employment. *Grandison Mather* proves too that Harland's change was deliberate when we read the criticism of a great American novel which had portrayed a tragedy of human decay:

"That cheap cleverness, that vulgar unscrupulous readiness, and that sordid, cynical materialism of thought and purpose,—it's wonderful, the way Northrup makes you see and hate it."

"Well, of course, I haven't read the book," Tom replied, "but still I don't quite understand—"

Harland did not at once achieve his mastery of the idealistic romance in which he was to shine. *Two Women in One* (1890), a story of a woman who is made to forget her miserable past by an operation, only to recall it later, is too melodramatic, and *Two Voices* (1890), containing accounts by men who are about to die of their innocence or guilt, is too full of the philosophy of determinism to be good fiction.

During the next decade Harland published three volumes of short stories, *Mademoiselle Miss* (1893), *Grey Roses* (1895), and *Comedies and Errors* (1898). They grow in artistry, those in the first volume being a bit sentimental, for it is almost impossible to believe in the ignorance of "Mademoiselle Miss" concerning her companions in the "Hôtel de l'Océan" in the Latin Quarter, even if one concedes her innocence. The characters are in general well drawn, especially in *Grey Roses*, and the cosmopolitan touch is effective. Sometimes, as in "Merely Players" and "Flower O' the Clover," they are preliminary sketches for his later novels. Harland knew the Latin Quarter, and the reckless, improvident, sordid life of the "Left Bank" is given its only real glamour, that of independence, while he draws with a realistic touch the many failures which seek in middle life a refuge there.

In 1900 Harland wrote his masterpiece, *The Cardinal's Snuff-Box*. It does not matter at all that Peter Marchmont is an English novelist and that Beatrice is an English widow, the Duchessa di Santangiolo. He is her tenant for the time on her estate in Lombardy and he wins her ultimately because of his novel in which he has painted her from the few opportunities which chance had given him to see her at a distance. Peter is well born, but she is a great lady; yet the barriers of wealth, position, and religion fall before the power of love, with the sympathetic help of her uncle, the Cardinal Udeschini. This gentle elderly patrician belongs with the Abbé Constantin among the delightful churchmen of fiction. Harland's description of him illustrates the dexterity of his method:

That was his title ecclesiastical. He had two other titles. He was a Prince of the Udeschini by accident of birth. But his third title was perhaps his most curious. It had been conferred upon him informally by the populace of the Roman slum in which his titular church, St. Mary of the Lilies, was situated: the little Uncle of the Poor.

As Italians measure wealth, Cardinal Udeschini was a wealthy man. What with his private fortune and official stipends, he commanded an income of something like a hundred thousand lire. He allowed himself five thousand lire a year for food, clothing, and general expenses. Lodging and service he had for nothing in the palace of his family. The remaining ninety-odd thousand lire of his budget . . . Well, we all know that titles can be purchased in Italy; and that was no doubt the price he paid for the title I have mentioned.

When the inevitable misunderstanding between Peter and Beatrice occurs, the Cardinal leaves his snuff-box on Peter's table and thereby brings him to the castle for the reconciliation. The Cardinal's liberality, his urbane disregard of Peter's creed, all fit into Harland's conception of the essential similarity of all real Christians. A characteristic passage occurs after the Cardinal has gone away from Peter's house:

It was in the afternoon, and he had just conducted the Cardinal and Emilia to their carriage. He stood at his gate for a minute, and watched the carriage as it rolled away.

"What a heavenly old man, what a heavenly old man," he thought.

Then, still looking after the carriage, before turning back into his garden, he heard himself repeat, half aloud—

> "Nor knowest thou what argument
> Thy life to thy neighbour's creed hath lent."

The words had come to his lips, and were pronounced, were addressed to his mental image of the Cardinal, without any conscious act of volition on his part. He heard them with a sort of surprise, almost as if some one else had spoken them. He could not in the least remember what poem they were from, he could not even remember what poet they were by. Were they by Emerson? It was years since he had read a line of Emerson's.

As usual in Harland's best fiction, the minor characters are etched with skill. The conversations between Peter and his cook Marietta are almost perfect examples of the revelation of character to the reader by means of words which one of the characters does not understand. But the greatest charm of all lies in the sentences which reveal the harmony of English sounds and the fine distinctions of which the language is capable in the hands of a master. It was a cheering comment upon taste in America that the book became one of the most popular novels of its day.

The Lady Paramount (1902) was concerned with the search of an Italian countess in England for her cousin who is really the heir to her little country, but whose great-grandfather had been dispossessed. Harland drew well the contrasts caused by the mingled blood of the two races, Italian and English, in both the man and the girl. It is all sheer romance, and neither Anthony Craford nor the Countess of Sampaolo rise to the clarity of the characters in *The Cardinal's Snuff-Box*.

But in *My Friend Prospero* (1904) Harland wrote a novel that rivals his earlier artistic triumph. Again the love story of John Blanchemain, the heir to an English peerage, and Princess Maria Dolores, of Zelt-Neuminster in Austria, is laid against the background of Italian landscape. If they remind us of Peter and Beatrice, it is partly because these represent the eternal lovers of romance. Harland had come to the romantic-idealistic manner by conviction. As John Blanchemain says:

> "The world is still, is always, young and romantic," said John, sententious. "I can't admit that an age of prose and prudence is possible. The poetry of earth is never dead, and no more is its folly. The world is always romantic, if you have the three gifts needful to make it so."
>
> "*Is* it a woman?" repeated Lady Blanchemain.
>
> "And the three gifts are," said he, "Faith, and the sense of Beauty, and the sense of Humour."

There are also enough new characters to make any criticism of Harland for imitating himself beside the question. The little girl, Maria Annunziata, is a creation of the first rank. She acts as a link for the lovers, both of whom she adores, but it is the innate spiritual life of this frail little girl, made up of her devout belief in the beautiful phases of her faith, shot through with the echoes of pagan fancies of long ago, that make her a shining spirit. Her lack of fear of death is expressed in just the form an imaginative child might employ:

". . . You ask me, what is Death? It is exactly like a transformation-scene. At the pantomime the scene was just like the world. There were trees, and houses, and people, common people, like anyone. Then suddenly click! Oh, it was wonderful. Everything was changed. The trees had leaves of gold and silver, and the houses were like fairy palaces, and there were strange lights, red and blue, and there were great garlands of the most beautiful flowers, and the people were like angels, with gems and shining clothes. Well, you understand, at first we had only seen one side of the scene;—then click! everything was turned round, and we saw the other side. That is like life and death. Always, while we are alive, we can see only one side of things. But there is the other side, the under side. Never, so long as we are alive, we can never, never see it. But when we die,—click! It is a transformation-scene. Everything is turned round, and we see the other side. Oh, it will be very different, it will be wonderful. That is what they call Death."

If the characters, with the exception of Winthorpe the Puritan, the lines about whose mouth "were clearly the footprints of smiles," are foreign, Harland never loses the American point of view; and indeed Peter Marchmont and John Blanchemain have an American flavor even if he calls them English.

His last novel, *The Royal End* (1909), has an American heroine, Ruth Adgate, a young orphan and an heiress, who, after living in Europe since childhood and, being asked to form a morganatic marriage with the son of a Grand Duke, returns in disgust to visit her uncle at Oldbridge, in New England. The plot, as usual, does not matter much. Her love for Henry Pontycroft, an English gentleman whose religion forbids his obtaining a divorce from his worthless wife, is stated early, and one knows that sooner or later the wife will die. The charm of the book lies in Ruth's spirited reception of the blow fate has dealt her, her refusal to be abashed at artificial glory of rank, and her sense of the destruction of the older New England landscape and life, even while she recognizes its limitations.

The Royal End was published four years after Harland's death, completed by Mrs. Harland. He died in his beloved Italy, after years of suffering from tuberculosis. He remains an illustration of the imaginative artist, beginning with realistic depiction of life in New York and gradually through European influence becoming enamored of an older civilization, social and religious, which he understood well and which he used as the background for characters whose urbanity is a directing force, not merely an accomplishment. He labored hard to select the exact word and the incisive phrase, but the labor is not apparent in the limpid prose style through which his delightful characters came into being.

At first glance, Henry Blake Fuller (1857–1929) presents two irreconcilable facets to the critic, but in reality they reflect the same impulse, his love for ordered beauty and his distaste for the unsettled conditions of his native city, Chicago. His life was that of a recluse at times, and his participation in the literary movements of Chicago was always critical.

His first novel, *The Chevalier of Pensieri-Vani,* was begun in 1886 while Fuller was working in "a business office" and was inspired by nostalgia for his beloved Italy, which he had visited in 1879–1880 and again in 1883. The account found among his manuscripts,[1] addressed to "Benigno Lettore," is the revelation of a sensitive nature working slowly for three years to perfect one of the most charming excursions into the fancy ever written under the spell of Italy. It is a collection of episodes, connected by the Chevalier, a fairly young Italian who is a wanderer, a bachelor, and a lover of art. Through his adventures we meet other people, his friend Hors-Concours, a gentleman of restricted means; the Prorege of Arcopia, a skilfully drawn nobleman; the Contessa; Mr. Occident, from "Shelby County," in America; and the Duke of Severn and Avon, a delicious caricature of a British nobleman who squeezes his tenants at home to bestow charity in Italy or to buy art treasures. Through the various Italian towns, Pisa, Rome, Florence, Venice, and Siena we are taken by one who knows and loves them. There is no story of moment, but there are delightful episodes. "The Margravine and the Iron Pot" is one of the most penetrating satires upon

[1] For this account see the biography of Henry Blake Fuller by Constance M. Griffin, in preparation.

pretence in art that has ever been written. Fuller's own philosophy of life is expressed through different characters. The predicament of the American, Occident, who wants to know the best of European culture and yet feels his own limitations, is put keenly:

He felt his position one of peculiar hardship. Birth and habit drew him in one direction; culture and aspiration, in another; but he had never been a good American, and he feared he should never make a good European. He was between two fires, both of which scorched him; between two stools, neither of which offered him a comfortable seat; between the two horns of a dilemma, each of which seemed more cruelly sharp than the other.

Through the Prorege, Fuller reveals the philosophy of leisure; through the Chevalier, he paints his social ideal:

It was his way to bite off the two ends of society and to throw the middle part away, and here he had had the extremes of the social scale: on the one hand the simple, unsophisticated, uncontaminated peasantry, with hearts to be moved and stirred; and on the other hand some representation from the urbane, cultivated circles of the *cognoscenti*, possessed of trained perceptions and equipped with the ability to formulate their impression of his powers.

This is, of course, as far removed from the social organization of Fuller's day, based upon the triumph of the middle class, as well could be.

The Chevalier turns, as for a tonic, to the medieval, to the powerful figures who did great things. He compares them with the men of his own day:

Before this great clan, who could dare and do, who could will and have, he shrank away as a very weak, pitiful, forceless creature. The stippling technique of his own day seemed immeasurably poor and paltry compared with the broad, free, sketchy touch with which these men dashed off their stirring lives; and he stood abashed before that fiery and robust intensity which, so gloriously indifferent to the subtilties of the grammarian, the niceties of the manicure, and the torments of the supersensitive self-analyst, could fix its intent upon some definite desire and move forward unswervingly to its attainment. Poor moderns! he sighed, who with all our thinking never know what we really think, after all.

The Chevalier, written on the backs of old envelopes and published in 1890 under the pen-name of Stanton Page at the author's expense, was recognized at first only by the discriminating like Lowell and Norton. Republished with additions in 1892, it has become one of the realities of American literature. It is not a "travel book"; it is an excursion of personified taste and knowledge, feeding upon beauty as an inspiration. As Fuller says in his own account of the book's creation:

Yet that I had not seen a particular town or district seemed no valid reason why that town or district should not go into my book. One sometimes writes with a freer hand for lack of positive knowledge and definite experience: besides there was always the future, with its chances to make freedoms and audacities good.[2]

The Chatelaine of La Trinité (1892) was meant, according to Fuller, to do for the Alps, French, German, Swiss, and Italian, what its predecessor had done for Italy. It is a delightful book in which Fuller flicks with apparent lightness, but really flays with penetrating phrases, several varieties of pretence. Miss Aurelia West, the young American girl who accompanies Bertha, the Chatelaine of La Trinité, is a means of satirizing American love of titles and European assumptions; but it is done so dexterously that the book never descends to mere satire. One gets to know the two women and the pleasant "Governor," Bertha's godfather, who might have been an Elector if things had gone differently. The "trinity" of younger men, Count Fin-de-Siècle, Baron Zeitgeist, and the Marquis Tempo-Rubato are more distinctly types, but each has some individuality, and they are really European. Beginning with the Governor's attempt to find Roman remains in a structure which his own grandfather has built, the pretence of the noble amateur antiquary is treated amusingly. Then the Governor, the Chatelaine and Aurelia go through Switzerland, Salzburg, the Dolomites, Verona, Bellagio, and finally reach La Trinité itself—which Aurelia tries to reconstruct according to her American ideas of what constitutes grandeur. Fuller's descriptive power is shown in such scenes as the one in which Tempo-Rubato discovers a talented dancer in a second-rate place in Paris and joins her in the tarantella:

But to Tempo-Rubato, and to his partner as well, the onlooking circle was a matter of comparative indifference. When he had lightly thrown back the lapels of his coat he felt himself dressed out in ragged sheepskin, and the lustrous hat that he had snatched from his head changed to a tambourine before his arm could even extend it. The hand that thrust back a straggling lock from the temples of his vis-à-vis had placed a striped and folded cloth above them, and the shake she had given to the disordered front of her gown had

[2] Manuscript account of his work.

put a long apron there, wide-barred in barbaric stripes of color. As he danced around her with an indulgent and confident grace, the tired and callous musicians in shabby dress-coats became a band of blithesome, tangle-haired pipers; and when she in her turn circled about him, with increasing confidence in every step and a more open gratitude, the anemones of Pæstum burst into bloom all over the wide reach of the waxen floor, the low, painted ceiling rose to the height and semblance of the blue sky itself, the battered columns of Ceres and of Neptune advanced in stately fashion through flimsy panelings and tawdry mirrors, and the free, pure, blessed air of heaven seemed to blow abundantly and refreshingly through the tarnished atmosphere of the place. And when they had ended their performance he had given her a vogue.

Fuller can change to the tragic note with ease as he does in the powerful imaginative picture of the delusion of an inmate of the madhouse at Thorheim who relives before the eyes of the travelers the agony of being caught by the frozen horror of an avalanche.

It was with this broad conception of life and its verities that Fuller turned to Chicago to examine and criticize it. His attitude differed from that of his friend Garland; it was eclectic and cosmopolitan. *The Cliff Dwellers* (1893) was developed from an earlier unpublished novelette, *Between the Millstones*. It is a realistic story of Chicago life, whose symbol is the tall office building, the property of Arthur Ingles. Nearly all the characters are associated, either directly or indirectly, with this building. In it is the bank of Erastus Brainard, the self-made rich man, hard and domineering; his family represent the variety often found in an American city: the older son, Burt, hard and aspiring; Abbie, fine and self-sacrificing; Mayme, who is silly and runs off with a worthless scamp, Vibert; Marcus, the weak younger son, who at the end kills his father and hangs himself. As a contrast, there is presented George Ogden, who comes from the East, enters Brainard's bank and should have married Abbie, who loves him, but marries instead Jessie Bradley, who ruins him by her desire to keep up with Cecelia Ingles. Cecelia never appears in person until the last page of the book but is, according to Fuller, the reason for the tragedy. Ogden, driven by Jessie's extravagance, takes money from the bank and is about to be prosecuted when Brainard is stricken. After Jessie's death, he and Abbie find solace in each other. The characters are too many for complete fusion, and the final tragedy hardly achieves inevitability, but the conversation is good, and the style is direct and pictorial. The description of Burt Brainard's rude stare when Ogden called at the house—"a glance that turned a person into a thing"—

illustrates Fuller's ability at phrase-making; and the description of the way Chicago has become a kind of faith to the inhabitant shows Fuller's understanding:

"Why not?" returned Fairchild. "Does it seem unreasonable that the State which produced the two greatest figures of the greatest epoch in our history, and which has done most within the last ten years to check alien excesses and un-American ideas, should also be the State to give the country the final blend of the American character and its ultimate metropolis?"

"And you personally—is this your own belief?"

Fairchild leaned back his fine old head on the padded top of his chair and looked at his questioner with the kind of pity that has a faint tinge of weariness. His wife sat beside him silent, but with her hand on his, and when he answered she pressed it meaningly; for to the Chicagoan—even the middle-aged female Chicagoan—the name of the town, in its formal, ceremonial use, has a power that no other word in the language quite possesses. It is a shibboleth, as regards its pronunciation; it a trumpet-call, as regards its effect. It has all the electrifying and unifying power of a college yell.

"Chicago is Chicago," he said. "It is the belief of all of us. It is inevitable; nothing can stop us now."

With the Procession (1895) is a picture of the social progress of the Marshall family in Chicago. Jane, the eldest daughter, has a real aspiration toward an achievement of finer things, but she confuses this achievement with social recognition by those whose wealth has given them earlier opportunities of establishment. Jane achieves a marriage for her younger sister with an Englishman of some slight rank and an acceptance of her brother, Truesdale, by Mrs. Granger Bates, the symbol of social success. The best figure is David Marshall, the father, who dies just as they enter the new house on the South Side, worn out by worry over Truesdale's unsatisfactory love affair and by the business troubles which his partner, Belden, has brought on him.

It is interesting also to see Fuller's prophecy of the organized criminal demands upon legitimate business, in view of later conditions in Chicago. The weakness of the novel is that the characters are not as alive as the background.

In 1898 Fuller brought together four stories laid in Europe or on an ocean liner. The best, "Pasquale's Picture," was the first story written and published by Fuller.[3] It is a poignant tragedy of Assunta, the mother

[3] *The Current,* July 11, 1885.

of the handsome gondolier of Murano, who after his death worships his photograph, which gradually fades and leaves her no memento of him. Next came *The Last Refuge* (1900), one of the very best of his books. It is a study of aspiration, with a hope but not a fulfillment. The Freiherr of Kaltenau, Theodor Egmont, tries to recreate in himself a sense of enjoyment in the beauty of places he has visited before. He hopes to do this through the eyes of a younger man, Bruno. He travels, and the two find adventures. In several places he meets other travelers, each of whom is seeking the "Last Refuge," which will bring them happiness. They place it in Sicily, and eventually they all meet there. But the city of Happiness is only a delusion, and they all hesitate to enter it, for as long as they do not, they can still hope. Donna Violante, the young patrician, knows the city, since it is her birthplace, and she tells them not to enter it. She and Bruno finally discover the only city of Happiness, in their mutual love. Freiherr von Kaltenau has the satisfaction of knowing that he has helped them.

Under the Skylights (1901), which includes three clever stories dealing with literary and artistic life in Chicago, is especially interesting because of its picture of Hamlin Garland in "The Downfall of Abner Joyce." This story describes the gradual weakening of the resisting power of a strong young farmer who has written *This Weary World*, a realistic book about the woes of his people:

Abner's book comprised a dozen short stories—twelve clods of earth gathered, as it were, from the very fields across which he himself, a farmer's boy, had once guided the plough. The soil itself spoke, the intimate, humble ground; warmed by his own passionate sense of right, it steamed incense-like aloft and cried to the blue skies for justice. He pleaded for the farmer, the first, the oldest, the most necessary of all the world's workers; for the man who was the foundation of civilized society, yet who was yearly gravitating downward through new depths of slighting indifference, of careless contempt, of rank injustice and gross tyranny; for the man who sowed so plenteously, so laboriously, yet reaped so scantily and in such bitter and benumbing toil; for the man who lived indeed beneath the heavens, yet must forever fasten his solicitous eye upon the earth. All this revolted Abner; the indignation of a youth that had not yet made its compromise with the world burned on every page. Some of his stories seemed written not so much by the hand as by the fist, a fist quivering from the tension of muscles and sinews fully ready to act for truth and right; and there were paragraphs upon which the intent and blazing eye of the writer appeared to rest with no less fierceness, coldly printed as they were, than it had rested upon the manuscript itself.

The way the social leaders and the writers of romantic fiction each try to include him in their circles; his resistance and gradual appreciation of comfort and the restriction of fashionable life—until he marries Medora Giles, sister of Stephen Giles, the decorator—all are well done. Abner's power, his youthful conceit, his ignorance of the miseries of the city dweller, his narrowness, all are portrayed by an artist who can view realism with a proper perspective.

In the next collection, *Waldo Trench and Others* (1908), the scene is laid in Italy and the stories have an international flavor. The American is usually satirized, either for his attempt to assimilate everything in a hurry, or for his introduction of modern methods with dire results. "Addolorato's Intervention" in its picture of two writers, one who appeals to the few and the other to the many, may reveal the two aspects of Fuller's interest.

In 1918 he returned to Chicago in the novel *On the Stairs*, a study of two men who go down and up the stairs of economic and social life. It begins in 1873, when they were boys, and brings them to maturity. The characters are well portrayed, especially that of Raymond Prince, the individualist who is too proud to be a follower of anyone else and yet is not great enough to lead. *Bertram Cope's Year* (1919) is a story of a young instructor at the University of Chicago who parries with some skill the interest of his feminine admirers and has a great friendship with a young man, Arthur Lemoyne, so intimate indeed that it subjects them both to that form of criticism which is especially rampant in contemporary conversation. An older man, Randolph, tries to help Cope without much success. Fuller was himself fond of associating with younger men, and the pictures of undergraduate life are quite realistic at times. But the novel seems the weakest of all his fiction, and the indication of perversion is irritating rather than tragic.

At the very end of his career, Fuller wrote two books which represent the two different backgrounds against which he had set his work. They showed no decline in his power. *Gardens of This World* was published shortly after his death in 1929. He started the Chevalier and his friend, Hors-Concours, from Paris on a search through France, Italy, Algiers, and Greece, looking for gardens, which are of course symbolic. They meet Aurelia West, now the Countess de Feuillevolante, the Freiherr von Kaltenau, the Chatelaine, of course, and other characters from the early books, and, as before, it is the pungent comment on over-organized life and the plea for the preservation of the individual that make the book delightful:

It is now well recognized that conferences are best held in Swiss towns with Italian names. These towns necessarily begin their names with an L, and should be situated on some Alpine lake. The site must not be too low for hot weather, nor too high for cold. There must be warm breezes from the Lombard Plain, and cool winds from the nearer Alps. Blow hot, blow cold; such is the proper atmosphere for conferences.

Who but Fuller could have created that delightful scene in Verona where the municipal council defend themselves for having placed Romeo in Juliet's tomb, so that the visitors can have the satisfaction of paying their tribute to both lovers at once!

Fuller did not live to see the proof sheets of *Not on the Screen* (1930), his last novel. Irritated apparently by the futility of the moving picture, he wrote a novel of Chicago life [4] which proceeds as differently as possible from the methods of the screen story. The love of Embert Howell, a young broker, for Evelyn Trent proceeds in a leisurely manner, and Howell is known rather by his effect on others than by his own words, which are few. While the novel is realistic, it was probably a mistake to connect it, even as a departure, with the moving picture.

While Fuller is important in the realistic criticism of life in the Middle West, and later writers like Theodore Dreiser have paid tribute to the inspiration they received from his novels of Chicago, he was following here the methods established by Howells. He wrote these novels deliberately, as part of a movement, but *The Chevalier, The Chatelaine,* and *The Last Refuge* were the children not only of his fancy but of his heart. It is idle to speculate on what he might have done if material considerations and the quiet heroism of assumed family duties had not kept him in Chicago, far from the Italy he loved. Perhaps the very difference between the grimy office buildings in which Fuller worked and the scenes of beauty through which the Chevalier moved made the wanderings of that spiritual epicure possible. Certainly Fuller's correspondence while he was writing his last books show that while *Not on the Screen* was somewhat of a task, *Gardens of the World* flowed spon-

---

[4] While no mention of a city is made in the book itself, see his letter in *Henry B. Fuller,* edited by Anna Morgan, p. 138.

taneously from his pen. He was one of the chief representatives in our fiction of the literature of escape, and the growing critical estimation of his art is only another indication that a fine spirit may have to wait for recognition but the final judgment is secure.

CHAPTER XX

THE DEVELOPMENT OF REALISM

WHILE the idealistic treatment of locality was winning wide acclaim, the roots of realism had been planted securely by the wide influence of Howells and never ceased to bear fruit. In 1883, a year after *A Modern Instance* was published, the first important story of Mary Wilkins, "Two Old Lovers," appeared in *Harper's Bazaar*. Mary Wilkins was born in Randolph, Massachusetts, in 1852, and her heredity and education developed in her a deep understanding of the rural life in Vermont, where her girlhood was spent. Her first volume of short stories, *A Humble Romance and Other Stories* (1887), followed by *A New England Nun and Other Stories* (1891), established her reputation. It was not that she marked any advance upon Howells or James in the truthful portraiture of character or in the analysis of the inmost motives of conduct. What attracted attention was the art with which she proceeded to take the very humblest forms of life and interest her readers by imbuing these characters with some quality which made them memorable.

First she represented the uncompromising courage, self-respect, and honesty of the women. There is little glamour in their lives, even in their love-making. Sally, in "A Humble Romance," is as undistinguished as any household drudge, and she marries Jake Russell, the peddler, to escape from a life without horizon. What makes her important is the courage with which she accepts his apparent desertion and carries on his trade, hoping against hope that he will return. One of the best is "Old Lady Pingree," the last of a race that had once "seen better days," who clings to the consolation that she has money saved to bury her and who then gives it to a young girl whose mother will otherwise have to be buried by the town. She does it without much graciousness, but with an innate delicacy which removes from it any implicit patronage. Miss Wilkins knew that it is not the amount of the sacrifice which counts; it is the fact that Old Lady Pingree gives all she has.

Allied to this personal self-respect is the pride of the women in their own property and home. In "A Mistaken Charity" two elderly women, Harriet and Charlotte Shattuck, are taken from their abject poverty by charitable neighbors to a comfortable Old Ladies' Home and run away to return to their *own* poverty. One of the most delightful, "An Independent Thinker," is a merciless satire of the small-town mind. Esther Gay, who declines to attend church because she is deaf, is ostracized, even by Lavinia, whom she is secretly supporting. But finally Lavinia has to come to live with Esther and, since Lavinia is bedridden, Esther will not be able to leave her on Sunday. As Esther says, "It's all settled right, and there don't none of 'em suspect that I'm a-carryin' out my p'int arter all." This note is struck again in "Persistence." When Candace, the church soprano, has been supplanted by a younger woman, she tries to drown the latter's voice and then on her death bed she repents and asks her rival to sing for her "Jesus, Lover of My Soul." Just as this atmosphere of peace has been established, Candace remarks quietly, "But you flatted a little on 'soul.' "

Miss Wilkins is not limited to women in her depiction of character, but her women are better than the men. Through them the note of revolt is sounded, sometimes in delightful comedy. One of the best is "The Revolt of Mother," in which Sarah Penn, having been refused a new house by her husband who prefers to put up a barn on the spot, seizes the occasion of his absence to move the family over to the new barn. On his return, he capitulates.

This strong note of individualism is carried even to rebellion against God, into a disbelief that demands a sign under suffering. In "The Bar Light House" a helpless woman, believing that her husband will be killed, drags herself up to the lighthouse top and, finding to her surprise the lamp is lighted, believes that divine interposition has come at her demand. In reality another woman has lighted it. The church in Miss Wilkins' stories is a social organization. The glance across the meeting-house between the boy and girl is so often the beginning of a love story that it becomes a mannerism. The delightful comedy, "In Butterfly Time," which illustrates Miss Wilkins' terse style, lays bare the passions that surge below the serene surface of a prayer-meeting:

Old Mrs. Wheat, in her corner, on her knees, listened with an outward show of reverence, but she was inwardly torn with jealousy. She was the last one called upon to take part; even old Mrs. Dill was preferred before her.

But she had her revenge; when she did get her chance to speak, long and weary was the time she kept her devout sisters on their aching knees.

She had been storing up a good deal to say while the others were praying, and now she said it. For church and town and commonwealth, for missions at home and abroad, her shrill cry went up. Lastly she prayed, with emphatic quavers, for old Mrs. Dill. "O Lord," pleaded she, "remember, we pray thee, this aged handmaiden at my side. May she long enjoy what blessin's are left to her in her age an' decrepitood. Sanctify her trials unto her, an' enable her to look away from the feebleness an' want of strength which is now her lot on this airth, to that better country where the wicked cease from troubling and the weary air at rest."

The tragedies of childhood, so real while they last, provide the material for her collection *Young Lucretia* (1892). In the next year her first novel, *Jane Field*, was published. It is a remarkable study of the character of a woman who, distraught with the fear that her daughter, Lois, is dying from tuberculosis, seizes a chance to secure property which has been left to her dead sister Esther, whom she exactly resembles. Miss Wilkins' realism was rarely seen to better advantage than in the scene in the lawyer's office, when he greets Jane Field as "Mrs. Maxwell." She has not quite made up her mind to the fraud, but his mistake determines her. The growing horror in her mind at the loss of the one thing she has kept even in her poverty—the consciousness of her upright life—culminates in the final revulsion of feeling which leads her to go from house to house in the village pounding on the doors and calling out, "I ain't Esther Maxwell!" *Pembroke* (1894) is even better. Here are the iron wills, the steadfast fidelity, the indomitable pride, the bitter cruelty and even the meanness, of different types of New England nature. The central theme is the fidelity of Charlotte Barnard to Barnabas Thayer, after the quarrel between Barney and her father. Barney has inherited his stubbornness from his mother, Deborah, a remarkable picture of a woman obsessed with a love of power, which has led to the shame of her daughter and the death of her little son. Those who write of Mary Wilkins' novels as lacking in structure must have neglected to read the last scene of *Pembroke*, when Barney, ill with rheumatism, tells Charlotte, who has come to nurse him, to go home because the town is gossiping about her, and then hobbles up to her cottage, which he had vowed years before he would never enter again. It ties the novel together as securely as can be imagined, for the conquest of pride by unfaltering love has rarely been better expressed. Another finely conceived character is Sylvia Crane, who has spent her last cent and has to go to the poor-house, the final depths of tragedy. Concealing this from her relatives, she determines to finish in style, gives a high tea to her sisters and sends her prized silver to her niece as a wedding present. Such characters prevent the novel from being merely a drab picture of uninteresting life, as is so often the case with Russian fiction. They present contrast, the life of any form of art, and it is just because Mary Wilkins provides even in such a town as Pembroke, where selfishness and ruthlessness rule, some redeeming characters, that the novel is not only more interesting but is also closer to reality. Another form of contrast appeared in *Madelon* (1896), between Madelon Hautville, of mixed French, English, and Indian blood, and the two men, Burr and Lot Gordon, who each loves her in his own way. There are melodramatic elements which make it inferior to *Pembroke* or *Jane Field*, but there is decided skill in the development of Lot Gordon's love and Madelon's passion for Burr.

While *Jerome, a Poor Man* (1897) is still realistic, the influence of the romantic-idealistic impulse which became triumphant about that time begins to show itself. Always a sympathizer with the underdog, Miss Wilkins depicted skilfully the small boy who shoulders responsibility early and chokes back the love which his poverty forbids him to express. Lucinda Merritt belongs to a more well-to-do stratum than appeared in the earlier novels, and she fails to understand Jerome's silence or her own physical restlessness. There is a striking passage in which Lucinda sees him asleep on the ground:

Love, even when it has apparently no past, is at once a memory and a revelation. Lucinda saw the little lover of her innocent childish dreams asleep there, she saw the poor boy who had gone hungry and barefoot, she saw the young man familiar in the strangeness of the future. And, more than that, Lucinda, who had hitherto shown fully to her awakening heart only her thought of Jerome, having never dared to look at him and love him at the same time, now gazed boldly at him asleep, and a sense of a great mystery came over her. In Jerome she seemed to see herself also, the unity of the man and woman in love dawned upon her maiden imagination. She felt as if Jerome's hands were her hands, his breath hers. "I never knew he looked like me before," she thought with awe.

The romantic flavor is apparent in *Silence and Other Stories* (1898), for these deal with the past of New England, such as the burning of Deerfield. They are not so distinctive as the earlier short stories, and her historical novel, *The Heart's Highway* (1900), laid in Virginia about 1682, is not one of her best. The hero has more of the Puritan than the Cavalier in him, and his sacrifice is really unnecessary. Much better was "The Love of Parson Lord," the title story of the collection of 1900. This clergyman, who dedicates his daughter to the service of the Lord and foreign missions, brings her up relentlessly, and gives her secretly the new doll and the pretty dresses which she thinks come from the Squire's wife, is a real creation. When Parson Lord refuses to marry his daughter, Love, to the Squire's grandson, the Squire tricks him by a clever device:

". . . Here is your daughter, an angel if ever there was one, loving this young man, and ready and willing to honor and obey him all the days of her life, comfort him in sorrow, and nurse him in sickness, are you not, sweetheart?"

Love nodded, sobbing.

"And here is my grandson, with all his heart set upon loving, cherishing, and protecting her in sickness or health, and cleaving to her for better or worse, are you not, Richard?"

"Yes, sir, I am," replied Richard, with a start of amazement.

"Then," said the squire, his voice changing suddenly from a tone of easy interrogation to one of solemn proclamation, "in virtue of the authority vested in me as justice of the peace of this township, I pronounce you man and wife."

This was probably the original of the ending of Jesse Lynch Williams' play *Why Marry?*, the first Pulitzer Prize winner.

The Portion of Labor (1901) belongs to the fiction of protest. While Miss Wilkins' sympathy was with labor, she did not allow her thesis to swallow the novel; her characters are concrete, especially Ellen Brewster, the girl who works in Robert Lloyd's shoe factory. The situation, as described by Miss Wilkins, which involved wage cuts and strikes, was hopeless, because Lloyd took the ground that, as owner of the factory, he was sole arbiter. This attitude may seem completely out of date, but it was omnipresent in 1901. The coal operators were about to receive a sharp lesson at the hands of Theodore Roosevelt when they declined to arbitrate while the country suffered. While Lloyd gives his workmen some concessions, it is only after he has won the strike; the idea of running his business at a loss for a time in order to keep his employees at work does not occur to him. *The Portion of Labor* is an accurate picture of conditions before the employer accepted social responsibility for those whom he employed, and Miss Wilkins' suggestion of the essential dignity of labor and the necessity on labor's part to realize this in a practical way is not badly wrought into the story.

In *Understudies* (1901) Miss Wilkins departed from her usual material to treat symbolically the nature of animals. These stories were varyingly successful; the ruthlessness of "The Cat," the kinship of the boy with "The Monkey," and the proprietary attitude of "The Squirrel" toward the nuts are well done. In the same volume are presented studies of human beings who partake of the nature of flowers. "Arethusa," the story of a girl who remains a maiden at heart even though she is married, and "Mountain Laurel," the tale of a man who lives happy on an illusion, are the best. They have a vein of poetic feeling which makes them charming.

In 1902 Miss Wilkins married Dr. Charles M. Freeman and lived from that time until her death in 1930 in Metuchen, New Jersey. Mrs. Freeman continued in 1903 in *The Wind in the Rose Bush and Other Stories of the Supernatural* to venture into new fields. In most of these stories she creates ghosts that cannot be seen, but may be apprehended by one or two of the other senses, and the result is usually impressive. Perhaps the best is "The Southwest Chamber," in which a woman recently dead objects to her room being used and causes the new occupant, her niece, to see her aunt in the mirror instead of herself and feel the emotions of hate and pride which her aunt had felt for her. Mrs. Freeman's sense for realism checks the extravagance which frequently spoils the supernatural, but it is of course not her particular province.

In *The Givers* (1904), a collection of short stories in which the central theme is concerned with the spirit of giving, there is some of her best work. The tragedy of "The Butterfly," in which a daughter discovers the frailty of her mother and her father's years of sacrifice, or the comedy of "The Givers," a delightful satire on the fundamental fact that people usually give not what the recipient needs but what they themselves fancy, showed Mrs. Freeman's great qualities of incisiveness and reticence. As a whole they are better than the stories in the subsequent collections, *The Fair Lavinia and Others* (1907) and *The Winning Lady and Others* (1909), though "Old Woman Magoun" in the latter volume is a strong story of devotion.

Mrs. Freeman's later novels are not upon the same high level as her earlier ones. *The Debtor* (1906), laid in a town near New York, is too long drawn out; the central character, Arthur Carroll, a man who lives by his wits, while real in some respects, is not credible in others. *Doc Gordon* (1906) is more direct, but the plot here strains any reader's credulity. To find one of the foremost realists of the 'eighties expecting us to believe that a wife would permit her husband to represent her for years as his widowed sister to save his niece from persecution is simply painful. The climax, in which the doctor is caught in the agony of a problem—whether he shall give his wife an overdose of morphine to save her pain, is not badly worked out and anticipated a somewhat similar situation in Mrs. Wharton's *Fruit of the Tree*. *By the Light of the Soul* (1907) is simply tedious, but it is noticeable that when Maria Edgham leaves New Jersey and lives in a New England village, the story begins to take on some life. *The Shoulders of Atlas* (1908) which is laid in New England is much better, and the way in which each character bears the burden which has been assigned to him gives a unity to the novel. The character of Mrs. Ayres, who hides from everyone the actions of her daughter, a neurotic, putting on the armor which good breeding can throw around a breaking heart, will alone repay any reader. *The Butterfly House* (1912) is an amusing satire on a woman with an itch for publicity, but while suburban life near New York is cleverly depicted, the novel is not important.

Mrs. Freeman's latest short stories, of which *Edgewater People* (1918) is a representative collection, rose almost to the level of her earliest work. By a curious reaction, she dealt more frequently with the representatives of families who had once been wealthier and more important but who retain great pride in their traditions. In other words, her material is more like that of Miss Jewett. "Sarah Edgewater" is a remarkably fine study of a woman who has been robbed of her lover by her own sister who hates her with "the hatred of the wrongdoer for the victim of the wrong." The final reconciliation of the sisters is told with a realistic absence of sentimentality that was Mary Wilkins' foremost quality and which she recaptured in these last stories. In "Value Received" Sarah Edgewater is again the center of interest through the revelation of her delicate understanding of the feelings of her two dependent aunts who have presented her with a bonnet of their own making which she bravely wears rather than hurt them.

If Mrs. Freeman's fiction is usually concerned with minor happenings like these, she attained distinction because in her best work she imbued these events with spiritual significance and therefore made them important. She was not an exponent of the heresy of little souls, for in the marked contrast between the artistic triumphs of *A Humble Romance, A New England Nun, Jane Field, Pembroke, Jerome,* and *Edgewater People,* and the dreariness of *By the Light of the Soul,* she proved within the limits of her own work that faithfulness to details is not enough. By themselves they are dull, but when a novelist possesses the insight that draws from them beauty, they become significant in terms of their fidelity to life. Being a woman, she was able to appreciate the power of little events in the shaping of a life. When she was young, she believed she could paint, and there is a pictorial power in her fiction. Her first writing was in verse, and after she had achieved success with stories in which apparently she stripped the glamour from life and locality, the essential quality of imagination provided another and an older splendor more universal than any local color fiction provides. It was the splendor of character, defying fate, fighting to the last for the right to independence, for the preservation of its own individuality. Her best stories were laid in New England, but she belongs, in the history of fiction, not to any local color school but to a wider field, that which reveals to the understanding the inner workings of the heart.

The change of manner which was noted in Mrs. Freeman's fiction becomes even more apparent in that of Alice Brown (1857–   ). Born in Hampton Falls, New Hampshire, she graduated from Robinson Seminary at Exeter, taught school and lived in Boston before she began to write. Her first novel, *Fools of Nature* (1887), was a study of the effects of spiritualism upon various characters. The sordid side of the séances is depicted realistically, but the characters are types and the construction is faulty. Yet Alice Brown's belief in the great power of human passion to order lives for good or evil was clearly expressed in her first novel. Her early short stories, collected in *Meadow Grass* (1895) and *Tiverton Tales* (1899), have a realism of the spirit rather than of locality. "Farmer Eli's Vacation" is a fine study of a man who is so overpowered by his first glimpse of the sea that he returns to his farm after one day because he felt the experience too deeply. "Told in a Poorhouse" is another story of deep feeling. The note of revolt which is one of Miss Brown's chief contributions is struck in "After All." This revolt is not against economic conditions, but is a protest against the control by other people of a soul who prizes her own individuality. "Heartsease" is a delightful story of a woman who protests against too much coddling by her son and daughter. In "Joint Owners in Spain," which later was dramatized by Alice Brown in a successful one-act play, she drew a picture of two difficult old women in an Old Ladies' Home who, forced to share a room, divide it by a chalk line and never speak to each other unless they cross it deliberately. It is a tragic picture of two individuals fighting hard to preserve the illusion that they have some place they can call their own. The conversation is as real as anything Mary Wilkins wrote, but the significance of the story lies not so much in the realism as in the imaginative conception. This imaginative quality is shown also in such stories as "The Mortuary Chest," in which a woman keeps the last things each of her relatives has worn; or in "A Second Marriage," in which the power of long association is powerfully depicted.

Alice Brown has never given herself completely to the ritual of realism. In her novel *Margaret Warrener* (1901) she puts into the mouth of Brandon, a playwright who dramatizes Margaret's own struggle to retain her husband's love and sees her play successfully in the stage version of her own tragedy, these words: "He felt anew the ignoble aspect of filching life to serve the purposes of art." To her fiction must be a portrait rather than a photograph. If her execution had always been as perfect as her theory, she would be one of the foremost novelists in America. But her work is distinctly uneven. The group of artists and writers in *Margaret Warrener* are a queer mixture of real people and literary figures, and their conversations are often stilted. Yet the flashes of insight are put into memorable sentences like "There is no cruelty like that of an admiration tempered by disdain."

Much better was her novel *Rose MacLeod* (1908), a story of individuals who must work out their own salvation in contrast with those who wish to give themselves to a "cause." Malcolm MacLeod, Rose's father, is a fine picture of a communist leader whose cause is really his device for satisfying his own sense of power. The way in which the women all look at matters from the personal standpoint is clearly indicated; and one of the happiest of the individualists, Mrs. Fulton, puts the matter concretely to her granddaughter, Electra: "You don't know anything about the truth. You've thought about it so much that now you only tell horrible facts."

Alice Brown's finest novel, *The Story of Thyrza* (1909), is the life of a girl, Thyrza Tennant, intensely proud, emotional, and, in her child-hood, irrational, who has a longing for beauty, and who rushes to meet experience and is hurt cruelly by her first encounter with passion. When Andy McAdam desires her for a moment, she believes he loves her and she gives herself freely and impulsively, thinking he will return and marry her. He does not love her, and indeed marries her sister Laura, his childhood's sweetheart, knowing that Thyrza will not betray him. Thyrza has a son, and the novel proceeds with her martyrdom, borne silently and bravely in payment for her one blind clutch at happiness. The emotional fire within her did not die into ashes but hardened into steel, and she remains in the memory not only as an individual, but as a symbol of an impulse which keeps the race alive. Not as great a figure as Hester Prynne, for her love had no such depth, she yet gains and keeps our sympathy like Hester for the dignity of her reparation. There are some remarkable passages in the book; the meeting of the two sisters after a lapse of years; the demand of her son that she represent herself as a married woman in order that he may win Angelica; Angelica's visit to her; the two occasions when Barton Gorse, who has always loved her, begs her to marry him. Through all she keeps her purpose steady, to tell the truth and bring no one else into her disgrace.

Miss Brown's next novel, *John Winterbourne's Family* (1910), seems unreal in characterization. But during the decade 1900–1910 she was writing some of her best short stories. The revolt of the individual is well done in "A Sea Change." [1] Here Cynthia, the farmer's wife, leaves her husband; and her reason is given succinctly: "He greases his boots so much. He leaves 'em by the oven door." The people in these stories are still real, but there is a touch of poetic fancy which keeps them from the stark verity of Mary Wilkins or Garland, and yet makes them at times very appealing. They were included in collections like *The County Road* (1906) or *Country Neighbors* (1910). In the latter, the best are "The Play House," "Flowers of Paradise" and "The Masquerade," in which the native country folk who have been given the proceeds of the masquerade balls which the summer visitors have conducted for their own amusement, decide to dress up in the costumes of their own an-cestors.

In *Vanishing Points* (1913) there are a number of stories about writers. "The Master" is a story of a dinner at which a group discuss their literary

---

[1] *Atlantic Monthly*, August, 1900.

inspiration, a novelist whose works do not sell well, but whom they have all imitated. As one of them remarks: "He's dug out the gold. They've minted it. They've put it in circulation." The description fits Henry James best, but there is not much apparent influence of James upon Alice Brown. "The Hands of the Faithful" is a very appealing story which shows how an author lives upon the appreciation of others.

Alice Brown has always possessed a dramatic sense in her fiction, and in 1915 she won the prize of $10,000 offered by Winthrop Ames for the best play submitted anonymously by an American. *Children of Earth* was produced and published in 1915, and while it did not succeed on the stage, the character of Ellen Barstow, the spinster who revolts against the domination of her men-folk, is allied to several of Miss Brown's fictional characters. Of this period, *The Prisoner* (1916) is the best of her novels. It is a study of the way in which all are prisoners of something, material or spiritual, either of their own or others' making. *Bromley Neighborhood* (1917) is interesting only because Miss Brown tried to represent the effect of the Great War, before we entered it, on a group of people in a quiet New England township. Some of it is quite real, such as Hugh Neale's joining the French Foreign Legion, but her vision of the clarifying effect of the European conflict upon the moral conflict of Ellen Brock, who has married one man while she loved another, is fantastic. Yet the spectacle of Thomas Neale, lying for months after his accident without speaking a word, but becoming articulate to bargain about the price of the woodlot he wishes to buy, is done in her best manner.

Her short stories, collected in 1918 as *The Flying Teuton and Other Stories*, illustrates how impermanent are the themes of woman suffrage and of the supernatural mixed not quite completely with war fever. But in "A Citizen and His Wife" there is an appealing story of a woman who has to choose between her loyalty to her country and to her husband, a German spy. That Alice Brown's real field lay in the primary relations of human beings, the story "Father" in this collection, or "The Wedding Ring" in the next volume, *Homespun and Gold* (1920), amply proves. Fanciful as she often is, she is at her satiric best when she reveals the instability of a feminine lecturer on mystic matters, and remarks that "you couldn't get anywhere when the ineffable sat in judgment on the obvious."

The struggle of individuals to adjust themselves to post-war conditions was not badly depicted in *Old Crow* (1922). The worldweariness of those who, like John Raven, a man of forty, return from France to find no place for them in the life in America is accurately and sympathetically portrayed. The remedy is not clear, for the solution has baffled others than Miss Brown. The most interesting portion of the novel, however, was the story of the Tenneys, husband and wife, farmers at Wake Hill, New Hampshire. Israel Tenney's insane jealousy of his wife "Tira," her devotion to her child, who was "not right," her refusal to leave Israel after he has murdered their child, and her ultimate suicide reveal a side of New England nature which Alice Brown knew well. Tira's worship of John Raven, who tries unsuccessfully to help her, ties the plot together skilfully. Miss Brown indicated well how Raven has been managed all his life by women who love him, and his final rescue by a younger woman ends one of the most interesting of her novels. *Dear Old Templeton* (1927) is not so powerful, but there is an illuminating passage in which Templeton, a novelist, criticizes the realistic movement:

"Mean?" said Templeton. "I meant to do something as near like life as I could. I took the people and the scenes I knew best. Small town life, that was what I knew. I'd an idea there was great virtue in realism. I didn't know then that the realist has got to be more than man, not less. I thought he could photograph his people and his locality and he'd be doing something of value when American literature came to be classified and mapped out by sections: some of 'em for New England, some of 'em for the west. I did the best work I could. I took people as I found 'em, and I didn't put any romance into 'em because there wasn't any there and it would simply have been painting a hippopotamus like a zebra. But I didn't get anything else into them— oh, that other thing that makes you laugh and cry and find there's something in humanity after all, even if it only walks on two sticks. . . ."

In her later novels Alice Brown has developed her interest in the supernatural which, consistent as it has been since *Fools of Nature*, is not her most successful theme. In *The Kingdom in the Sky* (1932), she describes the future life and falls into the pitfall which awaits anyone who tries to write of eternity in terms of human life. *Jeremy Hamlin* (1934) is better because the theme is subordinated to the study of the after effects of a strong personality who ruled the town in his lifetime. But neither in this novel nor in *The Willoughbys* (1935) are the people convincing. Miss Brown had a good theme in Hannah Willoughby's refusal to marry a man whose earlier love for her had been transferred to a young girl, crippled by an accident which forbade marriage. But it is a theme for a short story not a novel, and the episode of the mad girl, Ann Denison, might also have been a fine short story, provided in both cases there had been more edge to the characters.

Alice Brown should remain a permanent figure for her remarkable sympathy with those characters, especially women, who insist upon the preservation of their individuality, of the right to adventure on the sea of emotion, even if they wreck their lives in doing so. Their great tragedy is a loveless existence; marriage is not essential, if they have the memory of a passion shared by the man they have chosen. She knows that unhappy love is better for a woman than no love at all, and if her treatment of her men is at times a bit naïve, at other times she reveals a real insight into their weaknesses. Insight is, after all, her strongest characteristic; the poetic touches, at times imaginative, at times merely fanciful, are charming, and her style shows no deterioration in her long career. Her willingness to let her theme at times overshadow her characters is her marked defect. It prevented her prize play from being a stage success and it prevented her from being a great novelist. But when she is dealing with human relations only and has no abstract theme to impede her, she has given us novels and short stories which have every right to live.

Although Robert Grant (1852–   ) began to publish before Mary Wilkins or Alice Brown, and the influence of Howells upon him is clear, his best work was done in the twentieth century. His early books like *The Confessions of a Frivolous Girl* (1880) or *An Average Man* (1884) were not important.

Face to Face (1886) was published anonymously, as Grant believed its serious purpose might be hurt by the association with a writer whose success had been won by social satire of a light kind. The visit of Evelyn Pimlico, an English girl, to her cousins in Newport was probably inspired by Grant's marriage to Amy, the daughter of Sir Alexander Galt, a Canadian official, for Amy Galt had visited her own cousin at Newport in 1882. The book was also prompted by Grant's serious interest in the conflict of capital and labor; but the portions of the book devoted to these matters, are best described in Grant's own words in his autobiography, *Fourscore* (1934), as "padding." The best portions are those in which he portrays the life at Newport and reveals the similarity of the life there to one phase of the English social scene. He knew both and he was aware not only of their narrowness but also of their appeal.

Judge Grant's first important novel was *Unleavened Bread* (1900). Under the influence of Balzac and Flaubert he conceived the character of Selma White, a ruthless self-seeker and an unconscious hypocrite, who believes she is spiritual to the last degree and who looks like "a worried archangel." Beginning her married life in Benham, "a Western city with an Eastern exposure," she rapidly becomes dissatisfied with her first husband, a dealer in varnish, seizes the opportunity which his infidelity affords to divorce him, marries a New York architect and is bitterly disappointed at her lack of social progress in New York. Grant keeps her from becoming an abstraction by her feminine jealousy of other women who succeed, especially Flossie Williams, another well drawn character, who, starting with less ability but more money, outdistances Selma because she has a sense of humor and a willingness to learn. Selma returns to Benham, marries a lawyer politician and is again disappointed when she sees how relatively unimportant a place a new Congressman's wife takes in Washington. Once more she returns to Benham and when her husband becomes Governor she tries to solace herself with social recognition of a public nature. Grant shows well how hopelessly muddled such a woman becomes in a moral crisis such as that which confronts her husband when he has to choose between his political future and his promise to sign a bill granting a monopoly to certain interests. Nothing is clear to her but the sanctity of her ambitions. In Selma, Grant created a real person, a symbol of the urge for domination, the restlessness of a certain kind of woman who has become increasingly frequent in the twentieth century. The atmosphere, social, political, and economic, is correct. But notwithstanding the art which built up relentlessly through incidents which tingle with reality the slow moral degradation of Selma while she rises in public importance, *Unleavened Bread* is not a great novel, largely because, as Grant remarks in *Fourscore*, he "detested" his heroine. Consequently the reader has no sympathy for her and does not share in her disappointments. Howells did not detest Bartley Hubbard, and Thackeray did not detest Becky Sharp; it was Becky's sudden impulsive deviations from her program that made her a real and a sympathetic figure. The dramatization of *Unleavened Bread* in 1901, made by Leo Ditrichstein and Judge Grant, brought out even more clearly the lack of a hero and the unsympathetic quality of the heroine. Yet even with all its limitations, *Unleavened Bread* remains a valuable document in the history of the rise of the power of woman in public affairs, and Judge

Grant is deserving of the highest praise for his objective attitude and his courage, knowing that the fortune of a novel is made by its feminine readers, in portraying a woman who is a warning against the irresistible current of the time.

The Undercurrent (1904), a study of divorce, is too painfully detailed, and no character emerges as distinct as Selma White. Grant had permitted his theme to overshadow his characters, a fatal defect in fiction. Much more direct and suavely satiric was a novelette, *The Orchid* (1905), another study of the divorce question and the wide tolerance of a certain social group, provided the divorcée has plenty of money. Grant makes the conduct of his central character as revolting as possible, for she sells her baby to her husband for $2,000,000, as part of the divorce terms. The novel was based on a real incident, and it illustrates once more the principle that in fiction any act of a heroine which takes away the sympathy of the reader cannot be justified by its mere reality.

In 1909 Grant wrote his best novel, *The Chippendales*. With a thorough knowledge of the survivals of the Puritan conscience which had in general resulted in a sensitiveness to any outside criticism upon the standards of conservative Boston society, he drew the Chippendale family as representative of this last phase. "What a Bostonian will not do has ever been perhaps his highest title to distinction," or "Even her applause is always frigid, for her enthusiasm is a product of the brain, not the spontaneous tumult of the heart" are Grant's conclusions. The Chippendales are differentiated, not simply a group. Harrison Chippendale, the head of the family, is a courteous gentleman who had fought in the Civil War and lived upon his fortune. His son, Chauncey, is an example of the more active generation in the banking and investment business. The acquisitive sense has always been strong in them, especially in Harrison's maiden sister, Georgiana, and his bachelor brother, Baxter. But the best of the race is Henry Chippendale Sumner, Harrison's nephew, a young lawyer whose father had fallen at the head of his regiment in the Civil War, and who takes life seriously. In him the old spirit of that element in Boston which had denounced slavery and fought for great causes in the Revolution and the Civil War flared up at crucial moments, but expressed itself in daily life by a conscientious determination to do what was right, even if it made him ridiculous. His love for Priscilla Avery, the daughter of a Cambridge inventor, at first unsuccessful, wins out finally by her recognition of his innate nobility. She is a high-spirited young woman of Boston, not wealthy at first, who finds however no difficulty when fortune comes to her through her father's discovery of "Electric Coke" in fitting herself into the Chippendale group.

As a contrast to them Grant draws Hugh Blaisdell, a graduate of a country college, who by his own abilities rises to a high place in Boston finance. He is less fine in his feelings and his methods, and when his choice is made between Priscilla Avery and Lora, her stepsister, it is characteristic of a man who proceeds along the line of least resistance that he takes the girl who will not hold him up to too lofty standards. Blaisdell is not dishonest; he is adaptable, he does not even use his great financial power in revenge for the social barriers which the Chauncey Chippendales put up against Lora, since he believes that in the end he will gain more by preserving the outward appearance of friendship. He is one of Grant's best drawn characters in a novel replete with them and his second marriage with the younger Georgiana Chippendale is a delightful touch. One reason for the artistic success of *The Chippendales* lay in Grant's selection of ironic episodes which develop the relations of character. The stormy contest over the statue of the Bacchante which has been given to the Public Library and which is deemed improper for that place by the conservatives is delightful because it reveals how a city which once was swept by great causes can be disturbed by comparatively trivial events. It is this contest, however, which proves to Priscilla Avery that Henry Sumner and not Blaisdell is really her proper mate; and Henry Sumner's refusal to change his name to Chippendale, even to inherit his aunt's fortune, adds the final touch. Henry was drawn to a certain degree from Grant himself, and as a picture of Boston life, the novel is veracious and significant.

In *The High Priestess* (1915) Grant returned to Benham, and the problems of the married state complicated by a wife who insists upon her own career as a landscape architect. Mary Arnold is almost as sure of herself as Selma White; her introduction of Sybil Fielding as her substitute in her household duties leads directly to her husband's attempted infidelity. But Mary is a finer character than Selma, and the reader has more sympathy with her and more hope that she and Randall will reunite. Grant shows clearly the difficulties which children bring into such a situation; and when Mary's stern standards of virtue yield to temptation of another kind, she is revealed to herself as a human being and the reconciliation is brought about.

Judge Grant's later novels have not been on the same level as *The Chippendales* or *Unleavened Bread*. *The Bishop's Granddaughter* (1925) was a satirical picture of the absurdities of the divorce laws in America as seen through the eyes of a British bishop whose American granddaughter is prevented from divorce by his urbanity rather than by his arguments. The Bishop himself is satirized gently, for Grant recognized that in a time when satire had become more violent, his method of attack was not likely to be popular. *The Dark Horse* (1931) is a placid but at times understanding treatment of the interrelations of politics and social life in Boston. It is, according to the author, a sequel to *The Chippendales*, but it has not the scope or the vigor of that book. Robert Grant was never, even in his best period, a widely popular author. Like De-Forest, he depicted heroines who were too accurately painted to please the feminine audience that decides the fate of fiction. But his novels will remain a valid source of information to the social historian who wishes to read an account of the ferment of ideas at the turn of the century.

Like Mary Wilkins and Alice Brown, Harold Frederic (1856–1898) illustrates the realist who began under the influence of Howells but changed somewhat in method toward the end of his career. Born in Utica, New York, he had become by 1882 the editor of the *Albany Evening Journal* and later the London correspondent of the *New York Times*. He published a short story as early as 1879 in the *Utica Journal*, "Brother Sebastian's Friendship," a rather absurd tale, but his first novel, *Seth's Brother's Wife* (1887), is an excellent picture of the hard, bare life of a New York farm, of politics in upstate New York, and of the seamy side of journalism. All these were drawn from his own experience. The effect of the loneliness of the farm life upon Isabel Fairchild, her passion for Seth, her brother-in-law, and the way she interferes with the growing love between Seth and Annie Warren by absorbing the credit for saving Seth's life, are told with a realism and a directness that are admirable.

Frederic strips from the country a false glamour that is sometimes given to it. Apropos of the murder of Albert Fairchild by his hired man, the District Attorney remarks:

"You don't know the kind of murderers we raise here in the country. The chances are that your city assassin would be tortured by remorse, if he escaped discovery, and that he committed the deed in a moment of passion. But the rural murderer (I am speaking of native Americans, now) plans the thing in cold blood, and goes at it systematically, with nerves like steel. He generally even mutilates the body, or does some other horrible thing, which it makes everybody's blood boil to think of. And so long as he isn't found out, he never dreams of remorse. He has no more moral perspective than a woodchuck. But when detection does come, it knocks him all in a heap. He blubbers, and tries to lay it on somebody else, and altogether acts like a cur—just as this fellow's doing now, for instance."

The Lawton Girl (1890), a story of a girl who returns to her native village to live down the shame of her former life there, is faithful to the atmosphere of a small manufacturing town in New York; the conflict of capital and labor is not permitted to eclipse the interest in the central character. Jessica Lawton differs from the old-fashioned "wronged woman," for not only does she refrain from marrying the hero of the story but she also retains a certain amount of affection for her earlier betrayer and accepts a share of the responsibility for her own downfall. It is much better than Frederic's historical romance *In the Valley* (1890), laid in the Mohawk Valley before, during, and after the Revolution. The lack of incisive characters and his determination to prove that the defeat of St. Leger's campaign was the great fight of the Revolution are its principal defects. *The Return of the O'Mahony* (1892) is an amusing fantasy retailing the adventures of a false and a real heir, both from America, to a poverty stricken estate on the west coast of Ireland. The two Americans are real enough, but most of the novel is comic opera.

When Frederic returned to his native State of a more recent time, he did much more important work. The Civil War was near enough for him to write of it, not as a romance of heroism but as a bitter struggle of conflicting opinion in the North. In *The Copperhead* (1893) he drew a real character, Abner Beach, a farmer, a Democrat and an anti-abolitionist who refuses to change his opinions when war comes on. The hysteria of war, the intolerance that ostracizes Abner, first with petty tyranny and finally with the destruction of his house, is vividly portrayed. He is an individual who will not yield, and he pays the penalty meted out to many in that time. Frederic continued in his volume of short stories, *Marsena and Other Stories of the Wartime* (1894), to depict some of the less usual phases of the conflict. The scene in the surgeon's tent after Malvern Hill in which Julia Parmalee, an inconstant young woman whose war services are prompted by various motives, pulls her skirt away from a dying soldier because he is a mere private and then only dimly recognizes in the corpse a man with whom she had flirted quite violently at home, shows Frederic as a realist at heart.

It was in *The Damnation of Theron Ware* (1896), however, that Frederic wrote one of the best novels of the period. It was an ambitious theme, dangerous in fiction—the revelation of the fall of a Methodist minister from the simple sincere days of his early ministry until his degradation when, after a debauch, he is saved from utter ruin by Sister Soulsby, the revivalist, through her common sense, advice, and help. Frederic drew with skill the conflict between the emotionalism, the crudity, and the meanness of the small-town Methodist congregation, which even forces Ware's wife, Annie, to take the flowers out of her bonnet, and Ware's growing knowledge of his own ignorance and his desire to study and progress. But the novelist knew that this would not be enough. So he created in Celia Madden, the handsome, independent, pagan daughter of an Irish emigrant who has grown rich, the concrete influence which brings upon Ware his ruin. It is really his passion for Celia which makes him jealous of her friendship for Father Forbes, her pastor, and, while his admiration for the culture which Celia, Father Forbes, and his agnostic friend Dr. Ledsmar represent makes him discontented with his own limitations, Frederic shows well how Ware would and did square his ideals with the practical duty of earning a living. The forces which keep him from giving up his ministry, because of his disgust with the camp-meeting methods and emotional soul saving of the revivals, are represented by two well-sketched characters, Brother and Sister Soulsby. Sister Soulsby's conversation with Ware reveals the character of a woman who has been an actress and has almost been indicted for illegal practices, but who can influence a crowd of people through her dramatic appeal and who, moreover, believes she is doing an important job. It is, of course, the moral contrast again. Hearing that Father Forbes and Celia are going to New York, Ware jumps at the conclusion that they have illicit relations. He follows them, and realism has rarely gone farther than the description of his sordid ride in the day coach and his futile helpless pursuit of them to the Murray Hill Hotel, where they are trying to save her young brother from the consequences of his drunken debauch. Then when he forces his way into Celia's "parlor" she tells him the whole truth:

"It is all in a single word, Mr. Ware," she proceeded, in low tones. "I speak for others as well as myself, mind you,—we find that you are a bore."

Frederic's understanding of racial and theological ideas is at times penetrating; for example, his analysis of the conflicting elements in the Irish character and his contrast of the Greek and the Hebrew ideal of life in Christianity. Frederic's picture of the Catholic Church is very interesting, but he is drawing with sympathy only one element in it, that of the man who loves its artistic side and is not concerned with dogma. He leaves out the devotional side of all the churches, and he seems to be the coiner of the phrase that in the Episcopal Church "nobody seems to have to believe particularly in anything except the beauty of its burial service." The general effect of this book is to paint religions as necessary concessions to human weakness. But, being an artist, he does this without descending into crude caricature as Sinclair Lewis does in *Elmer Gantry*. His people are real, and he never allows them to become shrill or disgusting, however he may be turning their souls inside out. His satire is therefore all the more effective. While *Elmer Gantry* is so obviously overdrawn that the instinctive reaction even by those who may dislike Methodism is a feeling in its favor, *Theron Ware* produces just the opposite effect.

In his last stories Frederic drew upon his knowledge of English life. *March Hares* (1896) is a charming romantic novelette, with an illusion of reality. *Gloria Mundi* (1898) is more important because, through the career of Christian Tower who by a series of sudden deaths becomes heir to the dukedom of Glastonbury, Frederic represented the strength and weakness of the English patrician system and the materialistic basis of its social structure, without satire, but as a contrast to the truer democracy of the Middle Ages. *The Market Place* (1899), a story of the interrelations of English society and the stock market, contains a very real character, Joel Thorpe, the promoter, who makes a fortune by a clever trick and proceeds ruthlessly to buy and force his way into the position of a country gentleman, only to be bored by a life for which he is not suited. While Frederic wrote at times with the easy facility of a journalist, he rose above it in his best work; his charming style, his natural dialogue, and his sympathy with the individual who is fighting against odds make his novels far above the average. *Gloria Mundi* and *The Market Place* were both published after Frederic's early death.

It was only natural that the impulse toward realism should find material in the Middle West. True as Mark Twain was to reality in details, he was at heart a romantic-idealist, a creator of types. In 1839 Mrs. Caroline Kirkland had published her accurate picture of life in Michigan, and her son, Joseph Kirkland (1830–1894), who though born in New York grew up in Michigan and Illinois, wrote in *Zury* (1887), a realistic story of the pioneers in Illinois, beginning in "the first quarter of the 19th century" and continuing until the 'fifties. The central character, Usury Prouder, who is a boy when his father, Ephraim, "takes up" a section of the public land, grows up among bitter hardships. How could extreme poverty be more simply described than in the passage which tells of the death of Zury's little sister?

Ephraim called Zury in from the path which his trampling had kept open in the snow, and both men sat by the fireside till morning, while Selina straightened the wasted limbs, put on the poor girl's poor best clothes, tied up the sharp chin and closed the eyes with—something. They had no coins to lay on the lids.

The whole family had not money enough, nor even credit enough, to provide a coffin for the child.

Zury is not a rebel against conditions for he behaves ruthlessly when he has the power, especially in his relations with his two wives and with Anne Sparrow, the school teacher, and he wins whatever he tries for by whatever means he has at hand. There are sentimental and conventional episodes in *Zury* such as Anne's marriage with McVey, after she realizes she is with child by Zury but the impression is that of real life, and Garland has acknowledged Kirkland's influence.

In the sequel to *Zury*, *The McVeys* (1888), Kirkland told of the lives of Philip and Margaret McVey, the twin children of Zury and Anne, born of their one night together on the cliff, and he attempted the unusual experiment of writing of a period which he had already covered in *Zury*. He had the courage, unusual at that time, of killing Philip and leaving Margaret to her old-maidhood. But perhaps he felt that Anne was the real center of interest, and surely she remains an unusual picture of a woman who makes one great mistake and atones for it. There is a quietly effective scene at Philip's death, when Zury refrains under great temptation from telling him of his fatherhood, knowing that it will destroy Philip's reverence for his mother. Kirkland wrote also *The Captain of Company K* (1891), a realistic picture of the Civil War; especially the attack on Fort Donelson and the battle of Corinth. The picture of Captain Fargeon's first skirmish, in which he is afraid but conquers his fear, rivals those of DeForest and was based on Major Kirkland's own experiences in the Civil War. The sordid side of camp life is given without concealment, and the way the regiment and Company K were left to their own devices in crucial moments reveals one of the reasons for the Union defeats in the early days of the war.

There was nothing of the reformer in Kirkland, but Hamlin Garland (1860–   ) was filled with the crusading spirit. Born in Wisconsin, he knew farming life there and in Iowa and South Dakota. Repelled by that life, he went to Boston, studied and taught at the Boston School of Oratory, and came under the inspiration of Howells. A visit to his family in 1887 suggested the use of the life of the Mississippi Valley for fiction, and he wrote from 1887 to 1890 a number of short stories, representing usually with an uncompromising realism the hardships of the farmer's lot. Six of these stories were published in 1891 as *Main Travelled Roads* and, while five others were added in later editions, and two other collections, *Prairie Folk* (1892) and *Wayside Courtships* (1897), were combined with some judicious omissions in 1910 as *Other Main Travelled Roads,* the stories were all composed during the period of 1887 to 1890,[2] and should be considered together.

The tragic stories are the best. In "The Return of a Private" there is a vivid picture of the unromantic nature of the solitary homecoming of a soldier, racked with fever, to his family. No flags are waving, even his own people are away for the moment at a neighbor's, and his youngest child does not know him. He is no hero to the neighbors and in their quick forgetting of the martial feeling there is something very American. For, as a people, we dislike war; when it is necessary we will fight, but we look upon war as an interruption. The ending of the story is masterly:

The common soldier of the American volunteer army had returned. His war with the South was over, his fight, his daily running fight with nature and against the injustice of his fellow men was begun again.

It is the way Garland frames this protest against injustice of any kind that makes these stories important in our literature. "Under the Lion's Paw" is a bitter story of the renting farmer who has to pay more to the grasping owner for the very improvements he has made by his own grinding toil. "Up the Cooly" surges with the hate of the farmer for his

[2] Statement of Mr. Garland to the writer.

brother who has become successful in the theatrical business and who has neglected his own people. Garland does not usually suggest a remedy, which makes the tragedy more dramatic. But in "A Branch Road," when the man who has left the girl he loved, for a fancied slight, returns to find her married to his rival who ill-treats her, he takes her away in defiance of moral law. In this story and in "Lucretia Burns" Garland vies with Mary Wilkins in the picture of the hopeless monotony of farm life, especially for the women. "Where in this wide earth, with its forthshooting fruits and grains, its fragrant lands and shining seas, could this dwarfed, bent, broken middle-aged woman go? Nobody wanted her, nobody cared for her."

The evils which result from the frenzied emotional reactions created by the revivalist are graphically treated in "Elder Pill, Preacher" and "A Day of Grace." On the other hand, in "A Preacher's Love Story" he shows the difference between real and false religion. What lifts many of these stories, especially the earliest, into distinction is the hard fight the people make. He does not give us misery just for its own sake, as E. W. Howe did. Even "Daddy Deering," a man who has lost his health and has no resources left, goes out into the snow and dies "with a frown of resolution on his face, as if he had fancied Death coming and had gone defiantly forth to meet him." Garland is best in the stories of the Middle West, and already in *Wayside Courtships* he showed the unevenness of his art when he attempted to describe the clash of caste in the Far West in "A Meeting in the Foothills."

In his first novels Garland the reformer overshadowed Garland the artist. *A Spoil of Office* (1892) gives an accurate picture of the rise of the Grange and the Farmers' Alliance; the way the people rebel against the Republican party and yet hesitate to join the Democratic because it has been the party of secession is of interest to the political historian. But Garland himself realized later that these matters are not sufficient to make a novel. In *Roadside Meetings* he remarks, "The stories which live, the poems we still quote, had nothing to do with the political unrest." In *A Member of the Third House* (1892), he drew a picture of the methods of influencing railroad legislation in a State capitol. But again the people are merely types. Much better was his novelette, *A Little Norsk* (1892), in which against the bitter cold and the hardships of the Dakota farm life is set a story of two farmers who bring up a little girl whom they have saved from freezing, only to have her marry a worthless chap who deserts her. The characters are individualized, and the distinction between the loves of the two men for the girl is quite well drawn.

Garland's first long novel of importance, *Rose of Dutcher's Cooley* (1895), had been written in Chicago and Boston in 1892 and 1893. It is a real portrait of a Wisconsin girl who, revolting against the ceaseless toil and hopeless monotony of the life on a farm, studies at the University of Wisconsin and goes to Chicago, trying to write. Garland draws a good picture of the beginnings of literary interest in Chicago, where he was the founder of the "Cliff Dwellers." It is possible that Warren Mason, the newspaper man, drifting, cynical, and disillusioned, may reflect some of Garland's own experiences. Her struggles not only to find a vocation but also to find herself make Rose a very appealing character, and her marriage with Mason is the result of no sudden infatuation but of a gradual realization of their need for each other, recognized after hesitation on both sides. Here again Garland is a realist, and his dramatic sense was evident in the description of the storm on Lake Michigan. The incident of the captain sailing his ship on the rocks in order that he might remain in control until the very end represents Garland's style at its best. Garland put his critical theories into a series of essays, *Crumbling Idols* (1894) which have now a certain historical interest because they reveal the strength and the weakness of the provincial point of view. He was possessed by the belief that Americans should write only of the American scene, not seeing that this theory is a limitation, not a widening, of the borders of art, and that if it had been applied to English literature we should lose, among other masterpieces, *Hamlet* and *Othello*. Shakespeare, incidentally, is one of the idols that is crumbling! With Garland's pleas for sincerity and originality one cannot help sympathizing, but his fallacy lies in these words, "the question for America to settle is not whether it can produce something *greater* than the past, but whether it can produce something *different* from the past." Since the same mistake is sounding from critical journals today it is necessary perhaps to emphasize the stern fact that mere "difference" is never of importance. It all depends on what the difference consists in. Garland is right when he says that the Middle West of the 'nineties was the most conservative and imitative portion of America in its literature and art, and he did a real service in treating his section in a fresh and vigorous way. But he failed to see that the very "universality" against which he was inveighing was the reason for the superiority of his early work to the fiction that came from him after 1900. It was not so much the fact that "The Return of a Private" was laid in the Middle West that clutches at the heartstrings of the reader. It is the spectacle of the lonely man returning to his home after making a supreme sacrifice, not for Wisconsin but for the Union, and finding no reward for his service, that makes the story. It could as a matter of fact have been laid anywhere, North or South, with equal truth. It is the *way* Garland told it that mattered.

By a seeming paradox, but one that is easily explainable, Garland's work declined in importance as it became more popularly successful. He is not correct, however, when he attributes his decline as an artist wholly to the insidious temptations of the popular magazine. It is true that, spurred on by his first financial success, *The Captain of the Gray Horse Troop* (1902), he let his art grow more superficial and depended for his results more upon the selection of striking incidents than upon insight into character. But it was also his theory that new material and new locality would necessarily prove inspiring which led him to the Far West in search of it. He knew the Sioux Indians by observation, at least, and *The Captain of the Gray Horse Troop* became a rambling story whose hero is determined to treat the Indians properly, and who is hampered by political interference and the white settlers on the Indian lands. It was spoiled partly by propaganda, but its great lack was that of character drawing. This element is somewhat stronger in *Hesper* (1903), a story of the Cripple Creek labor troubles, in which he makes the three conflicting elements, the mine owners, the unionized miners, and the independent miners, more concrete than is usually the case with capital and labor stories. Matt Kelly, who represents the independent miners, is especially well done, because Garland, who is an individualist, is most sympathetic with the man who wishes to preserve his independence. But as usual, the theme overshadows the personalities, and the conversations are at times hopeless. *The Light of the Star* (1904), a romance of the theatre in New York, has a certain reality in the difficulties which a playwright with high ideals experiences, but also an unreality in the relations of the leading actress and the dramatist. In 1907 he returned to Colorado in *Money Magic*, a study of a self-made woman, the daughter of a boarding-house keeper at Sibley Junction. Garland, as before in his Far Western stories, creates a highly romantic situation, in which Bertha marries a gambler, Mort Haney, on his supposed death-bed, and then tries to work out their married life together in a realistic manner, with only fair success.

Cavanagh, Forest Ranger (1910) is probably the best of the Far West novels of Garland. Conservation of the natural resources of the United States had been much in the public eye during Theodore Roosevelt's administration, and Garland wished to represent the conditions in Wyoming, Colorado, and Montana as they formed the background for the conflict between the old cattle barons and the power of Federal law. Ross Cavanagh, an Englishman who has for some time been in the United States, is the protagonist in the struggle. There are descriptions of the West as it really was, stripped of romance. As one of the characters describes it:

"The cowman was conceived in anarchy and educated in murder. Whatever romantic notions I may have had of the plains twenty-five years ago, they are lost to me now. The free-range stock-owner has no country and no God; nothing but a range that isn't his, and damned bad manners—begging pardon, Miss Wetherford. The sooner he dies the better for the State. He's a dirty, wasteful sloven, content to eat canned beans and drink canned milk in his rotten bad coffee; and nobody but an old crank like myself has the grace to stand up and tell the truth about him."

By 1914 Garland relapsed into the conventional melodrama of *The Forester's Daughter*, a story of Colorado. But already he was preparing something much more significant. In 1898 he had begun to write a narrative of his own and his family's experiences in their pioneer life, and after many revisions it was published in 1917 as *A Son of the Middle Border*, having appeared as a serial in 1914. Strictly speaking, it is not fiction, since the events are real, but Garland has dramatized the movements of the pioneer from the return of his father, Richard Garland, from the Civil War, until the family, often separated, comes together once more in Wisconsin about 1893. The interest of the narrative, which seems like a return to reality after his excursions into the idealistic romance of the Far West, and the similarity of his material to that of his earliest stories is illustrated by the very first episode, which had been the inspiration of "The Return of a Private" in *Main Travelled Roads*. In *A Son of the Middle Border* the roving spirit which prompted his father to move on from Wisconsin to Iowa and thence to Dakota becomes the symbol of a great movement in our national life. It is told, too, with a charm that is missing in *Main Travelled Roads*, a charm that comes from the softening influence of memory. Garland does not ideal-ize the picture into untruth, however, for he never hesitates to tell of the sufferings his mother faced, or how little chivalry existed in the relations of the sexes, and even the animals are pictured as the unfeeling brutes they appeared to be to the boy who had to tend them. The description of the rush of the steers after they have scented blood has a fine note of the primitive about it.

Garland continued in *A Daughter of the Middle Border* (1921) with his life after his marriage, but while his account of Chicago and his rela-tions with writers there is interesting, it has not the significance of the first book. In the third number of the series, *Trail Makers of the Middle Border* (1926), he adopted more definitely the methods of the novel, giving fictitious names to the older generation of pioneers who left New England and settled the Middle West. The disguise is thin, however; Richard Graham is his father, and the most vivid portions of the book are those of which Garland knew at first hand. *Back Trailers from the Middle Border* (1928) is the least important of the series, for while there is a certain significance in the retracement of the Western family to the East, a movement which is affecting our economic and financial life to a greater extent than is usually recognized, Garland does not paint that return in as large a manner as he did the earlier invasion of the West. The four books, however, form an epic of migration, of struggle and discouragement, of the conquest of unfriendly nature, and of hu-man indifference which no historian of literature or of life may neglect.

Of this group of realists who began in the 'eighties, Margaretta Wade Campbell Deland (1857–   ) drew characters with the firmest strokes. She was born in Manchester, now a part of Allegheny, Pennsylvania, but then an attractive small town. It is probably the origin of "Ashurst" and "Old Chester," where so many of her novels are laid.[3] Her educa-tion at Cooper Institute, which led to her instructorship in drawing and design at what is now Hunter College, New York City, probably helped in giving to her fiction that sense of construction for which she rightly became noted. Since her marriage to Lorin F. Deland in 1880, she has lived in Boston or in Cambridge.

She began as a poet with *The Old Garden and Other Verses* (1886), but she first attracted marked attention by her novel, *John Ward, Preacher* (1888). It appeared in the same year as Mrs. Humphry

---

[3] See her charming account of her childhood, *If This Be I* (1935).

Ward's *Robert Elsmere*, and it was a striking coincidence that these two literary daughters of George Eliot should have chosen to treat of the conflict between conservative and liberal ideas in religion. Such discussion was of course in the air. To read Huxley, Herbert Spencer, and John Fiske was to be a bit dangerously progressive, and the heroine of James A. Herne's play *Shore Acres* was forbidden by her father to scan Howells' *A Hazard of New Fortunes!* In order to make the contrast as strong as possible, Mrs. Deland created in John Ward a nineteenth-century Jonathan Edwards, gentle in spirit, but relentless as a preacher of the most extreme Calvinistic doctrines. There is no struggle in John Ward's soul concerning the truth of these dogmas. The conflict occurs between his doctrines and his love for Helen Jeffrey, who has been brought up by her uncle, the Episcopal rector of Ashurst, without any strong interest in dogma, but with a positive disbelief in hell. Again Mrs. Deland makes the issue as definite as possible by the narrow-minded parishioners of John Ward in Lockhaven, where he and Helen live after their marriage. Finally, in order to save her soul, John Ward refuses to allow her to live with him until she believes as he does. It is only on his death-bed that he sends for her, and apparently he raises then no question of her disbelief. Mrs. Deland revealed in her first novel the limitation of such a conflict as material for fiction. Despite the great love that is said to exist between John Ward and Helen, it is irritation rather than sympathy that is excited, for the reader feels that the whole matter could so easily have been settled. But in two of the minor characters, Mr. Denner, the little elderly lawyer, and Dr. Howe, the easy going rector of a somnolent town, where gentility is the only important creed, Mrs. Deland showed the promise of her later achievement. Mr. Denner, whose whole life has been pale and insignificant flashes into one moment of heroism when he stops the runaway horses of Mrs. Forsythe and Lois Howe, but he loses his own life. The death scene of the quiet little man when he appeals to Dr. Howe for the certainty of immortality that his friend cannot give him is remarkable, both for what it states and what it omits. Too long to quote entire, the last few paragraphs will show its quality:

The rector was silent.
"I have wondered about it often," the other continued. "I have expected —this, for some days, and I have wondered. Think how strange: in a few

days—almost a few hours, I shall know all, or—nothing! Yes, the mystery of all the ages will be mine!" There was a thrill of triumph in his feeble voice. "Think of that, doctor. I shall know more than the wisest man that lives,—I! I was never a very clever person, never very wise; and yet, here is a knowledge which shall not be too wonderful for me, and to which I can attain."

He held up his little thin hand, peering at the light between the transparent fingers. "To think," he said slowly, with a puzzled smile, "to think that this is going to be still! It has never been any power in the world; I don't know that it has ever done any harm, yet it has certainly never done any good; but soon it will be still. How strange, how strange! And where shall I be? Knowing—or perhaps fallen on an eternal sleep. How does it seem to you, doctor? That was what I wanted to ask you; do you feel sure of anything—afterwards?"

The rector could not escape the penetrating gaze of those strangely bright brown eyes. He looked into them, and then wavered and turned away.

"Do you?" said the lawyer.

The other put his hands up to his face a moment.

"Ah!" he answered sharply, "I don't know—I can't tell. I—I don't know, Denner!"

"No," replied Mr. Denner, with tranquil satisfaction, "I supposed not,— I supposed not. But when a man gets where I am, it seems the one thing in the world worth being sure of."

In *Sidney* (1890) Mrs. Deland continued her study of temperaments and moral questions. The great fact of love is the animating force of the book, and the futility of Major Lee's effort to keep his daughter Sidney from any deep experience because it will lead to unhappiness is clearly shown. Even if her love for Alan Crossan has only a short time for its expression, "it was worth while," and the faith that her father would also have kept from her comes to comfort her. As before, some minor characters like Mrs. Paul, a terrible old woman, and Robert Steele, a study in a morbidly active conscience, are etched sharply, and the tragedy leaves one with no feeling of depression.

Philip and his Wife (1894) is a searching study of married life, even if the central situation is a bit strained. Philip Shore is an idealist and, knowing that he has ceased to care for his wife, Cecil, he proposes to separate from her rather than continue in what he feels is an immoral relation. Cecil has no objection, but the consequent legal details bring into the novel a disturbing element in the lawyer, Roger Carey. Mrs. Deland shows clearly, through Carey, how a man may love one woman and know that she will make him an admirable wife, while at the same

time he has an infatuation for another. The novel is a powerful arraignment of selfishness in many forms, especially those subtler aspects like
Philip's moral qualms. As Cecil says in the end to Dr. Lavendar, "Tell
Philip, Cecil says 'You saved yourself, so you could not save anyone
else.'"

Throughout this early period Mrs. Deland had been publishing short
stories which were distinctly preparatory to later achievements. The best
can be found most easily in *Mr. Tommy Dove and Other Stories* (1893)
and *The Wisdom of Fools* (1897). There is the note of sacrifice to ideals
and at times of their shattering in the clear light of reality. In "Elizabeth" a woman tries to keep a widower true to the memory of his dead
wife, even though she herself loves him, only to find him turning for
comfort to less vigorous spiritual tonic. Mrs. Deland's humor, one of her
strongest claims to attention, shows delightfully in "The Fourth Class
Appointment." Many problems are proposed. Is it necessary for a forger
who has lived an upright life for twenty years to confess his crime to his
fiancée? Is it right for a dependent widow to live upon money given to
her by a brother who is grinding it out of his employees? Is it wise to
save a woman who has "gone wrong" if she really does not want to be
straight? Mrs. Deland does not attempt to solve these problems; being
an artist, not a sociologist, she is content to show them concretely.

The quality of Mrs. Deland's short story reached its highest expression in the two collections *Old Chester Tales* (1898) and *Dr. Lavendar's
People* (1903). While Dr. Lavendar had already appeared in her fiction, it was in these stories that he became established as one of the
real contributions to American character portraiture. If she had painted
the easy-going rector in Dr. Howe, she could also draw the positive but
kindly parson, the embodiment of good sense, narrow in some of his
views, but with a great knowledge of the material he has to work with,
that is, the people of his village. Everyone loves and respects him. His
sympathy is quick and yet he is never sentimental. He does not believe
much in organized or impersonal charity, but he does believe in a sinner's
being saved and he thinks that a sinner can often be saved best through
punishment. He is the concrete exponent of Mrs. Deland's belief that
there is a higher law than human law, a Divine Equity in which the
fatherhood of God is emphasized quite as much as the brotherhood of
Christ. In "The Child's Mother," in which Dr. Lavendar prevents a
worthless woman from taking the child she has abandoned from the wo-

man who has become her spiritual mother, Mrs. Deland speaks of the situation of the little waif as appealing "profoundly to this old man who had never known the deep experience of paternity." Here she has recognized the reason why some of the finest fictional portraits of clergymen, Emanuel Bayard, Cardinal Udeschini, or Dr. Lavendar, have been childless men.

Many of the stories present problems to Dr. Lavendar, and his solutions are prompt and go to the root of the matter. He disposes of the wife who wishes to ease her conscience by telling her husband of her past unworthiness without realizing that it will give him more pain than such a relief of her distress is worth. He summons a girl home from her convent to take the place of an older sister who has postponed her happiness too long through her quiet sacrifice for her family. The scene of his labors, Old Chester, is not definitely placed. It is in the western part of Pennsylvania, "too near Mason and Dixon's line for economical housekeeping," easy-going, conservative. Old Chester is not so much a place as a number of people and a state of mind, for newcomers did not belong to it. The principal characters are feminine, either like Martha King, whose "common sense" and sharp tongue drive her sister Lucy out of her home, or gentle women whose problems are solved by matrimony. Much of the interest of the stories lies in the pungent remarks of Mrs. Deland. The chessboard kept just as its dead owner had left it is not sentimentalized; it is "that pathetic effort of grief to find permanence." The Jay sisters, whose great-grandfather had been a bishop, were filled with "that gentle condescension which is the ecclesiastical form of Christian humility."

Two striking stories, both in *Dr. Lavendar's People*, illustrate Mrs. Deland's constructive power. In "The Note" she creates a situation in which Dr. Lavendar, in order to prevent injustice, commits a legal crime and lies without hesitation. Having been told by his old friend John Gordon to destroy a promissory note given to Gordon by his son-in-law Algy Keen, and knowing that John's son Alexander will demand the full payment out of revenge for the disgrace of the earlier seduction of his sister and her hasty marriage to Keen, Dr. Lavendar learns of John Gordon's sudden death. The power of attorney John Gordon has given him is worthless, but Dr. Lavendar, knowing also how Algy Keen has been struggling to live decently after his wife's death, decides that he must carry out John Gordon's wishes. So he burns the note. But while Dr. Lavendar is willing to place equity above the law for others, he holds himself to the strictest obligation. So he sends the following letter to Alexander Gordon:

My dear Alexander,—I owe your father's estate to the amount of the enclosed check. No papers exist in regard to it, as the matter was between ourselves. I will ask you for a receipt.

Yours truly,
EDWARD LAVENDAR.

He is rather an accessory than a principal in "An Exceeding High Mountain," but his influence is clearly shown. The story is based on a profound knowledge of human nature, to which the preservation of a cherished illusion is so precious. Robert Gray has married abroad an English girl, Alys Winton, who had been abandoned suddenly by the family in which she had been the governess. She dies after giving birth to a daughter, Alice, and Robert idealizes her memory. When Rebecca Jones, a plain young woman who worships him, is finally rewarded for her devotion by being married by him, she becomes, with some reason, insanely jealous of the worship he still cherishes for his first wife. Alice learns through her fiancé, a young editor, that an inheritance of £5000 awaits "the child of Alys Winton," and Mrs. Deland admirably portrays the varying emotions of joy and wonder which first fill the minds of the young people, to whom the bequest means happiness. Then comes the realization, when the lawyer in charge of the estate arrives in Old Chester, that the acceptance of the bequest from the former employer of Alys Winton means the recognition that she was his mistress and that Alice is not Robert Gray's child. Robert Gray is away on his vacation, and Alice is inclined to accept the bequest. Rebecca at first is filled with an unholy joy that at last the woman she could never supplant will be dethroned and perhaps her husband will turn to her at last. Her moral struggle through the night, her decision to keep the knowledge from Robert Gray at the cost of the money, her domination of Alice, build a character into spiritual greatness. Through all the struggle Dr. Lavendar enters at just the right moments to support Rebecca and Alice in their sacrifice.

Dr. Lavendar plays a major part in Mrs. Deland's best novel, *The Awakening of Helena Richie* (1906), a superb study of the moral and spiritual growth of a selfish woman. Mrs. Deland puts the case for rebellion against the moral code strongly and yet shows the weakness of the doctrine that individual happiness is all important and that passion makes any situation sacred. Helena Richie is married to a drunkard who has been responsible for the death of their child, and when she leaves him for her lover, Lloyd Pryor, her husband refuses to divorce her. Some time during the 'sixties she comes to Old Chester where she represents Pryor as her brother. Charming, reserved, a woman of breeding, she is suspected only by old Benjamin Wright, who has himself had experiences that make him competent to judge her correctly. His revelation to his grandson, who worships her, and the boy's suicide savor a bit of melodrama, but the main story, which concerns the cooling of Pryor's passion and the breakdown of a relation which has been built upon selfishness, is told with the relentless surety of a realist who produces her effects concretely and whose characters talk like human beings. One of the best characters is that of the village physician, Dr. King, through whom she is placed in charge of a little orphan boy, David. Dr. King, like all the men, is fascinated by her, but he never lets her see it, and her confession to him of her relations with Pryor is a magnificently quiet scene. She grows to love David deeply, and the child's absorption in his own concerns provides some delightful humor. Naturally and inevitably, David brings the situation to a climax. When Helena's husband dies, Pryor, a widower with a young daughter he adores, wishes to avoid a marriage with Helena, and makes her choose between him and David. She chooses David, for she has really ceased to love Pryor, and he has become only a means by which she can put an end to her anomalous situation. Then there occurs the remarkable scene with Dr. Lavendar:

"You thought it would make everything right if you married this man?"

"Right?" she repeated, surprised; "why, of course. At least I suppose that is what good people call right," she added dully.

"And you gave up doing right, to have David?"

She felt that she was trapped, and yet she could not understand why; "I sacrificed myself," she said confusedly.

"No," said Dr. Lavendar; "you sacrificed a conviction. A poor, false conviction, but such as it was, you threw it over to keep David."

She looked at him in terror; "It was just selfishness, you think?"

"Yes," said Dr. Lavendar.

"Perhaps it was," she admitted. "Oh, how frightful life is! To try to be happy, is to be bad."

"No; to try to be happy at the expense of other people, is to be bad."

"But I never did that! Lloyd's wife was dead;—Of course, if she had been alive"—Helena lifted her head with the curious pride of caste in sin which is so strongly felt by the woman who is a sinner;—"if she had been alive, I wouldn't have thought of such a thing. But nobody knew; so I never did any harm,"—then she quailed; "at least, I never meant to do any harm. So you can't say it was at anybody's expense."

"It was at everybody's expense. Marriage is what makes us civilized. If anybody injures marriage we all pay."

She was silent.

"If every dissatisfied wife should do what you did, could decent life go on? Wouldn't we all drop down a little nearer the animals?"

"Perhaps so," she said vaguely. But she was not following him. She had entered into this experience of sin, not by the door of reason, but of emotion; she could leave it only by the same door. The high appeal to individual renunciation for the good of the many, was entirely beyond her. Dr. Lavendar did not press it any further.

He tells her she is not a fit woman to bring up David, and she agrees to give him up. Through her consequent suffering and conflict with herself, Dr. Lavendar watches her, knowing she must win her own fight, and finally she goes off to begin life again in a distant city. Then, just as keenly as he had put aside the confusions of her moral judgments, he recognizes that David needs her and she needs him, and they go on together.

The Iron Woman (1911) brings Helena Richie to Mercer, evidently based on the Allegheny City of the late 'sixties, and David grows up in the company of Blair and Nannie Maitland, son and stepdaughter of Mrs. Maitland, the "Iron Woman" who directs the iron works which have been left to her by her husband. She is so busy making money that she has no time to bring up Blair properly; she is a fine picture of a woman whose only recourse in any trouble is to give someone a check. The selfishness of Blair Maitland is balanced by the selfishness of Elizabeth Ferguson, niece of Robert Ferguson, the manager of "the Works." Of the new characters, she is the best drawn. Her frightful tempers, her ruthlessness to herself as well as to others, her inherited tendency to lawlessness produce a woman who wrecks the lives of both Blair and David Richie. When David, whom she really loves, hesitates to marry her until he is able to support her, in a moment of intense resentment she agrees to run off with Blair and repents at once. The novel, which has dragged somewhat during the details concerning Mrs. Maitland's death, rises to a fine climax in the midnight journey of Elizabeth to David, and in Helena Richie's pursuit to save her son from the ruin of his career as a physician which the consequent scandal will produce. After every other argument has broken down against the passion of David and Elizabeth's response to it, she destroys the ideal which David has built up through the years of her devotion to him:

As she stood there a slow illumination grew in her face—the knowledge, tragic, and triumphant, that if Love would save others, itself it cannot save! . . . "I'm not afraid that he will tire of me," Elizabeth had said; and David's mother, looking at him with ineffable compassion, said, very gently:
"I was not afraid of that, once, myself."
That was all. She was standing up, clinging to the table; her face gray, her chin shaking. They neither of them grasped the sense of her words; then suddenly David caught his breath:
"What did you say?"
"I said—" She stopped. "Oh, my poor David, I wouldn't tell you if I could help it; if only there was any other way! But there isn't. I have tried, oh, I have tried every other way." She put her hands over her face for an instant, then looked at him. "David, I said that I was not afraid, once, myself, that my lover would tire of me." There was absolute silence in the room. "But he did, Elizabeth. He did. He did."
Then David said, "I don't understand."
"Yes, you do; you understand that a man once talked to me just as you are talking to Elizabeth; he said he would marry me when I got my divorce. I think he meant it—just as you mean it, now. At any rate, I believed him. Just as Elizabeth believes you."
David Richie stepped back violently; his whole face shuddered. "You?" he said, "my mother? No!—no!—no!"
And his mother, gathering up her strength, cringing like some faithful dog struck across the face, pointed at him with one shaking hand.
"Elizabeth, did you see how he looked at me? Some day your son will look that way at you."

This scene is powerful because it is based on something elemental which has survived even the sophistication of a later generation. Here the desire of woman for the desire of man comes in conflict with the desire of woman for the respect not only of the man she loves but also of the son she may bear. Helena Richie saves David and Elizabeth from folly and, from the point of construction, the novel should have ended there. For the conclusion is unsatisfactory, as indeed it had to be, perhaps, with no Dr. Lavendar to tell them what to do.

While she was writing her two most important novels, Mrs. Deland continued her short stories, the best of which are included in *R. J.'s Mother and Some Other People* (1908) and *Around Old Chester* (1915). In the first collection "The Black Drop" puts definitely and forcibly the tragedy of mixed blood, and contrasts favorably with the sentimentality of Howells' "An Imperative Duty." "The White Feather" approaches Mrs. Wharton in its treatment of the novelist who is driven to publish inferior work by his wife's insistence. In *Around Old Chester,* Dr. Lavendar is bringing his career to a close by straightening out tangles of petty tyranny in "An Encore" or by stripping a self-deceiver of his pretences in "The Thief." Many of these stories are comedies; there is delightful irony in Dr. Lavendar's efforts to help his young Presbyterian rival to win the girl he loves. The stories are usually laid before or during the Civil War, but the interest is not definitely historical. Mrs. Deland tended more and more to the very long short story which had separate publication, such as *Partners* (1913), a comedy of a small-town post-office, or *The Hands of Esau* (1914), an ethical problem of a young man's premarital concealment of his father's criminal record. These were not in her best manner, and her novels, *The Rising Tide* (1916), a story of a militant suffragette, and *The Vehement Flame* (1922), an absurd love story of a boy of eighteen and a woman about forty, made Mrs. Deland's admirers feel that her significant period was over. But among the three novelettes published together in 1924 as *New Friends in Old Chester,* "The Elliots' Katy" is a fine story of the devotion of an English servant, first to the family of her mistress and later to her own daughter, who is ashamed of her. Katy denies her child in a scene that at once brings *Madame Delphine* to mind, and the superiority of Cable's story proved again that for an heroic situation the dialect of the Creole octoroon is much better adapted than that of an illiterate Englishwoman, if only on account of its unfamiliarity. There is some power in *The Kays* (1926), in the character drawing of a New England woman, a hard taskmistress to herself and to her husband, who, like many of Mrs. Deland's citizens of Old Chester, is a hard drinker. The sacrifice of Agnes Kay in keeping a demented mistress of her husband in her own home would have been more effective as a motive if it had not been so incredible. Mrs. Deland had drawn the Puritan conscience in a novelette, *The Promises of Alice* (1919), and in 1932 *Captain Archer's Daughter* is laid in a Maine seaport at an indefinitely past time. The contrasts among the Archers, native descendants of the old shipping families, the "summer people," and the Caseys, representative of an earlier invasion, have a flavor of her best period.

Among the classic realists who began in the 'eighties, Mrs. Deland remained constant to her method and was unswayed by the romantic idealistic wave of the late 'nineties. She proceeded through the method of insight rather than that of selection. Life in a small town or a grimy city was to her a rich mine of human joy or sorrow, of patience and struggle, of character growth and decay. It is usually growth: tragedies come but the characters grow spiritually. Usually she retains an objective attitude toward the social, ethical and religious problems she presents. No one could tell from her fiction what her own creed may be, but her liberality is not mere tolerance. Tolerance always implies the conquest over a prejudice and is itself an assumption of superiority. Liberality, however, is a quality of the spirit, and it is because she incarnates that spirit in Dr. Lavendar that he is so fine a creation. This liberality shows itself in her treatment of the question of divorce. At times her novels show its futility, at other times she seems to favor it, recognizing the possibility that those who may condemn it as a general proposition may see mitigating circumstances in individual instances.

This avoidance of a final judgment on marriage and divorce is quite in keeping with her code of ethics. Nothing to her is all black or all white. In "The Note" she makes Dr. Lavendar say, "In fact . . . as I get older there is nothing more constantly astonishing to me than the goodness of the Bad;—unless it is the badness of the Good." Here, in brief, is the moral contrast of Bret Harte again, one of the most certainly successful motives of fiction. It is a tribute to its perennial appeal that it could be used both by an artist who refrained from moral judgements and by one whose stories are shot through with moral and ethical implications.

It was an evidence of her artistry that Mrs. Deland during her best period kept these ethical motives from becoming abstract by her power of character portrayal. Dr. Lavendar, Helena Richie, Mrs. Maitland, Elizabeth Ferguson, Mr. Denner, Rebecca Gray, Mrs. Paul, Dr. King are among the best portraits in our fiction. She had a wide knowledge of the motives of action, not probing beneath the surface for evil, but content to reveal hidden springs of conduct which, while not always redounding to the credit of her creations, still made for the better understanding of human nature. As she says in *Sidney:*

Those promises of pardon which we bestow so readily are apt to be given without thought of this terrible and inescapable power of memory. The lover or the husband, the mother or the child, may love as deeply as before the quarrel or the crime, but the remembrance of one bad and cruel word, the color of a tone, the meaning in the glance of an eye, will too often linger in the soul;

such a recollection will start up between two kisses, force itself beneath the hand that blesses, be renewed in vows of renewed tenderness. No assertions of forgiveness or of love can blot it out; it is as immortal as the soul.

In the same novel Alan says to Steele: "I tell you, Bob, there is a point where concern about right and wrong becomes the subtlest kind of egotism." She has no patience with finely spun theories of conduct. "Where two duties jostle one another," Mary Alden tells her niece, "one of them isn't a duty." To Dr. Lavendar, "Virtue is just temptation overcome."

While her satiric gifts and her genial and humorous outlook keep her books from being solemn, Mrs. Deland is serious in her art. She likes to paint lives in which there is no glory to keep up the spirits but in which some middle-aged, uninspired person, usually a woman, plays a great part with no reward but her invincible self-respect. Every life, moreover, is worth while; to have worked hard, to have suffered in silence, to have given up for an ideal or for some other human being the favorite object of their desires, all this was worth while. There is no railing at conditions, social or economic, no bitter arraignment of divine or human law, but a series of pictures of real people,.often provincial and frequently narrow-minded, but with a capacity for letting other people manage their own affairs, and for playing the game according to the rules, as characteristic perhaps of Pennsylvania as the Puritan conscience is of New England.

That these novelists do not exhaust the long list of those who, beginning in the 'eighties, have held up the spiritual, moral, and economic institutions of the United States to the observation of their fellow countrymen goes without saying. Criticism of American life was to take other directions than those pursued by the writers treated in this chapter, whose unifying quality was their serious concern with their material even if they covered that concern at times with the glamour of poetry. Their material was not so much local as moral and ethical. Problems were faced and faced squarely, and this group of writers like their great leader Howells, were earnest in their clear-sighted love of justice. They did their best work usually in the late 'eighties, in the 'nineties, or in the first decade of the twentieth century. To the 'eighties belong *A Humble Romance, John Ward, Preacher,* and *Seth's Brother's Wife;* in the 'nineties, *Jane Field, Pembroke, Tiverton Tales, The Damnation of Theron Ware, Old Chester Tales, Main Travelled Roads* and *Rose of Dutcher's Cooley,* while the new century had to its credit *The Story of Thyrza, Unleavened Bread, The Chippendales, The Awakening of Helena Richie, Dr. Lavendar's*

People, The Iron Woman and *A Son of the Middle Border.* These are only the most notable contributions of the movement, but even more important was the steady progress toward the realistic presentation of familiar life.

CHAPTER XXI

JAMES LANE ALLEN AND THE NOVEL OF THE SPIRIT

WHILE he began his work with descriptions of Kentucky life, James Lane Allen (1849–1925) is to be distinguished from the other writers of Southern romance by a steady progression through different methods of treatment, by a more conscious artistry and by a more universal note. He was born near Lexington, Kentucky, graduated in 1872 from the University of Kentucky, known before and after his undergraduate course as Transylvania University, and taught school until 1880, mainly in Kentucky. Three years were spent at Bethany College as Professor of Latin and Higher English; then he returned to Lexington and founded the Allen Grammar School. Feeling that his real interest lay in fiction, he went to New York City in 1884, determined to conquer a place for himself. He had already published some critical articles, the first being upon *The Portrait of a Lady*, for the *Critic* and the *Continent*, but recognition came slowly. The struggle in New York becoming desperate, he was on his way to the railroad station to return to Kentucky and teaching when, as a last resort, he called at the *Evening Post* and proposed a series of articles dealing with Kentucky life. Receiving the commission, he continued on his way, to collect material. These sketches led to his being asked by *Harper's Magazine* to write similar articles, which were ultimately published in 1892 as *The Blue Grass Region of Kentucky*. In the meantime he had been writing short stories. His first, "Too Much Momentum," [1] a satiric account of the marital attack of a Kentucky widow upon her neighbor, is not important. But his second, "Part of An Old Story," [2] is much more significant. Here Allen's imagination produced a powerful and original conception. Two lovers, Angelo and Francesca, beg the magician Cagliostro to give them a draught of the liquid which will permit them to relive the two years since their marriage, which they believe have been happier than any future can be. But when the draught has been taken, they

[1] *Harper's Magazine*, April, 1885.
[2] *Century*, February, 1887.

begin to lose little by little the artistic power and the mental growth they had acquired, and the joys they had experienced together begin to fade. More terrible, neither they nor Cagliostro know whether the elixir will not carry them back past the time of their union into that part of their life before they loved each other. The description beats with the very rhythm of approaching doom. Allen skilfully carries the story to the night of their marriage, when they perish, since the elixir had really ended their natural life at the moment they had taken it and they had been living only by its power for the two years past. It is one of those studies of the fate which awaits those who defy the inexorable laws of Nature which Hawthorne might have created.

It seems strange that Allen did not include "Part of an Old Story" in his first volume, *Flute and Violin* (1891), which contained stories written during the preceding three years. They are the expression in romance of the scenes he describes in *The Blue Grass Region of Kentucky*. "Two Gentlemen of Kentucky" is an appealing character contrast between Colonel Fields, a landholder who could not adjust himself to the conditions after the Civil War, and his devoted servant Peter, formerly his slave. This should be read in conjunction with the descriptive sketch "Uncle Tom at Home," for in both sketch and story Allen has tried to draw a Negro as he was and not as Mrs. Stowe sentimentalized him. "King Solomon of Kentucky," a tale of a white vagrant who rises to heroic heights during the pestilence of 1833, indicates that Allen had read the moral contrasts of Bret Harte; and "Flute and Violin," proves that he knew how to draw pathos from the sufferings of a boy who could not conform to the code of a Kentucky town of 1809. Allen had not achieved complete mastery as yet in his fiction. "The White Cowl," a story of the rebellion of one of the Trappist monks, when compared with "A Home of the Silent Brotherhood" in *The Blue Grass Regions*, shows a tendency to melodrama that is not entirely absent from a story exquisite in some of its phases, "Sister Dolorosa."

It is over forty years since, as a college undergraduate, I read *A Kentucky Cardinal* when it first appeared in *Harper's Magazine* for May and June, 1894, yet I can still remember the impression that was made upon me that here was something that rose out of the mass of magazine writing because it had those qualities which men have agreed to call literature. The novelette was laid in Kentucky in 1850, but there was no note of the provincial in it. It was laid in the universal land of the spirit, and in the dramatic conflict that hovered over the two neighboring gardens where Adam Moss and Georgiana Cobb met, hesitated before they made that self-surrender which is the preface to all great love stories, and finally achieved the triumph which comes only from that self-surrender, Allen epitomized what a lesser artist would have taken a volume to tell. The characters are ideal, but are not merely types. Georgiana has a wilful quality that separates her from the usual sugary heroine of romance. Her test of Adam's love by demanding that he trap the cardinal bird for her and her rejection of him because he has done it lead to the unusual love scene in which Adam tells her some home truths:

". . . If you think a man will not do wrong for a woman, you are mistaken. If you think men always love the wrong that they do for the women whom they love, you are mistaken again. . . .

"You fear I might sacrifice you to something else. It is possible. Every man resists temptation only to a certain point; every man has his price. It is a risk you will run with any. . . .

"I make no defence—believe all that you say. But had you loved me, I might have been all this, and it would have been nothing."

It was in *A Kentucky Cardinal* that Allen revealed through his description of birds and flowers his deep understanding of nature, and his remarkable ability at the choosing of colorful and definite words. Notice how the cardinal is set against the background:

With almost everything earthly that he touches this high herald of the trees is in contrast. Among his kind he is without a peer. Even when the whole company of summer voyagers have sailed back to Kentucky, singing and laughing and kissing one another under the enormous green umbrella of Nature's leaves, he still is beyond them all in loveliness. But when they have been wafted away again to brighter skies and to soft islands over the sea, and he is left alone on the edge of that Northern world which he has dared invade and inhabit, it is then, amid black clouds and drifting snows, that the gorgeous cardinal stands forth in the ideal picture of his destiny. For it is then that his beauty is most conspicuous, and that Death, lover of the peerless, strikes at him from afar.

Or how birds in general are placed in their relation to the fading of the day:

The last hour of light touches the birds as it touches us. When they sing in the morning, it is with the happiness of the earth; but as the shadows fall strangely about them, and the helplessness of the night comes on, their voices seem to be lifted up like the loftiest poetry of the human spirit, with sympathy for realities and mysteries past all understanding.

Aftermath (1896) was a sequel to *A Kentucky Cardinal,* in which the early married life of Adam and Georgiana, the birth of their son and Georgiana's death are told with a delicacy which keeps the pathos within the proper bounds of restraint. The book closes with a description of the unobtrusive comfort of Nature:

To-day, for the first time, I went back to the woods. It was pleasant to be surrounded again by the ever-living earth that feels no loss and has no memory; that was sere yesterday, is green to-day, will be sere again to-morrow, then green once more; that pauses not for wounds and wrecks, nor lingers over death and change; but onward, ever onward, along the groove of law, passes from its red origin in universal flame to its white end in universal snow.

There is a rare humor in these early books, which was not so apparent later, provided usually by the young girl Sylvia and the widow "Mrs. Walters," who was never really married but has assumed the name. As Adam says:

Indeed I have gone so far, when she has asked for my sympathy, as to lament with her Mr. Walters's death. After all, what great difference is there between her weeping for him because he is no more, and her weeping for him because he never was?

In June, 1892, *John Gray* appeared in *Lippincott's,* which at that time made a feature of printing complete novels in each issue. It was revised in 1897 as *The Choir Invisible,* laid in Kentucky in 1795. Yet while there is established a true atmosphere of the mingled roughness of pioneer life and the culture that came from Virginia and Maryland, the historical interest is not the main one. The characters and the scenery dominate. The love of John Gray, the school teacher, first for a woman unworthy of him and then for Mrs. Falconer, wife of his friend Major Falconer, is the chief motive. John Gray goes away without telling Mrs. Falconer of his passion for her, and the stern sense of duty and decency are in keeping with a character that is not made a prig. This feeling for a woman who in reality has grown to love him also was deepened in the revision, and John Gray's later marriage in the East is not made so much a matter of gratitude as it was in the earlier version. *The Choir Invisible* was one of the most popular of Allen's novels, yet it has certain definite faults. It is too long drawn out, and the analysis of motives too frequently overshadows the action.

A Summer in Arcady (1896), published in *The Cosmopolitan* as *But-*

terflies, marked Allen's first change in material and method. For this novel he chose simpler farmer folk, and the passion of Hilary and Daphne is more earthy and superficially more realistic. Both came from stock that is passionate and narrow-minded, especially in matters of theology. Hilary is rather unmoral than immoral in his sex relations; Allen showed clearly how the power of self-control may be developed in a young man who has been stripped by his neighbors' intolerance of any human aid in his effort to do right. It is in fact by his reverence for the instinct of purity which he sees in Daphne and part of which he imagines that they are saved from disaster. In 1900 *The Reign of Law,* published in England as *The Increasing Purpose,* confirmed Allen's realistic reaction. It is an epic of the Kentucky hemp fields in 1867 from which a farmer boy, great-grandson of a pioneer, goes to the university which is a goal of his dreams. He finds there, however, sectarian intolerance and returns disillusioned to his farm. There is a delightfully ironic touch in his parents' total inability to understand why he cannot go on toward his career as a minister simply because he has ceased to believe in their own narrow creed. David is eventually comforted by the love of a young school-teacher, but, fine as is the central theme, the hatred of intolerance, it is too often permitted to overshadow the characters to prevent the flagging of interest.

Much better, especially in its character drawing, was *The Mettle of the Pasture* (1903). In the first place, the spirited people of the Kentucky town were more worth writing about. Taking his inspiration from Shakespeare, in the speech of King Henry [3] to his yeomen before the battle, he creates figures who illustrate the high mettle of those who cannot live below their own standards of conduct. Rowan Meredith, on the very night of his acceptance by Isabel Conyers, feels that he has to tell her of his illegitimate child by a woman he had met while at college in the North, of his offer of marriage to the woman and of her refusal, her later marriage, and her desire above everything else to keep her relations with Rowan secret. Isabel refuses to marry him, since the shock which has been given to her ideal of him is too great. She confides in no one, and Allen indicates clearly how helpless are those who care for both the lovers, before their unbreakable pride. The best drawn character, however, is Mrs. Conyers, Isabel's grandmother. She is one of the finest examples in modern fiction of the well-bred she-devil, a woman upon whose bosom even flowers soon wilt. Proceeding always under the cover of good manners,

[3] *Henry V,* Act III, Scene 1.

she has sown scandal for years against those she hated. One of the most
sardonic touches is the picture of Judge Morris, whose life she had ruined
years before, calling upon her in the twilight of their lives each Sunday
evening, in ignorance of the harm she had done him. Since Isabel will not
confide the reason for her estrangement, preferring to leave town, Mrs.
Conyers begins to suggest various explanations, all damaging to Rowan's
character. She does not love her granddaughter, but her instinct is to attack anyone who has injured a member of her tribe. The effect of these
rumors is to bring Isabel back to defend Rowan from injustice, and ultimately to marry him, but too late, for he dies shortly after their son is
born. There are more finely etched characters than in any other novel of
Allen's, from the Meredith family, "who were a reserved household, inclined to the small nobilities of silence," the serious, kindly Professor
Hardage and Judge Morris, to the charming young girl, Marguerite,
whose worship of Rowan also helps to bring Isabel back. Through his
description of Pansy, a farmer's daughter, Allen reveals his democracy.
It is the democracy of Howells, not of Page. Allen had come from farming stock, which, while well connected, had not owned slaves.

This was Pansy, child of plain, poor, farmer folk, immemorially dwelling
close to the soil; unlettered, unambitious, long-lived, abounding in children,
without physical beauty, but marking the track of their generations by a path
lustrous with right-doing. For more than a hundred years on this spot the land
had lessened around them; but the soil had worked upward into their veins, as
into the stalks of plants, the trunks of trees; and that clean, thrilling sap of the
earth, that vitality of the exhaustless mother which never goes for nothing, had
produced one heavenly flower at last—shooting forth with irrepressible energy
a soul unspoiled and morally sublime. When the top decays, as it always does
in the lapse of time, whence shall come regeneration if not from below? It is
the plain people who are the eternal breeding grounds of high destinies.

Even in his realistic period, Allen had not lost the poetic insight, which
had manifested itself first in his early verse and animated his prose. *The
Last Christmas Tree* (1914) published serially in 1908 is a prose poem
dealing with the final conquest of the earth by the snow. It is dedicated
to "those who know they have no solution of the Universe, yet hope for
the best and live for it." The story is carried on by the conversation of two
fir trees, and Allen's study of the symbolism of the tree bore fruit in his
next fiction.

In 1909 Allen announced a trilogy to begin with *The Bride of the Mis-*

tletoe. Since the artistic purpose of the book was not understood, Allen's own explanation, given to me orally in 1911, should be considered in any critical appraisal. He had begun with romantic material treated idealistically; he had next proceeded to treat familiar life in a realistic manner, to deal with facts. He hoped in this trilogy to portray "an ideal truth, made up of facts," and thus to take a third step which should deal with more profound motives of human conduct, those which do not appear on the surface and are often not revealed by human beings to anyone. Believing that such fundamental impulses have descended from primitive times, he made an exhaustive study of such works as Frazer's *Golden Bough* and decided to take as his main theme "the desire of a middle-aged husband for another *young* wife." This theme is never expressed so frankly in the book, and of course Allen made no claim that it was new: his originality came in the method by which it was developed. Frederick Ousley, a professor of botany in a Kentucky college, prepares as a present to his wife Josephine on their wedding anniversary, which falls on Christmas Eve, a story of the mystic relation of man and the tree. Through this entire section of the book, "The Wandering Tale," Allen describes in prose that keeps a shining level of distinction, the symbols that decorate the Christmas tree. When Ousley omits a description of the mistletoe, his wife insists upon an interpretation, and he finally pictures for her an imaginary scene in Druidical times, of the testing of the virgin under the mistletoe:

Then the shrubbery is tremblingly parted at some place and upon the scene a young girl enters—her hair hanging down—her limbs most lightly clad—the flush of red hawthorn on the white hawthorn of her skin—in her eyes love's great need and mystery. Step by step she comes forward, her fingers trailing against whatsoever budding wayside thing may stay her strength. She draws nearer to the oak, searching amid its boughs for that emblem which she so dreads to find and yet more dreads not to find: the emblem of a woman's fruitfulness which the young oak—the Forest Lover—reaches down toward her. Finding it, beneath it with one deep breath of surrender she takes her place—the virgin's tryst with the tree—there to be tested.

Such is the command of the Arch Druid: it is obedience—submission to that test—or death for her as a sacrifice to the oak which she has rejected.

Again the shrubbery is parted, rudely pushed aside, and a man enters—a tried and seasoned man—a human oak—counterpart of the Forest Lover—to officiate at the test.

Josephine understands that he is telling her implicitly the story of his waning passion, that the Forest Lover is a symbol of himself, and she demands:

"The friend of your youth—the friend of your middle age—the children—your profession—the world of human life—this house—the dogs of the house—you care more for them all as time passes?"

"I care more for them all as time passes."

Then there came a great stillness in the room—the stillness of all listening years.

"Am I the only thing that you care less for as time passes?"

There was no reply.

"Am I in the way?"

There was no reply.

"Would you like to go over it all again with another?"

There was no reply.

She had hidden her face in her hands and pressed her head against the end of the sofa. Her whole figure shrank lower, as though to escape being touched by him—to escape the blow of his words. No words came. There was no touch.

Allen believed that Frederick's refusal to reply, his coming to her bedroom as usual that night, was due to his feeling that she must work through the crisis alone, and that it was a tragedy for her husband as well as herself. After a time of bitter regret, Josephine resumes life as usual. Allen deliberately avoided any third person in the usual triangle, and kept the novel on a high plane in consequence. It became not merely a celebration of illicit desire; it was a symbolic representation of the longing of middle age for youth, a universal emotion.

If *The Bride of the Mistletoe* puzzled the critics, *The Doctor's Christmas Eve* (1910) brought down upon Allen a chorus of disapproval. This was partly justified and partly unjustified. The story of Dr. Birney, who as a young physician falls in love with Mrs. Ousley and, realizing the hopelessness of his passion for her, marries a woman whom he does not love, has no central character with whom the reader can sympathize as he could with the wife and husband in *The Bride of the Mistletoe*. Allen seemed not to recognize that a deliberate wrong, even if done in what Dr. Birney thought was self-protection, is quite a different matter, in fiction, from a buffet of Fate or the slow erosion of Nature. The relations of the children of the two households are not very convincing, either. The little boy's relation to his father is well brought out, but it is difficult to see just how Allen would have proceeded with his plan for the trilogy. In the third book, he told me, "the children of these two marriages were to have been brought together on a high plane of spiritual relationship." But Allen was so discouraged by the reception of the two first members that he never completed the trilogy. It was a pity he did not, for he was at the height of his creative power, and the accusations of morbidity which were hurled at him were beside the point. There is much keen insight into human nature in *The Doctor's Christmas Eve*, and Allen's theory that fiction based upon a truth fused out of facts is an advance upon the mere relation of facts, is completely sound. One passage seems like a prophecy:

On one side of them lay the thinning shadow of man's ancient romance with Nature which is everywhere most rapidly dying out in this civilization—the shadow of that romance which for ages was the earliest ray of his religion: in later centuries became the splendor of his art; then loomed as the historic background of his titanic myths and fables; and now only in obscure valleys is found lingering in the play of superstitious children at twilight before darkness engulfs them—the latest of the infants in the dusk of the oldest gods.

On the other side blazed the hard clear light of that realism of human life which is the unfolding brightness of the New World; that light of reason and of reasonableness which seems to take from man both his mornings and his evenings, with all their half-lights and their mysteries; and to leave him only a perpetual noonday of the actual in which everything loses its shadow.

Allen called his next book, *The Heroine in Bronze; or, a Portrait of a Girl* (1912), a pastoral of the city. It differed from his earlier work in being laid in New York and was told by a young writer whose struggles paralleled Allen's own. Donald Clough wins the girl he loves because he refuses to let her dictate the development of his story. The book may be looked upon as a reaction of Allen against a criticism that would not take from him serious probing of the darker side of human conduct. "If they want charming love stories from me," he said in 1911, "they will have them." Charming love stories, after all, are not so easy to write, and there is something very appealing in Donald Clough's struggle to maintain his own artistic standards when he believes they mean the failure of his suit. There is more body to Allen's novelette of the Civil War, *The Sword of Youth* (1914). Once more the standards of conduct are upheld, and there is something very human in the brave but pitiful efforts of a Kentucky boy, who has deserted from the Confederate army on hearing from the girl he loves that his mother is dying, to persuade himself that he has returned for that reason only. When he finds that his mother has died, he saves his self-respect by refusing to go to Lucy's house and returns to Lee's army to risk disgrace and death. There is a good description of the last days of Lee's struggle, after the fall of Richmond. Allen's father and brother had fought for the Confederacy, and he was probably writing from information given by those actually in the conflict.

Allen's constant interest in Nature led to the writing of *The Kentucky Warbler* (1918), a novelette revealing the growth of an interest in bird life on the part of a Kentucky boy. The life of Alexander Wilson, the ornithologist, is the background of the book. Neither of these, nor a comedy told by letters, *The Emblems of Fidelity* (1919), approach in power *The Alabaster Box* (1923), one of the most sardonic ironies upon human nature in our fiction. Through the comments of various people in a Southern town at the funeral of a prominent citizen who had been noted for his charitable deeds, Allen showed how a really selfish man receives more thanks for one act of benevolence than the dead man had obtained from his constant benefactions, because the town had begun to look upon them as its right. Even his family look upon his death as an unpardonable interruption to the benefits to which they are accustomed. It belongs with Mark Twain's "The Man That Corrupted Hadleyburg" because it does not deal with superficial manners or caricatures but touches upon a universal weakness of humanity. Another universal note is struck in a short story, "The Ashcan," published with some other significant stories in the year of Allen's death, under the title of *The Landmark*. The title story reveals the unruly nature of some of the early settlers of Kentucky. Perhaps the best of these stories is "Miss Locke," a subtle study of the relations of a young man with a young woman who, desiring to express real emotions with which her physical appearance is at odds, lays herself open to the charge of insincerity.

Allen's most distinct contributions to fiction were his creations of characters who live according to their own standards, usually high ones; his profound interpretations of the relations of man and nature, and his ability to portray American life which had roots in Kentucky, but was in no sense parochial. Adam Moss, Georgiana Cobb, John Gray, Rowan Meredith, Isabel Conyers, Frederick Ousley, Josephine Ousley, Donald Clough, Joseph Sumner work out their own salvation. There is no "happy ending"—in fact Allen often closes his novels with death. But he is not concerned with happiness in the usual sense. Death is simply a development and man, like nature, is a unit in a universal process of change. Nature is a counter claimant to love for the soul of man, and how well Allen understood her claims is reflected in the descriptions which stud the pages of his books. In fact, they sometimes though not often impede the narrative unduly. But the nature painter who could give us the bird life of *The Kentucky Cardinal* or *The Kentucky Warbler* or those magnificent passages in *The Bride of the Mistletoe* which describe man's worship of the forest might be forgiven.

This descriptive power is shown in his character painting often in a sentence or in an illuminating comparison. When David comes to Gabriella in his theological troubles, she replies, "There is not a dogma of my church that I have ever thought of for a moment: or of any other church," and Allen continues: "In those simple words she had uttered a long historic truth: that religion, not theology, forms the spiritual life of women." For a bachelor, Allen understood the nature of his heroines remarkably well. They are practically never mere recipients of passion, and in the quality of his analysis of love he was ahead of his time. From the comedy of *The Kentucky Cardinal* to the tragic parting of Isabel and Rowan when she passes her fingers over his face in the dark before she bids him what she believes to be farewell, he was able to portray a spiritual as well as a passionate love in which the man is not merely a gallant suppliant but is giving and knows that he is giving as well as receiving a gift worth cherishing.

While Allen lays great stress upon the persistent "Anglo-Saxon" tradition in Kentucky life, at times attributing to their "Saxon" ancestors traits which came as a matter of fact from the Norman conquest, he insists rightly upon the development of an American type. In *The Bride of the Mistletoe* he represents Frederick Ousley looking at his ancestors:

As he stood there—the man beside the Tree—into the picture entered three other men, looking down upon him from their portraits on the walls.

One portrait represented the first man of his family to scale the mountains of the Shield where its eastern rim is turned away from the reddening daybreak. Thence he had forced his way to its central portions where the skin of ever living verdure is drawn over the rocks: Anglo-Saxon, backwoodsman, borderer, great forest chief, hewing and fighting a path toward the sunset for Anglo-Saxon women and children. With his passion for the wilderness—its game, enemies, campfire and cabin, deep-lunged freedom. This ancestor had a lonely, stern, gaunt face, no modern expression in it whatsoever—the timeless face of the woods.

Near his portrait hung that of a second representative of the family. This man had looked out upon his vast parklike estates in the central counties; and wherever his power had reached, he had used it on a great scale for the destruction of his forests. Woods-slayer, field-maker; working to bring in the period on the Shield when the hand of a man began to grasp the plough instead of the rifle, when the stallion had replaced the stag, and bellowing cattle wound fatly down into the pastures of the bison. This man had the face of his caste—the countenance of the Southern slave-holding feudal lord. Not the American face, but the Southern face of a definite era—less than national, less than modern; a face not looking far in any direction but at things close around.

From a third portrait the latest ancestor looked down. He with his contemporaries had finished the thinning of the central forest of the Shield, leaving the land as it is to-day, a rolling prairie with remnants of woodland like that crowning the hilltop near this house. This immediate forefather bore the countenance that began to develop in the Northerner and in the Southerner after the Civil War: not the Northern look nor the Southern look, but the American look—a new thing in the American face, indefinable but unmistakable.

His lack of parochial feeling is shown in his fair treatment of the Civil War and his democratic attitude already noted. Finally, his distinction of style, the product of hard labor and of comparatively slow production, gave to his fiction those magnificent phrases which are not mere fine writing but which illuminate character. In *Aftermath*, he gave a key in one sentence to the nature of the life he chose to portray. "She was of a soft heartedness that ruled her absolutely—but only to the unyielding edge of honor."

"The unyielding edge of honor." How can the English language hold four words which say more about that quality of American life which manifests itself not in the glare of public contest, but in those quieter moments of decision where character is finally established?

CHAPTER XXII

THE ROMANCE OF HISTORY AND POLITICS

ONE of the most striking qualities of fiction is the persistence of the type. The impulse to portray a past epoch, one of the earliest among native writers, never ceased, and allied to this impulse was that which told a romantic story with a background of political institutions of a more contemporary nature. The subjects with which the elder romance was concerned, the Colonial conquests and settlements, native and foreign, the Indian, the Revolution and the frontier were treated again, and other themes, especially the Civil War and the newer frontier of the Far West. There was a wider use of European history and at times a better understanding of it, but the main currents ran into native moulds.

No completely satisfactory definition of an historical novel has been given. Marion Crawford's analysis in *The Novel—What It Is* has already been mentioned,[1] and surely his statement that when an historical novel fails to be a great book it will probably be an absurd one was amply justified at the end of the century. He also remarks:

It is doubtful whether any genuine historical novel has ever yet been written for the sake of the history it contains. In nine cases out of ten the writer has selected his subject because it interests him, because it has dramatic elements, and possibly because he hopes to interest his readers more readily by means of characters and events altogether beyond the reach of the carping critic.

Paul Leicester Ford believed that an atmosphere could be as historical as an occurrence and attributed the popularity of historical romance to that "atmosphere of truth which is conveyed to the mind of the reader by mention of real persons and places and events." [2] Brander Matthews was of the opinion that "the really trustworthy historical novels are those which were a-writing while the history was-a-making," [3] and distinguished himself by prophesying correctly that "Mr. Ford will never write

---

[1] See p. 398.

[2] "The American Historical Novel," *Atlantic Monthly*, December, 1897.

[3] *The Historical Novel and Other Essays*, 1901. The essay on the historical novel was first published in 1897.

an historical novel having a tithe of the historical value possessed by his suggestive study of the conditions of contemporary politics in New York City, *The Honorable Peter Stirling.*" For *Janice Meredith* appeared within two years to justify him!

The difficulty arises, of course, from the two standpoints from which a novel may be viewed, that of the writer and that of the reader, and from the fact that what will be history fifty years from now is not history today. Matthews' definition would make almost every novel an historical one, and Ford's conception would make *The Scarlet Letter* an historical novel, although its real artistic purpose is spiritual and moral. Yet although Ford and Matthews widen perhaps unduly the scope of the historical novel, the reason they do so is clear. The impulse which leads a novelist to paint an epoch in the past and the impulse which causes him to depict the political scene of his own time are akin. Both spring from a desire to portray characters swayed by forces which have governed men in earlier days or are determining their lives in the present. It becomes appropriate, therefore, to treat these two phases of fiction together, more especially since it permits the unified treatment of certain of the novelists and makes possible a consideration of their work as a whole.

In the interest of clarity it is necessary to point out that the real historical novel is one in which the characters and incidents are true to the period and place in which they are laid. This period should be far enough in the past for a proper perspective to blur mere details and color the striking and dramatic events, which it thus brings into relief, with the dignity which the past fittingly assumes in the eye of the present. It is not so much a question of years which decides the suitability of material for historical treatment. If a civilization or an epoch is completed by profound changes such as those which swept the real Western cowboy out of existence, it is possible to write objectively of that time, or if there is a definite beginning and end, as in the case of the Civil War, twenty or thirty years are quite sufficient to make an historical novel possible.

While John Esten Cooke, the last of the romantic school of Simms, was still writing, General Lew Wallace (1827-1905) published in 1873 *The Fair God,* a successful attempt at the romance of the conquest of Mexico. Wallace depended upon Prescott, of course, but he also read the account purported to have been written by Bernal Diaz del Castillo, one of the Conquistadores, and he consulted other authorities [4] with his usual care.

[4] See his *Autobiography,* Vol. I, p. 90.

While the novel was begun in 1843, Wallace knew Mexico through his service in the Mexican War, and it was not completed until after his later mission in behalf of the Juarez régime. His very real ability as a story-teller is revealed when his novel is compared with its sources. It was necessary for him to excite the reader's interest in the "lost cause" of the Aztecs. But as Montezuma deserted his people at the end, and was weak when he should have been strong, Wallace created a character, Guatamozin, who becomes the leader of the forlorn hope and naturally the lover of Montezuma's daughter. Love, however, is not the main interest; the racial conflict leading to the stirring climax which describes the retreat of Cortez from the capital keeps the center of the stage. There is no great advance, however, upon the Mexican romances of Bird, and the speeches are full of bombast.

General Wallace learned much about the art of fiction before he wrote his next novel, *Ben-Hur* (1880). From the magnificent opening scene when the three wise men meet and proceed on their way to the birthplace of the Saviour, the novel is conceived on a large scale. In its pages, crowded with incident, the dramatic struggle of three great forces, Judaism, Christianity and the Roman Empire, is pictured with a power and a clarity that captured and held alike the admiration of millions and the critical judgments of the discriminating. Wallace knew that the figure of Christ must be kept in the background in fiction, but without pietism he drew an unforgettable picture of His influence winning its spiritual victory in the change that passes over the character of Ben Hur. To the Jewish patrician, cruelly dealt with by Messala, the Roman soldier, revenge was a sacred duty, and his hate, nurtured in the galleys and brought to its climax in the spirited chariot race, was a unifying force of great appeal. The narrative power is of a high order, based as it is upon phrases singularly well chosen and arranged, not only in the opening scene, but also in the rescue of Ben Hur's mother and sister from the leper's cell, or in the naval victory over the pirates. It is easy to criticize the thrilling chariot race as rhetorical; it is not so easy to better it. But the incidents alone would not have made a great novel. *Ben-Hur* surpasses any other story in English fiction dealing with the time of Christ not only because of the thorough study Wallace made of places and races,[5] but because of his character drawing. To

---

[5] *Autobiography*, Vol. II, pp. 926–937. Wallace had not been in the Holy Land when he wrote *Ben Hur*, but he visited the scenes of his novel later when Minister to Turkey.

a reading public surfeited with caricatures of Jewish lower-class merchants, the figure of the well-born son of the race of Hur with the ambitions and passions of his caste was a revelation. Simonides, the steward who from his chair, to which Roman torture and his fidelity to the house of Hur have condemned him, sends out his ships to provide the money which helps Ben Hur to secure his revenge, is a real person, and Ilderim, the Arab sheik, is another. The women are not so clearly drawn, but Messala is a faithful picture of a Roman of his day. The art of Wallace is shown also in the way he makes every other character derive its importance from its relation to Ben Hur. This unity of impression was carried over to the dramatization in 1899 by William Young, which became one of the perennials of the theatre. *Ben-Hur* has been translated into German, French, Swedish, Bohemian, Italian, Spanish, Turkish, and Arabic. General Wallace wrote, however, only one great novel. *The Prince of India* (1893), a story based upon the legend of the wandering Jew, was too involved and confused, and no characters emerged from it. But the fact that *Ben Hur*, which by 1933 had sold 1,950,000 copies, will keep Wallace from being forgotten by a nation generally unconscious of his services as the saviour of Washington from the Confederate Army in 1864, needs perhaps no comment from an historian of fiction.

Ben-Hur, not at all to its discredit, had a touch of the grand manner of the earlier romance. Through the 'seventies and 'eighties and 'nineties, the interest in historical romance added its flavor to new impulses in fiction. Most important was the combination of history and character analysis in Weir Mitchell's *Thee and You* (1876), *Hephzibah Guinness* (1878), *In War Time* (1885) and *Roland Blake* (1886). With Eggleston's *Circuit Rider* (1874), *Roxy* (1878) and *The Graysons* (1887), Cable's *Old Creole Days* (1879) and *The Grandissimes* (1880), Miss Murfree's *Where the Battle was Fought* (1886), Frederic's *In the Valley* (1890) and *The Copperhead* (1893), and Allen's *John Gray* (1892), sectional or racial interest was enhanced by the glamour of the past. These romances of American locality have already been analyzed, as well as Crawford's *Zoroaster* (1885) and *Khaled* (1891), Hardy's *Passe Rose* (1889) and Mrs. Ward's *Master of the Magicians* (1890) and *Come Forth* (1891), in which the scene was foreign. Several of these romances appeared in serial form and if anyone doubts the persistence of romantic fiction he has only to turn the pages of a typical magazine like *Scribner's Monthly* and the *Century* and note how the long serials usually include one story of contemporary life and one romance either of history, of the frontier, or of pure fancy.

The popularity of the historical romance of the 'eighties may be illustrated by the success of the novels of Jane G. Austin (1831–1894), whose *A Nameless Nobleman* (1881) ran through over thirty editions. The early portions of the book which send François "Le Baron" from the court of Louis XIV to America are conventional, but there is a certain reality in the delineation of New England characters of the late seventeenth century, especially Mary Wilder, who saves Le Baron, a wounded fugitive, in her attic, and marries him in defiance of Puritan objections. Mrs. Austin followed this book with three others, *Standish of Standish* (1889), dealing with the settlement at Plymouth; *Dr. LeBaron and his Daughters* (1890), a sequel to *A Nameless Nobleman;* and *Betty Alden* (1891), a sequel to *Standish of Standish,* in which the figure of Sir Christopher Gardiner once more appeared to plague the Pilgrims. A good deal of research went into the making of these books, but Mrs. Austin was a bit too anxious to prove her ancestors' greatness to permit them to remain normal, Miles Standish being placed upon an especially high pedestal.

With more vigor and sweep in the narrative and with more colorful a background, Mary Hartwell Catherwood (1847–1902) took for her province the colonies of France in the New World. *The Romance of Dollard* which appeared in the *Century* in 1888 and 1889 with a foreword by Parkman is a romance of Canada under Louis XIV. Adam Daulac, Sieur des Ormeaux, called "Dollard," the hero of the attack on the Iroquois, was a real person, but Mrs. Catherwood provided him from her imagination with a wife in Claire de Laval-Montmorency, whom he had loved in France and who had come over with the ship bearing French girls for the marriage market, at which the coureurs-de-bois were provided with helpmeets. The novel has considerable movement, and the death of Claire and Dollard in the fight against overwhelming odds is told with spirit. But Mrs. Catherwood seems more interested in her background than in her characters and spends too much time upon incidents which have no bearing on the plot. *The Lady of Fort St. John* (1891) is laid in Acadia during the reign of Louis XIII and deals with the heroic defence of Fort St. John made by Marie de la Tour while her husband is away, and the treacherous murder of the garrison by his rival, D'Aulnay, after the surrender. There is atmosphere and action, but not much character drawing, except for the curious dwarf, "Le Rossignol," a woman who rides out at night on a swan and learns thereby of the plans of the enemy. Her description of the death of D'Aulnay in the quicksand while she mocks him from a safe distance, checking off each wave as the tide comes in on him with the name of one of the murdered garrison, is done with skill. Even better, from the point of view of style, are Mrs. Catherwood's short stories. The best of these are found in *The Chase of Saint Castin and Other Stories* (1894), especially "The Windigo," a tale of a female flesh-eater. *Mackinac and Lake Stories* (1899) have not the same appeal, although those dealing with the strange power of "King Strang," the ruler of the Mormon settlement on Beaver Island are valuable for their picture of a curious episode in the history of the Northwest. *Lazarre* (1901) is one of the many attempts to tell the story of the Dauphin, Louis XVII, who is in this novel his own narrator. It is based on the adventures of the Reverend Eleazar Williams, but departs easily into the realms of sheer romance.

It is not surprising, in view of what has been said concerning the relations of the historical novel and the novel of politics, that Henry Adams (1838–1918), one of the best of our historians, should have given us in *Democracy* (1880) a bitter satire upon the corruption of politics in Washington, and the interrelations of society and government. It is written with the polished style and delicate understanding of verbal nicety which made Adams' other writing so distinguished, but its merit lies in the picture of that period, among the most corrupt in our history, rather than in the structure of the novel. Adams knew the warped state of morals which made possible Senator Ratcliffe of Illinois, his courtship of Mrs. Lightfoot Lee, and even her hesitation before her final refusal. Lovers of keen satire may still read with delight the description of the ball given by the English ambassador to the Grand Duke and Duchess of Saxe-Baden-Hambourg, at which the mutual dislike of the Duchess and of the President's wife tested the resources of the masters of diplomacy, male and female. But Adams fails to differentiate between the methods of the politicians then in power and the institutions of democracy, and his novel remains interesting chiefly as a protest of the patrician against a system which was soon to meet its challenge from the leadership of Grover Cleveland. *Democracy* is a much better novel, however, than John Hay's one effort at fiction, *The Breadwinners* (1884). This was an attack upon organized labor laid in the city of "Buffland" in 1877.

The characters are all types, and the realism occurs only in the description of the riots. But Hay, like Adams, failed as a novelist because he showed only one side of the conflict. His labor leaders are caricatures, and the strikes are called apparently by accident. The ending, too, is hopelessly sentimental, and Hay's description of Andrew Jackson "as the most injurious personality in American history" is sufficient to show his incapacity to understand the fundamentals in any contest between employers and employed. Had Adams or Hay represented both sides of the conflict at their best there would have been more real contrast and therefore a finer novel. But they were more interested in their themes than in their characters. DeForest had written a better novel of politics in *Playing the Mischief*, and Mrs. Burnett showed in *Through One Administration* (1881) how a natural story-teller could use the complicated interrelations of social, financial, and political life of Washington for their proper function of developing characters. Bertha Herrick, who marries Richard Amory on account of his charm and who realizes too late that she loves Colonel Philip Tredennis, is a remarkable picture of a woman of breeding who surmounts every danger that lurks for a pretty, vivacious matron, because she has first won a victory over herself. Mrs. Burnett knew supremely well how to draw the involved web in which Bertha was enmeshed by her husband's eagerness to make use of her social gifts to promote one of those nefarious land schemes with which the time was crowded. She could paint equally well the splendid scene at the ball, in which those who came prepared to witness the ruin of Bertha's reputation stayed to watch her triumph. Briefly as they appear, the gracious gentlewoman who is known simply as "the wife of the Secretary of State" and Senator Blundell, the shrewd but honest friend of Bertha, seem to be living and speaking in the short time in which, at their command, the tide of scandal ebbs and turns into acclaim. The tragic ending, after the death of Colonel Tredennis, which leaves Bertha facing the relentless "tomorrow and tomorrow" of life with a husband she has ceased even to respect, but with whom she will live for their children's sake, gives Mrs. Burnett a right to claim a place with the most logical of the realists.

It is not surprising either that the most popular of the romances which portrayed a future state should have been written by a man who began with a novel of the past. The impulse which led Edward Bellamy (1850–1898) to write *The Duke of Stockbridge* was akin to that which created *Looking Backward,* a deep and at the same time a romantic interest in problems of human happiness. *The Duke of Stockbridge* was published first in a newspaper in Great Barrington, Massachusetts, in 1879, and appeared in book form only in 1900. It is a veracious and interesting story of the revolt of the distressed farmers of the Berkshires after the Revolution, commonly known as Shays' Rebellion. Bellamy's research resulted in a picture of the revolt which is fairer to the rebels than that usually given in history. The hopelessness of their repaying debts when there was no money, the flow of gold abroad and the growth of unemployment are represented through living characters, several based on actual participants in the rebellion. Bellamy held the scales even, however, and did not hesitate to describe the evils that arose from mob government. He made the novel concrete through a likeable hero, Captain Hamlin, whose passion for Desire Edwards, granddaughter of Jonathan Edwards, ends with his death in one of the last skirmishes of the rebellion. *The Duke of Stockbridge* is especially interesting for its picture of the caste system in Massachusetts which separated the lovers, and which existed to a degree not usually recognized.

In 1880 Bellamy proved his imaginative power in a novelette, *Dr. Heidenhoff's Process,* in which Henry Burr, who is so deeply in love that he is willing to marry Madeline Brand, who has jilted him and been betrayed by her second lover, dreams that he conducts her to a Doctor Heidenhoff who can, through a galvanic shock, destroy the memory of a sinner so far as the crime over which he is brooding is concerned. So realistic is the description of the dream that the reader is completely deceived and believes that the cure has been accomplished. The awakening of Burr only to find that Madeline has killed herself rather than permit him to marry her, is also managed swiftly and dramatically. The choice of the name "Brand" suggests at once Hawthorne's "Ethan Brand," the story of the unpardonable sin.

Bellamy was, of course, of most significance for *Looking Backward* (1888) and yet notwithstanding the great vogue of that novel, his sincerity in endeavoring to call attention to social injustice was greater than his art as a novelist. His hero goes into a trance in Boston in 1887, wakes in the year 2000, and by his picture of a Utopia founded on state communism calls attention to the evils of his own day. Waking in the room in which his trance had commenced, he is horrified at the life he once lived, and then once more awakes to find that his return to the nineteenth century was the dream and that he can live on in the year 2000, wedded blissfully to the great-granddaughter of the girl he once had loved. It is quite easy to point to fatal lapses in the logic of *Looking Backward*. The very foundation of his scheme, the principle of universal service and equality of income is violated cheerfully by the conditions of the family into which he is brought, where the wife and daughter apparently do nothing at all, and all the disagreeable duties of life are waved aside by the provision that if any occupation had no volunteers, it would remain unperformed! The book is a curious mixture of unsound economic theories with utterances prophetic of things only now coming to pass. Bellamy's criticism of a financial system based "on the sign of a sign" and the substitution of one founded on actual commodities, and his picture of true life insurance, when man was "guaranteed against need of any sort, by a policy underwritten by one hundred million fellow countrymen" have a very contemporary sound. Naturally his criticism of the conditions of his own period, when labor and capital were at each other's throats, is more interesting than his picture of an ideal state in which greed and corruption vanish hand in hand with overproduction, depressions, and undernourishment, and also, it is to be feared, with ambition, charity, and the heroism of self-sacrifice. He could find much in the social and economic organization of the 'eighties that needed correction. As he pertinently asks, through Dr. Leete, the physician and expounder of the new order, "And, in heaven's name, who are the public enemies? Are they France, England, Germany, or hunger, cold and nakedness?" It was because of the clarity of his style and the sincerity of his hope for human betterment that millions of his countrymen read his book, and Bellamy Clubs were founded to study it. *Equality* (1897), the sequel to *Looking Backward*, endeavored to answer the many unfavorable criticisms of that book. But the details submerged the fiction. Bellamy, to judge from his short stories which date from the 'seventies in some instances and which appeared in book form as *The Blindman's World and Other Stories* (1898), was definitely interested in observing the probable effects on human beings when a natural law is violated. The title story describes the inhabitants of Mars in terms of their perfect knowledge of the future.

When the continuous production of historical romance is remembered, it is not hard to explain its development at the close of the century into a vogue. A fashion in fiction needs first, a great popular success to start the way and second, a receptive state of mind in the reading public. It was quite fitting that the novelist who had begun twenty years before with novels of the Civil War and of the early nineteenth century should write the book which still stands as the best of the romances of the Revolution. When *Hugh Wynne* began to appear in the *Century* in November, 1896, it was recognized at once for reasons that have already been given as a model and how often it was imitated in the next few years will be apparent to any critic familiar with the material. Its great merit can best be appreciated when it is compared with Frederic J. Stimson's *King Noanett*, which appeared in the same year. The stilted language and the interminable legal details of this romance of Colonial Virginia and New England illustrate what happens when a novelist fails to observe the necessary compromises in diction which have to be made between the actual speech of the past and that of today.[6] One of the best tests of an historical novelist lies in the ability to make such compromises, and the most severe criticism of many of the romances of the late 'nineties lay in their lamentable conversations.

Hugh Wynne came just at the right moment. The nation had been slowly recovering from the panic of 1893 and was feeling its oats. The Exposition at Chicago had brought about a better mutual understanding of the different sections. The Mason and Dixon line was growing fainter; Grover Cleveland's two terms had buried the "bloody shirt"; and even the new sectionalism of the West versus the East did not prevent a popular support to an imperialistic program. The Spanish-American war, which came in 1898, was a result rather than a cause of the national feeling, although in its turn it spurred the novelists on. A natural outlet was the survey of our past, especially of its most vigorous periods. It was not accidental then that in the two years following the publication of *Hugh Wynne* in book form there should appear *Red Rock, Prisoners of Hope, To Have and to Hold, Janice Meredith* and *Richard Carvel*, while *Via Crucis* and *The Adventures of François* revealed the two foremost historical novelists of the time at the height of their power.

The romance of Stevenson and his group in England helped also in the wave of romantic impulse, but it is easy to overemphasize the foreign element, for the historical novel in this country had a distinctly American flavor. And indeed, with the literary honesty characteristic of

[6] See Dr. Mitchell's clear explanation of this difference, quoted on p. 312.

Stevenson, he acknowledges in the introduction to *Treasure Island* his own great debt to Washington Irving.

This romantic wave inspired, sometimes to great popular success, a group of novelists who if not as fine in artistry as Mitchell, Crawford, Cable, Page, or Allen, yet rise above the great mass of story-tellers of the time, many of whom contented themselves with the production of juveniles. At the very close of his career James Maurice Thompson (1844–1901), the poet of nature who had to his credit a novel of sectional contrasts, *His Second Campaign* (1883), and an amusing novelette, *A Fortnight of Folly* (1888), in which fictional characters like Bartley Hubbard or Henrietta Stackpole are mixed up with real people at a mountain resort, turned to the historical novel. *Alice of Old Vincennes* (1900) is a vigorous romance centering on the capture of this key to the Northwest Territory by the British under General Hamilton, the "hair-buyer," and its recapture by George Rogers Clark. Thompson drew an accurate picture of the uncertainties of 1778 and the perils of an outpost. His best character, Father Beret, the priest who acts as a guardian angel of the heroine, was imaginary, but was probably based on Father Gibault, who aided Clark in securing the loyalty of the French inhabitants to the United States. Alice Tarleton is a typical romantic figure, who disarms trained soldiers with her rapier and is responsible for several theatrical situations. The book was vastly popular and may have suggested to Winston Churchill the romantic possibilities of the struggle for the Northwest.

It was again a trained historian, Paul Leicester Ford (1865–1902), who wrote in *The Honorable Peter Stirling* (1894) one of the very best novels of political life which, if not historical in any strict sense, is much superior to *Janice Meredith* (1899), his romance of the Revolution. It was, however, because Ford, in addition to his first-hand knowledge of the political conditions of his day, had the historian's understanding of the real distinction between the two great political philosophies which, under one party name or another, have existed in the Republic, that his novel of politics is so enthralling. He created Peter Stirling, coming from plain New England people, a graduate of Harvard and a lawyer, and placed him in New York City, slowly winning his way in politics. Ford avoided the mistake usually made by writers of American political novels who, fearing to give offence, speak vaguely of "the party." He made Peter Stirling a Democrat, because he is the exponent of that political thinking which lays stress not so much upon the preservation of certain institutions as upon the choice of a leader. Peter puts the case himself early in his career:

If a man's honest, the poorest thing we can do to him is to tie him fast to one course of action, when the conditions are constantly changing.

For the purposes of fiction it is best to select a hero who represents the Democratic ideal of a leader whose power rests upon his intimate knowledge of the people, first in his ward, then in his city, then in his State, who sympathizes with all sides, from the tenement-house children and the saloon-keepers to the millionaire who is willing to use his money as Peter suggests for the betterment of conditions. Ford knew too that satire upon political corruption is amusing, but that a "practical idealist" like Stirling, who is a fighter and tells the truth, may accomplish a great deal more than a reformer who fails to understand that feudalism is not extinct. Peter's defence of his kind of "boss" is made to Lenore D'Alloi, the young girl he loves:

"Don't you see how absurd it is to suppose that the people are going to take the opinions of the better element offhand? At the end of a three months' campaign? Men have come into my ward and spoken to empty halls; they've flooded it with campaign literature, which has served to light fires; their papers have argued, and nobody read them. But the ward knows me. There's hardly a voter who doesn't. They've tested me. Most of them like me. I've lived among them for years. I've gone on their summer excursions. I've talked with them all over the district. I have helped them in their troubles. I have said a kind word over their dead. I'm godfather to many. With others I've stood shoulder to shoulder when the bullets were flying. Why, the voters who were children when I first came here, with whom I used to sit in the angle, are almost numerous enough now to carry an election as I advise. Do you suppose, because speakers, unknown to them, say I'm wrong, and because the three-cent papers, which they never see, abuse me, that they are going to turn from me unless I make them? That is the true secret of the failure of reformers."

Peter Stirling was supposed to represent Grover Cleveland, and the tireless energy, the courage, and the truthfulness of Ford's hero may have been inspired by Cleveland's career. Stirling's sacrifice in accepting the responsibility for an illegitimate child in order to save Helen D'Alloi, whom he had loved, from a knowledge of her husband's infidelity, was also based upon the scandalous stories which made the Cleveland-Blaine campaign of 1884 the most disgraceful in our history.

But Peter Stirling is more than a copy of any one man. He is the concrete representation of the liberal as opposed both to the tory and the radical. Though he has no interest in liquor, he opposes prohibition because he knows "you can't strengthen humanity by tying its hands." When Peter Stirling, as colonel of his militia regiment, is ordered to disperse a gathering of anarchists, he would have preferred to let them talk instead of putting them out by the bayonet. Then, when the consequent explosion occurs, Ford shows the futility of violence in three brief sentences:

Underneath that great dun pall lay soldier and anarchist, side by side, at last at peace. The one died for his duty, the other died for his idea. The world was none the better, but went on unchanged.

The love story is not so happy and the minor characters, except Dennis Moriarty, the saloon-keeper, one of Stirling's henchmen, are not individualized. Ford knew he was writing romance, and he strenuously defends the right of the novelist to select from life rather than to depict what is sordid and mean. But Peter Stirling is a real person.

When Ford turned to the historical novel he wrote one of the "best sellers" of the day in *Janice Meredith*. The atmosphere is correct; the inertia, time serving, and even treachery of the inhabitants of the New Jersey town in which the heroine lived are portrayed with skill. But the characters persistently refrain from coming alive, and the various escapes of Janice Meredith from both armies are theatrical and unconvincing. Even more unhappy is the language, whose artificiality can only be fully appreciated if it is compared with the actual speech of the time as given in Sally Wister's *Journal* or any other Revolutionary diary. Of Ford's other fiction, *The Story of an Untold Love* (1897) alone needs mention and that is a more natural if a bit sentimental story of his own day.

After an amusing light social satire, *The Celebrity* (1898), Winston Churchill (1871–   ) devoted himself to the task of interpreting the institutions of the past and the present in the United States. To write *Richard Carvel* (1899), one of the most successful novels of its day, Churchill took the strong, hot-blooded young Whig with a Tory grandfather, animated him by a passion for a dazzling beauty who loves him from boyhood but who flirts with many others, gives him an extraordinary skill with the rapier, equal only to his stupidity in not recognizing Dorothy's love for him, and, after many adventures, brings him safe home to his inheritance at Carvel Hall. So far *Hugh Wynne*, somewhat altered, was the prototype. But for variety's sake Churchill borrowed Harry Warrington from *The Virginians* and plunged Carvel into the gaming tables of London society. It is perhaps unnecessary to point out that Weir Mitchell would not have written of Carvel's first meeting with Washington, "He stood regarding me a full minute, his eye seeming to penetrate the secrets of my life," or Thackeray would not have written the extraordinary scene in which a boy of nineteen kindles in the soul of Charles James Fox the seeds of his spiritual reformation! Yet these and other absurdities mark just the difference between historical novels of the first rank and those of the second. In *The Crisis* (1901) Churchill painted a picture of the confused conditions before and during the Civil War in Missouri, especially in St. Louis. Here Churchill could use the tradition and atmosphere of his native city to paint an authentic picture of the strong Confederate feeling, fortified by the instincts of a ruling caste, and could contrast with it the prompt action of the leaders who made use of the large German element in Missouri to save the State for the Union. He brings his hero, Stephen Brice, and his villain, Eliphalet Hopper, both from New England, and his heroine, a granddaughter of Richard Carvel, is just as naturally a strong secessionist. These are conventional romantic figures; and the contest between Stephen Brice and his rival, Clarence Colfax, is introduced by an auction scene in which Brice buys a young slave woman to give her freedom. Apart from the melodramatic episode, which dates from the time of Mayne Reid's *Quadroon* and the theatre of Boucicault, the action is entirely out of drawing so far as Churchill's picture of Stephen Brice in his other relations is concerned. It points to one of his main faults, his subordination of the characters to the incidents. The portraits of Lincoln, Sherman and Grant are not bad and they are given their proper place. Churchill introduces Lincoln through his Freeport speech in 1858, in which he asked the famous question which lost him the senatorship in 1858 but made him President in 1860. While the description of Lincoln stresses a bit too much his uncouth qualities, it is pictorial and is far better than many other fictional portraits of the great President.

In *The Crossing* (1904) Churchill attempted a large task and in part accomplished it. The story of the settling of Kentucky, of the conquest of the Northwest Territory by Colonel George Rogers Clark during the Revolution, is told by David Ritchie, who is one of those wonderful boys of romance whom Scott and Cooper loved to draw. It is his brain rather than his arm, however, which is remarkable. He settles questions of strategy or finance at the age of fourteen, and yet Churchill has managed to make his story appealing, for he has given him loyalty, courage and self-sacrifice and he does not talk too much. The action is rapid and the love-making mercifully brief. The historical figures, especially Clark, are well drawn, but the imaginary characters are properly kept in the foreground and are better, especially the men, than in *The Crisis* or *Richard Carvel*. That Churchill conceived *The Crossing* as a political document as well as an historical romance is shown clearly in his "Afterword." To him the novel is the celebration of the manifest destiny which took the borders of the United States westward. Churchill's knowledge of history is shown, too, in his description of the loyalty of the French settlers after Clark has shown them where liberty is to be found. Here again the traditions of St. Louis were helpful to him. *The Crossing* is much less conventional than *Richard Carvel*, and there is a certain epic quality in the picture of Clark and his small band of Americans and Frenchmen winning the Northwest against thousands of Indians and the power of England. For the purposes of historical fiction there is hardly any theme so fitting, whether it be laid at Thermopylæ or at Vincennes, as the conflict of brave men against overwhelming odds, in a struggle that is to decide the fate of a continent.

In *Coniston* (1906) Churchill illustrated the close connection of the historical and political novel and drew his best character, Jethro Bass, the political boss of a New England State. Beginning about 1830, in the era of Jacksonian Democracy, the main action comes after the Civil War. Bass starts his political life as a Democrat and changes with the times to the Republican party. But his significance lies, first, in the methods by which he secures his power. It is not only because of the fact that he holds mortgages upon a great many farms in his district; it is rather because of the strong personality of the man. He is the representative of feudalism, based upon individual leadership, and his great contest is with Isaac Worthington, who represents the impersonal rule of the railroad corporation. Jethro Bass is not an office-holder; he is in politics for the love of power, and his methods are not always savory. But he secures the sympathy of the reader because of a certain pride which makes him inarticulate in his own defence. Jethro's protecting care of Cynthia Wetherell, whose mother he had loved, provides the motive which brings about a fine climax. Another kind of politician might have planned the revenge upon Worthington when the latter interfered to separate his son from the obscure little school teacher. But what lifts Jethro Bass into fictional importance is his triumph over himself. With the fight against Worthington won, he sends for the railroad president and offers to permit his consolidation bill to pass if he will withdraw his opposition to the marriage. This interview is probably the best that Churchill ever drew for it brings into a dramatic conflict the two men who represent the personal and the institutional domination of politics. Knowing that his deal with Worthington will be misrepresented, he gives up what his whole life has been built upon, the joy of conquest and the reputation for success, in order to save Cynthia from unhappiness. In a novel as in a drama, the struggle within the soul of an individual has produced finer results than the struggle between individuals; and anyone familiar with American politics knows how often personal feeling has been allowed to decide the fate of important political and financial issues.

Mr. Crewe's Career (1908) is a study of the next page in political corruption, that in which the railroad monopoly controls politics in the same New England State. The forces that oppose this domination are made concrete in the person of young Austen Vane, the reformer, and Humphrey Crewe, the rich man who thinks he can win his ambition by the lavish use of money. Neither one succeeds in defeating the machine, and Churchill was optimistic in announcing through Austen Vane that the day of corporation dominance is over. There is no such outstanding character as Jethro Bass, however, probably because the growing impersonality of politics made such a picturesque figure less possible. Having shown one weakness of the railroad's machine, the neglect of personal loyalty on the part of the chief manipulator to his representative, Hilary Vane, Churchill failed to use it for a conclusive climax. But his description of the manipulation of a State legislature is delightful, for it is painted with a humor which makes the details bearable. Churchill knew the atmosphere of State politics in New England, for he represented the town of Cornish in the New Hampshire Legislature and was a candidate for the nomination as governor.

The interrelations of politics and finance form the background also of

A Far Country (1915) which, however, is laid in a middle western city. Here the conception is better than the execution. Hugh Paret, the lawyer who, beginning with some ideals, gradually submerges them through the pressure of professional opportunity until he arrives at a great material success, is a real picture of a man so wholly in love with the game he is playing that he neglects everything else for it. It is the intellectual accomplishment that appeals to him and in his services to corrupt financial deals he deliberately blinds himself to the injustice he is aiding because of his glory in the ingenuity with which he evades what seem to him antiquated laws. Churchill draws with sufficient clarity the early days of the holding companies and, being a liberal rather than a radical, does not become shrill in his criticism and is therefore more effective. Where he becomes at all concrete in his remedies, he proposes "acquiescence to developed leadership made responsible." Both the great parties seemed to him hopeless, for he was a progressive of the Theodore Roosevelt type, and he seemed not to realize that such a way out could hardly be through a third party, or through a party which had made the preservation of institutions rather than the development of leadership its cardinal principle.

Churchill's limitations as a novelist are shown clearly in those later books when the interest of history or politics is absent. *A Modern Chronicle* (1910) is an attempt to deal with the question of divorce. But Honora Leffingwell, through all her marital experiments, is never convincing. She is really three different women so far as she is alive at all, and the backgrounds of New York, Newport, or Paris are simply places. *The Inside of the Cup* (1913), a study of modern religion, is even less interesting. Churchill dealt with a real situation in the decline of faith on the part of the younger generation. But John Hodder, the clergyman who, although nearly forty, "is just learning about conditions of life in a modern city," who horrifies his parishioners by his advanced views on theology and who refuses to resign at Parr's bidding, is not nearly so real as Theron Ware, Emanuel Bayard or Dr. Lavendar. Harold Frederic, Mrs. Ward and Mrs. Deland at her best period knew that the novel is no place for theological arguments, and Hodder is simply an expression of Churchill's ideas of what Christianity should be. *The Dwelling Place of Light* (1917), a study of industrial relations in a manufacturing city in New England, has a certain verity in the drab picture of two girls' lives which drive them into illicit relations, but the story goes serenely to pieces at the end, and even the strike is won for no apparent reason by the I.W.W.

Churchill's merits include an instinct for selecting dramatic moments in history, a feeling for pageantry, a deep sympathy with the pioneer spirit in American life, a love of the country as a whole, and a belief in the ultimate triumph of the right. He worked without haste and evidently hoped to make a contribution first to the knowledge of his country's past and, second, to a solution of those problems which confronted his own age. No one can read his novels without respecting his industry and the sincerity of his utterance, and that millions of readers have enjoyed his competent narrative talents is beyond question. His faults are a prolixity of detail, a lack of constructive ability in plot-making, often resulting in feebleness or inconclusiveness in the ending, a weakness in character drawing, and a general tendency toward superficiality. When one looks at the illustrations for *The Crisis* by Howard Chandler Christy, they represent strikingly the essentially artificial quality of the characters of that period of romantic fiction. But above all Churchill lacks the distinction of style possessed by greater romancers like Mitchell or Crawford. There is usually no edge to his sentences, just as there is often no edge to his thinking. His naïve "Afterwords" read almost like the words of an amateur, conveying information which is or should be unnecessary. He appeals now as always to a young audience, who delight in his gallant figures and do not bother much with his theories of life. That is the reason *The Crossing*, which has a boy hero, is the most satisfactory of his historical novels. It has no character to equal Jethro Bass, however, who seems to be the one creation of Churchill who rises into a high rank.

The most consistently productive of the historical novelists, Mary Johnston (1870–1936), began in 1898 with *Prisoners of Hope*, which illustrates strikingly the merits and demerits not only of her twenty-two volumes, but also of the historical romance of the time. Miss Johnston, who was born in Botetourt County, Virginia, has written of various stages in the history of that State, but did her best work in her pictures of the Colonial period and that of the Civil War. She understood at the very outset of her career that romance demands vivid contrasts, the continued suspense of danger, and the story of a love to which time and space are merely incidental impediments. In order to provide contrasts, she made her first hero, Godfrey Landless, a convict, innocent of course, who had been shipped to the colonies and sold to a planter, Colonel Verney. He loves Patricia Verney, who promptly scorns him, and as a rival Miss Johnston created in Sir Charles Carew a type of the polished courtier who possesses everything Godfrey lacks. The novel proceeds in a whirl of insurrection, Indian attacks, treachery and heroism, culminating in Godfrey's rescue of Patricia from the Indians and their return together. With a courage rare in the historical romance, Miss Johnston separated the lovers, and Godfrey is left to his own devices in the wilderness, a victim to a social organization which made marriage with Patricia impossible, although she promises to remain true to him. All the emotions of the characters are keyed to a high pitch. There are constant improbabilities, and yet there are skilful touches which revealed Miss Johnston as a plot architect of no mean ability. One example is the way in which Carew's insolence thrusts Godfrey out of his boat when he begs permission to go with the expedition to save Patricia. This exclusion prevents Godfrey from going on the false trail with the others and brings him alone with Patricia at the end of the journey. In *To Have and to Hold* (1900) Miss Johnston inverted her first plot and brought a young English noblewoman to Virginia among the women sent over to be purchased as wives for the colonists. She comes to avoid a marriage with a man she loathes, and her purchaser, who is of course the "best swordsman in Virginia," treats her with a delicacy which finally wins her. The improbabilities are more daring than in *Prisoners of Hope*, and Ralph Percy, who tells his own story, is one of those irritating romantic heroes who turns pirate at a moment's notice and apparently learns seamanship overnight. Having spent several days on short rations in an open boat, he conquers three pirates by his skill with the rapier. This might have been overlooked, but when the third swordsman has faced him for a long time and Captain Percy calmly remarks, "Slowly but surely I wore him out," the bubble of illusion bursts and the masculine reader thinks with a sigh of the duelling scenes in *Saracinesca*, or the thrilling fight on the staircase in *The Adventures of François*. *Audrey* (1902) is much better. The mountain girl, whose parents have been killed by the Indians and who becomes an actress in that first theatrical company which played at Williamsburg in the early eighteenth century, has some reality. Miss Johnston's power to recreate an atmosphere is beyond dispute. Only an historian of the theatre perhaps can appreciate the skill with which she has made that playhouse of Charles and Mary Stagg, of which only a faint tradition remains, a living thing. We do not know even the plays they produced in 1727–1728, but she has selected just the ones they would probably have put on, and the attitude of the planter class toward the troupe, the easy transition from amateur to professional which makes possible Audrey's success—these are true to the time and place. With the courage of the romanticist, she does not hesitate to use older material, for the scene at the ball to which Howard takes Audrey is obviously modelled on a similar one in John Esten Cooke's *Virginia Comedians*. That Cooke's episode was still better done is only another illustration of the limitations of romance. And yet Cooke would probably not have had the courage to let his heroine die, as Audrey does, after the vivid scene in the theatre when she saves Howard's life.

In *Lewis Rand* (1908) Miss Johnston drew her best male character, the son of a "tobacco-roller," who rises to legal and political eminence amid the fierce partisan warfare of the first decade of the nineteenth century. The contrast here is between the Democrat, the man of the people, and the Federalist patricians, especially Jacqueline Churchill, whom he marries, and Ludwell Cary, his rival, whom he ultimately kills. The strong, passionate nature of Lewis Rand, his ruthless ambition, which involves him in Aaron Burr's conspiracy; his struggle with himself, which finally leads him to confess the murder, are depicted with a skill Miss Johnston never exceeded. The friendship between Ludwell Cary and Jacqueline, which leads him to force a duel on Rand in order to keep him from joining Burr, is pitched on a high plane of idealistic romance, yet it makes more intelligible Rand's intense hatred of a man whom he secretly respects and yet whose interference he bitterly resents. The actual historical characters are few. Jefferson is brought in briefly but effectively, and the trial of Burr for treason is vividly described.

The daughter of Major John W. Johnston of the Confederate Army, Mary Johnston naturally turned to the Civil War for material. *The Long Roll* (1911), which traces the war from the beginning to the death of Stonewall Jackson, and *Cease Firing* (1912), which carries the narrative close to the inevitable end, are based on careful research and are animated by that passion for self-government which might have been expected from a native of the county in which the famous Botetourt Resolutions were born. The wealth of detail concerning the campaigns clogs the action, however, and the fictional characters are submerged by the very effort at completeness. *The Long Roll* is more interesting than *Cease Firing* because in the first book the South is winning, while in the second there is a long record of defeat. Stonewall Jackson, whom Miss Johnston draws with considerable skill, disappears also, and Lee is not so well portrayed. But there is a reality in the atmosphere, a sense of tragic struggle against odds, which is very appealing. If Miss Johnston could have fused her facts into concreteness through imaginary characters, she might have written a great novel of the Civil War. Everything else, except this essential quality, is there.

Her later novels of Virginia, *Michael Forth* (1919), a vague story of post-Civil War conditions; *Croatan* (1923), a story of Raleigh's "lost colony"; *Hunting Shirt* (1931), a frontier story of the last quarter of the eighteenth century; and *Miss Delicia Allen* (1933), a leisurely novel of patrician life before and during the Civil War, show none of the sweep and vigor which made her earlier stories, with all their faults, interesting reading. Miss Johnston's historical romances based on foreign scenes are consistently inferior to those written about her native Virginia. Whether they deal with the Spanish main in *Sir Mortimer* (1904), the Jacobite uprisings of 1745 in *Foes* (1918), the rivalry of monasteries in Henry VII's time in *Silver Cross* (1922), they are conventional and need no analysis. The best of them is *The Fortunes of Gavin* (1915), a story of the "Ugly Princess" laid in the later twelfth century in France, where Miss Johnston represents with some fidelity the impulses of chivalry. With a better prose style than Ford or Churchill, especially in the purely narrative portions, she shares their faults when it comes to the conversations of her characters, who speak in that stilted artificial language which is the chief blemish of the minor writers of the historical romance.

It was only natural that the impulse to portray a civilization in the distant or immediate past should turn to the West for romantic material. Owen Wister (1860–   ) in his introduction to *The Virginian* (1902) claimed that it was an historical novel, and indeed it portrays a civilization that was past when the book was written. Wister had written a series of episodes dealing with the cowpunchers of Wyoming, which he combined into a connected story in *Lin McLean* (1898), and both it and *The Virginian* are interesting on account of some striking episodes rather than through any well-constructed plot. In this regard as in their other qualities, they stem directly from Bret Harte. The same "moral contrast" is the chief attraction of Wister's two heroes, who are indeed much alike. They are virility incarnate and are tenderly chivalric of the right kind of women. Each wins an Eastern girl, one from Kentucky, one from New England. Lin McLean tries vainly to save from the effects of the poison she has taken a woman who has tricked him into a bigamous marriage and who stands between him and his happiness. The Virginian sturdily refuses Mary Wood's plea on their wedding eve not to fight with his enemy and, having killed him, returns to her arms. Lin McLean's adoption of the boy Billy, the fruit of an earlier marriage of his transitory wife, is another Bret Harte touch. But Bret Harte would not have written the scene in which the Virginian sobs over the thought of the friend he has just hanged or that in which the worthless "Shorty" cries into the mane of the pony he has sold for thirty dollars. The great popularity of *The Virginian,* of which editions poured out for more than ten years, is only an indication of the continuous demand for vigorous romance with a theatrical flavor by which the grandson of Fanny Kemble came naturally. It was a form of fiction which the era of the "strenuous life" fostered rather than checked, as the continuous stream of Western fiction proves. But neither of the romances of the West had the charm of Wister's best novel, his sympathetic picture of Charleston life, *Lady Baltimore* (1906). Here the time is more recent, but the attraction of the novel lies mainly in the urbane tone with which Wister portrayed a city whose roots, like those of his native Philadelphia, rested deep in the past.

Distinctly below Wister's novels were the volumes in which Gertrude Atherton (1857–   ) attempted to paint a pageant of the life of California. In neither *The Californians* (1898) nor *The Splendid Idle Forties* (1902) does she succeed in making either the Spanish or the American inhabitants convincing. *Rezánov* (1906), a story of the Russian chamberlain who lays ambitious plans for the conquest of California in 1806, is slightly better, for the characters of Rezánov and "Concha" de Argüella, whom he loves so passionately and who returns his love with interest, are more clearly drawn than is usual with Mrs. Atherton. In most of her fiction, such as her later novel of San Francisco, *The Sisters-in-Law* (1921), the characters simply refuse to stay in the memory. Her political novel, *Senator North* (1900), is an example of the romance of Washington life by one who seems to have looked simply upon its surface. In fiction one cannot convey a sense of the permanent social life of the capital by simply stating that the heroine "is a member of the inner Washington circle" and then plunging her into a love affair with a sixty-year-old Senator who is attractive apparently because he has not lost his "sensuality"! To appreciate thoroughly the absurdity of this story, one has only to turn back to Mrs. Burnett's *Through One Administration*.

The most interesting of Mrs. Atherton's books is *The Conqueror* (1902), a dramatized history of Alexander Hamilton, based upon some research and animated by an admiration for a romantic figure. It was one of the earliest of the "new biographies," in which a man is made a hero not only by recounting his important contributions but also by misrepresenting his opponents. Jefferson is depicted as a coward, Madison as a creature of Hamilton, except when he differs with him, and then he is a traitor! This fatal habit of overstressing her plots, her emotions, and her language will keep Mrs. Atherton's fiction from permanent importance. How can any novelist be taken seriously when she begins a chapter with "The muscles in Doña Ignacia's cheeks fell an inch as she listened"? What Mrs. Atherton was really interested in was the relations between men and women in a state of intense emotional excitement, and it really made little difference as to their locality. When she lays the scene in Munich in *Tower of Ivory* (1910), for example, there is the same superficial treatment of characters who fairly swim in passion.

Notwithstanding the reasons already given for this vogue of romance, the vast popularity of second-rate fiction remains still its most surprising feature. *Eben Holden* (1900), by Irving Bacheller (1859–   ), one of the best sellers, is a sentimental account of the emigration from Vermont to New York, early in the nineteenth century, of an extraordinary orphan and his guide. It is not quite so bad, however, as *D'ri and I* (1901), a story of the War of 1812, for probably the proceedings of the British secret society which nobly releases its enemies after some queer tests of endurance reaches the high water mark of absurdity. Bacheller, like so many others, kept on steadily during the twentieth century, and the figure of Abraham Lincoln, which has often touched with dignity one production of novelists and playwrights, gave some interest to his *A Man for the Ages* (1919). The artistic necessity for understatement in dealing with epochs like the Reconstruction Period, to which Page had called attention in *Red Rock*, is revealed most clearly when such restraint is absent. The romances of Thomas Dixon, (1864–) such as *The Leopard's Spots* (1902) or *The Clansman* (1905) which he evidently believed to be answers to *Uncle Tom's Cabin* since Simon Legree and George Harris are resuscitated, are based, it is true, upon facts. But the horrors of slave domination are laid on with too lurid a brush for fiction, and the style is so faulty and the purpose so obvious that the books rarely approach the level of literature.

While the production and popularity of the romance of history did not remain at the peak they reached at the turn of the century, there was no sudden cessation of interest. Mitchell, Crawford, Cable, Page, Hopkinson Smith, and Allen continued throughout the first and in some cases the second decades to write of the past, either in the novel or the short story. It is true that a classic realist like Mrs. Wharton turned to other fields after one fine novel of eighteenth-century Italy, *The Valley of Decision* (1902). But Booth Tarkington, James Branch Cabell, Joseph Hergesheimer, Ellen Glasgow and Willa Cather all represent the historic impulse, with, however, variations in method which demand special critical treatment. A fine example of historic romance and the best American novel devoted to Greek themes was *The Coward of Thermopylæ* (1911) by Caroline Dale Snedeker, called in later editions *The Spartan*. Taking from Herodotus the account of the one man, Aristodemos, who returned from the battle of Thermopylæ, Mrs. Snedeker painted through his boyhood, his creative gift of song and his heroic struggle against the cruel injustice of Sparta, a remarkable picture of the qualities that upheld Greece in her struggle against the menace of Asia. Aristodemos is the son of an Athenian father and a Spartan mother, and one of the finest elements in the novel is the contrast between the intellectual and artistic flexibility of the Athenian democracy and the rigid uniformity of the Spartan autocracy. The writer seems to have caught from her study of Greek life the clarity and beauty of a style whose sustained strength closes in the exquisite tribute of Pindar to the dead son of his unforgotten friend. Mrs. Snedeker's later story of Greece *The Perilous Seat* (1923) hardly rose to the level of her earlier work. Theria the heroine seems more like a modern girl than a Grecian, and while there are fine episodes, the historical characters are not incorporated with the same skill into the novel. But it would be unfair even to the author of *The Coward of Thermopylæ* to expect her to recreate the serene beauty of that truly remarkable picture of a great civilization.

The persistence of the historic impulse in fiction has been illustrated by the artistic success made at times by those who began in other fields. John T. McIntyre (1871–   ), a Philadelphian, wrote as early as 1902 a realistic description of the seamy side of city life in *The Ragged Edge*. Devoting himself for a time to juvenile fiction, and to the short story, of which "The Three Wise Men" published in *McClure's Magazine* in 1907 was a brilliant example, he matured slowly. It was not until 1923 that his historical novel, *Blowing Weather*, a vivid picture of Philadelphia in 1793, revealed his power to recreate the atmosphere of the old shipping district when his native city was a great port of entry. The romance of the sea and of the slave ships in *Stained Sails* (1928), of old city streets and lanes in *Shot Towers* (1926), was established with a realistic wealth of detail which a keen sense of humor prevented from becoming oppressive. McIntyre has that unusual combination of realistic method and romantic material which keeps his imaginative creations from excess. His dramatic sense which has been evidenced by his work as a playwright shows in the poetic flight of *A Young Man's Fancy* (1925), originally written for the stage. The poet hero who falls in love with his own idealization of a model in a shop window is very appealing. McIntyre has not limited himself to the past, and *Steps Going Down* (1936) is, I believe, to be a realistic picture of life. It has been selected, in advance of publication, as the American representative in the All-Nations Prize Novel Competition, and it is a source of satisfaction to those who have known of the persistent determination of the author to maintain his own standards to learn of his wider recognition.

In the case of romance the progress is not easy to define, for methods and material remain much more constant than is the case with fiction which deals with contemporary life. Yet the novelists treated in this chapter belong together by reason of those virtues and faults that have already been sufficiently indicated. Moreover, in spite of the absurdities of the mass of historical romances, many of which it is not necessary even to mention, in its best examples it was a literary impulse that made for national self-respect as well as for national vanity, and by processes obscure yet real, prepared a public opinion that rendered more possible the social and political reforms of the twentieth century.

CHAPTER XXIII

LAFCADIO HEARN AND THE LATER EXOTIC ROMANCE

THE exotic romance had as one of its most striking exponents a strange genius who, while not native to America, spent so much of his creative life here that he must be included in any survey of our fiction or essay. Born in 1850 on the Isle of Santa Maura in the Ionian archipelago, of an Irish father and Greek mother, whose birthplace, Leucadia, gave him his name, he was educated in Ireland, England, and France and came to New York City in 1869. After various adventures, he went to New Orleans in 1877, apparently under the influence of Cable's fiction,[1] where he fortunately found an outlet through the *Item* and the *Times-Democrat* for his stories, sketches, and translations of foreign literature. From the beginning he said: "I have pledged myself to the worship of the Odd, the Queer, the Strange, the Exotic, the Monstrous." [2]

The *Fantastics*, which were published in book form only in 1914, are probably his earliest productions in New Orleans, dating from 1879 to 1884.[3] His own description of them as dreams of a tropical city with one twin-idea of Love and Death running through them all, is correct. The love has nearly always the touch of death or decay upon it. Some were evidently inspired by Poe, for "The Name on the Stone" is a prose rendering of "Ulalume," and the style is reminiscent either of Poe or of Poe's French imitators. Some are couched in phrases of marked verbal beauty, such as "Aphrodite and the King's Prisoner" or "The Night of All Saints." The yellow fever, of which Hearn had had a light attack in 1878, is described effectively; that his thoughts turned already to Japan shows in "A Tale of a Fan." But the *Fantastics* are interesting mainly as promises of better things to come.

[1] See his article, "The Scenes of Cable's Romances," *Century Magazine* (November, 1883).
[2] Letter to W. D. O'Connor, May, 1884, in *Life and Letters*, Koizumi Edition, Vol. XIII, p. 322.
[3] See Introduction by C. W. Hutson in Vol. II of the Koizumi Edition, concerning the identification of the *Fantastics* from the unique file of the *New Orleans Item*.

Hearn did not reprint the *Fantastics* but preferred to publish his translations or imitations of foreign literature in 1884 as *Strange Leaves from Strange Literature*. He frankly stated in his Introduction that they were "reconstructions of what impressed me as most fantastically beautiful in the most exotic literature which I was able to obtain." He also gives the sources, some of which were secondary, and he makes no claim to scholarly accuracy. Like Joel Chandler Harris, his aim was literary and he took liberties freely with his material. The best of the stories are from Indian and Egyptian originals. "The Book of Thoth" is a powerful tale of Egyptian sorcery. "The Making of Tilottama," in which Brahma, who has made two evil beings invulnerable except to each other, saves humanity by creating the most beautiful of all women, over whom the two Daityas promptly fall out, is typical of Hearn's method. He proceeds to create an atmosphere by a lusciousness of phrasing which appeals best in brief stories, but which palls somewhat in collections. "Bakawali," one of the best stories, tells of a love that passes the bounds of death. The fatalism of the Orient is strongly portrayed in several of the sketches. The stories of Moslem lands and those from the Kalewala and from the Talmud are not so interesting as the Hindoo or Egyptian stories, because there is not so much glamour. Glamour and situation are what Hearn could best create.

The spell of the Orient was upon him before he went to Japan, for *Some Chinese Ghosts* (1887) includes stories taken from Chinese legends, and through their fine understanding of the Oriental spirit raises the old questions as to whether imagination may not often be substituted for experience. Especially appealing is "The Soul of the Great Bell," in which a girl jumps into the molten metal to bring to it the fine tone which will save her father the bellmaker from death or disgrace.

Hearn spent some time on Grande Isle in 1884 and while there visited the sand bank which was all that was left of "Last Island," destroyed in 1856 by one of the terrible storms of the Caribbean Sea. *Chita: a Memory of Last Island* (1889) is a series of remarkable descriptions, united by the story of a lost child, with some good characters, especially Feliu the sailor, who saves Chita and his wife Carmen. Already Hearn showed his power of word painting:

But the pleasure-seekers of Last Island knew there must have been a "great blow" somewhere that day. Still the sea swelled; and a splendid surf made the evening bath delightful. Then, just at sundown, a beautiful cloud-bridge grew up and arched the sky with a single span of cottony pink vapor, that changed and deepened color with the dying of the iridescent day. And the cloud-bridge approached, stretched, strained, and swung around at last to make way for the coming of the gale—even as the light bridges that traverse the dreamy Têche swing open when luggermen sound through their conch-shells the long, bellowing signal of approach.

Then the wind began to blow, with the passing of July. It blew from the northeast, clear, cool. It blew in enormous sighs, dying away at regular intervals, as if pausing to draw breath. All night it blew; and in each pause could be heard the answering moan of the rising surf—as if the rhythm of the sea moulded itself after the rhythm of the air—as if the waving of the water responded precisely to the waving of the wind—a billow for every puff, a surge for every sigh.

His next important book, *Two Years in the French West Indies* (1890), reflected his residence there from 1887 to 1889. These sketches are partly essay and partly fiction, but he is best when he is building up an imaginative picture of terror, as in "La Guiablesse," a story of a Negro witch who leads her lover to a mountain top and sends him to his death when she reveals "the goblin horrors of her face." There is a remarkable description of a smallpox epidemic in "La Vérelte" and, in " 'Ti Canotié," a thrilling story of two little Negroes who are carried out to sea in their packing box, in which they paddle out to welcome the steamers. Sometimes, as in "Un Ravenant," the account of a famous missionary of 1693, Hearn reveals in his lack of sympathy with Père Labat's efforts to preserve white supremacy in Martinique his own lack of any sense of racial integrity. This quality, which had permitted him to establish a connection with a mulatto in Cincinnati in 1875 and even in a chivalric mood to propose marriage, brought upon him consequent ostracism but perhaps made it possible for him to understand the exotic as few have done. Of his other fiction dealing with Martinique, *Youma* (1890) is one of the very best. The devotion of Youma, a "da," corresponding to the "mammy" of the United States, is told without any sentimentality, and her sacrifice of her lover to her fidelity to her little charge, Mayotte, culminates in a dramatic death in the fire kindled by the slaves. "Youma" was a real person, although as usual Hearn included actions of other slaves. There is a remarkable picture of a slave insurrection in 1848; the slow gathering of the insurgent impulse throbs into action:

Even as the last vermilion light began to fade, there sounded from the Place du Fort a long, weird, hollow call, that echoed sobbingly through all the hills like an enormous moan. Then another—from the Mouillage;—another—from the river-mouth;—and others, interblending, from the pirogues and the gabarres and the sabas of the harbor: the blowing of a hundred lambi-shells—the negroes of the city calling to their brethren of the hills . . . So still, the fishers of sharks, from the black coast of Prêcheur, call the travailleurs of the heights to descend and divide the flesh.

And other moaning signals responded faintly—from the valley of the Roxelane and the terraces of Perrinelle—from the Morne d'Orange and the Morne Mirail and the Morne Labelle: the travailleurs were coming! . . . And from the market-place, where by lantern-light the sorcerer still gave out his *léssence-brisé-lenfè,* and his amulets and grease of serpents, began to reverberate ominously the heavy pattering of a tamtam.

The final scene also, when Youma's stoic quality is revealed as she stands at the window of the burning building, and the ironic note which tells of the needlessness of the slave rebellion show Hearn's mastery of phrases.

Hearn seems to have been inspired to visit Japan in 1890 by reading Percival Lowell's *The Soul of the Far East.* He remained there, became a Japanese citizen, married a Japanese, had children, and died in Japan in 1904. Mrs. Bisland, his best biographer, speaks of his function to interpret the childhood of a race that was becoming rapidly modern. Hearn's Japanese works were concerned largely with the tremendous hold of the past upon the Japanese, the subjection of the individual to the race. It happened that Hearn's first appointment as teacher in the school at Matsue in 1890 took him into a region where the older customs still lived to a remarkable degree, and his marriage to a daughter of one of the "samurai," the nobility which had lost their estates and power in the Japanese Revolution, naturally strengthened his interest in the patrician rather than the democratic life of Japan. Gradually his unfavorable reactions to the more modern cities, like Kobe or Tokio, where he became Professor of English in the Imperial University in 1896, threw him more and more into a world of his own imagining.

Much of what Hearn wrote in his twelve volumes about Japan is description, but since he frequently sets his fiction in a framework of essay, and since the finest element of his Japanese fiction is the description of place or mood, no useful distinction between fiction and essay can be preserved. The best stories are to be found in *Out of the East*

(1895), *Kokoro* (1896), *In Ghostly Japan* (1899), *Shadowings* (1900), *A Japanese Miscellany* (1901), *Kottō* (1902), *Kwaidan* (1904) and *The Romance of the Milky Way* (1905). But since there is no marked development in these volumes, the Japanese fiction of Hearn is best analyzed from the point of view of the themes he treats. More than half his stories deal with the supernatural. He assumes, like all great artists who deal with the occult, the reality of the life of a spirit world. One of the most exquisite of the tales is "The Nun of the Temple of Amida" in *Kokoro*. The tenderness which imbues all Hearn's stories of family relationships animates the few words which chronicle the end of the happiness of O-Toyo:

Then twice, within the time of three days, those masters of life and death whose ways belong to the eternal mysteries struck at her heart. First she was taught that the gentle husband for whom she had so often prayed never could return to her—having been returned unto that dust out of which all forms are borrowed. And in another little while she knew her boy slept so deep a sleep that the Chinese physician could not waken him. These things she learned only as shapes are learned in lightning flashes. Between and beyond the flashes was that absolute darkness which is the pity of the gods.

It passed; and she rose to meet a foe whose name is Memory. Before all others she could keep her face, as in other days, sweet and smiling. But when alone with this visitant, she found herself less strong. She would arrange little toys and spread out little dresses on the matting, and look at them, and talk to them in whispers, and smile silently. But the smile would ever end in a burst of wild, loud weeping; and she would beat her head upon the floor, and ask foolish questions of the gods.

O-Toyo calls back the spirit of her little son and he tells her:

"O mother, never weep for me! It is not kindness to mourn for the dead. Over the River of Tears their silent road is; and when mothers weep, the flood of that river rises, and the soul cannot pass, but must wander to and fro. . . ."

So she begins to build her life out of little things, spiritual and material, becoming a companion of the children and thereby living close to the spirit of her own child. Allied to this story is "Karma" in *In Ghostly Japan*, in which a woman and her servant return after death to her lover.

The supernatural was not limited to human beings, with Hearn. The idea of a picture possessing a soul, which refuses to pass into the ownership of one who steals it from its rightful owner, is portrayed effectively in the story of "Kwashin Koji." The supernatural is not always heroic.

Sometimes the shades torment the living people, as in "I Kiryō"; sometimes the spirit enters a living body to convict a thief, as in "Shiryō"; there is a vampire rather effectively portrayed in "The Story of Chugorō." These stories, all from *Kottō*, are brief and have not the stylistic beauty of the earlier stories. Yet in *Kwaidan* the supernatural is colored with dainty charm in "The Story of Aoyagi," in which a young samurai marries a tree maiden; and in *The Romance of the Milky Way* the supernatural is touched with great delicacy once more in "The Story of Itō Norisuke," a tale of a woman's devotion which lasts through long ages to find the lover whom she weds as a spirit. Sometimes the resemblance to the supernatural legends of other races is striking. In "The Dream of a Summer Day" in *Out of the East* the kinship with the Tannhäuser story or the legend of the voyage of Bran is apparent. Urashima weds the daughter of the Dragon King of the sea, lives with her for what he thinks is three years, and returns to find his own tombstone mouldering to decay. He opens the box which she has given him as a charm which will enable him to return to her, and dies.

In the group of "Strange Stories" in *A Japanese Miscellany* the supernatural is allied to another motive which Hearn frequently employs, that of personal honor. "Of a Promise Kept" tells of a samurai who has promised to return to his home on a certain day. Being imprisoned, he commits harakiri, knowing that the soul can travel great distances with rapidity, and he arrives in time to keep his word. Life is always at the service of an ideal. "Yuko, a Reminiscence," the tale of a young girl's suicide as an offering to the gods for the health of the emperor, is an instance of Hearn's use of contemporary material, for Yuso Hatekeyama actually killed herself in 1891.

The love stories are many, usually tinged with the supernatural, and in some respects they remind anyone familiar with the Middle English ballad of a life where "a may's love is easily won" and yet once won lasts forever. Hearn in his essays on Japanese life insists on the absence of love in the Occidental sense, a union of spiritual kinship and physical desire, and implies that Japanese passion is satisfied by the courtezan, while marriage is a family arrangement. It is true that devotion rather than passion is celebrated in his love stories, yet one of the best, "The Red Bridal" from *Out of the East*, is a realistic account of the joint suicide of two lovers, when the girl is to be forced to marry an old man for his wealth. They lie down calmly in front of an approaching express train, being sure that in the next life they will be united. Another story of sacrifice, "Kimiko," is a remarkable character study of a samurai woman who in order to support her mother and little sister becomes a geisha. When a young man of good birth and wealth wishes to marry her she becomes his mistress but postpones the wedding, and finally tells him why. Her disappearance and her message years afterward through his child, whom she passes at the gate of his house, are told with complete simplicity. Like most of Hearn's heroines, she has been of noble rank, and one feels his sympathy with the quiet acceptance of the inevitable on the part of a spirited race. Yet one of his most effective stories, "A Woman's Diary" in *Kottō,* is the record of the unconquerable courage of a woman of a poorer class in meeting the daily tragedies of existence, beginning with a loveless marriage to avoid the shame of being an old maid, and culminating in the deaths of her children for lack of prompt medical attention.

Hearn rarely deals in his fiction with the contrast of Japanese institutions and the activities of Christian missionaries. There is one remarkable story, however, in *A Japanese Miscellany,* "The Case of O-Dai." It is simply the account of a girl who becomes a Christian, throws away at the command of two English missionary women her ancestral tablets of worship, and is completely ostracized by her own race in consequence. Then, when she is dropped by the missionaries whom she has not satisfied in her clerical capacity, she has no recourse but prostitution. The final stroke of fate comes like a blow in the face:

Said the person who bought the body of O-Dai at a third of the price prayed for:

"My business is an exceedingly shameful business. But even into this business no woman can be received who is known to have done the thing that you have done. If I were to take you into my house, no visitors would come; and the people would probably make trouble. Therefore to Ōsaka, where you are not known, you shall be sent; and the house in Ōsaka will pay the money . . ."

So vanished forever O-Dai—flung into the furnace of a city's lust.

The qualities which make Lafcadio Hearn secure of his place in critical estimation are his extraordinary sensitiveness to impressions of beauty, and his power, in which he is allied to Poe, of translating those impressions into words and phrases filled with light and color. He celebrates the primitive virtues of courage and loyalty, the universal sentiments of pity and tenderness. He imbues these with a mysticism which unites the seen and the unseen, which sets at naught the limits of time and space. The result is a universality of motive and situation characteristic of permanent literature. That his major contributions to fiction deal with life in the West Indies and in Japan is no bar to his comprehension by any nation, for he passed his material in all cases through an imagination which selected what was beautiful and rejected the tawdry and the banal.

Of even greater importance than his material was the form of his fiction. He wrote and rewrote, often five times, until the final revision expressed in the most fitting terms at his command the thought he wished to convey. Here again he reminds us of Poe, for even his most exotic fancies were curbed by a simplicity and directness of language in which little trace of "fine writing" appears.

While Hearn is best known as an interpreter of Japanese life, I believe he was correct when he said, even after he had been in the Orient, "Ah, the tropics—they still pull at my heart strings. My real field was there—in the Latin countries, in the West Indies and Spanish America." [4] His most powerful writing is to be found in *Chita, Youma* and *Two Years in the West Indies*. No character equal to Youma emerges from the Japanese fiction. Charming as his stories of Japan may be, he was working in an atmosphere which his own letters prove was alien to him, and where intellectual kinship was almost unknown. In New Orleans, on the other hand, he was stimulated by the encouragement of American editors and writers who understood his peculiarities and gave him free scope. It was in American magazines, notably *Scribner's* and *Harper's*, that he found recognition at a later time. It is a pity that the plans he formed to return to the United States were shattered by his death, for by one of those seeming paradoxes, this wanderer through two hemispheres was most at home in the land of which he never even became a citizen.

If the exotic quality in Hearn was made authentic by observation, that of John Luther Long (1861–1927) was largely the product of his imagination, at times of a high order, and one that has not had proper appreciation either in fiction or drama. He was never in Japan, but inspired by information which he received from his sister, Mrs. Irwin

[4] See his letter quoted in Elizabeth Bisland's *Life and Letters*, Koizumi Edition, Vol. XIII, p. 99.

Currell, he established an atmosphere which has the illusion of reality, and from it he evolved one character at least, of supreme importance, who has passed into world literature. In his first novel, *Miss Cherry Blossom of Tôkyô* (1895), he drew a charming picture of a Japanese girl, Sakura-San, who has studied at Bryn Mawr College and has yet retained the Oriental standards of conduct which provide opportunities of contrast of which Long took advantage. The love-making of Sakura-San and Dick Holly, the American Secretary of Legation at Tokio, is made interesting through the misunderstandings which naturally arise, especially when a clever American woman is trying to keep them apart. But there is a melodramatic quality and an excess of detail in *Miss Cherry Blossom* which indeed is chiefly interesting as a preparation for his long short story, *Madame Butterfly*. *Madame Butterfly* is significant because it illustrates the difference between fiction that is merely charming and that which is great. It is because the love of Cho-Cho-San, a girl of the patrician caste, for Lieutenant Pinkerton, of the American Navy, fills her life to the exclusion of all other passions that she has become known to millions of people who have never known Japan. For him she has cut herself off from her relations, who disown her, and she has refused offers of marriage with her own race with a fine scorn which is incomprehensible to them. For the tragedy of Madame Butterfly makes its great appeal because her devotion is lavished upon a man who from the very beginning looked upon their relations as temporary. The very song he taught her:

> Rog-a-by, bebby, off in Japan,
> You jus' a picture off of a fan,

makes the tragedy inevitable. Her trust, her courage, her battle to keep her illusion, are touched with beauty because they all spring from her own heroic nature, without any real inspiration in Pinkerton's casual passion. Her infinite loneliness, her despair when she finds he has come and gone again with his American wife, her acceptance of the facts with Oriental fatalism lead swiftly to the scene in which she takes out her father's sword with the inscription "To die with Honor, when one can no longer live with Honor," and attempts to follow his example. Long's skill in handling the dialect is remarkable. He gives just enough to convey the atmosphere of the Japanese and, while the dialect adds through its quaintness a humor which keeps the pathos within bounds, it serves even more artistically as a mantle of courtesy under which Madame Butterfly hides her breaking heart.

The dramatic qualities of *Madame Butterfly*, apparent in the contrasts of races and the conflict within the soul of the heroine, attracted the attention of David Belasco, and the play which he and Long made of it was produced in 1900. Certain changes were made to preserve the unities of place and time, and Pinkerton was brought back to allow her to die in his arms. Through the play, but more especially through the opera with music composed by Puccini, Madame Butterfly has become known over the civilized world. But the conception of the character, and the artistic simplicity of the language belong to John Luther Long. She may be an ideal creation, but for purposes of fiction it is just this ideality which has made her intelligible to so many races. Earlier treatments of similar situations, such as Pierre Loti's *Madame Chrysanthème*, are probably more true to the actual circumstances of such relations between foreigners and Japanese, but Madame Chrysanthème has nothing like the vitality of Madame Butterfly because she is a passive agent, while Butterfly is an active force. As Hearn said of Loti, he keeps on the surface of things. With *Madame Butterfly* in 1898 were published other short stories of Japan. These were poignant tragedies like "Purple Eyes" and "Glory" and comedy in "A Gentleman of Japan and A Lady." This story, in which an American lad who has learned by heart a speech from a newspaper for his birthday hears the clergyman who is introducing him making the same speech and is saved from disaster by his Japanese sweetheart, who takes his place, has been the model for at least one very successful scene in the theatre.

Long continued his exotic romance in *The Fox Woman* (1900), an imaginative novel of a crippled Japanese artist and his worship of a beautiful but soulless American woman to whom he is just a passing whim. She is the "Fox Woman" of the Japanese, who is without a soul. For her own pleasure she models him after the hideous Ni-O figures, and in order to please her he tries to look like these grotesques until he grows as bestial as they and his soul becomes subject to his body, just as before his ugly body had been made noble in the eyes of his wife, "Jewel," by the splendor of his soul. Long uses effectively the utter submission of a Japanese wife to her husband's will in Marushida's present to Miss Carroway of Jewel for her body servant. The inevitable discovery on the artist's part of his abandonment by the goddess and the return of Jewel are told simply and naturally.

In *The Prince of Illusion* (1901), *Sixty Jane* (1903) and *Heimweh* (1905) Long's short stories dealt with romantic situations, uneven in plot or treatment, but sometimes rising to a high level through the sympathy with which he revealed the natures of those whom life has treated hardly but who meet misfortune with unshaken courage. Most of the characters are foreign, or of foreign extraction. Long was born in Hanover, Pennsylvania, although he lived during his creative period in Philadelphia, and he knew the inarticulate quality of the Pennsylvania German, which he portrays so well in "Ein Nix-Nutz" or "Heimweh." The Italian is equally well treated in "Dolce" or *Felice* (1908), a delightful comedy of legal inconsistencies in Philadelphia, where Long practised law. Best of all, however, is "The Prince of Illusion," a heart-rending tale of a blind and crippled boy whose mother has built up an illusion of beauty in his surroundings and even in his own person. Her devotion is matched by his own courage, when his sight is suddenly restored, for he keeps from her his knowledge of his sordid surroundings and his own deformity. Long, like all romantic artists, needed curbing at times, as his curious novel *Naughty Nan* (1902) proved, but at his best, when his imagination had free scope, as it did in *Madame Butterfly* or in his plays, like *The Darling of the Gods* or *Adrea*, he could strike a note of magnificence few writers of his time have surpassed.

The exotic life which is set in an American locality is illustrated in the short stories of Chester Baily Fernald (1869–   ), who lived from 1889 to 1894 in California and later visited China and Japan. Since 1907 he has lived abroad, mainly in England, and has written plays rather than fiction. "The Cat and the Cherub," which appeared first in the *Century* in 1895, gave the title to his collection of short stories in 1896, which, with his *Chinatown Stories* (1899), make up his contribution to Oriental themes in fiction. Through Hoo Chee, a small child who with One-Two, his cat, has remarkable adventures, Fernald gave an apparently authentic picture of an exotic civilization, with its own laws and rules, which operate in secret defiance of the laws of the United States. The wars of the Tongs, or secret societies, are revealed through the attempts at abduction of Hoo Chee, but they are usually kept from melodrama by Fernald's restrained, humorous treatment and by a certain indirection which at times makes for confusion. "The Gentleman in the Barrel" is one of the best of the stories, for the character of Doctor Wing Shee is quite real.

Fernald's stories of the sea, *Under the Flagstaff* (1903), are not so distinctive, although evidently based upon his travels, which took him to Alaska. Sudd Lannigan, the sailor, is real enough, and Fernald's style always had a certain distinction, but his taste for the dramatic led him into improbable situations.

CHAPTER XXIV

THE JOURNALISTS

IN a period when so many writers of fiction had their early training in the field of journalism, it may seem impossible to select a few that exhibit to a special degree the influence of this profession. Of course Mark Twain, Bret Harte, Howells and others grew up in the editorial office or the printing house. But they either passed out of this phase or became editors of magazines. The influence of the great monthlies, *Harper's*, the *Atlantic*, *Scribner's Monthly*, the *Century* or *Scribner's Magazine*, under the skilled direction of men like Lowell, Howells, Aldrich, Gilder, W. L. Alden, or E. L. Burlingame, was invaluable in the encouragement of American fiction, and in the sympathetic direction of new talent. Toward the close of the nineteenth century there developed however a form of fiction more vitally affected by the great competition among newspapers for special correspondence, in all quarters of the globe, for stories of so-called "human interest" in large cities, for startling tales of strange countries, in short for glorified reporting. It is apparent that the vast mass of such writing has no relation to literature, but there were a few men who rose into importance either because they combined imagination with experience, because the very demands of their careers afforded them opportunities denied to others, or because the fact that they wrote often for daily newspapers developed a sense of immediate contact with millions of readers which carried with it an inspiration of its own.

It is perhaps natural that there should be a wide variety of critical opinion concerning the permanent importance of those who so frequently wrote for the interest of the moment. Thus Ambrose Bierce (1842–1914) has been compared to Poe and has been by another standard of judgment completely ignored. Certainly the four biographies of Bierce which appeared in 1929 were prompted more by the picturesque career of a man who fought through the Civil War on the Union side and continued to attack throughout his journalistic career in California and in England anyone or any institution he disliked, than by his actual accomplishment in fiction. His early books, *Nuggets and Dust* (1872) and *Cobwebs from an Empty Skull* (1874), belong not to fiction but to sardonic humor. Bierce came to the writing of the short story comparatively late, his *Tales of Soldiers and Civilians* (1891) and *Can Such Thing Be?* (1893) being collections of fiction which had appeared a short time before in *The Examiner* of San Francisco and other papers. Although he industriously edited and published fourteen volumes in 1910, his important contribution to fiction is limited to these two collections of short stories, for *The Monk and the Hangman's Daughter* is a translation of a German novelette by Dr. Richard Voss and is not worth all the discussion that has raged as to its authorship. In December, 1913, Bierce took his provocative personality to Mexico and disappeared, and through the various and differing accounts of his death, all contributed by so-called eye witnesses, he has become a romantic legend. He was probably killed at the Battle of Ojiniga, in January, 1914.

Bierce wrote sixty-eight short stories, many of which are simply brief journalistic accounts of incidents. Of these sixty-eight, all but two deal with death, and probably no one has written so much with such definite limitations of theme. The best of the stories are based on his Civil War experience. Here he was on ground he knew well. His descriptions of the rapid movements of armies, of gallant charges and stubborn defences are given often with clarity and force, and usually with an avoidance of tiresome detail and an understanding of the essential point of conflict, which he transmits to the reader. He could paint also the emotions of the soldier, both the exaltation of conflict and the fear not only of the enemy but also of his own cowardice which leads him to despair and suicide. War is rarely glorious with Bierce; it is usually terrible, and he paints its repulsive side with skill. His own feeling about it is probably given even more definitely in his autobiographical accounts of his campaigns, in which he speaks of "the criminal insanity that we call war." But he is no pacifist. To him a battle was a grim necessity, to be endured and finished, but not to be stopped so long as the enemy was fighting. The war stories vary greatly in merit. Among the best is "One Kind of Officer," in which the fatal outcome of the military code of unswerving obedience to the orders of a superior officer turns the guns of a battery upon another Union regiment and mows them down in heaps. Bierce knew how to bring the climax of the story to personal tragedy in the arrest of Captain Ransome, who has protested against the orders of General Cameron, has been overruled, and, since the general is dead, must bear the blame for a stupidity not of his own making. "An Occurrence at Owl Creek Bridge" is an effective *tour de force*. A Confederate civilian is about to be hanged as a spy, upon the bridge which he has tried to destroy. During the instant in which he falls from the bridge into the river, he loses consciousness, then awakes, and it seems to him that he has escaped the shots of his pursuers and has actually reached his home and greeted his wife. The descriptions of his emotions during this escape, especially while swimming under water and toiling for a day and night toward his home are vivid. Then:

As he is about to clasp her he feels a stunning blow upon the back of the neck; a blinding white light blazes all about him with a sound like the shock of a cannon—then all is darkness and silence!

Peyton Farquhar was dead; his body, with a broken neck, swung gently from side to side beneath the timbers of the Owl Creek bridge.

This story has been justly praised for its suspense, but the surprise ending, of course, was not new, and Bierce used it too often, so that it became almost a mannerism. He did not seem to understand that a surprise ending is artistic only when it causes the reader to reconstruct his conception of the relations of the characters or remoulds the situation into sudden tragedy or comedy. In "An Occurrence at Owl Creek Bridge" or in "A Horseman in the Sky," where we suddenly become aware that the Confederate officer has been shot by his own son, there is such a reconstruction. In "The Coup de Grâce," the tragic situation at the end is terrific. Captain Madwell is the devoted friend of a soldier, Sergeant Caffal Halcrow, and is the enemy of Major Creede Halcrow, brother of his friend. When the Captain finds his friend mortally wounded and begging to be put out of his agony, he struggles for a time and then runs him through the heart. Just at that moment Major Halcrow appears with a stretcher, also looking for his brother, and the Captain is placed in the hands of his enemy. Bierce's merits and demerits show clearly in this story. The reader has forgotten Major Halcrow, and yet it was quite probable that he also would be looking for his brother, so that his appearance is logical. Bierce makes no speculation on the effect upon Captain Madwell, and so leaves the climax unspoiled. But in the description of the condition of Sergeant Halcrow, who has been partially eaten by swine who are prowling over the battlefield, he passes beyond the limits of art in the creation of horror and produces a revulsion of feeling. He did not seem to understand that such details even if based upon actual facts [1] in such a case destroy the effect tried for, for no tragic situation can stand the creation of disgust.

Many of the stories fail because of melodramatic elements, for Bierce again did not seem to understand the difference between the mere state-ment of facts which bear no relation of cause and effect, and the de-velopment of a story in which each event or character revelation is the product of something that has come before. Here the effect of journalis-tic training shows clearly, for every reporter has come in contact with accidental happenings which the creative artist knows he cannot use be-cause they are so improbable that he cannot secure the reader's belief. This defect ruins many of the supernatural stories of Bierce, of which there are a large number both in the war stories and in those of civil life. Sometimes, as in "The Damned Thing," he almost arrives, by reason of his suggestion of a color that cannot be seen by human eyes, just as there are sounds that cannot be heard by the human ear. In "A Fruitless Assignment" the attitude of the reporter who has been sent to a haunted house piques the reader to some interest. But usually Bierce simply states that a dead person has appeared, and the story carries no illusion of the supernatural.

Very rarely does he create an imagined situation and then follow the logic of that situation. In "Night Doings at Deadman's," for example, it is Bierce and not the earlier situations who brings the ghosts into the hut. Sometimes there is no way out, as in "A Psychological Ship-wreck"; sometimes he explains too much, as in "The Middle Toe of the Right Foot." There are laws of supernatural fiction and the most im-portant is to provide a possible natural explanation without obtruding it.

Any classification of Bierce with Poe is absurd. That he had read Poe is evident, from the plot of "Moxon's Master," or the quotations like "his lines 'in the tragedy Man' had all been spoken," in "John Morton-son's Funeral." But Poe's methods are so different that it is difficult even to draw a contrast between them. When Poe produces supernatural events by the denial of a natural law, the supernatural overpowers the natural and our judgment is for the moment surrendered. But with Bierce the judgment remains awake because the natural law is simply

[1] See "On a Mountain," *Works*, Vol. I, p. 232.

denied by the author. Bierce's pseudo-scientific stories are more after the manner of Fitz-James O'Brien than of Poe and rarely are impressive.

The Western stories savor often of Bret Harte, but in one, "The Famous Gilson Bequest," occurs a delightfully sardonic situation which anticipates Mark Twain's "The Man That Corrupted Hadleyburg" by several years. Gilson, who is hanged for horse-stealing, leaves his considerable property to Brentshaw, on whose charge he has been convicted, on condition that if anyone of those citizens who have accused Gilson of robbing their sluices of gold will prove their assertions, the property will go to them. The result is a large number of false claims, which totally corrupt the moral sense of the community and age Brentshaw long before his time.

So far as his stories of civil life are concerned, it is for this sardonic revelation of human weakness that Bierce will be remembered, rather than for his tales of horror. And this mocking, jesting note of his is simply cleverness, and by its very nature cannot be profound. Occasionally there are flashes of insight, such as the description of grief in "The Boarded Window," but they are rare. No character emerges from his stories; they are filled with types. His most important contribution was his picture of the Civil War, where even through the monotonous pattern of the stories we gain a picture of the stern response to duty of the soldiers of the Union, after the first flush of enthusiasm had passed away and they settled down to the bitter struggle against the only adversary that has ever held them long at bay.

Perhaps the next member of this group illustrates most strikingly the advantages and disadvantages of the journalistic career. Richard Harding Davis (1864–1916) was born in Philadelphia and grew up in an atmosphere whose tone was set by his father, L. Clarke Davis, editor of the *Philadelphia Public Ledger*, and his mother, Rebecca Harding Davis. To their home came some of the leading writers and actors of the day, and the love of the theatre shows throughout all Davis's fiction as well as in his plays. In his college career at Swarthmore, Lehigh, and Johns Hopkins he began to write fiction, his first published book being a collection of short stories, *The Adventures of My Freshman* (1883). It was of no importance except as it reflected his determination to write. His newspaper career began in Philadelphia in 1886 with the *Record* and later with the *Press*, and it gave him the material for his first important story, "Gallegher." Soon, however, he joined the staff of the

New York *Sun,* and in 1890 became managing editor of *Harper's Weekly.* There is something very appealing in the correspondence about this time between Davis and his mother, combining sympathy with his joy in his first check for a story [2] in *St. Nicholas* with the revelation that he had received the same sum, fifty dollars, which had been paid her for "Life in the Iron Mills" in 1861. He received practical advice from her also, of an invaluable nature; and even more important, he inherited from her a feeling for reality which, in spite of his own penchant for romantic material, clothes his most significant stories with surety and distinction.

His first important story, "Gallegher," appeared in *Scribner's* in August, 1890. To those who like myself read it as we were entering college, it seemed to be perfection. Gallegher, the office boy of the *Press,* is a real character. "All Gallegher knew had been learnt on the streets . . . and Gallegher had attended morning and evening sessions." The little member of the "Black Diamond" gang of wharf rats never steps out of his proper rôle. He is not merely a type; he is an individual with all the characteristics of his type used with skill to make probable the stirring adventures of a day, beginning with his recognition of Hade, the murderer, through Gallegher's escape from the police at the prize fight with the sporting editor's story in his pocket, to that thrilling race against time from Torresdale down Broad Street and Chestnut Street to the *Press* office "to beat the town." The very faltering of the boy, "so very young and so very old for his years," in his driver's seat on the old cab that bitter night only makes more vivid the grim courage that persists. Pluck, brains, devotion to his business—these are the qualities that make "Gallegher" a remarkable story. It was soon translated into German and French with appreciative comments.[3] Davis published his first collection, *Gallegher and Other Stories,* in 1891. At least one other memorable character came to life on these pages. Cortlandt Van Bibber, the wealthy clubman, who has no visible occupation and goes about breaking laws, social and municipal, but doing generous and quixotic things, is often melodramatic but always interesting. The original suggestion for Van Bibber came from Arthur Brisbane, editor of the New York *Sun,* who found him in a character of a French clubman created

---

[2] "Midsummer Pirates," August, 1889.
[3] See especially *Gallegher, scène de la vie de journal aux États-Unis,* reprinted from *La Revue Hebdomadaire* (Paris, 1894).

by Manchecourt, a writer of no especial prominence.[4] But the bibulous nature of the hero is about all Davis took from his original, and that is reflected only in the name. In his hands Van Bibber became the epitome of courtesy, especially to those weaker than himself. Something of Davis's own nature shines through Van Bibber, for he was constantly taking other people's concerns upon his own shoulders. *Van Bibber and Others* appeared in 1892, and *The Exiles and Other Stories* in 1894. He was on the road to great popular success, perhaps too much so for his own good. Opportunities to act as correspondent for leading dailies took him to battlefields in the Spanish-American War and later in Greece, Mexico, South Africa, France, and other places. But his work as a writer of short stories is best analyzed not through the volumes which were issued regularly, but rather in terms of the characters and motives he established.

He had an instinct for contrasts, especially the moral contrast, and he combined it with the contrast of civilizations in one of the very best short stories in the language, "The Exiles," which appeared in *Harper's Magazine*, May, 1894. Holcombe, an upright reform district attorney, to whom everything is black or white, goes on a vacation to Tangier, where there are no extradition laws. The first people he meets are Meakin, a corrupt police commissioner whom he has driven from New York, and Carroll, who was co-respondent in a divorce case in which Holcombe had represented the injured husband, Thatcher. The way the atmosphere grows on him and loosens his tense moral fiber is indicated in a masterly fashion. When Allen, an absconder, who has robbed an elderly woman, Miss Field, who had taught Holcombe's sister and "everybody's sister," comes to Tangier, Holcombe forces him at the point of a pistol to give him Miss Field's money. The concern of Carroll and Meakin about what Holcombe is going to do is a masterly touch. They want him to go back with his record unsmirched, for they have all grown to like each other, since they have known each other as human beings, not as members of differing castes and professions. The relapse of the highly civilized man into primitive methods, the way Holcombe dominates Allen not only by his gun but also by his force of character, while practically robbing him, might have made even Bret Harte a bit envious. To this group of stories belongs "A Question of Latitude," [5] which describes the way the Congo changes Everett, a newspaper man, who goes out to report on the evils of the Congo and ends by falling in love with Mme. Ducret, the wife of a trader and gambler, who repulses him. In "My Disreputable Friend, Mr. Reagan," Davis used the character of a New York criminal to establish the moral contrast.

Naturally the contrasts arising in the newspaper life were used by him after "Gallegher" had won him fame. The reasons he was not only a good journalist but also more than a journalist are shown in "A Derelict." [6] He describes Keating, the correspondent of the Consolidated Press, who sent only bare facts, as he was directed by the policy of the corporation, "which was death to the literary strivings of the Consolidated Press correspondents." Davis wrote only for newspapers which would permit him to tell the story in his own way. He contrasts with Keating, Channing, an irregular genius, who is down and out in Cuba just before Cervera's fleet comes out of the harbor. Keating has one weakness—drink; while half-sober he takes Channing on his despatch boat as a stoker. When the Spanish fleet makes its dash, Keating is dead-drunk; Channing writes the story and wires it to New York, then collapses with fever. There is a delightfully sardonic ending in New York, when Channing arrives just in time to hear the newspaper men cheering Keating at the testimonial dinner given him as a tribute to the man who has written "*the* story of the war."

The picture of the ships coming out of the harbor shows Davis's terse, vivid descriptive style:

Out through the crack in the wall of mountains, where the sea runs in to meet the waters of Santiago Harbor, and from behind the shield of Morro Castle, a great, gray ship, like a great, gray rat, stuck out her nose and peered about her, and then struck boldly for the open sea. High before her she bore the gold and blood-red flag of Spain, and, like a fugitive leaping from behind his prison-walls, she raced forward for her freedom, to give battle, to meet her death.

A shell from the *Iowa* shrieked its warning in a shrill crescendo, a flutter of flags painted their message against the sky. "The enemy's ships are coming out," they signalled, and the ranks of white-clad figures which the moment before stood motionless on the decks, broke into thousands of separate beings who flung themselves, panting, down the hatchways, or sprang, cheering, to the fighting-tops.

Heavily, but swiftly, as islands slip into the water when a volcano shakes the

[6] In *Ranson's Folly* (1902).

ocean-bed, the great battle-ships buried their bows in the sea, their sides ripped apart with flame and smoke, the thunder of their guns roared and beat against the mountains, and, from the shore, the Spanish forts roared back at them, until the air between was split and riven. The Spanish war-ships were already scudding clouds of smoke, pierced with flashes of red flame, and as they fled, fighting, their batteries rattled with unceasing, feverish fury. But the guns of the American ships, straining in pursuit, answered steadily, carefully, with relentless accuracy, with cruel persistence. At regular intervals they boomed above the hurricane of sound, like great bells tolling for the dead.

It was just that quality of imagination which Davis celebrated in Channing that lifted him above so many writers of his time. His "Invasion of England" [7] reads now as a prophecy both of the unpreparedness of England before the Great War and also of the qualities which rose to meet the emergency. Davis knew thoroughly the limitations of mere reporting. In "The Mind Reader," he makes a distinction of importance:

"There are two kinds of men who succeed in writing fiction—men of genius and reporters. A reporter can describe a thing he has seen in such a way that he can make the reader see it, too. A man of genius can describe something he has *never* seen, or any one else for that matter, in such a way that the reader will exclaim: 'I have never committed a murder; but if I had that's just the way I'd feel about it.' . . ."

And in "The Reporter Who Made Himself King" he gives another aspect of the matter:

If you train up a youth in this way, he will go into reporting with too full a knowledge of the newspaper business, with no illusions concerning it, and with no ignorant enthusiasms, but with a keen and justifiable impression that he is not paid enough for what he does. And he will only do what he is paid to do.

Now, you cannot pay a good reporter for what he does, because he does not work for pay. He works for his paper. He gives his time, his health, his brains, his sleeping hours, and his eating hours, and sometimes his life, to get news for it. He thinks the sun rises only that men may have light by which to read it. But if he has been in a newspaper office from his youth up, he finds out before he becomes a reporter that this is not so, and loses his real value. He should come right out of the University where he has been doing "campus notes" for the college weekly, and be pitchforked out into city work without knowing whether the Battery is at Harlem or Hunter's Point, and with the idea that he is a Moulder of Public Opinion and that the Power of the Press is greater than the Power of Money, and that the few lines he writes are of more value in the Editor's eyes than is the column of advertising on the last page, which they are not.

[7] In *The Red Cross Girl* (1912).

This story, which Kipling admired so much, is sheer joyous invention, in which Davis created an island, a people, two kings and a grave international situation, all through the actions of a young reporter who had determined to be a war correspondent.

From the beginning of his career Davis presented contrasts of a more subtle nature through situations which his knowledge of social values made authentic. The effectiveness of "An Unfinished Story," [8] for example, lies not only in the fact that the famous explorer tells, in the presence of the woman whom he has loved and who has deserted him for another, the story of his great devotion as though it were the tragedy of another man. It is principally because she hears this bitter arraignment at a dinner party where every faculty must be strained to conceal her emotion. The moral contrast of "His Bad Angel" [9] is all the more effective because we are not dragged through any sordid details of the party which breaks up only at dawn. "The Other Woman" still rings true to masculine and feminine nature, and amid all the sentimentalities which the discussion of the so-called "double standard" has evoked, it shows relentlessly the truth.

This knowledge of social values makes his stories of diplomatic life abroad, like "The Writing on the Wall," [10] almost up to the level of Marion Crawford, who must have been to some degree his model. Like Crawford he gives one the impression of knowing the international situation. When he came to write stories of the Great War, like "Somewhere in France" (1915), he showed no loss of power to keep up suspense and used effectively the double surprise ending.

Davis was always urban. His amusing story "The Nature Faker" shows his disbelief in the return to primitive conditions by those, even animals, who have escaped from them. He knew the city thoroughly; his stories of politics like "The Frame-Up" or "A Wasted Day" prove this as conclusively as the Van Bibber stories. He loved the city because its life is more complex and rapid, because in it there is more for the reporter to see.

Davis was essentially a writer of short fiction. His novels were extremely popular and found their way on to the stage and later to the moving pictures. But there is a looseness of texture in them, a melo-

[8] In *Van Bibber and Others* (1892).
[9] In *The Exiles and Other Stories* (1894).
[10] In *The Exiles and Other Stories*.

dramatic touch which is not so often present in his short stories. All his novels deal with the international scene. *The Princess Aline* (1895) had a motive based on reality, even though Carlton's journey across the ocean and through Europe in pursuit of a Princess whom he never meets is fantastic. The deeper hold which the American woman has upon the American man, even in the midst of his infatuation for a foreign princess, made the book appealing, especially to those who have had an opportunity to contrast the natural relations of man and woman in the United States with their more artificial relations on the continent of Europe. *Soldiers of Fortune* (1897) is a good yarn dealing with a revolution in Venezuela, thinly disguised as "Olancho," in which an American engineer performs heroic actions and wins a young girl, Hope Langham, who has some reality and would have more if Davis could have managed a love story better. It was the weakest element in his fiction, for his people proceed to make speeches to each other as soon as they fall in love.

White Mice (1909) is another good yarn, dealing again with a revolution in Venezuela. The plot is comic opera, but again the flavor of reality is there in the way in which Roddy Forrester breaks through the complicated strands of intrigue simply because of his courage and the singleness of his purpose. Archie Gordon, the American journalist who upsets the schemes of the royal adventurers and blackmailers in *The King's Jackal* (1898), is like a breath of fresh air in a hothouse. Curiously enough, *Captain Macklin* (1902), in which Davis attempted to draw a less usual character, and which he thought was his best novel, did not succeed so well. He tried to represent a man who understresses his emotions and who unconsciously is revealing qualities of conceit and self-esteem. Davis's readers had grown to expect more dash and color in his novels of South American revolutions, and perhaps he had given them a right to establish such a standard for him. It is the penalty which any author pays for popularity.

It is easy to criticize Davis for superficiality and improbability which at times were present in his fiction, and it is necessary, of course, to differentiate between the melodrama of "The Lost House" or "The Spy" and the tense dramatic values of "An Unfinished Story" or "The Exiles." But on reviewing his short stories, it is astonishing how well they stand the test of interest, and even, in speaking of the curious lapses in "The Bar Sinister," in which a mongrel dog is made to use words like "exquisite," it seems a carping criticism to call attention to defects in a rattling good story. The critic who is honest with himself knows that he likes the work of Richard Harding Davis better than he thinks he should, and in such cases he must cease to insist upon standards which are perhaps more artificial than the stories he is attempting to judge. Certainly the artist in words who could make Moyamensing Prison stand out like an etching in "Outside the Prison" and who created Gallegher, and the "Derelict" needs none of the usual hesitating acknowledgements of his talent to establish his rank in American fiction.

If Davis was an expression of his time, Stephen Crane (1871–1900) was distinctly a rebel against the conventional critical canons of the day. He was born in Newark, New Jersey, spent one year at Lafayette College and one at Syracuse University, where he became a correspondent for the New York *Tribune*. His college training, which ended in 1891, seems to have made little impression upon him. His experiences as a reporter for the New York *Herald* and the *Tribune* were also intermittent, for during his brief career he persistently arranged his life to suit himself and disregarded patterns of all kinds. Naturally there arose accounts of dissipation, usually unfounded and always exaggerated, and there has grown up a Stephen Crane myth which the testimony of those who knew him has not been able to correct. His admirers have also done him harm by indiscriminate praise, and the critical estimate of his accomplishment needs adjustment even more than the record of his personal history.

He wrote fiction during his undergraduate days, but his first serious attempt was *Maggie, A Girl of the Streets* (1893), which shocked the magazine editors and was finally printed by himself in paper covers and almost completely ignored. Crane had from the very beginning a theory of art that truth is to be found in the depths, and *Maggie* is laid in as sordid an atmosphere as a large city can provide. Maggie grows up with a drunken father and mother, makes a feeble effort at supporting herself, and succumbs to the seductions of a barkeeper. She is expelled by her mother, with the assent of her brother, whose attitude is as ironic as her mother's hysterical "forgiveness" when Maggie commits suicide. The situation and the background are old, and the importance of *Maggie* rests upon its treatment. The conversation has the exactitude of the dull repetitious speech of half-drunken boasters, and Crane is responsible for the fictional theory that such repetition is realistic art. It shares, however, the journalistic fallacy that places mere observation on too high a pedestal. As Crane first wrote it, the novelette gave no names to the characters of the mother and brother, and while they are provided with labels in the printed form, the earlier omission is significant for it shows that in Crane's mind they were born as abstractions rather than individuals. They are forces of evil, puppets of fate. This is not denying, of course, that they might assist in the creation of literature, for the old morality plays deal with such forces. But with realism in its highest form they are not concerned. Moreover, even as a type Maggie's mother is not consistent. While her hypocrisy after the suicide is grimly ironic, her surprise when she discovers Maggie's seduction is simply absurd. Yet the writing of *Maggie* was important to Crane, for it brought him the practical friendship of Hamlin Garland, who introduced him to Howells. That apostle of realism was impressed by Crane's sincerity, and soon both he and Garland were justified by something much better than *Maggie*.

Crane read little and was probably ignorant of the descriptions of the Civil War by DeForest, Mrs. Davis, and Weir Mitchell, although he may have been acquainted with the stories of Bierce as early as 1895. In any event, after diligently reading *Battles and Leaders of the Civil War*, he painted a remarkable picture of the feelings of a young soldier during his first battle. The battle is not named, although according to his later story, "The Veteran," it became Chancellorsville, and the name of the hero, Henry Fleming, is found with difficulty. For he also is not an individual person. He is a representative of the untried soldier in general; one of the best elements of the book is the sense it gives of the boy's being a mere pawn in a game of which he does not know the rules. DeForest had printed a more accurate picture in his essay, "The First Time under Fire," but Crane's greatest achievement lay in his power to place himself in an imagined situation and then tell objectively of the spiritual baptism of fire through which a man is purged of the original sin of cowardice. The self-pity of the new recruit and the sudden panic of the regiment in the face of the enemy are remarkably depicted:

To the youth it was an onslaught of redoubtable dragons. He became like the man who lost his legs at the approach of the red and green monster. He waited in a sort of horrified listening attitude. He seemed to shut his eyes and wait to be gobbled.

A man near him who, up to this time, had been working feverishly at his rifle suddenly stopped and ran with howls. A lad whose face had borne an expression of exalted courage, the majesty of him who dares give his life, was, at an instant, smitten abject. He blanched like one who has come to the edge of a cliff at midnight and is suddenly made aware. There was a revelation. He, too, threw down his gun and fled. There was no shame in his face. He ran like a rabbit.

Others began to scamper away through the smoke. The youth turned his head, shaken from his trance by this movement, as if the regiment was leaving him behind. He saw the few fleeting forms.

He yelled then with fright and swung about. For a moment, in the great clamour, he was like a proverbial chicken. He lost the direction of safety. Destruction threatened him from all points.

Directly he began to speed toward the rear in great leaps. His rifle and cap were gone. His unbuttoned coat bulged in the wind. The flap of his cartridge box bobbed wildly, and his canteen, by its slender cord, swung out behind. On his face was all the horror of those things which he imagined.

The lieutenant sprang forward bawling. The youth saw his features wrathfully red, and saw him make a dab with his sword. His one thought of the incident was that the lieutenant was a peculiar creature to feel interested in such matters upon this occasion.

The terrible exhaustion of the men and the way the fighting becomes automatic are signally well portrayed, and one especially good touch is the contrast between the tremendous distance the regiment thinks it has gone in its charge with the short space it really has covered when viewed after the retreat. Most important, however, is the change in the boy's nature. His shame when he joins the men who are really wounded, in their procession to the rear, and the ironic incident by which he receives a slight wound from a fleeing soldier which enables him to rejoin his regiment without loss of prestige lead naturally to the climax. He fights like a wildcat without knowing it and seizes the colors of the regiment in the charge which reëstablishes its reputation. Finally he passes from active heroism of action to the more permanent courage of character:

With this conviction came a store of assurance. He felt a quiet manhood, non-assertive but of sturdy and strong blood. He knew that he would no more quail before his guides, wherever they should point. He had been to touch the great death, and found that, after all, it was but the great death. He was a man.

So it came to pass that, as he trudged from the place of blood and wrath, his soul changed. He came from hot ploughshares to prospects of clover tranquilly, and it was as if hot ploughshares were not. Scars faded as flowers.

It rained. The procession of weary soldiers became a draggled train, despondent and muttering, marching with churning effort in a trough of liquid brown mud under a low, wretched sky. Yet the youth smiled, for he saw that the world was a world for him, though many discovered it to be made of oaths and walking-sticks. He had rid himself of the red sickness of battle. The sultry nightmare was in the past. He had been an animal blistered and sweating in the heat and pain of war. He turned now with a lover's thirst to images of tranquil skies, fresh meadows, cool brooks—an existence of soft and eternal peace.

Over the river a golden ray of sun came through the hosts of leaden rain clouds.

The style of *The Red Badge of Courage* is at times a curious staccato, at others almost ornate. Crane's weaker side is illustrated by a few lines:

The youth turned, with sudden, livid rage, toward the battle-field. He shook his fist. He seemed about to deliver a philippic.
"Hell—"
The red sun was pasted in the sky like a wafer.

The last line, so often praised, is artificial both in itself and in the careful placing for effect at the end of a chapter. But the great advance over *Maggie* is apparent. The characters in Crane's first book had no power to elicit sympathy, for they had no spiritual importance, but Henry Fleming represents one of the most appealing motives of fiction, victory for a great cause won first by a victory over one's self.

In *George's Mother* (1896) Crane returned to the manner of *Maggie* in a study of the emotional reactions of a young workingman and his mother. The tone is more truly realistic and the petty tyranny of the feminine urge to arrange life in all its details is accurately described. Conversation is once more represented in its repetitions and its vacuity, but no great interest is excited in either of the characters. Much more successful were his stories included in *The Little Regiment and Other Episodes of the American Civil War* (1896). Again the unheroic is made interesting because it is set against a background of importance. The inarticulate affection of· two brothers who behave in an unusual but very human way is developed as a motif through the stirring description of a battle. The collapse of the charge against the Confederate intrenchments is a fine piece of word-painting. Crane's ironic method was usually successful. In "A Mystery of Heroism" the soldier who risks his life to bring water to his comrades is in a state of utter fright during his venture. Then when he returns the bucket is found to be empty, as he has spilled most of it in giving a drink to a wounded officer on the way.

The Third Violet (1897), a novelette, is partly autobiographical in its love story of an artist whose adventure with a girl he meets in the mountains is in any event pure journalism. The girl is hardly alive, but the ménage of the painters in New York City is sufficiently accurate. It has nothing like the importance of *The Monster*, which first appeared in *Harper's Magazine* in August, 1898. This is a powerful attack upon the stupidity and intolerance of a town that is ruled by the psychology of the herd. A Negro saves a little boy from being burnt and, falling, overcome by the fumes in the laboratory of Dr. Trescott, the boy's father, has his face eaten away by an acid falling upon it. At first he is a hero, but his deformity makes him an object of horror; finally even the Doctor's practice is affected by his refusal to abandon the Negro. The description of the accident goes to the very edge of art in its realism of horror:

Johnson had fallen with his head at the base of an old-fashioned desk. There was a row of jars upon the top of this desk. For the most part, they were silent amid this rioting, but there was one which seemed to hold a scintillant and writhing serpent.

Suddenly the glass splintered, and a ruby-red snakelike thing poured its thick length out upon the top of the old desk. It coiled and hesitated, and then began to swim a languorous way down the mahogany slant. At the angle it waved its sizzling molten head to and fro over the closed eyes of the man beneath it. Then, in a moment, with a mystic impulse, it moved again, and the red snake flowed directly down into Johnson's upturned face.

Afterward the trail of this creature seemed to reek, and amid flames and low explosions drops like red-hot jewels pattered softly down it at leisurely intervals.

Through one character, that of an old maid, who alone refuses to follow the herd, Crane conveys the acid comment of an uncompromising individualist upon the brutal instinct of the small-town mind. This is her function in the book, but by a curious critical stupidity she has been celebrated by his adulators as a study of starved sexual instincts.

One of Crane's finest short stories gave the title to his collection *The Open Boat and Other Tales of Adventure* (1898). "The Open Boat" was based upon his own experiences on his way to Cuba as a correspondent during the filibustering expeditions preceding the Cuban War. The emotions and reactions of four men in an open boat after a wreck are given with an insight and a fidelity to fact that makes the story memorable. It begins, "None of them knew the color of the sky. Their eyes glanced level and were fastened upon the waves that swept toward them." Their preoccupation with the things immediately around them, varied by occasional flashes of the distant horizon where may lie their safety, is finely wrought. The quiet acceptance of fate, the longing for rest, yet the constant response when their turn comes to row, all these are vividly told. One of the most realistic touches comes when the land is near but the breakers forbid them to run close to the shore. The correspondent, who tells the story, speaks of his lack of emotion at the supreme moment of danger. "It merely occurred to him that if he should drown it would be a shame." This sentence rang a responsive chord in my memory, for it represented exactly my impression when I was about to go down for the third time. No past life came to my mind, as the romantic accounts of drowning would have us believe. I simply had that sense of irritation which Crane puts so adequately yet so simply. The comedy of the filibusters is told delightfully in "Flanagan and His Short Filibustering Adventure." Crane's experiences in Nebraska, Texas, and Mexico come into the stories in this volume. In "A Man and Some Others" there is a good description of the way a man feels when he has killed a human being for the first time. The Western stories, however, while good journalism, treat of shooting affrays which Bret Harte had used to much better advantage, and the stories of Mexico are usually incidents which reveal no profound knowledge of Mexican nature.

Out of his experiences as a correspondent in the Greco-Turkish War came his novel *Active Service* (1899). It is a satire upon the place a correspondent plays in a situation where he is welcomed only as an audience. Some of the characters descend into burlesque, especially the college professor Wainwright and his daughter. Crane finished it under the strain of his more strenuous experiences in Cuba during the Spanish American War. The actual knowledge of war, curiously enough, added little to Crane's fiction, for none of the stories in *Wounds in the Rain* (1900) equals *The Red Badge of Courage*. The journalistic smartness tinges most of them, and the imitation of Kipling is evident, especially in "The Kicking Twelfth," a section added in later editions. The best of the stories are "The Price of the Harness," an appreciative analysis of the feelings of the regular army, both officers and privates, and "Virtue in War," which strikes something of the same note and has some vigorous fighting in it. There is a sardonic satire of the politicians who made the Spanish American War a playground for nepotism and an example of incompetency in "The Second Generation." But when Crane is not describing the emotions of the fighting man he is reaching for something he cannot attain, as in the love story in "The Clan of No-Name."

Crane's last work shows a marked decrease in power. His health never recovered from the exposure of the campaigns in which he had shared. *Whilomville Stories* (1900) reveal a rather bitter knowledge of boy psychology, but they are once more the contrast of the mob and the individual boy who does not fit into the pattern. How cruel the child mob can be to this type Crane well knew. His last novel, *The O'Ruddy*, was unfinished at his death in 1900 and was completed by Robert Barr. It is an amusing romance of a young Irishman of ancient but impoverished family, laid in an indeterminate time, but it can hardly be treated more seriously than Crane himself treated his material.

It would seem that it is time to dispel the haze which the shocked editors of 1893, the impatient lion-hunters of his brief day of fame, and the enthusiastic creators of a cult which has sent his first editions to high prices have all conspired to build up around the name of Stephen Crane. He is no supreme genius towering above men of talent; he is one of them, better than most, but still one of them. Occasionally in *The Red Badge of Courage*, in *The Monster*, in "The Open Boat" he rose out of rhetoric into imaginative prose. But these do not make a great contribution to literature, and the twelve volumes of his collected edition contain much work that is sketchy and immature or shows the strain of his approaching end. That he went down into the depths so often would not have mattered if, like Eugene O'Neill, he had had the power to draw beauty from the struggles of dwarfed souls striving upward to the light. But Crane too often left them in the mud, content to describe them in that state which has no justification in art except as a place from which to rise. It must be remembered, of course, that his creative period in normal health was limited to about seven years, and that he died before he was thirty. Yet it must also be remembered that he created no single character whose name is remembered, and that his method did not lead to the development of character. What he gave us was the vivid description of the psychology of fear amid the panorama of war.

In a recent report upon the materials for historical and social research, it was suggested that the best way in which a true picture of a community could be obtained would be through a journal kept by an editor of the principal newspaper, who could not only record incidents but could also interpret the motives that swayed the people. Such a record of a Middle

Western town has been written by two Kansas journalists and a comparison of their fiction is illuminating. Edgar W. Howe (1853–   ) was
editor of the Atchison *Daily Globe* when *The Story of a Country Town*
(1883) was written. There is a certain power in the narrative of Ned
Westlock, who as boy and man revolts against the stern rule of his father, the Reverend John Westlock, a domestic ecclesiastical tyrant who
tries to atone by his unyielding industry for his secret dreams of emotional adventures. The savage jealousy of Ned's uncle, Jo Erring, for his
wife, Mateel, and his murder of the man to whom she had once been engaged could easily be paralleled in the history of morbid crime.

But to speak of the novel as a great specimen of realistic art, as is often
done, is to misunderstand the meaning either of realism or of art.
Neither Fairview, the country village, nor Twin Mounds, the town in
which John Westlock's paper is published, ever existed except in the
pessimistic imagination of their chronicler. "There was never a happy
man in Fairview," he remarks, and the inhabitants live in an atmosphere
of perpetual misery, hopeless of achievement and animated by the meanest suspicion of the motives of their neighbors. Moreover, they are self-
contradictory. Jo grows up, we are told, lonely and without sympathy,
yet of the three people with whom he lives as a young man, his sister
loves him deeply and Ned is "the truest friend man ever had"!

The plot is manipulated by the author in a way which nettles any
lover of probability. John Westlock returns for no reason on the very
night his deserted wife dies. The father of the heroine, Agnes, Damon
Barker, a sea captain who has disappeared years before and has come to
the neighborhood entirely by accident, announces himself after his wife's
death just like the "heavy man" of a melodrama. The characters, in the
moments when great emotion would have made them inarticulate, deliver long orations, filled with sentences like Jo's utterance: "The fresh
and innocent affection which I should have had was given to Bragg—
he had the fragrance of the rose: I have the withered leaves, after he
tired of its beauty, and tossed it away."

Even more distressing is the cheap cynicism, sometimes put in the
mouth of Ned Westlock, as "I have never formed a good opinion of a
man there that I was not finally told something to his discredit by another citizen." As if these utterances were not sufficient, Howe created
Lytle Biggs, through whose supposed philosophy he attempts to strip
humanity of every shred of decency and succeeds only in boring the

reader. The book would not be worthy of much notice except that it illustrates the critical stupidity which praises a sordid picture of life as necessarily true and, in a natural reaction against sugary optimism, is deceived into a belief that such productions as *The Story of a Country Town* are important. Such criticism forgets that the fiction which presents life as entirely and completely hopeless is just as false as that which portrays it as perpetually happy. Howe's inability to construct a novel was proved completely by his succeeding books. *The Mystery of the Locks* (1885) is an absurd story of a mysterious stranger who comes to a small town where it apparently always rains. Howe conjured up a secret but utterly failed to provide motives for his characters' actions. The snarls at life and marriage continue, however, and in *A Man Story* (1889) plot disappeared completely.

The journalist submerged the novelist in Howe, but in William Allen White (1868–   ) this has not taken place to so great an extent. Some of his work is purely descriptive, but among his fiction the novels *A Certain Rich Man* (1909) and *In the Heart of a Fool* (1918) are important. *A Certain Rich Man* is a study of John Barclay, a Kansas boy who makes money a god and is successful, only to find he has no real happiness. His ultimate conversion through the midnight vision of a text, and his death while saving a woman of the town, are done rather in the vein of emotional symbolism, but there is a reality in the picture of the times through which he lives that is greater than the reality of the character portrayal. John Barclay, as a boy of ten, is wounded in the Civil War, and later loses the girl he loves by death. He marries and is apparently content, but he forces all those with whom he is associated into shady dealing, even into crime, and he himself is saved only by the bribery of a Federal judge. Barclay is an attempt to write of the typical American. He is not, however, fused into a character like Silas Lapham; he is, instead, told *about* by the author—the characteristic mark of the journalist. The method by which White introduces Molly Culpepper and tells his reader she is to be the heroine is typical. Most of the characters remain merely names. White, who was a follower of Theodore Roosevelt, is a liberal. He is not a muck-raker. His treatment of Barclay is sympathetic, and his solution, by which Barclay returns to the principles which his mother had preserved and for which his father had died, is after all perhaps the only solution.

In the Heart of a Fool (1918) is also a picture of life in a Kansas town, beginning in the 'seventies and continuing practically to the time of writing. There is a good character contrast between the idealist, Grant Adams, a mine worker and labor organizer, who is finally killed in a strike, and Tom Van Dorn, the successful judge, a sensualist, who divorces his wife to marry without knowing it the woman who had been in her youth the mother of Grant Adams' child but had refused to become his wife. The book is long drawn out, however; most of the characters remain names, and, while White often makes a penetrating observation concerning the essential selfishness of illicit passion, or the cloak of materialism that covers the idealism of Americans, one has to wade through a great deal of detail to obtain them. White's shorter fiction, some of which is included in *God's Puppets* (1916), is melodramatic and at times, as in the story "The One a Pharisee," shows the influence of Bret Harte. His fiction, if it lasts, will interest the social historian more than the historian of literature.

If it is a mark of the journalist to write too hastily and too often, Jack London (1876–1916) is a brilliant example. Forty-nine books in sixteen years tell the story of a virile personality who acquired experience rapidly and had the power of observation that hard knocks give more often than regular education. Before he entered high school in 1894, he had known the sea, seen Japan, tramped over the United States, been put in jail for vagrancy, and won a prize for his descriptive article, "Typhoon off the Coast of Japan," from the San Francisco *Call*, in November, 1893. His half year at the University of California could have made little impression, but the year in the Klondike made a deep one. How hard a time he had in establishing his footing as a writer is told in his novels *Martin Eden* and *John Barleycorn*, and even when he made his first success with *The Call of the Wild*, he received small financial return. Consequently he wrote too fast and, while his service as a war correspondent in the Russo-Japanese War in 1904 and in the Mexican campaign in 1914 are not reflected in his fiction to any great degree, the rapid transference of the picturesque to paper remained a characteristic of Jack London's fiction.

It is significant that his first short stories of any importance should have appeared in the *Overland Monthly* and the *Atlantic*, which had afforded Bret Harte his opportunity. For to Bret Harte and his disciple, Rudyard Kipling, London owed much, although his earliest idol had been Washington Irving. Already in his first volume, *The Son of the*

Wolf (1900), the note of violence is struck in the title story in which a woman is taken by her lover against the racial antipathy of her tribe. The best of these stories is "An Odyssey of the North," a powerful tale of the revenge of Naass, an Indian, upon the Scandinavian giant, Axel Gunderson, who had taken his wife from him by force years before. London could draw well the endless patience of Naass as he lures Axel and Unga by the promise of a gold mine into a wild region, going back each night to move the "cache" of provisions, so that Axel will starve on the return trip; the Indian's grim pleasure as his foe dies before his eyes of hunger; his realization after all his years of waiting that Unga has forgotten him and has come to love her husband with a devotion that makes her refuse to return with Naass; and finally the fidelity which brings him back through incredible hardships to the cabin of the white man who had bought his freedom from the service of the Canadian police and made it possible for him to pursue his revenge. The story, which appeared in the *Atlantic* in January, 1900, is more carefully written than much of London's later work.

In *The Call of the Wild* (1903) he made his first distinct impression upon a wide public. London pictured in a great dog, mixture of St. Bernard and shepherd, a response to the primitive call of the wolf pack from which he had originally come. The love of Buck, the dog, for John Thornton, who saves him from an ignorant master who was driving his dogs beyond endurance, is quite natural. But London endows Buck with human qualities which no dog has shown. For example, "He linked the past with the present, and the eternity behind him throbbed through him in a mighty rhythm to which he swayed as the tides and seasons swayed." The best scenes are those in which Buck fights for the supremacy of the pack, or in which he revenges himself upon the Yeehat Indians who have killed Thornton. Here Buck follows his instincts. But in the description of the dog's motives, London is often absurd. What made the book attractive was the direct, forcible style, the celebration of primitive force, and the new setting of the Alaskan gold fields.

In *White Fang* (1906) London attempted to repeat the success of *The Call of the Wild,* and, so far as popularity goes, he was successful, for the novel was translated into French as late as 1923.[11] But artistically it is not the equal of the earlier book. White Fang is one-quarter dog and three-quarters wolf; he reverses the career of Buck by being reabsorbed

[11] *Croc-Blanc,* translated by Paul Gouger and Louis Postif (Paris, 1923).

into civilization. The fights, as usual, are the high spots of the book, especially the contest of White Fang and the bull dog. But fights cannot make a novel; while the accounts of White Fang's parents, Fiche and One Eye, are interesting because they are imaginative, the relations of the wolf dog and his white masters are tinged with that sentimentality which London seemed unable to avoid. Worst of all is the confusion caused by the narrator's speaking at times through the feelings and instincts of a wolf dog and at times with his own mental processes. It is at least startling to have White Fang apparently think that "The wall seemed to him as permeable and yielding as light." And when London speaks of the call of man as "one which it has been given alone of all animals to the wolf to answer," the critic who does not claim to be an expert naturalist is at least puzzled.

To the same group of London's novels belongs *Before Adam* (1906), a picture of the primitive life of man, told in a series of dreams by a boy who, as London acknowledges, breaks the first law of dreams, which is that we do not dream of anything of which the elements have not been in our experience. It was evidently inspired by Kipling's *Jungle Books*. There is a certain cleverness in the description of the processes by which human beings learn to sail boats and defend themselves against the beasts. It is all sentimentalized, however, especially the delicacy of "Big Tooth," who remains unmated for a long time on account of his feelings for the "Swift One." London described primitive man not as he was or thought, but as London gave him thoughts and emotions.

The Alaskan experiences of Jack London are reflected in several of the novels and many of the short stories. Those which deal with human beings are not so important as the animal stories. *Burning Daylight* (1910) is a wild yarn. *Smoke Bellew* (1912), a succession of short episodes, is better, because the races against time to win untold gold, while too highly keyed, still give clearly the sense of desperate effort against the deadly cold of the North. Some of the episodes, such as the scurvy camp, are based on his own experiences. But when Labiskwee, the "white Indian" maiden, dies after her long trail with her lover, and he finds the food she has saved for him although she has starved to death, our memory recalls instantly Mother Shipton in "The Outcasts of Poker Flat." Among his short stories "The Love of Life," the title story of a collection of 1906, is a powerful study of the struggle of a man to win through to safety in the northern wilds.

Jack London's fictions of the sea were also based on his own knowledge but are not so original as the dog stories. *The Sea Wolf* (1904) is a strenuous story of Humphrey Van Weyden, a man of refinement, who is picked up by a sealer in San Francisco harbor and forced to serve as a cabin boy and later a mate by a demoniac captain. The narrative is not bad, but the conversations are unnatural and when Maud Brewster is also picked up, the old situation of a man and a woman alone on an abandoned island is worked over. London's heroes, like Van Weyden or Pathurst, the cabin passenger of *The Mutiny of the Elsinore* (1914), who quells the mutiny after the captain and mates are dead, either learn navigation with a rapidity that is startling or else sail a boat cheerfully without it. In the later novel, London exploits his theory of the supremacy of the blond races over the brunette, which just at that time had become an obsession of the pseudo-anthropologist. In the shorter fiction, "The Seed of McCoy" is a vigorous account of the governor of Pitcairn Island who pilots a burning ship to safety and subdues the mutiny. He is descended from McCoy of the *Bounty*.

Jack London's own experiences play a large part in his fiction, but at least two are definitely autobiographical. His early struggles in authorship make *Martin Eden* interesting, and *John Barleycorn* is a vivid account of his experience with alcohol. His early dislike for it, his gradual yielding to it for companionship among the sailors and oyster pirates of the coast of California, and his later dependence upon it for mental stimulus are told with a sincerity which even the too evident propaganda cannot spoil.

Jack London had a deep sympathy with the underdog which his own hard life had fostered. This led to his novel *The People of the Abyss* (1903), which is a description of the East Side of London, told in the autobiographical manner. Disguised by his clothing and general appearance, he lived in a boarding house for seven weeks and wrote his book. While the novel reveals such understanding of conditions as he could obtain in this inadequate time, there is even more evident the reporter's instinct for a good news story. It is better than *The Iron Heel* (1908), his imaginary account of events during the period 1912 to 1918, during which the Iron Heel, a vaguely described oligarchy consisting of plutocrats, mercenaries, and a selected group of labor unions, takes over by force the government of the United States. It is supposed to be written sometime after 1932 by the widow of the leader of the Social Revolution which, "through carnage and destruction brought lasting peace and happiness on earth." Apparently, the manuscript is found nine centuries later. The book is amusing now on account of what London prophesied and what actually happened in 1912, 1918, and 1932. Among other delightful bits is the martyrdom of Mr. William R. Hearst after he had captured the Democratic party! There is no constructive program, the novel consisting largely of denunciation of conditions, many of which have since been changed by the progressive social legislation of Wilson's first administration. The climax of absurdity is reached in the "premature Revolution" of 1917 in Chicago, in which the Iron Heel and the Socialists destroy most of the city.

Jack London made a mistake when he left imaginative fiction for lengthy recitals of detail, such as *The Valley of the Moon* (1913), in which a prize fighter and his wife leave the city on account of labor troubles and seek a haven in the country. It is a dull story, less interesting than *The Game* (1905), for the prize fighting in the earlier book was kept free of sociological propaganda, in which London is weakest.

It is almost certain that his vogue is passing, for there is something impermanent in the very nature of the literature of violence. But the frequent translations into continental languages give him a definite importance, and a far greater artist, Eugene O'Neill, has stated that it was the reading of Conrad and Jack London that gave him "the urge for the sea." [12]

Perhaps the most striking example of the influence of journalistic standards may be found in the fiction of William Sidney Porter, or "O. Henry" (1862–1910), as he is usually known. Born in Greensboro, North Carolina, where he varied his experience as a drug clerk by drawing caricatures, he went to Texas in 1882 and knew ranch and city life in the West. He became teller in the First National Bank of Austin and in 1896, when accused of embezzlement, he fled to Honduras in Central America. Returning, on account of his wife's illness, he was convicted and spent three years in the Ohio Penitentiary at Columbus. His first short story, "The Miracle of Lava Cañon," appeared in 1898. He had been a columnist for the *Daily Post* of Houston, Texas, but his real work as a short story writer began during his days in prison. On his release

[12] Letter to the present writer, June 13, 1922.

in 1901 he took the name "O. Henry," went to New York City in 1902, and there made his reputation, first as a writer for the popular magazines and later for the New York *World*.

His first book *Cabbages and Kings* (1904), was ostensibly a novel, but it is really a series of short stories connected by the general scheme of life in a Central American seacoast town. There is a certain amount of skill in his introduction of consuls, revolutionaries, blackmailers, and grafters who glide in and out, and the ending is a cleverly fabricated surprise. But there is no character development and no novel, and O. Henry must be judged as a writer of short stories.

It is amazing, when we reread his volumes now, to think how seriously he was taken at the time of his death in 1910. Even historians of literature who should have known better spoke of him as a great master of the art of fiction. But any study of O. Henry's stories becomes at once an exercise in discrimination. Neither the arrangement in volumes nor the date of serial appearance is very helpful, since some of the earliest stories appear in the later collections, and almost from the beginning O. Henry's method was established. That method he learned from Bret Harte. "Whistling Dick's Christmas Stocking," which appeared in *McClure's Magazine* in December 1899, is a story of moral contrast in which a tramp nobly declines to help rob a house because a young girl has called out "Merry Christmas" to him. In another early story, probably written during his prison term, "Georgia's Ruling," the influence of a dead child, another favorite theme of Bret Harte, sways a land-office decision. In "A Blackjack Bargainer" (1901) a drunken Southern lawyer, who sinks so low that he sells the rights to his feud, dons the coat and hat of his traditional enemy when he knows that if he does so, death is waiting for him at the turn of the road. When reading these stories the critic cannot help wishing he could have Bret Harte's opinion on the plot and the characters; it would be illuminating. The most definite impression is akin to that which is given by a melodrama on the stage. There is to be a "big scene" and everything else is built up to it. In "A Retrieved Reformation" (1903) a burglar, Jimmy Valentine, has reformed and, under another name, is about to marry the daughter of the president of the bank. When the new time vault is shown to them all, the president's little niece is shut in accidentally. Jimmy Valentine cuts his way into the vault with his burglar kit and walks calmly out to the spot where a detective is waiting for him. So far the thing is not badly done, although its inspiration in Jean Valjean's revelation of his identity to Javert, the detective, in *Les Misérables* is perhaps obvious. But O. Henry spoils the effect by having his detective refuse to recognize the convict! This story became a successful play, *Alias Jimmy Valentine,* dramatized by Paul Armstrong in 1909, in which the melodrama, of course, came into its own.

What lifts O. Henry at times above his general level was his deep sympathy for the under dog, for youth striving for a taste of joy before the humdrum of existence settles down, for the loyalty of true love, illumined by sacrifice. If his prison term had only made him acquainted with "gentle grafters" and noble-minded burglars, he would not be of any significance except as a humorist. But in the life of New York City he saw the pathos of the daily struggle of those whose margin is small, who live on the seacoast of insecurity, and he wrote in consequence of their few pleasures, magnified by their drab existence into great joys, of their temptations, sometimes overcome and sometimes submerging them, and finally but not often of the suicides which put an end to a struggle too bitter to be borne. Out of this sympathy came an instinctive art which respected the characters he had created, for however low they fall in fortune, in the really fine stories they are never futile.

What could be better of its kind than "The Gift of the Magi" (1905), a tender and compelling story of two young people who live on twenty dollars a week and who give their most cherished possessions—Della her hair and Jim his grandfather's watch—in order that they may buy a Christmas present for each other? Then when Jim buys the hair combs and Della the glorious watch fob, neither of which can be used, the story closes:

> The magi, as you know, were wise men—wonderfully wise men—who brought gifts to the Babe in the manger. They invented the art of giving Christmas presents. Being wise, their gifts were no doubt wise ones, possibly bearing the privilege of exchange in case of duplication. And here I have lamely related to you the uneventful chronicle of two foolish children in a flat who most unwisely sacrificed for each other the greatest treasures of their house. But in a last word to the wise of these days let it be said that of all who give gifts these two were the wisest. Of all who give and receive gifts, such as they are wisest. Everywhere they are wisest. They are the magi.

O. Henry called the volume in which "The Gift of the Magi" appeared *The Four Million,* in answer, according to the introduction, to

Ward McAllister's remark that there were only four hundred people in New York City who were worth knowing. If there is any distinction to be made among his collections, *The Four Million* contains perhaps the best stories. There is to be found "An Unfinished Story," in which Dulcie, a shop girl who has six dollars a week and lives in a hall bedroom, breaks the engagement she has made with a wealthy roué because of the look in the eyes of the portrait of General Kitchener, her idol. Here the best features of the story are the descriptions of her life. "Twice she has been to Coney Island. . . . 'Tis a weary thing to count your pleasures by summers instead of by hours." The story is saved from sentimentality by the implication that next time she may not resist. The natural longing of a girl who is not attractive for a little romance made two good stories, "The Coming Out of Maggie" and "The Brief Début of Tildy." O. Henry did not hesitate to repeat the motives of his stories, for "A Service of Love" strikes the same note of sacrifice with touching reality that sounded through "The Gift of the Magi." In "The Furnished Room" (1904) the interest of the story lies not in the fact that a lover takes unwittingly the same room to commit suicide as that in which the girl he has been seeking had also taken her life. This is sheer melodrama. But there is a sardonic power in the reproduction of the conversation of the landlady with her friend, which reveals how she has recognized the description of the girl that her new lodger had given, but had deliberately deceived him because she wished to conceal the suicide for business reasons. And all the time, unknown to her, he lies dead up in the room. This story illustrated another quality in the best of O. Henry's fiction—that which makes places and localities articulate. The cheerlessness of the room, its complete inhospitality and the pathetic impersonality of the relics of former feminine occupants are as real as can be. O. Henry had a remarkable knowledge of women, good and bad, and in "The Trimmed Lamp," the title story of one collection, there is a vivid contrast of two types of working girl in the city. The shop girl is not always idealized by any means. In "A Lickpenny Lover" Maizie is incapable of knowing honest love from dishonest, and she is in consequence one of his least interesting women.

Next to his stories of New York City, those laid in the South are best. One of these, "A Municipal Report" in *Strictly Business* (1910), was prompted evidently by a remark of Frank Norris that there were only three "story cities" in the United States, New York, New Orleans, and San Francisco. So O. Henry drew a picture of Nashville, Tennessee, where "nothing happens after sundown," and then tells of the Negro cabman who supports his white mistress, who in turn is robbed by her worthless husband until in sudden revolt the Negro kills the wretched drunkard and boaster. The murder is not described, and the excellence of the story is due to the way in which the cab driver is never permitted to step out of his natural rôle, even to the narrator. His loyalty and devotion, his wrath and vengeance are only implied. When the narrator tries to find out something of the circumstances of "Miss Adair," the Negro simply says: "She ain't gwine to starve, suh; she has reso'ces, suh; she has reso'ces." It is the older and romantic South about which O. Henry writes, but the figures in "The Duplicity of Hargraves" or "The Rose of Dixie" are touched sympathetically and will be good fictional material for many years to come.

New York City attracted O. Henry because it is too multiform to be epitomized. In "The Voice of the City" he tries to show this, with only moderate success. But when he depends simply on humor and shows the weaknesses of humanity without any spiritual redeeming spark, he seems cheap and often dull. When he tries to imitate Frank Stockton in "Thimble, Thimble" he falls down completely. Perhaps the compelling necessity of turning out a story every week for the *World* accounts for the fact that the greater part of his fiction is second-rate. In the nine volumes of completed stories there are two hundred and six, out of which about a dozen are first-rate and another dozen creditable. Many more are entertaining, but the entertainment is of the quality furnished by the Sunday supplement. Facility, brevity, and economy of the reader's attention, some devices he had learned from past masters of the form like Harte, Maupassant and Kipling, and the human sympathy life had taught him—these were not enough to make an artist of the first rank.

CHAPTER XXV

EDITH WHARTON

WITH Edith Wharton the supreme artist in modern American fiction emerges, belonging to no movement or group, following her own standards and, while assimilating more richly than any other American novelist except Crawford the culture of France and Italy, remaining essentially American in her choice of material and in her artistic point of view.

Born in New York City in 1862, Edith Newbold Jones grew up in that atmosphere of assured social and commercial values which she analyzes with such clarity in her autobiography, *A Backward Glance* (1934). Early foreign residence, the knowledge of French, German, and Italian as a child, and reading in her father's well selected library, gave her the education in the expression of ideas and the linguistic facility which have helped to make her the coiner of more magnificent phrases than any other living American or British novelist. The very prohibition which kept her as a child from the fiction of the day threw her into the company of the greater historians and poets of the eighteenth and early nineteenth centuries. Among the Americans, Irving, Longfellow, Prescott, and Parkman were the chief, and Keats and Shelley were the awakeners of a new world to her. For it was as a poet she began to write. Four of her lyrics, written when she was fifteen, were published through Longfellow's recommendation in the *Atlantic* in 1880.[1] Mrs. Wharton refers to them as "babblings." Truly, it is hard to see the author of *The Age of Innocence* in "The Parting Day" or "A Failure." But "Patience," beginning "Patience and I have travelled hand and hand," and "Wants," with its natural cry, "We women want so many things," show already that clarity and directness which have remained with their author after fifty-six years. Distinctly better were such sonnets as "Euryalus"[2] and

---

[1] The verses appear anonymously in February, April, and May, 1880.
[2] *Atlantic Monthly*, December, 1889.

"Happiness," [3] or "The Last Giustiniani," [4] in which Mrs. Wharton's narrative gift begins to show clearly.

After her marriage in 1885 to Edward Wharton, of Boston, there were several years of living at Newport, with annual travel in Europe and a growing interest in Italian art and architecture. Through the charming pages of her autobiography one can sense the deepening influence of beauty—in landscape, in architecture, in painting, in literature —and the growth of a discriminating taste which has kept her serenely unmoved by temporary fashions in fiction.

This taste was ruthlessly shown when she came to the selection of her short stories for publication in book form. She rejected her earliest stories in *Scribner's Magazine*, yet they were far better than those written and collected by writers who were popular when her name was still known only to the discriminating. "Mrs. Manstey's View," her first short story, which appeared in *Scribner's Magazine* for July, 1891, is an appealing story of a widow and invalid of limited means who has built up her life on the pleasure she receives from the long vista down the back yards which she sees from her bedroom window. When the extension is to be put up on the house next door which will put an end to this vista, she tries to burn it up and dies of consequent exposure. In her first story Mrs. Wharton dealt with a character in modest surroundings, but one who, instead of lamenting her lot, lived on the resources within herself. It was an earnest of what was to come in *Ethan Frome* or in *Bunner Sisters*.

Another of the rejected stories, "The Fulness of Life," [5] is also of special interest because it deals with the supernatural, one of the fields in which she has achieved such distinction. A woman dies and is introduced in Heaven to the Kindred Spirit whom she has missed upon earth. There is a fine description of her love of beauty, which had been born in a moment in the Church of Or San Michele in Florence, where she recognizes "the light of the Middle Ages, richer, more solemn, more significant than the limpid sunshine of Greece." Another element that has ever been present in Mrs. Wharton's work shows in this story, for the wife refuses to go with the Kindred Spirit because she cannot be satisfied until she knows what will become of her husband when he arrives. It is

---

[3] *Scribner's Magazine*, December, 1889.
[4] *Scribner's Magazine*, October, 1889.
[5] *Scribner's Magazine*, December, 1893.

this ethical sense which has given body to Mrs. Wharton's fiction just as her love of beauty gave it spirit. It animates another unreprinted story, "That Good May Come," [6] which is a preliminary sketch for *The Touchstone*, and also "The Lamp of Psyche," [7] in which a wife's ideals of her husband are shattered because he had not fought in the Civil War. Mrs. Wharton's remarkable gift for ironic compression was revealed in "The Valley of Childish Things and Other Emblems," [8] a series of brief parables in which she did not hesitate to point a moral. The moral, however, is always a universal one:

A thinly clad man, who was trudging afoot through a wintry and shelterless region, met another wrapped in a big black cloak. The cloak hung heavily on its wearer, and seemed to drag him back, but at least it kept off the cold.

"That's a fine warm cloak you've got," said the first man through his chattering teeth.

"Oh," said the other, "it's none of my choosing, I promise you. It's only my old happiness dyed black and made over into a sorrow; but in this weather a man must wear what he's got."

"To think of some people's luck!" muttered the first man, as the other passed on. "Now I never had enough happiness to make a sorrow out of."

Any one of these early stories could have been included without criticism in *The Greater Inclination* (1899), her first volume of fiction, but there is a sense of more perfect form in those selected which show the critic as well as the artist. While there are slight traces of the influence of Henry James, Mrs. Wharton distinguished herself from him at once by the fact that her manner of expression never hinders the understanding of the reader, whose attention is always economized. Her Americans abroad, as in "Souls Belated," are not contrasted with Europeans from the social point of view. They are secure, and therefore the conflict lies between the human beings and the universal moral law and social code they have defied. The stories are all about Americans, sometimes in international relations, more often on native soil. One of the best is "The Muse's Tragedy," a masterly study of a woman who was supposed to have had a love affair with a famous poet who had really been simply an intellectual and spiritual comrade. She hungered in consequence for the passion she had never experienced. "It had been soul to soul, but never hand in hand, and there were no little things to remem-

[6] *Scribner's Magazine*, May, 1894.
[7] *Scribner's Magazine*, October, 1895.
[8] *Century*, July, 1896.

ber him by." "A Coward" is a fine story of a man who had spent his life in the hope of living down an episode in his youth in which he had abandoned a friend in danger and yet who had stood up for years under the daily torture of his wife's "smile of unforgiving sweetness" because he is paying his dead brother's debt of honor. "The Portrait" is of interest because of its possible relation to Henry James' "The Liar." In Mrs. Wharton's story the painter deliberately loses the opportunity to bring out the real nature of Vard, the corrupt politician, because of Miss Vard's worship of her father. In this story occurs a significant sentence, "In fighting shy of the obvious one may miss the significant," which marks again the difference between Mrs. Wharton's standard and that of Henry James.

The tone of the short stories in her second collection, *Crucial Instances* (1901), is much the same. Two stories, "The Angel at the Grave" and "The Recovery," reveal her knowledge of New England. It is intellectual and artistic New England, not the New England of *Ethan Frome;* the contrast of the painter, Keniston, before he has known the masterpieces of European art and afterwards is as fine an arraignment of the provincialism of that section as has been written. Two stories of Italy, "The Duchess at Prayer" founded on Balzac's "La Grande Bretêche," and "The Confessional," while well done, of course, seem less important to me than those which deal with her own countrymen, though the patrician note is sounded with surety.

To this early period belong two novelettes, *The Touchstone* (1900) and *Sanctuary* (1903). Both state ethical problems. In the first, Glennard sells, after her death, the love letters a celebrated woman has written him. He does this in order to make money which will permit him to marry the woman he really loves. His remorse and despair, and his salvation through his wife's understanding of his suffering are told with the skill Mrs. Wharton always has shown in depicting such a crisis. *Sanctuary* is even better. Here a woman, Kate Peyton, faces the moral dishonesty first of her fiancé and later of her son. She cannot help the first, for he does not understand, but she marries him nevertheless. In the second episode, her son is tempted to use the plans of a friend for a great architectural competition. Her boy, Dick, has lost the chance to finish his own plans through his devotion to his dying comrade, and the latter has definitely told him to use the plans, which are far better than any Dick could have made. The art of the story shows best in the way Mrs. Peyton does not say anything to Dick, even though she knows his fiancée's influence is working against her. *Sanctuary* is a moral tonic. Kate Peyton is a woman who sees right through subterfuges that affection or cowardice create and brushes them aside. The reader is lifted to a high moral altitude and invited to stay there.

Mrs. Wharton's first long novel, *The Valley of Decision* (1902), grew out of her knowledge of her beloved Italy. She gives her sources of information clearly,[9] but, as she says, it was not definite study but a long process of assimilation that gives the book its authority. She chose the end of the eighteenth century, a dramatic period; her hero, Odo, who becomes Duke of "Pianura," under which name Lombardy is thinly disguised, fails because he is a liberal in a day of revolution. The opposing forces of radical and conservative are made concrete by the conflict in his own heart between his mistress, Fulvia, and his wife, widow of the former Duke, whom he has married for reasons of state. Both women love him, and their characters are etched skilfully. The novel came just at the crest of the vogue of the historical romance, but compared with the flimsy quality of most of those romances its solid structure makes it of a different order. *The Valley of Decision* shows how the deadly inertia of inherited privilege fought against Odo, but how his worst enemies were not the nobility and clergy but the tradesmen who lived upon the higher orders. She paints with sympathy the efforts of a prince who is ahead of his time in reforming conditions which were the outgrowth of centuries and whose abuses in many cases had their roots in reforms of the past. The Duke had expected to find the tories against him; he had not expected that the radicals, whom all his changes were to benefit, would suffer themselves to be misled by carefully planned intrigues of the nobility and would block his schemes of reform and permit the murder of the one woman he loved. The novel is a warning to all reformers how little reliance can be placed

---

[9] The truth is that I have always found it hard to explain that gradual absorption into my pores of a myriad details—details of landscape, architecture, old furniture and eighteenth century portraits, the gossip of contemporary diarists and travellers, all vivified by repeated spring wanderings guided by Goethe and the Chevalier de Brosses, by Goldoni and Gozzi, Arthur Young, Dr. Burney and Ippolito Nievo, out of which the tale grew. I did not travel and look and read with the writing of the book in mind; but my years of intimacy with the Italian eighteenth century gradually and imperceptibly fashioned the tale and compelled me to write it; and whatever its faults—and they are many—it is saturated with the atmosphere I had so long lived in. (*A Backward Glance*, p. 128.)

upon popular feeling, and how Odo would have done better if he had depended upon his own sense of right. There is a fine touch when Gamba, the leader of the revolutionists, in the very act of dethroning Duke Odo, gives the ruler, whom he personally loves, the password which will lead him to safety. Mrs. Wharton never lets the background submerge the characters; the story has many dramatic episodes, such as the meeting of Fulvia and Odo at her gate, when she flings her arms around his neck in order that the spy who is following him will think it is a love intrigue that brings him to her father's house instead of the liberal meetings which would send her father to death or exile. Another fine scene is that in which Trescorre, the minister of state, proposes to Odo that he marry the Duchess, who is supposed to be Trescorre's mistress.

The Valley of Decision is a better novel of Italian life than any which have been written in English except those of Marion Crawford. It surpasses *Romola* because Mrs. Wharton, like Crawford, was a lover of Italy rather than a critic of it, and because it never, as Henry James said so truly of *Romola,* "smells of the lamp." Mrs. Wharton's treatment of the Church is characteristic. She paints the abuses of a clerical system which was hampered by political interference and of a monastic life which many of its votaries had selected by a process of social convenience rather than as a sincere vocation, but she understood far better than George Eliot the hold which their faith had upon the people, and she pays more than one tribute to the vitality of an institution which her own insight rather than her inherited instincts led her to appreciate. It was in *The Valley of Decision* that Mrs. Wharton showed for the first time her ability to work on a large canvas, to conceive an ambitious plan and complete it by serious effort. It is above all things a novel, not a mere romance. Though it is laid in the past she does not take refuge in any mistiness of effect. The result is clear cut and brilliant, but the brilliancy is the product of the file and not of the blowpipe.

Before her next novel appeared, Mr. and Mrs. Wharton had established their winter residence in New York City, and the social life which she knew so well became the background for *The House of Mirth* (1905). In this novel Mrs. Wharton created the character of Lily Bart, the product of modern life, endowed with beauty, exquisite in her physical charm, keen to seize advantages, alert in social crises, calmly preparing her campaigns to marry for the power and luxury that money gives, yet impelled toward Lawrence Selden, a lawyer of moderate means, by everything that is fine in her nature. The art of Mrs. Wharton showed in Lily's naturalness. She is not a mere type; she does not proceed with her conquests with mathematical exactitude. She is impulsive, one of those natures that must have their moments of relaxation from a purely intellectual program. Akin in one way to the greater souls who make one supreme sacrifice for their own self-respect, she is more human because she returns after her loftier moments to her program of self-indulgence. As her friend Carrie Fisher, the social middleman, says:

". . . That's Lily all over, you know: she works like a slave preparing the ground and sowing her seed; but the day she ought to be reaping the harvest she oversleeps herself or goes off on a picnic."

Mrs. Fisher paused and looked reflectively at the deep shimmer of sea between the cactus-flowers. "Sometimes," she added, "I think it's just flightiness —and sometimes I think it's because, at heart, she despises the things she's trying for. And it's the difficulty of deciding that makes her such an interesting study."

Around this character Mrs. Wharton grouped many others only slightly less striking. Lawrence Selden, who belonged to Lily's set, yet was above it:

Not that he was notably brilliant or exceptional; in his own profession he was surpassed by more than one man who had bored Lily through many a weary dinner. It was rather that he had preserved a certain social detachment, a happy air of viewing the show objectively, of having points of contact outside the great gilt cage in which they were all huddled for the mob to gape at. How alluring the world outside the cage appeared to Lily, as she heard its door clang on her! In reality, as she knew, the door never clanged: it stood always open; but most of the captives were like flies in a bottle, and having once flown in, could never regain their freedom. It was Selden's distinction that he had never forgotten the way out.

The group of rich people of which Gus and Judy Trenor are the chief, Bertha Dorset, her evil genius, the aspiring climbers of various degrees, especially Rosedale, the rich Jew whose intervention provides some of the most striking scenes, are all alive. The plot too is woven with great skill. Even seeming accidents, such as Selden's passing Trenor's house just as she is leaving it at midnight after Trenor had tricked her for a moment into his power, would not have damaged her in Selden's eyes if her own urgent need for money had not led her to use Trenor to speculate for her. The terrible half truth always played her false and her pride that kept her from explanations keeps our sympathy for her. There is something infinitely tragic in Lily's situation, a girl motherless, with no roots in any soil of home traditions:

She herself had grown up without any one spot of earth being dearer to her than another: there was no centre of early pieties, of grave endearing traditions, to which her heart could revert and from which it could draw strength for itself and tenderness for others.

She is thrown into a struggle against a selfish society with its own standards established for its self-protection, ready to applaud her if she amused it, and condemn her or ignore her if she was no longer of use to it. She was too generous to meet it on its own ground; too pleasure-loving to take a plane above it.

Mrs. Wharton took her place in this novel as our chief social satirist. She was thoroughly at home in the life she described, and she presents the mockery of it all with a skill which only Thackeray has rivaled in the English novel. She is not unaware of the hold of such a life. The physical appeal of its well-ordered luxury she represents through Lily Bart's enjoyment of it. The better side of this social stratum is shown through Selden or even in Gus Trenor's response to Lily's appeal when they are alone in his deserted house. But these occasional glimpses of light only serve to set off in deeper relief the heartlessness of the women, even her own kin, who let Bertha Dorset ruin her without lifting a finger; the sordid exchange by which the guests pay their tributes to hospitality; but, best of all, the purely external quality of its amusements, the lack of personality or of intellectual resources. Mrs. Wharton's analysis of the real source of social power is unerring, when she speaks of Bertha Dorset's attempt to take away even the climbers through whom Lily is forced to earn her living: "That influence, in its last analysis, was simply the power of money. Bertha Dorset's social credit was based on an impregnable bank account."

Mrs. Wharton remarked truly in her autobiography that "a frivolous society can acquire dramatic significance only through what its frivolity destroys," and the tragedy of Lily Bart was inevitable.

There can be no greater critical stupidity, however, than to speak of *The House of Mirth* merely as a social satire. What lifts it into greatness is the love story of Lily and Selden, one of the most exquisite in literature. The book begins with her visit to his rooms and ends with his visit to her death-bed. From the first mention of her affection for him, delicate in its indirection, through their different interviews at Bellomont, where they talk with a frankness which veils the hesitancy with which all deep love approaches its avowal, and the brief scene at the party in which she begs him not to tell her of his love, to the last poignant tragedy when the longing to see him once more takes her to his rooms, the love motive sounds from the depths of their being. In all the episodes some touch of beauty unites them, until there comes the farewell:

She looked at him gently. "Do you remember what you said to me once? That you could help me only by loving me? Well—you did love me for a moment; and it helped me. It has always helped me. But the moment is gone—it was I who let it go. And one must go on living. Goodbye."

She laid her other hand on his, and they looked at each other with a kind of solemnity, as though they stood in the presence of death. Something in truth lay dead between them—the love she had killed in him and could no longer call to life. But something lived between them also, and leaped up in her like an imperishable flame: it was the love his love had kindled, the passion of her soul for his.

In 1907 Mrs. Wharton established her residence in Paris. Her taste turned naturally to a country where her work was being appreciated and was soon regularly translated. In *Madame de Treymes* (1907), a novelette in which a crisis in the lives of three people is developed, Mrs. Wharton showed how much better she knew the Faubourg St. Germain than did Henry James. It is a contrast between French and American standards of honor. John Durham, much as he loves Madame de Malrive, whom as Fanny Frisbee he had known before her marriage to a dissolute marquis, cannot accept the invitation to bribe her sister-in-law, Madame de Treymes, in order to win the latter's aid in obtaining the divorce which will secure his own happiness. At first Madame de Treymes misunderstands his reason; then when she grows to see that it was because he could not degrade that happiness by founding it on a sordid bargain, for the money was needed to save her rascally lover from disgrace, Madame de Treymes betrays her family's plans to him. They have agreed to the divorce because they know that French law, while it has permitted Madame de Malrive to keep her son, will give him back to his father's family if she marries again. Once more Madame de Treymes has misunderstood the American point of view. She has warned him so that he will be prepared to comfort his wife for her loss. But when she finds that Durham's code requires him to tell Madame de Malrive, knowing that she will sacrifice them both to keep her boy, the French woman tries to convince him that she has lied to him and that he can go on safely with the proceedings. No American has so well portrayed the French position which places the continuance and the unity of the family above all other considerations, and yet which assumes the gratification of passion as inevitable. Even our sympathy for Durham cannot prevent Madame de Treymes from holding the center of interest, for her gallant effort, in the midst of her own trouble, to help a man through whom she has caught a glimpse of a standard of honor as inflexible as the social code of the Faubourg St. Germain.

The Fruit of the Tree (1907) was concerned with the struggle that goes on in a man's being between the claim of his chosen work and the more personal claims of the two women he loves. It might also be called a study of the marriage relations, since Bessy Westmore and Justine Brent are two absolutely different types, and each in her own way affects John Amherst. Each, also, fails to make herself the one supreme object of his existence, being pushed into the background by the Westmore factories, through which, in each case, she was led into his life. The novel, though it deals with the problems suggested by the ownership of a large industrial establishment, is not in any sense a "labor novel." The "Works" are useful only as a means to the establishment of human relations. The problems with which Mrs. Wharton is concerned are always personal; one is not so much interested in the well-being of the factory hands as in the question whether John Amherst is to pursue his life work or to give it up, either by reason of his first wife's extravagance and personal demands, or through the consequences of his second wife's action. John Amherst is by all rules of fiction the central figure; he is on the stage always, and yet he never excites our sympathies as Justine Brent does, nor are we as sorry for his frustrated ambitions as we are for Bessy Westmore's unanswered appeal for a larger share in his life. Amherst is one of those men who should never have married. He could not realize that in such a relation generosity is needed sometimes more than justice. It was not so much his absence from her that Bessy objected to; it was his willingness to be absent. Tact and he were strangers, it is true, but that might not have mattered if there had been anything in his nature to take the place of it.

During this period Mrs. Wharton produced some of her most notable short stories. In *The Descent of Man and Other Stories* (1904) a masterpiece of irony, "The Other Two," brings into intimate relations the three husbands of Alice Waythorn, until she is left serving tea to all of them. The ironic implications of this final scene are not spoiled by one word of comment. The futility of divorce is revealed in another striking story, "The Reckoning," which shows relentlessly the havoc which the theory that divorce is to be secured whenever one is tired of the bargain plays in the lives of both men and women. The supernatural is established adroitly in "The Lady's Maid's Bell." Mrs. Wharton wisely chose a woman for narrator whose limitations provide the possibility of natural explanation. But the power of the story arises from the way the devotion of the former lady's maid reaches across the barriers of death to summon her successor to the help of the mistress she had loved. In *The Hermit and the Wildwoman* (1908) the title story is not altogether successful in its interpretation of the impulses which led to the hermit life of the Middle Ages. The ironic touch is much better established in the modern stories, all of which deal with Americans, though in one, "The Last Asset," the scene is foreign. Here the shabby husband who has long before left his wife for reasons easily guessed is dragged out of his retreat to make his daughter's wedding possible, and the full flavor of Mrs. Wharton's satire is felt. The prevailing tone of the stories is that of disillusionment, artistic or personal. Sometimes, as in "The Pretext," the logic of the situation is not quite so inexorable as in Mrs. Wharton's best moments. In "The Best Man," one of her few ventures into the field of politics, she shows her understanding of such situations by having the Governor of "Midsylvania" meet an attempt at blackmail by publishing the facts before the attack appears, and thus taking the ground from under his enemies.

In *Tales of Men and Ghosts* (1910), "The Bolted Door" is a keen analysis of the emotions of a man who ten years before has committed murder in order to secure an inheritance that would mean leisure to write. Failing to succeed, he determines to confess the murder and leave a life he no longer enjoys. To his surprise, no one believes him, all deeming him insane, and the gradual development of his insanity makes a powerful if gruesome story. "His Father's Son" is an appealing story of the pride and affection which a plain man with a poet's soul finds in the son who is all that he had dreamed of being. There is delicious satire in "The Legend" of a cult in which the leader fails to recognize the great man around whom the cult is built. In this collection there is a very effective supernatural story. In "Afterward" the supernatural is at first atmospheric and hovers around a haunted house in Dorsetshire which has been rented by an American couple, Ned and Mary Boyne. The ghost who comes for Ned and with whom he disappears is not a wraith. He looks to Mary when she first sees him like a real person, and to her everlasting remorse she sends him in to her husband. She finds much later that he was a man whom her husband had wronged and who had killed himself. Mrs. Wharton knew well how to establish an atmosphere which permits the supernatural:

No, she would never know what had become of him—no one would ever know. But the house knew; the library in which she spent her long lonely evenings knew. For it was here that the last scene had been enacted, here that the stranger had come, and spoken the word which had caused Boyne to rise and follow him. The floor she trod had felt his tread; the books on the shelves had seen his face; and there were moments when the intense consciousness of the old dusky walls seemed about to break out into some audible revelation of their secret. But the revelation never came, and she knew it would never come. Lyng was not one of the garrulous old houses that betray the secrets entrusted to them. Its very legend proved that it had always been the mute accomplice, the incorruptible custodian, of the mysteries it had surprised. And Mary Boyne, sitting face to face with its silence, felt the futility of seeking to break it by any human means.

Early in the century, Mrs. Wharton had begun to write *Ethan Frome* as an exercise in French, but had abandoned it. Then a few years later Ethan reappeared in her mind as material for fiction,[10] and the complete novelette was published in 1911. Since *Ethan Frome* is often referred to as her finest story—a critical error which appears to have justly "bored and even exasperated" Mrs. Wharton—[11] it is important to place it correctly among her fiction. To those who think of her only as a social satirist and who have not read the many stories which, from "Mrs. Manstey's View" to *Bunner Sisters*, deal with the lives of simple peo-

[10] Edith Wharton, "The Writing of Ethan Frome," *Colophon*, Part XI, Vol. 3 (September, 1932).

[11] Edith Wharton, *A Backward Glance*, p. 209.

ple, or to those who forget how intimately through her residence at Lenox and elsewhere she knew New England, *Ethan Frome* may seem a departure from her prevailing manner. It is, of course, nothing of the kind. Her introduction to the novelette makes clear her selection of the theme because it gave her an opportunity to deal with the inarticulate granite of New England character. She is in error, however, in saying that the "New England of fiction bore little resemblance to the harsh and beautiful land." It is unnecessary to repeat in this place the record of earlier successes in this field. But it is significant that Mrs. Wharton felt that "it was the first subject I had ever approached with full confidence in its value," [12] and the further enlightening remark that while "an air of artificiality is lent to a tale of complex and sophisticated people which the novelist causes to be guessed at and interpreted by any mere looker-on, there need be no such drawback if the looker-on is sophisticated, and the people he interprets are simple." In short, and this point seems to have been overlooked by her critics, to the artist who had created *The House of Mirth* and who was to create *The Age of Innocence*, *Ethan Frome* was an easier task.

Her art is shown most clearly in the manner of the telling. With apparent disregard of the element of suspense, she introduces Ethan Frome as a broken man of fifty-one, as his neighbors see him, and then returning to his youth she relates his tragedy through the eyes of a visitor from a larger world, but really, of course, through her own imagination. For we forget the constructing engineer who is telling the story, and Ethan Frome, his wife Zeena, and her young cousin, Mattie Silver, form that triangle of one man and two women which so often engaged Mrs. Wharton's attention. Ethan Frome elicits our sympathy because he has had to sacrifice his ambitions to take care, one after another, of his father, his mother, and his wife, Zeena Frome, a woman seven years his senior, whom he has married in a reaction of fear at the loneliness of the life he has lived. She is a professional invalid whose terrible grasp upon Ethan is tightened with the power that comes from utter selfishness when it fastens itself upon a generous nature. When she notices the growing affection of Ethan for Mattie, whom she has brought into the house to help her, she pursues ruthlessly her plans for ridding herself of her rival. One of the chief claims of the novel to importance lies in the skill with which the petty circumstances of life bind

[12] "Confessions of a Novelist," *Atlantic*, CLI (April, 1933), 385.

Ethan into helplessness. Through his poverty and his incapacity for a mean action, which prevent him from leaving Zeena and going off with Mattie to begin a new life, the long slow decay of the New England farm, the bitter winters that have sapped the strength from body and will, finally have their way with Ethan. There is magnificent writing as the novel rises to its tragic close in the last coast of Ethan and Mattie together and the crash into the big elm tree that leaves her a helpless invalid and him a twisted survivor. Then with the ironic touch that Mrs. Wharton knows best how to lay upon her situations, she makes Zeena Frome rise from her invalidism to take care not only of Ethan, but also of Mattie, whose broken back takes her out of the reach of Zeena's physical jealousy. But in "that lonely New England farm house that makes the landscape lonelier" the three people face their misery together. It is not misery, however, that makes *Ethan Frome* a fine novel. It is the struggle of Ethan to taste one moment of happiness, and the iron logic of the situation in which a nature like his could not abandon a duty, even if it wrecked his life. There was a potential greatness in his soul, otherwise there would be no reason for the story. How intensely dramatic, too, were the relations of the characters was clearly revealed in the play by Owen and Donald Davis in 1936.

It was a far cry from the stark simplicity of *Ethan Frome* to the complicated issues of *The Reef* (1912). It is an instance of the art with which Mrs. Wharton takes what might be the plot of melodrama and develops it to a powerful novel whose interest lies in the continued interplay of character. The postponement of George Darrow's visit to Anna Leath at her late husband's chateau in France leads to one of those chance meetings with another woman, Sophy Viner, which ends in a week's adventure in Paris, and which wrecks the lives not only of Darrow and Anna but also of Sophy and of Owen Leath, Anna's stepson, who falls deeply in love with Sophy Viner when she becomes established as a governess to his little sister. The title is particularly relevant, for the current of the love of Darrow and Anna is made up of deep and shallow places, and Anna Leath's emotions are complicated to a degree that approaches uncertainty too closely for complete vitality. Yet she is human and feminine, and her horror at the revelation of the passionate interlude between George Darrow and Sophy Viner is measured in terms of her peculiar devotion not only to him but to her conception of their mutual love. This makes all the more effective her sudden gift of herself to Darrow, in her determination to know with him all the experiences of which Sophy has been the mistress. Yet after all Sophy Viner remains most vividly in the memory, for her pluck, her directness of purpose, and her final unselfish plunge into the insecurity which awaited her.

While the scene of *The Reef* is foreign, the characters were all Americans, and in 1913 Mrs. Wharton returned to her native soil in *The Custom of the Country*. This penetrating study of the absurdities of divorce is marred by the utter selfishness of the central character, Undine Spragg, a girl of great physical beauty, whose three marriages and divorces lead her finally back to her first husband, Elmer Moffatt, a fit mate for her. There are some passages as realistic as anything Mrs. Wharton has done, and some of the minor characters, especially Undine's father, who has made money in "Apex" somewhere in the Middle West, are extraordinarily lifelike. The contrast between Undine and the standards of a French patrician, her third husband, Count Raymond de Chelles, is also veracious. But somehow, notwithstanding her great physical beauty, Undine Spragg is unconvincing as the choice of either Ralph Marvell or Count de Chelles. Mrs. Wharton for the first time in her novels permitted the theme to overshadow her characters, and Undine Spragg remains a symbol of perpetual discontent rather than a living woman.

Mrs. Wharton's services to France and Belgium during the Great War belong to history and have been recognized officially by those nations. Her organization of work relief for the destitute began at the commencement of the war and is described modestly in *A Backward Glance*. By 1918 she had five thousand refugees permanently cared for in Paris, four colonies for old people and children, four large sanatoria for tuberculous patients. This work brought her constantly to the front, and her experiences there resulted in her book *Fighting France* (1915). During this war activity she found a certain relaxation in writing *Summer* (1917), a grim novel of New England village life, with a heroine, Charity Royall, the child of a degenerate race that live on "the Mountain," who has been rescued and brought up by "lawyer Royall" in the town of North Dormer. There is no question of the reality of the picture. Every detail of the hopeless misery of the promiscuous group of outlaws was given her by the rector of the church at Lenox, who had ventured on just such a journey as Mrs. Wharton describes in the climax of the novel. The sordid relations of Charity and her guardian, the coming of her child by a man already engaged to be married, her desperate impulse to go back to her mother's people on "the Mountain" and her rescue by Royall are all told with unrelenting realism. But the fact remains that while *Ethan Frome* is a great novel, *Summer* is not. The details of squalor and misery, of characters like Royall and Charity, caught in the toils of moral weakness and inherited evil, rarely, if ever, have made the material for a great novel. Such details are useful only as a background out of which great characters emerge, and they do not emerge in *Summer*. What made *Ethan Frome* a fine novel was not the meanness of Zeena Frome and the petty limitations of poverty. It was the truth that there are human souls so brave, so tender, so generous that neither the chill terror of the lonely winter nor the ceaseless nagging of a bitter woman can conquer them.

In 1916 the publication of *Xingu and Other Stories* revealed the constant power of Mrs. Wharton in the short story. "Xingu" is a delightful satire upon the woman's club and the visiting celebrity. But it has not the power of "Autre Temps," one of the best if not the best of her social studies. This story is based upon the profound truth that society will not take the trouble to revise its judgments. Mrs. Lidcote, who years before had fled with another woman's husband and been tabooed by her generation, learns that her daughter has committed a similar error and rushes home from Europe to stand by her. To her surprise she finds her daughter divorced, remarried, and in the midst of a large house party. But the delicious irony comes in the gradual discovery that her daughter is ashamed of her, and that instead of a comfort she has become a social detriment to her child. She returns to Europe, leaving behind a man who wishes to marry her and live abroad, but is a bit restless at being seen with her in New York! There is a fine war story, "Coming Home," and a strong story of the supernatural, "Kerfol," laid in France in the seventeenth century. But the most remarkable story of this collection is *Bunner Sisters*, a novelette of almost the same length as *Ethan Frome*. To those who have never read "Mrs. Manstey's View" or "That Good May Come," it might seem that Mrs. Wharton was venturing into unfamiliar ground in this story of two obscure maiden sisters in a little millinery shop on a shabby street off Stuyvesant Square in the days of horse cars. But Mrs. Wharton's insight and her sympathy for those who hold to their own standards of conduct has never been limited by economic, social, or geographical distinctions. Ann Eliza Bunner is kin to Ethan Frome, through their deep love and their self-sacrifice. She is a great soul, and her petty surroundings are used properly to dignify her through contrast. To her and to her sister Evelina comes one touch of romance in the unheroic figure of Herman Ramy, the clock-maker. Ann Eliza puts her chance by, although he asks her first, for Evelina's sake. Tawdry as her romance was, it was her only one:

That night, after the light had been put out, the elder sister knelt longer than usual at her prayers. In the silence of the darkened room she was offering up certain dreams and aspirations whose brief blossoming had lent a transient freshness to her days. . . . Grief held up its torch to the frail fabric of Ann Eliza's illusions, and with a firm heart she watched them shrivel into ashes; then, rising from her knees full of the chill joy of renunciation, she laid a kiss on the crimping pins of the sleeping Evelina and crept under the bedspread at her side.

The return of Evelina after her brief but bitter days with a drug fiend for a husband is told with that reticence which marks the artist. How a certain school of fiction would have revelled in the details of Evelina's tragedy, and how unnecessary it would have been! Just enough is told of these days and of Evelina's death to leave Ann Eliza homeless and without resources, to face the emptiness of her future. But never even then does she lose her self-respect.

It was in *The Age of Innocence* (1920) that Mrs. Wharton rose serenely to the unquestionable priority among the novelists writing in English during the twentieth century. Looking back to the days of her girlhood, she recreated the tribal solidarity, the intense clan feeling of New York society of the 'seventies, and against that dull background she drew in vivid flashes the romance of Newland Archer and Ellen Olenska. Archer hears the finer overtones of art and literature to which his clan is deaf, and when the Countess Olenska returns in flight from her intolerable life with her Polish husband, their two natures strike that instant spark which makes their few hours together the source of the real life they live apart. To these hours they bring their deep love, their judgments, and their visions. But Mrs. Wharton understood that this love must not conflict only with a convention or a clan. Just as Ellen Olenska returns, Archer's engagement to May Welland is announced. She is the concrete expression of the period and the place and is as remarkable a character as her cousin and her fiancé. In each of the crises in their love story she strikes surely but relentlessly to prevent the loss of the man she loves. She fights with the weapons forged from her innocence, never letting Newland know that she suspects him, but with perfect good breeding shutting from him all avenues of escape. In that first scene of avowal, when Archer tells Ellen that he cannot go through with his engagement, come the two telegrams from May, agreeing to the advancement of her marriage date, for which he had appealed in vain. When Count Olenski makes overtures to his wife, it is May's fine hand which shuts Archer out of the family's efforts to persuade Ellen to return. When Ellen has promised to come to him once and then leave him, May tells her of her coming child, and keeps them once more apart. But so adroit is she that it is not until his boy, Dallas, tells his father long after May's death that his mother knew of her husband's passion, that he realizes how firm her hold upon his life had been. In each event she counted not only upon her husband's honor but also upon Ellen's generosity, and she had never counted in vain.

One source of May Welland's strength lay in the standards of the life they all knew. That life is delightfully satirized, but its less obvious currents were never lost upon Mrs. Wharton. When the van der Luydens come to the rescue of the Countess Olenska on her return to New York to make a difficult fight against a code that as yet shunned the divorcée, how well Mrs. Wharton puts the older American point of view:

> The dinner was a somewhat formidable business. Dining with the van der Luydens was at best no light matter, and dining there with a Duke who was their cousin was almost a religious solemnity. It pleased Archer to think that only an old New Yorker could perceive the shade of difference (to New York) between being merely a Duke and being the van der Luydens' Duke. New York took stray noblemen calmly, and even (except in the Struthers set) with a certain distrustful *hauteur;* but when they presented such credentials as these they were received with an old-fashioned cordiality that they would have been greatly mistaken in ascribing solely to their standing in Debrett. It was for just such distinctions that the young man cherished his old New York even while he smiled at it.

But the social satire is merely the background. In *The Age of Innocence* Mrs. Wharton painted scene after scene with a surety of touch, a magnificence of phrasing and a splendid control of the resources of the language. How perfect is the first description of the Countess Olenska:

In the middle of the room she paused, looking about her with a grave mouth and smiling eyes; and in that instant Newland Archer rejected the general verdict on her looks. It was true that her early radiance was gone. The red cheeks had paled; she was thin, worn, a little older-looking than her age, which must have been nearly thirty. But there was about her the mysterious authority of beauty, a sureness in the carriage of the head, the movement of the eyes, which, without being in the least theatrical, struck his as highly trained and full of a conscious power.

She becomes to Archer the romance that his life had missed, and she loves the qualities in him that keep him from her:

"At least," she continued, "it was you who made me understand that under the dullness there are things so fine and sensitive and delicate that even those I most cared for in my other life look cheap in comparison. I don't know how to explain myself"—she drew together her troubled brows—"but it seems as if I'd never before understood with how much that is hard and shabby and base the most exquisite pleasures may be paid."

How could language strip away more clearly the sentimentality with which fiction has clothed illicit passion than this passage:—

The carriage had crossed Forty-second Street: May's sturdy brougham-horse was carrying them northward as if he had been a Kentucky trotter. Archer choked with the sense of wasted minutes and vain words.

"Then what, exactly, is your plan for us?" he asked.

"For us? But there's no us in that sense! We're near each other only if we stay far from each other. Then we can be ourselves. Otherwise we're only Newland Archer, the husband of Ellen Olenska's cousin, and Ellen Olenska, the cousin of Newland Archer's wife, trying to be happy behind the backs of the people who trust them."

"Ah, I'm beyond that," he groaned.

"No, you're not! You've never been beyond. And I have," she said, in a strange voice, "and I know what it looks like there."

But the last scene of the novel surpasses all else in its power. Twenty-six years after their separation Newland Archer and his son Dallas come to the apartment of Madame Olenska in Paris. Then, instead of going up himself, he sends his youth in the person of his son, keeping to himself the memory of her as she was and preserving for her unchanged a picture he believes she cherishes:

The father glanced away at an empty bench under the trees.

"I believe I'll sit there a moment," he said.

"Why—aren't you well?" his son exclaimed.

"Oh, perfectly. But I should like you, please, to go up without me."

Dallas paused before him, visibly bewildered. "But, I say, Dad: do you mean you won't come up at all?"

"I don't know," said Archer slowly.

"If you don't she won't understand."

"Go, my boy; perhaps I shall follow you."

Dallas gave him a long look through the twilight.

"But what on earth shall I say?"

"My dear fellow, don't you always know what to say?" his father rejoined with a smile.

"Very well. I shall say you're old-fashioned, and prefer walking up the five flights because you don't like lifts."

His father smiled again. "Say I'm old-fashioned: that's enough."

Dallas looked at him again, and then, with an incredulous gesture, passed out of sight under the vaulted doorway.

Archer sat down on the bench and continued to gaze at the awninged balcony. He calculated the time it would take his son to be carried up in the lift to the fifth floor, to ring the bell, and to be admitted to the hall, and then ushered into the drawing-room. He pictured Dallas entering that room with his quick assured step and his delightful smile, and wondered if the people were right who said that his boy "took after him."

Then he tried to see the persons already in the room—for probably at that sociable hour there would be more than one—and among them a dark lady, pale and dark, who would look up quickly, half rise, and hold out a long thin hand with three rings on it. . . . He thought she would be sitting in a sofa-corner near the fire, with azaleas banked behind her on a table.

"It's more real to me here than if I went up," he suddenly heard himself say; and the fear lest that last shadow of reality should lose its edge kept him rooted to his seat as the minutes succeeded each other.

He sat for a long time on the bench in the thickening dusk, his eyes never turning from the balcony. At length a light shone through the windows, and a moment later a man-servant came out on the balcony, drew up the awnings, and closed the shutters.

At that, as if it had been the signal he waited for, Newland Archer got up slowly and walked back alone to his hotel.

To the credit of the playwright, Margaret Ayer Barnes, and the star, Katherine Cornell, in the dramatization of the novel, this scene was played as it was written although it kept the leading actress from the stage.

Mrs. Wharton's experiences in France during the war found their next expression in a novelette, *The Marne* (1918), an account of the desire of an American boy to fight for France, culminating in his being wounded in the rush of the early days of the fighting. There is a touch of the supernatural, and the story, brief as it is, is vivid and discriminating. More elaborate is the novel *A Son at the Front* (1923). This is a remarkable picture of the war, as Mrs. Wharton truly says, from the rear, "with its unnatural sharpness of outline and overheightening of colour." The frantic efforts of an American artist to keep out of danger his son who, having been born in France, is subject to military service, and the more successful attempt of the boy, who is on the fighting line, to prevent his father's finding out this fact, form a thread on which Mrs. Wharton hung tragic and comic details of the social intrigues of life behind the lines.

Mrs. Wharton's thorough understanding of the difference between a real marriage and the make-believe was shown in *The Glimpses of the Moon* (1922). It is a good study, also, of the way in which a woman like Susy Lansing will "manage," even to the sacrifice of her ideals, in order to secure luxuries for herself and Nick when they agree to marry on almost nothing a year. His revolt at paying for their Italian villa by pandering to Ellie Vanderlyn's illicit affair is natural, and the consequent separation of the two married lovers gives Mrs. Wharton a good opportunity to show the strength of a true passion. The prospect of divorce and remarriage to "Streffy," their old friend, who becomes the Earl of Aldringham, tempts Susy for a time, and the advantages of a similar remating for Nick with a wealthy woman are also tempting, but, as Mrs. Wharton puts it:

"Married . . . Doesn't it mean something to you, something inexorable? It does to me. I didn't dream it would, in just that way. But all I can say is that I suppose the people who don't feel it aren't really married—and they'd better separate; much better."

The effectiveness of *The Glimpses of the Moon* lies in the fact that Nick and Susy are not simple-minded young people. They know thoroughly the things they are giving up and have felt their appeal, yet know also that there is something deeper. The scene is foreign, but the contrast is not simply international; it is spiritual. It is noteworthy, too, that while their American friends illustrate the flexible attitude of the easily divorced, and their British and Continental friends the inflexible relation of marriage to property, the only ones who understand their higher personal standards are also Americans.

In 1924 Mrs. Wharton returned to the American scene in a series of four novelettes, dealing with New York life in the 'forties, 'fifties, 'sixties and 'seventies, and called together *Old New York* (1924). The first, *False Dawn*, while revealing Mrs. Wharton's knowledge of Italian art, is not so significant as *The Old Maid*, which is one of the very best pieces of character portrayal in her fiction. Here the dramatic conflict is between two cousins, Charlotte Lovell and Delia Lovell Ralston, both of whom have loved Clem Spender, a charming person who has solaced himself with Charlotte when Delia married Jim Ralston. The quality of this book, which carried it into a stage triumph when dramatized by Zoë Akins in 1934, lay in the manner in which Delia Ralston breaks off the engagement of Charlotte and Joseph Ralston, takes Tina, Charlotte's child by Spender, and brings her up as her own, and dominates the lives of all around her. Like May Welland, she conquers by her singleness of purpose, and sacrifices Charlotte to the tribal instinct that forbids such a stain coming into the Ralston family, of which she is now a member. The fierce jealousy of Charlotte for Delia's power over her child flares out on the night before her daughter's wedding, and she accuses Delia of robbing her of her own child's love because Tina was the daughter of the man Delia could never forget. Delia acknowledges to herself the truth of the accusation, and "she saw that it was a terrible, a sacrilegious thing to interfere with another's destiny, to lay the tenderest touch upon any human being's right to love and suffer after his own fashion."

The story of the 'sixties, *The Spark*, is least important of the series, but it shows how strong an impression Walt Whitman had made upon Mrs. Wharton's critical appreciation, culminating in the title of her autobiography, but never showing in her method. *New Year's Day* is next to *The Old Maid* in merit, probably because it is laid in the 'seventies, and because it is more unified than *False Dawn* or *The Spark*. The life of a widow with few mental resources, but with enough money to entertain young and old men with consequent taboo from women, is extremely well done.

The Mother's Recompense (1925) was a distinct drop from Mrs. Wharton's standard. The situation was at fault, notwithstanding the realistic description of Kate Clephane's aimless life on the Riviera and the consistency of her conduct as a woman who has framed her life upon impulse and has made a wreck of it. For the reappearance of her lover, younger by nine years than herself, as the lover of her daughter, has no originality, and the conduct of all three deprives them of sympathy. *Twilight Sleep* (1927) has a well-drawn central character, the managing woman with her incessant routine of important trifles. But the relations of her family end in melodrama. *The Children* (1928) was much better, for while the complications consequent upon the divorces and remarriages of Cliffe and Joyce Wheater forbid retelling, the character of Judith, the eldest child, a girl of sixteen, who mothers the rest and to whom the responsibilities of life come too early, is among the best of Mrs. Wharton's later creations. The story is told through the eyes of a civil engineer, Boyne, and his final recognition that there is a gulf between Judith and himself that cannot be bridged, and yet that his love for the child has separated him from the woman he had thought he loved, is brought home simply and naturally. The book is a scorching satire upon "the incurable simplicity of the corrupt" in its picture of the eternal sameness of the doings of the Wheaters' crowd. But there is much more than satire. There is also the insight that could write: "For jealousy to excite sympathy must be felt by someone who also inspires it. Shared, it was part of love: unshared, it made love impossible."

In *Hudson River Bracketed* (1929) Mrs. Wharton drew a contrast between the ideals of the Middle West, personified in Vance Weston, a young writer from Illinois, and the older civilization of the East. She had usually avoided Western characters, except in *The Custom of the Country*, and little was made of their place of origin. But Weston becomes a symbol of those qualities which his civilization lacks, just as Halo Tarrant, a young married woman in New York, becomes an inspiration to him through her instinctive knowledge of artistic and social values. The novel gains rapidly when it leaves Euphoria, for Mrs. Wharton's description of it has no such authority as her pictures of New York or New England. "Paul's Landing," the New York country town, she knew, and the old house, "The Willows," becomes vocal to him, as he writes within it, of the generations who had lived there. To Vance, whose people had moved constantly from place to place, "it sometimes seemed that they had left the rarest of all behind," the continuity of life, flowing like a tide from the hills to the sea. There are vivid pictures of the difficulties of a young writer in New York, of the accidents of publishing, of all the mechanics which get between the writer and his public. The book is in a sense a tragedy of a boy with a dream but insufficient background, and the grinding poverty, the death of his young wife, and his love for Halo Tarrant all are a part of his preparation to write.

Mrs. Wharton evidently felt that one novel was too brief for the development of Vance Weston's character, for *The Gods Arrive* (1932) is a sequel to *Hudson River Bracketed,* the title revealing her remembrance of Emerson as that of the earlier book showed her knowledge of architecture. Halo has not waited for her divorce from Tarrant but departs for Europe with Vance, and the book becomes an implicit argument against love without marriage. Tarrant refuses at first to divorce her, and the very effort she made to let Vance feel free caused the chains to be more apparent to him. Mrs. Wharton shows the absurdity and yet the strength of the social conventions which shut out the woman who does not play the game according to the rules. She was not "Mrs. Vance Weston," that was all. There is of course much delightful satire of the various celebrity hunters; Mrs. Wharton has hardly done anything better in this vein than the party at Lorry Spear's in Paris, including Mrs. Glaisher "who has seen almost everything and understood nothing." The various literary groups in London are differentiated clearly also. The best parts of the book, however, are concerned with the artistic processes of Vance Weston. He is unable to appreciate his first vision of Chartres because his mind and soul are in the first stages of the creation of his new book, and the creative soul is as blind to a situation where it should be receptive as the receptive soul that cannot become creative. Through a French critic, Savignac, Mrs. Wharton criticizes the philosophy of the little soul:

"It's the scale of the pattern. It's all part of a pattern, subject and characters. It's to be an attempt to deal microscopically, with the infinitely little of human experience, incalculably magnified, like those horrid close-ups of fever microbes, when you don't know whether you're looking at a streptococcus or the villain of a Chinese drama. Till I can find a reason why the meanest physical reflexes should have an aesthetic value equal to the windows of Chartres, or the final scenes of Faust, I shall refuse to believe that they may be legitimately treated as if they had."

While *The Gods Arrive* is not one of her very best books, it shows no marked decline in power. The age-long conflict between those who create without background and those with background who cannot create is represented skilfully, by one who has both ability to create and the background too. Few but Mrs. Wharton could draw this contrast, and no one can do it better.

Mrs. Wharton's later short stories, found most conveniently in the volumes *Here and Beyond* (1926), *Certain People* (1930), *Human Nature* (1933), and *The World Over* (1936), include several powerful studies of the supernatural. The vampire theme in "Miss Mary Pask" has just the right touch of horror. "Bewitched" gives effectively the sense of New England belief in witchcraft, heightened by the dread of madness hovering over people in lonely farms, and made impressive by the brief and telling dialogue. In "Pomegranate Seed" the messages to a man from his dead wife are all the more effective because all we know of them is through the recital of her successor. The "granite" of New England character crops out in another story, "The Young Gentlemen," a moving recital of the stubborn pride of Waldo Cranch, who keeps the secret of the existence of his two boys, forty years of age but still children in mind, and kills himself when they are discovered. In this story, one of her finest efforts, Mrs. Wharton showed her power to heighten tragedy, as she had done in "The Lady's Maid's Bell," by telling of the sacrifice of a proud and complicated nature through the simple language of the nurse who had sheltered through her devotion the master she loved and the helpless dwarfs she cherished. The self-respect of this English servant who always speaks of the boys as "my young gentlemen" turns the horror into dignity.

New scenes appear in "The Seed of the Faith," but although the scene is Morocco, the interest lies in the Americans. But the mistress of irony does not desert her own field of artistic and social life, and in the delightful satire of "A Glimpse" or "The Temperate Zone" the artistic temperament lives in the flesh or in its effect upon the survivors. The realism of "After Holbein" builds up a striking picture of the elderly diner-out, going, after a very slight stroke, to the house of his old friend Mrs. Jaspar, who is really insane, and solemnly sitting down to dine because he has forgotten where he was going. The aura of a past civilization hovers over them. The Great War inspired "The Refugees," a blistering satire of the way certain English people seized upon the Belgian refugees as social assets at the beginning of the war, and the humor of the situation in which a helpless American teacher is mistaken for a refugee and rushed off to a country house in triumph is irresistible. *Her Son*, included in *Human Nature*, is really a novelette, and there is something very attractive in the affection of the teller of the story for a woman, slightly older than himself, which is not love but that instinct of protection which flowers best in America. Here, too, is revealed again the power of an illusion which keeps a woman happy. In one of the latest and the best stories, "Roman Fever," Mrs. Wharton brings a placid conversation between two women to a sudden dramatic climax which shatters for each a precious memory.

It is significant that a novelist whose insight is so keen and delicate should emphasize so often in her critical writing the necessity of selection. The old distinction between "the method of insight and the method of selection" vanishes in the understanding that insight in a more exact yet broader sense is most active in the very moment of the selection of the material. Her description of the "slice of life" theory of fiction is relentless. As she shows clearly in *The Writing of Fiction*, it has been an attempt

. . . to refurbish the old trick of the early French "realists," that group of brilliant writers who invented the once-famous *tranche de vie,* the exact photographic reproduction of a situation or an episode, with all its sounds, smells, aspects realistically rendered, but with its deeper relevance and its suggestions of a larger whole either unconsciously missed or purposely left out. . . . It seemed necessary to revert to the slice of life because it has lately reappeared, marked by certain unimportant differences, and relabelled the stream of consciousness; and, curiously enough, without its new exponents' appearing aware that they are not also its originators. . . . The stream of consciousness method differs from the slice of life in noting mental as well as visual reactions, but resembles it in setting them down just as they come, with a deliberate disregard of their relevance in the particular case, or rather with the assumption that their very unsorted abundance constitutes in itself the author's subject.

And she adds appropriately: "the art of rendering life in fiction can never, in the last analysis, be anything, or need to be anything, but the disengaging of crucial moments from the welter of existence."

With the exception of Poe, Howells, and James, no American writer of fiction has been so thoroughly aware of the basic laws that govern the art, or so conscious of his own relations to them. In her volume *The Writing of Fiction* (1925) and in her critical articles [13] she has

---

[13] "The Criticism of Fiction," *London Times,* May 14, 1914; reprinted in *Literary Digest* (July, 1914).

"The Great American Novel," *Yale Review,* XVI (July, 1927), 646–656.

"Visibility in Fiction," *Yale Review,* XVIII (March, 1929), 480–488.

"Confessions of a Novelist," *Atlantic Monthly,* CLI (April, 1933), 385–392.

established the sources from which she drew her inspiration just as in her fiction she proved her significance by becoming independent of them. References to Balzac, Stendhal, and Flaubert, Tolstoi and Turgenev are frequent, and yet with the exception of a few definite obligations such as are found in her early story "The Duchess at Prayer," the resemblances between her fiction and that of the French and Russian novelists lies not in specific imitation but in general realistic power and the ease with which she handles a complicated social scene. To Jane Austen, Thackeray, and Trollope, whom she mentions most frequently among English novelists, she shows no greater debt. Her canvas is broader than Jane Austen's, her method is more objective than Thackeray's, and she is incapable of achieving the dullness of Trollope. That she could not draw a Colonel Newcome is, of course, apparent, but she never tried, and what she might have learned from Thackeray in the portraying of intricate social interrelations she could have learned also from her own observations. The master who taught her most was Henry James, but she soon outgrew his tutelage. Rarely has a novelist who was so steeped in literature assimilated so thoroughly what she read. To the feminine receptivity which shows in her remarkable acquaintance with painting and architecture as well as poetry, fiction, and drama, she added a sustained power of creation which it would be naïve to call masculine, but, unlike certain novelists who in their first fiction attracted attention by the discovery of new material, she developed gradually and rose to her greatest heights thirty years after her first story appeared in *Scribner's Magazine*.

The first principles of Mrs. Wharton's critical canon stated in "The Criticism of Fiction" seem obvious, and yet need constantly to be restated. "There seem to be but two primary questions to ask in estimating any work of art: what has the author tried to represent, and how far has he succeeded?—and a third, which is dependent on them: was the subject chosen worth representing—has it the quality of being what Balzac called 'Vrai dans l'art'?" So much fiction has been written in recent years with a different standard, which, put briefly, insists that it matters little what is written about, so long as it is photographically represented, that Mrs. Wharton's restatement of a dictum old as art itself is constantly necessary. She never leaves us in doubt as to what she is trying to represent, she usually succeeds in representing it, and she practically never descends to the treatment of material which is unworthy, in the artistic sense, of being represented.

While Mrs. Wharton's fiction is as far removed from the flavor of didacticism as possible, she knew nevertheless that "a good subject must contain in itself something that sheds a light on our moral experience," otherwise it remains "a mere irrelevant happening, a meaningless scrap of fact torn out of its context." She has no doctrine to preach, but she knows that characters who struggle between a temptation to break human or divine laws and an instinct to obey them, whether it be innate, inherited, or acquired, are inherently more interesting than those who have no standards of conduct except personal desire. They are more interesting because they provide that inner conflict and contrast which are the very life of art, while the completely unmoral man or woman is limited to achievements without importance, like those of Mr. Erskine Caldwell's poor whites, or to the equally stupid happenings by which readers of certain contemporary magazines are introduced to the atmosphere of so-called fashion.

It is remarkable that, dealing with moral questions so often, her characters should so seldom become abstract. It is true that in the short stories we frequently forget their names, although we remember the men and women. But that is due partly to Mrs. Wharton's habit of choosing names that are a bit precious or at least unusual, and partly to her own belief that "situation is the main concern of the short story; character of the novel." [14] Yet in "The Other Two," the three husbands are clearly individualized; we fail to remember their names because the situation is so delightfully ironic that we forget everything else in the appreciation of the final picture. The lover who sells the letters in *The Touchstone* remains clearly in the memory as a real person, but "Glennard" is a hard name to remember. And after all, there is less time to fix a name in a short story by the constant repetition which a novel permits, and I would be unwilling to agree with Mrs. Wharton that her characters in the short story are obscured except by the very power of the situation with which they are concerned. In both the novel and the short story she follows her own critical rule concerning the business of the novelist:

[14] *The Writing of Fiction*, p. 48.

He must, above all, bear in mind at each step that his business is not to ask what the situation would be likely to make of his characters, but what his characters, being what they are, would make of the situation. . . . The moment the novelist finds that his characters are talking not as they naturally would, but as the situation requires, are visibly lending him a helping hand in the more rapid elucidation of his drama, the moment he hears them saying anything which the stress of their predicament would not naturally bring to their lips, his effect has been produced at the expense of reality, and he will find them turning to sawdust on his hands.[15]

One of the reasons why Edith Wharton rises so definitely above her contemporaries in the novel lies in her skill in making her characters dominate the situations, which yet in their turn illuminate both the past and the future of her characters. When Fulvia sends Duke Odo back to his duty, when Mrs. Peyton keeps her son from dishonor, when Madame de Treymes betrays her family for the sake of an ideal she has never before known, when Lily Bart puts temptation in the fire for Selden's sake, when Sophy Viner takes herself out of the picture, when Ellen Olenska sends the key of Archer's rooms back to him, unused, when May Welland tells Ellen Olenska of her coming child, when Delia Ralston takes command of Charlotte Lovell's life, when Ann Eliza Bunner refuses her one chance of romance, the characters are active, potent forces, behaving like real people whom earlier incidents have brought before us in flesh and blood reality. It is because Lily Bart has won our sympathy that we watch her sacrifice with such concern; the incident is not in itself new, as any reader of *Henry Esmond* knows, but no one just like Lily Bart has acted in this way before, and the placing of Bertha Dorset's letters in the fire is but a gesture which prepares us for a much more important scene.

It will be noticed that these great moments are dominated by the nature of Mrs. Wharton's heroines; it cannot be denied that her women are on the whole better drawn than her men. There are, to be sure, Newland Archer, Ethan Frome, Duke Odo, and, to a less degree, John Amherst, George Darrow, and Vance Weston, but even these heroes are to a certain extent controlled by more insistent feminine forces. Not that this is in itself an unfavorable criticism, since Mrs. Wharton's fiction is concerned largely with personal relations and the steady clutch of feminine hands shapes, as in real life, those situations. Her male char-

[15] *The Writing of Fiction*, pp. 140–141.

acters are usually professional men with some leisure, often, especially in the short stories, painters or writers. It has been a critical mistake to attribute this limitation to the influence of Henry James. She grew up in a circle where men usually lived upon their incomes, and she knew in later years artists in words and colors. She could draw a business man, as her picture of Mr. Spragg amply proved, but she does not follow him into his deals; she is weakest when she attempts the description of business relations, but she had the acumen to avoid these as often as possible. Ethan Frome is a farmer, but his farming is used only to establish his hopeless poverty. In other words, she wrote of what she knew.

She knew well, indeed, the American woman, young and old, rich and poor, patrician and plebeian, urban and rural. No American novelist has given us a greater variety of feminine characters, from the luxury-loving heroines of *The House of Mirth* and *The Glimpses of the Moon,* and the tragic figures of Ellen Olenska and Charlotte Lovell, to those other women, like Delia Ralston and May Welland and Anna Leath who from their strongholds of matrimony and respectability dominate others, yet have always the inner consciousness that the very women they control or combat have had a rapture they have never known. There are the women who have yielded to temptation of various kinds, like Sophy Viner, Justine Brent, Mrs. Lidcote or Madame de Treymes; the remarkable dowagers, Mrs. Mingott and Mrs. Peniston; the ruthless forces of evil, Bertha Dorset and Zeena Frome, so different yet so alike in their tyranny over a husband too weak or too strong to free himself from the yoke.

They are nearly all American, although the portraits of the French women who assume minor rôles, usually social, are painted with knowledge and discrimination. The Italians are usually medieval or of the eighteenth century, and, with the exception of Fulvia and the Duchess of Pianura, seem not so authentic or so significant as the others.

Mrs. Wharton's variety is shown not only in the characters, but also in her background. In New York life, old and new, she is completely at home, with a metropolitan tone and a sense for its social values no other American has equaled. In her fiction, New York is not a province or a mere locality; it is a town with traditions, but it is a city where many American strains meet and merge. She watched the social fortress of the old commercial and financial New York being stormed by new forms of wealth, and undermined by the steady pressure of new forces which could supply diversion to a society dependent upon outside stimulation. Through her long residence she knew New England, intellectual, artistic, and rural. To it she turned largely for tragedy. She had no real sympathy for the Middle Western civilization and used it simply for contrast with the East. She was too great an artist to descend to mere caricature for its own sake, and even Elmer Moffatt has some reality, though just how he learned to become so quickly a discriminating collector of objects of art is a puzzle. But one of her finest strokes is the endowing of Mr. Spragg, from "Apex," with the same simple and rigid attitude toward divorce as that which was held by the older members of Ralph Marvell's family in New York. For, after all, differences in moral outlook in America are chronological rather than geographical.

Her European scene is again authentic. She knew the Faubourg St. Germain in its unity and its variety, and the more fluid life of Paris in the social atmosphere that is pictured in *A Son at the Front*. Life on the estates of the French landholder are a background in *The Reef* and *The Custom of the Country*, and of course the more obvious side of French life she could describe at will. Her Italy is largely historic, unless, as in *The Glimpses of the Moon*, it is a background for Americans. Her English scenes are few in number, and Morocco is again only a contrast for American evangelists.

Her supernatural stories have usually some local habitation, and in those laid in New England the nature of the people enters into the fiction. Usually, however, the locality is chosen simply because it is remote, and the variety arises from her choice of plot and the method of narration. Her supernatural appearances are not mere wraiths; they are the results of the working of emotional forces, often mystic or criminal. Usually she leaves a way out through a natural explanation, but she never intrudes this upon the reader.

Finally, she clothed her unflagging invention, her remarkable character drawing and her unswerving reality of situation in a style so distinguished that we read and reread her fiction for the sheer joy of tasting again the magnificent phrasing which fits its theme with the unobtrusive nicety of great art. Her own phrase baffles competition. By the "mysterious authority of beauty" she has won her secure place, not only in American fiction but in that of the world, as one who has touched real life with the imaginative magic of a poet and who, amid the shifting standards of a disturbed and disjointed time, has steadily refused to depart from that conception of art which from the days of the Greeks has been the highest. She belongs to no school, for she is her own master. She follows no fashions because she has become herself a standard by which the writers of American fiction of this period must ultimately be judged. Like Balzac, she has looked upon life as a great spectacle, and it has been the certain proof of her genius that she has seen through its surface into the more profound chambers of character and drawn from them the beauty she only could find because she alone could put it there.

CHAPTER XXVI

ANNE DOUGLAS SEDGWICK

ANNE DOUGLAS SEDGWICK, like Mrs. Wharton, demands, because of the individual quality of her fiction and her refusal to follow any literary fashion, a special critical treatment. She represents the novel of international relations, not only in the contrast of American with English, but also of English with French characters and life. Like Mrs. Wharton and unlike Henry James, she never lost the American point of view. Born in Englewood, New Jersey, in 1873, she was taken abroad by her parents at nine years of age and, with the exception of two years spent with her grandmother in Ohio and occasional visits to this country, she lived principally in England or France. After her marriage in 1908 to Basil de Sélincourt, she lived in Oxfordshire until just before her death in 1935.

When she was eighteen she began the study of painting at the Academy Julien and under Amanjean, and exhibited at the Champ Mars. The visualizing power and the sense of form which this training must have developed, showed at once when she turned to fiction. Her knowledge of painting led also to her first short story, "Miss Jones and the Masterpiece," [1] a clever comedy of contrasted artistic and moral values.

Her first novels, *The Dull Miss Archinard* (1898) and *The Confounding of Camelia* (1899) were promising rather than important. Laid in England, they were love stories in which the delicacy of feeling and the finish of style compensated for a thin plot and, in *The Dull Miss Archinard*, a central situation in which it is difficult to believe. In *The Rescue* (1902) Miss Sedgwick wrote a novel of the first rank. It is a study of the relations of a mother and daughter, seen largely through the eyes of an Englishman, Eustace Damier. Damier is attracted by the photograph of Madame Vicaud, who as Clara Chanfrey had run off in the late 'sixties with a French artist, and seeks her out in

[1] *Scribner's Magazine*, June, 1898.

Paris. The international contrast here lies between the passionate, bitter nature of the daughter, Claire Vicaud, half-French and half-English, and her mother, who, beginning by distrusting her daughter, ends by hating her, and with good reason. In one sentence Miss Sedgwick describes Claire—"Her father explained her; her mother reclaimed her." If Damier's financial sacrifice to save Claire's reputation seems a bit too chivalric, it is the only blemish upon a book fraught with exquisite scenes of mutual understanding between Damier and Madame Vicaud, linked together in their efforts to save a girl not worth saving except as she affects that self-respect which in Clara Chanfrey survived her husband's callous treatment and her daughter's sullen bitterness.

Paths of Judgment (1904) has a more crowded canvas, and an English rather than an international scene. Skilfully Miss Sedgwick introduces the heroine, Felicia Merrick, bored by inaction and ready to fall in love with the weak but charming Maurice Wynne, a character Miss Sedgwick must have known, for he appears in more than one of her stories. Their love is wrecked after their marriage by a remarkable woman, Lady Angela Bagley, a horrible egotist, who dramatizes herself as a benefactor of the human race. Her self-deception, feeding upon Maurice's baseness and striking into Felicia's happiness, is uncanny in its reality, and the ensuing tragedy is logical and inevitable. Miss Sedgwick's next novel, *The Shadow of Life* (1906), a study of a pale and ineffective man, shows too much the influence of Henry James' later manner. But *A Fountain Sealed* (1907), her first novel to be laid in America, contained two of her best characters. Valerie Upton is a Bostonian who has been repressed by her life with her serious, noble but ineffective husband, and quietly arranges her existence so that she escapes to England as often as possible. Her daughter Imogene is even better done. Her serene self-content, buttressed by her confident belief in her dead father's greatness, her harsh judgment of her mother, her quick reaching out for her mother's English lover, Sir Basil, when her own fiancé awakens to her real nature, make her so vivid that the reader feels a constant desire to shake her. But she is not just an annoyance. She brings out qualities in Valerie that establish that charming person, and she is an admirable picture of the Puritan strain developing into new channels which Miss Sedgwick was able to discover. *Amabel Channice* (1908) is one of the most direct of her novels and one of the most dramatic. Her heroine lives, with her son, a life of comparative seclusion on her estate in England, visited occasionally by her husband, Sir Hugh. Miss Sedgwick proved how clearly she understood the financial basis of English morality and English social life. Sir Hugh had married Amabel for her money, had neglected her, and in her unhappiness Amabel had run off with a young novelist. In the account of their relations and Amabel's recognition of the futility of their adventure, whose enchantment lasted only a week, Miss Sedgwick puts the case tersely:

She saw that laws were not outside things; that they were one's very self at its wisest. She saw that if laws were to be broken it could only be by a self wiser than the self that had made the law. And the self that had fled with Paul Quentin was only a passionate, blinded fragment, a heart without a brain, a fragment judged and rejected by the whole.

Lady Channice is not pictured as living a life of shame. When she returned to England after that brief escapade, Sir Hugh had been quite ready to save her reputation and even to father the child that comes, in return for her willingness to provide him with the money necessary to carry on the various affairs with which he solaced himself. She builds up an illusion concerning him, but their amiable relations are interrupted by her son Augustine, and she has to tell him the truth. One of the best scenes is occasioned by the visit of her husband's mistress, Lady Elliston, who breaks Amabel's illusion concerning Sir Hugh in order that Amabel may not sacrifice Augustine to that illusion. There has rarely been plainer speaking than in Lady Elliston's conversation. But the best passage is that in which the fallacy of the "sacredness of illicit passion" is attacked:

"And," Augustine went on after a little pause of reflection, "I especially hate him in that form;—romance and blind love: because what is that, really, but the animal at its craftiest and most dangerous? What is romance—I mean romance of the kind that jeopardizes 'goodness'—what is it but the most subtle self-deception? You don't love the person in the true sense of love; you don't want their good; you don't want to see them put in the right relation to their life as a whole: what you want is sensation through them; what you want is yourself in them, and their absorption in you. I don't think that wicked, you know—I'm not a monk or even a puritan—if it's the mere result of the right sort of love, a happy glamour that accompanies the right sort; it's in its place, then, and can endanger nothing. But people are so extraordinarily blind about love; they don't seem able to distinguish between the real and the false. People usually, though they don't know it, mean only desire when they talk of love."

Miss Sedgwick was not, of course, always at her highest level. In *Franklin Winslow Kane* (1910) she attempted a difficult task and only partially succeeded. It is a study of what happens to two Americans, Althea Jakes, rich and a good deal of a fool, and Franklin Kane, a physicist who has loved her unsuccessfully all his life, when they are brought under the spell of two charming but impecunious and self-centered English people, Gerald Digby and Helen Buchanan. Portions of the book are finely wrought, especially the passages describing Helen's passion for Gerald, who treats her like a sister. The novel is ironic, for after much engaging and re-engaging, Franklin and Althea are left together, with the consciousness that they have been singed by a flame that has discarded them. There are delightful touches, like Kane's careful provision for Helen's financial future, and her calm acceptance of it. But neither Kane nor Gerald acts naturally in the climax of the novel, and the too involved analysis of all their emotions leaves the reader gasping. Yet somehow irritated as one is with them all, the figure of the plain little scientist, who "had an air of finding no one beneath him, and at the same time seemed unaware of superiority" remains as a creation of no mean significance.

It was in *Tante* (1911) that Miss Sedgwick rose unquestionably to the high rank she still retains among modern novelists. It is a study in the psychology of genius, with its power not only to sway multitudes of admirers, but also to prey upon the lives of those nearest to the shrine. In that remarkable opening of the novel, Mercedes Okraska, the great pianist, is depicted with the discrimination which only an artist in fiction could summon to her triumphant interpretation of a master in another art:

To criticize with the spell of Madame Okraska's personality upon one was hardly possible. Emerged from the glamour, there were those, pretending to professional discriminations, who suggested that she lacked the masculine and classic disciplines of interpretation; that her rendering, though breathed through with noble dignities, was coloured by a capricious and passionate personality; that it was the feeling rather than the thought of the music that she excelled in expressing, its suffering rather than its serenity. Only a rare listener, here and there among her world-wide audiences, was aware of deeper deficiencies and of the slow changes that time had wrought in her art. For it was inspiration no longer; it was the memory of inspiration. The Nemesis of the artist who expresses, not what he feels, but what he is expected to feel, what he has undertaken to feel, had fallen upon the great woman.

But it is the personal life of Mercedes von Marwitz which pervades the novel. Daughter of a Pole and a Spanish Creole from New Orleans, she inherits the selfish cruelty of her father and the sensuous nature of her mother. Her craving for admiration, her determination to be always right, her desperate anger when crossed, her diabolical skill in putting her adversaries in the wrong, are relentlessly developed through their effects upon the love story and marriage of her protégée, Karen Woodruff with Gregory Jardine. Viewing both sides objectively, Miss Sedgwick drew the inevitable clash between the social conventions of the British gentry "like boxes one inside the other" to which Gregory belonged, and the queer but less firmly rooted standards of the artistic *milieu* in which Karen had been brought up. With the same mixture of impulse and calculation which had driven her first husband to despair and her second to suicide, Mercedes deliberately sets out to win back Karen to her position as appendage, not that she really wants her, but just because she cannot bear that anyone shall take away one of her possessions. A man less proud and a little less stupid might have circumvented her, but Karen, through her mingled American and Norse inheritance, has a rocklike pride of her own which helps to bring on the catastrophe. Memorable are the scenes when "Tante," as Mercedes is called by Karen, finally declares war upon Gregory, or when Karen waits through the night, hoping in vain that her husband will come to her, or when after her flight to Tante, her protectress turns on her in a rage of jealousy over the young writer who is her latest devotee. Especially fine are those passages in which swords are crossed in a gathering where passions have to be controlled:

"Ah, come," said Gregory. "You can't shatter the conceit of a happy husband so easily, Madame von Marwitz. You ask too much of me if you ask me to believe that Karen makes confidences to you that she doesn't to me. I can't take it on, you know," he continued to smile.

He had already felt that the loveliness of Madame von Marwitz's face was a veil for its coldness, and hints had come to him that it masked, also, some more sinister quality. And now, for a moment, as if a primeval creature peeped at him from among delicate woodlands, a racial savagery crossed her face with a strange, distorting tremor. The blood mounted to her brow; her skin darkened curiously, and her eyes became hot and heavy as though the very irises felt the glow.

"You do not accept my word, Mr. Jardine?" she said. Her voice was controlled, but he had a disagreeable sensation of scorching, as though a hot iron had been passed slowly before his face.

But fine as these passages are, the supreme joy in *Tante* to the critic comes from the character of Mrs. Talcott, the New England woman who has watched over Mercedes ever since her birth and who alone is able to cope with her. Clear sighted, with few words to say, but those direct and telling, she breaks the long silence of her fifty years with Mercedes and tells Karen the truth. All those years, first in poverty and then in luxury, Mrs. Talcott has looked life in the face, undismayed by pretence, devoted to the daughter of the woman she had loved, and bound to Mercedes by the strongest tie, that of the one who has cherished and forgiven much, and loves without illusion, held by the inner chains of memory and of perils faced together. Through the dramatic scenes that follow Karen's flight from Madame von Marwitz and her guardian's pursuit and recapture of her, Mrs. Talcott moves, the mistress of the situation. When she strikes, she strikes hard, and her uncompromising honesty, her shining integrity, bring Gregory and Karen together even after Tante has raised an almost impregnable barrier between them. Through a maze of falsehood, false pride and misunderstanding, this indomitable old woman succeeds by the sheer power of truth and sincerity, and by a tact that is as undismayed by the armor of Gregory Jardine's cool aloofness as it is by Karen's feverish despair or Mercedes' "stage talk." No one but an American could have conceived Mrs. Talcott; no one but a great novelist could have avoided the temptation to caricature and could have finished a portrait so life-like and so potent.

In *The Encounter* (1914) Miss Sedgwick painted another genius, this time a German philosopher, Ludwig Wehlitz, whose love for a young American girl is developed against a background of his narrowing group of disciples in a small German watering-place. With less dramatic quality than *Tante*, there is a keen insight into the composite nature of Wehlitz, with his flashes of power, his piteous weaknesses, his jealousy of any falling off in the devotion of his followers. These live the curious life of satellites, much more frequent in Europe than in America, and are extremely well drawn, especially Conrad Sachs, the cripple, and Ludenstein, the genial rake. Persis Fennamy is an admirable picture of a girl of nineteen whose impulses are not clear to herself and who is willing to wreck her life for Ludenstein more because of boredom than passion. The best character again is that of her mother. Mrs. Fennamy is the epitome of common sense and the contrast of her shrewd insight into character with the vague temperamental outlook of the German philosopher and his admirers, gives a tang to the book which shows Miss Sedgwick's continued understanding of one kind of American.

In 1913 Miss Sedgwick chose from her short stories five examples to form the volume called *The Nest*. They are mainly comedies, and even in the title story, with its sympathetic interpretation of a man's sensations when he thinks he has only one month to live, there is an ironic note. Miss Sedgwick excluded from this collection a story of considerable power, "Madeline Tristram," [2] evidently feeling it was not in the same tone. But this objection could hardly apply to a clever social satire, "A Lion Among Ladies," [3] also omitted from the volume. Miss Sedgwick's later collection, *Christmas Roses* (1920) appeared while she was at the height of her creative power. It is a series of stories in which the main characters have some relations with flowers, but this symbolism is the least important element. The best of the stories, "Daffodils," illustrates the power of illusion in the establishment of character. A young English soldier, Marmaduke Follett, is dying in a French hospital. None of his family has come to visit him: he has always been the runt of his race and he grimly takes comfort in the thought that the Victoria Cross will tell them of their error. For despite their neglect, his pride in being a Follett is keen. Then a visitor, an elderly man, is announced, whom Marmaduke barely remembers as a tutor years before, and after a while, the man blurts out that he is the boy's father, through an amour with his mother, who soon tired of him. The quality of the story arises from the manner of Marmaduke's reactions. Hating the man who has destroyed his precious belief in his patrician origin, the very *noblesse oblige* inground through years makes him treat with courtesy the father for whom he feels nothing but loathing. It is a fine study in the triumph of a noble habit over the sordidness of fact.

The Third Window (1920) marked Miss Sedgwick's triumphant conquest of a field, that of the supernatural, which might have seemed alien to her talent. But as had been the case with James and Mrs.

[2] *Century*, March, 1905.
[3] *Century*, July, 1901.

Wharton, the classic realist proved once more that the master of a more difficult medium could succeed in an easier task. *The Third Window* is the story of the attempt of a woman to prevent by supernatural means the remarriage of the widow of the man she had herself worshipped. Cicely Latimer believes that her dead cousin, Malcolm Wellwood, will be vitally hurt if his widow Antonia marries Captain Bevis Saltonstall. Being a mind-reader, Cicely is able to see in Bevis's mind during a table rapping, what neither she nor Antonia knew, that Malcolm's face had been badly disfigured by his death wound. This enables her to pretend that she has seen Malcolm's ghost in the garden "at the fountain," and to convince Antonia he is unhappy. Bevis tricks her into disclosing this mind-reading to him, but it does him no good with Antonia. Over Antonia's death-bed, however, he has the satisfaction of telling Cicely what he thinks of her. The distinction of the story lies in the establishment of the supernatural, and the explanation of it in terms of the abnormal. It is not the situation so much as the characters which give force to the supernatural effects. They all sense Malcolm's presence, but in different ways, Antonia as his wife, Cicely as the hopeless but faithful lover, Bevis as the old friend and rival. The bleak atmosphere is suited for the supernatural effects—even the "stone curlews whose call sounds like the cry of a creature who has been forgotten by its mate."

If *Tante* was a great novel, *Adrienne Toner* (1922) was a masterpiece. Through the central character, an American girl not remarkably beautiful but with a voice which always "said things to the end," Miss Sedgwick drew a contrast between the civilizations of her native and of her adopted country which reveals not only their strength, but also their weakness. Adrienne is always the center of the group, through the force of her character, through her serene belief not only in her own rightness but also of the rightness of others, if they only allow themselves to follow the better instincts of their nature. With an art which rivaled the subtlety of Henry James' later manner without its fatal indirection, Miss Sedgwick introduces Adrienne through the eyes of Roger Oldmeadow, a disillusioned English man of letters; her final conquest of him is not only personal, it is the triumph of sturdy faith in human nature over the negation of critical scepticism. The novel is by no means a study of abstract forces, however; it is a thickly woven pattern of action, making use of the Great War as a background and an opportunity for Adrienne Toner to prove her power when her marriage to Barney Chadwick, a charming English country gentleman, is shattered. The contrast of Adrienne with the Chadwicks and their friends is masterly. She is no crude type of wealthy American; her power is fortified, not bestowed by her money. Cultivated by travel and by study, and aided by a serene self-confidence, she is unabashed by any situation, and her handling of the transplanted American woman, Mrs. Aldesey, is swift and telling. Mrs. Chadwick, Barney's mother, is a remarkable picture of a woman whose inconsequent conversation sheds a ray of delicious comedy over the novel. To every member of the Chadwick family Adrienne Toner is a disturbing factor. She captures Barney, who should have married his neighbor, Nancy Averil. When Meg Chadwick is about to enter into a hole-and-corner affair with a married man, Adrienne helps her to the more open flight which horrifies the family because it is public, and brings on the quarrel that wrecks the life of Barney and Adrienne. When Palgrave Chadwick becomes a conscientious objector, she supports him in the course that leads to his tragic death. Caught at first by her spell, this conventional English family end by hating her, but they take her gifts at all times and even accept the fortune which she leaves to them through Palgrave, with that comfortable acquiescence in the reception of wealth which permits them to forget its source through the dignity it gains by their acceptance of it.

Adrienne is not spared by her creator in her less admirable qualities, especially in her determination to control the fates of others, but through Roger Oldmeadow's gradual recognition of the nobility and generosity of her nature, the reader is led on to sympathize with her tragic fate. Her good impulses recoil upon her, and Barney's leaving her to follow Meg's flight, which brings on the death of Adrienne's child, precipitates the bitter misunderstandings which lead to their separation. To the Chadwick family it was only natural that he should pursue his wayward sister rather than stay at his wife's request, and the sublime unconsciousness of the tribal instinct which eliminates the outsider from consideration is as clear as the English sky. The war is used skilfully not only to bring Adrienne and Roger together as nurse and patient, but also to provide her with an outlet for her powers of hypnotic healing and organization. Through the stress of her own suffering and of curing pain in others, Adrienne learns the humility which she needs to bring her finally to peace. Her quixotic offer to Oldmeadow to go through the form of living together in order to free Barney so that he can marry

Nancy, is quite in keeping with her character, just as her refusal of Roger's love and their departure on their several ways is logical. To her, who broke conventions easily, the fundamental laws were sacred, and while she still loved Barney, she could be the wife of no other man. Through Roger Oldmeadow's words to Mrs. Aldesey, Miss Sedgwick makes Adrienne a symbol of one aspect of the American character:

"I feel," he went on, "since knowing her, that I understand America, her America, better than you do. You're engaged in avoiding rather than in understanding it, aren't you? What you underrate, what Americans of your type don't see—because, as you say, it's so oppressively usual—is the power of her type. If it is a type; if she is as ordinary as you say. It's something bred into them by the American assumption of the fundamental rightness of life; a confidence unknown before in the history of the world. An individual, not an institutional or social, confidence. They do, actually, seem to take their stand on the very universe itself. Whereas the rest of us have always had churches or classes to uphold us. They have all the absurdities and crudities of mere individualism. They have all the illusions of their ignorance. Yet I sometimes imagine, after I've seen her, that it's a power we haven't in the least taken into our reckoning. Isn't it the only racial thing that America has produced—the only thing that makes them a race? It makes them independent of us, when we've always imagined, in our complacency, that they were dependent. It enables them to take what we have to give, but to do with it what they, not we, think best."

The art of *Adrienne Toner* shows in the careful establishment of the minor characters as well as in the major figures. Much could be said of the verity of the young English girl, Nancy Averil, and it is characteristic of Miss Sedgwick that she permits us to observe for ourselves that it is the youngest of the English group, like Nancy and Palgrave Chadwick, who understand Adrienne best. She is, after all, the incarnation of youth although in years she is as old as Barney. The force, the virility, the blindness of youth, the perennial hopefulness, the realization of her mistakes, the insistent courage to accept the inevitable but to conquer by the refusal to see the barriers to progress, all these make Adrienne Toner a character truly American.

Miss Sedgwick's sense of the international contrast was turned in *The Little French Girl* (1924) upon the fundamental differences between French and English manners, morals, and general philosophy of life. But she is never too abstract; she makes that contrast live through the persons of Alix de Mouveray and Giles Bradley, two of her best characters. The opening of *The Little French Girl* is an almost perfect introduction of a girl, nearly sixteen, through her sorrow, not quite understood, which the shadow of her mother's life casts over her. Her maturity in some things, her childishness in others, her great love for her mother, even while she is beginning to judge her, above all her logical faculty, are so justly French. She comes, on her father's side, from a family with generations of breeding and with inflexible conventions. But her mother has broken with them, and after her divorce and remarriage, Madame Vervier lives with a succession of lovers. Among these, Captain Owen Bradley, whose engagement to an English girl "Toppie" Westmacott has not prevented his falling under Madame Vervier's spell, has spoken so often of his desire to have his family know Alix, that after his death, Madame Vervier sends her to visit them. Alix has not become aware of her mother's relation to Owen and she sees no inconsistency in her being sent to visit his family in England. Miss Sedgwick chose to present her contrast through an English family whose men are scholars and stock brokers, modest in circumstances, and whose life is normal and healthy. The most dramatic scenes are introduced through the quiet processes of family life. Through a natural question of Mrs. Bradley to Alix, the little girl suddenly realizes that Owen Bradley had concealed his frequent visits to her mother in Paris. Then looking at Giles Bradley, she sees, as she frames the lie that saves Mrs. Bradley's peace, that Giles knows of his brother's actions. The brave way she carries the matter off lightly, the manner in which she shows Giles next day that she does not understand the real significance of Owen's liaison with her mother, and her appeal to Giles in her mother's defence are poignantly touching. For Alix is a soldier, fighting for a cause she loves but does not quite understand. The climax of this scene is a brilliant example of the art by which a novelist creates a new relation between her characters.

Equally skilful is the description of the life at Madame Vervier's country house in France, with her former and present lovers, to which Alix brings Giles. Here is unrolled the tragedy of the attempt of Madame Vervier to save Alix from her own fate "in the jungle." Miss Sedgwick makes the situation clear through its effects upon Giles, and gradually his pity and affection for Alix begin to replace in his heart the hopeless passion for his brother's fiancée which has clouded his life. It is difficult to do justice to the art with which the relation of Giles and Alix is interwoven with the dawning horror of Alix's realization of her mother's character. The climax of the novel comes in the great scene in which Alix tells "Toppie" the truth about Owen's relations with her mother, so that the older girl's illusion will be dispelled and Giles will have his chance. To do this, Alix must sacrifice her mother, and when "Toppie" turns upon her and denounces Madame Vervier, and Alix for the first time sees clearly how her mother is regarded by the respectable and the secure world, she stumbles blindly back across the fields to Giles, and out of the emotional tension is born their deep love for each other.

Miss Sedgwick's sense of social values, in which she rivals even Mrs. Wharton, is revealed by the high comedy of the episodes of Lady Mary Hamble's efforts to prevent her son's marriage with Alix, while her tolerance of Madame Vervier is delicately distinguished from the more direct condemnation of Mrs. Bradley. Lady Mary "made Giles think of a soft white hand, withdrawing itself, while avoiding all danger of a rent, from a glove that has proved a misfit." Through Lady Mary, Alix begins to see the difference between French and English standards:

Lady Mary resembled Giles in that; and Toppie and Mrs. Bradley; and if they swallowed you down, asking no questions, was it because they were so extraordinarily kind, or because they were so sure of themselves and of their conditions that they could not conceive of your doing them any harm? The difference—how often Alix had meditated these differences—was that the French were so sure of themselves and of their conditions that they couldn't conceive of your doing them any good. The English, certainly, were more kind.

The Old Countess (1927) was another contrast of French and English characters, but of a quite different nature. It is a tragic story of two French women, in Normandy. The Countess Lamouderie, a sinister figure, making one last clutch at life in her love for Graham, the young English painter, and Marthe Ludérac, set apart because she is the daughter of a woman who has killed her husband, are two striking portraits. The vampire note is resolutely kept in its place, but Miss Sedgwick makes it strike relentlessly when the old Countess senses Graham's infatuation for Marthe. The flood that sweeps Marthe to her death is only part of the vivid depiction of the gloomy house and the barren Norman cliffs which brood over the tragedy. In *Dark Hester* (1929) Miss Sedgwick drew a striking contrast between the older and younger generations. Monica Wilmott and Hester dislike each other not only because of their relation as mother-in-law and daughter-in-law, but also because of the greater subtlety in the older woman and the fierce directness of the younger. The story is told through Monica's eyes, but Miss Sedgwick holds the scales even and her understanding of Hester's standards is ample. The additional complication caused by the appearance of Captain Ingpen, Hester's former lover, is managed dexterously through the attraction which Monica feels for him. Miss Sedgwick does not make the mistake of permitting this mature love story to develop too far: it is one of the reasons for her high rank as a novelist, that she nearly always knows when an element in the story has been completed. There are tense dramatic scenes when the two women fight for Clive and also when they come to a better understanding after Hester prevents Monica's attempted suicide. The weak spot in the novel is its conclusion, because it should have been Clive and not Monica who persuaded Hester not to break up the marriage. Marvelously as she has pictured the women in their varying moods, Miss Sedgwick did not understand that Clive would not welcome Monica's triumph over his wife's determination, after he had failed.

Miss Sedgwick's last novel, *Philippa*, (1930) was a study of the selfish daughter of a selfish man. Both Philippa and her father, Aldous Wyntringham, are those who take life, demand things from it, and get what they demand. Happiness does not always come to them, but they are quite direct and almost primitive in their methods. In contrast to them Beth Wyntringham, wife and mother, sacrifices herself to both of them and gets nothing in return. Aldous leaves her for Cosima Brandon, a very well-drawn character, the poseuse, who swims in a veritable atmosphere of self-pity and self-appreciation. Philippa's own love story is not so important, although the young American, Challoner Day, whom she loves, is an exception to the general rule that Miss Sedgwick's men are not as well drawn as the women. Eventually Cosima is beaten in her struggle for Aldous's regard by Philippa, who is *his* child and whom he seems to think more of than anything else in the world. It is, however, his own nature in Philippa that eventually controls him and brings him around to her.

If the characters do not make the same appeal as in her greater books, Miss Sedgwick had not lost the power to reveal them. Her description of the change in Philippa showed her still the mistress of the harmonies of language:

The child had changed since Cosima had last seen her, only a fortnight before. Even then it had been absurd to call her child; but now one of those transformations that take place in the young, making them suddenly strange to eyes that see them freshly, showed her as what she was to remain until age came to wither or distort her meaning. Anything can happen to the face of seventeen years old, unexpected heredities sweeping away in one fell season the sweet uncertainties of youth. But for Philippa the mists of dawn had lifted to reveal happiest fulfilment. She was beautiful; simply beautiful; and she knew it. Her security breathed from her like the fragrance from a flower, a challenge, a menace to rival loveliness.

Miss Sedgwick showed also through Challoner Day that she retained her understanding of America. His security of tone and his appreciation of the beautiful, are qualities which an English novelist would hardly have insisted upon.

Miss Sedgwick was noteworthy for her steady resistance to the lure of mere popularity and the blighting influence of the periodical. With a keen sense for the dramatic, which was reflected in the adaptations of *Tante* and *Dark Hester* for the stage, she combined a restraint which shines in those quiet scenes where her characters grow luminous before our eyes. Her disciplined art imparts to her very characters a maturity which meets the chances of life bravely and without self-pity. Adrienne Toner, Alix de Mouveray, Karen Woodruff, Philippa Wyntringham, varying in age, know instinctively the right values of life. Her older women, Madame Vicaud, Valerie Upton, Mrs. Fennamy, and Mrs. Talcott, add to this quality of maturity the authority of experience. Perhaps it is this sense of authority, of keen insight into the motives that sway complex characters, which remains Miss Sedgwick's most striking quality. With the exception of Mrs. Wharton, no American novelist of her generation had such varied experience in the study of international types. Her American origin enabled her to treat English and French characters with objectivity as well as insight. It made it possible also for her to draw her American characters not only in contrast to Europeans but usually as dominating forces and never as mere caricatures. This complete control over her characters is matched by the mastery over those delicate shades of expression which distinguish the great artist from the lesser. It is not mere surface brilliancy but an imaginative power which fuses her images through metaphor and simile until they glow with light and color.

CHAPTER XXVII

BOOTH TARKINGTON AND THE LATER ROMANCE

ASIDE from his personal achievement, Booth Tarkington is significant because he illustrates the constant conflict which, during the end of the nineteenth and the first two decades of the twentieth centuries, was being waged among both the creators and the critics of American fiction. He began to write when the idealistic treatment of romance was in fashion and he has never lost his love of it. But another impulse, to paint the life of the Indiana he has known so well, has at times seemed to lead him into the ranks of the realists. That these impulses are in his case not so contradictory as they appear I shall try to show a little later, but in any event, he has steered a middle course between those who stripped life of its illusions and those who covered it with a layer of unreasoning optimism. That he was able to maintain the poise of an artist is the more to his credit since his gift for satire would have made the first path easy, but his fundamental belief in human nature has continued ever since he concluded his first published novel with the question of his heroine, "Aren't they good, dear people?", and the hero answered, "The beautiful people!" The more obvious danger lay in the roseate vision that led him to write such lines. But the more subtle temptation is implied in an earlier sentence of the same hero as he gazes on Main Street in the little Mid-Western town. "I used to think it was desolate, but that was long ago." It was Booth Tarkington's sense of humor that saved him from both dangers.

It was also his lack of provincialism, for though he was born in Indianapolis in 1869, he came of New England ancestry and was educated in part at Phillips Exeter and Princeton, where, like John Harkless in *The Gentleman from Indiana,* he seemed to his classmates to be destined for great things. Success came slowly, however; five years of constant rejections preceded the acceptance of *The Gentleman from Indiana* by *McClure's Magazine,* varied only by occasional publication of verses and a one-act play, "The Kisses of Marjorie," for a short-lived periodical, *John-a-Dreams,* in 1896.

Tarkington illustrated some of these early efforts,[1] and one of the sketches of an eighteenth-century gentleman may be the original of *Monsieur Beaucaire.* This story was written before *The Gentleman from Indiana,* though it was not published until 1900. It is heroic romance of an unusual quality. In a brief compass, for it is a long short story, Tarkington compressed a contrast between eighteenth-century French and English standards of honor. The Duke of Orleans, a prince of the blood royal, who masqueraded first as a barber and then as "le duc de Chateaurien" is not a mere type. Tarkington's reading of Daudet, Dumas, and Balzac, but above all, his imagination, gave him the power to create a French nobleman who defeats his rival, the Duke of Winterset, not only by his remarkable sword play but more important, by his better brain and his sense of the dramatic. Tarkington leaves "Beaucaire" triumphant over his enemies and over his passion for Lady Mary Carlisle whom he has tested and who has not trusted him in the moment of his apparent unmasking by the Duke. Sheer romance as it is, the form is remarkable for a first book; the conversation is direct and the situations almost perfect of their kind. The essentially dramatic quality of the story was revealed in the success of the play, although the stage version, written in collaboration with Evelyn Sutherland, was marred by an illogical reconciliation between Beaucaire and Lady Mary.

The triumph of personality over circumstances, which constituted the charm of *Monsieur Beaucaire,* was the prevailing note of *The Gentleman from Indiana* (1899). John Harkless, the editor of a country newspaper in a small Indiana town, wins the hearts and the respect of nearly all its citizens by that intangible quality of leadership which an individualist like Tarkington loves to give his characters. Harkless is epitomized in a sentence; "He was the only man the old darky, Uncle Xenophon, had ever addressed as 'Marse,' since he came to Plattville, thirty years ago." The attempt of the "White Caps" to tie him and whip him in revenge for his crusade against their sordid and cowardly type of persecution would have been as great a desecration as the effort of the English nobles to lash the sacred body of the Duke of Orleans in *Monsieur Beaucaire.* This quality of leadership makes probable the political events in the novel, for it is by just such personalities that the rule of organized and

---

[1] See reproductions in Barton Currie's *Booth Tarkington, A Bibliography.*

impersonal corruption has often been beaten in American politics. The heroine is pure romance, however, and her conduct of the newspaper during Harkless' illness is laid not in Indiana but in Tarkington's fancy.

The general impression so far as the background is concerned is one of accuracy. Yet Tarkington tells in *The World Does Move* how strenuous were the objections of his neighbors to this picture of a Middle Western town. He had committed, they told him, the fatal error of representing them as "an absolutely uncultivated backwoods people," and he experienced a similar reaction to that which Cooper and Bret Harte or any critic of American social standards has had to face. Tarkington did not keep up to the level of his two first books in *The Two Van Revels* (1902), a story of "Rouen," an Indiana town in the early nineteenth century. It is charming but has no character to match that of his first books. Neither has *Cherry* (1903), a story of the eighteenth century, for the figure of the solemn young narrator, Sudgeberry, is too absurd even for satire, and the language is a bit precious.

Tarkington's early short stories, based upon his actual experience in politics, were published as *In the Arena* (1905). They reveal, as did *The Gentleman from Indiana*, the inspiration of Bret Harte in the moral contrasts within the characters. This inspiration shows even more clearly in *The Conquest of Canaan* (1905), a novel of an Indiana town. The hero, Joe Louden, the bad boy of Canaan, who has to leave because of his wildness and who returns, a lawyer, to become one of its leading citizens, has that interest which the story of the returned prodigal so often evokes. Tarkington's knowledge of mob psychology is correct as usual, and there are good dramatic moments, among them Joe Louden's walking coolly into the crowd that is threatening to tar and feather him, and dominating them by his personality. But the ending, with even the villain forgiven, is too sugary.

Tarkington was at home in the long short story, especially when it gave his romantic impulse room. *His Own People* (1907) has a fine comic situation in the story of an American boy who feels the charm of Europe for the first time and believes the adventurers he meets are "his own people." Later he finds of course that they are card-sharpers and that even their titles are assumed. *Beasley's Christmas Party* (1909) [2] is a charming account of a man of forty who, to please a crippled child

[2] Published originally as "Beasley and the Hunchbergs," *Cosmopolitan Magazine*, December, 1905.

left to him by a friend, impersonates the queer kinds of people whom the little fellow imagines. It is better than *The Beautiful Lady* (1905) which is couched too much in superlatives, and in which the figures, Italian and American, are conventional. Tarkington was still following his romantic impulse. *The Guest of Quesnay* (1908) a modern novel laid in France with American characters, is an amusing but hardly important account of the recapture of a divorced husband. Briefer and much better was the long short story in play form, *Beauty and the Jacobin* (1912) laid in France at the time of the Revolution. Tarkington is best in romance when he is dealing with the heroic, and with a past that permits him liberties.

During 1913 and 1914 there appeared in various magazines stories concerning a boy of eleven, which were published in book form as *Penrod* (1914). In creating this character, Tarkington at once challenged comparison with Tom Sawyer, for Penrod is a natural, mischievous, adventurous boy, and the book is frankly humorous. But Penrod is no slavish imitation of Tom Sawyer; he is a real person. The most striking quality is his imagination; he secures the reader's sympathy because of his efforts to write a romance, and through such flights of fancy as his dream at school that he is flying in the air. All imaginative children have such dreams, and Tarkington knew instinctively that Penrod would never tell his teacher of the dream, for the dread of being laughed at is the inalienable sign of the boy like Penrod.

The Negro boys, Herman and Verman, who is tongue-tied, are delightful creations, and Tarkington introduced a new note into boy fiction in their fight with the bully in which they use every weapon from a rake to a mowing machine. But after all, the charm of *Penrod* for elders lies in the artful incongruity of language, and the remarkable comparisons. Penrod's despair at his approaching performance of "the Child Sir Lancelot" in a children's pageant is a good example of Tarkington's felicitous choice of words.

After each rehearsal he had plotted escape, and only ten days earlier there had been a glimmer of light: Mrs. Lora Rewbush caught a very bad cold, and it was hoped it might develop into pneumonia; but she recovered so quickly that not even a rehearsal of the Children's Pageant was postponed. Darkness closed in. Penrod had rather vaguely debated plans for a self-mutilation such as would make his appearance as the Child Sir Lancelot inexpedient on public grounds; it was a heroic and attractive thought, but the results of some extremely sketchy preliminary experiments caused him to abandon it.

There was no escape; and at last his hour was hard upon him. Therefore he brooded on the fence and gazed with envy at his wistful Duke.

The dog's name was undescriptive of his person, which was obviously the result of a singular series of mésalliances. He wore a grizzled moustache and indefinite whiskers; he was small and shabby, and looked like an old postman. Penrod envied Duke because he was sure Duke would never be compelled to be a Child Sir Lancelot. He thought a dog free and unshackled to go or come as the wind listeth. Penrod forgot the life he led Duke.

The sequels, *Penrod and Sam* (1916) and *Penrod Jashber* (1929) are entertaining, but hardly come up to the standard of the first book. In *Seventeen* (1916) Tarkington created another character, Billy Baxter, the adolescent boy whose calf love is amusing but who has not the sharpness of outline of Penrod.

The uncertainty of Tarkington's philosophy of composition is seen in *The Flirt* (1913), a study of a ruthless young woman, Cora Madison, who rules her family and her lovers by her charm and her immediate recognition of what will be to her own advantage. She is the first of those remarkable pictures of women which have elicited the admiration and even wonder of their own sex at Tarkington's insight. Yet the plot of the novel is loose and melodramatic, and the other characters are vague.

It was in *The Turmoil* (1915), however, that Tarkington began that trilogy of novels dealing with life in a large Middle Western city, evidently Indianapolis, which make up his most significant contribution to fiction. *The Turmoil* begins with a vitriolic protest of a lover of beauty against the American wish for mere "bigness." To illustrate his theme he created the Sheridan family, the dominating father, who is real, his two elder sons and daughter who are types of what such a father will produce, and finally the youngest son "Bibbs," who longs to write and who is the most interesting character. He is the individual soul, hating the smoke and the crudity of the bigness and yet in some miraculous way learning to run a complicated business in about a month. Tarkington shows here that he is still an idealist. Mary Vertrees, the flower of a race that had once been strong but had atrophied in her father's generation, is the best of the women and her quick recognition of the finer qualities of both Bibbs and his father is natural enough. Tarkington is too much of an artist to let his criticism of life overwhelm his characters. But his opening essay and his final optimistic vision of the giant of big business struggling through the smoke until he reaches the sky, are inserted into the novel instead of becoming an integral part of it.

Perhaps Tarkington had in mind when he wrote *The Magnificent Ambersons* (1918) the criticism of his *Gentleman from Indiana* for its representation of Middle Western life as lacking in standards of culture. Or perhaps it was because in *The Turmoil* he had placed a *nouveau riche* family in the center of the picture that he emphasized in the portrayal of the Amberson family its social security. It is true that the principal character, George Amberson Minafer, representative of the third generation of Ambersons, is an insufferable snob, but his snobbery does not consist in attempts at climbing to loftier regions. He is perfectly satisfied with himself and his family; his snobbery reveals itself in his constant watchfulness for any lack of appreciation on the part of others of his royal rights. But George's very faults set out more clearly the contrast with the good breeding of his grandfather, his mother, his uncle George, and of Eugene Morgan, the inventor of the "horseless carriage" and the father of the heroine, Lucy. Through his picture of these earlier generations, Tarkington expressed his nostalgia for a simpler life of more true distinction, and by dating this distinction in the past time, he established, of course, a more solid substructure for his implicit social defence of the Middle West. But it was of the Middle West as it might have become, not as it is. His picture of the present is almost as gloomy as in *The Turmoil*—bigness and boasting are everywhere. The Amberson estate, however, when the old Major dies, is nowhere; its disappearance is a symbol of the passing of the older Midland.

The plot, as usual, is the weakest element. George Minafer's ruthless interference with his mother's marriage with Eugene Morgan, even though he believes it will end his own love story with Lucy, is consistent with his character; and his quiet if unpleasant assumption of all the family responsibilities including his Aunt Fanny, and his buckling down to hard work are also natural, for he has gone at everything hard. But the ending, especially Eugene Morgan's visit to the medium, where he talks to Isabel's spirit, and the scene at the hospital after George's accident, let down into melodrama the tone of what might have been one of the finest of American novels. Tarkington was best, as always, in his comments upon human weakness. George Amberson's remarks to his nephew upon gossip are delightful:

"Gossip is never fatal, Georgie," he said, "until it is denied. Gossip goes on about every human being alive and about all the dead that are alive enough to be remembered, and yet almost never does any harm until some defender makes a controversy. Gossip's a nasty thing, but it's sickly, and if people of good intentions will let it entirely alone, it will die, ninety-nine times out of a hundred." . . .

". . . I dare say it isn't so much so now as it used to be, because the town got too big long ago, but it's the truth that the more prominent you are the more gossip there is about you, and the more people would like to pull you down. Well, they can't do it as long as you refuse to know what gossip there is about you. But the minute you notice it, it's got you! I'm not speaking of certain kinds of slander that sometimes people have got to take to the courts; I'm talking of the wretched buzzing the Mrs. Johnsons do—the thing you seem to have such a horror of—people 'talking'—the kind of thing that has assailed your mother. People who have repeated a slander either get ashamed or forget it, if they're let alone. Challenge them, and in self-defense they believe everything they've said: they'd rather believe you a sinner than believe themselves liars, naturally. Submit to gossip and you kill it; fight it and you make it strong. People will forget almost any slander except one that's been fought."

In one volume, *Growth*, Tarkington has included with *The Turmoil* and *The Magnificent Ambersons*, as a third member of the trilogy, *The Midlander* (1923). It is a contrast of the Mid-West and the East, made concrete in the persons of Dan Oliphant, of Amberson Boulevard and Lena McMillan, of New York. The book falls far below its predecessors because Lena is not a representative of New York, except in a very limited sense. Her conduct at the reception given in her honor is as unbelievable as Dan's real estate transactions are superficial, and there are no characterizations such as those which made the first two of the trilogy memorable.

Tarkington had made his contribution to war fiction in *Ramsey Milholland* (1919). He wisely made no attempt to describe the war in Europe, but contented himself with tracing the impulse which beginning with Ramsey's grandfather, who had been a Colonel in the Civil War, flowers in Ramsey's enlistment in the Great War. It is a sympathetic account of the mental attitude of the college boy, but to anyone who was a college officer at that time it does not go very far below the surface. The other characters are merely types, especially Dora Yocum, the pacifist.

In 1921, Tarkington did something much better in *Alice Adams*, a penetrating study of a girl who had been "popular too soon," and who having no wealth or secure position, had to fight her way alone. The details of her one sincere but unhappy love story were given with a realism which won her sympathy, especially among women, who have appreciated keenly the agony of mortification into which her family's social errors plunge her. The advance, however, in Tarkington's art is most sharply marked in the ending. No happy accident occurs and no lover is provided, as had been the case in *The Turmoil,* for a heroine incapable of earning her own living. Alice Adams faces the future as millions of American girls have done, in real life, without heroics and without despair, matured, not soured, by experience, and secure in her own self-respect. Tarkington marked time with his next book, *Gentle Julia* (1922), for Julia Atwater is a copy of "the Flirt" with the sting left out, and the young people are more irritating than amusing.

Among his short stories of the early twenties, found in *The Fascinating Stranger* (1923), "The One Hundred Dollar Bill" is a fine ironic study. In *Women* (1925) Tarkington's uncanny knowledge of feminine nature is revealed more than once. The devices by which a young woman takes a man away from a much finer rival are almost blood-curdling in their realism.

In *The Plutocrat* (1927) Tarkington made another contribution to the fictional portraiture of the "American Self-Made Man." Tinker is a real person, powerful physically and financially successful, crude in manner and with abysmal lacks of understanding of the European scene through which the story moves. Tarkington brings him from the Middle West, and contrasts him with Laurence Ogle, a playwright from the East, whose horror at his countryman is intensified by their common interest in Madame Momoro, a French woman of distinct charm and comprehensive appreciation of the value of money. She has also an admiration for Tinker as a power, and her final dismissal of Ogle with the frank admission that it is power only which interests Europeans in Americans, power based upon wealth, is accurate enough in most cases. Tarkington tries to paint Tinker in Africa as a descendant of the Roman conquerors, but in this guise Tinker exists only in Tarkington's fancy. Tinker is not as truly representative of the self-made man as Silas Lapham, but he is less of a caricature than Lewis's Babbitt, and he remains one of the best of Tarkington's characters.

After *Claire Ambler* (1928), a rather sympathetic study of the character of a young girl who develops from a merely selfish person to an

604   AMERICAN FICTION

appreciation of the existence of other people, and a satirical trifle, *Young
Mrs. Greeley* (1929), Tarkington turned to New England, which he
knows well, and in *Mirthful Haven* (1930) drew a social contrast between the native citizen and the summer people of a town on the coast
near the borders of Maine. There are fine lines of distinction, too, within
the contrasted groups. The best characters are "Long Harry" Pelter, his
daughter Edna, and Captain Embury, a vigorous old relic of shipping
grandeur. The Pelters have a long ancestry at Mirthful Haven, but
they have sunk in the economic and social scale until he makes a living
by bootlegging and she has an unenviable reputation for "wildness."
Their independence not only of the summer people, but also of the local
village opinion is humorously and at times delightfully indicated. The
steady family pressure which separated Edna from Gordon Corning,
one of the summer colony, and the way the village, led by Captain Embury, rallies to Edna's support after her father is shot by the coast guard,
is told skilfully, even if the marriage of Captain Embury to Edna dates
back to a much earlier form of romance. Tarkington used the New England material in a lighter vein in *Mary's Neck* (1932) an amusing satire
upon a summer colony. But it has not the significance of *Mirthful
Haven*. Nor has his return to his earliest field, *Wanton Mally* (1932) a
romance of a Frenchman who comes to eighteenth-century England
through his disgrace with the King of France, the verve which made
Beaucaire notable. Tarkington tried to mix idealistic and realistic methods in this book with the result that the total effect partakes of neither.

In *Presenting Lily Mars* (1933), however, he combined his knowledge of the theatre, of which he had already given an example in *Harle-
quin and Columbine* (1918), with his insight into feminine nature.
Tarkington's instinct for romantic material is shown in the rapid change
of Lily from a hopeless incompetent to a star actress. He could defend
himself, of course, by quoting certain incidents in theatrical history, but
the point is that they are exceptional. Her personal character is much
more consistent than her theatrical progress except for her final sacrifice,
impossible for one so selfish. But the characters, especially the promoter,
who is easily recognizable by anyone familiar with the contemporary
stage, live in that artificial temperature which has become apparently
a necessity for most people connected with the theatre. Perhaps the best
touch is the differentiation between the playwright and the rest.

In *Little Orvie* (1934) Tarkington made the mistake of selecting too young a boy, and of making him too consistently disagreeable. The poisonous child is not interesting in himself, and the humor of *Little Orvie* falls flat compared with that of *Penrod*. The four long short stories published together as *Mr. White, The Red Barn, Hell and Bridewater* (1935), are studies of immortality. They are sincerely written but they are confused, as was perhaps inevitable. More realistic was *The Lorenzo Bunch* (1936), a study of a group of young married people in an apartment house. But outside of the gallant effort of one woman to save another from the consequence of her imprudence there was only Tarkington's satire upon a group of artistic pretenders to hold the interest.

The vacillation in Tarkington's fictional methods is partly real and partly only apparent. But the statement that he swings from romance to realism and back again only illustrates the usual inexactness in the use of these terms. His material he takes as he pleases, from his home town, from New England, or from abroad, and he chooses the present or the past at will. But with the sure instinct of a romantic artist, he selects the unusual character or an unusual situation for his central interest. He places this character and situation against a background, through which shine by contrast the most attractive qualities of the character or the dramatic values of the situation. The heroic nature of *Beaucaire* is brought out by the vices or faults of the English society that surrounds him. The personal charm of John Harkless is emphasized by the drab life of the little Indiana town. The spiritual grace of Bibbs Sheridan gains its potency because of the dullness of the family and the city in which he has to live. Our sympathy for Alice Adams arises from her social ostracism and the cruel tricks fate plays her. What makes Penrod so much the best of his adolescents is the spark of individuality which resents the deadly uniformity of the life his adventurous spirit despises. Obnoxious as George Amberson Minafer is, he stands out against the background of a society which he dismisses as "riff-raff," and also through his resisting power he stands alone when the rest of the "Magnificent Ambersons" have given up the struggle. Even the crudity of the Plutocrat, Tinker, is forgiven because of his power and the breadth of his attitude compared with the futility of the Easterner, Ogle, and the materialism of the Europeans. But these characters, which alone should keep him in remembrance, are not permitted to sink into their background or to be conquered by it. Even Alice Adams or George Minafer wins spiritually at the end.

In other words, the material is that of the romanticist, wherever the scene or time may be. But Tarkington uses both realistic and idealistic methods in the treatment of this romantic material. In his weakest efforts he descends into caricature, like "Little Orvie," or into an artificial atmosphere as in *Cherry*. But when through his remarkable insight into the natures of men and women, he treats realistically these characters which his romantic fancy has created, he produces results which have the stamp of permanence upon them.

In a sense, he occupies in the twentieth century a similar position to that of Bret Harte and Mark Twain in the nineteenth. Without the great vigor of Twain or the secure artistry of Harte, he has that quality of perpetual youth and that sense of moral contrast which those two great masters bequeathed to him. He caught also that delightful power of producing through incongruity a humor infectious and unquenchable, and a steady eye which enabled him to send shafts of priceless satire into human pretence and weakness. It is perhaps to his credit that living in our time he refrained from placing poison on the shafts.

What lifts him above so many of the novelists who came from his locality is his love of beauty. It would seem that this search for beauty leads him constantly away from those elements in American life which tend to stifle it, and that he seeks the past as an avenue of escape. But something also calls him back, the love of his own people, in whose essential rightness he believes, and out of whose higher spiritual ranks he has drawn his most significant inspiration.

The two impulses that swayed Booth Tarkington, the first toward the romance of escape and the second toward the romantic elements of his own section, may be illustrated by three novelists, one of whom was influenced by him while the others developed their own individual talents.

There is a sharp contrast between the finished manner of Tarkington and the staccato style in which Edna Ferber (1887–   ) has written of the Middle West. Born in Kalamazoo, Michigan, of Jewish parents, her training was gained in newspaper work; she has remained, in her fiction, essentially a reporter of life. Her first novel, *Dawn O'Hara* (1911) was simply an expanded newspaper incident, but in her short

stories, collected under the title of *Roast Beef Medium* (1913) she created a character, that of the traveling saleswoman, Emma McChesney.
She became through one short story after another, the representative of
the business woman, the worker who meets men on their own ground
and through whom Edna Ferber makes some very shrewd observations
about life. Yet while the details of the terrible loneliness of the hotel
life are realistic, the situations are romantic and the influence of Bret
Harte and of O. Henry is clear. Emma McChesney and her son continued to be the central figures of other collections, *Personality Plus*
(1914) and *Emma McChesney and Co.* (1915).

Cheerful, *By Request* (1918) contained some fine short stories like
"The Gay Old Dog," and "The Eldest," in which the futility of self-
sacrifice for those who do not appreciate it was told with a realism that is
in contrast with the sentimentality of "The Woman Who Tried to Be
Good." Her situations continue to be theatric, however, as in "Gigolo,"
the title story of the collection of 1922.

Edna Ferber's novels are built upon the same fictional philosophy as
her short stories. In *The Girls* (1921), a chronicle of three generations,
there is an excellent study of the women who make up a life without
marriage, yet there is a definite acknowledgment that they have missed
romance, and that romance is all important. When young Jesse Dick
comes to see the youngest Charlotte, we know at once that he is the
grandnephew of the first Charlotte's dead lover. So much happens in
Edna Ferber's fiction that is accidental that it becomes irritating, especially when she is dealing with contemporary life. She is best when she
lets her flair for the romantic and the theatric have full play, especially
in the past. *Show Boat* (1926), a story of the old life on the floating
theatres of the Ohio and Mississippi Rivers, is full of action and color.
Even though the method of telling the story leads backward and forward, and Gaylord Ravenel, the Adonis who suddenly becomes an actor,
is a woman's hero, Edna Ferber knows how to paint the lure of the stage
which brings Magnolia Ravenel back to the show boat at last. Of course
it is the exterior of life, but it is a fascinating exterior. I prefer it to
So Big (1924) although in that book a mother's devotion to her son is
truly developed, because the theatre is more interesting than truck gar-
dening and more suitable for the kind of fiction that Edna Ferber writes.
Show Boat was easily and successfully transferred to the stage, and Miss
Ferber's theatric instinct gave, in collaboration with George S. Kaufman,

a delightful play in *The Royal Family*, in which the central motive of *Show Boat* reappeared in different guise.

While Edna Ferber wrote most often of that territory of which Chicago is the center, she has not limited herself to it. Her novel of the rush to settle Oklahoma, *Cimarron* (1929), was a good picture of the time and place and the central character of the adventurer was another instance of her fortunate choice of a romantic figure. *Cimarron* was more successful than *American Beauty* (1931), a story of the blending of an old New England strain with the Polish immigration into Connecticut. It was not her material, and the pictures of both New Englanders and Poles are conventional. *Come and Get It* (1935), a novel of Wisconsin, both in its town life and in the logging industry, has some fairly well-drawn characters but is not one of her significant books. Here she should have been at home, but neither Barney Glasgow, the "virile," ruthless type, nor his self-centered daughter, nor even the Swedish logging family excite much interest. Her contribution to American fiction remains the romance of the business woman, the romance of the theatre, the romance of the Mid-Western city. Her sympathy with those who fail to catch from life some happiness, however brief, is her most attractive quality. Her deep appreciation of Tarkington's skill in depicting the pathos of Alice Adams at the dance reveals her kinship to one of the impulses which made him the leading example of the romance of his generation.

The wide variety in the romance of the twentieth century is illustrated in the sharp contrast between the work of Booth Tarkington and of James Branch Cabell (1879–   ). Rarely has there been such confusion of values as has pervaded the estimate of the latter. By his admirers he has been hailed as one of the incomparable romancers of his time; by his severest critics he has been condemned as an indecent, blasphemous portrayer of perversion. To the calmer judgment it seems incredible that his work should have been taken so seriously by either group. But as a phenomenon in American letters, illustrating the sudden rise and the early collapse of a vogue, he is extremely interesting. Born in Richmond, Virginia, of a well-established family, and educated at William and Mary College, where he taught French and Greek for a year, he served an apprenticeship at newspaper work before he devoted himself to fiction, criticism, and autobiography. His short stories began to appear in periodicals in 1902, and it must be understood at once that Cabell is essentially a teller of episodes. His bibliography makes clear that nearly all his books are collections of short stories, connected adroitly at times into a unity through a character whose adventures are there recorded. Cabell has also, through revision and rearrangement of his books in his latest editions, sought to connect his modern American characters like John Charteris and Felix Kennaston with his medieval creations, Jurgen and Manuel, into one cycle of romance. This effort makes a purely chronological discussion of his books less important than a classification based upon the romantic impulse they represent.

Yet chronology in Cabell's case is not without value in any appraisement of his significance. His first book, *The Eagle's Shadow*, (1904) is hardly more than an example of the lighter forms of romance then popular. As Cabell solemnly tells us, so that we shall not miss the moral, it is a study of various people as they are affected by the worship of money. At times he is undoubtedly satirizing the current style of romance. But he is never quite sincere in his satire, for he treats seriously the curious jumble of signed and unsigned wills, with a hero incredibly stupid and a heroine, supposedly of breeding, who talks at times like a fishwife. This story was laid in a modern Southern town, but already Cabell had published in magazines some of the stories which make up *The Line of Love* (1905), a series of love episodes beginning in 1293 and concerned mainly with medieval happenings. They represent the sophisticated romance of history, the other field in which Cabell has labored. Here he did his most artistic work. *Gallantry* (1907), a collection of short stories dating from 1902, begins with an episode of 1750. In these short fictions he caught fairly accurately the cold-blooded atmosphere of the eighteenth century. But no character remains like Tarkington's Monsieur Beaucaire, and the situations grow tiresome in repetition. Much better were the stories gathered together in 1909 as *Chivalry*, where the scenes are laid in England and the Continent during the fourteenth and fifteenth centuries. It is not necessary to discuss the various imaginary historical references with which Cabell apparently seeks to give an air of authority to his romances. He would be the last person, I imagine, to wish them taken seriously. But he has read widely in medieval history and in "The Story of the Tenson" he gave Edward I of England the personal courage, the military skill and the steadfastness which seated him firmly upon the English throne. The varying moods of Richard II and the audacity of Henry V are also correctly portrayed in *Chivalry*, but it is to be noticed that when Cabell deals with a character of his own devising as in "The Story of the Satraps," when he imagines an older brother for Richard II, he fails. When the characters are provided him from history, he can dress them up with a dramatic surrounding. But his own inventive powers are not strong, as his constant repetition of situations sufficiently indicates.

To the same group of his writings belongs *The Soul of Melicent* (1913), revised in 1920 as *Domnei*. It is a romance in which three persons, Perion of the Forest, Demetrios and Melicent, betrothed to King Theodoret, vie with each other to prove their standards of pride and honor. Especially in the final recognition by Perion of the spiritual quality of Melicent, transcending the physical beauty that lured him and other men, Cabell rises to at least a partial understanding of the medieval worship of "the lady" associated with the adoration of the Virgin. His remark in the "Afterword" that "it was also a malady and a religion" shows that he did not comprehend it completely. But *Domnei* is one of the best of his books, and the sly suggestiveness of his later work is happily minimized. *The Certain Hour* (1916) has less vitality and less unity, for the episodes run from the thirteenth to the twentieth centuries. There are some good ironical situations, especially in the stories which deal with Wycherley and Pope, but Cabell should have let Shakespeare alone.

The stories laid in America have not the interest of the medieval romances. The heartlessness of Robert Townsend in *The Cords of Vanity* (1909) is not as interesting as the ruthlessness of Perion. There is a fair picture of the emotional development of a writer who "has not been intimate with anybody" but the incidents and characters are forgotten as soon as the book is finished. *The Rivet in Grandfather's Neck* (1915) is characteristic of Cabell's uncertainty of method. Viewed as romance, it might be a celebration, through Colonel Rudolph Musgrave, of the gallant sacrifice of his reputation when he takes the blame for an illicit affair which really belongs to the writer, John Charteris, or of his attempted sacrifice when he is willing to give up Patricia Stapylton to a younger man. We are even invited to believe that he prevents Charteris from running away with Patricia for the sake of Anne, and the old romantic clichés are trotted out in the extraordinary monologue he delivers to the eloping pair when they are sneaking away in the early morning and the Colonel's "eyes were like chill stars." But all the time Cabell is inserting sly digs at the permanence of marital love and the worth of the ideals Musgrave represents. His satire upon the feminine psychology which forgets and ignores what it wishes to disregard and yet lashes the object of its regard with bitter upbraiding, belongs to an ironic manner which sits uneasily upon the foundations of romance. Cabell's attitude toward the South is equally inconsistent. He cannot make up his mind whether the loyalties which tradition and breeding have cherished and preserved are important, or whether Charteris, who is a coward and a liar but who has accomplished something, is the only important product of the town. He speaks as though Edward Musgrave, who has raped a Negro slave, is in the same category as the half-breed product of this liaison, who is hanged because he has treated a white woman as his father had treated his mother. In *The Cream of the Jest* (1917) Cabell attempted to join the modern and the medieval interests through Felix Kennaston, the writer who passes into dreamland in search of Ettare, the ideal of beauty. But as soon as he touches her, the dream vanishes. The last sentence of the book, "I reflected that it is only by preserving faith in human dreams that we may, after all, perhaps some day make them come true," represents Cabell in his most attractive mood. But it is not the mood of the book, which is sardonic. Its satire of pretence we can enjoy thoroughly, but the mummery about the mirror is boring because it leads nowhere.

With the publication of *Jurgen* (1919) Cabell entered into a new phase, both in his work and in his popularity. He became a "best seller" and the controversy that raged over the attempted suppression of the book secured him many readers. It is amusing now to remember the avidity with which *Jurgen* was purchased by the adolescents of all ages, and their consequent disappointment. The adventures of Jurgen, a pawnbroker of forty, who is restored by enchantment to his youth with the privilege of knowing what has already happened to him, need not be retold. The queer collection of beings whom he meets in his journeys are mere names where they are not symbols of a philosophy of frustration. His doings in Hell are stupid and in Heaven are absurd. The symbolism is used to satirize human weaknesses. Men and women are unfaithful as a matter of course. Loyalty, purity, and fidelity are illusions. Jurgen returns to his wife because he is no longer young, and he has never believed in his illusions, anyway. When we remember how much more artistically James Lane Allen had treated the theme of a middle-aged man's long-

ing for union with youth in *The Bride of the Mistletoe,* it seems hardly
to be doubted that the desire to be shocked had much to do with the sale
of *Jurgen*. And while, of course, the attempt to suppress *Jurgen* was
silly, there is an odor of decay about it which is repulsive to any healthy
minded reader. Cabell protests in the "Foreword" to the revised versions,
that such choice passages as those describing Jurgen's stay with Anaïtis
have no double meaning. If this be true and they are not implicit dab-
blings in perversion, they are nonsense. But in any event they are dull.

In *Figures of Earth, A Comedy of Appearances* (1921), the character
of Manuel of Poictesme, of whom much had been hinted in the earlier
books, especially in the revised versions, emerged. Elaborate maps have
been drawn of this mythical country, but its location does not really matter, nor does the plot. At first glance Manuel seems to be the symbol of
individualism in its protest against all restriction. "I am Manuel: I follow after my own thinking and my own desire, and if to do that begets
loneliness I must endure it." Even his ruthlessness in his various amours
are not incompatible with his return to Niafer, the woman whom he
idealizes, or his excursion through the magic third window into the sorcerer's land to win back the lock of hair of Melicent, his child, and his
final sacrifice to Death, to save Melicent. His quest for the unattainable
which drives him on, while not a new note in fiction, is also in keeping
with the character of Manuel. And there are some fine passages in
Figures of Earth, such as that in which Manuel tells Alianora that their
passion has not been love but only lust. Cabell spoils the book, however,
through the summing up by Manuel of his career:

Yet, looking back,—now that this famed Count of Poictesme means less to
me,—why, I seem to see only the strivings of an ape reft of his tail, and grown
rusty at climbing, who has reeled blunderingly from mystery to mystery, with
pathetic makeshifts, not understanding anything, greedy in all desires, and always honeycombed with poltroonery.

Manuel is a symbol of the complete pessimism of the bankrupt spirit,
more insidious than the objective criticism of the realistic school, for it
strikes at the roots of faith and of hope. He is the Byronic hero who is
weary because his inmost thoughts cannot be expressed even to the
woman he loves. It is perhaps this quality which caught the fancy of the
young generation who rebel against this inevitable law and have not
grown to an understanding that the very possession of these desires and

longings should be a resource that reconciles human creatures to their loneliness.

The parallelism of Manuel's career to that of Christ, beginning with his virgin birth and leading to his "Eucharist," including the spending of three days in a tomb before his resurrection, is offensive, of course, and in bad taste, but it is all the more inexcusable because it is dragged in. Cabell of course does not mention Christ, and he attempts to forestall criticism by a marshalling of characters to whom tradition has attached somewhat similar events. But the implication is clear enough. It is even clearer in *The Silver Stallion, A Comedy of Redemption* (1926), for the legend of Manuel the Redeemer is carried on by his wife and his apostles, and by Jurgen, in whose mouth are placed the actual words of Christ.[3] If there is a central idea which ties together the adventures of the companions of Manuel, it is the depiction of the gradual growth of a legend concerning a lofty character whose memory the people worship and who, in reality, was a murderer and an adulterer. Moreover, his resurrection rests upon the empty tomb and the unsupported word of the child, Jurgen, who, it is implied, has made up most of the story. Between *Figures of Earth* and *The Silver Stallion* had appeared *The High Place* (1924) another tale of Poictesme, but this rather stupid dream story of Florian de Puysange, descended from Manuel, hardly needs discussion.

After *The Silver Stallion*, Cabell seems to have lost completely the sense of standards once his. *The White Robe* (1928) is a fantastic account of a werewolf whose sexual adventures give the author an opportunity to pass the limits which divide beasts from men. So does *Something About Eve, A Comedy of Fig Leaves* (1927), a transmigration of one of the Musgrave family into peculiar regions where the curious in abnormality may find pleasure. *The Way of Ecben* (1929) repeats the earlier theme of the seeking after the unattainable, but the book adds nothing of importance except some quite pertinent observations upon Cabell's own generation of novel writers in America. Cabell is indeed quite penetrating in his criticism, which is distributed through his "Forewords" and has its most organic body in *Beyond Life* (1919) a series of essays. His creed is definitely that of a romanticist, and his scorn of realism, which he seems to think is the antithesis of the romantic, is complete. It is not necessary here to discuss his theories except to remark in passing

[3] P. 296, Storiesende Edition.

that a critic who believes Wycherley to have been the first example in English drama of "stooping to real life" is hardly a perfect guide.

Cabell's latest flair seems to be for autobiography, which it is to be hoped, is partly fiction. *These Restless Heads* (1932) is ostensibly a series of personal reminiscences written with ease and studded with epi- . grams. But the book is spoiled by the pitiful spectacle of an elderly gentleman gloating over his amorous successes of bygone days. Beneath these depths it is difficult to go. On the border land of fiction and personal history, *Special Delivery* (1933), a series of letters to various correspondents, first the one Cabell sent and then the one he might have written, and *Ladies and Gentlemen* (1934), letters to historic characters, have a certain cleverness, but that is all. Those who desire to read his own criticism of his books will find it most conveniently in *Preface to the Past* (1936).

If it were not for one quality in the fiction of James Branch Cabell it would be sufficient simply to note the passing of his vogue, established by the incorruptible testimony of the recession in the library demand for his books. That lack of popularity is no evidence of lack of merit hardly needs emphasis, but what is most striking is the quick decline of his vogue. It came, I believe, from an inherent flaw, a lack of sincerity, both moral and artistic. According to his own theories of art in *The Certain Hour*, "a book's subject is of extremely minor importance" and the only important quality is beauty. But beauty of form is not the only beauty in literature. There must also be beauty of conception, and one great element of that beauty is sincerity. A novelist must respect his own creations, and though he may make them capable of crime, even murder like Donatello, or adultery like Hester Prynne, he must never make them embodiments of a vice that leads a reader to despise them. Many great novels have been based upon the passionate relations of men and women, outside the conventions of society or the laws of marriage, but no great novel has been based upon those abnormal practices which take from man his manhood or woman her womanhood. And above all else, no novelist of sincerity will titillate his readers by such tricks as the carefully placed series of dots and dashes, or the eternally recurring phrase "then he did what was necessary," which are frequent mannerisms of Cabell. They are unworthy of any artist.

Cabell's fall from grace is to be regretted, because he had one quality of the artist, that of style. He had not much of a story to tell, but he had the gift, especially in his early work, of the well-chosen word, the charming phrase, and the sentence whose proportions are a delight. There were few writers of his generation who had such control over the resources of the English tongue. Had he chosen to clothe great historic figures with some salient quality as he did in *Chivalry*, or to personify an idea of beauty as he did in *The Soul of Melicent*, he might not indeed have become a great writer, but he would at least have retained the respect of the discriminating. But instead, he chose to pass into the cave of moral twilight with *Jurgen*, and he has never come out again into that clear light of artistic truth by which alone literature of importance can be written.

With the instincts of an artist and an ability to use words in some cases almost as a painter uses colors, Joseph Hergesheimer (1880–   ) illustrates the novelist who seeks romantic material anywhere but who varies in his methods of treatment. Born in Philadelphia and educated in part at the Academy of Fine Arts, his first novel, *The Lay Anthony* (1914) is an idealistic romance of a young man who is a symbol of chastity through fastidiousness and inexperience, and who ends by being shot in a brawl in a house of ill fame where the news of the death of the girl he loves has sent him. There are good moments in *The Lay Anthony*, especially the criticism of science and the dramatic discovery by a research botanist that the opening color of his new species of flowers makes useless his years of labor. But the characters remain types.

In *Mountain Blood* (1915) Hergesheimer conceived a fine romantic theme, the persistence of the traits of a Highland stock in the mountains of Virginia in contrast with the money-getting spirit of the average citizen of the place. George Mackimmon, who has sunk to the position of stage driver, which he loses by a chivalric defence of a girl, Lettice Hollidew, could have been made an appealing symbol of personality in its struggle against static conditions. But Hergesheimer tried to combine realistic with idealistic methods and produced an inconsistent hero, who marries Lettice for her money and yet loses his fortune by his generous and even careless loans to his fellow townsmen. Among the short stories of this early period, included in *The Happy End* (1919), "Tol'able David" is a good example of the unflinching courage of a mountain lad, who brings in safely the United States mail and leaves dead or dying three of the men who have broken his brother's body.

The Three Black Pennys (1917) was Hergesheimer's first novel of importance. Against the background of the iron industry in Pennsylvania, which he portrays in its picturesque phases, he set three men, representing the rise, climax, and decline of the race. Although the Pennys are usually fair, every few generations a "black Penny," an inheritance from their Welsh blood, appears, with opposition to control as the breath of life. Illegitimate passion sways Howat Penny of 1750 and Jasper Penny of the early eighteen hundreds, but in the twentieth century it is the woman Mariana who is the rebel against law. The setting as usual with Hergesheimer is painted with skill. Best of the three parts is the second, in which the Philadelphia of the early nineteenth century lives in the quiet streets and the atmosphere of solid standards of conduct. Jasper Penny's break with his sordid past, his abrupt wooing of Susan Brundon, the mistress of a "Select Academy," the way his will bends before the unyielding surface of her self-respect and gentility is admirable. I can see still the building in which my own grandmother ruled over just such an "Academy" in that time and place, and the atmosphere is absolutely correct. While the iron industry hardens into steel, the family of the Pennys loses its vigor and only the energy of the illegitimate branch brings it back into harmony with the new times.

Like most romantic artists, Hergesheimer loved to celebrate power even if it overflows the channels of law. *Gold and Iron* (1918) contained three novelettes, of which *Wild Oranges,* a story of the rescue of a girl from morbid surroundings on the Georgia Coast, does not quite arrive. But *Tubal Cain,* a study of a man's greed for power, and of his rise to a commanding position in the iron industry in western Pennsylvania during the early nineteenth century, has an intensity which carries the details into unity. And *The Dark Fleece,* laid in a New England seaport, contains a contrast between Jason Burrage, who returns from the gold fields, a rich man, and Honora Canderay, the last survivor of the leading family of the town, also rich and independent, which clothes the romance with reality. Her proposal of marriage to Jason because he is an avenue to variety in the drab town and his worship of her delicacy and refinement are very probable.

It is atmosphere that remains from a reading of *Java Head* (1919) rather than character. Hergesheimer recreated the dying glories of the port of Salem, from whose wharves had gone out the privateers that had swept the sea in 1812, and the stately East India trading ships of later days. These are symbolized in old Captain Jeremy Ammidon, who dies of rage when he hears that his son William has engaged in the opium trade. His other son, Captain Gerrit, brings back a Manchu wife from China, and her tragedy is or ought to be the climax of the book. But Gerrit's return to his first love leaves the whole episode of Taou Yuen without reality. For there is no tragedy, apparently, for Gerrit, either. Somehow Hergesheimer seems to have missed by a small margin a great opportunity in *Java Head* which he was artist enough to see but not to establish.

It was in *Linda Condon* (1919), however, that Hergesheimer rose to a level of achievement worthy of a great conception. Linda is the incarnation of beauty, whose shuddering reaction to the welter of corruption in which her mother lives brings her untouched to the early maturity in which she assumes control over her own life. She is like a Greek statue, cold, pagan, secured from the edge of evil in which she has been reared not by essential purity, but by a personal fastidiousness through which the care of her body becomes the only religion she knows. The art with which Hergesheimer brings her to a knowledge of the life her mother has been living without dragging us through all its sordid details is astonishing, for by 1919 the cult of the ugly was being established. It was a fine stroke also which released her from the environment of second-class fashion in New York to bring her to the home of her dead father's sisters in Philadelphia. Here in the narrow but impeccable surroundings of the Lowries she is suddenly explained, as soon as she enters the room where the picture of her father tells her at once why he had left her mother, without a word, before Linda was born.

Linda Condon's character is established by the two men who love her, Dodge Pleydon, the sculptor whose wooing alarms her, and Arnaud Hallet, her cousin, whom she marries as a refuge against a passion which threatens to engulf her. Both are older than she, and she gives to neither any return of rapture. She is one of the natures that is incapable of giving herself completely, not through selfishness, but because of a personal integrity which preserves an inner citadel to which no one is admitted. It is not a sanctuary, however, for Linda Condon is no saint. But her love of her own beauty is endurable because she uses it not as a seduction but simply for her own enjoyment. Her self-centeredness indeed becomes active for others, when she forces her husband to permit their daughter to choose her own happiness. Her relations with Arnaud are not unhappy but unfulfilled. Hergesheimer can flash a whole character contact in a few words:

> He put his book aside completely and gazed at her in patient thought. "Linda," he said finally, "I have never heard anything that stirred me so much; not what you said, my dear, but the recognition in your voice." A wistfulness of love for her enveloped him; an ineffable desire as vain as the passion she struggled to give him in return. She smiled in an unhappiness of apology.
> "Perhaps——" he stopped, waiting any assurance whatever, his face eager like a dusty lamp in which the light had been turned sharply up.

Unlike so many romances, the book moves upward to its conclusion. Pleydon has never made a bust of her but into his masterpiece, the statue of a pioneer, Downige, he has placed the beauty and the aspiration with which his love had endowed her. The painter in Hergesheimer shows in the conception:

> Linda . . . saw the statue, under life-size, of a seated man with a rough stick and bundle at his feet. A limp hat was in his hand, and, beneath a brow to which the hair was plastered by sweat, his eyes gazed fixed and aspiring into a hidden dream perfectly created by his desire. Here, she realized at last, she had a glimmer of the beauty, the creative force, that animated Dodge Pleydon. Simon Downige's shoes were clogged with mud, his entire body, she felt, ached with weariness; but his gaze——nothing, Linda discovered, but shadows over two depressions——was far away in the attainment of his place of justice and truth.

When the western city to which the statue has been given by Downige's descendants destroys it because it represents their founder as a tramp, Linda goes to Pleydon to give her life to him as a recompense. Then she finds that he no longer needs her bodily presence, that his possession of her must keep them always apart, and without telling him of her errand, she returns to Philadelphia. But the last scene of the novel takes her after his death to the little New England village where a replica of the great statue had been sent. When she sees it:

> She was choked by a sharp rush of joy at Dodge's accomplishment, an entire understanding of the beauty he had vainly explained, the deathless communication of old splendid courage, an unshaken divine need, to succeeding men and hope. This had been hers. She had always felt her presence in his success; but, until now, it had belonged exclusively to him. Dodge had, in his love, absorbed her, and that resulted in the statues the world applauded. She, Linda

thought, had been an element easily dismissed. It had hurt her pride almost beyond endurance, the pride that took the form of an inner necessity for the survival of her grace—all she had.

She had even asked him, in a passing resentment, why he had never directly modelled her, kept, with his recording genius, the shape of her features. She had gone to him in a blinder vanity for the purpose of stamping her participation in his triumph on the stupid insensibility of their world. How incredible! But at last she could see that he had preserved her spirit, her secret self, from destruction. He had cheated death of her fineness. The delicate perfection of her youth would never perish, never be dulled by old age or corrupted in death. It had inspired and entered into Pleydon's being, and he had lifted it on the pedestal rising between the sea and sky.

Then she turns after she has drunk in the significance of Pleydon's relation to her and the novel ends:

She gazed again, for a last view, at the bronze seated figure; and a word of Pleydon's, but rather it was Greek, wove its significance in the placid texture of her thoughts. Its exact shape evaded her, a difficult word to recall—*Katharsis*, the purging of the heart. About her was the beating of the white wings of a Victory sweeping her—a faded slender woman in immaculate gloves and a small matchless hat—into a region without despair.

The promise of *Linda Condon* has not been carried out. *Cytherea* (1922) was the picture of the disintegration of a man under the influence of illicit desire, a member of a group of middle-class minds in a suburban town, drinking heavily, and with the restlessness of post-war aimlessness. The background is accurately done, but Hergesheimer was unaware of the principle, clearly stated by Mrs. Wharton, that a futile society is of dramatic value only as a means of destroying something important, and the central figures of *Cytherea* are unimportant. The theme of a man of forty breaking up his married life for another love must rise to the dignity of tragedy, if it is to be of significance, but the flight of Randon and Savina is simply a physical adventure in passion, too frequent in its occurrence to be of interest. If Hergesheimer had carried out his intention, evident at times, to treat the matter ironically, the result would have been at least intelligible, but the effort to combine the symbolism of the vampire doll and a dissatisfied woman, with no excuse of youthful enchantment, results in a confusion which the style only emphasizes. How can anyone take seriously a heroine who cries out "I want to be outraged!"?

The best part of *Cytherea* had been the realistic picture of the death of Savina in the dreadful blue room at the Cuban hotel. Hergesheimer continued in *The Bright Shawl* (1922) to try to capture the exotic atmosphere of the West Indies. But the recollections of the old man who, forty years before, had gone down to help on the freedom of Cuba, fails to thrill the reader whose sympathy for that land is tempered by events of recent occurrence. There is more directness in *The Bright Shawl* than in *Cytherea*, and there is vigor in the final scene in which the young American, striving to keep himself free of the complications which his warning of his Cuban friend in the café will bring upon him, nevertheless finds himself at his friend's side before the latter is murdered. But such a story would have been better if it had been told as objective romance. *Tampico* (1926), Hergesheimer's romance laid in Mexico, in which he brings back a virile figure, Govett Bradier, to the scenes of his earlier triumphs in the oil fields, has more power because Bradier is a picturesque survival of the personal conqueror of material difficulties, eventually pushed aside by the equally ruthless procedure of a corporation.

In *Balisand* (1924) Hergesheimer had a better subject in Richard Bale, a typical Virginia planter, who had fought in the Revolution, and was a great admirer of Washington. The novel is told through Bale's consciousness, and Hergesheimer succeeds in presenting the courage, the intolerance, the overbearing qualities of Bale, who drinks excessively and who is left behind by the march of political happenings which he scorns to understand. He takes whatever he wants, but his swift wooing of Lavinia Roderick at the party at which her engagement to Gavin Todd is announced is not only improbable from the point of view of passion, both on his part and hers, but is unlikely under circumstances which would have made such a breach of hospitality unthinkable to a code of which Bale is drawn as a representative. Events follow time rather than motives, and Lavinia's accidental death, Bale's marriage with Lucia Mathews, his final duel with Gavin Todd seem arranged by Hergesheimer rather than by fate. The historical events from 1783 to 1801 are nearly all seen through Bale's memory and Hergesheimer did not seem to recognize that historical romance cannot be made lively through a man who retires from events out of disgust.

In *Quiet Cities* (1928) Hergesheimer recreated the past of nine American cities with varying success. Sometimes the atmosphere is all that remains, but in "Charleston" at least, the character of Colonel John

Fearnes is carried along with it into life. His sacrifice for the sake of his native city is greater than that of his friends who simply gave up their lives in the Civil War. During the terrible days of reconstruction, Colonel Fearnes descends into the depths of Negro voodooism, brings a quadroon woman into his own home and, through her, drives out of the city the Negro leader who menaces its existence. Hergesheimer in a brief space creates a hero who, for the sake of the racial supremacy of his people, loses his own racial integrity and lives, a fluttering shadow of himself, with a horror in his memory.

The Limestone Tree (1931) is an attempt, at times markedly successful and at other times distinctly irritating, to tell a romance of Kentucky from about 1776 to 1890. There is enough material for several novels in it and the number of characters forces Hergesheimer to repetitions and explanations which leave a reader puzzled or bored. He does succeed in bringing down through several generations the love of the Kentucky land and the Federalist-Whig feeling of an aristocracy devoted to the Union, and merging into Democracy through the Civil War and Reconstruction. The episodes are uneven in merit. The best are those dealing with the Civil War, the separation of families, and the stubborn stand of the Confederates under Morgan. But the utter absurdity of one of the earlier incidents in which James Sash on his first meeting with a nun, "Sister Euphemia," calmly rips her veil off her head and announces that she is to marry him, calls sharply to our attention how much better Allen dealt with a somewhat similar situation in *Sister Dolorosa*. Insufficient motivation runs all through the book, but perhaps the final scene in which old Gabriel Sash goes over the entire history in order apparently to keep one of the youngest generation from abandoning another, after he has seduced her, is too absurd for words. There are limitations, too, in the method which Hergesheimer had used with such success in *The Three Black Pennys*. About three generations are enough for one volume.

Hergesheimer used the same method in *The Foolscap Rose* (1933), and described the progress of a family in Pennsylvania which had founded a paper mill in 1790, and ramified into banking and politics by the early twentieth century. There are several good character sketches, especially Jacob Kinzer, the German journeyman whose shrewdness captures the mill about 1820, but the details grow tedious; there are too many characters that remain only names, and the final marriage of one of the family to a young German paper-maker is so obvious that it is almost painful. Hergesheimer did not seem to realize that paper-making affords none of the romantic possibilities of the iron industry, and while his style is somewhat clarified, it still remains affected by the staccato movement of his later novels.

These historic novels, however, are more worthy at least in conception than the *The Party Dress* (1929) and *Tropical Winter* (1933), in which the doings of people whose dissipation is without distinction are chronicled with a growing stylistic incoherence that leaves the books a mere blur in the memory. The unfortunate indirection, which began to show in *Cytherea* and become established in *Balisand*, was deliberate and may be attributed to the influence of foreign models or the general tendencies of one brand of fiction since the Great War. It may also have been due to the circumstance of periodical publication. But in any event it was most unfortunate. It matters little to American fiction if certain popular novelists persist in writing in a language in which interjections have taken the places of nouns and verbs. But Hergesheimer is, or was, an artist. Up to 1919 his fiction, while not always on the same high level, was marked by artistic sincerity and was written in a style which few of his contemporaries could match. His creation of vivid phrases, with their singular fitness for the objects described, added that charm of the individual sentence to the distinction of the whole composition which separates fiction of high rank from the rest.

That the creator of the *Three Black Pennys*, of *Java Head* and of *Linda Condon* could descend to his later incoherent thinking and writing is in every sense of the word a calamity. For at his best Hergesheimer had an unusual power of visualizing an historic period and of making it live, and he showed at times an objective power which was distinctly refreshing. Moreover, he possessed, at one time, a love of beauty which was as he implies in his autobiographic chapters of *A Presbyterian Child,* a reaction against the undue strictness of the atmosphere in which he was reared. Like Tarkington, he turned to the past for relief, but it was in the past of his native State, not of eighteenth-century Europe, that he found his best material.

CHAPTER XXVIII

CRITICS AND SATIRISTS—THE LIBERALS

As THE twentieth century began, the criticism of American life which had been an element of fiction since the days of Hopkinson and Brackenridge and which rose to intensity in Cooper, became more insistent. It was only natural that at the turn of the century, American fiction should concern itself with a scrutiny of existing institutions, economic and social, with a view to their improvement. In cheerful disregard of the fact that the human race does not mark its forward steps by the calendar, many looked to the new century for a solution of the problems arising from the struggle between capital and labor which had shaken the country during the 'eighties and 'nineties. Hope sprang again that the new century would bring a better understanding on the part of employers of the rights of the employed, and on the part of the employee, more appreciation of the weight of responsibility upon those who direct production.

Scrutiny, too, of the relations of the individual to his community, and of the state to its citizens, hope for political reform that would not be merely sporadic, but would establish itself in the principles as well as the platforms of political parties, were characteristic of the time. Some went further and demanded for all a share in those rational forms of entertainment in leisure time which make the labor of life bearable and fruitful. It is a matter of record now that under the leadership of the personality of Theodore Roosevelt, and later, of the character of Woodrow Wilson, some of these things were achieved or started upon the way of achievement. Then came the dislocation of the Great War, the reaction following it, and the progress of a new liberalism, of which it is yet impossible to prophesy the results.

From the historian's point of view, the fiction of protest has its value in its representation of the feeling of the times. But its importance as literature rests upon other considerations. If criticism of life is to be significant, it must be written by a man who has a broad knowledge not only of the surface but also of the fundamental springs of human con-

623

duct. However just his imagination may be, however generous his motives, his work will not endure if he submerges his characters to his desire for reform. Charles Dickens and Charles Kingsley both attacked the abuses of their day. But Dickens used the Courts of Chancery and the slums of London simply as a background for the creation of character. That is why *Bleak House* is a great novel and *Alton Locke* is not. Propaganda usually means bad art, for in order to drive home a projected reform, a novelist generally overstresses the evil he is describing in relation to the complete picture of life. Everything he says may be correct, in detail, yet it may present an untrue picture of life because other elements in the picture are omitted. Nothing can be more untrue than a fact when the fact is distorted. And the fiction of protest must stand or fall by its reality in this larger sense.

It will naturally be impossible to treat here the vast mass of so called "muck-raking" fiction. Most of it is now forgotten, for there is nothing so dead in literature as an economic or social evil that has been reformed. But certain of the novelists through their real achievement or through the amount of critical discussion their work has aroused, demand inclusion in this survey. In some cases their very limitations and failures are of interest in the analysis of that elusive but important element in the history of fiction, the reaction of the general reader.

The first group of critics include the liberals, of whom Frank Norris, Robert Herrick, Brand Whitlock, and Ernest Poole are most significant. Frank Norris (1870–1902) was born in Chicago, but went to San Francisco in 1885 when he began the study of painting which took him in 1888 to Paris. Being convinced that this was not his forte, he entered the University of California and later spent a year at Harvard, where he came under the inspiration of Lewis E. Gates, to whom so many students of the 'nineties have paid tribute. After a trip to South Africa in 1895, where he became involved in Jameson's Raid, he returned to San Francisco, writing for *The Wave*, in which he had published a short story "The Jongleur of Taillebois" as early as 1891, and of which he was assistant editor from 1896 to 1898.[1]

Among these early stories, "Miracle Joyeux" [2] is a poetic conception of Christ's love for children. The stories are of interest, however, mainly

---

[1] See *Frank Norris of the Wave*, edited by C. G. Norris (San Francisco, 1931), for these early stories; also *The Third Circle* (1909).

[2] *The Wave*, October 9, 1897. Printed in book form, 1906 as *The Joyous Miracle*.

as preliminary sketches for later work. "Judy's Service of Gold Plate" appears in *McTeague,* and "Fantasie Printanière" uses the names "McTeague" and "Trina" in a grim story of two women who fight over their respective husbands' prowess as wife-beaters.

In one of these stories, "His Sister," itself of little importance, Norris indicates through a criticism of the journalistic novelists, especially Davis and Crane, and his clever parodies of certain mannerisms of Kipling, Harte, Crane, and others, the artificial quality of certain of their effects. He was also a journalist, but he is to be distinguished from Davis, Crane, London, and O. Henry because he was concerned with reform, while they were either unconcerned with it or were definitely more interested in other phases of fiction. Norris, too, while affected somewhat by his journalistic experiences, shows this influence less than the others. While he went to Cuba during the Spanish American War for the McClure Syndicate, the magazine did not publish his articles and the trip resulted mainly in the collapse of his health. His reading for McClure and later for Doubleday, Page and Company is of interest because he discovered Dreiser's *Sister Carrie* which was published on his recommendation. But as soon as his novels made him independent, he gave up his magazine connections. His death as a result of an attack of appendicitis cut him off just as he was planning a European trip to collect material for *The Wolf.*

Although *Vandover and the Brute* was not published until 1914, it was written in 1894–1895, and must be judged as an unfinished novel, which he would certainly have revised.[3] It shows definite influence of Stevenson's *The Wrecker* and of *Ben Hur,* and in general of Zola, but it has unmistakable power. It is a study of the growth of the brutish nature of a man who tries to be a painter but becomes involved with a girl whose suicide brings on him disgrace, until his final state of nervous degeneration reduces him to the lowest depths. It is naturally an uneven production: the spectacle of Vandover barking like a dog is unimpressive, but the description of his loss of power to paint is well done.

Moran of the Lady Letty (1898) showed fewer of the youthful faults of *Vandover* but also less of its promise. It is a romance of the sea, with Stevenson as a model, and a remarkable heroine, who is found overcome by coal gas on a derelict, and between whom and the hero, a man of good family who has been shanghaied, there develops a love story

---

[3] Charles Norris edited the novel, with additions and subtractions, made necessary by the incorporation of certain scenes in later books.

which is ended by her death. Norris rather than fate takes her out of the story, because of her unfitness for the life which Wilbur represents.

Norris's first important novel, *McTeague* (1899), had existed in its earliest stages as far back as his year at Harvard and was finished in 1897. It is a celebration of force—huge, stupid and animal. McTeague, first a miner, becomes a dentist without adequate training, and Norris depicts with fidelity his squalid love story with Trina, his miserly wife whom he kills under alcoholic excitement, although he is not actually drunk. So far the book would have simply been a photographic account of an unimportant matter. But in the flight of McTeague from pursuit through the mining regions and the alkali desert, Norris added the imaginative touches that lifted the book into significance. Like the animal that he is, McTeague feels instinctively the approach of his pursuers, and Norris, unlike London, does not overdo the primitive motive but translates it effectively into terror. When the dentist believes he has thrown his pursuers off the track, he is traced by the personal hatred of Marcus, from whom he has won Trina, and who has joined the sheriff's posse. McTeague kills Marcus but in the struggle Marcus has caught his wrist with the handcuff and, a hundred miles from water, McTeague is lost. The picture of the huge inarticulate figure, chained to the body of the man he hates, and waiting for death by thirst, has an epic quality.

Blix (1899) is autobiographical, for the adventures of Condy Rivers in winning his way as a writer and his gradual love story with "Blix" parallels to some extent Norris's own life. The comradeship of Rivers and "Blix" in their wanderings around San Francisco while he is looking for material strikes just the right note. Love that comes to life while a woman is helping a man build the foundations of his creative career, a love that is based on friendship and understanding, is a far more important subject for fiction than the morbid analysis of temporary infatuation. It is more important because it is more real and permanent, and because it exists in America more frequently than is generally supposed. Norris used some of the material he had treated but not printed in *Vandover*. "Blix" was drawn from Jeannette Black, the girl he married. *A Man's Woman* (1900) was not very important. It is the story of a vigorous, brutal man, who returns from an Arctic expedition through sheer force of will, and marries by the usual recipe in such fiction a woman who ultimately sends him back to the Arctic regions. Norris himself knew it was poor.

In *The Octopus* (1901) Norris came into the maturity of his power, under the inspiration of a lofty conception. He determined to write the epic of the wheat, the universal food of man, and planned a trilogy to deal with the production, the distribution, and the consumption of American wheat. In order to provide a conflict, he chose as his central characters a group of wheat-growers of south-central California—Magnus Derrick, his son, Harran, and their associates, Annixter, Osterman, and others. They represent the struggle of the creators of a world necessity against the greed of a corporation, the "Pacific and South Western" Railroad, which takes a ruinous toll from the labors of the farmers, and which ultimately leads to the death of many, fighting in desperation for their homesteads. Norris did not permit this conflict to remain abstract. The power of the corporation is made concrete through the character of S. Behrman, banker and railroad representative, who is extremely well drawn.

The opening of *The Octopus* showed conclusively Norris's power of conception and his ability to express that conception concretely and dramatically. The railroad enters the novel through the massacre of the sheep which have wandered on the track and are flung aside, broken and bleeding, by the fast passenger locomotive speeding relentlessly on its appointed way, with the track cleared for its special purpose. This imaginative picture is established through the character of Presley, the poet, whose longing to write an epic of the West is greater than his ability to express his feeling. Through him, Norris brings the novel back to the large conception with which he started. After the stormy meeting in which the treachery of Derrick's other son, Lyman, who had been elected railroad commissioner by the wheat-growers, is established, Presley turns to the landscape for relief.

And there before him, mile after mile, illimitable, covering the earth from horizon to horizon, lay the Wheat. The growth, now many days old, was already high from the ground. There it lay, a vast, silent ocean, shimmering a pallid green under the moon and under the stars; a mighty force, the strength of nations, the life of the world. There in the night, under the dome of the sky, it was growing steadily. To Presley's mind, the scene in the room he had just left dwindled to paltry insignificance before this sight. Ah, yes, the Wheat—it was over this that the Railroad, the ranchers, the traitor false to his trust, all the members of an obscure conspiracy, were wrangling. As if human agency could affect this colossal power! What were these heated, tiny squabbles, this feverish, small bustle of mankind, this minute swarming of the human insect, to the great, majestic, silent ocean of the Wheat itself! Indifferent, gigantic, resistless, it moved in its appointed grooves. Men, Liliputians, gnats in the sunshine, buzzed impudently in their tiny battles, were born, lived through their little day, died, and were forgotten; while the Wheat, wrapped in Nirvanic calm, grew steadily under the night, alone with the stars and with God.

There are fine elements in *The Octopus* in addition to the major conflict. The vision that comes to a herder, Vanamee, of the girl he had loved, who had died in childbirth, a vision in all probability of her living daughter, is exquisitely told. And the growth of a real love in Annixter, out of the roots of his sensual passion, is interwoven artistically with the new birth of the wheat in the spring. Throughout all the novel the passion of the sowing and ploughing, the coming fruitfulness of the rain, the eternal renewal of the seasons, run like a *motif* just as Egdon Heath played its part in *The Return of the Native* or the hemp fields in *The Reign of Law*.

Norris had not arrived at complete control of his material in *The Octopus*. It is at times loose and repetitious. The conflict between the wheat-growers and the railroad could have been compressed. The chicanery of the road, even although it was based on the Mussel Slough affair, down to the very prices the farmers were forced to pay for their land by the Southern Pacific Railroad in 1880, is described in too much detail, and the propaganda hurts the novel inevitably as a work of art. In fact, the methods are idealistic quite as often as they are realistic, and many of the characters run into types. But the dramatic incidents are often skilfully handled, especially the drowning of Behrman, in the rush of the loose wheat into the hold of the ship. And the conception of the issue is on large lines, much larger indeed than the facts warranted. If Norris had not made the railroad so completely black, he would have made his story more convincing.

The final note of optimism—that whatever evils come, the wheat remains, perennially growing and sustaining life—lifts the novel into imaginative surety.

The second novel of the trilogy, *The Pit* (1903), is more compact and unified, and the central character, Curtis Jadwin, the speculator in the wheat market of Chicago, is as sharply defined as any of the characters in *The Octopus*. He corners the wheat market, but in an endeavor to maintain his corner, he is ruined. Norris has shown with skill how it is not the bear operators who ruin him; it is Nature herself and the inexorable laws of supply and demand. By forcing up the price of May wheat earlier in the year, he has prompted the farmers to sow more wheat, and the rush of wheat in July swamps him and forces the price down.

It was the Wheat, the Wheat! It was on the move again. From the farms of Illinois and Iowa, from the ranches of Kansas and Nebraska, from all the reaches of the Middle West, the Wheat, like a tidal wave, was rising, rising. Almighty, blood-brother to the earthquake, coeval with the volcano and the whirlwind, that gigantic world-force, that colossal billow, Nourisher of the Nations, was swelling and advancing.

Again the wheat has triumphed, as it did over Behrman in *The Octopus*. In *The Pit*, however, we have a sympathy for Jadwin we did not have for Behrman. His love story with Laura Dearborn illustrates his dogged persistence, but Norris's women are never very effective. Laura is not sure of herself and, while the picture of her dissatisfaction with life because she has no interest left when Jadwin begins to neglect her for the wheat pit is well done, one has no real sympathy with her because she is essentially selfish.

The evil that the corner on wheat accomplishes in financial ruin, in starvation in Europe, and in the high price of bread in this country is shown clearly, and the advantage it has been to the farmers is also indicated sufficiently. What prevents *The Pit* from being as important as *The Octopus* is first the lack of any really interesting character except Jadwin. He is so much more distinct than the others that there is a temptation to forget that it is his relative rather than his absolute merit that makes him remembered. There are at least three characters in *The Octopus*, Magnus, Annixter, and Behrman, that are quite as well drawn as he. But perhaps even more important is the lack of that brooding poetical insight into the relations of man and the earth that distinguishes *The Octopus*. The Chicago grain pit cannot by its very nature strike the epic note which rises from the vast acres of wheat in California. The forces of Nature that bring to fruition the seed sown months before are titanic compared to the struggle between the bulls and bears of a grain exchange. The latter produce nothing, the former everything.

It was a loss to literature when Norris's early death prevented the third of the trilogy from being written. It was to have been called *The Wolf*, and would have dealt with the relieving of a famine in Europe. Here Norris might have had an opportunity to rival *The Octopus*.

That Norris was essentially a critic of economic and social conditions is shown in his essay "The Novel with a Purpose." [4]

> Every novel must do one of three things—it must (1) tell something, (2) show something, or (3) prove something. Some novels do all three of these; some do only two; all must do at least one.
>
> The ordinary novel merely tells something, elaborates a complication, devotes itself primarily to *things*. In this class comes the novel of adventure, such as "The Three Musketeers."
>
> The second and better class of novel shows something, exposes the workings of a temperament, devotes itself primarily to the minds of human beings. In this class falls the novel of character, such as "Romola."
>
> The third and what we hold to be the best class, proves something, draws conclusions from a whole congeries of forces, social tendencies, race impulses, devotes itself not to a study of men but of man. In this class falls the novel with the purpose, such as "Les Misérables."

It is to be noticed that all three of his illustrations are romances, although in *Romola* and in *Les Misérables* George Eliot and Victor Hugo used realistic methods at times. Norris began his career with romantic impulses, and after the writing of *McTeague*, he returned to romance in *Moran* and *The Man's Woman*. There are romantic incidents in *The Octopus* and *The Pit*. But the sincerity of Norris, his love of the oppressed and his liberality, even at times to the institutions he was attacking, make him an engaging figure. His conception of the function of the novelist reads even yet like a bugle call:

> To make money is not the province of a novelist. If he is the right sort, he has other responsibilities, heavy ones. He of all men cannot think only of himself or for himself. And when the last page is written and the ink crusts on the penpoint and the hungry presses go clashing after another writer, the "new man" and the new fashion of the hour, he will think of the grim long grind of the years of his life that he has put behind him and of his work that he has built up volume by volume, sincere work, telling the truth as he saw it, independent of fashion and the gallery gods, holding to these with gripped hands and shut teeth—he will think of all this then, and he will be able to say: "I never truckled; I never took off the hat to Fashion and held it out for pennies. By God, I told them the truth. They liked it or they didn't like it. What had that to do with me? I told them the truth; I knew it for the truth then, and I know it for the truth now."
>
> And that is his reward—the best that a man may know; the only one really worth the striving for.

[4] *The Responsibilities of the Novelist* (1903), p. 25.

Robert Herrick (1868–   ) illustrates both the strength and the weakness of the critical attitude. At first, a survey of his many novels, from *The Man Who Wins* (1897) to *Sometime* (1933), seems to include a large variety of themes, written with knowledge of the conditions of American life, scornful of wrongdoing, and yet with a liberal attitude which permits him to see the inevitability of the evils against which he inveighs. But there is an aloofness, a narrowness of outlook, a lack of that warmth of feeling without which no novelist can achieve greatness. Objective quality is important in a critic of life, but when that objectiveness seems to be manifested not so much in the creation of his plots and characters as in a remoteness from life itself, it becomes a defect. It would be easy to explain this quality by calling it "academic" and attributing it to his career in the English Department at the University of Chicago from 1893 to 1923. But Herrick's friend and colleague in that department, William Vaughn Moody, was as deep a sympathizer with human joy and suffering as anyone of their day. Perhaps a New England birth, a Harvard education, and what seems to Herrick to have been an exile in Chicago, may account for the chill in Herrick's fiction. Perhaps it was an overdose of the Russians.

In any event, there is a certain sameness in Herrick's fiction which makes classification rather than strict chronology fruitful. His major purpose has been a criticism, through a man or woman, of the conditions which forbid the free exercise of their personality. In the cases of the men, their development is closely interwoven with their profession or business. Jarvis Thornton in *The Man Who Wins* (1897), Dr. Sommers in *The Web of Life* (1900), Dr. Holden in *The Healer* (1911) are physicians. Dr. Thornton is kept from devoting himself to research by the demands of his wife and her family. Dr. Sommers gives up the woman he truly loves for another woman who is already married. Dr. Holden, who is the best drawn of these three, is prevented from living the free life in the Canadian forest by the insistent claims of his wife for the social organization she craves. Herrick's criticism of the medical profession for commercialism is far from justified, and his solution, the establishment of an Institute by private benefaction, was hardly a new one, even in 1911. In *The Real World* (1901) Jack Pemberton faces problems of legal ethics more clearly, largely because he keeps himself freer of responsibilities. In *The Common Lot* (1904) it is an architect, Francis Hart, who gradually loses his professional ideals under the pressure of temptation and of family necessities. Here his wife is a moral tonic, but Herrick unlike Howells in *A Modern Instance* misses an opportunity to let the plot work out logically. Hart is saved from the immediate legal consequences of his corruption by personal influence, and while he pays the penalty in loss of professional standing, his return to the ranks, which Herrick seems to think is a solution, is no solution at all.

Herrick's middle-of-the-road attitude is shown in *A Life for a Life* (1910) in which the hero, Hugh Grant, a banker, fights a power trust headed by a corrupt financier whose son illustrates, on the other hand, the hopelessness of the anarchist's position. In *One Woman's Life* (1913), it is a painter who loses his power to create, through his wife's extravagance. Herrick did not spare his own profession, and in *Chimes* (1926) he drew a picture of the University of Chicago in which his satiric gift rather than his sense of fairness is in evidence.

Another major theme with Herrick which obviously enters also into the novels already discussed, is a study of the change that came into the relations of men and women during the new century. *The Gospel of Freedom* (1898) is the story of a discontented woman, with education and wealth, who roams over Europe, marries, lives in Chicago, leaves her husband and arrives nowhere. Herrick shows that she is never free because she has never thought of anyone but herself, yet he seems to put most vigor into her denunciations of the dullness of life in general. It is only fair to Herrick, however, to quote the recipe for living which he puts into the mouth of Jennings, a young teacher: "To accept the world as it comes to our hands, to shape it painfully without regard for self, that brings the soul to peace."

The Gospel of Freedom shows clearly the influence of Howells and Fuller, but in *Together* (1908) Herrick developed a manner more in keeping with the fiction of the decade 1900–1910, a manner which on the whole was not an improvement. If the analysis of married life which is the theme of *Together* makes an attempt at a keener realism by stripping the characters of all reserves and penetrating to their inmost thoughts and emotions, the final result is a blurring of these characters, who are overshadowed by the theme. The novel begins with the wedding of John Lane and Isabelle Price and not only is their marriage unhappy, but all her bridesmaids and some of her other friends go through a similar experience. Marriage, as an institution, seems to be hopeless, but Herrick was not able in *Together* to make us care much about the characters in these relations. His use of Lane, a railroad man, to attack the methods of larger roads in their mergers, and in their discrimination in freight rates against the short haul, is also not dramatized.

By 1924 Herrick had lost all sense of proportion, and in *Waste* he drew a picture of the utter hopelessness of American life. Jarvis Thornton begins life in a collegiate town in New England, and is taken through college, through the Great War, and through most of the United States, and everything is futile. Herrick's picture of the Great War is pessimistic but seems drawn from the outside. The women Thornton loves are all simply drags upon him, and if the book has any meaning it is a wail against the very existence of the other sex. *One Woman's Life* (1913) while not as ambitious as *Together* is more interesting, because Milly Ridge is kept constantly before the reader and her main fault, her absolute failure to understand the value of money, is not incompatible with a certain charm that Herrick rarely gives to his heroines.

It is significant that the two novels which are unquestionably Herrick's best, depart to a certain degree from his usual, almost stereotyped method. *The Memoirs of an American Citizen* (1905) is a straightforward account of the rise of Van Harrington, a man not too scrupulous, from the farm, through the meat-packing business, to the office of senator. The autobiographic method, in which Harrington tells the story in language which a man of his type would use, is partly responsible for the high position the novel takes in Herrick's work. By this method we are spared the author's comments, often in his other fiction too solemn and sometimes laughably banal. Herrick has also been able in a masterly way to indicate through Harrington's narrative his lack of any real understanding of right and wrong. The picture of life in Chicago is accurate, and the interrelations of politics and business are sufficiently indicated.

In *Clark's Field* (1914) the importance arises from the originality of the conception. This lot of ground in Chicago becomes an active force in shaping the lives of the people who own it. When, through the operation of the trust, arranged by a well-drawn character, Judge Orcutt, it arrives at a value of $5,000,000, it becomes the property of Adelle Clark, who is, so far as she knows, the sole heir. Her marriage, her divorce, and her discovery of her cousin, who is also an heir, in California, make up a novel in which Herrick does not clutter up the book with characters and in which the field acts as a unifying force. There is a largeness of conception in this novel, and a sense of inevitability which is missing in so much of Herrick's fiction.

Herrick's third theme, which showed more definitely in his later books, is a realistic analysis of the physical aspects of sex. *Homely Lilla* (1923) is an unimportant story of a girl of animal instincts, whose marriage is incredible and whose husband's objection to children is naïve when it is not silly. In *Wanderings* (1925) a series of long short stories, laid in the United States or in the Caribbean Sea, lawless passion of rather mature people forms the staple of discussion. They were preliminary studies apparently for the novel *The End of Desire* (1932). This is a study of the gradual cooling off of two persons, both physicians and both nearly fifty. Herrick protests in this book against the contemporary obsession in literature and science with sex, yet the minute details of the physical relations of Serena Massey and Arnold Redfield leave little to the imagination; and the Negro orgy which they visit in the Caribbean region and the interest of Serena in the Negro cook are certainly illustrations of the tendency which Herrick deplores.

In *Sometime* (1933) Herrick wrote one of the most absurd of all the novels which have satirized modern life through the picture of a Utopia. He lays the scene in Khartoum, some centuries after America and Europe have been destroyed by an ice pack. In this delightful land, where the dark races have finally come into their own, nobody sells anyone anything; lawyers, priests, soldiers, and business men have been done away with; and no one is allowed to produce offspring except by permission of the state. It would be amusing to record the various misstatements of facts concerning our present civilization, but it is not worth while. It would seem as though Herrick had concentrated all his dissatisfaction and blown one blast of denunciation upon the ruins. His remedies are also delightful. The disasters of sex are avoided by sterilizing all those who are not permitted by the state to have children, and then they are turned loose to do as they please, their morality being no longer a matter of interest! The voyage to North America where excavations are being conducted, and the deposit of certain young women among the Indians of Mexico to teach birth control and sterilization winds up one of those books which a man of Herrick's intelligence should have left in the inkstand.

It seems remarkable now to think of the discussion which raged in women's clubs over Herrick's novels about 1910. For his criticism was on the whole destructive, and in none of his novels did he solve the questions he discusses. Life is wrong, and the only way out is to withdraw from it as Dr. Holden does in *The Healer*. His program was an ambitious one, for he attempted to deal with the problems of several industries, and nearly all professions, and if he had had the skill, he might have created a *Comédie Humaine* that would remain at least of value as a picture of the times. But the trouble is that his picture is usually one-sided. *Together* does not portray American marriage, even in the average; *Waste* is not a fair picture of the effect of women upon men. Even his liberalism is based not upon a broad view of life, but upon the very hopelessness of even radical measures to improve it. Finally, as an artist he created characters that are hard to remember, because something is left out of their composition. Certainly sympathy is not there; neither is the love that he is always talking about, the union of spiritual and physical passion, but which he seems not to understand. He is an irritating example of the novelist whose sincerity determined him to look life squarely in the face, but who had not the vision to see it as it really is.

With a broader outlook on life than either Norris or Herrick, the liberalism of Brand Whitlock (1869–1934) expressed itself in fiction through his sympathy with those who suffer through their lack of adjustment to human law. He is not indignant like Norris, or scornful like Herrick, and his criticism of conditions is all the more effective because he is content to let the characters and incidents establish the criticism. Born in Urbana, Ohio, he became a reporter, studied law, and had a distinguished career as the reform mayor of Toledo for four terms. He was elected on an independent ticket, and his experience in defeating the bi-partisan combination gave him a keen insight into politics.

His first novel, *The Thirteenth District* (1902), is, in consequence, one of the best treatments of American politics in fiction. It is laid apparently in Illinois, in the 'nineties, and describes the rise and final defeat of a congressman, Jerome Garwood. The political philosophy of Garwood is based upon selfishness, and he goes down to defeat because he fails to understand the feudalism that is still the most potent force in American political life. He is defeated by his earlier friend and supporter, to whom he has been ungrateful, and he finds himself deserted because he has not been quite loyal to his own party associates. Whitlock does not paint Garwood as a traitor by any means; he is contrasted favorably with some of the other political types who proceed by blackmail and even less savory devices. He is simply an average, human politician, with good and evil tendencies, and in spite of his shortcomings, Whitlock secures enough sympathy for his central character to make the reader want him to win. Whitlock's own experiences as a political correspondent in Toledo for the Chicago *Herald* are probably reflected in an amusing light novel, *Her Infinite Variety* (1904) in which woman suffrage is used as material for the comedy of politics. Even more distinctly autobiographical was *The Happy Average* (1904) laid in the town of "Macochee" in Ohio, for it parallels Whitlock's own struggles to become established in journalism and law.

It is not so effective, however, as *The Turn of the Balance* (1907) which is a realistic story of the condition of the criminal in modern society and his inter-relations with other forms of life. As Whitlock tells in his autobiography and in the preface to the revised edition of 1924, the novel had its origin in his own experiences when he undertook the defence of poor prisoners before the criminal courts. He avoids all sentimentality by making the offenders like Archie Koerner guilty of the crimes with which they are charged, but his indictment is not so much of the courts as of the treatment of the criminal. His description of the prisons, which he knew thoroughly,[5] proves that there had been little improvement since the days when Charles Reade fulminated against the English jails, and *The Turn of the Balance* was a potent force in bringing about prison reform in this country. Yet Whitlock kept steadily before him the necessity of subordinating his thesis to the characters, and he makes the defence attorney, Gordon Marriott, a real person. Through him the accidental nature of court proceedings is brought out clearly, the liberty of a prisoner depending so much upon the ability of his counsel, the health of a juror, or the convenience of a judge. The moral contrast is used skilfully also through Marriott who saves a weak but not hopeless embezzler by intimidating the banker who intends to prosecute him, using a receiver of stolen goods in the process, and running the risk of disbarment.

After the publication of a volume of short stories, *The Fall Guy* (1912), dealing mostly with sacrifices of a romantic nature, Whitlock's writing of fiction was interrupted by his career in diplomacy. Appointed Minister to Belgium in 1913, and later Ambassador in 1919, he played

[5] See *Forty Years of It*, p. 122.

an important part in the history of the Great War, which was recognized by signal honors from Belgium, France, and other nations.

In 1923, he returned to "Macochee" in *J. Hardin and Son*, a study of two men, both hard and dominating, who afford an opportunity for the contrast of two generations. The father is uncompromising; he is a bitter advocate of Prohibition because it allows him to make other people good in *his* way. Paul Hardin, the son, has more of a struggle between his sense of duty and his illicit desires. Whitlock's criticism in this book is more subtle than the usual denunciation of the herd instinct of the intolerant. Paul Hardin represents the Puritan inheritance fading out into a conscience not strong enough to prevent sin but powerful enough to put an end to it.

In 1928, Whitlock returned to the field of politics in *Big Matt*, an appealing story of contrasted loyalties. Whitlock showed his liberal understanding of human nature in this novel. Independent Democrat as he was, the hero of the book is Matt Holt, the Republican State Chairman, who has made John Blake Governor, and who as Commissioner of Public Utilities takes a bribe which leads to his imprisonment. Holt knows only one duty, to be true to his friends, and when Governor Blake visits him in prison to offer him a pardon, he refuses without heroics because he knows it would wreck his friend's political future. He possesses the interest which in fiction a simple, direct nature often wins. John Blake, on the contrary, is also a machine politician, but has ambitions to serve the State which are not realized because he is continually compromising between his conscience and his desire for reëlection. He is well drawn but he takes the second place in interest. There are some very realistic scenes, especially the interviews between Matt and Blake, in which the Governor feels himself in the presence of a will stronger than his, and in which the knowledge of the many deals they have arranged together prevents him from taking the lofty tone of patriotism that he strikes in public. But the finest note is that of the quiet insistence on Matt's part that the Governor will prove a greater man than he really is, and the response on Blake's part to that appeal. Whitlock's very avoidance of preachment makes the book one of the best criticisms of the standards of State politics in fiction.

Whitlock's European experiences led to the writing of two international novels. In *Uprooted* (1926) he placed Betty Marsh of Macochee, Ohio, who had been a war worker in France, back in that country after a brief stay in the United States. Betty's restlessness and independence are quite well drawn, and while her innocence is hard to reconcile with her experience, she is more credible in this respect than Daisy Miller. Leslie Waldron, the painter whose protecting attitude toward Betty does not carry him far enough to marry her, is a real figure, with the bachelor's reluctance to give up his freedom, even for his old love, Dorothy, the Countess of Granvallon, whose appreciation of the position her marriage has brought her is also a deterrent. There are other well-drawn American types, particularly Mrs. Richardson who lives in the skirts of international society, and for contrast, Lady Agnes Drayton, an English woman of determination, who helps Betty at a time of need. The solidarity of Americans in Europe is particularly well established.

Whitlock tried a curious experiment in *Transplanted* (1927). Having introduced the Countess of Granvallon in *Uprooted* as a widow, he makes her the central figure of the later novel, but places the time before the war. *Transplanted* is a contrast between American and French standards. Dorothy Manning, of New York, has married Count Georges de Granvallon, partly for his handsome presence but more for his position as a member of a family secure in the traditions of the Faubourg St. Germain. Her struggle against the power of the family unit, of a system of morals which refuses to acknowledge her husband's infidelity, but takes her money to buy off the husband of Georges' mistress, is quietly but vividly depicted. Dorothy's final absorption into the family unit through her son is a climax to which Whitlock gives the sense of inevitability. He writes about the society of the Faubourg as though he knew it, but he is concerned with the domestic and moral contrasts quite as much as the social aspects of the matter. Except for Leslie Waldron who is brought in as a disturbing element, the characters are all French, and Whitlock's liberality is shown in his understanding of a system which the American usually dismisses impatiently without trying to comprehend it.

Neither of his stories of modern Europe, however, has quite the stylistic charm of *Narcissus, a Belgian Legend of Van Dyck* (1931). In this novelette Whitlock threw around the painting of Van Dyck's masterpiece, "St. Martin Dividing his Cloak," a glamour of love, possession, and "the persistent illusion of the future," and made of the relations of Rubens and Van Dyck one of those rare incidents in fiction in which a master touches the universal note in his warning to his successor. Rubens' counsel applies not only to painting but to any form of art.

"Ah! His dream! Yes! But a dream is quite another thing; don't delude yourself by imagining that your reverie is a dream. And even a dream is worthless unless it is captured and realized. To do that means hard thinking—and hard work. Reverie is enervating. A dream—the artist's dream—is stimulating. How rarely it comes! We paint the same picture over and over, again and again. The first part of one's career is but a preparation for the supreme achievement, the solitary masterpiece—if there ever is one; the rest is but a dwindling imitation of it. Fortunately the public does not know when that moment has come—and gone. No more do we."

Whitlock's last novel, *The Stranger on the Island* (1933), was laid on Beaver Island, in Lake Michigan near Mackinac, which Mrs. Catherwood had treated in her short stories. That strange personality, "King Gorel" in this novel, who ruled absolutely, and annexed a plurality of wives, meets his death at the hands of a Frenchman whose sceptical attitude toward the religion of King Gorel is developed skilfully.

In the pages of Whitlock's autobiography, *Forty Years of It* (1914), can easily be read the struggle between the lover of art and the lover of politics. Writing was evidently his earliest ambition, and he looked at first upon the demands of politics as an interruption. It is of course idle to speculate on his accomplishment if he had devoted himself entirely to fiction, but certainly of all of this group of critics he had the best command of style and the farthest vision. His warm feeling for humanity, his recognition that time and infinite patience are needed for the reform of social and political evils make his fiction glow with a wisdom that came from his wide experience. The firmness and integrity which brought him safely through the devious byroads of Ohio politics and gave him later his diplomatic triumphs in the most difficult of all the posts of Europe, show in his fiction in pity and tenderness for those who possessed neither courage nor integrity. His understanding of the people's needs was complete. As he says in his autobiography:

. . . but the great emancipations will not come through the formulæ of Independents, Socialists, or single-taxers, nor through Law and Order Leagues, nor Civic Associations. Down in their hearts these are not what the people want. What they want is a life that is fuller, more beautiful, more splendid and, above all, more human. And nobody can prepare it and hand it over to them. They must get it themselves; it must come up through them and out of them, through long and toilsome processes of development; for such is democracy.

Among the liberal critics, Ernest Poole (1880–   ) deserves attention because of his humanity and his restraint. Born in Chicago, and educated at Princeton, he spent three years in social work in New York City. After writing two plays, he turned to fiction and won the Pulitzer Prize with his first novel. *The Harbor* (1915) is one of the rare novels that is possessed by a large idea. The great harbor of New York, in its actual being, in its possibilities for extension of trade, in its function as a gateway for all nations, and as a beginning from which goes out over the world the spirit of America, is made the symbol through which characters grow into life. Beginning with his childhood in the house on the Heights of Brooklyn which overlooks the East River through which his father's ships sail to distant ports, Billy learns through the seamy side of life in the streets below to hate ugliness and love beauty. His experiences in Paris, his study of Maupassant and Flaubert, kindle his aspirations to write. Through his magazine work and his love for Eleanore Dillon he becomes acquainted with her father, who has a great vision of the harbor of New York in the future and plans from his lofty office the remodeling of the mistakes of the past. Billy learns, too, through a friend, Joe Kramer, to know the stokers, and dockers, the underdogs; one of the most vivid passages is the account of the life of an anarchist, Jim Marsh, through the bitter story of his wife. Keeping the story concrete, Poole describes the strike on the docks through Billy's eyes, and there is the note of regret for an earlier and cleaner life of the sailing ships before steam brought about the dark conditions of the stoke-hole. In a way, it is a preparation for the dramatic treatment of the theme in O'Neill's *The Hairy Ape*. The strike is crushed, but it leaves in the mind of the writer who has taken his part in it "one tremendous burning passion for the freedom of mankind." He has seen his friends jailed for their part in it, he has lost himself the market for his work, but he is never shrill or bitter in his denunciation of capital. He feels the great power of the workers when a mass idea inspires them, but he doubts whether the time has come for the mass to take over the leadership.

Being a novelist first, Poole preferred to describe the changes and problems without attempting to settle all the questions raised by the struggle between capital and labor. As he makes his hero say: "I have seen three harbors, my father's which is now dead, Dillon's harbor of big companies which is very much alive and Joe Kramer's, which is struggling to be born." There is a warm sympathy for the mass of workers whose margin is small, and yet an equal sympathy for those individuals who, like Dillon, depend for the fulfilment of their visions upon those who have large resources they are willing to risk. *The Harbor* appeared after the Great War had begun and Poole ventured upon prophecies some of which have been realized and others which have not. But the book remains one of the most intelligent and one of the most liberal criticisms of life. "To each age a harbor of its own."

In *His Family* (1917) Poole's criticism of life was not framed on so large a scale as in *The Harbor*. It was, however, in a sense, more constructive, for it presented a picture of the effort of a man to face the problems of complex modern life in the only way in which they can be solved. When the novel begins, Roger Gale is a widower nearly sixty years old, living in New York City. He has a prosperous business, and three daughters. Edith is married and has five children; Deborah is the principal of a large school in the tenement district; Laura, who is soon married to a young broker, is almost completely selfish. Roger Gale has a hope that he will live in his children, but his children naturally insist upon living their own lives. There is real insight into feminine nature in the way the three women disagree. Edith is willing to sacrifice everyone else for her own children. Deborah postpones her lover's happiness for her large family in the tenements and her own personal satisfaction in her job. Laura pursues her own way ruthlessly until it comes to divorce and what to Roger is disgrace. Not only do they fight for their own way, but woman-like, they try to arrange the lives of others. As Poole puts it briefly through Bruce, Edith's husband, in speaking of Laura and her husband:

"Young Sloane is not a bad sort of chap. The way he lives—well it isn't mine —and mine isn't his—and we both let it go at that. But the women can't, they haven't it in 'em. Each sits with her way of life in her lap. You can't see it over the table cloth, but my God, how you feel it."

Of the three, Deborah is painted with most sympathy, a result probably of Poole's own work in the University Settlement in New York City.

Blind (1920) is partly autobiographical, for Poole's experiences as a war correspondent in Germany and France in 1915 and in Russia in 1917, as well as his earlier play-writing, give authority to this survey of a man's life, beginning in 1875 and coming up to 1920. An officer blinded in the Great War tells through the eyes of a reporter of the crowded life of New York City, from the tenement houses where the ignorance of the inhabitants as well as the selfishness of the owners bring continual re-infection, to the hectic life of rehearsals on Broadway where he loses a sense of artistic values in the rush for success. The picture of the war in Germany and in Russia is without doubt accurate. The Russian scene is most interesting, for though it is an old story now, the calm account of the evershifting phases of the Revolution in Russia forms a valuable picture. Poole remarks in describing a Russian family whose estate was being abandoned by the peasant workers, "They were my kind of people. They were liberals." And it is as a plea for liberality that the book is most appealing. Unfortunately it appeared in October 1920, when the generous flood of feeling that united Americans in the War was ebbing into the indifference of Harding "normalcy," and the truth of Poole's portrait and the sanity of his opinions are a requiem, not a prophecy, of that international coöperation which alone could have secured a permanent peace. His very title indicates that he felt this himself. *Blind* is too much of a reporter's narrative to be great fiction. The canvas is too crowded with details, and the characters are dwarfed in consequence. But it was a brave book to write in 1920.

Poole next treated the post-war conditions in *Danger* (1923), a novel painting realistically the devastation which a woman, made neurotic by her experiences in France, could work in the lives of her brother and his wife. The story moves on relentlessly to the death of her brother and her own suicide, a grim piece of work and more unified than is usual with Poole. In *The Avalanche* (1924) Poole described a conflict between the scientific ideals of a young neurologist and the urge for material success which his wife, who has a flare for publicity, has had implanted in her through her success in the Liberty Loan drives during the War. Dr. Llewellyn Dorr is a real character; his mysticism, implanted through his childhood in the mountains, lifts him above the ordinary physician, but the powers which raise him also wear him out. Poole knew thoroughly the pitiless methods of publicity which reacts upon the subject of adulation, and the death of Llewellyn Dorr is a logical outcome even if the sudden shifting of his wife's love is hardly so probable.

The mountain country near Sugar Hill in New Hampshire which Poole knows well comes in several times in his fiction as a refuge for the city dweller who may there be cured of his ills, real or imaginary. Sometimes, as in *Great Winds* (1933), the complicated life of well-to-do people is emphasized by the New Hampshire setting. Again in *One of Us* (1934), the story deals with simpler types, and is told through the eyes of a storekeeper in New Hampshire who reviews the many changes that have transformed the country in forty years. Without any striking plot, there is a sincerity which makes it one of his quietly satisfactory novels, for the spirit of true Americanism is in it.

Poole's work is uneven, and his first novel, *The Harbor*, remains his best. But even his minor fiction, like *Millions* (1922), has an ironic quality in the family group waiting for the death of a man who has really lost his fortune, and there is a touch of fantasy in *The Hunter's Moon* (1925) that makes it worth while. What he did best was to describe the joys and tragedies of New York City life, with a sane and sympathetic attitude toward both rich and poor, a pity for the wrecks the Great War had left behind it, and a deep appreciation of the comfort of the hills of New England where a simpler and more sincere life prevailed. The weak element in his fiction lies in the lack of distinction in his style, especially in the conversations. He is more of an observer than a creator, and he seems more interested in his material than in his characters. But he also seems to have written only of what he knew and to have had the courage to avoid the easy path of caricature.

CHAPTER XXIX

CRITICS AND SATIRISTS—THE RADICALS

Usually, in life as well as in literature, the radical attracts more attention than the liberal. His promise to "go to the root" of the matter, whether he kills the plant or not, is more appealing to those seeking a new sensation than any calm discussion of the problem. In fiction, the group of novelists, Theodore Dreiser, Upton Sinclair, Sherwood Anderson, and Sinclair Lewis, who determined to write of "life as it is," stripped of sentimentality and void of reticence, have met with violent opposition and received equally violent acclaim. They have been translated freely into foreign tongues, and to many Europeans they represent the most significant developments in our fiction. It is important, therefore, to examine critically the claim that they have represented American life with reality, and that their work has in it those qualities which will secure its permanence. It is a fitting time to do this, since, with one exception, their careers as novelists seem drawing to a close.

Before discussing the work of the four leading exponents of this school, a few words are necessary concerning a novelist who represented the radical impulse at its height during the first decade of the twentieth century. Beginning in 1901, David Graham Phillips (1867–1911) satirized the newspaper publisher, the British fortune-hunter, the industrial magnate, Wall Street, the political boss, and other types and institutions which were just then under fire. The transitory nature of his work is so apparent now that it is hardly necessary to speak of any of his novels except *Susan Lenox, Her Fall and Rise*, which was completed in 1908, but was not published till 1915, four years after Phillips' death. Even then it raised a storm of protest during its serial publication; after it had appeared in book form in 1917, the first edition was withdrawn and some passages to which the Society for the Suppression of Vice objected were deleted. *Susan Lenox* illustrates the change in public taste which had already begun by 1917, but in judging the book, it must be remembered that it was preceded in its composition by *Sister Carrie*, and that its preface is dated in the year in which *The Easiest Way* was provoking discussion upon the stage. It is the story of the courtesan, a girl who starts life in the Middle West under the shadow of her mother's illegitimacy and is taken through the lowest depths of prostitution in New York City. There is no doubt that the details of her struggle, especially those describing her employment by a man who lives on the earnings of street-walkers, are based on actual life. The fallacy in *Susan Lenox*, however, and in books of its type, lies in the inconsistency of the central character. In order to preserve the interest of the reader, Susan is drawn as a girl who preserves, through all these degrading incidents, a purity of soul and a delicacy of feeling which take the novel out of the category of realism. We can easily believe in her first downfall, but to expect us to believe that such a girl will leave a man she loves "for his sake," and yet become a street-walker, or that she will give herself to a commercial buyer for "the sake of the house" which employs her, yet leave the store the next day; or that she will refuse nobly the offer of protection made by a dramatic agent and yet continue her street-walking, is absurd. *Susan Lenox* is based upon the sentimental fallacy that evil leaves no trace on the character of a woman who sells her body promiscuously. Perhaps even more irritating is her feeling about Palmer with whom she goes to Europe. He is, she thinks, "a big man and a big man couldn't possibly be a bad man." Palmer is the gentleman who has been living on her earnings and those of other women! It is this muddy thinking, on the part of the author, that makes *Susan Lenox* and its imitations such bad art. Bret Harte could draw the generosity or the courage of a prostitute, but he would have smiled at *Susan Lenox*.

Theodore Dreiser (1871–   ) has given ample information of an autobiographic nature especially in *Dawn, A Book About Myself,* and *A Traveller at Forty.* He was born at Terre Haute, Indiana, of parents who were German by birth or descent, spent a year at the University of Indiana and from 1892 to 1910 was a newspaper reporter in St. Louis, or Chicago, or a magazine editor in New York, his career culminating in the editorship-in-chief of the Butterick Publications. The early poverty of the family is reflected in his fiction, and together with a religious training of a rigid nature, was responsible presumably for a lasting resentment against economic conditions, social caste, or religious orthodoxy. We are concerned with his naïve revelations of his emotional development, especially in the matter of sex, only because they explain the curious abnormality of some of his characters. To a writer who, according to his own statements, desired sex experiences but for a long period had not the courage to attempt them, there will come a time when he will find it necessary to dramatize these desires in his characters. And that he will overdo the matter is almost inevitable.

Sister Carrie, Dreiser's first novel, was published in 1900 on the recommendation of Frank Norris who was reading manuscripts for Doubleday, Page and Company. According to the *Publishers' Weekly,* the book was carried on Doubleday's list at least till 1905. It was re-published in England in 1901, in the United States in 1907, 1908, 1912, and 1917, and has therefore been continuously available since its original publication; and while its first reception was unfavorable, it was not suppressed as is usually stated.[1]

To present standards, *Sister Carrie* seems so tame that we are likely to forget how different were the standards of American taste in 1900 when the police stopped the production of Daudet's *Sapho* because Olga Nethersole was carried upstairs by her lover. Dreiser believed he was doing something significant when he conceived the idea of telling what might easily happen to a girl of eighteen who in 1889 went to Chicago, without experience, to find employment. Since the question of Dreiser's importance rests first upon the reality of his characters and incidents, *Sister Carrie* demands more attention than its intrinsic merits deserve. For it was one of the first of those twentieth-century American novels which piled detail upon detail of a sordid nature, in order to present a picture of "life as it is." That Carrie should become the mistress of a salesman whom she does not love, simply because she is hungry and bored, is natural enough. It is not improbable that she should leave Drouet for Hurstwood who promises her more.

---

[1] So many misleading statements have been made concerning the matter that the statement of the firm (September 30, 1935) is of interest:

Sister Carrie was recommended for publication by Frank Norris, then reader to the company, and it was accepted on his recommendation. It was then read in manuscript by other members of the firm who felt that its general content was not in keeping with the company's list. Such a matter has very little relationship to censorship, since a publishing list to be successful must have a character of its own and must not overstep that character to too marked a degree. This disagreement with the readers' recommendations was brought to Mr. Dreiser's attention. He requested that the book be published, even though it were done without advertising or promotion. It was, therefore, published and offered for review. The early criticisms were not good; there were few orders and the larger part of the edition remained for some time in the stockroom of the company. It was, however, neither suppressed nor withdrawn.

But that she should fail to inquire whether he is married is unlikely. And that when she has found out this fact she should solemnly go through a useless marriage ceremony with him is incredible. Equally unreal are the actions of Hurstwood. This gentleman is the manager of a fairly large retail liquor business, and while it is difficult to visualize him in Dreiser's words as "a very acceptable individual of our great American upper class—the first grade below the luxuriously rich," he presumably has a fair salary, for he owns a house, a horse and carriage, and supports a wife and two children. Yet he throws all this away for ten thousand dollars, which he takes from the safe, knowing that it is the end of any business career of importance. Even this amount he returns under fear of prosecution, so he really ruins himself for a woman whose standards would have presented no insuperable obstacle to his wishes even if he had not run away with her to Montreal and later to New York. Here Carrie, by some miraculous process more in keeping with the romantic melodrama, jumps without any training from the chorus of a musical show to the position of leading lady. Hurstwood loses the money he invests in a saloon, and sinks in the economic scale until suicide closes his career. There is more reality in this decline than in any other part of the novel. But it is not enough to save the book, for no one cares about Hurstwood; in fact, there is no reason to care about Carrie. Dreiser tries at the end to depict her as a seeker after beauty, but nothing she does or says indicates it. Her aspirations are purely material, and she lets Hurstwood starve while she has plenty without a thought.

What made *Jennie Gerhardt* (1911) vastly superior to *Sister Carrie* is the imaginative nature of the heroine, and her quiet self-sacrifice for others. She becomes the mistress of Senator Brander and later of Lester Kane because she is caught in the grip of circumstances and she sees no way out for her family than in her acceptance of the protection of these men. She cares also for Lester Kane and grows to love him deeply. With a sense of the value of reticence in art, which later left him, Dreiser does not dwell unduly upon the sexual relations of Jennie and Lester; in fact it is the establishment of their comradeship and domestic happiness which lasts after passion has subsided which makes their final separation tragic. If Dreiser had let this picture speak for itself, if he had made the reader think—here is a true marriage in everything but a ceremony—he would have written a far finer novel. The visit of Jennie to Lester's death-bed, her silent triumph when she hears him say that she is the only woman he has ever truly loved, are good touches. Even better is the scene at the funeral, when his wife and his family naturally resume their control and Jennie sits unheeded in a corner of the church. Dreiser should have stopped there of course, but he had to express his own interpretation of the puzzle her life presented in an absurd epilogue.

The moral values in *Jennie Gerhardt* are confused. That would not make so much difference—so they are in life—but Dreiser is so much interested in *proving* that the standards of the world are wrong that the thing becomes irritating. If a writer wishes to use moral contrasts, he should either, like Bret Harte, keep them as dramatic material, irrespective of their moral significance; or if he wishes to weave the moral issues into the story, then like Howells or Mrs. Deland he must *think clearly*. But Dreiser cannot think clearly. His solemn defence of Jennie's first liaison with Brander is a delightful example of this muddled philosophy. It is not necessary perhaps to refute his arguments. The biological laws to which he appeals have refuted them for centuries, and the social laws which he regards as accidental will continue to operate as long as men prefer to know that their children are their own, and women continue to recognize that Nature, which has given them that certainty, has placed upon them, in consequence, a responsibility which they reject at their own peril. But the criticism of his preaching rests after all upon its very introduction into fiction, and the reception of it by a type of critic who seemed to think it was new was most amazing.

Dreiser next turned his attention to the evils of financial corruption, and built upon the career of the speculator Charles Yerkes two novels, *The Financier* (1912) and *The Titan* (1914). The central character, Frank Cowperwood, is a type, with the reality of a newspaper biography. His ruthless shrewd instinct for money-getting, which brings him at first success, then failure and prison for embezzlement of public funds, then once more success during the Jay Cooke panic, and, in *The Titan*, control for a short time over the street railway systems of Chicago, is established by an interminable series of incidents. Dreiser worked hard to collect facts, and especially in *The Financier* there is fidelity to scenes and conditions in Philadelphia before and after the Civil War. The interrelations of politics and finance in the process of combining the street railways of Philadelphia and Chicago are described with sufficient ac-

curacy. But we read about Cowperwood's rise and fall without any sympathy and with only the faint interest that arises from watching a game
in which we care little which side wins. The issues are entirely material,
Cowperwood remains the same impersonal type and there is no spiritual
development through the hundreds of pages. Dreiser showed too in
these books his growing obsession concerning the sex relations of his
characters. Cowperwood passes from one woman to another with an
indifference to any natural affection such as made Lester Kane in *Jennie
Gerhardt* tolerable, an indifference which is shared by the reader, for
none of the women comes alive. As an example of inanity in conversation
the utterances of one of his mistresses in Chicago, Rita Sohlberg, is priceless, and yet we are told she has a remarkable spiritual attraction for him.
Another mistress, Stephanie Platow, who has already been the mistress
of two men, is "an innocent untarnished jewel"!

In *The Genius* (1915) Dreiser lost completely his sense of proportion. The book is supposed to be the account, beginning in the 'eighties,
of the career of a painter who starts in the town of Alexandria, Illinois,
and becomes a magazine editor in New York. But it is really a chronicle
of his relations with women who yield to his ardor with a regularity
which at first is startling but soon becomes ridiculous. At the fifth or
sixth of these episodes, he addresses his beloved:

"Open your eyes," he pleaded. "Oh, God! That this should come to me! Now
I could die. Life can hold no more. Oh, Flower Face! Oh, Silver Feet! Oh,
Myrtle Bloom! Divine Fire! How perfect you are. How perfect! And to think
you love me!"

If this be realism, the word has ceased to have any meaning.

About a year after its publication, *The Genius* was withdrawn by its
publishers on account of the protest of the New York Society for the
Suppression of Vice. It was republished in 1923. No one acquainted with
the history of fiction can support censorship of this nature, of course,
but the salacious quality of *The Genius* is not its most definite weakness.
It is simply inconceivably dull.

For some years Dreiser confined himself largely to autobiographical
volumes or to shorter fiction, collected in 1918 as *Free and Other Stories.*
They have little distinction either of subject or form. "The Lost
Phoebe," a story of an old demented man who searches for his dead
wife until he follows her image over a cliff to his death, has some power.

Dreiser's passion for detail was even less at home in the short story than the novel. Of all his shorter fiction, the best is "Sanctuary," found in his second collection, *Chains* (1927), a tale of a girl who "goes wrong," is taken in by the Sisters of the Good Shepherd, relapses, is brutally treated by her lover and finds her way back to the shelter of the Sisters. There is a sympathy for suffering which makes the sordid story better than his usual work.

In 1925 came *An American Tragedy*, in two volumes. The most sympathetic interpretation of this work is as an attempt to take a boy below the average, intellectually and spiritually, handicap him with poverty and show how life grinds him into fragments and tosses him aside. It is quite conceivable that a great artist might have made a great novel starting with such material. But he would have proceeded quite differently from Dreiser. He would have kindled in such a character a spark which the hardships of life would have fanned into a glow that defied them, and whether he won or lost there would have been a conflict that made the book significant. But Dreiser could not do this. Clyde Griffiths is fired by no higher ambition than to make a better salary and satisfy his passions. When he decides to murder Alberta, his mistress, in order to be free to court a girl whose people are wealthy, he plans the deed in the most absurd manner. Here Dreiser's admirers might contend that this is just the way such a weakling, with "a temperament that was fluid and unstable as water" would proceed. But such a person does not *plan* murder at all. He might commit it in a moment of rage, but the long cogitation preceding the murder is so obviously built up to provide details which, later, in the hands of the District Attorney, will convict Clyde that it becomes unbearable. Probably the high point of absurdity is reached when this District Attorney is provided with a "psychic sex scar" which causes him to prosecute Clyde more vigorously because he has been repressed in his own sexual desires! Unbearable for another reason are the horrors of the death cell where Clyde waits for execution. Dreiser's criticism of this element of the prison system is not unfair and the novel might have a slight justification if it drove home the barbarity which makes each murderer live through the agonies of his predecessors. But the long drawn out detail defeats its own purpose, while a few swift strokes would have been impressive. Nothing arises from Clyde's agony of impatience, no tragedy, that purges through pity or terror, for we have long since ceased to care what becomes of him.

According to the list of Dreiser's books in *Dawn*, his *A Gallery of Women* (1929) is fiction. It is to be hoped that the autobiographic method employed in it is therefore objective, for it is apparently an account of the author's various adventures with women of easy virtue, commonplace and without interest. Dreiser's philosophy of life by this time seems to have become completely pessimistic. In "Rella" [2] he arrives at this conclusion.

If I were less convinced that life itself is anything but a game, arranged for as well as motivated by the greedy, the arrogant, the lecherous, and the heartless, with dullards and beggars and nincompoops at the bottom as their tools and pawns, I would be prepared to assail the members of the joyous profession of which she was a part. There is little that is too sharp or uncomplimentary, I assure you, that might be said of them—mercenary, covetous, sycophantic, lax, dissolute, malevolent, brutal— But why go on? You may find lists that apply in Trent and Walker. Yet having said all this, I am still compelled to ask myself wherein they are so much worse than the members of any of the other professions that eventually and perforce, via related compulsions find themselves in authority in life. If any one òr anything is to be indicted, let it be Life.

With a philosophy of life such as this, Dreiser's failure to write great literature hardly needs explanation. The only wonder is that he has been taken so seriously by a school of criticism which believes that he did a service to American literature by his encyclopedic revelation of the lives of male or female sensualists whose standards have an aroma of the barnyard. That there are such people is beyond question; that they are worth writing about is another matter. But that Dreiser and his imitators have widened the scope of American fiction is incorrect. Any such imitation of a certain school of Continental fiction is a limitation, not a broadening of art, at least so far as the interpretation of American life is concerned. Howells said the right thing long ago about the sense of proportion which the normal American keeps in matters of illicit passion. He does not devote a major portion of his time to such affairs, because he has other things relatively more important to which to attend. Dreiser's fiction represents therefore the introduction of a foreign standard generally unrepresentative of life in America.

Even if his view of life were sane, Dreiser's pedestrian style, labored and undistinguished, would keep his work from being first class. He writes, as Fuller said with much less justice of Garland, with his fist

[2] Vol. II, p. 529.

rather than with his hand. The poverty of Dreiser's vocabulary and the bareness of his style may be seen if we compare his description of Moyamensing Prison with that of Richard Harding Davis, who, whatever his limitations, could at times lift journalism into literature. But except for *Jennie Gerhardt*, Dreiser has never done this.

In the fiction of Upton Sinclair (1878–   ), propaganda reached its ultimate. Born in Baltimore and educated in New York City, he has lived in various parts of the United States and has been active in the politics of California. It is not necessary to chronicle all of Sinclair's novels. His earliest work was romantic melodrama. *King Midas* (1901), for example, is an inane novel in which a poet loves a maiden to madness, and finds that the man she marries is his father, who has betrayed his mother many years before. Being presented in this extraordinary manner with a stepmother, he passes into a comparatively peaceful state. *The Journal of Arthur Stirling*, (1903) is supposed to be the expression of Upton Sinclair's own protest against the lack of opportunity for a poet to obtain a hearing. His struggles with publishers will elicit the sympathy of any young aspirant, but, on his own showing, he received quite fair treatment. The novel is too long drawn out; there is about enough material for a short story. The explanation of his failure to become an artist is given in this novel first when he says, "My soul is centered upon the *thing*," and later on when he says: "An artist, as I understand the word, is a man who has but one joy and one purpose and one interest in life,—the creating of beauty." Since Sinclair has not created beauty, he fails by his own standard.

From whatever he has touched, Sinclair has endeavored to strip illusion. In *Manassas* (1904), his novel of the Civil War, nearly every one is incompetent or a coward. With cheerful disregard of facts, Stephen A. Douglas "is a representative of the lowest classes of the cities of the North. When he first came to Washington he brought with him the manners of the barroom." Douglas is denied any moral perception, and Lincoln is represented equally unfairly. His speeches on the way to Washington "were full of flippant and tactless remarks." The man who quietly put Seward in his place and assumed the leadership of his party in a letter whose language is one of our classic utterances, is represented as dismissing Charles Francis Adams with the sentence: "It was the Governor's choice, you understand, so it's him you have to thank."

The cheerful disregard of facts, illustrated by a picture of the characters singing "Dixie" nine years before it was written by Dan Bryant, and the breathless career of his hero who is whirled around to any place in which his creator desires to have him, reveal the basic weaknesses of Sinclair.

His most successful novel, *The Jungle* (1906) is a socialistic treatise rather than a novel. It is written with a burning sense of injustice and a sympathy with those whose margin is small and who have no economic security. Evidently Zola and other European naturalists influenced Sinclair, and he took as hero a Lithuanian, Jurgis Rudkus, and his relatives, especially Ona, his wife. They are chosen among the employees of the packing industry because they do not understand the language and have the European instinct of not objecting to the oppression of an upper class. While the description of the methods of the packers was based upon facts, and the exposure of their wanton disregard of public health led to the pure food crusade of the Theodore Roosevelt era, the cure Sinclair proposed as a panacea, the creation of another political party, that of Socialism, has been proved to be inadequate. Occasional sentences in *The Jungle* are well worth remembering, such as:

"To do that would mean, not merely to be defeated, but to acknowledge defeat—and the difference between these two things is what keeps the world going."

The weaknesses are the sentimentalizing about the hogs, and the utter lack of probability of all the ills happening to *one* person or *one* family. Jurgis might be thrown out of work. It is hardly likely that a woman like Ona would become the mistress of a brute like Connor, that she would die of utter neglect in childbirth in a big city like Chicago, that their child would drown in the street puddle, and her little brother would be eaten alive by rats. When a novelist piles on the misery too much, one ceases to believe in it; the book therefore loses in appeal, or one continues to read it through curiosity to see what form of misery Jurgis will escape. From the child who has scarlet fever, mumps and measles all in his first year, to his father who is laid up for three months with a pulled tendon, the characters succumb not to fate or circumstances but to the novelist himself, and one simply refuses to follow the stream of misery with sympathy.

The fanciful economics of Sinclair, by which the only cost of a product is the labor involved, or the suggestion of a world in which the labor of one hour a day is to provide sustenance for all the world, leave the reader cold, for such theories were disproved a century ago. As art, *The Jungle* fails entirely, because the material, not the characters, is the important thing in Sinclair's eyes. Sinclair was probably right in feeling that a novel might help the cause of the pure food crusade more than a volume of documented facts, but after all, the facts, not the fiction, called the book to Theodore Roosevelt's attention and resulted in its popularity. Much less effective than *The Jungle* was Sinclair's attack upon the methods of financial operation in Wall Street in *The Money Changers* (1908). The methods by which steel companies and railroads were refinanced from solvency to insolvency were sufficiently accurate in detail, but the lack of motivation in the actions of the hero, who is as naïvely credulous at times as he is inconceivably reckless at others, ruins the book as a novel. Sinclair's magnates act at times like fiends, and at times like children, for a reader has little belief in the power of a capitalist to shake the foundations of national credit when he neglects to give a simple order which would have prevented the hero from invading his yacht to save the young woman the magnate yearned to possess.

Another phase of Sinclair's work, the recounting of his own career and the revelation of his struggles, is illustrated by *Love's Pilgrimage* (1911), a thinly veiled autobiography dwelling mainly upon the cruel hardships imposed upon a creative writer when he has to support a wife. This extraordinary genius, who "had stayed at the university until he taught himself French and Italian, as well as German, and had read all the best literature in those languages" and who lives with his wife as "brother and sister" for months, until it is time to describe their sensations when they consummate their union, is a source of irritation rather than sympathy. The curious may check the autobiographic details with Sinclair's later attack upon journalism in *The Brass Check* (1919), but in both books, the hunger for publicity is apparent and explains much of Sinclair's writing.

After the Great War, Sinclair relieved his mind on the subject of the treatment of pacifists and conscientious objectors during that struggle. *Jimmie Higgins* (1919) is one of his weakest attempts. Through this little Socialist machinist Sinclair tried to show the evils of war, and the confused mental processes of such a man were described with an accuracy which might be important if the details were interesting. But when Jimmie finally goes into the war as a machinist and, being sent to the front as a courier, takes command of a gun and wins the battle of Chateau Thierry, the thing becomes so absurd that even the later fantastic adventures in Russia where he is tortured by the American Army of Occupation for his sympathy with Bolshevism, arouse only a languid interest. In *100%, the Story of a Patriot* (1920) Sinclair's main character, Peter Gudge, is a weakling who becomes a spy upon the Communist and Socialist groups. The Mooney Case in San Francisco provides the opportunity for Peter to exercise his talents, and the hysteria of intolerance which war engenders is at times rather vividly described. But Sinclair by his exaggeration spoils the effect as usual. No one who coöperated with members of the Federal Intelligence Service during the Great War and remembers the care that was taken to be sure of their ground before acting against the nation's enemies, can read the book with anything but a smile. As a novel, it simply does not exist, for it is a series of episodes, and the character of Peter Gudge is so inconsistent that he becomes a mere name. Any group of Communists who placed their trust in him for a moment, are inconceivable. Sinclair adds an appendix in which he attempts to establish his facts, but by that very effort indicates that his object is propaganda and not art.

None of Sinclair's recent books has attained the popularity of *The Jungle. Oil!* (1927), a story of the California oil fields, has some good moments in the description of a father's love for his son and the boy's reciprocal affection, but the welter of details which makes all capitalists criminals and all laborers heroes, submerges this thin thread of interest. *Boston* (1928) is a long drawn out account in two volumes of the Sacco-Vanzetti Case. While it is true that the trial and the consequent action of the Governor of Massachusetts were indecisive and bungled almost beyond belief, Sinclair's book is written entirely from the propagandist's point of view, which is, of course, fatal to both truth and art. Any unprejudiced person is so wearied by constant repetitions that he loses interest in the characters or their fates. Sinclair does not understand that in a novel of this kind, the reader is inclined to judge of the truth of what he does not know at first hand, by the treatment of other matters on which he is well informed. Anyone familiar with recent history who comes across such absolutely incorrect statements as those concerning the conduct of President Wilson at the Peace Conference, or the absurd discussion of the Federal Reserve System, hesitates to believe what Sinclair states concerning the trial itself. His efforts at prophecy in *The Millennium* (1929) "a comedy of the year 2000," in which the last capitalist is starved to death, showed his weakness when he matched his strength against *Looking Backward*. *The Wet Parade* (1931), an involved defence of prohibition, is, of course, now as dead as the Eighteenth Amendment.

If Upton Sinclair is remembered at all in the history of fiction, it will be by *The Jungle*, and then only because of the journalistic dexterity in the depiction of horrors. No character emerges from his fiction, and his exaggerations leave us with a distrust of his intellectual honesty. It is not by such writing that the many who wish to work, and cannot, will find the justice they demand instead of the charity from which they shrink.

Like Dreiser, Sherwood Anderson (1876–　　) has taken his own career seriously, and not only in his autobiographical books, *A Story Teller's Story* (1924) and *Tar, a Midwest Childhood* (1926), but also in his fiction he reverts constantly to his own experiences, and to his father, whom he pictures as a dreamer and "a ruined dandy from the South." It is necessary to be careful not to take Anderson's conception of his heritage as a decline from a patrician South too seriously, for he warns us himself in *Tar* that he is dramatizing his life. Born in Canton, a small town in Ohio, he was a wanderer, working as a mechanic, conducting a small factory, taking part in the Spanish-American War, and writing publicity for the moving pictures. If *A Story Teller's Story* is at all accurate, he wrote hundreds of pages before he began to publish short stories in *Masses, The Little Review*, and other magazines.

His first novel, *Windy McPherson's Son* (1916) is the story of a boy who begins life in a small, drab, Iowa town in the 'eighties and proceeds by ruthless methods to become the owner of a large munitions trust. He gives this up, however, "to find truth," wandering around among working people, helping on strikes, till the workers betray him, or the union leaders stop him. Anderson's solution of Sam's problem is, as always with him, inconclusive. He brings home the three children of a profligate woman and presents them to his wife. But even this somewhat drastic action does not satisfy him. In his first novel Anderson revealed certain traits which have remained characteristic. The story is confused and fumbling in its method. Life is not rightly planned, and nothing much can be done about it. Like other writers of this group, he describes certain isolated aspects of life correctly, but he lacks any sense of proportion. His sweeping denunciation of women, "mothers of half mankind," who spend their days gossiping meanly on porches, represents accurately a certain type of woman. But it does not include "the mothers of half mankind." He evidently believes that fiction must shock the reader if it is to make an impression, and his picture of McCarthy in the jail calling out to the public the names of the twelve married women in town with whom he has lain, is made more offensive by his remark that "if it had not been for a quirk in his brain, Mike McCarthy might have been a kind of Christ with a pipe in his mouth." Great literature never shocks: it often thrills or startles the reader, but the essence of good art forbids a sudden dislocation of ideas except for the purposes of humor.

In *Marching Men* (1917) the animating force of his hero Norman MacGregor, is a hate for injustice, instilled into him by his father's sacrifice in trying to save the lives of fellow miners trapped in a burning mine in a Pennsylvania coal town. His vague yearnings to be great, to lead the workers in their struggle, come to nothing. Thousands of men are trained to march in squads as Anderson had learned to do in the war, but nothing comes of it. Nothing arises either from his love affairs, and the scene in which he brings the little milliner with whom he has been living to the rich social worker to explain to her that though he loves her better, he will continue with the milliner, is old fashioned melodrama of the purest type.

Inspired probably by *The Spoon River Anthology* of Edgar Lee Masters, Anderson had been publishing short prose sketches of people in a small town which were collected in *Winesburg, Ohio* (1919). The characters are lonely, frustrated, futile, and abnormal. Anderson explains in the introduction that he intends to draw grotesques, and it is quite probable that in a small town there might be found an insane person with hands which loved to fondle small boys, another who thinks everyone is Christ, a woman who takes a pillow to bed with her instead of a man, a minister who peeps through a hole in a stained glass window at a woman in her bedroom across the way, to mention only a few of the eccentrics. But why in the name of sanity and maturity, without which art is sterile, should anyone write about them? These aberrations occur mostly among adolescents, and to record them is to place one's self on the level of the small boy who relieves his mind with a piece of chalk on a back fence.

Much the same notes are struck in the stories which make up *The Triumph of the Egg* (1921). Married philanderers who kiss young girls and solemnly dismiss them with their blessing, or for variety murder their wives in order to possess a maiden whom they fail to secure, are celebrated. Perhaps the most unhealthy is "Out of Nowhere into Nothing" in which a wife decides that heaven is "a sexless, quiet, windless place where mankind lived in a state of bliss" from which man had been thrown because of "the sin of sex." The fumbling is continued in *Poor White* (1920). Hugh McVey, a descendant of the poor Southern whites who have refused to compete with the slaves and have lost their energy, is at first an interesting figure. Through the inspiration of a New England woman who has come to that small town in Missouri, Hugh breaks away from his drunken father and later from the town itself, and arrives at an Ohio town where he becomes an inventor. The inarticulate nature, struggling to find his place in the scheme of things, has possibilities. But after having been presented over night by Anderson with $100,000 with which he does nothing, Hugh meets the heroine, Clara, and then the novel goes to pieces. Anderson's picture of Clara's sexual awakening had been sufficiently uninteresting with its slant at perversion in her friendship with another woman. But for utter futility, the description of the fright into which Hugh falls on their wedding night, and his fear of consummating the marriage until Clara gently but firmly leads him to his duty, is almost unmatched in fiction. The worst of it is that the frequent adjournments of the consummation seem arranged by the author to whet the appetites of adolescent readers, and beneath this level it is difficult to go. Certainly the book goes nowhere, and the narrative method by which each character, at a moment when he is about to push the action forward a little by some decision, goes back and reviews his earlier life, reminds one of the French and British romances of the seventeenth century, when each character tells his life story as an introduction. It is only artificiality of another nature. Nor is it necessary to analyze his short stories, *Horses and Men* (1923), in which Anderson's experiences with the race track find expression. The pathologist might find some interest in one amiable yarn, "The Man Who Became a Woman," but it would lie rather in the study of the author than in the plot of the story, which continually postpones the delightful climax, as had been done in *Poor White*.

In *Many Marriages* (1923) Anderson went completely mad. Into the purlieus of this story it is not necessary to enter in detail, but the crowning scene, in which the hero brings an image of the Virgin and two candles and setting them up in his room, walks up and down naked before them, planning his career, and then elaborates to his wife and daughter who come in, his philosophy of marriage, takes Anderson out of consideration as a novelist of any significance. Leaving aside the question of taste, the incident leads nowhere, and could lead nowhere. *Dark Laughter* (1925) was another study of restless people dissatisfied with life. Some variety was introduced by a description of an orgy at the Quat'z-Arts Ball in Paris through which an American woman passed unscathed, apparently much to her regret. The central character, Bruce Dudley, is another one of those heroes of Anderson who marches manfully into the heroine's bedroom in her husband's absence and is said to possess a charm which is nowhere indicated by his conversation or his actions. He is not as badly drawn, however, as the husband, who sits down and cries when he discovers the relations of his wife and his gardener. Having exhausted the potentialities of the Middle West, Anderson laid in Georgia his scene of *Beyond Desire* (1932), another dull book of frustration in which the hero is killed in a conflict between a Communistic group and the militia. Nothing results, however, from the economic clash. His later short stories are included in *Death in the Woods* (1933). They deal with the low lights of existence as before, and have only the merit of brevity. Most of them revolve about sex, one choice example "These Mountaineers" dealing with a girl of twelve who is already with child, and yet has "a look of breeding, of aristocracy." Another charming young woman describes, with the aid of her husband, the physical lures by which she secured him.

The most astonishing circumstance connected with Sherwood Anderson is the fact that he has been taken seriously. Even the late Stuart Sherman in a moment of critical blindness, compared the first chapter of *Dark Laughter* to the first chapter of *Pride and Prejudice!* It was the form, apparently, which led him to this strange statement, and yet the form of that opening chapter illustrates one of Anderson's worst faults, the deliberate indirection of approach. The first sentence begins with a statement about Bruce Dudley, but immediately we are led off to an analysis of another character, and one has to reread the opening paragraph before he gets his bearings. Compare that with the delicate art with which Mr. Bennet is made to stand out clearly by Jane Austen and is kept in the center of the picture. This indirection infects the conduct of Anderson's novels, which proceed by a series of spirals, where progress becomes a lost art, and the story finally fades away into thin air.

But the most striking quality of Anderson's fiction is its lack of just that reality for which it has been at times celebrated. These monsters of lust, of perversion, of frustration, are not real people. They are shells surrounding obscure and futile forces, pale incarnations of idle thoughts which, if they come to normal human beings, are rarely translated into action. For their very nature forbids action, and in Anderson's fiction they are longings of abstractions reviewing the record of lost opportunities of evil which they had not even the courage to grasp. There is no promise for the future of American fiction in such writing, although I am not unaware of his successors in the anatomy of sex relations.

When such a writer is taken seriously, it is time to remind ourselves of that fable of Hans Christian Andersen in which the King orders a robe from visiting tailors whose work is praised highly by the courtiers, although they see nothing, but who are afraid they will not be considered up-to-date unless they admire it. Then a child enters and simply says: "But the King has nothing on!", and the illusion is dispelled.

The youngest of this group and one of the most interesting phenomena of recent years, Sinclair Lewis (1885–   ), was born in Sauk Center, Minnesota, educated at Yale, and spent some time as a free lance writer and a reporter, during which he traveled widely through the United States. From 1910 to 1915 he filled various positions in publishing houses in New York City, until his short stories and serials began to free him for more travel and the writing of novels. His early novels made no distinct impression. The most appealing, *Our Mr. Wrenn* (1914) puts into fiction Lewis's own love of adventure, and there is a wistful note in the character of the little clerk who goes to England, finds it cold, and returns to the safety of his mediocre life. Adventure is also the theme of *The Trail of the Hawk* (1915), but the romantic career of an aviator who covers most of the country is preceded by a satire on the small western denominational college which foreshadows the Lewis of later years. He is not visible, however, in *The Innocents* (1917), a gentle tale of an elderly couple who also travel widely, this time on foot. *The Job* (1917) is a success story of a girl in New York who leaves her work to be supported by a man whom she finally loathes and divorces. It is tiresome in detail and has no appealing characters. Neither does *Free Air* (1919), a race across the western part of the United States in an automobile, which reads, like all these early stories, as though it were planned for a moving picture.

With the publication of *Main Street* (1920) Sinclair Lewis arrived. Many novelists had written about the Main Street of a small town. As early as 1839 Mrs. Kirkland had pictured realistically the crudity of a frontier town, and in 1918 Zona Gale had drawn an accurate portrait of the Main Street of a small Wisconsin village in *Birth*. But Lewis made Gopher Prairie, a town of three thousand inhabitants in Minnesota, the symbol of a national disease, the small-town mind.

It is an unimaginatively standardized background, a sluggishness of speech and manners, a rigid ruling of the spirit by the desire to appear respectable. It is contentment . . . the contentment of the quiet dead, who are scornful of the living for their restless walking. It is negation canonized as the one positive virtue. It is the prohibition of happiness. It is slavery self-sought and self-defended. It is dullness made God.

With this loathing for the petty tyranny of an oligarchy of opinion which tries to reduce all the lives within its reach to one deadly level and spreads uniformity like a plague, every liberal must sympathize. Lewis's attack upon the active obstruction to progressive ideas, the grudging consent to civic improvement, the terror of a few more taxes for schools and libraries, struck a welcome note. In Lewis's conclusion that "not individuals but institutions are the enemies" of progress, he seemed to recognize the basic political cleavage between those who vote to preserve some institution like the tariff or prohibition, and those who trust to leadership which is flexible enough to meet the issues as they arise.

The pictures of the stupid parties, of the village gossips, of the Thanatopsis Club, which dealt with all English literature in two sessions, are deadly in their accuracy. They read as though some unusually acute reporter had been present taking notes. But a great novel cannot be built up on satire alone; it must have character as its ultimate. Lewis attempted to provide this interest through the central character, Carol Kennicott, a college-trained librarian, who marries Dr. Kennicott without any great love, and who vainly endeavors to bring beauty into the town. But Carol fails, and, incidentally, the novel fails, because she has no real source of beauty in herself. She makes no effort to understand the people, to approach them gradually by capitalizing their better instincts, and they resent the attitude of superiority she takes toward them. Her rebellion takes the form of a tawdry love affair, and a calm abandonment of her husband for two years of clerking in Washington. Consequently we lose interest in her, and wonder why her husband bothers to bring her back. *Main Street* has to be judged, therefore, entirely upon its merit as a caricature of a small town, and like all caricature, it depends for its success upon exaggeration. This lay not so much in the description of Gopher Prairie itself, as in Lewis's explicit statement that "Nine-tenths of the American towns are so alike that it is the completest boredom to wander from one to another." It is not necessary or important to prove that Gopher Prairie is representative of only a limited number of American towns, for the wide sale of the book showed conclusively that millions of Americans could smile at the satire of a state of mind which they did not share.

Having met with much popular approval in his satire of a small community, Lewis selected for his next effort, *Babbitt* (1922), a city of three hundred thousand, called Zenith, and vaguely located in the Middle West. But his central character, George F. Babbitt, is no contrast to the city: he is the expression of its most tiresome qualities. Again he is a caricature, this time of the eternal "booster," who, not very secure in his social vision, tries to climb through his fussy activity in matters of church and club, of university-alumni relations, of any avenue to prominence. So coarse, so crude is Babbitt, so well chosen is his name, that he became a symbol and has given, for the time at least, an expression to the language. But the attempt, especially of foreign criticism, to make of him a victim of excessive conservatism is mistaken. The last minute feeble revolt of Babbitt not only collapses, but is entirely out of keeping with his character throughout the rest of the novel, and seems to have been inserted in a desperate effort to find a climax. But the most serious criticism of *Babbitt* lies in its structure. It is, in reality, hardly a novel at all. Babbitt has no life of his own, the book is simply a series of interviews of Babbitt with life. He is brought in contact with liquor, with the Church and Sunday School, with social life, with the Booster's Club, with an illicit love affair, with his family difficulties. Lewis, the skilled reporter, tells us how Babbitt reacted to these phases of his existence, dresses up the interviews with implicit headlines, and when he thinks there are enough of them, closes his notebook. But Babbitt is not a real man; he is only the symptom of a social and economic disease. Such vividness as he possesses is relative; the other figures are so definitely filled with sawdust that he achieves a spurious life by his contrast to them.

Notwithstanding the popular acclaim of *Main Street* and *Babbitt*, Lewis's first important novel was *Arrowsmith* (1925). Again his hero comes from the Middle West, the town of Winnemac, probably in Wisconsin, and the description of his life at the Medical School of the University is dull indeed. But when Dr. Arrowsmith is launched on his career, the whole tone is changed, because for the first time Lewis writes about a character of spiritual significance. *Arrowsmith* is the celebration of the pursuit of *truth* as opposed to the mere making of money. The interference of the world in its various aspects, the necessity of making a living for his wife Leora, the commercialized atmosphere in the Rouncefield Clinic, the jealousies in the McGurk Institute, the most subtle temptation, that of anticipating discoveries in order to forestall possible rivals and to bring glory to the Institute, are surmounted by Dr. Arrowsmith one by one. Finally the supreme temptation arises in the plague stricken Island of St. Hubert in the West Indies. Arrowsmith has discovered what he believes to be a cure, the "phage" as it comes to be known. But with the true spirit of the scientist he wishes to inoculate half the population and leave the other half without the injections, in order to test the results in both cases. It is not only the desire of the governor and the other officials; it is the call of humanity itself, the pleading of thousands for the chance that the inoculation brings to them, which beats down Arrowsmith's resistance and ultimately makes his results uncertain. But the plague disappears and the Institute receives its credit from the public.

Lewis did not continue on this high level. *Mantrap* (1926) is a rather ordinary melodrama laid in Canada, with the ancient plot of an extremely urban New York lawyer flying with the wife of an honest son of the woods at her request, and being pursued by the husband, and later by the forest fires. It seems to have been framed from the point of view of the moving picture, but in any event is negligible. In *Elmer Gantry* (1927) Lewis returned to satire, this time upon Evangelical religion.

Elmer Gantry, a sensual, half-educated Baptist minister who becomes a Methodist because he has been dropped from the rolls of the Baptist Church on account of drunkenness and immorality, is so grotesque a caricature that he is completely unconvincing. Moreover, he is not important enough to make a book. Dickens painted the hypocritical evangelist in the Reverend Mr. Chadband perfectly, but he knew that such a characterization was useful only as a minor figure. All that is necessary to place *Elmer Gantry* properly is to compare it with *The Damnation of Theron Ware,* by the side of which it sinks into insignificance. Nor are Lewis's reproductions of smoking car conversations in *The Man Who Knew Coolidge* (1928) more than amusing satires on the Kiwanis type of "booster."

In *Dodsworth* (1929) however, Lewis rose almost to the level of *Arrowsmith,* and for the same reason. Sam Dodsworth is no caricature: he is a real person, and he has qualities that make him worth writing about. He sells his automobile business and goes to Europe to enjoy the leisure he has earned, and to please his wife. Dodsworth is usually bored by his European experiences, and although he is curiously limited for a university graduate, Lewis has the right to portray him in this guise and had the good taste to make Dodsworth a product of his own college. "Fran" Dodsworth is drawn with great care but not with great skill. She is really not worth bothering about, for she is wholly selfish, and her ambitions are for external social opportunities and for sentimental excursions. She is of value, however, merely as a means of revealing Dodsworth, and her treatment of him which leaves him a lonely wanderer on the Continent while she has an affair with Kurt von Obersdorf, an Austrian Count, brings to him our sympathy. He grows in dignity through his quiet sacrifice, and when he finally abandons her and finds comfort in Ethel Cartright, justice is done. As usual, the novel is too detailed, especially in the descriptions of European life which hardly penetrate farther than Baedeker. But the main character is there, and in the hands of Sidney Howard, the playwright, and Walter Huston, the actor, he came into reality upon the stage. The published form of the play contains a joint introduction by Howard and Lewis, extremely valuable not only in its revelation of Howard's skill in dramatizing the novel, but also of Lewis's limitations as a novelist. With a courage that redounds greatly to his credit, Lewis reprints thirty-eight pages of the novel for which Howard has substituted nine pages of play, practically all of which is new. Instead of Dodsworth's wanderings, including an illicit affair, Howard substituted a brief scene in an express office which brought together Dodsworth and Ethel Cartright. It proved conclusively that Dodsworth's infidelity was unnecessary to the progress of the story and that the descriptions of Venice impeded, rather than helped it. But if Howard pruned relentlessly he knew as well when to expand. In the novel, a letter from Fran tells in a few sentences about the visit of Kurt's mother, the Countess. Out of these few sentences Howard wrote that memorable scene between the Viennese patrician and Fran Dodsworth, which put an end to the latter's hope of marriage with her son, and which through the acting of Madame Ouspenskaya became one of the most glorious moments of the contemporary stage. Not a word of the dialogue is in the novel, but more important, the whole spirit of the interview is changed. In the novel, "Kurt's mother was pretty rude to me" and "wailed at Kurt and ignored me." In the play, the Baroness conquers Fran with the weapons of courtesy, and overpowers her resistance by sending Kurt from the room and then saying:

"I am so much older than you, my dear! . . . You will forgive me if I observe that you are older than Kurt. . . . I should think of my own happiness, if I were you."
Fran. "I am thinking of that."
Baroness (*leaning forward and speaking with great deliberation*) "Have you thought how little happiness there can be for the old wife of a young husband?"

It is not unfair to Lewis to remark that he has never indicated in his fiction the ability to draw characters whose standards and training enable them to help, to warn, or to stab others less secure, who are subdued by a force they only dimly understand. Lewis would probably reply that he is not interested in such contrasts, but if not, he should have kept away from situations which demand such an ability. But after all, the comparison, which might be extended much farther, would only establish the fact that Sidney Howard, the playwright, is a far finer artist than Sinclair Lewis, the novelist.

Up to this point in his career Lewis had mercifully spared us the details of the sexual irregularities of his characters. But in *Ann Vickers* (1933) he lost his sense of proportion and wrote a futile piece of propaganda against organized society, decency, self-control, or that restraint upon the animal instincts which gives them, incidentally, their keenest poignancy. Ann Vickers is a girl who is brought up in Waubanakee, Illinois, goes to college in Connecticut, where we are dragged through a satirical description of the introverted life of a girl's college without men. After having been put in jail for helping on a disturbance in favor of woman's suffrage, which, being a closed issue, is no longer interesting, Ann has a tawdry affair with a Jewish captain of infantry. We are then dragged through her abortion and ever afterward we are led to believe that she lives in a sentimental ecstasy concerning her daughter that might have been. After an unpleasant homosexual chapter or two, concerning two friends of hers, she becomes a criminologist and goes down to a prison in Copperhead Gap. A long description of the ill treatment of convicts follows. Lewis usually works hard in collecting his facts and the picture may be correct, but its very intensity defeats its purpose, as a comparison with Whitlock's *The Turn of the Balance* will easily prove. Ann's later marriage with a stout sociologist and her affair with a grafting judge by whom she has a child, are absurd, especially in her husband's actions concerning the child. None of the characters are alive in any event. *Ann Vickers*, however, did not reach the depths of dullness achieved by *Work of Art* (1934). These lengthy adventures of a hotel man defy retelling, much less analysis, and the spice injected by the sordid affairs of his patrons is as unworthy of the author as his cheap remarks like "It was 1904 and God and William Jennings Bryan were still alive and popular." Lewis's *Selected Short Stories* (1935), in which he gathered together a number of short pieces of fiction going back to 1917, do not rise above the ordinary magazine story. There is a certain grim humor in "The Letter from the Queen," and a touch of irony in "Young Man Axelbrod" that any college graduate will appreciate. But in general they are incidents which have been worked up for periodical publication.

Perhaps the most feeble of Lewis's novels is his attempt at prophecy in *It Can't Happen Here* (1935). This picture of what will occur in 1936 after a Fascist president, Berzelius Windrip, establishes a tyranny, based upon force and oratory, is so absurd that its impossibilities and inconsistencies need no detailed criticism. Such a novel, to be effective, must proceed with some degree of probability, and the methods by which he secures his nomination and election are as improbable as the measures by which he builds up his power. Nothing that he says or does would have impressed a child. The novel is told mainly through the eyes of a newspaper editor, Doremus Jessup, who is apparently an example of the failure of the liberal to meet the dangers created by the extremes of Capitalism and Communism. But while Lewis is quite correct in his statement that the liberal is the only hope of society, Jessup is completely unrepresentative of liberalism in the United States. If the novel is to be taken as a warning that Doremus is a type of the average citizen who will be helpless before such a tyrannical windbag as Berzelius, there is no answer except to point to the liberalism of Cleveland, Wilson, and both Roosevelts, with its unyielding edge of iron. As a novel the book is hopeless because no character is established, and the entire volume is simply a newspaper report of outrages which, being imaginary, fail to interest us. Its beginning is impossible, its details are unconvincing, and its ending is inconclusive.

One limitation that prevents Lewis, notwithstanding the award of the Nobel Prize in 1930, from taking a high rank among novelists is the undistinguished, at times hopeless, quality of his style. It has the hall marks of the reporter, not the artist, but in addition to the bareness and staccato jerkiness, there are mannerisms which spell mediocrity. One of these is his constant habit of describing a character by means of epithets, usually in threes or multiples of threes, which depend upon incongruity for their effect. "Mr. Wrenn was talking to an American who had a clipped moustache, brisk manners, Knights of Pythias pin, and a mind for duck shooting, hardware selling and cigars." In the first paragraph of *Main Street*, Carol "was meditating upon walnut fudge, the plays of Brieux, the reasons why heels run over." In *Babbitt*, a character "believed that the earth is flat, that the English are the lost ten tribes of Israel, and that the United States is a democracy," with two more triplets of the same nature in the next two paragraphs. In every novel of Lewis, hundreds of such sentences occur, until any reader with a sense of form and variety literally begs for mercy. This mannerism has more than usual significance because it springs from the reporter's instinct for seeing things as individual instances rather than as parts of an organic unit. That it can be used occasionally for burlesque humor Mark Twain proved in *Roughing It*, but to make it the basis of character delineation is another matter.

That Lewis is not a realist he has recognized in his preface to his *Selected Stories*, although I fancy his description of himself as "a romantic Medievalist" is hardly to be taken seriously. He is primarily a caricaturist, and his characters are usually the incarnations of some virtue or vice, with other human qualities omitted. It is a weakness of the average reader of fiction that a caricature makes more immediate impression upon him than a well-rounded portrait. It would be idle to protest against this tendency when one remembers how Dickens received more credit for Sairy Gamp and Mrs. Jellyby than for the finely etched picture of an English gentleman in John Jarndyce. But it is necessary to insist that caricature is an easier form of art, and that while both novels were published in the same year, *Main Street* is of 1920 and *The Age of Innocence* is timeless. *Arrowsmith* and *Dodsworth* alone are of any real importance among Lewis's novels, and his later works show a marked decline in power. It seems a pity that the crusading spirit which saw the narrowness of the provincial life, the stupid self-praise of the charlatan of business, and the dangerous power of the hypocrite in religion should not have had the artistic power to make them the background of larger and finer figures, beside whom they would have taken their proper place, and whom, by their contrast, they would have helped to establish.

It has perhaps become apparent that the work of this school of writers fails in just those aspects of fiction for which they have received the most indiscriminate praise. They are not realists, for they have the fatal defect of the photograph; they do not know what to leave out. Selection is usually a lost art with them; details clog the action, and when a selection is made, it is nearly always of some character or event that is peculiarly unrepresentative of life as a whole. Moreover, by a curious paradox, this school of writers, who have been lauded by each other and by a critical stupidity hard to understand, as pioneers in the crusade to represent American life as it really is, are as a matter of fact, quite foreign in their philosophy of composition. Anyone who has lived on the Continent of Europe will recognize in their conception of the relations of the sexes a point of view which is not American. European fiction and European life, to a certain extent, take the satisfaction of passion as a matter of course, and the possibility of men and women being more interested in other phases of life is hard for a Continental to understand. It is apparently equally hard for this group of novelists, and the wide reception of their work abroad is perhaps thus accounted for. But the normal American does not live like the people in *The Genius* or *Poor White* or *Ann Vickers*. It is not so much a matter of morality as it is a question of proportion, and it cannot too often be repeated that it is not American fiction that is limited in its choice of subject, it is rather Continental fiction that is limited by its insistence upon only one function of mankind.

This school of writing fails also of greatness by the supreme test, that of the creation of character. No character of Sinclair or of Anderson lives in the memory, of Dreiser only Jennie Gerhardt, of Lewis only Arrowsmith and Dodsworth. The rest are names, and even the names are quickly forgotten unless, like Babbitt, they are associated with caricature. Finally, there is not one single passage, much less a chapter, which has added by its potency, its brilliancy, or its charm, to the resources of their native tongue.

CHAPTER XXX

ELLEN GLASGOW AND THE NEW SOUTH

THE group of novelists who had endowed Southern life with the charm of a romantic civilization, were still writing when Ellen Glasgow began her career in 1897. But she belonged to a new generation, and, while her material is selected at times with an eye to romance, it was in the main a different South that she portrayed, a South that was the result, and not the cause of the Civil War. Born in Richmond in 1874, she comes from a stock that had fought in the Revolution and had moulded the guns of the Confederacy. From the Scotch-Irish strain of the Glasgows came her respect for the "vein of iron" so often referred to in her novels, and finally to become the title of one of them. Judging by her own account of her methods as a novelist,[1] she was an imaginative child, and had begun to invent characters long before she wrote. Her statement that her scenes are limited by her impressions and recollections of her early childhood, is significant in properly estimating her strength and her limitations.

Her first novel, *The Descendant*, (1897) was built upon a situation to which she returned several times, the invasion of New York City by a Virginian. It is also a contrast between those who sacrifice themselves for love and those who accept the sacrifice, a constantly recurring theme in her fiction. While the general tenor of the novel is romantic, even, at times, becoming melodrama, as in the murder her hero Michael Akershem commits, Miss Glasgow proved herself a realist in her relentless portrayal of the effect upon Michael of Rachel Gavin's surrender to his passion. But *The Descendant*, like her next book, *Phases of an Inferior Planet* (1898), also laid in New York City, is interesting simply as an early promise of finer things.

The Voice of the People (1900), her first novel of importance, was

---

[1] See her "One Way to Write Novels," *Saturday Review of Literature*, XI (December 8, 1934) 335.

laid in Virginia, where she is thoroughly at home. It struck one of the notes for which she has become justly distinguished, the emergence of a character, heavily handicapped in youth, into spiritual triumph. Nick Burr is the son of a poor farmer, whose struggle upward to reach high political office and to win the love of Eugenia Battle, a girl of breeding, is told with great sympathy. Miss Glasgow permits him to become Governor and run for Senator before he meets death at the hands of a mob, but Eugenia marries in her own class, and both Nick and she learn that life can go on without the rapture they might have known. Miss Glasgow's realistic development of this theme is to be contrasted with its treatment in the historical romance by Mary Johnston, in *Lewis Rand,* seven years later. *The Battleground* (1902), which begins before the Civil War and continues through it, is not among her best efforts. The people are types rather than individuals, and such reality as exists lies rather in the description of the suffering of the troops than in the relations of the central characters. Yet the picture of the little boy, Dandridge Mountjoy, walking two hundred miles to his grandfather's house, from which his mother had been exiled, is drawn with the skill which Miss Glasgow usually shows when she portrays courage and determination.

The Deliverance (1904) is one of the strongest of her stories. In it she contrasts the old and the new civilizations in the South. While in several of the other books she expresses her sympathy with the new order, here she draws inspiration from the survival of gentility. It is true that through her characters she reveals still her democratic breadth of view: "Good Lord! It's such a little thing to make a fuss about," said Tucker, "when you remember, my dear, that our levels aren't any bigger than chalk lines in the eyes of God Almighty."

But the characters she lavishes the strength of her art upon are patricians like Christopher Blake, who as a boy of ten, has had to stop school to work upon his dwindled acres, and especially his mother, who is blind, and for whose sake the Blakes have kept up a gallant lie for twenty years. She has never known, sitting in her chair, that the old hall had been sold. Every day she has had her chicken and port, though the rest went hungry. There is a fine scene when she dies, and frees Boaz, the old servant, thinking that slavery still exists and that the Confederacy won the war. Her code is put briefly, without comment, for it needs none:

"One never knows, my son, and at least I am only doing my duty in speaking to you thus. I am a very old woman, and I am not afraid to die, for I have never to my knowledge done anything that was unbecoming in a lady. Remember to be a gentleman, and you will find that that embraces all morality and a good deal of religion."

The humor which is usually ironic in Miss Glasgow's work is conveyed often through the conversation of the uneducated characters. The remarks of Mrs. Spade, the wife of the store-keeper, are delightful:

"It ain't sense, it's natur," returned Mrs. Spade, sitting squarely down on the bench from which Christopher had risen; "an' that's what I've had ag'in men folks from the start—thar's too much natur in 'em. You kin skeer it out of a woman, an' you kin beat it out of a dog, an' thar're times when you kin even spank it out of a baby, but if you oust it from a man thar' ain't nothin' but skin an' bones left behind."

After an unsuccessful attempt to write of a curious mixture of literary and fashionable types in New York City, in *The Wheel of Life* (1906), Miss Glasgow portrayed one of her best male characters in Daniel Ordway of *The Ancient Law* (1908). She is always best when she represents people struggling to build or rebuild their lives, and in Ordway's effort to win back his place after serving a jail sentence for embezzlement, the details of his struggle are in themselves interesting. That he fails through his daughter's inherited weakness, and his wife's inability to rise above her resentment at his first offence, shows clearly Ellen Glasgow's determinism, bred in her through her Scotch-Irish Presbyterian ancestors.

In *The Romance of a Plain Man* (1909) she varied her method by having Ben Starr, the hero, tell his own story. He is a boy of poor parentage, living in Richmond about a decade after the Civil War, and his first inspiration arises from Sally Mickleborough's remark that he is "a common boy." There is a mixture of romantic and familiar material in the novel. Ben makes money in the miraculous manner in which heroes proceed in romantic fiction, but, on the other hand, the character of Ben's mother, hard-worked and driven, remains as one of the most vivid of Miss Glasgow's women, and her qualities of pluck and persistence come out in her son.

Miss Glasgow's democracy is always conscious of caste; it proceeds by obliteration of lines, not by ignoring them. One of the most dramatic scenes occurs when Ben's elder brother, a miner, suddenly appears while

Ben and Sally are giving a dinner party. Sally rises and greets him with courtesy, but Jessy, his own sister, sits crumbling bread ashamed of him, though he has given her the means of her education. Here one feels Miss Glasgow's sympathy for the patrician point of view.

As usual, her humor proceeds through her comments on life and through the characters. Mrs. Cudlip's remark is a typical example:

". . . She was the death of him, Benjy; I ought to know, for I lived next do' to 'em to the day of his burial. As to that, anyway, ma'am," she added to Sally, "my humble opinion is that women have killed mo' men anyway than they've ever brought into the world. It's a po' thought, I've al'ays said, in which you can't find some comfort."

So is the conversation at the funeral:

"So you've brought yo' little boy along, Mrs. Starr," remarked a third from the opposite seat, in an aggressive voice.

"Yes, he had a cold an' I thought the air might do him good," replied my mother with her society manner.

"Wall, I've nine an' not one of 'em has ever been to a funeral," returned the questioner. "I've al'ays been set dead against 'em for children, ain't you, Mrs. Boxley?"

Mrs. Boxley, a placid elderly woman, who had already begun to doze in her corner, opened her eyes and smiled on me in a pleasant and friendly way.

"To tell the truth I ain't never been able really to enjoy a child's funeral," she replied.

The Miller of Old Church (1911), is another contrast of the new and old South, made concrete by Abel Revercomb, the young miller whose people have been of the poorer class, but who has fought his way up by industry, and Jonathan Gay, easy-going, pleasure-loving, whose uncle, the older Jonathan Gay, had promised years before to marry Janet Merryweather, the daughter of his overseer, Reuben Merryweather, but had been persuaded not to do so by Angela Gay, his brother's widow, the mother of young Jonathan. Mrs. Gay is a brilliant example of the professional invalid who rules by her weakness. Through her baleful influence, Miss Glasgow frames the unity of the plot. The illegitimacy of Molly Merryweather, her trifling with Abel's love, the tragic end of both Jonathan Gays, all have their beginning in Angela Gay's complete selfishness. All the characters are well established, and the delightful loquacity of the rustics, who supply the comedy, is sharply contrasted with the inarticulate quality of Abner Revercomb, the grim elder brother who had killed the elder Jonathan Gay as the betrayer of his sister, and who shot the younger Jonathan, his daughter's husband, because he believed him to be her seducer.

Miss Glasgow knows well how to characterize a race or an individual. In her description of old Reuben Merryweather she puts with admirable clearness the condition of the poorer white:

Past seventy now, his youth had been trained to a different civilization, and there was a touching gentleness in his face, as if he expressed still the mental attitude of a class which had existed merely as a support or a foil to the order above it. Without spirit to resent, he, with his fellows, had endured the greatest evils of slavery. With the curse of free labour on the land, there had been no incentive for toil, no hire for the labourer. Like an incubus the system had lain over them, stifling all energy, checking all progress, retarding all prosperity save the prosperity of the great land-owners. Then the soil had changed hands, and where the plough had broken the earth, the seeds of a democracy had germinated and put forth from the very blood of the battlefields. In the upward pressure of class, he had seen the stability of custom yield at last to the impetus of an energy that was not racial but individual. Yet from the transition he had remained always a little apart. Reverence had become for him a habit of mind, and he had learned that respect could outlive even a belief in the thing upon which it was founded.

Equally pungent is her description of Sarah Revercomb, Abel's mother:

. . . for it was Sarah's fate that an excess of virtue should have wrought all the evil of a positive vice. From the days of her infancy, when she had displayed in the cradle a power of self-denial at which her pastor had marvelled, she had continued to sacrifice her inclinations in a manner which had rendered unendurable the lives around her. Her parents had succumbed to it; her husband had died of it; her children had resigned themselves to it or rebelled against it according to the quality of their moral fibre. All her life she had laboured to make people happy, and the result of this exalted determination was a cowed and resentful family.

In her next two novels, Miss Glasgow presented through studies of two characters, a contrast between the passive and the active strength of the Southern gentlewoman. *Virginia* (1913) is a fine picture of a woman who sacrifices herself for her husband and children, until he ceases to be interested in her, and turns to an actress who can give him the inspiration for his creative work. Miss Glasgow has no hesitation in turning her epigrammatic skill upon Southern institutions. "Just as the town had battled for a principle without understanding it, so she was capable of dying for an idea, but not of conceiving one." Miss Glasgow here, as elsewhere, shows how those who sacrifice themselves are permitted to do so, while those who demand much from life often receive it. There is an especially fine scene in which Virginia visits the actress in New York with the intention of telling her what she is doing to her husband, and finds herself unable to speak.

Then because it was impossible to say the things she had come to say, because even in the supreme crises of life she could not lay down the manner of a lady, she smiled the grave smile with which her mother had walked through a ruined country, and taking up her muff, which she had laid on the table, passed out into the hall.

In contrast with Virginia, the heroine of *Life and Gabriella* (1916) refuses to submit to circumstances. When her husband, whom she has married through that purely physical infatuation which attacks so many of Miss Glasgow's heroines, goes off with another woman, Gabriella successfully takes charge of a millinery and dressmaking establishment in New York. Gabriella is much more of a force than Virginia, and yet somehow she seems less of a person.

Miss Glasgow's picture of the New South has been a progressive one. In *The Builders* (1919) she interwove through the central character, David Blackburn, personal and national problems which the Great War precipitated. Miss Glasgow, through her hero, shows herself to be an idealist, deeply concerned with these problems and with her hope that the New South may once more be a leader in the nation. Her belief that the United States may be helped through the preservation of such personal leadership in combination with the solidarity of the North may, after all, not be so idealistic a dream as it seemed in 1919. As usual, there are some remarkable characters, especially Angelica Blackburn, a woman fundamentally wrong, yet putting others at a disadvantage through her beauty and her appeal to sympathy. She is almost as good as Weir Mitchell's Octopia Darnell. Mattie Timberlake, an elderly relative who keeps house for her and who looks like "a freckled engraving of Hecuba gazing over the Ruins of Troy" is a sheer delight in her biting analysis of the evil some good women do.

The struggle between personality and the inertia of the settled institution was also pictured in *One Man in His Time* (1922), through the life of Gideon Vetch, an independent Governor of Virginia. Miss Glasgow does not dwell too much on details of strikes or politics. She feels instinctively that the fundamental cleavage in politics and economics is between those whose interest lies in humanity and those who prefer the sanctity of an institution, although she does not state the problem in just those terms.

Miss Glasgow has not indulged frequently in the writing of short stories, and her collection *The Shadowy Third* (1923) included probably all she wished to preserve. The prevailing tone is that of the supernatural, which she strikes effectively in the title story, or in "The Past," which has to do with the appearance of a first wife and the havoc it works upon a second marriage. But that her real interest lies in the actual is shown by the superior merit of "A Point in Morals," which seems to have been her first short story,[2] and "Jordan's End," a powerful study of a Southern family with a streak of insanity. Both stories state a moral problem—shall one human being aid or prevent another from taking his own life if he is better out of the world? The figure of the young wife who has promised her husband that she will not let him live as his father has done for twenty years, plaiting straw endlessly in the hopeless desolation of Jordan's End, is of heroic stature.

It was amusing to those who had followed Miss Glasgow's career to find *Barren Ground* (1925) hailed by a certain type of critic as a realistic departure from Southern fiction. It is, in truth, a powerful somber epic of the farm lands of lower Virginia, where the "good people" whom Miss Glasgow carefully differentiates from the gentry of the higher altitudes, and from the poor whites, have degenerated in the struggle against the impoverishment of the soil and the menace of the "broomsedge" which closes in upon the fertile fields. The entire novel is told from the point of view of Dorinda Oakley, child of a poor white father and a mother whose ancestry has been Scotch-Irish and Presbyterian. Dorinda is a very human figure, from her first grasp at happiness through her love for Jason Greylock, a weak but charming man, through her courageous battle against fate when he marries another woman, and her return from New York to the farm determined to wring a living from the soil. Miss Glasgow lavished her skill in the depiction of human agony upon this novel, but unlike certain of her contemporaries, she gives us the misery not just for its own sake, but as a means of establishing the "vein of iron" to which she refers so often in speaking of Do-

[2] *Harper's Magazine*, May, 1899.

rinda. Dorinda, unlike her neighbors, is unconquered by the land. Her life is absorbed by the daily claims of the farm, but her spirit remains mistress of itself. When she has buried both her husband and the lover who had betrayed her, and whom she had taken from the poor house in the pity that is a distant kin to love, she remains unconquered:

Strange how her courage had revived with the sun! She saw now, as she had seen in the night, that life is never what one dreamed, that it is seldom what one desired; yet for the vital spirit and the eager mind, the future will always hold the search for buried treasure and the possibilities of high adventure. Though in a measure destiny had defeated her, for it had given her none of the gifts she had asked of it, still her failure was one of those defeats, she realized, which are victories. At middle-age she faced the future without romantic glamour, but she faced it with integrity of vision. The best of life, she told herself with clear-eyed wisdom, was ahead of her. She saw other autumns like this one, hazy, bountiful in harvests, mellowing through the blue sheen of air into the red afterglow of winter; she saw the coral-tinted buds of the spring opening into the profusion of summer; and she saw the rim of the harvest moon shining orange-yellow through the boughs of the harp-shaped pine. Though she remembered the time when loveliness was like a sword in her heart, she knew now that where beauty exists the understanding soul can never remain desolate.

The difference between the material of *Barren Ground* and *The Romantic Comedians* (1926) illustrates the variety which is a marked characteristic of Ellen Glasgow's work. For her next three novels she turned to the urban life to which she belongs, and irradiated it with the ironic insight which had always been hers, but which grew even keener with the years. *The Romantic Comedians* is packed with epigrams— "Judge Honeywell, an upright, even a religious man," who "was disposed to encourage liberty of thought as long as he was convinced that is would not lead to liberal views," is not as interesting a hero as many of her other central characters because a man of sixty-five who marries a young girl is a ridiculous, rather than a tragic figure. His young wife also is so callous in her relations with him and accepts money from him after her flight with a younger lover with such nauseating promptitude, that she also fails in interest. The book forms a striking contrast in this respect with *They Stooped to Folly* (1929). Virginius Littlepage, a lawyer of fifty-seven feels, like Judge Honeywell, that his marriage has not given him everything of which he had dreamed. But his wife, Victoria, is still alive, and her eternal domination through the power of

habit and inertia, makes a reader sympathize with his adventures in ro-
mance, especially since his reception of the advances of the widow, Mrs.
Dalrymple, are pure comedy, written with a remarkable insight into a
man's character. The younger people also are much better done. Mary
Victoria, Littlepage's daughter, who has a war record and goes to the
Balkans to reform everybody, is a delightful satiric figure, and Milly
Burden, his secretary, who has had a child by Martin Welding while
Martin is in France ignorant of his parenthood, is a good picture of the
new generation who refuses to be ashamed of her baby and does not even
tell Martin for fear of worrying him. This concealment precipitates one
of the best ironic situations in modern fiction, for Mary Victoria returns,
married to Martin because she has been so sorry for him, after she has
saved him from a nervous breakdown, that she insists upon continuing
her rescue. The helplessness of the Littlepages before this situation, and
especially the comments of Mrs. Burden, Milly's mother, who is a creation worthy of Dickens, add to the humor of a book which brings out
human beings in sharp contrast to each other and to the shifting conditions of the time. The only unfavorable criticism that may be directed at
the novel is its inconclusive ending. Martin's flight from a world which is
filled with women who are determined to control him is amusing, but it
is hardly a termination. Yet the death of Victoria, after writing an unfinished letter to her husband which enshrines her forever in his memory, leaves the older generation, at least, in permanent peace. And the
brilliancy of the dialogue and Miss Glasgow's comments on the characters set a new high standard in her work. She never hesitates to criticize
her own generation, as in the picture of the puzzled outlook of Miss
Louisa, a maiden lady who had kept her love for Littlepage concealed
for thirty years:

"Certainly, it is the trend of the age," assented Louisa, who was an authority upon trends, ancient and modern, and had found them to be of inestimable
value in the dissemination of culture. Ancient trends were naturally more in-
structive because they were less pushing than modern ones, but all were equally
useful as warning examples. Never, indeed, in an historical survey, which,
though adequate to her purpose, was brisk rather than thorough, had she been
able to discover a trend that moved in a proper direction. All flowed, however
rapidly or sluggishly, over an immovable obstacle, which was revealed by the
ebbing tide of progress as a bulwark of the best minds. Take, for instance, this
bold modern trend toward loose behaviour in love. To Louisa, who was nothing if not compact in principle, and who disapproved of looseness in any form,

even in her attire, the present impetus toward indecency appeared far less pronounced than similar trends in Babylon (if you could judge a whole civilization by the biased ejaculations of prophets) or even in Rome, where one could rely, of course, upon the impregnable reputation of Gibbon.

Miss Glasgow showed no sign of weakening in another novel dealing with Richmond, *The Sheltered Life* (1932). Here again are vivid characterizations. General Archbald, who has been kept from the adventures he most desired, by his daughters and his daughter-in-law, is described with remarkable insight:

"But I don't need anybody. I am able to go alone." No man needed protection less; but because he had lived a solitary male among women, he could never escape it, and because these women depended upon him, he had remained at their mercy. It was impossible to wound the feelings of women who owed him the bread they ate and the roof over their heads, and so long as he did not hurt their feelings, they would be stronger than he was. Always, from his earliest childhood, he mused, with a curious resentment against life, he had been the victim of pity. Of his own pity, not another's. Of that double-edged nerve of sympathy, like the aching nerve in a tooth, which throbbed alive at the sight of injustice or cruelty. One woman after another had enslaved his sympathy more than his passion, and never had she seemed to be the woman his passion demanded.

This theme of feminine dependence is interwoven skilfully with that of womanly love and jealousy through the demands of Mrs. Birdsong, a great beauty, and of Jenny Archbald, a young girl, upon George Birdsong, whose weakness of character leaves him, dead at his wife's hands, at the end of the novel. Miss Glasgow has rarely done anything better than the weaving of the nets which hold in their meshes these men whose strength or weakness has made them helpless before their womankind.

In 1935 Miss Glasgow returned in *Vein of Iron* to the rural life of Virginia. Through the characters of Ada Fincastle, her father and her grandmother, she celebrated once more that unbreakable courage and self-respect, that pitiless and unswerving judgment upon one's self and upon others, that came down into Virginia with the Scotch-Irish pioneers. In Grandmother Fincastle, who rode at night over the mountains to bring healing to the helpless, the iron predominates; in John Fincastle, who loses his pulpit because his philosophical works do not square with orthodox Presbyterian theology, the vein of iron takes another turn. In Ada it manifests itself in her brave fight, first against the village pity when her lover, Ralph McBride, is taken from her by another girl's lie, later against the village scorn when she has yielded to Ralph's love and given birth to his child. There is a certain lack of motivation in the plot, for Ralph's agreement to break his engagement with Ada under the circumstances, seems incredible and certainly weakens our interest in him. The later post-war scenes in Richmond when, after their marriage, misery descends in waves upon Ada and Ralph, are realistic pictures of the depression, and are justified in their development of Ada's character. But they have not the power of the earlier portions of the book, laid in Ironside, or of the last great scene when John Fincastle goes back to his early home to die. It is in Ironside that the unforgettable incidents are laid. As Ada lies dreading the ordeal of childbirth, turned into agony by her grandmother's refusal to speak to her while she was carrying a child of shame:

Suddenly arms were about her. She was pressed to a bosom as stout as oak, as sustaining as fortitude. A hand, large, strong, knotted, healing, pushed the damp hair back from her forehead, and looking up, she saw her grandmother's face bending over her. The old woman must have risen at the first stir; the bunch of black ribbon nodded over her left eyebrow, the cameo brooch pinned her collar together.

"Hold tight to me, Ada," she said. "Hold tight as you can. I won't let you go."

"Grandmother! Oh, Grandmother!" The steadfast life of the house, the strong fibers, the closely knit generations, had gathered above, around, underneath. She might sink back now, cradled in this blessed sense of security. "Now pain may have its way, and I may give up. Grandmother will know what to do."

Vein of Iron has not the charm of *They Stooped to Folly* or *The Sheltered Life,* but it has a great theme and great characters. It illustrates like so many of her other novels, that combination of unity and variety which has placed Ellen Glasgow in the first rank of modern novelists. Through a significant theme such as the triumph of a human soul in its struggle against fate or circumstances, treated most effectively in *The Voice of the People, The Deliverance, The Ancient Law, The Romance of a Plain Man, The Miller of Old Church, Virginia, The Builders, One Man in His Time, Barren Ground,* and *Vein of Iron,* she has secured the unity of the novel. Yet she has not forgotten that unity alone may become monotony; not only in the different novels, but within each novel she has provided sufficient variety to make each book a new creation. Her characters are sharpened, not dulled or absorbed by the theme of which they are the concrete expression. And with an inventive power fertile within the limits of her special field, she never fails to provide characters enough to produce those contrasts that are essential.

In her penetrating analysis of her own work to which reference has already been made, she makes a statement which is illuminating, but only half true: "I have never wanted for subjects," she says, "but on several occasions, when because of illness or from external compulsion, I have tried to invent a theme or a character, invariably the effort has resulted in failure." She probably refers to novels like *The Wheel of Life*, or the others laid in New York City, when she was dealing with themes which seem only partly established. But she certainly has invented characters, or at least has taken characters from her own experience and made them live in fiction. Her Southern gentlemen and gentlewomen, of the older or newer régime, are a varied flock; so too are her farmer folk, her store-keepers, her dressmakers, all her rustic and village characters. Her women are on the whole better drawn than her men, and no one has pictured more relentlessly the feminine tyranny which seems in her novels to make even infidelity excusable. No one has, on the other hand, surpassed her in the portraits of women whose whole life has been a generous daily sacrifice, often to the weakness of man.

Ellen Glasgow has shown a remarkable receptivity to new ideas. She began to publish when the idealistic treatment of the romantic material of Southern life had reached its climax of popular approval. She did not break sharply with the traditions of that school, but she took the best lessons it had to teach, and turned them into a new achievement. Through her the Puritan strain, always present in Virginia, which had animated Bacon's rebellion in the seventeenth century and had reached its height in the iron tenacity of Stonewall Jackson, came into its proper place in the panorama of fiction. While Miss Glasgow knows well the patricians, easy-going or heroic, and has drawn brilliant pictures of them like Mrs. Blake in *The Deliverance,* she reserved her finest strokes for those who, like Abel Revercomb or Dorinda Oakley, were trying to build up a New South not on "the ashes of the past" but through industry, intelligence, and recognition of improved methods of agriculture. Their refusal to continue in the recurrent impoverishment of the soil is symbolical of their independence in all matters of tradition. Sometimes they are from the poor white class, but more often from the lower middle class and frequently are survivals of a race once higher in the social and economic scale, and their consequent struggle upward is a return to an earlier status. Most important, they are indigenous to Virginia; they have always been there, waiting for attention. Of course, they had not been entirely neglected, Kennedy had drawn "Horse-Shoe" Robinson from this same group. But with Ellen Glasgow they became the central figures, the hope of the New South, emerging at last into their own.

It was only natural that her method in treating such material should be realistic. The poverty, the hardships of the small farmer, or of the young lawyer, or the widow with children, do not lend themselves to the glamour of romance so easily as does the planter, even in his decay. In the older Southern fiction, the loyalty of one race to another gave distinction even to slavery. But Miss Glasgow's people are, with few exceptions, drawn from a class that did not own slaves, and their loyalty is not so much to a person as to a standard of conduct, or to an obligation, inherited or assumed. Here again the Calvinistic vein of iron appears, in its capacity for abstract thinking, in its rejection of the symbol, in its subjection of beauty to duty.

Here finally is an artist who, steadily expanding rather than changing in her method, has followed no temporary fashions. Like her own characters, she has enriched a field that seemed to be exhausted by the insight and imaginative power that drew new inspiration from a vein too long neglected, but rich with reward for the vision which could perceive it. Her own words, written in 1933 in the introduction to *The Voice of the People* [3] reveal her understanding of the novelist's art. "Whether I wrote history or fiction, I would write of the South not as a lost province but as a part of the larger world; I would touch the universal chords beneath the minor variations of character."

[3] Old Dominion Edition, p. x.

CHAPTER XXXI

WILLA CATHER

It is the usual critical mistake to speak of Willa Cather as though her main significance lay as a representative of the Far West. While she has represented life in that region with unusual insight and sympathy, she has not been limited to that locality, nor indeed is locality an element of supreme importance in her fiction. She is quite unprovincial, and her significance lies much more in the artistry of her method than in her material. Yet by a paradox that is only apparent and not real, some of her most remarkable effects are the result of a power of visualization rare in the annals of our fiction.

Born in Virginia, near Winchester, in 1876, of farming stock, of English, Irish, and Alsatian inheritance, she was taken by her father as a girl of eight to a farm near Red Cloud, Nebraska. They went out during a time of great expansion in the West, but soon came a long period of drought and disaster. As another novelist has observed in speaking of Willa Cather's girlhood, "This dismal period full of disappointment and bitterness began when Willa Cather was about twelve. . . . She lived in the midst of one of the greatest disillusionments the American pioneer movement has ever known." [1]

Here among a population largely of Scandinavian, German, or Bohemian extraction, she was educated by wide reading and by private instruction until she entered the University of Nebraska, from which she graduated in 1895. During the next ten years she traveled widely, taught school in Pittsburgh, and wrote for the newspapers. In 1900 she published her first short story and her first poem, and it is significant that the verses "Grandmither, think not I forget" are better than "Eric Hermannson's Soul." [2] This story is of interest, however, because it is laid in

---

[1] Fisher, Dorothy Canfield, "Daughter of the Frontier," *New York Herald Tribune,* May 28, 1933.
[2] *Cosmopolitan,* April, 1900.

Nebraska and because it deals with the struggle in the soul of a musician, between his love for his fiddle and his emotional evangelicism. Thus the greatest theme of Willa Cather, the contest of the artist with the limitations of the West, is definite from her beginning.

Miss Cather's severe critical taste, exercised most relentlessly in judging her own work, is shown in the selection of her verse for her volume *April Twilights* (1903), and in *The Troll Garden* (1905), her first collection of short stories. *April Twilights* revealed the singular ability in the choice of words and the love of beauty that have animated her prose, but it contained only twenty-four poems. Even more selective was her judgment in *The Troll Garden*. From it she omitted "The Professor's Commencement," [3] an appealing story of the high school teacher who had labored for thirty years to bring beauty into the manufacturing city and had accomplished so little, except in those intangible influences upon the lives of his scholars that are his only reward. The other stories are interesting mainly as preliminary sketches for later work. In "The Treasure of Far Island," for example, the return of a great playwright to his western home is an idealistic treatment of a theme which she developed realistically in a much more powerful story included in *The Troll Garden*. "The Sculptor's Funeral" is a contrast between the drab life of a small Kansas town and the creative instinct of a great sculptor who was born there and who is brought home to be buried. The complete failure of his family and his townspeople even to apprehend his great accomplishment, is brought out by their audible regrets that he had not remained an honest farmer. In this way Miss Cather produces an even more vivid picture of the hopelessness of the life the sculptor had escaped than she does in the conversation between the disciple who has brought the body home and the one man who had understood the dead artist. "Paul's Case" is a remarkable study in the temperament of a boy who revolts at his life in Pittsburgh. "A Death in the Desert" is an equally impressive story of a singer who is dying in Colorado and is comforted in the mistaken belief that her lover has returned to her.

Henry James was a strong influence upon Miss Cather in these early short stories. "The Profile," [4] for example, a subtle study of a painter's love for a woman who has a horrible scar on one side of her face, revealed her power in interpreting the artist's mind. "The Enchanted

---

[3] *New England Magazine*, June, 1902.
[4] *McClure's Magazine*, June, 1907.

Bluff" [5] contains the first description of that city, high in the air, which was to become Outland's story in *The Professor's House*. Neither of these short stories has been reprinted in her later collections. It was through her short stories, however, that she became associate editor of *McClure's Magazine*. This position she resigned in 1911 to devote herself to creative work. Fine as some of these short stories were, it was in her novelette, *Alexander's Bridge*, (1912) that Miss Cather revealed that power of character analysis, that compact control of her material and that ability at revelation of the more profound impulses in the natures of men and women, that have won her the secure place she now holds. This book has a special place in my esteem, for it was because of it that I experienced that delight that comes to a critic when, to quote her own verse,

> "To the old, old ports of Beauty
> A new sail comes home."

I was so enthusiastic about the novel that in a public address in 1914, I selected Miss Cather as one of three of the younger American novelists who were destined to great achievement. I have less hesitancy in referring to this prophecy since the two others, Theodore Dreiser and Henry Sydnor Harrison, have failed to justify my prediction!

Alexander's Bridge was remarkable, first because of Willa Cather's understanding of a man's point of view. Other women had been able to realize that a man may love two women at the same time, but no one had drawn with such sympathy the disintegration of character which this dual life occasions. The rivalry between Bartley Alexander's wife, Winifred, and Hilda Burgoyne, whom he had loved twelve years before, when he was a struggling young engineer and she had not yet won her place on the stage, is not only a contest of personalities. It is a struggle between the love that encloses and enriches a man's life and the passion inspired by present charm and linked through memory with a grace and a fragrance that come only with youth. His hesitation to seek her in London, because "remembering Hilda as she used to be, was doubtless more satisfactory than seeing her as she must be now" is a flash of insight written eight years before Mrs. Wharton developed from the same idea the great last scene of *The Age of Innocence*.

Bartley's death by the collapse of his great bridge is symbolical, of

---

[5] *Harper's Magazine*, April, 1909.

course, of the flaw in his own nature, but the symbolism is not obtrusive. And the contrast of his love for Hilda, tortured by remorse, and of her single-hearted devotion to him, is developed through scenes masterly in their restraint as well as in their expression. Her decision to marry someone else is put into a few telling words: "I never used to understand how women did things like that, but I know now. It's because they can't be at the mercy of the man they love any longer." The scenes of *Alexander's Bridge* lie in London, in Boston, in New York, or in Canada, but the scene is not important. It is the clashing of human natures and the conflict of character that are vital.

In the same year, 1912, Miss Cather wrote a long short story, "The Bohemian Girl," [6] a tale of Swedish immigrants in the Northwest, in whose life a Bohemian girl, Clara Vavrika, is a disturbing element. It is inconclusive and has not been reprinted. She succeeded much better with her novel of Nebraska, *O Pioneers!* (1913). The Nebraska of the 'eighties which had filled her girlhood with love for its magnificent distances was the inspiration. To her it had been a land "with its own fierce strength, its peculiar savage kind of beauty, its uninterrupted mournfulness." The story is not an heroic saga of the pioneers; she knew and depicted the Bergsons, who were not meant to be pioneers, and the bitter struggle of John Bergson, ending in failure, is very real. So, too, is the happier struggle of his daughter, Alexandra. Willa Cather, much as she loved the land, knew that background alone is not enough. Like Cooper, she keeps the scene where it belongs. The weakness of *O Pioneers!* however, lies in its structure. It is a series of episodes, not too well tied together. The later portions of the novel, laid about sixteen years after the beginning, shift the interest away from Alexandra to characters who are never quite established, and Alexandra's own love story is too placid to be inspiring. The racial contrast of the stolidity of the Swedes and the quicker mentality of the French and Bohemian settlers, is well drawn but it is in essay rather than narrative form. And while there are fine passages, the writing is distinctly below that of *Alexander's Bridge*.

My Ántonia (1918) has the same general scene as *O Pioneers!* and belongs to the same phase of Miss Cather's work. In it she tried an experiment, difficult for a woman, to write through the eyes of a boy, Jim Burden, a novel in which the central figure is a Bohemian girl, Ántonia

[6] *McClure's Magazine*, August, 1912.

Shimerdas. *My Ántonia* is not one of her best novels, but she has painted admirably the friendship of a boy for a girl a little older than himself, a friendship that lives more vitally because of his long absences from her. It brings him back, twenty years after her elopement, her disgrace and her marriage with another Bohemian, to view her large brood of children with equanimity. The fault with *My Ántonia* lies once more in the structure, which is too episodic, and the lack of any very interesting story to tie the episodes together. The descriptions of hardship on the farms, of the drab, dull life of the town, are too detailed because they really lead to nothing important in the lives of the characters. At the very beginning of the story the small boy's remark as he sits in the train is significant: "The only thing very noticeable about Nebraska was that it was still, all day long, Nebraska." Those who still believe that Willa Cather's major achievement has been the picture of the West, should notice how the story of the blind Negro's passion for music, which transforms him from a being near to idiocy into something remarkable, shines out from the pages of the book. To be sure, it has nothing to do with the plot, but it shows where Miss Cather's real strength lies.

That power had already been shown in her short stories and in *The Song of the Lark* (1915). In this novel Willa Cather portrayed the soul of an artist in her struggle to enter into her heritage. The story begins in Moonstone, Colorado, but the town is simply a point of departure. Thea Kronborg begins to live when, after her difficulty in adjusting herself to the confusing life of Chicago, her great gift is discovered. Her inspiration from "The Song of the Lark," a picture of a girl in the early morning fields, is a fine example of the use of one art to stimulate another. But this incident is only a preliminary to the climax of character when Thea hears Dvořák's "New World Symphony." First there is the bursting of new sense impressions upon her:

There was home in it, too; first memories, first mornings long ago; the amazement of a new soul in a new world; a soul new and yet old, that had dreamed something despairing, something glorious, in the dark before it was born; a soul obsessed by what it did not know, under the cloud of a past it could not recall.

Then, when out in the street after the concert, the confusion seems to be trying to take the spell away from her, there is the fight to keep what she has won:

All these things and people were no longer remote and negligible; they had to be met, they were lined up against her, they were there to take something from her. Very well; they should never have it. As long as she lived that ecstasy was going to be hers. She would live for it, work for it, die for it; but she was going to have it, time after time, height after height. She could hear the crash of the orchestra again, and she rose on the brasses. She would have it, what the trumpets were singing! She would have it, have it,—it! Under the old cape she pressed her hands upon her heaving bosom, that was a little girl's no longer.

Her growth through love, sorrow, and professional success which leave her not happy but with a workable scheme of life, proceeds steadily through one of the finest of Miss Cather's novels.

Her knowledge of artist life was revealed also in her collection of short stories, *Youth and the Bright Medusa* (1920). "Coming Aphrodite," the best of the new stories, is an episode in the life of a painter and an opera singer, both young and struggling, who occupy adjoining rooms in Washington Square. It has both the romance and the reality of such associations. Singers are the heroines of "The Diamond Mine," of "Scandal," and "A Gold Slipper," with excellent characterizations. As Miss Cather reprinted four [7] of the stories from *The Troll Garden* in this volume, it probably represents her judgment as to the stories she considers most important. She did not include "The Bookkeeper's Wife" [8] or "Ardessa" [9] which reflect her knowledge of business and editorial offices in New York City, realizing probably that, while they are above the level of magazine fiction, they are not upon her own level.

One of Ours (1922), although it won the Pulitzer Prize, is not one of her best novels. The life in the West is too detailed and Claude Wheeler becomes symbolic of a prosaic life which can be of interest in art only when it provides contrast. Even when he escapes into the Great War, he does not challenge interest, and Miss Cather showed no especial capacity for the description of the skirmishes in which he figures. Her very broadmindedness which kept her either from the spread eagleism or the bitter cynicism of later writers on the Great War, made the novel undramatic.

It was only a temporary lapse, however, for in *A Lost Lady* (1923)

[7] "The Sculptor's Funeral," "Death in the Desert," "Paul's Case," and "A Wagner Matinée."
[8] *Century*, May, 1916.
[9] *Century*, May, 1918.

she created some of her finest characters. In Marian Forrester she drew the eternal courtesan, a woman in whom passion was an active, not merely a receptive, force. With a profound consistency, beside which *Sister Carrie* and *Susan Lenox* seem shallow and superficial, Miss Cather with rapid strokes established this woman, who held by her charm and her courage, even the men who knew her for what she was. "If she merely bowed to you, merely looked at you, it constituted a personal relation." "Never elsewhere had he heard anything like her inviting musical laugh, that was like the distant measures of dance music, heard through opening and shutting doors." If at times she seems to change her nature, it is because she possesses "the magic of contradictions." It was a master stroke to reveal her through the eyes of the men who loved her. Through Niel Herbert, the boy who worships her as his ideal, through her husband, Captain Forrester, who knew "all there was to know about Marian Forrester," through her lovers, Frank Ellinger and Ivy Peters, she turns to us the facets of her character, shining with devotion or dark with disloyalty. When Miss Cather strips bare the illusion Niel had built up concerning Marian, she does it with one swift stroke. He has come up in the freshness of the morning to Marian's house to bring her a tribute of flowers and to look after her in Captain Forrester's absence:

After tying his flowers with a twist of meadow grass, he went up the hill through the grove and softly round the still house to the north side of Mrs. Forrester's own room, where the door-like green shutters were closed. As he bent to place the flowers on the sill, he heard from within a woman's soft laughter; impatient, indulgent, teasing, eager. Then another laugh, very different, a man's. And it was fat and lazy,—ended in something like a yawn.

Niel found himself at the foot of the hill on the wooden bridge, his face hot, his temples beating, his eyes blind with anger. In his hand he still carried the prickly bunch of wild roses. He threw them over the wire fence into a mudhole the cattle had trampled under the bank of the creek. . . . In that instant between stooping to the window-sill and rising, he had lost one of the most beautiful things in his life.

With rare insight into a man's nature, of which she had given an earnest in *Alexander's Bridge,* Miss Cather brings Niel back to Marian's service in their common devotion to Captain Forrester after his stroke. For the understanding of her higher qualities is meted out to each man in terms of his own finer feelings. The men who have satisfied her physical craving leave her, but those who judge her not by the usual moral standards, but as one man judges another, keep her memory fragrant till the end. She is not, however, the only character of distinction. In Captain Forrester, a pioneer who had built the railway from Omaha to Denver, Miss Cather drew a magnificent personality. "Something in the way he uttered his unornamented phrases gave them the impression of inscriptions cut in stone." When he tells how he and his fellows "had dreamed the railroads across the mountains," there is heard in his voice "the lonely defiant note, that is so often heard in the voices of old Indians." His treatment of his wife is that of a protector who knows the weakness of the citadel. Even his tolerance for her frailty is like an offering he places upon the scale to balance the twenty-five years difference between them. Through him Miss Cather draws a vivid contrast with the newer owners of the soil:

The Old West had been settled by dreamers, great-hearted adventurers who were unpractical to the point of magnificence; a courteous brotherhood, strong in attack but weak in defence, who could conquer but could not hold. Now all the vast territory they had won was to be at the mercy of men like Ivy Peters, who had never dared anything, never risked anything. They would drink up the mirage, dispel the morning freshness, root out the great brooding spirit of freedom, the generous, easy life of the great land-holders. The space, the colour, the princely carelessness of the pioneer they would destroy and cut up into profitable bits, as the match factory splinters the primeval forest. All the way from the Missouri to the mountains this generation of shrewd young men, trained to petty economies by hard times, would do exactly what Ivy Peters had done when he drained the Forrester marsh.

The scene of *The Professor's House* (1925) is again the West, but once more it is the character study which is most important. It is a masterly picture of the gradual disenchantment with life of Godfrey St. Peter, a professor of history in a State university within sight of Lake Michigan. Through this disillusionment is born a criticism of life itself, but in the spirit of acceptance, not of rebellion. With the acceptance comes the triumph of the individual, the recognition that to a man who can become his own best companion, one solution at least of the problem of living has been reached. His wife and daughters, he knows, can do without him; not that he has ceased to love them, but that each in her way has arrived at much the same conclusion without seeing the matter through so clearly. Miss Cather wisely chose to limit his family to two daughters, whose absorption in their husbands is natural. But there is one of her keenest flashes of insight in the sentence: "A man, she knew, could get from his daughter a peculiar kind of hurt—one of the cruellest that flesh is heir to." Into *The Professor's House* Miss Cather inserted through the story of Tom Outland, a protégé of St. Peter, a remarkable description of a city, high up in the cliffs of New Mexico, the home of a lost race, which had been foreshadowed in the short story, "The Enchanted Bluffs":

Far up above me, a thousand feet or so, set in a great cavern in the face of the cliff, I saw a little city of stone, asleep. It was as still as sculpture—and something like that. It all hung together, seemed to have a kind of composition: pale little houses of stone nestling close to one another, perched on top of each other, with flat roofs, narrow windows, straight walls, and in the middle of the group, a round tower.

It was beautifully proportioned, that tower, swelling out to a larger girth a little above the base, then growing slender again. There was something symmetrical and powerful about the swell of the masonry. The tower was the fine thing that held all the jumble of houses together and made them mean something. It was red in colour, even on that grey day. In sunlight it was the colour of winter oak-leaves. A fringe of cedars grew along the edge of the cavern, like a garden. They were the only living things. Such silence and stillness and repose—immortal repose. That village sat looking down into the canyon with the calmness of eternity.

My Mortal Enemy (1926), while not undistinguished at times in its portrait of a passionate and wilful woman, created no character that was on the level of Marian Forrester or St. Peter.

In 1927 Willa Cather rose to her greatest height, so far, in the picture of the dramatic struggle of two unconquerable souls in their contest with the hostility of nature and the racial prejudices, personal ambitions, and rock-like traditions that threatened the success of their mission. *Death Comes for the Archbishop* (1927) is an epic of the pioneer, but of a pioneer not of material things, but of the spirit. Bishop Jean Latour and his vicar, Father Joseph Vaillant, are French missionaries sent out in 1848 to organize the diocese of New Mexico. Their very contrasts of character bring out the finer traits of each. Bishop Latour is the patrician, intellectual enough to doubt at times the usefulness of his own mission, but spiritually great enough to overcome that doubt. Without Father Vaillant's power to form new ties easily, he brings his vast territory into order through the sheer power of character. One of the finest elements in the novel is the establishment of the loneliness of the Archbishop, not through the desertion of his people, but through an innate spiritual serenity with which he faces the end which is only the beginning of a greater beauty. If he is the soul of the mission, Father Vaillant is the body, active, untiring, warm with love for human kind.

Contrasted with these French missionaries are the survivals of an earlier Spanish occupation, Padre Martinez and Padre Lucero. They represent personal domination, sensuality, avarice, and the resistance to new ideas. It is a delightful ironic touch when, after their suspension from their priestly functions by Bishop Latour, they found a schism which they call the Old Holy Catholic Church of Mexico, denouncing the Bishop's church as an American institution. It is interesting that Maxwell Anderson in his play *Night over Taos* presents Father Martinez as a believer in the coming democracy! Miss Cather showed again in this novel her remarkable power of observation, not only of isolated scenes, but also of profound racial traits.

In the working of silver or drilling of turquoise the Indians had exhaustless patience; upon their blankets and belts and ceremonial robes they lavished their skill and pains. But their conception of decoration did not extend to the landscape. They seemed to have none of the European's desire to "master" nature, to arrange and re-create. They spent their ingenuity in the other direction; in accommodating themselves to the scene in which they found themselves. This was not so much from indolence, the Bishop thought, as from an inherited caution and respect. It was as if the great country were asleep, and they wished to carry on their lives without awakening it; or as if the spirits of earth and air and water were things not to antagonize and arouse. When they hunted, it was with the same discretion; an Indian hunt was never a slaughter. They ravaged neither the rivers nor the forest, and if they irrigated, they took as little water as would serve their needs. The land and all that it bore they treated with consideration; not attempting to improve it, they never desecrated it.

That Miss Cather's eminence is not due to her Western material alone, was proved conclusively by *Shadows on the Rock* (1931), for she translated into terms of another race and land, that of Colonial Quebec, the qualities which had made her stories of the West living and breathing realities. Again it is the characters that shine, through their loyalty to family ties or to their king and country, or to a hopeless passion. Beginning with a remarkable picture of Quebec in 1697, which paints vividly the fort and the churches of the Upper Town, some of which still stand guard over the cluttered streets of the Lower Town, Miss Cather builds up through the eyes of an apothecary, Auclair, and his young daughter, Cécile, a pageant of characters from the little outcast she befriends to Governor Frontenac himself, and the two Churchmen, Bishop Laval and Bishop de Saint-Vallier. Her understanding of the French nature is revealed with even more depth and variety than in *Death Comes for the Archbishop*. That untranslatable Gallic trait, the love for *la gloire*, made manifest in Governor Frontenac, the force of Monseigneur Laval which shows itself through courage and sacrifice, the less stable, though more brilliant, nature of Bishop de Saint-Vallier, the mysticism of the devotée, Jeanne Le Ber, the dashing recklessness of her lover Pierre Charron, the *coureur de bois*, are brought out through swift flashes of description and narration. All have that spirit of the pioneer which Miss Cather understood so well:

Inferretque deos Latio. When an adventurer carries his gods with him into a remote and savage country, the colony he founds will, from the beginning, have graces, traditions, riches of the mind and spirit. Its history will shine with bright incidents, slight, perhaps, but precious, as in life itself, where the great matters are often as worthless as astronomical distances, and the trifles dear as the heart's blood.

Cécile and her father represent that other stratum of French nature, the *bourgeoisie*; he an exile from a beloved France, she with roots deep in her adopted country. The character of Cécile is one of Willa Cather's finest creations. Inheriting from her dead mother "the little shades of feeling that make the common fine," this girl of thirteen is a gallant figure of mingled childhood and maturity. The Mother Superior, whom she loved, recognized that Cécile "had no vocation" for a cloistered life. To Cécile life was something to be lived actively; even as a child, she loved the dramatic quality of the miraculous legends, but wanted no moral "applications." As usual, Miss Cather inserts some dramatic episodes, but they are more closely woven into the story than in some of her earlier books. The scene in which Pierre Charron watches at midnight in the church for the woman he has vainly loved to keep her nightly vigil at the altar, not only puts an end to his hopes, but prepares the way for his later growth of love for Cécile. The tales of hardship in the woods make more keen the atmosphere of Quebec, the outpost of French civilization in the New World. One brief recital of Frontenac's visit to King

Louis explains the puzzle which disturbs every visitor to Quebec who wonders why France lost, without a real struggle, a land which is still so Gallic in its spirit.

In *Obscure Destinies* (1932) Miss Cather returned to the West with three stories, two of which are really novelettes. The best, *Old Mrs. Harris,* laid in a Colorado town, is a fine picture of a grandmother who had come from Tennessee, who is the household dependent, and who wishes above all not to be pitied. She is neither the conventional Southern patrician nor the mountaineer; she represents the great mass of Southerners who prized independence above all other things, but who had always been accustomed to plenty of service. Miss Cather establishes firmly and dextrously the contrast between this easy civilization and "the snappy little Western democracy, where every man was as good as his neighbor and out to prove it." The conversation between her granddaughter, who longs to go to college, and her neighbor, Mr. Rosen, is worth recording:

"Why do you want to go to college, Vickie?" he asked playfully.
"To learn," she said with surprise.
"But why do you want to learn? What do you want to do with it?"
"I don't know. Nothing, I guess."
"Then what do you want it for?"
"I don't know. I just want it."
"Then if you want it without any purpose at all, you will not be disappointed." Mr. Rosen wished to distract her and help her to keep back the tears. "Listen; a great man once said: '*Le but n'est rien; le chemin, c'est tout.*' That means: The end is nothing, the road is all. Let me write it down for you and give you your first French lesson."

In "Two Friends" there is a vivid contrast between R. E. Dillon and J. H. Trueman, the Celtic and Teutonic types of successful men in a Western town, who break their friendship over politics in 1896.

Lucy Gayheart (1935), while written with charm and with understanding of a girl whose nature was warm and impulsive, was hardly up to the standard of *Shadows on the Rock*. The characters run in parallel lines, rather than in a woven pattern, and while Lucy's worship of the great singer whom she accompanies is not inconsistent with her continued affection for the younger man whom she had always known in their Nebraska town, her conduct is not consistent. One kind of girl would have told Harry Gordon falsely that she had become Sebastian's mistress;

another kind would have wished above all things to preserve Harry's respect for her by telling him she had lied. But they would not be the same woman. The deaths of both Lucy and Sebastian are accidental, and consequently there is no inevitability in the tragedy. In *Lucy Gayheart* Miss Cather created a character with fine possibilities, but did not make the most of her.

The most distinct impression that a general survey of Willa Cather's fiction leaves, is that of her breadth of vision and her understanding of different points of view. Some of her finest characters, like Captain and Mrs. Forrester, are native Americans, but no one before her had represented so sympathetically the foreign elements that make up so much of the West. Garland in *A Little Norsk* had painted a real portrait of the Norwegian immigrant, but Miss Cather went farther and revealed the artistic quality of the Northern races in *The Song of the Lark*. Even more striking was her comprehension of the differences between the Swedish and the Norwegian elements in Thea Kronborg. Usually the American lumps them together as "Scandinavians." Her Indians, as has been indicated by quotation, are interpreted without sentimentality, but she had been preceded in this field by Mrs. Jackson and others. Perhaps the most penetrating insight is reflected in her characters like the Bohemians and the Mexicans, who have usually been treated conventionally, except by men like Janvier, or disregarded as beneath the notice of an Anglo-Saxon. Her Bohemian characters are sharply differentiated from their Norwegian or Swedish neighbors, and their racial instinct for color and their love of beauty are established by action as well as by description. Her Mexicans are portrayed as through their own eyes, not the eyes of an alien. Even the most irregular in their habits, like "Spanish Johnny" in *The Song of the Lark* have their *raison d'être:*

"He is always fooled,"—the Mexican woman spoke rapidly and tremulously, her long under lip quivering. "He is good at heart, but he has no head. He fools himself. You do not understand in this country, you are progressive. But he has no judgment, and he is fooled." She stooped quickly, took up one of the white conch-shells that bordered the walk, and, with an apologetic inclination of her head, held it to Dr. Archie's ear. "Listen, doctor. You hear something in there? You hear the sea; and yet the sea is very far from here. You have judgment, and you know that. But he is fooled. To him, it is the sea itself. A little thing is big to him." She bent and placed the shell in the white row, with its fellows. Thea took it up softly and pressed it to her own ear. The sound in it startled her; it was like something calling one. So that was why Johnny ran away. There was something awe-inspiring about Mrs. Tellamantez and her shell.

This understanding of the profounder difference of races extends to the French characters in her later books, as has been shown sufficiently. This breadth of vision came, of course, like all liberality, from knowledge. Willa Cather had traveled widely, at home and abroad, before she wrote of the races I have mentioned. In her introduction to the 1922 edition of *Alexander's Bridge*, she says:

> One of the few really helpful words I ever heard from an older writer, I had from Sarah Orne Jewett when she said to me: "Of course, one day you will write about your own country. In the meantime, get all you can. One must know the world *so well* before one can know the parish."

It is apparent to any close student of Willa Cather's work, that it is just because she knows the world so well that she not only wrote with sympathy of the life of Nebraska, but that she could pass beyond that life into larger regions. This introduction reveals much of her philosophy of composition, but one can easily be misled by its emphasis upon the importance of the impression made upon a novelist by the scenes of early life. That step into the experiences which in youth "lie at the bottom of his consciousness and continue to feed him, but . . . do not stimulate him" was a necessary step forward in Willa Cather's progress, but it must be remembered that her greatest books came after 1922, and that none of them owe their power to the description of the farming life of Nebraska.

It is that universal quality, the distinguishing mark of the artist of high rank, that is Miss Cather's most distinct claim to consideration. Marian Forrester would have had much the same nature, no matter where she lived. If Bishop Latour had been sent to Africa, his greatness would have been established by the same qualities. The American scene gave the Bishop a splendid background, but the background never obscures the character. Human nature is, after all, human nature wherever it is found, and especially are the great traits the common property of humanity. Miss Cather knows the evil, the weakness and the pettiness of life, but while she never hesitates to describe them, she is not primarily concerned with them. Her primary interest is the pursuit of beauty, whether in the soul of an archbishop, or of a Norse immigrant, or a Mexican ne'er-do-well. Often she finds it in the spiritual heritage of a race. In *Shadows on the Rock,* with a remarkable understanding of a faith to which she does not belong, she speaks of the effect of the traditions of the Canadians:

The people have loved miracles for so many hundred years, not as proof or evidence, but because they are the actual flowering of desire. In them the vague worship and devotion of the simple-hearted assumes a form. From being a shapeless longing, it becomes a beautiful image; a dumb rapture becomes a melody that can be remembered and repeated; and the experience of a moment, which might have been a lost ecstasy, is made an actual possession and can be bequeathed to another.

Sometimes it is the beauty of early memories, often the beauty of places dear to the beholder's heart. Often it is the beauty that springs out of the agony of creation, from the outpouring of the artist in words, in painting, in music, or in sculpture. Her artists, like all those who can create what few around them can understand, are usually in conflict with their environment. So far as they spring from the West, they leave it as soon as possible. In "The Sculptor's Funeral," she pictures "the yearning of a boy, cast ashore upon a desert of newness and ugliness and sordidness, for all that is chastened and old and noble with tradition."

Her greatest pioneers are pioneers of the spirit, bringing beauty and order and the fragrance of sacrifice to the outposts of civilization. From her own poetry again comes the best final characterization of her prose. In it, without any taint of the provincial, there are found:

"The thoughts of men, which are eternal,
In which, eternal, men remain."

CHAPTER XXXII

THE CELEBRATION OF THE INDIVIDUAL

ONE of the prevailing notes in the fiction of the twentieth century is that of rebellion against the restriction of personal freedom. It is concerned not so much with economic conditions as it is with the limitations imposed by traditional barriers of convention, and just as the fiction which criticized the economic and political conditions was written largely by men, so this other phase was developed principally by women. One of the earliest to publish, Mary Hunter Austin (1868–1934), was born in Carlinville, Illinois, but lived during her creative period in California, in both the ranch country and in Carmel. In her autobiography, *Earth Horizon* (1932), she reveals a curious restless personality, probably hard to live with. Her unhappy marriage, the tragedy of her defective child, her later divorce, all were symptoms of a deeper dissatisfaction, perhaps of a power never fully ripened.

She began with glowing descriptions of that region, lying in her own words "between the high Sierras south from Yosemite—east and south over a very great assemblage of broken ranges beyond Death Valley and on illimitably into the Mojave Desert." In *The Land of Little Rain* (1903) she interpreted the spell of this region and in *The Flock* (1906) she gave a vivid picture of the sheep-herding of California. While these books are not, however, fiction in any real sense, they represent Mrs. Austin in what will probably be her most permanent contribution to literature. Her visualizing power was her greatest asset, and the care with which she documents her earliest fiction with footnotes reveals at once her accuracy and her limitations as a novelist.

Isidro (1905) is an historical romance of what is now New Mexico, before the Franciscan missions were secularized. No historical figures emerge, however; what remains are the descriptions of the country. In *Lost Borders* (1909) the short stories are often dramatic and there are flashes of insight such as the explanation why the primitive woman frequently takes men away from her more civilized rivals. But Mrs. Austin reveals the limitation of her material in "The Woman at the Eighteen Mile," when she says: "Here in the borders, where the warp runs loose and wide, the pattern has not that richness it should show in the close fabric of civilization."

Santa Lucia (1908) represents another phase of Mrs. Austin's fiction, the analysis of marriage. Here she attacks the problem of marriage through three women. One is quite happy in her love story; one comes to tragedy and suicide through no reason except her restlessness and her selection of a husband, a professor of biology in Santa Lucia College, who tries to create some intellectual comradeship in her and fails. The third passes through unhappy times, partly on account of her husband's financial dishonesty and partly because she does not recognize that he regrets his yielding to the temptation of economic pressure. The last pair work out their salvation through their children and mutual interest in his work. At the last, the wife, Serena, seems content "as the pang of unfulfilment of romance passed in the sense of saving commonness." She realized, too, that her husband whom she had at first condemned because he was not on her moral level, "was a representative of the undaunted male attitude which begat great achievement in the West. She felt herself shamed by its largeness forever out of the complicated futility of her moral conventions." In such moments Mrs. Austin was a realist, and she continued this phase in *A Woman of Genius* (1912) which is laid in a small town in the Middle West, during the 'seventies and 'eighties. Again the heroine is dissatisfied with her marriage and finds an outlet through her stage career. There is some realism in the description of her difficulties in finding employment; little, however, in the record of her ultimate success.

The mystical side of Mrs. Austin's nature which is revealed positively in her autobiography is shown in a brief novel, *The Lovely Lady* (1913), a spiritual romance, describing with sympathy the dream life of a boy and man. More daring was her romance *Outland* (1919) written in collaboration with the poet, George Sterling, and published first in London under the pen name, Gordon Stairs. Here they imagined a primitive people, still living in California and visible only to the few, who pay the penalty of drinking the cup of forgetfulness which deprives them of memory. There was the possibility of a fine symbolical romance in *Outland*, but while it has some tense moments and the characters are more vivid than is usual with her, there is an attempt to square the relations of the Outlanders with reality which precipitates it into artificiality. Such a story must frankly rest upon a dream. Her last novel, *Starry Adventure* (1931) had also a mystic tinge. She conveys well the feeling of the boy Garth that there is a relationship between himself and the landscape.

Mrs. Austin's one attempt at criticism of economic injustice, *The Ford* (1917) proved that this was not her forte. The details of the struggle for a water supply are too long drawn out. *26 Jayne St.* (1920) which she thought her best novel, and which "aimed to uncover the sleazy quality of current radicalism," failed because the confusion of pre-war conditions was too close to her in 1920 to interpret them correctly.

Mary Austin made important contributions to our knowledge of the Indian, the Mexican, and the Spanish civilizations, especially in their literary monuments. It is paradoxical that being such an ardent advocate of a woman's right to her individual and personal career, she is least truly a novelist when she deals with problems of that nature. When she forgot herself and painted the land and the people among whom she labored, she interpreted the primitive and the foreign elements in western civilization with knowledge and sympathy. The final impression of her work is one of irritation that a writer who could do some things so well could descend to weakness, even banality, in the conversations of her characters and even in the body of her narrative.

The fiction of Zona Gale (1874–   ) is at first glance difficult to classify, for her earliest novel, *Romance Island,* (1906) and *Papa La Fleur* (1933) seem like the work of different people. Yet the very changes in her work are not unrepresentative of the insistent effort of women during the twentieth century to find a satisfactory solution of life which would preserve their individuality, in or out of the marriage relation. Born in Portage, Wisconsin, she graduated at the University of Wisconsin in 1895 and spent some years on the staffs of newspapers in Milwaukee and New York City. Zona Gale's first published short stories date from her freshman year at college in 1892, but these early efforts appeared in newspapers. Neither these nor her earlier magazine stories, dating from 1903, have been reprinted by her. In 1904 she returned to Wisconsin and in 1928 married William L. Breese, of Portage.

Her first novel, *Romance Island* (1906), was sheer fantasy, in which a New York newspaper man and an heiress are transported by a submarine to an imaginary island, a queer mixture of Anthony Hope and George MacDonald. *The Loves of Pelleas and Ettare* (1907) was also idealistic romance, but these stories of an elderly pair of married lovers in New York had much more verity, even if they were reminiscent of *Prue and I*. Beginning in 1908 Miss Gale found the material in her native Wisconsin for several volumes of short stories and more than one novel. *Friendship Village* (1908) was an idealistic treatment of familiar life, a defence of the small town for its "kindly brooding companionship." Through the various complications of village loves, ambitions, jealousies, generosity, and selfishness, she built up a picture in which the community is an active force for kindness and good will. In this volume and its successors, *Friendship Village Love Stories* (1909) and *Neighborhood Stories* (1914) she laid little stress upon the narrowness or the petty tyranny of the small town except to use them as enemies to be put to rout. Her picture is therefore one-sided just as *Main Street* is one-sided in the other direction. Yet there are real characters, such as Calliope Marsh, the shrewd old maid whose caustic remarks provide much of the humor. A more serious criticism of these stories might be directed at the belief of their author that the great virtues are chiefly feminine. Her effort to build up a novel, *Mothers to Men* (1911), upon a romantic social philosophy which, among other accomplishments, forces the tradesmen of the town to clean up their stores by methods that are frankly blackmail, is saved from absurdity only by that humor which describes one of the town Tories as "a place in the atmosphere where a citizen ought to be and ain't." To this same period in Miss Gale's work belongs *A Daughter of the Morning* (1917), a novel dealing with the struggles of a country girl to make her living in New York. Miss Gale was still proceeding according to the well-worn paths of romance by which lucky accidents rather than her own character win success for her heroine.

The celebration of comradeship and good will led to such a novel as *Heart's Kindred* (1915), in which the protest against war was represented through a conventional California miner who is converted to feminine peace propaganda by those methods which spell death to fiction. After the war this same impulse for peace and good will was represented with more success in *Peace in Friendship Village* (1919). The later stories in this collection still appeal to those who have not forgotten the large impulses for permanent peace which soared up at Versailles under President Wilson's leadership, only to fall dead under the wave of materialism and partisan politics. Most of the stories, however, had been published before the Great War and belong to Zona Gale's earlier manner.

In *Birth* (1918) Miss Gale made a distinct advance in the sharpness and vitality of her fiction. Instead of the pleasant portrait of the small Wisconsin village of her earlier stories, she drew a realistic picture of the town against whose lack of understanding a fine soul in an insignificant body struggles in vain. There could hardly be imagined a more hopeless hero than Marshall Pitt when he enters Burage, a pickle salesman, under-sized, inarticulate, uneducated, but with a great longing to rise spiritually and intellectually. Miss Gale with fine insight presented at once a contrast between the recognition which Rachel Arrowsmith, the woman of breed-ing, accords to those qualities of Pitt which lie beneath his unattractive surface, and the lack of understanding of the commonplace girl, Barbara Ellsworth, whom he marries. What wins and keeps the sympathy for Pitt is his humanity, beginning with marriage to a woman whose father's death has left her with nothing but debts, and ending with his own rescue of a dog at the cost of his life. Even when his wife deserts him and their little son for a flashy bandmaster—or when years later his son Jeffrey shows how ashamed he is of his father's insignificance, Pitt rises to the supreme degree of charity in attributing to both of them motives higher than those by which they are really actuated. Quietly he takes the blame upon himself. Pitt's growth in spiritual stature is unperceived by anyone except Rachel Arrowsmith, and even her efforts to help him are not persistent. The comments of the citizens, male and female, after his death, are ironic bits of complacent misunderstanding:

"Say," said Mis' Barber, "did you ever see anybody pick up the way Jeff-rey has since his father died?"

"Ain't he?" said Mis' True. "I've thought of that myself."

"Why, my land," said Mis' Miles, "he's a different person. It looks like what he'd needed was to get rid of that little man—honestly."

They wove this in small patterns, and when Mis' Hellie came back they all reverted to an old design.

"Jeffrey ain't a bit like his father, is he?" Mis' Hellie observed with satis-faction.

They gave their negatives without restraint and Mis' Monument Miles took up the whole story, from the first, rocking slowly and looking out upon the Burage Street.

"Pitt never was much good," she began.

Burage is etched mercilessly but fairly. The picture of the town at six o'clock is better than Sinclair Lewis's description of Main Street because it gives both sides of the shield:

Burage breathes deep, all the tension of the day dissolves. A new air permeates the village. It relaxes, expects. It is as if some great brooding, wistful face, so close to all, changes expression; and every one replies. A creative moment, spiritual, tender, human. All Burage either goes home or welcomes home. Meetings, supper, complaints, tenderness, irritations, control. An impressive and spectacular and glorious moment, and a terrible moment.

Whether Lewis had read *Birth* before he wrote *Main Street* I do not know, but it is significant that he chose the surname of Rachel Arrowsmith for the leading character in one of his later novels.

Zona Gale's next novel was founded on an episode which she cut out of *Birth*, on account of the length of that story. At first it concerned Jeffrey Pitt as a failure in love. He became Bobby in *Miss Lulu Bett,* changed, of course, but the greatest change was the building up from a casual aunt in *Birth* of the leading character of *Miss Lulu Bett* (1920). In this novel Miss Gale portrayed the urge of the individual to revolt against the petty tyranny of the family. Taking again an undistinguished figure, a woman of thirty-four, the unconsidered beast of burden "who was not strong enough to work anywhere else," Miss Gale depicted remorselessly one of the most poisonous households in recent fiction, dominated by Dwight Deacon, dentist and magistrate, whose idea of humor consists of apparent jokes upon his sister-in-law, which taunt her with her helpless dependence upon him. The selfish children, the grandmother, whose visits to her bed-ridden neighbor next door were "as good as a dose of medicine," the flabby wife, are reality itself. But in themselves they would be unimportant; it is because they provide a cause for Lulu's revolt that they become interesting. It was a mistaken criticism that praised Zona Gale for daring to write about stupid people. Dwight Deacon is not stupid at all; his knife-like thrusts are clever in themselves, and the use Miss Gale makes of these worthless persons to provide occasion for her own humorous comments marks her out from those novelists who drag us through pages of repetitious conversation without reward. Even the banal foolery of the mock wedding between Lulu and Ninian Deacon, which turns out to be legal, is not accidental. Lulu would not have grasped at the opportunity Ninian offered her if she had not been desperate, and if that other Lulu, hidden beneath the surface, had not risen to the stimulus to her pride in at last being wanted by a man. When she returns from the wedding trip with the news that Ninian had confessed to another wife who had left him six-

teen years before, and Dwight at once suggests that this is a lie to enable
Ninian to get rid of her, she begins that fight to secure her own self-respect
which makes her a personage. She insists upon proof of this earlier marriage, because Ninian was to her only a symbol which made her significant
not so much to the others as to herself. She could stand the position of a
deserted wife, but she could not stand the thought that she had consented
to marry a man who did not want her. Her later marriage to Niel Cornish
is not merely a romantic concession, it is rather an incident in Lulu's triumph over Dwight Deacon, for it makes it necessary that he should reveal his brother's bigamy which he was desperately anxious to conceal. It
is seldom that a reader has such a savage joy in seeing shattered the respectability of a hypocrite. The dramatic qualities of *Miss Lulu Bett* were
made apparent in the play which Zona Gale constructed from the novel
in 1920, and which won the Pulitzer Prize for the best play of the year.

The same note of revolt is struck in *Faint Perfume* (1923), but Leda
Perrin has not the sharp veracity of Lulu Bett. Her cousins, the Crumbs,
are just as terrible a ménage as the Deacons, especially Richmiel, the
daughter, who has divorced Barnaby Powers. Her utter selfishness and
her willingness to let her husband take their little boy away is quite consistent with her refusal to keep her word when she finds Leda and Barnaby
are planning to marry. Miss Gale had the courage to leave the lovers with
a bleak prospect of waiting, which in the play of the same name is changed
into a happy ending. But Barnaby, like Leda, is a shadowy creature, and
as Richmiel's husband, he is unexplainable.

The Preface to a Life (1926) started well with its grim picture of the
way in which circumstances keep a young man from pursuing his chosen
career. But when the hero returns from the War and tries to see through
the appearances of things into their reality, the novel becomes muddled.
This is a theme for idealistic fiction, but Miss Gale has so cluttered it
around with realistic details that she succeeds in making it neither one nor
the other. Reality is more apparent in the short stories gathered together
under the title *Yellow Gentians and Blue* (1927). The futility of life is
the general theme, but it is the brief compressed form of the tales which
makes the best of them striking. The cruelty of a farming community
which drives a man to suicide through its curiosity, is revealed in "The
Charivari" and the ironic ending in "Belnap" is original and effective.
Several of the characters are abnormal, and so is the heroine of the novel

Borgia (1929) in which the contest of two forms of abnormality is treated in an unusual manner. While *Borgia* is not one of Miss Gale's most important books, the rescue of the hero from his sister who is gradually absorbing his entire life, by a woman who has become morbid in the belief that her influence is certain to be evil, is based upon an accurate knowledge of the feminine need for emotional activity.

Miss Gale's later short stories in *Bridal Pond* (1930) deal with a woman's strength of character, among them "White Bread" and "The Cobweb" being notably good. "The Need" is a realistic picture of the desperate loneliness of a woman who has moved into a new neighborhood. In *Old Fashioned Tales* (1933) Miss Gale shows clearly the futility of those advanced ideas which are based not upon independence but upon mere restlessness. A good touch occurs in "Whippoorwill" when an older woman who is invited to represent a character in an historical pageant appears just as she is, without costume, and wins her triumph as the American woman of the Victorian Age. Miss Gale is by no means a Tory, however. In her novelette *Papa La Fleur* (1933) she draws with sympathy the point of view of a daughter who has left the home village on the same train with a man from Chicago. When she returns and her father and lover both try to forgive her, she naturally resents their attitude and does not let them see that nothing has happened to her. The conversation between Linnie, her father, and her lover puts the case for all sides:

"Well then," said Linnie, "I refuse to talk about it. All this isn't the language of my generation."

Her father looked at her, and as he looked, he seemed taller and of a dignity greater than any that he had borne. And curiously his face softened as if he were regarding a child.

"Then can't ye be merciful," he said, "to your father's generation—and try to make him understand what, in God's name, is in your heart?"

With that he turned abruptly and entered the house. Myron Lettish rose and was gone too, walking unevenly towards the gate, muttering under his breath as he went. Milo was left there, and suddenly he was standing close beside Linnie and saying, without his will:

"Linnie—Linnie. You know how I love you . . . God help me—I can forgive you anything—anything! That's how I love you, Linnie . . ."

To his utter, extravagant amazement, Linnie cried:

"Forgive me? For what? Don't you belong to this generation either, Milo?"

He took her by her arms and held her fiercely. His face was that of a man

suddenly adult, and suddenly showing all the patience and wisdom of the
world for the youth of the world.

"God Almighty," he said, "if you're so wise, can't you understand that
cruelty belongs to no generation?"

The fiction of Zona Gale has been progressive in matter and in form.
Beginning with the idealistic treatment of romantic material, she proceeded to realistic pictures of familiar life. She has never lost, however,
a sense of the distinction between the merely external analysis and the
more searching synthesis which builds up a story that in her own words
"does something to you." There is a poet's touch constantly in her prose,
and while at times it has led to unreality, and even absurdity, it has been
responsible also for flashes of insight which atone for them. Her plays
and her dramatic interests undoubtedly sharpened her later fiction, but
she is a novelist rather than a playwright. It did not need the publication
of the play *Miss Lulu Bett,* with its alternate third acts, one of which followed the novel and the other which yielded to the necessities of production, to prove that she works best when she has her material under her
own control.

She had her own theories of fiction, found in "The Novel and the
Spirit" and "The Novel of To-morrow" in her volume of essays *Portage,
Wisconsin and Other Essays* (1928). She objected to the school of thinking which believes that the novel of economic struggle includes all the elements of conflict, and stated correctly: "The novel in which a crude moral
struggle, either lost or won, is the highest motif as is primitive in art as
is the economic struggle in life." She also remarked hopefully that: "The
chief concern of the American novel of tomorrow will be to uncover the
beauty of our essential commonplace living as the novel of today has triumphantly uncovered its ugliness." In this belief she may be an optimist,
but there can be no question that in her own fiction she has sought beauty
in many forms, and has at times achieved it.

In the fiction of Dorothy Canfield Fisher (1879–   ) the rights of the
individual are emphasized but his duties to others are never forgotten.
Her New England ancestry and her father's activities as a college president probably account for the broad social consciousness which has resulted in volumes upon educational topics, with which we are not here concerned. She was born in Lawrence, Kansas, while her father was teaching
at the University of Kansas, and she graduated at Ohio State University
in 1899 at the close of his term as president. Her graduate study at Co-

lumbia was in preparation for a career as a teacher of modern languages, but in 1904 she began to publish short stories in *Everybody's*, *Munsey's*, and other magazines. The summer of 1905 she spent in Norway and many of the stories published later in *Hillsboro People* were written at this time. While some of her early fiction like "Jerusha and Guiseppe" [1] has significance for its suggestion of a way out for the decaying families of New England in the union with the foreign invaders, the best of these early stories are found in the collections, *Hillsboro People* (1915) and *The Real Motive* (1916). "An Academic Question," dating from 1910, is an amusing satire upon social pretence in the faculty circles of a Middle West university, and "An April Masque" is a very human and well-told story of the conspiracy of a group of French painters to save an old copyist from starvation by buying his atrocious reproductions of a patriotic painting without hurting his *amour propre*. The very best of the tales deal with New England, and the best are very good indeed. Others had written before, of course, of New England pride and self-respect, but Mrs. Fisher strikes fresh notes out of situations which had still fine echoes to resound. The supreme content of the artist is the theme of "The Bedquilt," an appealing story of a woman, pushed aside by her family, who lends her quilt to the Fair and then when she is permitted as a great treat to go to see the many attractions, spends all her time sitting before her own work. "The Artist" depicts the struggle between duty and the creative spirit. The individual struggle for expression is revealed in "The Heyday of the Blood," "Adeste Fidelis," and "Piper Tim." "Petunias—That's for Remembrance" is a strong contrast between the horizons of the farmers and that of a girl, college-bred and traveled, who returns to her native heath. She thinks them stupid—they think she has seen nothing. But their questions have all been economic, and of the gifts which Italy might make to the imagination, they know little. Best of all is "Portrait of a Philosopher," one of the finest short stories in the language. The conflict here is between the immortality of art and the immortality of the soul. A great French painter has painted the portrait of Professor Gridley, the foremost scholar of a little New England college. His life had been austere, in sharp contrast to that of his father whose moral derelictions had been notorious. Mrs. Fisher draws a perfect picture of the college function at which the portrait is to be presented. No one but Professor Gridley's aunt

[1] *Everybody's Magazine*, July, 1905.

sees what the Frenchman has done. Out of the dead man's eyes shines the longing for the fleshpots which he has inherited but which he has stifled for the sake of something higher. The theme had been treated before, notably by Henry James in "The Liar." But Mrs. Fisher gave a new aspect to it. In "The Liar" the man whose inner nature has been betrayed by his enemy, returns to destroy the portrait to save himself. But in "Portrait of a Philosopher" the old aunt destroys the portrait with her crutch, because to her the picture was a libel. Great painter as he was, the Frenchman had seen beneath the surface, but he had not seen the moral strength which had triumphed over nature. To the painter, the subject had no rights, the portrait as a work of art was all important. To the woman who had loved and understood the great scholar, the portrait was of little account compared with the tradition of his moral beauty. How real such traditions can be after they have hardened into certitude, every American knows. These stories are interesting also as celebrations of the village as opposed to the city.

Dorothy Canfield's first novel, *Gunhild* (1907), was laid in Norway. It was a contrast between the simple straightforward nature of a girl, who though born in Kansas had returned with her family to Norway, and a group of Americans held for some time in Gunhild's little village. The chief interest of the novel lies in the ironic situation of Henry Fox, an over-sophisticated young American whose delicate sense of values has prevented his accomplishing anything of importance, but who finds his prejudices undermined by his passion for Gunhild. Then when he finally decides to marry her, he has been forestalled by a very eligible Norwegian officer who has swept her off her feet. The rival suitor is simply told about, and Gunhild's feelings are interpreted to us through others' eyes. But the character-drawing, especially of Miss Fox, the chaperon, is adequate; the descriptions of Norwegian scenery are at times brilliant; and the separation of two people who were really not fitted for each other is indicated by an insight into the relations of men and women which declined to over-estimate a minor tragedy. There was a clarity and directness of thought in this first novel that was not quite so evident in *The Squirrel Cage* (1912), a study of an average American marriage, laid in Ohio. The picture is realistic, but Mrs. Fisher had not yet learned that to create sympathy for a woman who feels that her marriage is unsatisfactory, a novelist must provide a character strong enough to hold the center of the stage. Lydia Emery is one of those women who belong in the background of fiction. While a heroine may sin as much as she pleases and still remain a heroine, she must never be simply ineffective. *The Bent Twig* (1915), Mrs. Fisher's first important novel, is a study of American family life, beginning in a Middle Western State university town, where Professor Marshall and his wife bring up their daughters with an indifference to the petty social creed of the place that causes them to pay the penalty of all independent souls. In Sylvia, the oldest daughter, Mrs. Fisher evidently made an attempt to portray a girl whose instincts for luxury struggle constantly with her conscience, and the two men whom she grows to love in different ways, are brought in not unskilfully to make that struggle concrete. It is the New England conscience, vivified into Austin Flint's broad social plans for the betterment of his coal-miners, which wins Sylvia in the end. He is more real than his sybarite rival, and, indeed, the men are backgrounds for the women, especially Mrs. Marshall, who is again of New England. *The Bent Twig* is not by any means Mrs. Fisher's best novel. There is too much argument and analysis, but Sylvia is quite human in her indecision as to her own feelings, and her criticism of social uplifters—"It always seemed to me it was bad enough to be poor without having other people with a little more money messing around in your life" must strike a responsive chord in many breasts.

In 1907 Dorothy Canfield was married to John Redwood Fisher. The deep interest in France, which both Mr. and Mrs. Fisher knew so well, led them to volunteer their services in 1916. Mr. Fisher entered the French ambulance service and Mrs. Fisher assisted in organizing an establishment for printing books for blinded soldiers. She also directed the camp commissary when Mr. Fisher was placed in charge of an American Ambulance Field Service Training Camp. The first literary result of this service in France was a collection of short stories, *Home Fires in France* (1918). While the great enthusiasm that welcomed these fine revelations of the indomitable spirit of the French people has inevitably cooled with the decline of war fever, they are still important as fiction. The characters of the peasant in "The Permissionaire," of the patrician in "The Eyes of the Blind," and of the shopkeeper in "La Pharmacienne," reveal Mrs. Fisher's clear understanding of Gallic nature. The stories form one of the earliest pictures of the cruelty and the futility of war. There is no glorification of contest, the grim results in suffering and devastation are given relentlessly, without the bitterness and cynicism which made some of the later writing about the war less effective. *The Day of Glory* (1919) contains only one story, "On the Edge," a vivid picture of a Frenchwoman's struggle to keep her family alive, the return of her husband for a few hours' leave, her belief that it has been an illusion, and then the proof that he actually has been with her. The descriptive articles have the dramatic methods of fiction, however, especially "The Day of Glory," a brief but telling picture of Armistice Day.

The Brimming Cup (1921) was a disappointment. It is another study of married life, laid in New England, and is largely concerned with the analysis of Marise Crittenden's emotions when, although she is apparently happily married, with children, a disturbing force in the shape of another man appears. She works out her problem with satisfaction to herself after many months of struggle which are unduly prolonged. Mrs. Fisher did an unusual thing in writing as a sequel to *The Brimming Cup* a story of the early life of Neale and Marise Crittenden in *Rough Hewn* (1922), but while this was published last, it had been thought out before *The Brimming Cup* was written. It is much more interesting than *The Brimming Cup* because there is more contrast and because the reader has more sympathy with the struggles of Neale and Marise as children and as young people to find out what they really wish to make of life. The quiet, normal life of Neale's parents in New York and the tragic life of Marise's mother and father in France explain both his solid sensible character and her dread of marriage. There is an admirable picture also of the way Neale mistakes friendship for love in his earlier engagement. Thousands of men and women drift into marriage as Neale and Martha are in danger of doing, and it is not usually the woman who saves them from making a mistake. Both novels are stories of intensely individual characters, but there is more sympathy for the younger Neale, the "lone wolf" in college, and Marise, the young girl driven in upon herself in a foreign land, than with the older woman whose responsibilities have been of her own making. In *The Brimming Cup* her feeling that marriage has not given her perfect satisfaction is, of course, a reflection that comes to many women of thirty-eight, but she would be a more interesting heroine if she had not had an experience of passion which should have given her more poise in meeting the inevitable "mid-channel" of married life. *Rough Hewn*, too, has more minor characters of interest; the Basques who serve Marise and her family are admirably drawn. The dawning of artistic interest in Marise, her experience at Lourdes, her sudden plunge into maturity when her mother dies, are paralleled by Neale's growing interest in things that are worth while. His discovery of Dickens and of Emerson, which develop his interest in humanity, and his individualism, will appeal to anyone who has passed through similar experiences.

In *Raw Material* (1923) Dorothy Canfield states that she presents only the material for fiction, but the volume really contains short stories of New England life—not as finely wrought as those in *Hillsboro People*. The situations are, as she implies, the compelling interest, especially that of "old man Warner" who would *not* be looked after, and who died in his own kitchen, independent to the last. Mrs. Fisher departed from her studies of the relations of husband and wife in *Her Son's Wife* (1926), to create one of her best characters, Mrs. Bascomb, a dominant woman who tried to control the lives of her son, her daughter-in-law, and her grand-daughter. The scene is laid either in New York or Pennsylvania, but the scene does not matter much. Mrs. Bascomb, a widow and a school-teacher, could be duplicated almost anywhere. A mixture of self-pity and conscientious devotion to duty, she quenches all tendency to independence in her son's nature, and when he marries Lottie, a commonplace woman, instead of the girl she has selected for him, she at first seeks refuge in another town. But the love for her little granddaughter brings her back and she plans a unique method of salvation for the girl. By playing upon Lottie's laziness, she convinces her that she is an incurable invalid, and she devotes herself to the bedridden woman she dislikes in order that she may bring up the girl she adores. Then Mrs. Fisher conceived a delightfully ironic situation whose possibilities she did not fully develop. With the departure of "Dids," the granddaughter, to college, and a change in her son's business, Mrs. Bascomb is left with Lottie on her hands. Here the novel should have ended, but Mrs. Bascomb's passage through remorse to pity and finally to love of Lottie, leaves the book on a lower level of sentimentality.

It was in *The Deepening Stream* (1930) that Mrs. Fisher made her most distinct contribution to American fiction. In a way, all her earlier studies of married life seem to have been a preparation for this novel. Be-binning in the West, in a university town, she describes, through the eyes of a young girl, Matey Gilbert, the desperate struggle for control between her father and mother. She had to endow the girl with an almost uncanny insight into the subtle methods by which the conflict is carried on. But the dramatic scene at Professor Gilbert's death bed needs only a loving heart to understand it. Matey Gilbert is a distinct advance beyond

Marise Crittenden in *Rough Hewn* because the morbid idea of married life which Marise has gained from the relations of her parents is modified in Matey's case by her comprehension of the spiritual kinship between the husband and wife which came to the surface in a great crisis. Contrast, the life of fiction, is next established by Matey Gilbert's life in the little village on the Hudson River, where she meets her husband, Adrian Fort. Mrs. Fisher's real preference for the East is revealed by her sympathetic picture of Rustdorf, with its long-settled tradition, which comes as a revelation to a girl whose constant changes of residence have prevented the growth of roots of any kind. The Great War, to which Adrian goes as an ambulance driver, taking with him Matey and their two children, is painted without glamour. Out of Mrs. Fisher's own experience rise some very striking scenes; the description of the arrival of the first American troops, the roughneck regulars, with their proficient, professional swing; the effect upon the French of President Wilson's statement concerning the real meaning of the war; the picture of the materialists, who went over during the Peace Conference to make sure that his idealistic program would be upset; and most of all, the complete apathy that took possession of Adrian and Matey, as compared with the enthusiasm with which they went to the aid of France in 1915. In *The Deepening Stream*, Mrs. Fisher has accomplished the rare feat of making a happy marriage interesting and of depicting the growth of a woman's character consistently and naturally.

On the same high level, her short stories, *Basque People* (1931), revealed her understanding of that primitive pre-Aryan race who have survived among European conquerors, keeping their own institutions and being content with the fundamental realities of life: love, family, affection, faith, courage, and strength drawn from the past. Mrs. Fisher had spent almost a year in 1918 in the Basque country of southern France, where she established a convalescent home for children, so that she knew the race at first hand. But the book is not just a picture of a civilization. There are dramatic stories, tragedies and comedies, told usually through the eyes of a teacher, Mlle. Etchegaray. Among the best are "Vive Guignol," the story of an old puppet man, and "The Saint of the Old Seminary," a story of moral contrast which Bret Harte might have conceived, and which portrays the relentless hate of the race. The most interesting is "An Ancestral Home," told through the eyes of a New England schoolteacher who visits her Basque relatives and falls under the spell of the place and people. Her discovery of the cave with its historic drawings, which explain the ancient customs of the Basques, like the fringe that hangs down over the oxen's eyes and the curious interwoven lines on the "makhila" or oxgoad, is only one of the incidents that change her point of view. She sees the Basques not as an ignorant unimaginative race who have not developed in art or literature, but as a race so old that they may have passed beyond the time when art seems important, and may have preferred to live a poetry of their own instead of writing it. It is the same theme, of course, that gave rise to the climax of her story "Portrait of a Philosopher." The most dramatic story, "The Majesty of the Law," is laid in 1609 during the witchcraft trials. The methods of the judges, who had the women of the district at their mercy while the men were away for months fishing on the Banks of Newfoundland, the heroic determination of two old men and two boys to sail across the Atlantic Ocean and bring the men back, the return of the fleet, and the charge of the returned fisherman upon the court, sweeping the judges out of the town and forcing them to walk miles for safety, is a triumph of description and narrative.

Bonfire (1933), a study of the havoc wrought in several lives by a girl who comes from one of those backward settlements in New England and is a combination of oversexed passion and shrewd ruthlessness, was hardly up to the standard of *The Deepening Stream*. The minor characters confuse the plot, and the ending seems weak.

Throughout all Dorothy Canfield's fiction the prevailing note is that of the individual who, never underestimating the disillusioning processes of life, nevertheless finds the struggle worth while. Thoroughly as she knew the limitations of the Western town without adequate knowledge of social values, or the Eastern village where tradition ruled with a power that verged upon stagnation, or the pettiness of the French provincial, or the immovable prejudice of the Basque farmer, she has had the insight to see below the surface, and discern the rich variety of character which in any place or time reward the student of human nature. In the introduction to her collection of short stories, *The Real Motive*, she describes the dying man who, knowing how weak and futile life can be, had pretended to an optimism he did not feel, who "had showered upon a wretched world a flood of reassuring thoughts, of inspiring phrases," and who knew and dreaded the unsparing mirror which death was about to hold before him, and in which he would at last see himself as he really was—and who trembled in an awful terror. "And yet those who were with him at the last, say that at the end he cried out in a loud voice of exceeding joy."

Like Miss Cather, her wide knowledge at first hand of many sections of the United States and of some of Europe, prevented her from making those superficial generalizations which weaken the work of the satirists like Lewis, Dreiser, or Sinclair, and her knowledge of adolescence gained through her experience as a teacher, spared her from the errors of those novelists like Anderson who picture youth as a quagmire of evil. If her material seems at times to overwhelm her powers of artistic assimilation and expression, her best fiction has an acuteness of insight which will keep her place secure.

Like Zona Gale, Susan Glaspell (1882–   ) won distinction as a playwright as well as a novelist, and her association with her first husband, George Cram Cook, in the establishment of the Provincetown Players, reveals that love of the theatre which has affected her fiction both fortunately and unfortunately. Born in Davenport, Iowa, and educated at Drake University and the University of Chicago, she became a reporter in Des Moines, Iowa, covering political assignments. As early as 1903 she began to publish in *Harper's Magazine* and elsewhere, short stories, which were collected in *Lifted Masks* (1912). Several of these deal with political situations, usually leading to a climax when a governor or a State senator sacrifices himself to prevent injustice to another person or simply for the good of the State. What seems to be her earliest story, "The Plea," [2] is a protest against the tyranny of public opinion which opposes the pardon of a boy murderer without considering the circumstances of his life. Thus, in the beginning of her career, Susan Glaspell celebrated the case of the individual against the general law. Perhaps the best of the political stories is "The Last Sixty Minutes" in which a retiring governor, who has been merely the mouthpiece of a boss, revolts at the very end of his term to save from disaster his successor who has the independence he himself had never dared to assume. Miss Glaspell's knowledge of the mixed motives which sway politicians is evident in these stories, and also her love for the unusual situation.

Her first novel, *The Glory of the Conquered* (1909), was an appealing story with an original idea, even if at times it was sentimentally expressed. Her inspiration came from Mercie's statue of "Gloria Victis," and the dead soldier's grip on his broken sword became the symbol of

[2] Published in *Harper's Magazine*, October, 1903, as "In the Face of His Constituents."

the brave struggle of a man and a woman to meet their tragedy. Miss Glaspell conceived one of the very hardest situations in modern life, the enforced idleness of a scientist upon the brink of a great discovery. It is not only that Karl Hubers, Professor of Biology at the University of Chicago, goes blind, but also the fact that the disease has been caused by his own carelessness that creates a situation for him almost unbearable. The description of his mental state while waiting for the verdict is masterly. Equally fine is the struggle in his wife's soul when she decides to give up her career as a painter to devote herself to learning the laboratory technique that will enable her to help him carry on his work. Ernestine Hubers is a great soul, capable not only of a momentary sacrifice, but of that harder task of facing unflinchingly the daily effort to save the man she loves from mental and spiritual disintegration. That he dies under an operation just as she is ready to begin her work, is not accidental; it is an ironic ending which the dramatic instinct of Susan Glaspell provided.

In *The Visioning* (1911), the theatrical rather than the dramatic instincts of Miss Glaspell resulted in a brave effort to reveal the narrowness of life when judged by inflexible standards. Again she chose her theme wisely, for the "army people" from which her heroine is drawn are good material from which to choose the maximum of conservatism. But the quixotic attempt of Kate Jones to insert into the life of an army post a chorus girl whose "past" is intimately connected with one of her own admirers, is fantastic. The old argument that such a girl has suffered no more change in character from her liaison with Major Darrett than he has, is another evidence of a sentimentality which seems perennial. Miss Glaspell's sincere dislike of war makes her army people hardly credible, but even she did not have the courage to describe the reactions of Kate's family when she presents as her husband a military convict whose offence of striking an officer seems hardly important enough to make a hero of him. So she closes rather than concludes the novel.

Fidelity (1915) is more intelligible, but even here the issues are not completely met. Each character is faithful to his or her standards, especially the heroine, Ruth Holland, whose elopement with a married man precipitates the situation. The attitudes of her own family and her friends are characteristic of those small cities where everyone is acquainted, and Ruth's refusal to marry Stuart Williams when his wife finally decides to divorce him, is at once a defence of her right to preserve her individual career, and also a comment on the endurability of a union which had passion alone for its foundation.

For the next thirteen years, Miss Glaspell was concerned with the writing and production of plays. In 1928 she returned to fiction with *Brook Evans* (1928). It is a study of two women, Naomi and Brook, her daughter, beginning in 1888 in Illinois, and coming down to the present day. To Naomi, passion comes early, and to Brook late, but in each case the woman forgets everything else. It is a disappointing book, for the motivation is not clear in several of the relationships, especially in Brook's devotion to the man who has married Naomi to save her good name.

Fugitive's Return (1929) was much better. It is also a study of passion, but the characters are more interesting. It is told through the eyes of Irma Shraeder, who, having lost her child and her husband's love, is sent off to Greece, and finds comfort and renewed interest in life through the place and the new people she meets. Miss Glaspell cannot resist the touch of the theatric, but the refusal or inability of Irma to speak is utilized quite effectively. *Fugitive's Return* is one of those novels frequent in contemporary fiction in which a heroine reviews her life, and Irma's memory of her girlhood in Iowa, her family's poverty, her marriage, and experiences in Boston and "on the Cape" are made more vivid by the surroundings of the Grecian scene. As usual with Miss Glaspell, the novel does not end; Irma is left with the prospect of taking with her to America a Greek girl she has saved, and of waiting for a new lover to come for her. Much of the story gains reality by Susan Glaspell's own experiences, as her biography, *The Road to the Temple* (1926), proves. What gives it distinction is the description of the various stages and kinds of passion, made concrete by the living characters, American and Greek.

Ambrose Holt and Family (1931) is in some ways the best novel Susan Glaspell has written. In it the problem of those to whom the supreme necessity is an escape from an environment which is deadening, is stated skilfully through characters that remain as clearly as any of her creations. Ambrose Holt, who had disappeared about twenty years before the story opens in a Middle Western town, his wife, a strong character who refuses to be pitied, her son Lincoln who hates his father for his desertion, and Lincoln's wife who resents the inability of her people to take her seriously, are all very real. When Ambrose Holt returns to his native place but not to his home, the recognition by himself and his daughter-in-law that they are kindred spirits is expressed through excellent conversation. Best of all is the flight of Lincoln and the visit of one of his Eastern friends who comes to find out what is preventing Lincoln, who is a poet, from doing the work of which he is capable. This critic has believed that Lincoln has been crushed by his environment, but he finds to his surprise that Lincoln's longing for an unrestricted life is entirely a dramatized situation. In reality the only restrictions of his life are those which he imagines.

The uneven quality in Susan Glaspell's work is due primarily to the high lights in which she paints emotion. When she succeeds, as in the picture of deep tenderness in *The Glory of the Conquered*, of the resurgent waves of passion in *Fugitive's Return*, or of the ironic contrasts of *Ambrose Holt*, she is a novelist of high rank. In other places these pictures seem unfinished or exaggerated. But of one who could write the stark tragedy of *Bernice* and the incoherent rhapsody, *The Verge*, which filled one of the maddest nights in the Provincetown Playhouse, it was to be expected that her fiction also should rise to the heights and broaden out to the absurd. At its best, however, it has a glow and a depth of feeling for those whom life has hurt which redeems its incoherence.

It is obvious that Mary Austin, Zona Gale, Dorothy Canfield Fisher, and Susan Glaspell are only in a special sense representative of the fiction which emphasizes the note of individual protest against the complexities of modern life. Fiction is full of it, but these four women, all born in the Middle West, have made, each in her own way, a signal contribution. It would be an error, however, to overstress the locality of their scenes, for they range from California to New England, and even across the Atlantic. Of more significance is their defence of the village or the town, for those qualities of independence and individuality which another school of fiction has depicted them as lacking. But to speak of these writers as part of the revolt from the village or even the defence of it, is a critical mistake. They are primarily concerned with the relations of women to the changing fashions of conduct. While their fiction deals, of course, with love and marriage, these are not the ending, but rather the beginnings of the story. The old feminine struggle for the single standard of morality for men is changed to a more modern conflict of personalities, a conflict not only for control, but for the right to retain independence of thought as well as action, without breaking the marriage tie. Divorce is no longer a panacea for marital ills; it occurs at times, but the most interesting situations, like those of *The Deepening Stream,* proceed upon the assumption that marriage is permanent, and that from the point of view of the novelist, the characters are most interesting when they try to work out their problems without the easy solution of separation just around the corner. That this view of marriage should be taken not only by this group but also by Mrs. Wharton, Miss Sedgwick, and Miss Cather, implies that women of intelligence have become aware that the freedom of divorce has not been a liberation, but a disaster to them. That the effort to find the right basis for the relations of men and women should engage the attention of women novelists, is natural, for the problem seems of more moment to them, and in some ways, is of more significance to women than to men. Of the four Mrs. Fisher has seen most deeply into the fundamental relations of married life, especially those strands of common interest which bind husband and wife into the real union to which passion has only been the preliminary.

CHAPTER XXXIII

RETROSPECT AND PROSPECT

We have seen how American fiction, rising out of its early imitative stages, was established by the penetrating if somber analysis of human passions in the work of Charles Brockden Brown, how through the artistry of Irving the short story came into being and the protesting cry of the liberal which has never ceased in our literature, animated them both. With the advent of Cooper, the novel spread upon a broader canvas, the high spirit of adventure carried heroic figures over sea and land, and the frontier became animate with the struggle of the coming and the fading race. Following the inspiration of Irving and Cooper, the romance of history and the frontier flourished from New England, South, and West, rising at times to a high level with Catherine Sedgwick, Bird, Kennedy, and Simms, and descending to the exaggeration and sentimentality to which the idealistic method of treatment so often leads.

Meanwhile the genius of Poe was brooding over fascinating problems of human identity, speculating on the supernatural, finding in the fiction of ratiocination new avenues for the short story to develop, and perfecting its form. Hawthorne, too, was not only widening its sphere in his reincarnation of American history and in the supernatural, but in his novels and short stories was dealing in a larger way with those human beings through whose sin and suffering the beauty of moral triumph was to be established. Almost isolated in his field of the exotic, Melville was creating an imaginative world in which the beasts of the sea rose to their contest with man.

By the middle of the nineteenth century, the American novelists were beginning to turn from the heroic to the material of familiar life, and the transition from an idealistic to a realistic presentation of that life. Characters drawn from humbler walks of life began to take their places as central figures, and the tragedies of economic oppression were portrayed. But the fiction of fantasy went side by side with this transition, and the 'sixties and 'seventies, which welcomed the moral indignation of Rebecca Harding Davis and Elizabeth Stuart Phelps were charmed, also, with the fancy of Aldrich and Harriet Spofford. Romance, too, was seeking for new fields and found them in the moral contrasts of Bret Harte and the humor of Mark Twain.

In the 'seventies and the 'eighties Howells brought the realistic treatment of the average American to its height, James struck the international note and Weir Mitchell brought the scientific observation of human psychology into American fiction. About the same time, the fictional possibilities of locality widely developed, especially in New England and the South, and racial traits were selected with a view to their romantic qualities. The folk-lore of Harris gave us, too, imperishable characters. In the 'eighties and 'nineties the influence of Howells reached its climax, stimulating novelists like Mary Wilkins in New England, Margaret Deland in Pennsylvania, and Hamlin Garland in the West to the revelation of ethical possibilities in fiction. During the same decades Marion Crawford painted the cosmopolitan scene, and the urbane fancy of Hardy, Fuller, and others found material abroad. Allen struck in the 'nineties his distinctive note in the spiritual romance, and Lafcadio Hearn led the romance into the exotic fields of the West Indies and Japan. All these novelists continued to write during the twentieth century. Toward the end of the nineteenth century, the romance of history, which had never ceased to be written, rose to a vogue and continued throughout the new century. The turn of the century witnessed also the best work of the journalists, like Davis, Crane, London and "O. Henry," usually in the short story.

The late 'nineties saw the first fiction of the great figures of the twentieth century. Edith Wharton has remained in her unquestioned supremacy, a realist dealing with varied scenes, at home and abroad, sharing only with Anne Douglas Sedgwick the complete understanding of the international. Ellen Glasgow has progressed steadily in her depiction of characters drawn from the New South. Coming into her own in the second decade, Willa Cather shares with these the distinction of high artistry. All have been realists, dealing with life as they know it, undisturbed by the beating of critical tom-toms, dealing with universal motives and fundamental human qualities.

During the twentieth century romance has continued with Tarkington and others to deal with the American scene or to escape from it into the historic past. There has also been a determined, at times a bitter criticism of American life. A group of liberals, of which Frank Norris was the first and Brand Whitlock the most definitely an artist, scrutinized the economic and social situation and proposed remedies for what they saw. At the same time a more radical group, of which Theodore Dreiser and Sinclair Lewis are the most prominent, have confined themselves to destructive criticism and have beclouded the issue, usually with a certain obsession concerning matters of sex. With a different outlook, Dorothy Canfield, Zona Gale, and others have celebrated the individual struggling against the pressure of uniformity and convention.

It would be a fascinating excursion into speculative criticism to estimate the present tendencies in American fiction, but here the historian warns the critic of danger. Since 1920 there has been much significant work done by those already in the field and this, I hope, has been sufficiently estimated. But while among the new writers there are at least fifty men and women with whose fiction I am conversant, there are very few of whose significance I am assured. Many have written one good novel and then relapsed into the treacherous quicksands of that mediocrity which seems to be the quality peculiarly demanded by the periodicals of today. Others have chosen their material under the mistaken idea that the backwaters of life are important. Still others, often competent in their workmanship, have defeated their efforts by a labored insistence upon minute details of no significance. Still others, animated often by a sincere hatred of injustice, have rendered their work futile by a style in which incoherence is a basic principle.

In 1926 when I wrote a chronicle of American drama, I was able to prophesy with some certainty that Eugene O'Neill, Philip Barry, Maxwell Anderson, Marc Connelly, and George Kaufman would become major figures. I can find no such outstanding group, I regret to say, among the writers of fiction. My continued optimism concerning the future of our fiction is based, therefore, not on our contemporary output, but upon the continuous achievement which I have recorded in this survey. Who that has lived in joy and sorrow with Rip Van Winkle and Ichabod Crane, with Harvey Birch and Leatherstocking, with Ligeia and William Wilson, with Hester Prynne and Donatello, with Huck Finn and Tom Sawyer, with John Oakhurst and "the Luck," with Elsie Venner and Marjorie Daw, with Silas Lapham and Basil March, with Isabel Archer and Emanuel Bayard, with Hugh Wynne and Count Saracinesca, with Ramona and Honoré Grandissime, with Mars' Chan and Colonel Carter, with Uncle Remus and Brer' Rabbit, with Mrs. Lecks and Mrs. Aleshine, with Theron Ware and Peter Stirling, with Dr. Lavendar and Sarah Maitland, with Ben Hur and Madame Butterfly, with Penrod and Alice Adams, with Ellen Olenska and Ethan Frome, with Adrienne Toner and John Fincastle, with Thea Kronborg and "the Lost Lady," can believe that the portrait gallery of American fiction has no frames waiting for the future?

Or who that has felt the salt spray on his cheek while the Pilot carried the "Ariel" through the British shoals; who that has seen the Red Death stalk through the hushed halls of the Prince Prospero; who that has watched the agony of Arthur Dimmesdale as he stood on the Boston scaffold with Hester and Pearl beside him; who that has heard Squire Gaylord make his last plea in defence of his daughter's name; who that has heard with a growing fascination of horror the voice of Peter Quint calling across the unknown to the little boy whom he would destroy; who that has seen Sip Garth hold up her dumb sister's fingers to God that he might answer the question she could not bear to see; who that has watched Gilbert Warde seize the bridle of Queen Eleanor with the unbreakable hold of the Norman race; who that has stood with François and the Marquis at the head of the staircase up which the Jacobin mob was soon to rush; who that has lived with Madame Delphine through the hour of agony when she denied her child in order that that child might marry a man of the race that despised her; who that has seen the look of horror come over David Richie's face as his mother bared her life secret; who that has been in Lawrence Selden's room when Lily Bart puts her future in the fire rather than bring into an hour's scandal the name of the man she loves; who that has risen in spirit with Dorinda Oakley as she gazed with quiet triumph over the barren ground where she had turned life's defeat into the soul's victory; who that has watched Death come for the Archbishop, can believe that the masters of narration and description that made the past live and the present glow with action are to have no great successors? For my part I am confident that just as every great epoch in our national life has evolved a leader to direct its progress, so the multiform, interesting life of today will develop minds and hearts capable of interpreting and revealing it.

When the renascence of the American novel comes it must proceed upon the principles laid down by the foremost living American novelist. Writing upon "The Great American Novel" in 1927, Edith Wharton said truly: "Its scene may be laid in an American small town or in a

European capital. It may deal with the present or the past, with great events or trivial happenings; but in the latter case it will certainly continue to relate them to something greater than themselves."

Freedom to choose a subject anywhere in space or time, provided it is significant, and to treat it by any method through which characters speak the language which the heart understands and remembers—that freedom is the right of the artist in fiction. There is one law, however, he must obey: his conception and his execution must have beauty as their aim, that beauty which moulds facts into truth, which draws hope from terror, and which clothes the weaknesses of humanity with the charity that turns them into power.

BIBLIOGRAPHY

Owing to the vast mass of fugitive writing upon American fiction, this bibliography has been made strictly selective. I have recorded those productions which I have found most helpful. I have also included some which I believe to be misleading in their basic critical theory, but which, on account of the wide discussion they have caused, are to be expected in a bibliography. I have also included a few because they represent a fresh approach to the subject even if the approach does not seem to me the best one.

In the General Bibliography, I have included only those histories of American Literature which treat extensively or significantly of fiction. I have not repeated these references in the Chapter Bibliographies, presuming that the student will realize that in general the most helpful criticisms are to be found in books and not in periodical literature.

For the same reason, I have not, except in special instances, repeated references in each chapter to the extensive bibliographies of the *Cambridge History of American Literature*. These are extremely useful where they have not been superseded by the more complete bibliographies furnished in the critical monographs, which in several instances have taken their places as the standard biographies of American novelists.

In the Chapter Bibliographies, I have followed the usual order, placing, under each author, Bibliographies, Works, Biographies and Criticism. When the number of the items justified it, these headings have been indicated. In certain cases, it seemed best to separate the Biographies from the Criticism, in others they are grouped together. In every instance, the object of the Bibliography has been to furnish help to the student and not to sacrifice usefulness to mere uniformity.

GENERAL BIBLIOGRAPHY

THE AMERICAN NOVEL

Bibliographies

Baker, E. A., *A Guide to the Best Fiction in English* (London, 1913; New and enlarged edition, New York, 1932).

Baker, E. A., *A Guide to the Best Historical Fiction* (London and New York, 1914).

See Bibliographies in *Cambridge History of American Literature,* especially on "Early Fiction," Vol. I, pp. 525-546; "Irving," Vol. I, pp. 510-517; "Poe," Vol. II, pp. 452-468; "Hawthorne," Vol. II, pp. 415-424; "The Later Novel," Vol. IV, pp. 656-671, including Howells; "James," Vol. IV, pp. 671-675.

Firkins, Ina Ten Eyck, *Index to Short Stories* (New York, 1915 and 1923; Second Supplement, 1936).

Griswold, W. M., *A Descriptive List of Novels and Tales Dealing with American Country Life* (Cambridge, Massachusetts, 1890).

Griswold, W. M., *A Descriptive List of Novels and Tales Dealing with American City Life* (Cambridge, Massachusetts, 1891).

Griswold, W. M., *A Descriptive List of International Novels* (Cambridge, Massachusetts, 1891). [Contains other than American.]

Griswold, W. M., *A Descriptive List of Novels Dealing with the History of North America* (Cambridge, Massachusetts, 1895).

Johnson, J. G., *Southern Fiction Prior to 1860* (University of Virginia, 1909).

Manly, J. M. and Rickert, Edith, *Contemporary American Literature* (New York, 1922; Revised, 1929).

Nield, Jonathan, *A Guide to the Best Historical Novels and Tales*, Fifth edition (London, 1929).

Rusk, Ralph L., *Literature of the Middle Western Frontier*, 2 vols. (New York, 1925). [Complete bibliographies in Vol. 2.]

Wegelin, Oscar, *Early American Fiction* (Stamford, 1902; Revised, New York, 1913; 1929).

History and Criticism of American Fiction

See the *Dictionary of American Biography* for brief biographies.

Baskervill, William M., *Southern Writers: Biographical and Critical Studies* (Nashville, 1897).

726

Beach, Joseph Warren, *The Outlook for American Prose* (Chicago, 1926).
Beach, Joseph Warren, *The Twentieth Century Novel* (New York, 1932).
Blankenship, Russell, *American Literature* (New York, 1931).
Boynton, Percy H., *The Rediscovery of the Frontier* (Chicago, 1931).
Boynton, Percy H., *Some Contemporary Americans* (Chicago, 1925).
Boynton, Percy H., *More Contemporary Americans* (Chicago, 1927).
Canby, Henry S., *Classic Americans. A Study of Eminent American Writers From Irving to Whitman* (New York, 1931).
Cooper, Frederic Taber, *Some American Story Tellers* (New York, 1911).
Dondore, Dorothy M., *The Prairie and the Making of Middle America* (Cedar Rapids, Iowa, 1926).
Du Breuil, Alice J., *The Novel of Democracy in America* (Baltimore, 1923).
Dunlap, George A., *The City in the American Novel* (Philadelphia, 1934). [Privately printed.]
Erskine, John, *Leading American Novelists* (New York, 1910).
Flory, Claude R., *Economic Criticism in American Fiction* (Philadelphia, 1935). [Privately printed.]
Hartwick, Harry, *The Foreground of American Fiction* (New York, 1934).
Hatcher, Harlan, *Creating the Modern American Novel* (New York, 1935).
Hazard, Lucy Lockwood, *The Frontier in American Literature* (New York, 1927).
Josephson, Matthew, *The Portrait of the Artist as American* (New York, 1930).
Linn, James W. and Taylor, Houghton W., *A Foreword to Fiction* (New York, 1935).
Loshe, Lillie D., *The Early American Novel* (New York, 1907; 1930).
Lubbock, Percy, *The Craft of Fiction* (London, 1921).
Macy, John, *American Writers on American Literature* (New York, 1931).
Marble, Annie Russell, *A Study of the Modern Novel, British and American* (New York, 1928).
Michaud, Regis, *The American Novel Today* (Boston, 1928).
Mims, Edwin, "History of Southern Fiction," in Vol. VIII of *The South in the Building of the Nation*, 13 vols. (Richmond, 1909–1913).
Northrup, C. S., "The Novelists," in *A Manual of American Literature*, edited by Theodore Stanton (New York, 1909).
Novel of Tomorrow and the Scope of Fiction, by Twelve American Novelists (Indianapolis, 1922).
Overton, Grant, *An Hour of the American Novel* (Philadelphia, 1929).
Parrington, Vernon L., *Main Currents in American Thought* (New York, 1926–1930). Vol. II, *The Romantic Revolution in America* (1927). Vol. III, *The Beginnings of Critical Realism* (1930).
Pattee, Fred Lewis, *The Development of the American Short Story* (New York, 1923).
Pattee, Fred Lewis, *A History of American Literature Since 1870* (New York, 1915).

Pattee, Fred Lewis, *The New American Literature* (New York, 1930).
Pattee, Fred Lewis, *The First Century of American Literature, 1770-1870* (New York, 1935).
Perry, Bliss, *The American Spirit in Literature* (New York, 1919).
Rusk, Ralph L., *Literature of the Middle Western Frontier*, 2 vols. (New York, 1925).
Sherman, Stuart P., *Americans* (New York, 1922).
Sherman, Stuart P., *The Genius of America* (New York, 1923).
Sherman, Stuart P., *On Contemporary Literature* (New York, 1917).
Sherman, Stuart P., *Points of View* (New York, 1925).
Sherman, Stuart P., *Critical Woodcuts* (New York, 1926).
Sherman, Stuart P., *The Main Stream* (New York, 1927).
Sherman, Stuart P., *Shaping Men and Women* (New York, 1928).
Singer, Godfrey, *The Epistolary Novel* (Philadelphia, 1933).
Van Doren, Carl, "Fiction I, Brown, Cooper," and "Fiction II, Contemporaries of Cooper," *Cambridge History of American Literature* (New York, 1917), Vol. I, pp. 284–325. Valuable bibliographies, pp. 525–546.
Van Doren, Carl, *The American Novel* (New York, 1921).
Van Doren, Carl, *Contemporary American Novelists, 1900–1920* (New York, 1922).
Vincent, Leon H., *American Literary Masters* (Boston, 1906).
Vollmer, Clement, *The American Novel in Germany, 1871–1913* (Philadelphia, 1918).

THE AMERICAN SHORT STORY

Bibliographies, History, and Criticism

Firkins, Ina T., *Index to Short Stories* (New York, 1915 and 1923; Second Supplement, New York, 1936).
Haningan, F. J., *Standard Index of Short Stories 1900–1914* (Boston, 1918).
Canby, Henry S., *The Short Story in English* (New York, 1909). [For the short story in general.]
Canby, Henry S. and Dashiell, Alfred, *A Study of the Short Story*, Revised Edition (New York, 1935).
Hart, Walter Morris, *Hawthorne and the Short Story* (Berkeley, California, 1900).
Harte, Francis Bret, "The Rise of the Short Story," *Cornhill Magazine*, New Series, VII (July, 1899), 1–8.
Matthews, Brander, *The Philosophy of the Short Story* (New York, 1901).
Pattee, F. L., *The Development of the American Short Story* (New York, 1923). [General Bibliography, 377–378. Useful chapter bibliographies.]

Pattee, F. L., "The Short Story," *Cambridge History of American Literature,* Vol. II, Ch. VI, pp. 367–395; Bibliography, pp. 616–631.
Smith, C. Alphonso, *The American Short Story* (Boston, 1912).
Williams, Blanche C., *Our Short Story Writers* (New York, 1918).

Collections

Stories by American Authors, 10 vols. (New York, 1884).
Baldwin, Charles S., *American Short Stories* (New York, 1904). [In Wampum Series of American Literature.]
Becker, May Lamberton, *Golden Tales of New England* (New York, 1931).
Becker, May Lamberton, *Golden Tales of Our America, Stories of Our Background and Tradition* (New York, 1929).
Becker, May Lamberton, *Golden Tales of the Old South* (New York, 1930).
Burrell, Angus and Cerf, Bennett A., *Bedside Book of Famous American Stories* (New York, 1936).
Dashiell, Alfred, *Editor's Choice* (New York, 1934).
Gerould, G. H., *Contemporary Types of the Short Story* (New York, 1927). [American and English.]
Hibbard, Addison, *Stories of the South, Old and New* (Chapel Hill, North Carolina, 1931).
Howells, William Dean, *The Great Modern American Stories* (New York, 1920).
Jessup, Alexander, *Representative American Short Stories* (New York, 1923). [Contains a valuable list of American short stories, arranged by authors and also by years.]
Matthews, Brander, *The Short Story, Specimens Illustrating Its Development* (New York, 1907).
Meine, Franklin J., *Tall Tales of the Southwest; An Anthology of Southern and Southwestern Humorists, 1830–1860* (New York, 1930).
O'Brien, Edward J., *The Best Short Stories of 1915 and the Year Book of the Short Story* (Boston, 1915). [Issued annually since.]
Pattee, F. L., *Century Readings in the American Short Story* (New York, 1927).
Sherman, Stuart P., *A Book of Short Stories* (New York, 1914).
Trent, W. P. and Henneman, J. B., *Best American Tales* (New York, 1907).
Williams, Blanche Colton, *Best American Stories, 1919–1924* (New York, 1926). [Selections from O. Henry Memorial Prize Winning Stories.]
Williams, Blanche Colton, *Great American Short Stories* (New York, 1933). [Selections from O. Henry Memorial Prize Winning Stories, 1919–1932.]

CHAPTER I

THE FOUNDATIONS OF AMERICAN FICTION

JEREMY BELKNAP

Belknap, Jane Marcou, *The Life of Jeremy Belknap, D.D., with Selections from His Writings* (New York, 1847).

HUGH HENRY BRACKENRIDGE

Brackenridge, Henry Marie, *A Memoir of H. H. Brackenridge*, in *Modern Chivalry* (Philadelphia, 1846).

Brown, David Paul, "A Memoir of H. H. Brackenridge," *The Forum; or, Forty Years Full Practice at the Philadelphia Bar*, 2 vols. (Philadelphia, 1856), Vol. I, pp. 396–417.

Newlin, Claude M., *The Life and Writings of Hugh Henry Brackenridge* (Princeton, 1932). [Good Bibliography.]

WILLIAM HILL BROWN

Brayley, A. W., "The Real Author of *The Power of Sympathy*," *The Bostonian*, I (1894–1895), 224.

Ellis, Milton, "The Author of the First American Novel," *American Literature*, IV (1932–1933), 359–368.

HANNAH WEBSTER FOSTER

Dall, Mrs. C. H., *The Romance of the Association; or, One Last Glimpse of Charlotte Temple and Eliza Wharton* (Cambridge, Massachusetts, 1875).

Shurter, R. L., "Mrs. Hannah Webster Foster and the Early American Novel," *American Literature*, IV (1932–1933), 306–308.

BENJAMIN FRANKLIN

McMaster, John Bach, *Benjamin Franklin as a Man of Letters* (Boston, 1887). [American Men of Letters.]

FRANCIS HOPKINSON

Hastings, George E., *The Life and Works of Francis Hopkinson* (Chicago, 1926).

Gilbert Imlay

Emerson, Oliver F., "Notes on Gilbert Imlay—Early American Writer," *P. M. L. A.*, XXXIX (1924), 406–439.

Hall, James, "Imlay's Account of Kentucky," in *Sketches of History, Life, and Manners, in the West* (Philadelphia, 1835), Vol. II, pp. 97–106. Reprinted in *The Romance of Western History* (Cincinnati, 1857), pp. 257–265.

Rusk, R. L., "Adventures of Gilbert Imlay," *Indiana University Studies*, Vol. X, No. 57 (23 pp.)

Wyatt, Edith Franklin, "The First American Novel," *Atlantic Monthly*, CXLIV (1929), 466–475.

Charlotte R. Lennox

Small, M. R., *Charlotte Ramsay Lennox* (New Haven, 1935).

Sarah Wentworth Morton

Littlefield, Walter (ed.), Introduction to *Power of Sympathy; or the Triumph of Nature Founded in Truth* (Boston, 1894). Also in *The Bostonian*, I (1894).

Pendleton, Emily and Ellis, Milton, *Philenia, the Life and Works of Sarah Wentworth Morton* (Orono, Maine, 1931). *University of Maine Studies*, Second Series, No. 20.

Susanna Haswell Rowson

Cobbett, William, *A Kick For a Bite; or Review upon Review: with a Critical Essay on the Works of Mrs. S. Rowson; in a Letter to the Editor, or Editors of the American Monthly Review, by Peter Porcupine* (Philadelphia, 1795).

Halsey, F. W. (ed.), *Charlotte Temple. A Tale of Truth*, Latest Edition with introduction (pp. xix–cix) and a Bibliography of Editions of *Charlotte Temple* (New York, 1905).

Knapp, S. L. (ed.), *Charlotte's Daughter; or, The Three Orphans. A Sequel to Charlotte Temple. To which is prefixed, a Memoir of the Author* (Boston, 1828.)

Nason, Elias M. A., *A Memoir of Mrs. Susanna Rowson, with Elegant and Illustrative Extracts from her Writings in Prose and Poetry* (Albany, 1870).

Vail, R. W. G., *Susanna Haswell Rowson, the Author of Charlotte Temple, a Bibliographical Study* (Worcester, Massachusetts, 1933).

ROYALL TYLER

Tupper, Frederick, "Royall Tyler, Man of Law and Man of Letters," *Proceedings Vermont Historical Society* (1928), 65–101.
Tupper, Frederick and Brown, Helen Tyler (eds.), *Grandmother Tyler's Book; the Recollections of Mary Palmer Tyler (Mrs. Royall Tyler) 1775–1866* (New York, 1925).

CHAPTER II

CHARLES BROCKDEN BROWN
AND THE ESTABLISHMENT OF ROMANCE

Works

The Novels of Charles Brockden Brown, 6 vols. (Boston, 1827).
The Works of Charles Brockden Brown, 6 vols. (Philadelphia, 1827).
The Works of Charles Brockden Brown, 6 vols. (Philadelphia, 1887).
Alcuin, a Dialogue, Parts 1 and 2 (New York, March, 1798). Partly reprinted in *The Weekly Magazine,* March 17–April 7, 1798 as *The Rights of Women, a Dialogue.* In the foreword of E. H. Smith, a continuation is promised, and this, introduced by some sentences identical with Part I, is given in Dunlap's *Life of Brown,* Vol. I, pp. 71–105.
Memoirs of Carwin the Biloquist, Literary Magazine and American Register, Vol. 1 (Nov., 1803), pp. 100–104, 181–184, 255–259, 332–335, 412–416; Vol. II, pp. 1–7, 89–93, 248–252 (July, 1804); Vol. III, pp. 110–114, 210–214 (Feb. and March, 1905).
Wieland, or The Transformation, together with Memoirs of Carwin the Biloquist, edited with critical introduction by F. L. Pattee (New York, 1926).
Edgar Huntly; or, Memoirs of a Sleepwalker, ed. with an introduction by David Lee Clark (New York, 1928). [The Modern Readers Series.]
Alcuin; a Dialogue: a typefacsimile reprint of the first edition, introduction by L. E. Kimball (New Haven, 1935).

Biographies

Clark, Dana L., *Charles Brockden Brown, a Critical Biography.* N.p; n.d. [1923].
Dunlap, William, *The Life of Charles Brockden Brown: Together with selections from the rarest of his printed works, from his original letters, and from his manuscripts before unpublished,* 2 vols. (Philadelphia, 1815). Contains the second installment of *Alcuin;* the "unfinished romance"; Sketches of a History of Carsol; Sketches of the History of the Carrils and Ormes; Adini; Thessalonica; Memoirs of Carwin the Biloquist; The Scribbler; Memoirs of Stephen Calvert.

Dunlap, William, *Memoirs of Charles Brockden Brown, the American Novelist* (London, 1822).

D[unlap], W[illiam], *Charles Brockden Brown*. In *National Portrait Gallery of Distinguished Americans*, conducted by J. B. Longacre and James Herring, Vol. III (1836).

The Diary of William Dunlap, 3 vols. (New York, 1930).

Prescott, W. H., *Charles Brockden Brown, the American Novelist*, in Sparks' *American Biography* (1834). Reprinted in Prescott's *Biographical and Critical Miscellanies* (1845, 1875).

Vilas, M. S., *Charles Brockden Brown. A Study of Early American Fiction* (Burlington, Vermont, 1904).

Criticism

Anonymous, "Charles Brockden Brown," *The American Review*, I (March, 1848), 260–274.

Blake, W. B., "Brockden Brown and the Novel," *Sewanee Review*, XVIII (1910), 430–443.

Garnett, Richard, "The Minor Writings of Charles Brockden Brown," *Cornhill Magazine*, n.s. XIII (1902), 494–506.

Higginson, T. W., "Charles Brockden Brown," *Carlyle's Laugh and Other Surprises* (Boston, 1909).

Sickels, Eleanor, "Shelley and Charles Brockden Brown," *PMLA*, XLV (1930), 1116–1128.

Solve, M. T., "Shelley and the Novels of Brown," *Fred Newton Scott Anniversary Papers* (Chicago, 1929), pp. 141–156.

Tuckerman, Henry T., "Charles Brockden Brown, the Supernaturalist," *Essays Biographical and Critical; or, Studies of Character* (Boston, 1857), pp. 369–378.

Van Doren, Carl, "Early American Realism," *Nation*, Nov. 12, 1914.

—— "Minor Tales of Brockden Brown, 1798–1800," *Nation*, Jan. 14, 1915.

—— "Fiction I: Brown, Cooper," *Cambridge History of American Literature*, Vol. I, pp. 284–306. Bibliography, Vol. I, pp. 527–529.

Wilkens, F. H., "Early Influence of German Literature in America," *Americana Germanica*, III (1900–1901), 110–136.

CHAPTER III

WASHINGTON IRVING AND OTHER PIONEERS

TIMOTHY FLINT

Kirkpatrick, J. E., *Timothy Flint, Pioneer, Missionary, Author, Editor* (Cleveland, Ohio, 1911).

Flint, Timothy, *Recollections of the Last Ten Years* (Boston, 1826).
—— *Recollections of the Last Ten Years,* edited with an Introduction by
    C. Hartley Grattan (New York, 1932). [Americana Deserta.]

WASHINGTON IRVING

Bibliographies

Langfeld, William R. and Blackburn, Philip C., *Washington Irving: A
    Bibliography* (New York, 1933).
Williams, Stanley T. and Edge, M. E., *A Bibliography of the Writings of
    Washington Irving* (New York, 1936).

Works

The Works of Washington Irving, Author's uniform revised edition, 21 vols.
    (New York, 1860–1861).
The Works of Washington Irving, Spuyten Duyvil edition, 12 vols. (New
    York, 1881).
The Works of Washington Irving, New Knickerbocker edition, 40 vols.
    (New York, 1896).
[For other Editions, see Williams' *Bibliography.*]

Biographies

Boynton, H. W., *Washington Irving* (Boston, 1901).
Bryant, William Cullen, *A Discourse on the Life, Character, and Genius
    of Washington Irving* (New York, 1860).
The Diary of William Dunlap, 3 vols. (New York, 1930).
Hellman, George S., *Washington Irving, Esquire, Ambassador at large from
    the New World to the Old* (New York, 1925).
Hellman, George S. (ed.), *Letters of Irving to Henry Brevoort,* 2 vols.
    (New York, 1915; 1 vol., 1918).
Hill, D. J., *Washington Irving* (New York, 1879).
Irving, Pierre M., *The Life and Letters of Washington Irving,* 4 vols. (New
    York, 1862–1864).
Laun, Adolph, *Washington Irwing* [sic]—*Ein Lebens und Charakterbild,* 2
    vols. (Berlin, 1870).
Trent, W. P. (ed.), and Hellman, G. S. (ed.), *The Journals of Washington
    Irving from July, 1815 to July, 1842,* 3 vols. (Boston, 1919).
Warner, Charles Dudley, *Washington Irving* (Boston, 1881). [American
    Men of Letters.]
Williams, Stanley T., *The Journal of Washington Irving, 1823–1824*
    (Cambridge, Massachusetts, 1931).
Williams, Stanley T., *Washington Irving and the Storrows. Letters from Eng-
    land and the Continent, 1821–1828* (Harvard University Press, 1933).

Williams, Stanley T., *The Life of Washington Irving*, 2 vols. (New York, 1935).

Criticism

Curtis, George W., *Washington Irving, a Sketch* (New York, 1891). Reprinted in *Literary and Social Essays* (New York, 1895).
Ferguson, John deLancey, *American Literature in Spain* (New York, 1916).
Goggio, E., "Washington Irving and Italy," *Romanic Review*, XXI (January–March, 1930), 26–33.
Howells, W. D., *My Literary Passions* (New York, 1895).
Morris, G. D., *Washington Irving's Fiction in the Light of French Criticism* (Bloomington, Indiana, 1916). [Indiana University Studies, No. 30.]
Penney, Clara L. (ed.), *Washington Irving Diary, Spain 1828–1829* (Hispanic Society, 1926), Vol. 43.
Pochmann, Henry A., "Irving's German Sources in *The Sketch Book*," *Studies in Philology*, XXVII (1930), 477–507.
Pochmann, Henry A., "Irving's German Tour and Its Influence on His Tales," *Publications Modern Language Association*, XLV (December, 1930), 1150–1187.
Russell, Jason Almus, "Irving: Recorder of Indian Life," *Journal of American History*, XXV (1932), 185–195.
Sprenger, Robert, *Über die Quelle von Washington Irvings Rip Van Winkle* (Northeim, 1901).
Thackeray, W. M., "Nil Nisi Bonum," in *Roundabout Papers*, 1863.
Thompson, John B., "The Genesis of the Rip Van Winkle Legend," *Harper's Magazine*, LXVII (September, 1883), 617–622.
Williams, Stanley T., "The First Version of the Writings of Washington Irving in Spanish," *Modern Philology*, XXVIII (November, 1930), 185–201.
Williams, Stanley T., "Washington Irving and Fernán Caballero," *JEGP*, XXIX (1930), 352–366.

JOHN NEAL

Neal, John, *Wandering Recollections of a Somewhat Busy Life. An Autobiography* (Boston, 1869).

JAMES KIRKE PAULDING

Bibliography

Wegelin, Oscar, *A Bibliography of the Separate Publications of James Kirke Paulding, Novelist, Humorist, Statesman, 1779–1860*. Reprinted from *Papers of the Bibliographical Society of America*, XII, Vol. 2 (January–April, 1918).

Works

Collected Works, 15 vols. (New York, 1834–1839).

Biographies

Herold, Amos L., *James Kirke Paulding, Versatile American* (New York, 1926). Bibliography, pp. 148–160.
Paulding, W. I., *The Literary Life of James K. Paulding* (New York, 1867).

CHAPTER IV

JAMES FENIMORE COOPER

Bibliography

Spiller, Robert E. and Blackburn, Philip C., *A Descriptive Bibliography of the Writings of James Fenimore Cooper* (New York, 1934).
Cambridge History of American Literature, Vol. I, pp. 530–534.

Works

Cooper's Novels, New edition (New York, 1852–1854), 65 vols. in 33.
Cooper's Novels, Illustrated by F. O. C. Darley (New York, 1859–1861), 32 vols.
J. Fenimore Cooper's Works, Household edition, with introductions by Susan Fenimore Cooper (Boston, 1876, 1881–1884), 32 vols.
The Works of James Fenimore Cooper, Mohawk edition (New York, 1895–1896, 1900), 33 vols.
The American Democrat (Cooperstown, New York, 1838); Reprinted, with an introduction by H. L. Mencken (New York, 1931).
Gleanings in Europe, edited by Robert E. Spiller. Vol. I, *France;* Vol. II, *England* (New York, 1928, 1930).
A History of Cooperstown. Including "The Chronicles of Cooperstown," by James Fenimore Cooper, "The History of Cooperstown, 1839–1886" by Samuel M. Shaw, "The History of Cooperstown, 1886–1929" by Walter R. Littell (Cooperstown, New York, 1929).
Notions of the Americans Picked up by a Travelling Bachelor, 2 vols. (Philadelphia, 1828).
The Lake Gun, with an introduction by Robert E. Spiller (New York, 1932).
New York: Being an introduction to an unpublished manuscript, by the author, entitled *The Towers of Manhattan.* Limited edition, with an introduction by Dixon Ryan Fox (New York, 1930).
Correspondence of James Fenimore Cooper, edited by his grandson, J. F. Cooper, 2 vols. (New Haven, Connecticut, 1922).

Biographies

Boynton, Henry W., *James Fenimore Cooper* (New York, 1931).
Bryant, W. C., *A Discourse on the Life and Genius of James Fenimore Cooper* (New York, 1852).
Clymer, W. B. S., *James Fenimore Cooper* (Boston, 1900). [Beacon Biographies.]
Lounsbury, Thomas R., *James Fenimore Cooper* (Boston, 1883). [American Men of Letters.]
Phillips, Mary E., *James Fenimore Cooper* (New York, 1913).
Spiller, Robert E., *Fenimore Cooper: Critic of His Times* (New York, 1931).

Criticism

Adkins, Nelson F., "James Fenimore Cooper and the Bread and Cheese Club," *Modern Language Notes*, XLVII (1932), 71–79.
Balzac, Honoré de, "Fenimore Cooper et Walter Scott," *La Revue Parisienne*, July 25, 1840.
Barba, P. A., *Cooper in Germany*, Indiana Univ. Studies, Vol. 21 (Bloomington, 1914). Also, *Ger. Amer. Annals*, 1914.
Bosset, Georgette, *Fenimore Cooper et le roman d'aventure en France vers 1830* (Paris, 1928).
Brownell, W. C., "James Fenimore Cooper," *Scribner's*, XXXIX (1906), 455–468. Also in *American Prose Masters* (New York, 1909).
Goggio, Emilio, "Cooper's *Bravo* in Italy," *Romanic Review*, XX (1929), 222–230.
Matthews, James Brander, "Fenimore Cooper," *Atlantic Monthly*, C (1907), 329–341. Reprinted in *Gateways to Literature* (New York, 1912).
McDowell, Tremaine, "James Fenimore Cooper as Self-Critic," *Studies in Philology*, XXVII (1930), 509–516.
McDowell, Tremaine, "The Identity of Harvey Birch," *American Literature*, II (1930), 111–120.
Morris, G. D., *Fenimore Cooper et Edgar Poe d'après la critique française du dix-neuvième siècle* (Paris, 1912).
Oakley, Kate Russell, "James Fenimore Cooper and *Oak Openings*," *Mich. Hist. Mag.*, XVI (1932), 309–329.
Paine, G., "Cooper and *The North American Review*," *Studies in Philology*, XXVIII (1931), 267–277.
Palfrey, Thomas R., "Cooper and Balzac: *The Headsman*," *Modern Philology*, XXIX (1932), 257–341.
Spiller, Robert E., "Fenimore Cooper and Lafayette. Friends of Polish Freedom, 1830–1832," *American Literature*, VII (March, 1935), 56–75.
Winterich, J. T., "Romantic Stories of Books, Second Series, XXII, *The Spy*," *Publishers' Weekly*, CXIX (1931), 2882–2886.

CHAPTER V

EDGAR ALLAN POE AND THE ESTABLISHMENT OF THE SHORT STORY

Edgar Allan Poe

Bibliography

Campbell, Killis, in *Cambridge History of American Literature*, Vol. II, pp. 452–468.

Campbell, Killis, in *Short Stories of Edgar Allan Poe* (New York, 1927).

Harrison, James A., Bibliography in Virginia Edition of Poe, Vol. 16, pp. 355–379.

Heartman, Charles F. and Rede, Kenneth, *A Census of First Editions and Source Materials by Edgar Allan Poe in American Collections*, 2 vols. (Metuchen, New Jersey, 1932).

Robertson, John W., *A Bibliography of the Writings of Edgar A. Poe*, 2 vols. (San Francisco, 1934).

Stedman, E. C. and Woodberry, G. E., Bibliography in Vol. 10 of *Works*.

Works—Collected Editions

The Works of the Late Edgar Allan Poe. With a Memoir by Rufus Wilmot Griswold and Notices of his Life and Genius by N. P. Willis and J. R. Lowell, 4 vols. (New York, 1850–1856; 1858; 1861; etc.).

The Works of Edgar Allan Poe, edited by John H. Ingram, 4 vols. (Edinburgh, 1874–1875; 1880, etc.).

The Works of Edgar Allan Poe, edited by R. H. Stoddard, 6 vols. (New York, 1884; 1894).

The Works of Edgar Allan Poe, edited by E. C. Stedman and G. E. Woodberry, 10 vols. (Chicago, 1894–1895; New York, 1914).

The Complete Works of Edgar Allan Poe, edited by C. F. Richardson, 10 vols. (New York, 1902).

The Complete Works of Edgar Allan Poe, with Biography and Introduction by Nathan Haskell Dole, 10 vols. (London and New York, 1908).

The Complete Works of Edgar Allan Poe, Virginia Edition, edited by James A. Harrison, 17 vols. (New York, 1902).

—— Monticello Edition, Large Paper (New York, 1902).

Works—Separate Editions

Tales of the Grotesque and Arabesque, 2 vols. (Philadelphia, 1840).

The Prose Romances of Edgar A. Poe, Uniform Serial Edition. Each Num-

ber Complete in Itself. No. 1 (Philadelphia 1843). [Contains "The Murders in the Rue Morgue" and "The Man That Was Used Up." The only number issued.]

Tales (New York, 1845; London, 1845).

Poe's Short Stories, edited with Introduction by Killis Campbell (New York, 1927). Contains valuable list of all Poe's short stories, with dates of first magazine publication.

Tales of Edgar Allan Poe, edited by James S. Wilson (New York, 1927).

Edgar Allan Poe: Representative Selections, with Introduction, Bibliography and Notes, edited by Margaret Alterton and Hardin Craig (New York, 1935).

Doings of Gotham, Collected by Jacob E. Spanneth, with Introduction and comments by T. O. Mabbott (Pottsville, Pennsylvania, 1929).

The Gold Bug, Foreword by Hervey Allen, Notes on the text by Thomas Ollive Mabbott (Garden City, New York, 1929).

Edgar Allan Poe and the Philadelphia Saturday Courier, Facsimile reproductions of the First Texts of Poe's Earliest Tales (Charlottesville, 1933).

Last Letters of Edgar Allan Poe to Sarah Helen Whitman, edited by J. A. Harrison (New York, 1909).

Edgar Allan Poe Letters Till Now Unpublished in the Valentine Museum, Richmond, Virginia, edited by Mary Newton Stanard (Philadelphia, 1925).

Biographies

Allen, Hervey, *Israfel. The Life and Times of Edgar Allan Poe,* 2 vols. (New York, 1927).

Gill, William F., *The Life of Edgar Allan Poe* (London, 1877; 1878).

Graham, George R., "The Late Edgar Allan Poe," *Graham's Magazine,* March, 1850.

Griswold, R. W., Memoir in Poe's *Works* (New York, 1850).

Harrison, J. A., *Life and Letters of Edgar Allan Poe,* 2 vols. (New York, 1903). Revision of Vols. 1 and 17 in Virginia Edition.

Ingram, John H., *Edgar Allan Poe, His Life, Letters and Opinions,* 2 vols. (London, 1880; 1 vol., 1884).

Krutch, Joseph Wood, *Edgar Allan Poe, a Study in Genius* (New York, 1926).

Lauvrière, Emile, *Edgar Poe. Sa vie et son œuvre* (Paris, 1904).

Lauvrière, Emile, *The Strange Life and the Strange Loves of Edgar Allan Poe* (Philadelphia, 1935).

Lowell, James Russell, "Edgar Allan Poe," *Graham's Magazine,* February, 1845.

Nichols, Mary Gove, "Reminiscences of Edgar Allan Poe," *Sixpenny Magazine,* February 1, 1863. Privately printed, with introductory letter by T. O. Mabbott (New York, 1931).

Phillips, Mary E., *Edgar Allan Poe, the Man*, 2 vols. (Philadelphia, 1926).
Pope-Hennessy, Una, *Edgar Allan Poe* (New York, 1934).
Robertson, J. W., *Edgar Allan Poe, A Psychopathic Study* (New York, 1923).
Smith, C. A., *Edgar Allan Poe* (Indianapolis, 1921).
Stanard, Mary Newton, *The Dreamer, The Life Story of Poe* (Philadelphia, 1925).
Stedman, E. C., *Edgar Allan Poe* (Boston, 1881). Revised in *Poets of America* (Boston, 1898).
Ticknor, Caroline, *Poe's Helen* (New York, 1916).
Willis, Nathaniel Parker, "Death of Edgar A. Poe," *Home Journal*, October, 1849.
Woodberry, George E., *Edgar Allan Poe* (Boston, 1885). [American Men of Letters.]
Woodberry, George E., *The Life of Edgar Allan Poe, Personal and Literary, with his Chief Correspondence with Men of Letters*, 2 vols. (Boston, 1909).

Criticism

Baudelaire, C., *Edgar Poe, sa vie et ses œuvres* in *Histoires Extraordinaires par Edgar Poe* (Paris, 1856).
Betz, L. P., "Edgar Poe in der Französischen Litteratur," in *Studien zur vergleichenden Litteraturgeschichte der neuren Zeit* (Frankfurt, 1902).
Brownell, W. C., "Poe," in *American Prose Masters* (New York, 1909).
Cambiaire, Celestin P., *The Influence of Edgar Allan Poe in France* (New York, 1927).
Campbell, Killis, "Poe," in *Cambridge History of American Literature*, Vol. II, 1918, pp. 55–69.
Campbell, Killis, *The Mind of Poe, and Other Studies* (Cambridge, Massachusetts, 1932).
Clark, David Lee, "The Sources of Poe's *The Pit and the Pendulum*," *Modern Language Notes*, XXIV (1929), 349–356.
Cobb, Palmer, *The Influence of E. T. A. Hoffmann on the Tales of Edgar Allan Poe* (Chapel Hill, North Carolina, 1908).
Ferguson, J. D., *American Literature in Spain* (New York, 1916), pp. 55–86, 229–236.
Jackson, David K., *Poe and the Southern Literary Messenger* (Richmond, 1934).
Lemonnier, L., "Edgar Poe et le Roman scientifique français," *La Grande Rev.*, XXXIV (1930), 214–223.
Lemonnier, L., "L'Influence d'Edgar Poe sur quelques conteurs realistes," *Rev. de Litt. Comp.*, XI (1931), 451–465.
Lemonnier, L., *Edgar Poe et la critique française de 1845 à 1875* (Paris, 1928).

Mabbott, Thomas Ollive, "Poe and The Philadelphia *Irish Citizen*," *Am. Irish Hist. Soc. Annual*, XXIX (1931), 121–131.

Morris, G. D., *Fenimore Cooper et Edgar Poe d'après la critique française du dix-neuvième siècle* (Paris, 1912).

Ransome, Arthur, *Edgar Allan Poe, A Critical Study* (New York, 1910).

Studies in Philology, Poe Number, Vol. 20 (Chapel Hill, 1923).

Wilt, Napier, "Poe's Attitude Toward His Tales," *Modern Philology*, XXV (1927), 101–105.

JAMES HALL

Works, 4 vols. (Philadelphia, 1853–1856).

Biography and Criticism

James, Davis L., "Judge James Hall, a Literary Pioneer in the Middle West," *Ohio Archeological and Hist. Society Pub.*, XVIII (1909), 468–483.

Eckert, Robert P., Jr., "The Path of the Pioneer," *The Colophon*, New Series, I (Winter, 1936), 404–421. [Check List of Hall's Writings, 420–421.]

AUGUSTUS BALDWIN LONGSTREET

Wade, J. D., *Augustus Baldwin Longstreet, a Study of the Development of Culture in the South* (New York, 1924).

FITZ-JAMES O'BRIEN

The Poems and Stories of Fitz-James O'Brien, collected and edited with a sketch of the author, by William Winter (Boston, 1881).

The Collected Stories of Fitz-James O'Brien, edited by Edward J. O'Brien (New York, 1925).

The Diamond Lens and Other Stories, with an Introduction by G. Seldes (New York, 1932).

CHAPTER VI

THE DEVELOPMENT OF IDEALISTIC ROMANCE

ROBERT MONTGOMERY BIRD

Bibliography

See Foust below under Biography.

Works

Nick of the Woods: or The Jibbenainosay: A Tale of Kentucky (New York, 1928). [An American Bookshelf.]

Biography

Foust, Clement E., *The Life and Dramatic Works of Robert Montgomery Bird* (New York, 1919). [Bibliography, pp. 161–167.]

WILLIAM ALEXANDER CARUTHERS

Holliday, C., "William Alexander Caruthers," in *Library of Southern Literature*, edited by E. A. Alderman (1908), Vol. II, pp. 753–757.

LYDIA MARIA CHILD

Higginson, T. W., "Lydia Maria Child," in *Contemporaries* (Boston, 1899).
Whittier, John G., editor, *Letters of Lydia Maria Child, with a Biographical Introduction* (Boston, 1883).

JOHN ESTEN COOKE

Wegelin, Oscar, *A Bibliography of the Separate Writings of John Esten Cooke* (Metuchen, New Jersey, 1925).
Beaty, John O., *John Esten Cooke, Virginian* (New York, 1922).

ROBERT HARE

Smith, Edgar F., *The Life of Robert Hare, an American Chemist* (Philadelphia, 1917).

CHARLES FENNO HOFFMAN

Barnes, Homer F., *Charles Fenno Hoffman* (New York, 1930).

JOHN PENDLETON KENNEDY

Works

Swallow Barn, edited by J. B. Hubbell in American Authors' Series.

Biographies

Tuckerman, Henry T., *The Life of John Pendleton Kennedy* (New York, 1871).
Gwathmey, Edward M., *John Pendleton Kennedy* (New York, 1931).

Criticism

Moore, John Robert, "Kennedy's *Horse-Shoe Robinson:* Fact or Fiction?" *American Literature,* IV (1932), 160–166.

JOHN LOTHROP MOTLEY

Holmes, Oliver Wendell, *John Lothrop Motley. A Memoir* (Boston, 1879).

BIBLIOGRAPHY

ANNA CORA MOWATT

Mowatt, Anna Cora, *The Autobiography of an Actress; or, Eight Years on the Stage* (Boston, 1854).

FRANCIS PARKMAN

Farnham, Charles W., *A Life of Francis Parkman* (Boston, 1900).
Sedgwick, Henry Dwight, *Francis Parkman* (Boston, 1904). [American Men of Letters.]

CATHERINE MARIA SEDGWICK

Dewey, Mary E., *Life and Letters of Catherine M. Sedgwick* (New York, 1871).

WILLIAM GILMORE SIMMS

Bibliography

Wegelin, Oscar, *A List of the Separate Writings of William Gilmore Simms of South Carolina, 1806–1870* (New York, 1906).
Wegelin, Oscar, *Bibliography of William Gilmore Simms, American Book Collector* (1933). [A revision of the 1906 ed.]

Works

The Works of William Gilmore Simms, Caxton Edition, 17 vols. (Chicago, 1890).

Biography

Trent, W. P., *William Gilmore Simms* (Boston, 1892). [American Men of Letters.]

Criticism

Jarrell, Hampton M., "Simms' Visits to the Southwest," *American Literature*, V (1933), 29–36.
Russell, J. Almus, "The Southwest Border Indian in the Writings of William Gilmore Simms," *Education*, LI (1930), 144–157.

RICHARD PENN SMITH

McCullough, Bruce W., *The Life and Writings of Richard Penn Smith* (Menasha, Wisconsin, 1917).

DANIEL PIERCE THOMPSON

Flitcroft, J. E., *Daniel Pierce Thompson: The Novelist of Vermont* (Cambridge, Massachusetts, 1929).

Nathaniel Beverley Tucker

The Partisan Leader, edited with an Introduction by Carl Bridenbaugh (New York, 1933).

Susan Warner

Warner, Anna B., *Susan Warner* (New York, 1904).

Nathaniel Parker Willis

Beers, Henry A., *Nathaniel Parker Willis* (Boston, 1885). [American Men of Letters.]

CHAPTER VII

NATHANIEL HAWTHORNE, THE ROMANCE OF THE MORAL LIFE

Bibliography

Browne, Nina C., *A Bibliography of Nathaniel Hawthorne* (Boston, 1905). [Invaluable.]

Cathcart, Wallace H., *Bibliography of the Works of Nathaniel Hawthorne* (Privately printed by the Rowfant Club, Cleveland, Ohio, 1905).

Erskine, John, in *Cambridge History of American Literature*, Vol. II, pp. 415–424.

Ferguson, J. D., Bibliography of Spanish items on Hawthorne in *American Literature in Spain* (New York, 1916).

O'Connor, E. M., *Analytical Index to Works of Nathaniel Hawthorne* (Boston, 1882).

Works

The Complete Works of Nathaniel Hawthorne, with Introductory Notes by George P. Lathrop, Riverside Edition, 12 vols. (Boston, 1883; 13 vols., 1890–1891).

Writings of Nathaniel Hawthorne, Old Manse Edition, 22 vols. (Boston, 1904). [Has some stories not in Riverside Edition. Some of these are falsely attributed to him.]

The American Note-Books by Nathaniel Hawthorne, edited by Randall Stewart (New Haven, 1932).

The Heart of Hawthorne's Journals, edited by Newton Arvin (Boston, 1929).

"Hawthorne and Politics: Unpublished Letters to William B. Pike," by Randall Stewart, *New England Quarterly,* V (1932), 237–263.

Nathaniel Hawthorne. Selections, edited by Austin Warren (New York, 1935). [American Writers Series. Excellent bibliography.]

Biographies

Arvin, Newton, *Hawthorne* (Boston, 1929).
Clarke, Helen A., *Hawthorne's Country* (Boston, 1910).
Conway, M. D., *Life of Nathaniel Hawthorne* (London, 1890). [Great Writers Series.]
Fields, J. T., *Hawthorne* (Boston, 1876).
Gorman, Herbert, *Hawthorne: A Study in Solitude* (New York, 1927).
Hawthorne, Julian, *Nathaniel Hawthorne and His Wife,* 2 vols. (Boston, 1885).
Hawthorne, Julian, *Hawthorne and His Circle* (New York, 1903).
James, Henry, *Nathaniel Hawthorne* (London, 1879). [English Men of Letters Series.]
Lathrop, G. P., *A Study of Hawthorne* (Boston, 1876).
Lathrop, Rose Hawthorne, *Memories of Hawthorne* (Boston, 1897).
Morris, Lloyd, *The Rebellious Puritan: Portrait of Mr. Hawthorne* (New York, 1927).
Ticknor, Caroline, *Hawthorne and His Publisher* (Boston, 1913).
Woodberry, G. E., *Nathaniel Hawthorne* (Boston, 1902). [American Men of Letters Series.]

Criticism

Brownell, W. C., "Hawthorne," *American Prose Masters* (New York, 1909).
Curtis, G. W., "The Works of Nathaniel Hawthorne," *Literary and Social Essays* (New York, 1895).
Erskine, John, "Hawthorne," in *Cambridge History of American Literature,* Vol. II, pp. 16–31. Bibliography, pp. 415–424.
Gates, Lewis E., "Hawthorne," *Studies and Appreciations* (New York, 1900).
Howells, W. D., in *My Literary Passions* (New York, 1895).
——, "The Personality of Hawthorne," *North American Review,* CLXXVII (December, 1903), 872–882.
Hutton, R. H., *Essays in Literary Criticism* (Philadelphia, 1876).
Longfellow, H. W., "Hawthorne's Twice Told Tales," *North American Review,* XLV (July, 1837), 59–73; or *Prose Works,* Riverside Edition, Vol. 1, pp. 360–367.
Melville, Herman, "Hawthorne and His Mosses," in *The Apple-Tree Table and Other Sketches* (Princeton, 1922).
Perry, Bliss, "The Centenary of Hawthorne," *Atlantic,* XCIV (August, 1904), 195–206.
Poe, Edgar Allan. "Twice Told Tales. By Nathaniel Hawthorne." *Graham's*

Magazine, XX (April–May), 1842. Reprinted in Virginia Edition of Poe (1902), Vol. XI, pp. 102–113. Revision with additions, *Godey's Lady's Book,* Nov., 1847. Reprinted in Virginia Edition, Vol. XIII, pp. 141–155.

Stephen, Sir Leslie. "Nathaniel Hawthorne," in *Hours in a Library* (London, 1874).

Sherman, Stuart P., "Hawthorne; a Puritan Critic of Puritanism," in *Americans* (New York, 1922).

Trollope, Anthony, "The Genius of Nathaniel Hawthorne," *North American Review,* CXXIX (September, 1879), 203–222.

Whipple, E. P., "Nathaniel Hawthorne," in *Character and Characteristic Men* (Boston, 1886).

CHAPTER VIII

HERMAN MELVILLE AND THE EXOTIC ROMANCE

Bibliography

Minnigerode, Meade, Bibliography in *Some Personal Letters of Herman Melville and a Bibliography* (New York, 1922).

Sadleir, Michael, "Herman Melville, Essay and Bibliography," *Excursions in Victorian Bibliography* (London, 1922).

See also bibliographies in Weaver and Mumford, below.

Works

The Works of Herman Melville, Standard Edition, 16 vols. (London, 1922–1924).

The Collected Writings of Herman Melville, Pequod Edition, 5 vols. (New York, 1924–1925).

Romances of Herman Melville (New York, 1928). [Contains all of Melville's novels except *Pierre.*]

The Apple-Tree Table and Other Sketches with an Introductory Note by Henry Chapin (Princeton, 1922).

Benito Cereno, with pictures by E. McKnight Kauffer (London, 1926).

Journal up the Straits. October 11, 1856–May 5, 1857, edited by Raymond Weaver (New York, 1935). [With biographical introduction.]

Moby Dick or The Whale, illustrated by Rockwell Kent (New York, 1930).

Pierre; or, The Ambiguities, with a Preface by H. M. Tomlinson, and an Introduction by John B. Moore (New York, 1929).

Pierre; or, The Ambiguities, edited by Robert S. Forsythe (New York, 1930). [Americana Deserta.]

Sea Tales of Herman Melville, edited by Arthur Stedman (New York, 1892).

Shorter Novels of Herman Melville, edited by Raymond Weaver (New York, 1928).

Some Personal Letters of Herman Melville and a Bibliography, edited by Meade Minnigerode (New York, 1922).

Biographies

Freeman, John, *Herman Melville* (London, 1926). [English Men of Letters.]
Mumford, Lewis, *Herman Melville* (New York, 1929).
Smith, J. E. A., *Biographical Sketch of Herman Melville* (Pittsfield, Massachusetts, 1891).
Weaver, Raymond, *Herman Melville, Mariner and Mystic* (New York, 1921). [Good bibliography.]

Criticism

Morris, Lloyd, "Melville: Promethean," *Open Court*, XLV (1931), 513–526; 621–635.
O'Brien, F. J., "Our Authors and Authorship," *Putnam's Magazine*, IX (April, 1857), 384–393. [Melville and Curtis.]
Riegel, O. W., "The Anatomy of Melville's Fame," *American Literature*, III (May, 1931), 195–204.
Scudder, Harold H., "Melville's *Benito Cereno* and Captain Delano's Voyages," *Publications Modern Language Association*, XLIII (June, 1928), 502–532.
Simon, Jean, "Recherches Australiennes sur Hermann [sic] Melville," *Revue Anglo-Americaine*, XIII (December, 1935), 114–129.
Thomas, Russell, "Melville's Use of Some Sources in the Encantadas," *American Literature*, III (January, 1932), 432–456.

CHAPTER IX

THE TRANSITION TO REALISM

GENERAL CRITICISM

Brown, Herbert R., "The Great American Novel," *American Literature*, VII (March, 1935), 1–14. [Résumé of critical articles in the 70's, 80's and 90's.]
[DeForest, John W.], "The Great American Novel," *Nation*, VI–VII (1872), 27–29.
Perry, T. S., "American Novels," *North American Review*, CXV (1872), 366–378.

REBECCA HARDING DAVIS

Works

Bits of Gossip (Boston, 1904). [Autobiographical.]

Biography

Downey, Fairfax, "Portrait of a Pioneer," *The Colophon*, Part XII (1932).

JOHN W. DEFOREST

Gordon, Clarence, "Mr. DeForest's Novels," *Atlantic Monthly*, XXXII (November, 1873), 611–621.
Howells, W. D., "The Heroine of *Kate Beaumont*," in *Heroines of Fiction*.

OLIVER WENDELL HOLMES

Bibliography

Ives, G. B., *Bibliography of Oliver Wendell Holmes* (Boston, 1907).

Biographies

Crothers, Samuel M., *Oliver Wendell Holmes. The Autocrat and his Fellow Boarders* (Boston, 1909).
Morse, John T., Jr., *Life and Letters of Oliver Wendell Holmes*, 2 vols. (Boston, 1896).

HARRIET BEECHER STOWE

Erskine, John, "Harriet Beecher Stowe," *Leading American Novelists* (New York, 1910).
Fields, Annie, *Life and Letters of Harriet Beecher Stowe* (Boston, 1897).
Stowe, C. E. and Stowe, L. B., *Harriet Beecher Stowe* (Boston and New York, 1911).
Stowe, Lyman Beecher, *Saints, Sinners and Beechers* (Indianapolis, 1934).
Wyzewa, Teodor de, "La Vocation de Mme. Beecher Stowe," in *Le Roman Contemporain a l'étranger* (Paris, 1900).

BAYARD TAYLOR

Smyth, Albert H., *Bayard Taylor* (Boston, 1896). [American Men of Letters Series.]
Taylor, Marie H. and Scudder, H. E., *The Life and Letters of Bayard Taylor*, 2 vols. (Boston, 1884).
Warnock, Robert, "Bayard Taylor's Unpublished Letters to his Sister Annie," *American Literature*, VII (March, 1935), 47–55.

JOHN T. TROWBRIDGE

Burroughs, John, "J. T. Trowbridge," *Scribner's Monthly*, IX (1874), 32–36.
My Own Story, John Townsend Trowbridge (Boston, 1903).

ELIZABETH STUART PHELPS WARD

Phelps, Elizabeth Stuart, *Chapters from a Life* (Boston, 1896).

THEODORE WINTHROP

Curtis, George W., Biographical Sketch of Theodore Winthrop in *Cecil Dreeme* (Boston, 1861).
Johnson, Laura W., *The Life and Poems of Theodore Winthrop* (New York, 1884).

CHAPTER X

THE FICTION OF FANTASY

THOMAS BAILEY ALDRICH

Bibliography

North, E. D., "A Bibliography of the Original Editions of the Works of Thomas Bailey Aldrich," *Book Buyer*, XXII (May, 1901), 296–303.

Works

Works of Thomas Bailey Aldrich, 9 vols. (Boston, 1896).

Biographies

Aldrich, Mrs. Thomas Bailey, *Crowding Memories* (New York, 1922).
Greenslet, Ferris, *The Life of Thomas Bailey Aldrich* (Boston and New York, 1908).
Perry, Bliss, "Thomas Bailey Aldrich," *Park Street Papers* (Boston and New York, 1908).

GEORGE WILLIAM CURTIS

Cary, Edward, *George William Curtis* (Boston, 1894). [American Men of Letters.]

EDWARD EVERETT HALE

Works of Edward Everett Hale, 10 vols. (Boston, 1898, 1901).

Biography

Hale, Edward Everett, *A New England Boyhood* (New York, 1893).
Hale, Edward Everett, *Memories of a Hundred Years*, 2 vols. (New York, 1902).
Hale, Edward Everett, Jr., *Life and Letters of Edward Everett Hale*, 2 vols. (Boston, 1917).

DONALD G. MITCHELL

Dunn, Waldo H., *The Life of Donald G. Mitchell* (New York, 1922).

HARRIET PRESCOTT SPOFFORD

Cooke, Rose Terry, "Harriet Prescott Spofford," in *Our Famous Women* (Hartford, 1883), Chapter 22.
Halbeisen, Elizabeth K., *Harriet Prescott Spofford. A Romantic Survival* (Philadelphia, 1935). [Complete Bibliography, pp. 223–263.]

FRANK R. STOCKTON

Bibliography

Stockton, Mrs. F. R., Bibliography in Vol. XXIII of Shenandoah Edition of *The Novels and Stories of Frank R. Stockton.*

Works

The Novels and Stories of Frank R. Stockton, Shenandoah Edition, 23 vols. (New York, 1899–1904).
Stockton, Frank R., "How I Wrote 'The Lady or the Tiger?' and What Came of the Writing of It," *Ladies' Home Journal,* X (November, 1893), pp. 1–2.

Biography and Criticism

Buell, Clarence Clough, "The Author of 'The Lady or the Tiger?'" *Century,* New Series, X (1886), 405–412.
Howells, W. D., "Stockton and His Work," in "Fiction, New and Old," *Atlantic Monthly,* LXXXVII (January, 1901), 136–138.
Pforzheimer, Walter L., "The Lady, the Tiger and the Author," *Colophon,* New Series, I, 261–270.
Pforzheimer, W. L., editor, *Stocktoniana* (New York, 1936). [Reprint of "The Lady or the Tiger?" with above article, and an introduction by W. L. Phelps. Privately printed.]
Stockton, Marian E., *Memoir of Frank R. Stockton with bibliographical list of his writings,* Vol. XXIII in the Shenandoah Edition.

CHAPTER XI

BRET HARTE AND THE FICTION OF MORAL CONTRAST

Bibliography

Stewart, George R., Jr., *A Bibliography of Writings of Bret Harte in the Magazines and Newspapers of California, 1857–1871, University of California, Publications in English,* (Berkeley, 1933).

Cambridge History of American Literature, Vol. II, pp. 622–625.

Works

Works of Bret Harte, Riverside Edition, 19 vols. (Boston, 1897–1903). [Vol. 19 contains index of characters.]
Harte's Complete Works, California Edition, 20 vols. in 10 (Boston, 1929).
Stories and Poems and Other Uncollected Writings of Bret Harte, Compiled by Charles M. Kozlay (Boston and New York, 1914).
Sketches of the Sixties by Bret Harte and Mark Twain, edited by John Howell (San Francisco, 1927).
Letters of Bret Harte, edited by Geoffrey Bret Harte (Boston, 1926).

Biographies

Boynton, H. W., *Bret Harte* (New York, 1903). [Contemporary Men of Letters Series.]
Merwin, Henry C., *The Life of Bret Harte* (Boston, 1911).
Pemberton, T. Edgar, *The Life of Bret Harte* (London, 1903).
Root, Sophie W., "Three Lost Years of Bret Harte's Life," *Overland Monthly,* XC (1932), 229–230 and 246.
Stewart, George R., Jr., *Bret Harte: Argonaut and Exile* (Boston, 1931).

CHAPTER XII

MARK TWAIN AND THE ROMANCE OF YOUTH

Bibliography

Johnson, Merle, *A Bibliography of the Works of Mark Twain, Samuel L. Clemens: A List of First Editions in Book Form and of First Printings in Periodicals and Occasional Publications* (New York, 1910; Revised edition, 1935).

Works

The Writings of Mark Twain, Authorized Uniform Edition, 25 vols. (New York and London, 1869–1910).
Mark Twain's Notebook, Prepared for Publication with Comments by A. B. Paine (New York, 1935).

Biographies

Brashear, Minnie M., *Mark Twain, Son of Missouri* (Chapel Hill, North Carolina, 1934).
Clemens, Clara, *My Father: Mark Twain* (New York, 1931).
Clemens, Cyril, "The True Character of Mark Twain's Wife," *Missouri Hist. Rev.,* XXIV (1929), 40–49.

Henderson, Archibald, *Mark Twain* (London, 1911; New York, 1912).

Howells, W. D., *My Mark Twain* (New York, 1910).

Leacock, Stephen, *Mark Twain* (New York, 1933).

Paine, A. B., editor, *The Autobiography of Mark Twain*, 2 vols. (New York, 1924).

Paine, Albert Bigelow, *Mark Twain. A Biography*, 3 vols. (New York, 1912; 2 vols., New York, 1935). [Chronological List of Mark Twain's Writings.]

Paine, Albert Bigelow, editor, *Mark Twain's Letters* (New York, 1917).

Sherman, Stuart P., "Mark Twain," *Cambridge History of American Literature*, Vol. III, pp. 1–20.

Wagenknecht, Edward, *Mark Twain; The Man and His Work* (New Haven, 1935).

Criticism

Brooks, Van Wyck, *The Ordeal of Mark Twain* (New York, 1920; Revised Edition, 1933).

Brownell, George Hiram, "Mark Twain and the *Hannibal Journal*," *American Book Collector*, II (1932), 173–176; 202–204.

De Voto, Bernard, *Mark Twain's America* (Boston, 1932).

De Voto, Bernard, "The Matrix of Mark Twain's Humor," *Bookman*, LXXIV (1931), 172–178.

Phelps, William Lyon, "The American Humorist—Mark Twain," *Some Makers of American Literature* (Boston, 1923), pp. 167–187.

Phelps, William Lyon, "Mark Twain," *Yale Review*, XXV (1936), 291–310.

Sherman, Stuart P., "The Democracy of Mark Twain," in *On Contemporary Literature* (New York, 1917), pp. 18–49.

West, Victor Royse, "Folklore in the Works of Mark Twain," *Studies in Language, Literature, and Criticism* (Univ. of Nebraska), No. 10, 1–87.

CHAPTER XIII

WILLIAM DEAN HOWELLS AND THE ESTABLISHMENT OF REALISM

Bibliography

Cooke, D. G., *William Dean Howells: A Critical Study* (New York, 1922). Bibliography, pp. 257–272.

Firkins, Oscar, *William Dean Howells: A Study* (Cambridge, Massachusetts, 1924). Bibliography, pp. 339–346.

Works

No collected edition of Howells has yet been made, but one is under consideration. The projected "Library Edition" contains only six items, two fiction. The chief novels up to 1885 are still available, but some of the best
since that date have been permitted to go out of print.

Heroines of Fiction (New York, 1901).
Literary Friends and Acquaintances (New York, 1900).
My Literary Passions (New York, 1895).
My Year in a Log Cabin (New York, 1893).
Years of My Youth (New York, 1916).
Life In Letters of William Dean Howells, edited by Mildred Howells, 2 vols.
(New York, 1928).

Biography and Criticism

Alden, H. M., "William Dean Howells," *Bookman*, XLIX (July, 1919),
549–554.

Brownell, W. C., "The Novels of Mr. Howells," *Nation*, XXXI (July 15,
1880), 49–51.

Cooke, D. G., *William Dean Howells. A Critical Study* (New York, 1922).

Erskine, John, "William Dean Howells," *Bookman*, LI (June, 1920), 385–
389.

Firkins, O. W., *William Dean Howells: A Study* (Cambridge, Massachusetts, 1924).

Follett, H. T. and Follett, Wilson, "William Dean Howells," in *Some Modern Novelists* (New York, 1918), pp. 99–123.

Garland, Hamlin, "Howells," in *American Writers on American Literature*
(New York, 1932).

Harvey, Alexander, *William Dean Howells. A Study of the Achievement of a
Literary Artist* (New York, 1917).

James, Henry, "William Dean Howells," *Harper's Weekly*, XXX (June,
1886), 394.

Matthews, Brander, "Mr. Howells as a Critic," *Forum*, XXXII (January,
1902), 629–638.

Perry, Thomas Sargent, "William Dean Howells," *Century*, New Series I
(March, 1882), 680–685.

Phelps, W. L., "William Dean Howells," *Essays on Modern Novelists* (New
York, 1910).

Quinn, A. H., "The Art of William Dean Howells," *Century*, LXXVIII
(September, 1920), 675–681.

Robertson, John M., "Mr. Howells' Novels," in *Essays Toward a Critical
Method* (London, 1889).

Tarkington, Booth, "Mr. Howells," *Harper's Magazine*, CXLI (August,
1920), 347–380.

Taylor, Walter F., "William Dean Howells and the Economic Novel," *American Literature*, IV (May, 1932), 103–113.

Trent, W. P., "Mr. Howells and Romanticism," in *The Authority of Criticism and Other Essays* (New York, 1899).

Twain, Mark, "William Dean Howells," *Harper's Magazine*, CXIII (July, 1906), 221–225.

Van Doren, Carl, "The Later Novel—Howells," *Cambridge History of American Literature*, Vol. III, pp. 66–95. Bibliography, Vol. IV, pp. 663–666.

"America's Foremost Living Man of Letters," *Current Literature*, LII (1912), 461–463. [Contains a number of tributes to Howells.]

"William Dean Howells," *North American Review*, CCXII (1920), 1–20. [Contains Howells' response at the dinner in honor of his seventy-fifth birthday in 1912, a list of his writings for the *Review* and an Appreciation by W. L. Phelps.]

CHAPTER XIV

HENRY JAMES AND THE FICTION OF INTERNATIONAL RELATIONS

Bibliography

King, Frederick A., Chronological List of Novels of Henry James in *The Novels of Henry James* by Elizabeth L. Cary (New York, 1905).

Phillips, Leroy, *A Bibliography of the Writings of Henry James* (Boston, 1906; Revised, New York, 1930).

West, Rebecca, *Henry James* (New York, 1916). [Bibliographies of first editions.]

Works

Novels and Tales, New York Edition, 26 vols. (New York, 1907–1917).

The Novels and Stories of Henry James, 35 vols. (London, 1921–1923).

A Small Boy and Others (New York, 1913).

Notes of a Son and Brother (New York, 1914).

The Middle Years (New York, 1917).

Letters of Henry James, Selected and Edited by Percy Lubbock, 2 vols. (New York, 1920).

Henry James: Letters to A. C. Benson and Auguste Monod, edited by E. F. Benson (London and New York, 1930).

Theatre and Friendship. Some Henry James Letters with a Commentary by Elizabeth Robins (New York, 1932).

The Art of the Novel. Critical Prefaces by Henry James, with an Introduction by Richard P. Blackmur (New York, 1934).

Biography and Criticism

Beach, Joseph Warren, "Henry James," *Cambridge History of American Literature,* Vol. III, pp. 96–108. Bibliography, Vol. IV, pp. 671–675.
Beach, Joseph Warren, *The Method of Henry James* (New York, 1918).
Benson, A. C., "Henry James," in *Memories and Friends* (London, 1924).
Bradford, Gamaliel, "Henry James," in *American Portraits* (Boston, 1920–1922).
Brooks, Van Wyck, *The Pilgrimage of Henry James* (New York, 1926).
Brownell, W. C., "Henry James," in *American Prose Masters* (New York, 1909).
Cairns, W. B., "Character Portrayal in the Work of Henry James," *University of Wisconsin Series in Language and Literature,* No. 2, 1919.
Cary, E. L. *The Novels of Henry James, with Bibliography* (New York, 1905).
Conrad, Joseph, "Henry James. An Appreciation," *North American Review,* CLXXX (January, 1905), 102–108. Reprinted in *North American Review,* CCIII (April, 1916), 585–591. Also in Conrad's *Notes on Life and Letters* (New York, 1924).
Edel, Léon, *The Prefaces of Henry James* (Paris, 1931).
Edel, Léon, *Henry James: Les Années Dramatiques* (Paris, 1931).
Edgar, Pelham, *Henry James. Man and Author* (Boston, 1927).
Elton, Oliver, "The Novels of Mr. Henry James," in *Modern Studies* (London, 1907).
Follett, Helen T., and Follett, Wilson, "Henry James," in *Some Modern Novelists* (New York, 1918).
Fullerton, Morton, "The Art of Henry James," *Quarterly Review,* CCXII (April, 1910), 393–408.
Garnier, Marie Reine, *Henry James et La France* (Paris, 1927).
Gosse, Edmund, "Henry James," *Scribner's Magazine,* LXVII (April–May, 1920), 422–430; 548–557.
Grattan, C. Hartley, *The Jameses, A Family of Minds* (New York, 1932).
Hound and Horn, "Henry James Number," (April–June, 1934.) [Issue devoted to James. Gives a few newly established dates of short stories.]
Howells, W. D., "Henry James, Jr.," *Century,* New Series III (November, 1882), 24–29.
Howells, W. D., "Mr. Henry James's Later Work," *North American Review,* CLXXVI (January, 1903), 125–137. Reprinted in *North American Review,* CCIII (April, 1916), 572–584.
Hueffer, Ford Madox, *Henry James. A Critical Study* (New York, 1916). [Appendix has readings in *Daisy Miller* and *Four Meetings* from editions of 1888 and 1909.]

Alice James, Her Brother, Her Journal, edited by Anna Robeson Burr (New York, 1934).

Kelley, Cornelia Pulsifer. *The Early Development of Henry James* (Urbana, Illinois, 1930).

Pound, Ezra, "Henry James," in *Instigations* (New York, 1920), pp. 106–167.

Roberts, Morris, *Henry James's Criticism* (Cambridge, Massachusetts, 1929).

Sherman, Stuart P., "The Æsthetic Idealism of Henry James," in *On Contemporary Literature* (New York, 1917), pp. 226–255.

West, Rebecca, *Henry James* (New York, 1916).

CHAPTER XV

WEIR MITCHELL, PIONEER AND PATRICIAN

Bibliography

A Catalogue of the Scientific and Literary Work of S. Weir Mitchell, Privately Printed, 1894. [Prepared under the direction of Dr. Mitchell. Additional items were added in manuscript, bringing the record up to 1907, and two copies deposited in the Library of the University of Pennsylvania.]

Burr, Anna Robeson. Bibliography in *Weir Mitchell, His Life and Letters* (New York, 1929).

Works

Author's Definitive Edition, 16 vols. (New York, 1913–1914).

Biography and Criticism

S. Weir Mitchell, M.D., LL.D., F.R.S., 1829–1914. Memorial Addresses and Resolutions (Philadelphia, 1914).

Burr, Anna Robeson, *Weir Mitchell, His Life and Letters* (New York, 1929).

Burr, Charles W., *S. Weir Mitchell, Physician, Man of Science, Man of Letters, Man of Affairs* (Philadelphia, 1920).

Burr, Charles W., "S. Weir Mitchell, Physician," *General Magazine and Historical Chronicle* of the University of Pennsylvania (April, 1930).

Quinn, Arthur H., "Weir Mitchell, Artist, Pioneer and Patrician," *Century,* CXX (1930), 139–148.

Schelling, Felix E., "S. Weir Mitchell, Poet and Novelist," in *Proceedings of Mitchell Memorial Meeting of the Philadelphia Psychiatric Society* (Philadelphia, 1929).

CHAPTER XVI

PLACE AND RACE IN AMERICAN FICTION

GEORGE W. CABLE

Bikle, Lucy Leffingwell Cable, *George W. Cable, His Life and Letters* (New York, 1928). [List of Cable's Works, pp. 303–306.]
Hearn, Lafcadio, "The Scenes of Cable's Romances," *Century*, New Series V (November, 1883), 40–47.
Wykoff, George S., "The Cable Family in Indiana," *American Literature*, I (1929), 183–195.

KATE CHOPIN

Rankin, Daniel S., *Kate Chopin and Her Creole Stories* (Philadelphia, 1932). [Complete Bibliography, pp. 296–307.]

EDWARD EGGLESTON

Eggleston, George Cary, *The First of the Hoosiers* (Philadelphia, 1903). [Edward Eggleston.]
Nicholson, Meredith, *The Hoosiers* (New York, 1900).
Nicholson, Meredith, "Edward Eggleston," *Atlantic*, XC (December, 1902), 804–809.

HELEN HUNT JACKSON

Davis, Carlyle Chaning and Alderson, William A., *The True Story of "Ramona"* (New York, 1914).

SARAH ORNE JEWETT

Works

Works, 7 vols. (Boston, 1910).
The Best Stories of Sarah Orne Jewett, Selected and Arranged with a Preface by Willa Cather, 2 vols. (Boston and New York, 1925).
Letters of Sarah Orne Jewett, edited by Annie Fields (Boston and New York, 1911).

Biography and Criticism

Matthiessen, Francis Otto, *Sarah Orne Jewett* (Boston and New York, 1929).
Thompson, Charles Miner, "The Art of Miss Jewett," *Atlantic*, XCIV (October, 1904), 485–497.

Grace King

King, Grace, *Memories of a Southern Woman of Letters* (New York, 1932).

Mary N. Murfree, "Charles Egbert Craddock"

Parks, Edd Winfield, *Charles Egbert Craddock* (Chapel Hill, North Carolina, 1934).

Thomas Nelson Page

Works

The Novels, Stories, Sketches and Poems of Thomas Nelson Page, Plantation Edition, 18 vols. (New York, 1906–1918).

Biography and Criticism

Cable, George W., "Thomas Nelson Page," *Book News Monthly*, XXVIII (November, 1909), 139–141.
Kent, Charles W., "Thomas Nelson Page," *South Atlantic Quarterly*, VI (July, 1907), 263–271.
Mims, Edwin, "Thomas Nelson Page," *Atlantic Monthly*, C (July, 1907), 109–115.
Page, Rosewell, *Thomas Nelson Page. A Memoir of a Virginia Gentleman* (New York, 1923).
Quinn, Arthur Hobson, "Mr. Page in Fiction and Poetry," *Book News Monthly*, XXVIII (November, 1909), 142–144.

Francis Hopkinson Smith

Novels, Stories and Sketches of F. Hopkinson Smith, Beacon Edition, 20 vols. (New York, 1902–1911).

Albion W. Tourgée

Dibble, Roy Floyd, *Albion W. Tourgée* (New York, 1921).

Constance Fenimore Woolson

Benedict, Clara, *Five Generations*, comprising *Voices Out of the Past* (1929); *Constance Fenimore Woolson* (1930, 1932); *The Benedicts Abroad* (1930). (Privately printed, London.) [Contains letters and reprints and posthumous writings of Miss Woolson.]
Kern, John Dwight, *Constance Fenimore Woolson, Literary Pioneer* (Philadelphia, 1934). [Complete Bibliography, pp. 180–194.]
James, Henry, "Miss Constance Fenimore Woolson," *Harper's Weekly*, XXXI (Feb. 12, 1887), 114–115. In *Partial Portraits* as "Miss Woolson" (London and New York, 1888).

CHAPTER XVII

JOEL CHANDLER HARRIS AND THE FICTION OF FOLKLORE

Bibliography

Wooten, Katherine H., "Bibliography of the Works of Joel Chandler Harris," *The Monthly Bulletin of the Carnegie Library of Atlanta, Ga.,* (May–June, 1907).

Works

Joel Chandler Harris: Editor and Essayist; Miscellaneous Literary, Political, and Social Writings, edited by Julia Collier Harris (Chapel Hill, North Carolina, 1931).

Biography and Criticism

Harris, Julia Collier, *The Life and Letters of Joel Chandler Harris* (Boston and New York, 1918). [Bibliography, pp. 603–610.]

Wiggins, Robert Lemuel, *The Life of Joel Chandler Harris: From Obscurity in Boyhood to Fame in Early Manhood* (Nashville, 1918).

CHAPTER XVIII

FRANCIS MARION CRAWFORD AND THE COSMOPOLITAN NOVEL

Works

Complete Works, 32 vols. (New York, 1883–1904).
Works, 24 vols. (London, 1891).
Works, Sorrento Edition, 25 vols. (New York, 1894–1906).

Biographies

Chanler, Mrs. Winthrop, *Roman Spring* (Boston, 1934). [References to Crawford.]

Fraser, Mrs. Hugh, *A Diplomatist's Wife in Many Lands* (New York, 1910). Vol. I, Chap. 9. [References to Crawford.]

Fraser, M. C., "Notes of a Romantic Life," *Collier's Magazine* (April 23, 1910).

Howe, Maud Elliott, *My Cousin, F. Marion Crawford* (New York, 1934).

FRANCES HODGSON BURNETT

Burnett, Frances Hodgson, *The One I Knew the Best of All; A Memory of the Mind of a Child* (New York, 1893).

Burnett, Vivian, *The Romantick Lady (Frances Hodgson Burnett)* (New York, 1927).

CHAPTER XIX

THE URBANE NOTE IN AMERICAN FICTION

H. C. BUNNER

Collected Stories, 4 vols. (New York, 1916).

Matthews, Brander, "H. C. Bunner," in *The Historical Novel and Other Essays* (New York, 1901).

HENRY B. FULLER

Tributes to Henry B. [Fuller] from Friends in Whose Minds and Hearts He Will Live Always, Compiled and Edited by Anna Morgan (Chicago, 1929).

ARTHUR SHERBURNE HARDY

Hardy, A. S., *Things Remembered* (Boston, 1923).

In Memory of Arthur Sherburne Hardy, with portrait. Extract from 61st Annual Report of the Association of Graduates of the United States Military Academy (West Point, New York, June 11, 1930).

Marden, Philip S., "Arthur Sherburne Hardy," *Dartmouth Alumni Magazine,* XXIII (December, 1930), 97–101.

CHARLES DUDLEY WARNER

Complete Writings, Backlog Edition, edited by T. R. Lounsbury, 15 vols. (Hartford, 1904).

Fields, Annie Adams, *Charles Dudley Warner* (New York, 1904).

CHAPTER XX

THE DEVELOPMENT OF REALISM

MARGARET DELAND

If This Be I (New York, 1935). [Autobiographical.]

Mary E. Wilkins Freeman

The Best Stories of Mary E. Wilkins, Selected by and with an Introduction by Henry Wysham Lanier (New York, 1927).

Hamlin Garland

Works

Border Edition, 11 vols. (New York, 1895–1910).

Autobiographies

A Son of the Middle Border (New York, 1917).
A Daughter of the Middle Border (New York, 1921).
Trail Makers of the Middle Border (New York, 1926).
Back Trailers from the Middle Border (New York, 1928).
Roadside Meetings (New York, 1930).
Companions on the Trail (New York, 1931).
My Friendly Contemporaries (New York, 1932).
Afternoon Neighbors (New York, 1934).

Criticism

Howells, W. D., "Mr. Garland's Books," *North American Review,* CXCVI (1912), 523–528.

Robert Grant

Fourscore; An Autobiography (Boston, 1934).

CHAPTER XXI

JAMES LANE ALLEN AND THE NOVEL OF THE SPIRIT

Henneman, J. B., "James Lane Allen: A Study," in *Shakespearean and Other Papers* (Sewanee, Tennessee, 1911).
Knight, Grant C., *James Lane Allen and the Genteel Tradition* (Chapel Hill, North Carolina, 1935). [Bibliography, pp. 288–304.]
Townsend, John Wilson, *James Lane Allen* (Louisville, Kentucky, 1927).

CHAPTER XXII

THE ROMANCE OF HISTORY AND POLITICS

General References

Canby, H. S., "What Is Truth?", *Saturday Review of Literature,* IV (1927–1928), 481–482.

Cooper, Frederic Taber, "The Degeneration of the Historical Novel," *Bookman*, XII (1900–1901), 489–493.

Follett, Wilson, "The Novelist's Use of History," *Bookman*, LXVIII (1928–1929), 156–162.

Ford, Paul Leicester, "The American Historical Novel," *Atlantic Monthly*, LXXX (December, 1897), 721–728.

Gilder, Jeannette L., "The American Historical Novelists," *The Independent*, LIII (1901), 2096–2102.

Leisy, Ernest E., *The American Historical Novel Before 1860* (Published in part, University of Illinois Studies, 1926).

Matthews, Brander, *The Historical Novel and Other Essays* (1901). [Title essay reprinted from *Forum*, XXIV (1897–1898), 79–92.]

Speare, Morris E., *The Political Novel in England and America* (New York, 1924).

HENRY ADAMS

The Education of Henry Adams (Boston, 1906).

A Cycle of Adams Letters, edited by Worthington C. Ford, 2 vols. (Boston, 1920).

Letters of Henry Adams (*1858–1891*), edited by Worthington C. Ford (Boston and New York, 1930).

Adams, James Truslow, *Henry Adams* (New York, 1933). [Bibliography, pp. 213–229.]

GERTRUDE ATHERTON

Adventures of a Novelist (New York, 1932).

WINSTON CHURCHILL

The Novels of Winston Churchill, Uniform Edition, 10 vols. (New York, 1927).

JOHN HAY

Dennett, Tyler, *Life of John Hay; From Poetry to Politics* (New York, 1933).

Thayer, William Roscoe, *The Life and Letters of John Hay*, 2 vols. (Boston, 1915; 1 vol. edition Boston, 1929).

LEW WALLACE

An Autobiography, 2 vols. (New York, 1906).

OWEN WISTER

The Writings of Owen Wister, 11 vols. (New York, 1928).

CHAPTER XXIII

LAFCADIO HEARN AND THE LATER EXOTIC ROMANCE

Works

The Writings of Lafcadio Hearn, Koizumi Edition, 16 vols. (Boston, 1923).
[Contains biography by Elizabeth Bisland and a volume of letters.]
An American Miscellany, by Lafcadio Hearn, now first collected by Albert
Mordell, 2 vols. (New York, 1925).
*Letters from the Raven; Being the Correspondence of Lafcadio Hearn with
Henry Watkin,* with introduction and critical comment by the editor,
Milton Bronner (London, 1908).
Occidental Gleanings, by Lafcadio Hearn; sketches and essays now first col-
lected by Albert Mordell (New York, 1925).
Some New Letters and Writings of Lafcadio Hearn, collected and edited by
Sanki Ichikawa (Tokyo, 1925).

Biographies

Barel, Leona Q., *The Idyl: My Personal Reminiscences of Lafcadio Hearn*
(New Orleans, Louisiana, 1933).
Bisland, Elizabeth, *Life and Letters of Lafcadio Hearn,* 2 vols. (Boston,
1906).
Gould, George M., *Concerning Lafcadio Hearn* (Philadelphia, 1908). [Bib-
liography by Laura Stedman, pp. 336–416.]
Kennard, Nina H., *Lafcadio Hearn* (New York, 1912).
Koizumi, Kazuo, *Father and I. Memories of Lafcadio Hearn* (New York,
1935).
Temple, Jean, *Blue Ghost. A Study of Lafcadio Hearn* (New York, 1931).
Tinker, Edward Larocque, *Lafcadio Hearn's American Days* (London,
1925).

CHAPTER XXIV

THE JOURNALISTS

Ambrose Bierce

Bibliography

Starrett, Vincent, *Ambrose Bierce, a Bibliography* (Philadelphia, 1929).

Works

Collected Works, 12 vols. (New York, 1909–1912).
The Letters of Ambrose Bierce, edited by Bertha Clark Pope, with a memoir
by George Sterling (San Francisco, 1922).

Biography and Criticism

De Castro, Adolphe D., *Portrait of Ambrose Bierce* (New York, 1929).
Grattan, C. Hartley, *Bitter Bierce: A Mystery of American Letters* (New York, 1929).
Mahoney, Tom, "The End of Ambrose Bierce," *Esquire*, V (February, 1936), 62.
McWilliams, Carey, *Ambrose Bierce, A Biography* (New York, 1929).
Miller, Arthur M., "The Influence of Edgar Allan Poe on Ambrose Bierce," *American Literature*, IV (May, 1932), 130–150.
Neale, Walter, *Life of Ambrose Bierce* (New York, 1929).
Starrett, Vincent, *Ambrose Bierce* (Chicago, 1920).
Wilt, Napier, "Ambrose Bierce and the Civil War," *American Literature*, I (November, 1929), 260–285.

STEPHEN CRANE

Bibliography

Starrett, Vincent, *Stephen Crane, A Bibliography* (Philadelphia, 1923).
Stolper, B. J. R., *Stephen Crane: A List of his Writings and Articles About Him.* [Published for the Stephen Crane Association by the Public Library of Newark, New Jersey, 1930.]

Works

The Works of Stephen Crane, edited by Wilson Follett, 12 vols. (New York, 1925–1926).

Biography and Criticism

Beer, Thomas, *Stephen Crane, A Study in American Letters* (New York, 1923).
Garland, Hamlin, "Stephen Crane as I Knew Him," *Yale Review*, New Series IV (April, 1914), 494–506. [Also in *Roadside Meetings*. New York, 1930.]
Garnett, Edward, "The Work of Stephen Crane," in *Friday Nights*, First Series (London and New York, 1922).

RICHARD HARDING DAVIS

Bibliography

Quinby, Henry Cole, *Richard Harding Davis, A Bibliography* (New York, 1924.)

Works

The Novels and Stories of Richard Harding Davis, 12 vols. (New York, 1916).

From Gallegher to The Deserter. The Best Stories of Richard Harding Davis, selected with an Introduction by Roger Burlingame (New York, 1927).

Adventures and Letters of Richard Harding Davis, edited by Charles Belmont Davis (New York, 1917).

Biography

Downey, Fairfax, *Richard Harding Davis; His Day* (New York, 1933).

JACK LONDON

Works, 28 vols., Sonoma Edition (New York, 1919–1927).
London, Charmian, *The Book of Jack London,* 2 vols. (New York, 1921).
[Bibliography, Vol. II, pp. 397–414.]

WILLIAM SYDNEY PORTER—"O. HENRY"

Bibliography

O. Henry Papers, Containing Some Sketches of his Life together with an Alphabetical Index to his Complete Works (New York, 1924).

Works

O. Henry Novels, Watermark Edition, 12 vols. (New York, 1913–1920).
O. Henry's Works, Authorized Edition, 12 vols. (New York, 1920).
Complete Works of O. Henry, 1 vol. (New York, 1927).

Biographies

Davis, Robert H. and Maurice, Arthur B., *The Caliph of Bagdad: Being Arabian Nights Flashes of the Life, Letters, and Work of O. Henry— William Sydney Porter* (New York, 1931).

Jennings, A. J., *Through the Shadows with O. Henry* (New York, 1921).

Smith, C. Alphonso, *O. Henry Biography* (New York, 1916).

CHAPTER XXV

EDITH WHARTON

Bibliography

Davis, Lavinia, *A Bibliography of the Writings of Edith Wharton* (Portland, Maine, 1933).

Melish, Lawson McClung, *A Bibliography of the Collected Writings of Edith Wharton* (New York, 1927).

Writings

A Backward Glance (New York, 1934). [Autobiography.]
The Writing of Fiction (New York, 1925).
"The Great American Novel," *Yale Review*, XVI (July, 1927), 646–656.
"Visibility in Fiction," *Yale Review*, XVIII (March, 1929), 480–488.
"Confessions of a Novelist," *Atlantic*, CLI (April, 1933), 385–392.
"The Writing of Ethan Frome," *Colophon*, XI, Vol. 3 (September, 1932).
"Tendencies in Modern Fiction," *Saturday Review of Literature*, X (January 29, 1934), 1–2.

Criticism

Brown, E. K., *Edith Wharton: Étude Critique* (Paris, 1935). Bibliography, pp. 331–340.
Cross, Wilbur L., *Edith Wharton* (New York, n.d.). [Critical booklet, issued by D. Appleton-Century Company.]
Follett, Helen T. and Follett, Wilson, in *Some Modern Novelists* (New York, 1918).
Gerould, Katherine F., *Edith Wharton, a Critical Study* (New York, n.d.). [Critical booklet, issued by D. Appleton-Century Company.]
Gilbertson, Catherine, "Mrs. Wharton," *Century*, CXIX (October, 1929), 112–119.
Lovett, R. M., *Edith Wharton* (New York, 1925).
Lubbock, Percy, "The Novels of Edith Wharton," *Quarterly Review*, CCXXIII (January, 1915), 182–201.

CHAPTER XXVI

ANNE DOUGLAS SEDGWICK

de Sélincourt, Basil, editor, *Anne Douglas Sedgwick: A Portrait in Letters* (Boston, 1936).
Beach, Joseph W., in *The Twentieth Century Novel*.
Forbes, Elizabeth, "Anne Douglas Sedgwick and Her Novels," *Bookman*, LXIX (August, 1929), 568–574.

CHAPTER XXVII

BOOTH TARKINGTON AND THE LATER ROMANCE

JAMES BRANCH CABELL

Bibliography

Brussel, F. R., *A Bibliography of the Writings of James Branch Cabell* (Philadelphia, 1932).

Holt, Guy, *A Bibliography of the Writings of James Branch Cabell* (Philadelphia, 1924).

Works

Works, Storisende Edition, 18 vols. (New York, 1927–1930).

Criticism

Le Breton, Maurice, "James Branch Cabell, Romancier," *Revue Anglo-Americaine*, XI (December, 1933), 112–128, and XI (February, 1934), 223–238.

Mencken, H. L., *James Branch Cabell* (New York, 1927). [Critical booklet, issued by Robert M. McBride and Company, New York.]

Michaud, Regis, *Le Roman americain d'aujourd'hui* (Paris, 1926). Revised in *The American Novel Today* (Boston, 1928).

Van Doren, Carl, *James Branch Cabell* (New York, 1925).

EDNA FERBER

Dickenson, Rogers, *Edna Ferber. A Biographical Sketch with a Bibliography* (New York, 1925).

JOSEPH HERGESHEIMER

Bibliography

Swire, H. L. R., *A Bibliography of the Works of Joseph Hergesheimer* (Philadelphia, 1922).

Autobiography

A Presbyterian Child (New York, 1923).
From An Old House (New York, 1925).

Criticism

Cabell, J. B., *Joseph Hergesheimer* (Chicago, 1921).
Priestley, J. B., "Joseph Hergesheimer," in *Contemporary American Authors*, edited by J. C. Squire (New York, 1928).

BOOTH TARKINGTON

Bibliography

Currie, Barton, *Booth Tarkington, A Bibliography* (New York, 1932).

Works

The One-by-One Edition is now being published and will be the Standard Edition.

The Seawood Edition, 21 vols. (New York, 1932).
The World Does Move (New York, 1928). [Autobiographical.]

Biographies

Dickinson, Asa Don, *Booth Tarkington* (New York, 1926).
Holliday, Robert Cortes, *Booth Tarkington* (New York, 1918).

CHAPTER XXVIII

CRITICS AND SATIRISTS—THE LIBERALS

ROBERT HERRICK

Herrick, Robert, "The Background of the American Novel," *Yale Review*, New Series III (January, 1914), 213–233.
Herrick, Robert, "The American Novel," *Yale Review*, New Series, III (April, 1914), 419–437.
Howells, W. D., "The Novels of Robert Herrick," *North American Review*, CLXXXIX (1909), 812–820.
Lüdeke, H., "Robert Herrick, Novelist of American Democracy," *English Studies*, The Hague, XVIII (April, 1936), 49–57.

FRANK NORRIS

Bibliography

Gaer, Joseph, editor, *Frank Norris: Bibliography and Biographical Data* . . . [1935] Abstract from S. E. R. A. Project, 2–F2–132, California. Monograph No. 3.

Works

Complete Works of Frank Norris, 7 vols. (New York, 1903).
The Argonaut Manuscript Limited Edition of Frank Norris' Works, 10 vols. (Garden City, New York, 1928).
Frank Norris of "The Wave." Stories and Sketches from the *San Francisco Weekly,* 1893 to 1897; Foreword by Charles G. Norris; Introduction by Oscar Lewis (San Francisco, 1931).
The Responsibilities of the Novelist (New York, 1903).

Biography

Walker, Franklin, *Frank Norris* (Garden City, New York, 1932).

Criticism

Bixler, Paul H., "Frank Norris's Literary Reputation," *American Literature,* VI (May, 1934), 109–121.

Grattan, C. Hartley, "Frank Norris," *The Bookman*, LXIX (July, 1929), 506–510.
Howells, W. D., "Frank Norris," *North American Review*, CLXXV (1902), 769–778.
Peixoto, Ernest, "Romanticist Under the Skin," *Saturday Review of Literature*, IX (May 27, 1933), 613–615.
Walker, F., "Frank Norris at the University of California," *University of California Chronicle*, XXXIII (July, 1931), 320–349.

BRAND WHITLOCK

Whitlock, Brand, *Forty Years Of It* (New York, 1914; New Edition, 1925).
Howells, W. D., "A Political Novelist and More," *North American Review*, CXCII (1910), 93–100.

CHAPTER XXIX

CRITICS AND SATIRISTS—THE RADICALS

SHERWOOD ANDERSON

Sherwood Anderson's Notebook (New York, 1926).
Story Teller's Story (New York, 1924). [Autobiography.]
Chase, Cleveland B., *Sherwood Anderson* (New York, 1927).
Fagin, N. B., *The Phenomenon of Sherwood Anderson* (Baltimore, 1927). [Bibliography, 153–156.]

THEODORE DREISER

Bibliography

McDonald, Edward D., *A Bibliography of the Writings of Theodore Dreiser* (Philadelphia, 1928).

Biographies

Dreiser, Theodore, *A Book About Myself* (New York, 1922). [Autobiographical.]
——, *A Hoosier Holiday* (New York, 1916).
——, *A Traveller at Forty* (New York, 1913). [Autobiographical.]
——, *Dawn* (New York, 1931). [Autobiographical.]
Dudley, Dorothy, *Forgotten Frontier: Dreiser and the Land of the Free* (New York, 1932).
Rascoe, Burton, *Theodore Dreiser* (New York, 1925).

Criticism

Mencken, H. L., "Theodore Dreiser," in *A Book of Prefaces* (New York, 1917).

Sherman, Stuart P., "The Barbaric Naturalism of Theodore Dreiser," in *On Contemporary Literature* (New York, 1917).

SINCLAIR LEWIS

Addresses by Eric Axel Karlfeldt, Secretary of the Swedish Academy and Sinclair Lewis, Winner of the Nobel Prize in literature on the occasion of the award of the Nobel Prize. Stockholm, December, 1930. Reprinted by Harcourt, Brace and Company, New York, 1931.

Canby, Henry S., "Sinclair Lewis's Art of Work," *Saturday Review of Literature*, X (February 10, 1934), 465. [This issue contains also an unpublished chapter of *Work of Art*.]

Cabell, James Branch, "A Note as to Sinclair Lewis," *American Mercury*, XX (August, 1930), 394–397.

Jones, Howard Mumford, "Mr. Lewis's America," *Virginia Quarterly Review*, VII (July, 1931), 427–432.

Sherman, Stuart P., *The Significance of Sinclair Lewis* (New York, 1922). Reprinted in *Points of View* (New York, 1924). [Also published as a pamphlet by Harcourt, Brace and Company, New York. Contains sketch of Lewis' life.]

Van Doren, Carl, *Sinclair Lewis: A Biographical Sketch* (New York, 1933). [Bibliography by Harvey Taylor, pp. 76–185.]

DAVID GRAHAM PHILLIPS

Marcosson, Isaac F., *David Graham Phillips and His Times* (New York, 1932).

UPTON SINCLAIR

Sinclair, Upton, *An American Outpost; a Book of Reminiscences* (New York, 1932).

CHAPTER XXX

ELLEN GLASGOW AND THE NEW SOUTH

The Old Dominion Edition, 1929–1933, contains *The Deliverance*, *The Battleground*, *Virginia*, *The Voice of the People*, *The Miller of Old Church*, *Barren Ground*, *The Romantic Comedians* and *They Stooped to Folly*. To each volume Miss Glasgow wrote critical prefaces, of great value not only in interpreting her own work, but also in evaluating

Southern fiction in general. With a change of publishers the series was interrupted, but is still in print.

Clark, Emily, "Ellen Glasgow," *Virginia Quarterly Review*, V (1929), 182–191.

Field, Louise Maunsell, *Ellen Glasgow* (New York, 1923). [A pamphlet published by Doubleday, Page and Co.]

Sherman, Stuart Pratt, "Ellen Glasgow; the Fighting Edge of Romance," in *Critical Woodcuts* (New York, 1926).

Villard, Leonie, "Ellen Glasgow," in *Revue Anglo-Americaine*, XI (December, 1933), 97–111.

CHAPTER XXXI

WILLA CATHER

Willa Cather: A Biographical Sketch . . . with Bibliography (New York, 1927). [A pamphlet issued by publisher.]

Chamaillard, Pierre, "Le Cas de Marian Forrester," *Revue Anglo-Americaine*, VIII, No. 5 (June, 1931), 419–427.

Fisher, Dorothy Canfield, "Daughter of the Frontier," *New York Herald Tribune*, May 28, 1933. [Account of early life of Willa Cather.]

Rapin, René, *Willa Cather* (New York, 1930). [Bibliography, pp. 99–104.]

Sherman, Stuart Pratt, "Willa Cather and the Changing World," in *Critical Woodcuts* (New York, 1926), pp. 32–48.

Wagenknecht, Edward, "Willa Cather," *Sewanee Review*, XXXVII (1929), 221–239.

CHAPTER XXXII

THE CELEBRATION OF THE INDIVIDUAL

MARY AUSTIN

Gaer, Joseph, editor, *Mary Austin, Bibliography and Bibliographical Data*, Abstract from S. E. R. A. Project, 2–F2–132, California. Monograph No. 2.

Earth Horizon (New York, 1932). [Autobiography.]

DOROTHY CANFIELD

Williams, Blanche C., "Dorothy Canfield," in *Our Short Story Writers* (New York, 1920).

Wyckoff, Elizabeth, "Dorothy Canfield: A Neglected Best Seller," *Bookman*, LXXIV (September, 1931), 40–44.

Zona Gale

Gale, Zona, "The American Village Defended," *New York Times Magazine,* LXXX (July 19, 1931), 1–2, 21.

Follett, Wilson, *Zona Gale, an Artist in Fiction* (New York, 1923). [Pamphlet issued by D. Appleton Company.]

Susan Glaspell

The Road to the Temple (London, 1926; New York, 1927).

INDEX

Novels, novelettes, and collections of short stories are printed in Italics. Short stories are in roman type, quoted.

(1)